1 8 6 0 — 1 9 7 4

A CENTURY OF COMMENTARY
on the works of
WASHINGTON IRVING

This portrait of Washington Irving, an undated oil c. 50″ x 40″, is by Henry F. Darby (c. 1831–?) an American artist (fl. 1849–1859). It cannot be documented as done from life, and bears resemblance to the so-called Brady photograph of the author. In the possession of Sleepy Hollow Restorations, Darby's canvas (c. 1859–60) represents the Irving of the late 1850s, in the study at Sunnyside.

1860—1974

A CENTURY OF COMMENTARY ON THE WORKS OF WASHINGTON IRVING

Edited by Andrew B. Myers

SLEEPY HOLLOW RESTORATIONS

Tarrytown, New York

Library of Congress Cataloging in Publication Data
Main entry under title:
A Century of commentary on the works of Washington Irving, 1860–1974.
Bibliography: p.
Includes index.
1. Irving, Washington, 1783–1859—Addresses, essays, lectures.
I. Myers, Andrew B.
PS2081.C4   818'.2'09 [B]   74–7843
ISBN 0–912882–28–X

For information, address the publisher:
Sleepy Hollow Restorations, Inc.
Tarrytown, New York 10591

ISBN: 0–912882–28–X
Library of Congress Catalog Card Number: 74–7843

First Printing

Printed in The United States of America

DESIGNED BY RAY FREIMAN

iv

ACKNOWLEDGMENTS

Sleepy Hollow Restorations acknowledges with gratitude the authorization granted to reprint all or part of the following previously published selections:

"Washington Irving," from *A History of American Literature* by William B. Cairns. New York: Oxford University Press, 1912, 1930. Reprinted by permission.

"Irving," by George Haven Putnam, from *The Cambridge History of American Literature.* New York: Macmillan, 1917.

"Washington Irving," from *The Development of the American Short Story* by Fred Lewis Pattee. Copyright, 1923 by Harper & Row Publishers, Inc.; renewed 1950 by Fred Lewis Pattee. By permission of the publisher.

"Washington Irving," by Royal Cortissoz, by permission of The Hall of Fame for Great Americans at New York University.

"Washington Irving," from *Main Currents in American Thought* by Vernon Louis Parrington, copyright, 1927, 1930, by Harcourt Brace Jovanovich, Inc.; renewed, 1955, 1958, by Vernon Louis Parrington, Jr., Louise P. Tucker, Elizabeth P. Thomas. Reprinted by permission of the publishers.

"Washington Irving," by Henry Seidel Canby, from *Classic Americans* (1931) by permission of Courtlandt Canby.

"Introduction" to *Washington Irving—A Bibliography* (1933) by William R. Langfeld and Philip C. Blackburn, by permission of The New York Public Library.

"Introduction," from *The Life of Washington Irving,* Volume I by Stanley T. Williams. Copyright 1935, 1963 by Oxford University Press, Inc. Reprinted by permission.

"A Master of the Obsolete: Washington Irving in the Shadows," anonymous review article in *The Times Literary Supplement,* March 21, 1936. Reproduced from The Times by permission.

"Farewell to Spain," from *The Spanish Adventures of Washington Irving.* Boston: Houghton Mifflin Company, 1940. By permission of the publisher.

"William Dunlop and His Circle," from *The World of Washington Irving* by Van Wyck Brooks. Copyright 1944 by Van Wyck Brooks; renewal © 1972 by Gladys Brooks. Reprinted by permission of the publishers, E. P. Dutton & Co., Inc.

"Washington Irving," by Marcus Cunliffe, from *The Literature of the United States* (Pelican 1954), pp. 51–56. Copyright © Marcus Cunliffe, 1954, 1964, 1967. By permission of the publisher.

EPIGRAPH

"For Irving more than for most American authors, it seems literary history is inseparable from literary criticism, and until recently there was very little of the latter, *per se*. Even the "new critics" have not found Irving as discutable as for example, Hawthorne and Melville. So Irving, like Cooper, has remained in the special domain of the critical biographer and the literary historian. Much of what they have written is concerned with Irving's place in literary annals, with historical data concerning persons and places relative to his literary career, with his sources, and with the vogue and influence of his writings."

Henry A. Pochmann,
"Washington Irving," in
15 American Authors Before 1900,
Bibliographic Essays on Research and Criticism,
edited by Robert A. Rees and Earl N. Harbert
(Madison: University of Wisconsin Press, 1971)

CONTENTS

ILLUSTRATIONS

EDITOR'S NOTE

The present volume, as a collection of representative pieces all post-dating Irving's career and life, aims to help redress the imbalance described in the epigraph above, by a dean of Irving scholars. In this regard, many of the selections chosen from quite recent sources are of imaginative and incisive literary criticism, as such. All of the selections here printed were made on the basis of one man's judgment, that of the editor. I am grateful for the good advice, along the way, of Prof. Herbert Kleinfield, the supervising editor of the Center for Editions of American Authors edition, in progress, of *The Complete Works of Washington Irving*. However, any errors in fact or opinion are entirely my own responsibility.

The planned scope of this utilitarian work involved nineteenth as well as twentieth century choices, so that finally its length alone dictated the sacrifice of some justifiable inclusions, chiefly modern. The pieces actually decided on are in some cases parts of larger units, for example prefaces or even chapters from books. Other selections include independent articles, a number of speeches, and one important review. Inevitably there is some overlapping and repetition among pieces, however interesting in themselves, drawn from one hundred years and more of accumulated analysis and appraisal. As one result of this, initial efforts to add seemingly helpful cross references produced almost epidemic results. After emergency editorial treatment the hardy survivors are comparatively few in number. Similarly, footnoting by the editor has been kept to a practical minimum. In a few cases texts have been silently emended, chiefly to correct obvious printer's errors.

It is hoped that two overall purposes may be served. First, this anthology presents a cross section of commentary, both subjective and objective, which, since it is under one cover, will save users, especially students, the time and energy it would take to come by these widely scattered elements separately. Secondly, the cumulative effect of these readings should, at the least, be to outline the pattern of ups and downs of their subject's public esteem and literary influence. Worthy Reader (as Irving might have said), may the frame not distort the picture.

The Introduction does not, despite a fashion undoubtedly familiar to practiced users of workaday gatherings similar to this, attempt a capsulized version of each of the selections that follow, essentially because they are too numerous. Instead, an extended preface surveys the directions, including weathercock vagaries, that Irving's posthumous reputation has taken. The individual items chosen are then, with this as background, especially in cultural history, left largely to speak for themselves.

The contents are divided into four sections, each representing a more or less distinct phase in the evolution of Irving's reputation, after his passing on November 28, 1859.

PART   I   Nil Nisi Bonum* (1860–1890)
PART   II   The Long Sunset (1890–1920)
PART III   Slow Awakening (1920–1945)
PART IV   A New Day   (1945–1975)

Though, as it happens, each of these units covers roughly the same period, twenty-five or thirty years, no mere mechanical division was attempted. It is just a fact that every second generation or so a change of attitude and taste occurred, significant enough to affect the value of Irving's stock in the literary market place. During the decades immediately following his death it remained at an artificial high. Over the turn of the century it hovered at a lower but still respectable figure. Between the world wars it fluctuated, dropping to jarring lows followed by encouraging recoveries. Recent decades have witnessed a slow but sustained rise to the present, juster level.

* "Nothing but good"—from the Latin idiom, "De mortuis nil nisi bonum," which can be translated, "About the dead [say] nothing but good."

INTRODUCTION

This is the first modern collection of critical commentary on the long career of Washington Irving (1783–1859). It covers the period from his death to the present. Here in the mid 1970s, as a full-grown United States celebrates the two hundredth anniversary of the Revolution which gave it birth, it is more than time to ring the changes, in this fashion, on the contribution to our exceptional early history, of the republic's first unmistakably successful professional man of letters. That this has not been done before is an accurate reflection of the rise, and gradual fall, and then continuing rise of the reputation of so unique an American author.

It is, of course, easy enough to throw around the word unique, but it is chosen here with some care. Certainly it is not used to claim credit where it is not due. Washington Irving is not, in the habitual academic idiom, a "major" writer to rival, for example, a younger contemporary like Whitman. There is no Irving "industry" as there is a Melville. And no publisher seems likely to take a flyer on his "Living Thoughts" as has been done with Emerson and Thoreau. Nor does the fabled Common Reader often thumb clear through the Irving canon, if the latest *Books In Print* is an indication. However, despite these minuses, there remain pluses enough to justify the compliments explicit and implicit in the word unique.

For Washington Irving—or "Geoffrey Crayon" as his countrymen knew him best as the first half-century of independence was being rounded out in the 1820s—by a combination of natural talent as a storyteller in both fiction and fact, and a personality that lent dignity to his uncertain calling, made the first breakthrough in the extended struggle for widespread recognition of a genuine American literature. His *Sketch Book,* published first in parts during 1819–1820, was both a Continental and cisatlantic success. True, hot on his auctorial heels were James Fenimore Cooper and William Cullen Bryant, but accident of time or not, he was a "first," and almost monotonous repetition of the fact in textbooks should not, in justice, lessen that hard-won honor. For the *Sketch Book* had, and has, more than merely chronological value. Its literary qualities signified, for the self-conscious young nation impatient for encouraging signs of a cultural maturing, the emergence of *belles-lettres* for which it need not blush. From our twentieth century coin of vantage it is clear too that much was made then of an essentially uneven performance. Still, Crayon's portfolio of prose sketches and stories was a positive beginning—the extraordinary difference between zero and one.

It is well to remember that Irving was in his mid-thirties when he succeeded, with this miscellany, in an initial gamble as a professional. True, he had had one real triumph already, with his comic masterpiece, Diedrich Knickerbocker's *History of New York,* a bumptious hoax that Scott laughed at heartily then, as would Dickens years later. But this, in 1809, was still the work of an uncommitted amateur, a dilettantish lawyer-about-town. An overview of the career thus started shows that through a span of nearly sixty years, from the awkward teen-age efforts in *Jonathan Oldstyle* (1802–1803) to the center-table popularity of his five-volume *Life of Washington* (1855–1859), Irving demonstrated a staying power in creative endeavor that gave a momentum to the art (or craft, if you wish) of letters, from which many others quickly profited, and a select few thereafter increased far beyond his own powers.

In this regard, the encouragement which Irving's much bruited-about example was to the little-known Longfellow and the unknown Hawthorne, both in time readily confessed. However, in 1838 in a private letter, Edgar Allan Poe could write, "Irving is much overrated, and a nice distinction must be drawn between his just and his surreptitious and adventitious reputation—between what is due to the pioneer solely, and what to the writer." How ready Poe was to put this in print is another matter, but he made an adroit separation, and one which remains. This will be no surprise to those readers who have come to know Irving in the privacy of *his* letters and journals, because even as a graying academician he exhibited an equally candid ability to appraise his own literary limitations.

As for the pioneer, it is a helpful coincidence that scholarship today is turning to serious consideration of a previously neglected but fundamental aspect of our early world of words, the economics of authorship. The purpose is to document accurately the lessons to be learned from the difficult evolution of the American industry of printing and publication. With the financial success of George P. Putnam's fifteen-volume, Author's Revised Edition of Irving's works (1848–1851), our first ambitious project of its kind, coupling pragmatic business value with artistic vitality, a real highwater mark in American authorship was reached. Cooper's similar plans stalled, understandably, after the novelist's death in 1851. Poe's traumatic failures of income, before his sudden end in 1849, further served to underline the occupational hazards of timing and taste. The fact that at that late date, half a century after first breaking into print, dollars did not damn Irving, was for his inkstained peers a hopeful sign. Still, a devil's advocate could point to Melville's frustration in the same 1850s, and Whitman's struggles to get *Leaves of Grass* out, even as a lesser Irving, at twice their age, was settling into valetudinarian comfort as the beloved squire of Sunnyside.

As for Irving the writer, as a creative force, only two or three quick comments here, since so much follows about this subject in the present anthology. For one thing, his real genius was for shorter pieces—conversational essays, descriptive sketches, and compact tales. And this is stated in full consciousness of the thousands of pages in his histories, determinedly researched and written in the romanticized fashion of his age. Irving's favorite Pegasus was a pony. Moreover, as the author himself confessed, once distracted while composing he was easily unseated. As a result, except for a rare sustained performance such as Diedrich Knickerbocker's, his track records were for shorter distances. Also, Irving had a spontaneous gift for style, a crystalline, easy (somewhat old-fashioned even then), but rather elegant style. There was in this, alone, no substitute for impressive originality or penetrating insight, but it is still an uncommon quality, and the sensitive reader will respond to it by instinct.

Those several gifts notwithstanding, the rather diffident Irving worked hard at his manuscripts. Stanley T. Williams, in the section on Washington Irving in the now-classic *Literary History of the United States* (1948), summed this characteristic up with:

> no self-imposed discipline for the sake of image or sentence was, as the notebooks prove, too arduous. Ceaselessly he rewrote; indefatigably he revised; his was, in his best moments, the happy, blessed labor of the true artist.

And, for the host of readers he has addressed through soft-spoken apostrophes in his prefaces, just that kind of ultimately joyous effort has fashioned many a healthy laugh—with Irving, not at him. For this artist also enjoyed a gift of humor. True, as a jokester and satirist his characteristic touch was Horatian not Juvenalian, i.e., more mild than mordant. In this respect it may perhaps be argued (the crusading Cooper came close to it at the time) that Irving did not take his responsibilities to American society seriously enough. But if Irving's tolerant caricatures, his gentle ironies, and his light-hearted word play usually were more smiling than savage, this did not preclude a seriousness of purpose beneath the surface laughter. If characteristically he did not write to preach, he did often try to teach, though never with hickory switch in hand. This he did chiefly by telling stories, and consciously as an *American* yarnspinner. It is the American in him that much current criticism is rediscovering, and his lack of militancy hardly devalues the coinage of mirth which his best tales, such as "Rip" and the "Legend," have helped pass from hand to hand, from generation to generation.

In life his fame had another assist. Irving's quietly attractive personality, lost of course to us except by hearsay, was a factor of considerable importance in his unsought rise to prominence, about mid-century, as a kind of culture hero. His return in 1846 from successful diplomatic service as Envoy Extraordinary and Minister Plenipotentiary in Madrid was followed by a rarely disputed popularity as an elder statesman of the arts that increased with the years. Quietly gregarious but never pushy, sophisticated while at the same time essentially democratic, and ever the gentleman in manner and appearance, he saw his public image grow to that of a friendly, cultivated, unquestionably moral man whose real or imagined virtues made for a personal appeal so astonishingly widespread that we can only take it on faith. Then, however, the signs were clearly there.

For example, Brahmin littérateur James Russell Lowell, in the anonymous *A Fable For Critics* (1848), a poem presenting with occasionally acidulous wit a panorama of native writers, wrote enthusiastically:

What! Irving? thrice welcome, warm heart and fine brain,
You bring back the happiest spirit from Spain.

Aspiring "literary" societies sprang up soliciting his name and attendance; the first he politely acceded to, the second he resolutely declined. The transatlantic Train Line named one of its sleek McKay packets the *Washington Irving*. In 1854 the populace of Dearman, N.Y., in Westchester County, petitioned to change its name to "Irvington" in honor of its most famous resident. And in Manhattan a fashionable hotel bore his name, just as a newly organized "Irving Bank" similarly capitalized on the solidity of his wide reputation, even putting his picture on its house currency. A somewhat ironical end for the author who had, commenting on the unsettled economy of Jacksonian times, coined (apparently) the phrase "the almighty dollar."

The fact is, and numerous other examples are available to emphasize it, that in his final decade Washington Irving was virtually a national institution, with literary pilgrimages to Sunnyside, by both friends and strangers, a commonplace of life at his miniature Hudsonside estate. Published views proliferated of the overgrown and gothicized Dutch farm cottage there, witness the remarks of Dr. Oliver Wendell Holmes who, on a local visit in 1858 resolved to pay his respects, even if Irving, then ill, could not receive him, "At least, however, I might look upon that home of his, next to Mount Vernon, the best known and most cherished of all the dwellings in our land."

On Irving's death on November 28, 1859, in his seventy-seventh year, the America he had cherished, and gracefully adorned, slowed its busy pace to mourn. This was particularly true in his own New York, where by age and achievement he had become the dean of the "Knickerbocker School" of letters. William Cullen Bryant's *Evening Post* editorialized rhetorically:

> His rising on the world of letters was in what might almost be called the morning of our literature, and after completing his course, his setting takes place in the midst of a crowd of luminaries, among whom his orb shines with no less brightness than at its meridian.

The influential Board of Trustees of the new, free and public Astor Library, which for the decade past Irving had served as an active first President, in a parchment memorial united "in the general and wide-spread expression of the whole community, which deplores his death and loss to the Nation and to the Age." Further recognizing that added dimension to Irving's long writing career, the public service he rendered, as a conscious return to his countrymen for their applause, the municipal Common Council, also in Manhattan, passed a resolution, duly promulgated and complied with, to:

> recommend that his Honor the Mayor direct the bells in the several fire-alarm bell-towers to be tolled between the hours of one and two o'clock, on Thursday, Dec. 1, 1859, at which time the funeral will take place from his late residence; that the sextons of the several churches or places of Divine worship be requested to toll the bells of their several churches at the above-mentioned time; that the masters of vessels in the harbor, the proprietors of hotels and other public buildings be requested to display their flags at half-mast during the day.

Even subtracting ruthlessly for the traditional demands of eulogy, and also for uncritical local patriotism, enough sincere regret and admiration remains, for both the man and the artist, to make clear the remarkable reputation that was Irving's as he passed into history.

But what went up like this, over the tumultous next half century, as surely was bound to come down. The Geoffrey Crayon who had written shrewdly of the "Mutability of Literature" so long before, would not have been surprised at that result. Of course there was a time lag. It is this interim period which is covered in Part I of the Table of Contents. Household gods are not discarded overnight, even satellite ones. Case in point, the large canvas completed in oils in 1863 by Christian Schussele, "Washington Irving and his Literary Friends at Sunnyside," in which the painter, working from the basic drawing by F. O. C. Darley, included a score of "names" then renowned and, in a fashion familiar to the age, grouped them around the old master in an imaginary scene in Irving's study. Frequently reprinted, this gave continuing life to a contemporary legend. Longfellow's post–Civil War visit to the Irving family plot in Tarrytown Cemetery was personal, but the resulting poem, published in 1878, continued the public salute. The poet's line, "A simple stone, with but a name and date," (See p. 39, Part I) can lead, here, into the explanation that the gravestone he saw was in fact the second one erected, for the first, differently inscribed, had to be replaced because of damage from souvenir hunters who had badly chipped it. Albeit a ghoulish tribute, this took place again, so that sometime before

1897 a third stone (the present one) was necessary, rounded at the top in an apparent attempt to discourage further macabre depredations.

Numerous literary contemporaries of Irving lived on long enough to hear the September song of American Romanticism in the 1870s and '80s. Their elderly and genteel opinions still had influence, for one thing on school curricula and texts; so, for example, while Mark Twain's *Huckleberry Finn* was being banned by the Concord Public Library for unseemly colloquialisms, the durable *Sketch Book* was becoming entrenched as a classroom reader and guide for correct English style. In the early twentieth century, "Selections" from Irving's volume, with notes, etc., became a standard text in secondary schools in many parts of the country, especially as preparation for the old College Board examinations. In Europe it was equally familiar as a model for tutelage in "good" English usage.

All this while, periodic reprintings of sets of Irving's complete works continued to supply a demand which there would certainly not have been any attempt by Putnam's to meet, had there been doubt about sales. This habit reached an ultra-Victorian climax in the "Tappan Zee" Edition (circa 1890), in twelve volumes, "Sold in an oak case with a bronze bust of Irving by John Rogers." Unimpressed commentators have since suggested that the pages of few of such copies were ever opened, but even if partly true, this would really condemn that type of purchaser, and they exist in any age, who buys books as furniture.

As a cold-eyed Realism increased its hold on the taste of the time, one by one Irving's lesser works (as we can see them) were inevitably affected. As individual volumes, the once-praised *Oliver Goldsmith* all but dropped from sight, and the weak *Crayon Miscellany* faded into a mere title. *Bracebridge Hall* continued to please the stubbornly anglophile in the transatlantic audience, but the derivative *Mahomet* vanished. The *Washington* had scattered reappearances, including a school edition in 1887, abridged by the historian John Fiske, but after the turn of the century was harder to find. *Columbus* and *Conquest of Granada* hung on, sometimes splendidly illustrated and bound, but the uneven *Tales of a Traveller* and eventually the western books—now overrun by time—began to gather dust. However, to compensate to a degree for these more or less predictable casualties, there were constant victories by a corporal's guard of Irving stalwarts. In 1886 Knickerbocker's *History,* its author's best whole book, was handsomely reprinted by the bibliophiles of the newly founded Grolier Club. The more exotic *Alhambra,* widely translated, had become, as it continues, a tourists' *vade mecum.* And year by year the *Sketch Book,* justifying its original enthusiastic reception, added new readers to the old.

Of course by now, faded and tear-stained items in it like "The Broken Heart," which pleased even Byron, and a funereal "The Widow and Her Son" were out of fashion and just flipped past. But several components still charmed latter-day readers who adventured past the Augustan introduction of "The Author's Account of Himself." The five Christmas pieces continued as colorful perennials, frequently separated as single items or as a unit and printed as Yuletide gifts. A small library of these picturesquely illustrated volumes can still be collected, a mirroring of fashions in graphics and typography. Their influence on the evolution of American Christmastime customs may well have rivaled that of Clement Clarke Moore's verses and what Louis Cazamian later called Dicken's *"philosophie de Noël."* And many North Americans remained fascinated by "Westminster Abbey" and "Stratford-on-Avon," a reading interest less predictable today as Anglo-American contacts have, in a Jet Age, become almost routine. Then, stay-at-home pilgrims, in a U.S.A. still noticeably British in its mixed origins, daydreamed over Irving's reverential pages. Even in 1905 Brander Matthews could say the two sketches were catalysts for "an unending procession" of New World visitors to both sacrosanct shrines. Still today Irving relics are displayed in Stratford's modernized Red Lion Hotel. Tourist gimmicks? Perhaps. But even so, not unnoticed or unrecognized.

Best by far were "Rip Van Winkle" and the "Legend of Sleepy Hollow." The average reader did not pause to analyze carefully either form or content, search for hidden sources, or go myth-hunting, for these tales ("short stories" as a term being a post-Irving usage) were delightful for and in themselves. It was with undemanding responses on this simple human level that our legendary "Joe" Jefferson made nineteenth century theater history with his lively staging of *Rip,* bringing together in a domestic comedy a shrew-versus-sot conflict, sentimentally resolved, in which he starred for seemingly endless seasons. So much incisive comment is contained in the present text, on Irving's two most masterful stories, that it is necessary here only to attest to their sustained magnetic attraction, as the half century following his death critically tested the metal of his works, singly and together.

In 1883, the centenary of Irving's birth presented a natural opportunity for celebration. Clearly the memory had lingered on. Two years before, the influential Charles Dudley Warner, himself at one point a writer of popular Irvingesque essays, in a serious study that avoided the merely trendy, had reconsidered Irving's reputation, in sum sympathetically. However, as yet, our university community was unpracticed in hortatory exercises such as symposia and Festchriften; indeed, the composition of formal literary history on American writers had barely begun. So memorializing Irving became the work of the worthies of polite journalism, who took over, with the help of more amateur enthusiasts in Knickerbocker circles.

Published single articles and essays aside—and there was briefly a spate of them, even overseas—it was Tarrytown area leaders who organized the indigenous remembrance best recorded, because its proceedings appeared in book form (see Part I below). In these rites of 1883, graying veterans of the nation's literary wars were joined by first citizens of suburban Westchester communities, with many participants able to remember Irving in person. By now Sleepy Hollow country, its very name popularized by the *Legend,* and with collateral Irving descendants still inhabiting "Sunnyside," willingly accepted the unusual position it occupied on the American cultural scene. In the end, this hundredth anniversary combined aesthetic criticism, without boundaries, and uncritical veneration of a regional patron saint.

The last decade of the nineteenth century opened, for the nation, with the World's Columbian Exposition in Chicago in 1893, looking back with pride some four centuries to discovery, and ahead to an only guessed-at future, with buoyant optimism. As the American mood in general turned to widespread and excited expectancy, off in its own tidy Victorian corner the diminishing critical exegesis of Irving drifted into a patently nostalgic mood, which hardly matched the onracing tempo of a time that Howard Mumford Jones recently described as "The Age of Energy." Characteristic commentary from this transitional era makes up the selections from Part II which follow. In particular, the postgraduate Knickerbocker School was in an "I remember when" humor. George William Curtis, occupant of the "Editor's Chair" in *Harper's New Monthly Magazine* and a leader in the literary establishment, in his *Washington Irving, A Sketch* (1891), another elegant Grolier Club production, began with:

Forty years ago, upon a pleasant afternoon, you might have seen tripping with an elastic step along Broadway in New-York a figure which even then would have been called quaint. It was that of a man about sixty-six or sixty-seven years old, of a rather solid frame, wearing a talma—as a short cloak of the time was called that hung from the shoulders—and low shoes, neatly tied, which were observable at a time when boots were generally worn. The head was slightly declined to one side, the face was smoothly shaven, and the eyes twinkled with kindly humor and shrewdness. There was a chirping, cheery, old-school air in the whole appearance, an undeniable Dutch aspect, which in the streets of New Amsterdam irresistibly recalled Diedrich Knickerbocker. The observer might easily have supposed that he saw some later descendant of the renowned Wouter Van Twiller refined into a nineteenth-century gentleman. The occasional start of interest as the figure was recognized by some one in the passing throng, the respectful bow, and the sudden turn to scan him more closely, indicated that he was not unknown. Indeed he was the American of his time who was universally known. This modest and kindly man was the creator of Diedrich Knickerbocker and Rip Van Winkle. He was the father of our literature and at that time its patriarch. He was Washington Irving.

This introit suffered from a touch of Gothamitis, and thus ran the risk of self-limiting its subject, but in fact Irving was long since established, talma and all, as an actor on the stage of international affairs in the arts. Witness the account, in another volume put out in the same 1891, *Initial Studies in American Letters,* in which Yale professor Henry A. Beers offered the growing number of "Chautauqua Course" readers a more expanded, if syrupy, view,

> He is not the greatest of American authors, but the influence of his writings is sweet and wholesome, and it is in many ways fortunate that the first American man of letters who made himself heard in Europe should have been in all particulars a gentleman.

So much for a long look over the shoulder, backwards. As for an early twentieth century look ahead, for an increasingly self-confident American literature the next era opened with the still waters of our sluggish and superannuated Genteel Tradition already muddied by the crosscurrents of *fin de siècle* "decadence," and an increasingly aggressive Naturalism, this last both Darwinian and Zolaesque. However, as young literary rebels like Crane and Dreiser came to discover, efficient societal purifiers had already been installed and were vigorously functioning. These aesthetic safeguards would to an understandable degree be increased by the institutional strength of the newly founded Hall of Fame for Great Americans, based at the University Heights campus of New York University. In 1900 its hundred electors solemnly made a first, and fittingly idealistic, choice of, as it turned out, twenty-nine native worthies, four of whom were writers as such: Emerson (87 votes), Longfellow (85), Irving (85), Hawthorne (73).

Much more recently Prof. Jay B. Hubbell, in *Who Are the Major American Writers?* (1972), has examined historically the development and probable validity of such official popularity contests, and dispassionately noted sins of omission as well as commission, a number of each quite surprising. On the whole, however, he found that most such processes seem justifiably to represent a usually conservative but defensibly true national recognition. As for Irving's apotheosis in 1900, it eventuated despite a critical wheat-from-chaff separation going on among demanding readers, which for the nonce had discarded most of his non-fiction, and despite a growing tendency, mostly by commentators outside of the New York ambience, to consider Irving basically just a regional writer, and before all else an early local-colorist. That he was thus now hall-of-famous seemed to ratify the nostalgic judgment of myriad older readers who had learned to admire this author wholesale, half a century before. At the same time be it noted that schoolchildren of this new age, exposed chiefly to an Irving trimmed down to what seemed his best, chiefly in fiction, were agreeably joining grandsires in appreciation.

Nevertheless, the storm-tossed next half century saw even these sparse laurels thinned out, except as received opinion in the sturdy groves of Academe, and where Irving's memory was cultivated by the independent enthusiast. By a weary 1932, historian and critic Carl Van Doren in *The Nation,* looking "Toward a New Canon" of our finest authors, could list Irving among those past masters who had "shrunk and faded." In authorship, which Washington Irving had consciously striven to establish as both a respectable and a lucrative career, aggressive competition was the order of the day, indeed spectacular competition, as in the post-World War I years the Lost Generation (*soi-disant*) in a second literary renascence made overwhelming changes in matters of theme and stylistics. For many in this heyday of *The Green Hat,* a dusty Geoffrey Crayon was old hat. A professional, yes, but yesterday's reading. One of Hemingway's solitary references to his fellow hispanophile fits in here. Writing for *Esquire* in 1934 of the usually low level of Sunday-supplement story on the *corrida,* by "any newly arrived correspondent" in Madrid, the author of *Death in the Afternoon* (1932) punned on Irving's name, and that of popular humorist and newspaperman Irvin S. Cobb (1876–1944), with this mixed compliment:

> This was first sent, I believe, by Washington Irving who was then writing for the, then, New York Sun under the pen name of Irvin S. Washington. It was a story I always liked to write myself because you finally got so you could do it quicker than most stories; but no one ever improved on Irvin Washington's original dispatch.

Also, inexorably, by this time Irving's texts had, commercially speaking, moved into the public domain, with Putnam's vested interest as original publisher already lapsed. So our "first" author, constitutionally non-combative but yet a battle-scarred campaigner, had, this long after initial victories, to stand again the remorseless test of economic viability, under fire in the open field.

Approached from these several angles: the iconoclastic aesthetics of the hour, and the ageless profit-and-loss mentality of the moment's mandarins of publishing, Washington Irving's literary fortunes could be seen sliding toward an all-time low. Not to disappearance into backshelf oblivion, but down to uncommonly limited reader interest. Part III of this volume illustrates this decrescendo.

The mind that genuinely mourned a James in 1916 and a Howells in 1920 was ill-prepared for the emergence of an Eliot, a Faulkner, or an O'Neill. By extension, an admittedly more limited Washington Irving, born the year the British finally evacuated New York City, was bound to suffer. That Irving who had written in 1819, to his old Knickerbocker friend Henry Brevoort, "I seek only to blow a flute of accompaniment in the national concert, and leave others to play the fiddle & French horn," would have accepted philosophically his situation, 1919–plus. It must be emphasized, just at this point, that there was always another Irving, a hardheaded merchant for his own muse, with a clear head for business on his half-Hibernian shoulders. His commonsense business letters over three or four decades to booksellers, personal agents, and competing publishers, on both sides of the Atlantic, document the existence of this supportive alter ego, though headnotes in college anthologies seldom recognize this.

The composite Irving, long himself a shade by then, could about 1925 conceivably have dug with vigor into the ribs of the nodding Rip Van Winkle of his literary reputation, to call attention to more or less concurrent signs of remaining or reawakening interest. For example, though in 1909 William Crary Brownell excluded Irving from his six *American Prose Masters,* the nine chosen in 1916 by Norman Foerster in *The Chief American Prose Masters,* as "by general consent, the American prose classics," did include him. And our home-grown *Cambridge History of American Literature* in 1917 contained numerous, if measured, accolades. Various collected editions of his works, some even newly illustrated, as well as cheap reprints of sets, continued to appear, though at noticeably longer intervals than in palmier days. And in the second decade of the new century a process began, though regrettably uncoordinated, of editing for publication Irving's numerous and now scattered private papers—letters, journals, and notebooks.

In retrospect it is obvious that between the World Wars the most extensive concern with Washington Irving would be by biographers, collectors, editors, and literary historians. It was *his* story that received the principal attention. Only in more recent years has judicious literary criticism loomed larger in Irving scholarship, as his own *stories* took precedence. In 1919, for Boston's prestigious Bibliophile Society, Columbia professor William P. Trent, and New York bookman George S. Hellman, who himself in 1915 had edited Irving's numerous letters to Brevoort, brought out in three volumes *The Journals of Washington Irving.* Their joint preface to this first-in-time wide selection of diary material stressed the usefulness of such personalia as illustrating that the author who jotted them down, over decades, and in differing countries and circumstances, was "a man of flesh and blood, not merely a bookworm or an animated pen." Their textual transcriptions, as subsequent researchers have found, leave much to be desired in accuracy, but the overall endeavor was commendable, as a factual look at the daily life of one special exemplar of our usable literary past. Though the fact was not writ large by the editors, in the minds of the sponsors must clearly have been the anniversary of the *Sketch Book,* whose first numbers had appeared exactly a hundred years before.

This laudable, if less than ideal, scholarly effort was followed in 1921 by *Notes and Journal of Travel in Europe, 1804-1805,* published in a limited edition by the Grolier Club, wth transcriptions and some notes by its librarian, Miss Ruth S. Granniss, from manuscripts owned by Mrs. Isaac N. Seligman and Mr. William A. White. An introduction by Professor Trent emphasized how much of an adventure Irving's long Grand Tour was, especially for a sensitive and thoughtful young American of that time. Accompanying aquatints by Rudolph Ruzicka enriched the whole, so the boxed set remains a collector's item today.

To follow along this promising vein a bit, serious collecting was to be an important sustaining force for Irving's reputation over the next several decades, even as much potted commentary repeated the off-key, Jazz Age note that he was far out of fashion. In 1925, a most exceptional collection of Irvingiana was presented to the New York Public Library by Mrs. Seligman, in memory of her late husband who had carefully gathered it. Some of this ore for scholarly refining had been shown in 1920 in an NYPL loan exhibition, but it was henceforth to be a permanent holding. To this mass of manuscripts, published and unpublished, first and unusual editions, and divers memorabilia, shortly would be added many additional pieces, some conjugate, and also Irving family papers, including portraits, all owned by her nephew, the George Hellman mentioned above. The Library, through its Berg, Manuscripts and Archives, and Rare Book divisions in particular, has added judiciously to this Seligman-Hellman trove, so that, though other educational and research institutions have good and active Irving holdings too, i.e., Harvard at the Houghton, Yale at the Beinecke, and the University of Virginia in the Barrett Collection, the combined Irvingiana at Forty-Second Street and Fifth Avenue stand first in quantity and quality.

When George S. Hellman's biography *Washington Irving Esquire* appeared in 1925 it was the first fresh portrait in some half a century. Its author, full of ideas derived from professional knowledge gained as gentleman collector and sometime art dealer, spoke in his

Preface of an emerging "new visualization" of Irving, one that would regard him more seriously, as man and artist. Indeed Hellman's supportive evidence for his corrective if somewhat informal view, including official documents such as Minister Irving's dispatches from Madrid, suggested both character and intellect appreciably more interesting than that of the merely charming, intellectually lightweight "Geoffrey Crayon" of routine schoolbook identification.

This partisan interpretation had, however, to make an uphill fight against that bastion of Populist liberalism Vernon Louis Parrington's monumental three-volume *Main Currents in American Thought* (1927–1930). In the second, *The Romantic Revolution in America* (1927), Parrington found Irving, seen from one angle or another, though not primarily as a subject of aesthetic judgment, disappointingly conservative, if not apolitical, and incurably romantic. He all but wrote off six decades of creative effort and energetic application to the business side of his profession with, "An incorrigible *flâneur,* Irving's business in life was to loaf and invite the picturesque." Fortunately Henry Seidel Canby's *Classic Americans* (1931) took another tack, speaking seriously, it may be too seriously, of Irving's early Federalism as a wellspring of his attitude as an American artist.

The next year, 1932, saw the appearance in issues of the *Bulletin of the New York Public Library* of the first detailed bibliography of Irving, including published books and known contributions, unpublished writings, journals, and manuscripts. The work of a committed bibliophile and collector, William R. Langfeld, assisted by an experienced bibliographer, Philip C. Blackburn, their *Washington Irving—A Bibliography* cast a wide net, among other things considering items in certain private holdings, and gave a groundbreaking listing of numerous translations of Irving's works. This extensive material, published in book form in 1933, had a prefatory "Irving and The Collector," which enthused:

> His personality has an engaging charm; he possesses undeniable literary merits; his wit, his urbanity, his touches of quaint eighteenth-century style, his scholarship, the plots of his tales—all have a distinct appeal. To the bibliographer, the variations in the editions of his books, the occasional "points," the existence of little known items offer an absorbing study.

As professional scrutiny, solid though not infallible, "Langfeld and Blackburn" raised Irving's stock, particularly in the university community, and tangentially in auction rooms. Notwithstanding subsequent advances in bibliographical technique, their compilation remains a valuable elbow companion in research.

Thus far in the young century, those publications representing fresh stirrings of interest in Irving had focused as much on the person as on the author. Irving's own writings, however, had become less available to the new student, except in minimal selections in anthologies, and in rather weary editions in libraries. Today, with paperbacks pandemic, and reprint assembly lines kinetic, it takes something of a wrench in thought to visualize years when, except for comparatively isolated experiments like the Everyman and Modern Library series (or the Little Blue Books), all of which had some Irving, the inexpensive "pocket" book was something of a rarity. Luckily, in Irving's case this need was met by Henry A. Pochmann's *Washington Irving, Representative Selections* (1934). This volume in the American Book Company's "American Writers Series," compactly put together, with intelligent selections accompanied by a substantial life-and-works introduction, an up-to-date annotated bibliography of works of criticism, etc., set a standard by which, forty years later, any similar effort must be measured. Coming when it did, Pochmann's student edition served the Irving cause especially well.

Nineteen thirty-five saw the emergence, after years of close study and instructive travel, of *The Life of Washington Irving* by Stanley T. Williams, a careful two-volume biography which instantly superseded all previous endeavors. This Yale professor, already established as a serious Irvingite by the publication of a number of auxiliary editions of his subject's letters and journals, here added to familiar printed sources information drawn from a host of original manuscripts, tracked down on two continents. Reviewers widely applauded his efforts, as a model of scrupulous care in the creation of a full-length, precise, and colorful portrait. In his preface, and despite some negative passages elsewhere, the biographer himself summed up Irving's long career positively:

> Lacking force and concentration, his life experience, nevertheless, ranged freely over that past to which we now look back with mingled feelings of superiority and longing. Irving, as Poe

said, pioneered in the democracy—in literature, history, travel, politics, and diplomacy.

Looking back at Williams's definitive labor here, from the distance of the early 1970s, Pochmann would point out that by it Irving became "the first American man of letters to be honored by a full-length, modern, critical biography—for which Poe, Emerson, Hawthorne, Melville, Whitman, and others had to wait some years longer."

Closely following on this success, Williams, in collaboration with Mary Allen Edge, put out in 1936, *A Bibliography of the Writings of Washington Irving, A Check List*. Designedly a partner to the yardstick *Life*, this independent adjunct was:

> a check list of all his writings, a check list from its very nature imperfect and incomplete, but thorough, and extending from the year of Irving's first publication (1802) until the present time. Here exists in outline the literary career of our first man of letters.

Among the components, in a detailed volume, were specimens of criticism on Irving, both New World and Old, and an impressive range of foreign-language editions of the canon, wherever possible presented after personal examination. The Introduction, emphasizing that the evidence gathered demonstrated Irving's "insistent presence in the minds of the reading public" of his era, also paused to place him in perspective, with James Fenimore Cooper especially, as an American author enmeshed over a whole career in complications resulting from the "lack of international copyright law."

In these middle 1930s the biographer and critic Van Wyck Brooks had already begun, with *The Flowering of New England* (1936), the series "Makers and Finders," which presented a sanguine and idealistic synthesis of American cultural history, especially as exemplified in the lives and works of our writers. The next volume, the second published but the first in logical order would be *The World of Washington Irving* (1944). Though occasionally wearisome in minutiae, *The World*, alliterative title and all, depicted a bright scene as the young nation's early authors made adventuresome literary history, in prose and/or verse. Irving served, and deservedly, as a central though not controlling figure in a story which Brooks told, the more enthusiastically it would seem, for the echoes of World War II overseas clearly audible to patriotic stateside readers.

The ambitious *Literary History of the United States* (1948), carefully constructed by Robert Spiller, *et al.,* was, in the euphoria of the immediate postwar years, an instant success, and contained a full section (18) on Irving, inevitably by Stanley Williams. Soberly generous as a critic, simultaneously he made it clear that this author had importance for valid non-literary reasons as well. The *Literary History* was, it is obvious in retrospect, symptomatic of the onrush of interest in our own literary traditions that catapulted American Literature studies into unaccustomed academic prominence during these self-gratulatory years. Quickly thereafter in 1950, Williams repeated his emphasis on Irving's inherent strengths—without hiding concomitant weaknesses—in a penetrating essay that served the pragmatic purpose of Introduction to the paperback *Washington Irving, Selected Prose,* which he edited for Rinehart & Co. Expatiating on both the old-fashioned and the experimental in his cosmopolitan author, on the European muse that obligingly shared Irving's artistic affections with an equally vital American one, the influential Williams added force to freshets of "lit. crit." rising to swell a current of commentary about the old Knickerbocker frontier of American literature.

The next quarter century became a kind of second spring in Irving scholarship in particular and saw, as we continue to see, persistent reinforcement of the sum of Williams's sensitive, though not undiscriminating commentary. It is these years which have supplied the upbeat choices in Part IV here. This new interest has swelled into that intermittent yet impressive flow (of articles, books, dissertations, editions, monographs, reviews, and special studies) charted with a sure hand in Henry Pochmann's "Irving" essay, in 1971, in *Fifteen American Authors.* The epigraph to the present volume, a quotation from the conclusion of that most competent analysis, must suffice, at this point in an extended preface, to suggest the healthy admixture and the intrinsic value of the accumulated discussion of Washington Irving, artist as well as man.

A Century of Commentary is a gathering drawn from a hundred years, and a bit more, of informed though hardly uniform opinion. Open-minded consideration of a true sampling of it can help the serious reader (in an idiom that Irving would readily have recognized) to hold a clear, if slightly antique, mirror up to nature—in this case our complicated and adaptable American nature. To say this, is no mere grasping at passing relevance, for time has indelibly stamped a permanence on the best of Irving's work. And that best, and indeed also the worst of his extensive *oeuvre,* can be especially utilized to analyze the vicissitudes of authorship, in our formative years as an experiment in the hard-headed practicalities of being a New World republic.

Young Washington Irving had his dream and the realities to live with too. Even in his middle thirties, as from Britain in 1819 he dickered with Moses Thomas, the Philadelphia printer, over the transatlantic publication of the yet-untried *Sketch Book,* Irving had to write of his uncertain hopes to be able:

> to keep on quietly & regularly in the path I have marked out for myself, without the danger of being overtaken by want, on the way. *In the mean time continue to have faith in me.*

That act of faith so many contemporaries here and abroad would join in, that it sustained the nervous American author, in both spirit and body, for the next four decades.

Thereafter? In 1872, some dozen years after Washington Irving's death, John S. Hart of the Princeton faculty, one of the earliest organizers on a university level, of the concentrated study of American authors, celebrated Irving as "on the whole one of the brightest and dearest names in the annals of American literature." Some half a century later, H. L. Mencken, in the debunking mood of the literary iconoclasts of the 1920s, would counter with:

> American literature is chiefly remarkable, now as always, for its remarkable mediocrity. Its typical great man, in our time, has been Howells, as its typical great man a generation ago was Lowell, and two generations ago, Irving.

In 1971, Professor Pochmann, in the synoptic view of Irving studies referred to on the preceding page, could redress the balance by recording "a healthy revival of scholarly interest in Irving." This painstaking academic aside, and also the earlier feral critic (both equally committed men) the "last word" inevitably is the reader's, as it was from the beginning.

Diedrich Knickerbocker's *A History of New York,* and the best of the *Sketch Book* and *The Alhambra,* for example, hold their own against a kind of subsequent competition, in fact and fiction, which even Irving's romantic imagination could hardly have anticipated. So much, at present, for the artist. Add to this thoughts also of the man, and the steady stream of visitors, young and old, to "Sunnyside"—now a Registered National Historic Landmark under the direction of Sleepy Hollow Restorations—speaks cogently for itself.

It may well be best, in this advocatory volume, to let Irving speak a final candid word or two for himself. In November of 1859, within weeks of his death, in his seventy-seventh year, he remarked in an interview with a New York journalist, on his lifelong habits of work:

> . . . an essay or chapter that has been only *hammered out,* is seldom good for anything. An author's right time to work is when his mind is aglow—when his imagination is kindled. These are his precious moments. Let him wait until they come; but when they have come, let him make the most of them.

To what extent Washington Irving failed or succeeded in this, the present volume tries fairly to sketch out.

ANDREW B. MYERS
Fordham University
January 1976

PART I

NIL NISI BONUM

(1860–1890)

RESOLVED, That while we deeply deplore the death of our friend and associate, Washington Irving, we rejoice in the completeness of his life and labors, which, closing together, have left behind them so sweet a fame, and a memory so precious.

RESOLVED, That we feel a just pride in his renown as an author, not forgetting that, to his other claims upon our gratitude, he adds also that of having been the first to win for our country an honorable name and position in the History of Letters.

RESOLVED, That we hold in affectionate remembrance the noble example of his long literary career, extending through half a century of unremitted labors, graced with all the amenities of authorship, and marred by none of its discords and contentions.

RESOLVED, That as members of this Historical Society, we regard with especial honor and admiration, his Lives of Columbus, the Discoverer, and of Washington, the Father of our Country.

RESOLVED, That a copy of these resolutions be transmitted to his family, with the expression of our deepest and sincere sympathy.

Resolutions submitted by Henry Wadsworth Longfellow,
at a special meeting of the Massachusetts Historical Society,
in Boston, on Dec. 15, 1859

I

From "A Discourse"

BY WILLIAM CULLEN BRYANT

On April 3, 1860, which would have been Washington Irving's seventy-seventh birthday, the New-York Historical Society, of which he had for decades been a member, held a memorial meeting at the Academy of Music on 14th Street near Union Square. The principal speaker was William Cullen Bryant (1794–1878), editor and proprietor of the important *Evening Post,* and long established as poet and critic. In this selection on the young Irving, from a long address, Bryant's dutiful rhetoric cannot disguise, even yet, his personal regard for, and professional pride in, his fellow American artist. Bryant's "Discourse on the Life, Character, and Genius of Washington Irving," here reprinted from George P. Putnam's memorial volume, *Washington Irving* (New York, 1860), was also separately published. It is a *locus classicus* of mid-Victorian eulogy.

At the time that Washington Irving was born, the city of New York contained scarcely more than twenty thousand inhabitants. During the war its population had probably diminished. The town was scarcely built up to Warren street; Broadway, a little beyond, was lost among grassy pastures and tilled fields; the Park, in which now stands our City Hall, was an open common, and beyond it gleamed, in a hollow among the meadows, a little sheet of fresh water, the Kolch, from which a sluggish rivulet stole through the low grounds called Lispenard's Meadows, and following the course of what is now Canal street, entered the Hudson. With the exception of the little corner of the island below the present City Hall, the rural character of the whole region was unchanged, and the fresh air of the country entered New York at every street. The town at that time contained a mingled population, drawn from different countries; but the descendants of the old Dutch settlers formed a large proportion of the inhabitants, and these preserved many of their peculiar customs, and had not ceased to use the speech of their ancestors at their firesides. Many of them lived in the quaint old houses, built of small yellow bricks from Holland, with their notched gable-ends on the streets, which have since been swept away with the language of those who built them.

In the surrounding country, along its rivers and beside its harbors, and in many parts far inland, the original character of the Dutch settlements was still less changed. Here they read their Bibles and said their prayers and listened to sermons in the ancestral tongue. Remains of this language yet linger in a few neighborhoods; but in most, the common schools, and the irruptions of the Yankee race, and the growth of a population newly derived from Europe, have stifled the ancient utterances of New Amsterdam. I remember that twenty years since the market people of Bergen chattered Dutch in the steamers which brought them in the early morning to New York. I remember also that, about ten years before, there were families in the westernmost towns of Massachusetts where Dutch was still the household tongue, and matrons of the English stock, marrying into them, were laughed at for speaking it so badly.

It will be readily inferred that the isolation in which the use of a language, strange to the rest of the country, placed these people, would form them to a character of peculiar simplicity, in which there was a great deal that was quaint and not a little that would appear comic to their neighbors of the Anglo-Saxon stock. It was among such a population, friendly and hospitable, wearing their faults on the outside, and living in homely comfort on their fertile and ample acres, that the boyhood and early youth of Irving were passed. He began, while yet a stripling, to wander about the surrounding country, for the love of rambling was the most remarkable peculiarity of that period of his life. He became, as he himself writes, familiar with all the neighboring places famous in history or fable, knew every spot where a murder or a robbery had been committed or a ghost seen; strolled into the villages, noted their customs and talked with their sages, a welcome guest, doubtless, with his kindly and ingenuous manners and the natural playful turn of his conversation.

I dwell upon these particulars because they help to show here how the mind of Irving was trained, and by what process he made himself master of the materials afterward wrought into the forms we so much admire. It was in these rambles that his strong love of nature was awakened and nourished. Those who only know the island of New York as it now is, see few traces of the beauty it wore before it was levelled and smoothed from side to side for the builder. Immediately without the little town, it was charmingly diversified with heights and hollows, groves alternating with sunny openings, shining tracks of rivulets, quiet country-seats with trim gardens, broad avenues of trees, and lines of pleached hawthorn hedges. I came to New York in 1825, and I well recollect how much I admired the shores of the Hudson above Canal street, where the dark rocks jutted far out in the water, with little bays between, above which drooped forest trees overrun with wild vines. No less beautiful were the shores of the East River, where the orchards of the Stuyvesant estate reached to cliffs beetling over the water, and still further on were inlets between rocky banks bristling with red cedars. Some idea of this beauty may be formed from looking at what remains of the natural shore of New York island where the tides of the East River rush to and fro by the rocky verge of Jones's Wood.

Here wandered Irving in his youth, and allowed the aspect of that nature which he afterward portrayed so well to engrave itself on his heart; but his excursions were not confined to this island. He became familiar with the banks of the Hudson, the extraordinary beauty of which he was the first to describe. He made acquaintance with the Dutch neighborhoods sheltered by its hills, Nyack, Haverstraw, Sing Sing and Sleepy Hollow, and with the majestic Highlands beyond. His rambles in another direction led him to ancient Communipaw, lying in its quiet recess by New York bay; to the then peaceful Gowanus, now noisy with the passage of visitors to Greenwood and thronged with funerals; to Hoboken, Horsimus and Paulus Hook, which has since become a city. A ferry-boat dancing on the rapid tides took him over to Brooklyn, now our flourishing and beautiful neighbor city; then a cluster of Dutch farms, whose possessors lived in broad, low houses, with stoops in front, overshadowed by trees.

The generation with whom Irving grew up read the "Spectator" and the "Rambler," the essays and tales of Mackenzie and those of Goldsmith; the novels of the day were those of Richardson, Fielding and Smollett; the religious world were occupied with the pages of Hannah More, fresh from the press, and with the writings of Doddridge; politicians sought their models of style and reasoning in the speeches of Burke and the writings of Mackintosh and Junius. These were certainly masters of whom no pupil needed to be ashamed, but it can hardly be said that the style of Irving was formed in the school of any of them. His father's library was enriched with authors of the Elizabethan age, and he delighted, we are told, in reading Chaucer and Spenser. The elder of these great poets might have taught him the art of heightening his genial humor with poetic graces, and from both he might have learned a freer mastery over his native English than the somewhat formal taste of that day encouraged. Cowper's poems, at that time, were in everybody's hands, and if his father had not those of Burns, we must believe that he was no Scotchman. I think we may fairly infer that if the style of Irving took a bolder range than was allowed in the way of writing which prevailed when he was a youth, it was owing, in a great degree, to his studies in the poets, and especially in those of the earlier English literature.

He owed little to the schools, though he began to attend them early. His first instructions were given when he was between four and six years old, by Mrs. Ann Kilmaster, at her school in Ann street, who seems to have had some difficulty in getting him through the alphabet. In 1789, he was transferred to a school in Fulton street, then called Partition street, kept by Benjamin Romaine, who had been a soldier in the Revolution—a sensible man and a good disciplinarian, but probably an indifferent scholar—and here he continued till he was fourteen years of age. He was a favorite with the master, but preferred reading to regular study. At ten years of age he delighted in the wild tales of Ariosto, as translated by Hoole; at eleven, he was deep in books of voyages and travels, which he took to school and read by stealth. At that time he composed with remarkable ease and fluency, and exchanged tasks with the other boys, writing their compositions, while they solved his problems in arithmetic, which he detested. At the age of thirteen he tried his hand at composing a play, which was performed by children at a friend's house, and of which he afterward forgot every part, even the title.

Romaine gave up teaching in 1797, and in that year Irving entered a school kept in Beekman street, by Jonathan Irish, probably the most accomplished of his instructors. He left this school in March, 1798, but continued for a time to receive private lessons from the same teacher, at home. Dr. Francis, in his pleasant reminiscences of Irving's early life, speaks of him as preparing to enter Columbia College, and as being prevented by the state of his health; but it is certain that an indifference to the acquisition of learning had taken possession of him at that age, which he afterward greatly regretted.

At the age of sixteen he entered his name as a student at law in the office of Josiah Ogden Hoffman an eminent advocate, who, in later life, became a judge in one of our principal tribunals. It was while engaged in his professional studies that he made his first appearance as an author. I should have mentioned, among the circumstances that favored the unfolding of his literary capacities, that two of his elder brothers were men of decided literary tastes, William Irving, some seventeen years his senior, and Dr. Peter Irving, who, in the year 1802, founded a daily paper in New York, at a time when a daily paper was not, as now, an enterprise requiring a large outlay of capital, but an experiment that might be tried and abandoned with little risk. Dr. Irving established the "Morning Chronicle," and his younger brother contributed a series of essays, bearing the signature of Jonathan Oldstyle, of which Mr. Duyckinck whose judgment I willingly accept, says that they show how early he acquired the style which so much charms us in his later writings.

In 1804, having reached the age of twenty-one, Irving, alarmed by an increasing weakness of the chest, visited Europe for the sake of his health. He sailed directly to the south of France, landed at Bordeaux in May, and passed two months in Genoa, where he embarked for Messina, in search of a softer climate than any to be found on the Italian peninsula. While at Messina, he saw the fleet of Nelson sweeping by that port on its way to fight the great naval battle of Trafalgar. He made the tour of Sicily, and crossing from Palermo to Naples, proceeded to Rome. Here he formed the acquaintance of Washington Allston, who was then entering on a career of art as extraordinary as that of Irving in literature. With Allston he made long rambles in the picturesque neighborhood of that old city, visited the galleries of its palaces and villas, and studied their works of art with a delight that rose to enthusiasm. He thought of the dry pursuit of the law which awaited his return to America, and for which he had no inclination, and almost determined to be a painter. Allston encouraged him in this disposition, and together they planned the scheme of a life devoted to the pursuit of art. It was fortunate for the world that, as Irving reflected on the matter, doubts arose in his mind which tempered his enthusiasm, and led him to a different destiny. The two friends separated, each to take his own way to renown—Allston to become one of the greatest of painters, and Irving to take his place among the greatest of authors. Leaving Italy, Irving passed through Switzerland to France, resided in Paris several months, travelled through Flanders and Holland, went to England, and returned to his native country in 1806, after an absence of two years.

At the close of the year he was admitted to practice as an attorney-at-law. He opened an office, but it could not be said that he ever became a practitioner. He began the year 1807 with the earliest of those literary labors which have won him the admiration of the world. On the 24th of January appeared, in the form of a small pamphlet, the first number of a periodical entitled "Salmagundi," the joint production of himself, his brother William, and James K. Paulding. The elder brother contributed the poetry, with hints and outlines for some of the essays, but nearly all the prose was written by the two younger associates.

William Irving, however, had talent enough to have taken a more important part in the work. He was a man of wit, well educated, well informed, and the author of many clever things written for the press, in a vein of good natured satire and published without his name. He was held in great esteem on account of his personal character, and had great weight in Congress, of which he was for some years a member.*

When "Salmagundi" appeared, the quaint old Dutch town in which Irving was born had become transformed to a comparatively gay metropolis. Its population of twenty thousand souls had enlarged to more than eighty thousand, although its aristocratic class had yet their residences in what seems now to us the narrow space between the Battery and Wall street. The modes and fashions of Europe were imported fresh and fresh. "Salmagundi" speaks of leather breeches as all the rage for a morning dress, and flesh-colored smalls for an evening party. Gay equipages dashed through the streets. A new theatre had risen in Park Row, on the boards of which Cooper, one of the finest declaimers, was performing to crowded houses. The churches had multiplied faster than the places of amusement; other public buildings of a magnificence hitherto unknown, including our present City Hall, had been erected; Tammany Hall, fresh from the hands of the builder, overlooked the Park. We began to affect a taste for pictures, and the rooms of Michael Paff, the famous German picture dealer in Broadway, were a favorite lounge for such connoisseurs as we then had, who amused themselves with making him talk of Michael Angelo. Ballston Springs were the great fashionable watering-place of the country, to which resorted the planters of the South with splendid equipages and troops of shining blacks in livery.

"Salmagundi" satirized the follies and ridiculed the humors of the time with great prodigality of wit and no less exuberance of good nature. In form it resembles the "Tattler," and that numerous brood of periodical papers to which the success of the "Tattler" and "Spectator" gave birth; but it is in no sense an imitation. Its gaiety is its own; its style of humor is not that of Addison nor Goldsmith, though it has all the genial spirit of theirs; nor is it borrowed from any other writer. It is far more frolicsome and joyous, yet tempered by a native gracefulness. "Salmagundi" was manifestly written without the fear of criticism before the eyes of the authors, and to this sense of perfect freedom in the exercise of their genius the charm is probably owing which makes us still read it with so much delight. Irving never seemed to place much value on the part he contributed to this work, yet I doubt whether he ever excelled some of those papers in *Salma-*

*See a brief but well written memoir of William Irving by Dr. Berrian.

gundi which bear the most evident marks of his style, and Paulding, though he has since acquired a reputation by his other writings, can hardly be said to have written anything better than the best of those which are ascribed to his pen.

Just before *Salmagundi* appeared, several of the authors who gave the literature of England its present character had begun to write. For five years the quarterly issues of the "Edinburgh Review," then in the most brilliant period of its existence, had been before the public. Hazlitt had taken his place among the authors, and John Foster had published his essays. Of the poets, Rogers, Campbell and Moore were beginning to be popular; Wordsworth had published his Lyrical Ballads, Scott, his Lay of the Last Ministrel, Southey, his Madoc, and Joanna Baillie two volumes of her plays. In this revival of the creative power in literature it is pleasant to see that our own country took part, contributing a work of a character as fresh and original as any they produced on the other side of the Atlantic.

Nearly two years afterward, in the autumn of 1809, appeared in the "Evening Post," addressed to the humane, an advertisement requesting information concerning a small elderly gentleman named Knickerbocker, dressed in a black coat and cocked hat, who had suddenly left his lodgings at the Columbian Hotel in Mulberry street, and had not been heard of afterward. In the beginning of November, a "Traveller" communicated to the same journal the information that he had seen a person answering to this description, apparently fatigued with his journey, resting by the road-side a little north of Kingsbridge. Ten days later Seth Handaside, the landlord of the Columbian Hotel, gave notice, through the same journal, that he had found in the missing gentleman's chamber "a curious kind of written book," which he should print by way of reimbursing himself for what his lodger owed him. In December following, Inskeep and Bradford, booksellers, published "Diedrich Knickerbocker's History of New York."

"Salmagundi" had prepared the public to receive this work with favor, and Seth Handaside had no reason to regret having undertaken its publication. I recollect well its early and immediate popularity. I was then a youth in college, and having committed to memory a portion of it to repeat as a declamation before my class, I was so overcome with laughter, when I appeared on the floor, that I was unable to proceed, and drew upon myself the rebuke of the tutor.

I have just read this "History of New York" over again, and I found myself no less delighted than when I first turned its pages in my early youth. When I compare it with other works of wit and humor of a similar length, I find that, unlike most of them, it carries forward the reader to the conclusion without weariness or satiety, so unsought, spontaneous, self-suggested are the wit and the humor. The author makes us laugh, because he can no more help it than we can help laughing. Scott, in one of his letters, compared the humor of this work to that of Swift. The rich vein of Irving's mirth is of a quality quite distinct from the dry drollery of Swift, but they have this in common, that they charm by the utter absence of effort, and this was probably the ground of Scott's remark. A critic in the "London Quarterly," some years after its appearance, spoke of it as a "tantalizing book," on account of his inability to understand what he called "the point of many of the allusions in this political satire." I fear he must have been one of those respectable persons who find it difficult to understand a joke unless it be accompanied with a commentary opening and explaining it to the humblest capacity. Scott found no such difficulty. "Our sides," he says, in a letter to Mr. Brevoort, a friend of Irving, written just after he had read the book, "are absolutely sore with laughing." The mirth of the "History of New York" is of the most transparent sort, and the author, even in the later editions, judiciously abstained from any attempt to make it more intelligible by notes.

I find in this work more manifest traces than in his other writings of what Irving owed to the earlier authors in our language. The quaint poetic coloring, and often the phraseology, betray the disciple of Chaucer and Spenser. We are conscious of a flavor of the olden time, as of a racy wine of some rich vintage—

Cooled a long age in the deep-delvèd earth.

I will not say that there are no passages in this work which are not worthy of their context; that we do not sometimes meet with phraseology which we could wish changed, that the wit does not sometimes run wild and drop here and there a jest which we could willingly spare. We forgive, we overlook, we forget all this as we read, in consideration of the entertainment we have enjoyed, and of that which beckons us onward in the next page. Of all mock-heroic works, "Knickerbocker's History of New York" is the gayest, the airiest, and the least tiresome.

In 1848 Mr. Irving issued an edition of this work, to which he prefixed what he called an "Apology," intended in part as an answer to those who thought he had made too free with the names of our old Dutch families. To speak frankly, I do not much wonder that the descendants of the original founders of New Amsterdam should have hardly known whether to laugh or look grave on finding the names of their ancestors, of whom they never thought but with respect, now connected with ludicrous associations, by a wit of another race. In one of his excellent historical discourses Mr. Verplanck had gently complained of this freedom, expressing himself, as he said, more in sorrow than in anger. Even the sorrow, I believe, must have long since wholly passed away, when it is seen how little Irving's pleasantries have detracted from the honor paid to the early history of our city—at all events, I do not see how it could survive Irving's good-humored and graceful Apology.

It was not long after the publication of the "History of New York" that Irving abandoned the profession of law, for which he had so decided a distaste as never to have fully tried his capacity for pursuing it. Two of his brothers were engaged in commerce, and they received him as a silent partner. He did not, however, renounce his literary occupations. He wrote, in 1810, a memoir of Campbell, the poet, prefaced to an edition of the writings of that author, which appeared in Philadelphia; and in 1813 and the following year, employed himself as editor of the "Analectic Magazine," published in the same city; making the experiment of his talent for a vocation to which men of decided literary tastes in this country are strongly inclined to betake themselves. Those who remember this magazine cannot have forgotten that it was a most entertaining miscellany, partly compiled from English publications, mostly periodicals, and partly made up of contributions of some of our own best writers. Paulding wrote for it a series of biographical accounts of the naval commanders of the United States, which added greatly to its popularity; and Verplanck contributed memoirs of Commodore Stewart and General Scott, Barlow, the poet, and other distinguished Americans, which were received with favor. The Life of Campbell, with the exception perhaps of some less important contributions to the magazine, is the only published work of Irving between the appearance of the "History of New York," in 1809, and that of the "Sketch Book," in 1819.

It was during this interval that an event took place which had a marked influence on Irving's future life, affected the character of his writings, and, now that the death of both parties allow it to be spoken of without reserve, gives a peculiar interest to his personal history. He became attached to a young lady whom he was to have married. She died unwedded, in the flower of her age; there was a sorrowful leave-taking between her and her lover, as the grave was about to separate them on the eve of what should have been her bridal; and Irving, ever after, to the close of his life, tenderly and faithfully cherished her memory. In one of the biographical notices published immediately after Irving's death, an old, well-worn copy of the Bible is spoken of, which was kept lying on the table in his chamber, within reach of his bedside, bearing her name on the title page in a delicate female hand—a relic which we may presume to have been his constant companion. Those who are fond of searching, in the biographies of eminent men, for the circumstances which determined the bent of their genius, find in this sad event, and the cloud it threw over the hopeful and cheerful period of early manhood, an explanation of the transition from the unbounded playfulness of the "History of New York" to the serious, tender and meditative vein of the "Sketch Book."

In 1815, soon after our second peace with Great Britain, Irving sailed again for Europe, and fixed himself at Liverpool, where a branch of the large commercial house to which he belonged was established. His old love of rambling returned upon him; he wandered first into Wales, and over some of the finest counties of England, and then northward to the sterner region of the Scottish Highlands. His memoir of Campbell had procured him the acquaintance and friendship of that poet. Campbell gave him, more than a year after his arrival in England, a letter of introduction to Scott, who, already acquainted with him by his writings, welcomed him warmly to Abbotsford, and made him his friend for life. Scott sent a special message to Campbell, thanking him for having made him known to Irving. "He is one of the best and pleasantest acquaintances," said Scott, "that I have made this many a day."

In the same year that he visited Abbotsford his brothers failed. The changes which followed the peace of 1815, swept away their fortunes and his together, and he was now to begin the world anew.

In 1819, he began to publish the Sketch Book. It was written in England and sent over to New York, where it was issued by Van Winkle, in octavo numbers, containing from seventy to a hundred pages. In the preface he remarked that he was "unsettled in his abode," that he had "his cares and vicissitudes," and could not, therefore, give these papers the "tranquil attention necessary to finished composition." Several of them were copied with praise in the London "Literary Gazette," and an intimation was conveyed to the author, that some person in London was about to publish them entire. He preferred to do this himself, and accordingly offered the work to the famous bookseller, Murray. Murray was slow in giving the matter his attention, and Irving, after a reasonable delay, wrote to ask that the copy which he had left with him might be returned. It was sent back with a note, pleading excess of occupation, the great cross of all eminent booksellers, and alleging the "want of scope in the nature of the work," as a reason for declining it. This was discouraging, but Irving had the enterprise to print the first volume in London, at his own risk. It was issued by John Miller and was well received, but in a month afterward the publisher failed. Immediately Sir Walter Scott came to London and saw Murray, who allowed himself to be persuaded, the more easily, doubtless, on account of the partial success of the first volume, that the work had more "scope" than he supposed, and purchased the copyright of both volumes for two hundred pounds, which he afterward liberally raised to four hundred.

Whoever compares the Sketch Book with the History of New York might at first, perhaps, fail to recognize it as the work of the same hand, so much graver and more thoughtful is the strain in which it is written. A more attentive examination, however, shows that the humor in the lighter parts is of the same peculiar and original cast, wholly unlike that of any author who ever wrote, a humor which Mr. Dana happily characterized as "a fanciful playing with common things and here and there beautiful touches, till the ludicrous becomes half picturesque." Yet one cannot help perceiving that the author's spirit had been sobered since he last appeared before the public, as if the shadow of a great sorrow had fallen upon it. The greater number of the papers are addressed to our deeper sympathies, and some of them, as, for example, the Broken Heart, the Widow and Her Son, and Rural Funerals, dwell upon the saddest themes. Only in two of them—Rip Van Winkle and the Legend of Sleepy Hollow—does he lay the reins loose on the neck of his frolicsome fancy, and allow it to dash forward without restraint; and these rank among the most delightful and popular tales ever written. In our country they have been read, I believe, by nearly everybody who can read at all.

The "Sketch Book," and the two succeeding works of Irving, "Bracebridge Hall" and the "Tales of a Traveller," abound with agreeable pictures of English life, seen under favorable lights and sketched with a friendly pencil. Let me say here, that it was not to pay court to the English that he thus described them and their country; it was because he could not describe them otherwise. It was the instinct of his mind to attach itself to the contemplation of the good and the beautiful, wherever he found them, and to turn away from the sight of what was evil, misshapen and hateful. His was not a nature to pry for faults, or disabuse the world of good-natured mistakes; he looked for virtue, love and truth among men, and thanked God that he found them in such large measure. If there are touches of satire in his writings, he is the best-natured and most amiable of satirists, amiable beyond Horace; and in his irony—for there is a vein of playful irony running through many of his works—there is no tinge of bitterness.

I rejoice, for my part, that we have had such a writer as Irving to bridge over the chasm between the two great nations—that an illustrious American lived so long in England, and was so much beloved there, and sought so earnestly to bring the people of the two countries to a better understanding with each other, and to wean them from the animosities of narrow minds. I am sure that there is not a large-minded and large-hearted man in all our country who can read over the "Sketch Book" and the other writings of Irving, and disown one of the magnanimous sentiments they express with regard to England, or desire to abate the glow of one of his warm and cheerful pictures of English life. Occasions will arise, no doubt, for saying some things in a less accommodating spirit, and there are men enough on both sides of the Atlantic who can say them; but Irving was not sent into the world on that errand. A different work was assigned him in the very structure of his mind, and the endowments of his heart—a work of peace and brotherhood, and I will say for him that he nobly performed it.

Let me pause here to speak of what I believe to have been the influence of the "Sketch Book" upon American literature. At the time it appeared the periodical lists of new American publications were extremely meagre, and consisted, to a great extent, of occasional pamphlets and dissertations on the questions of the day. The works of greater pretension were, for the most part, crudely and languidly made up, and destined to be little read. A work like the "Sketch Book," welcomed on both sides of the Atlantic, showed the possibility of an American author acquiring a fame bounded only by the limits of his own language, and gave an example of the qualities by which it might be won. Within two years afterward we had Cooper's "Spy" and Dana's "Idle Man;" the press of our country began, by degrees, to teem with works composed with a literary skill and a spirited activity of intellect until then little known among us. Every year the assertion that we had no literature of our own became less and less true: and now, when we look over a list of new works by native authors, we find, with an astonishment amounting almost to alarm, that the most voracious devourer of books must despair of being able to read half those which make a fair claim upon his attention. It was since 1819 that the great historians of our country, whose praise is in the mouths of all the nations, began to write. One of them built up the fabric of his fame long after Irving appeared as an author, and slept with Herodotus two years before Irving's death; another of the band lives yet to be the ornament of the association before which I am called to speak, and is framing the annals of his country into a work for future ages. Within that period has arisen among us the class who hold vast multitudes spell-bound in motionless attention by public discourses, the most perfect of their kind, such as make the fame of Everett. Within that period our theologians have learned to write with the elegance and vivacity of the essayists. We had but one novelist before the era of the "Sketch Book;" their number is now beyond enumeration by any but a professed catalogue-maker, and many of them are read in every cultivated form of human speech. Those whom we acknowledge as our poets—one of whom is the special favorite of our brothers in language who dwell beyond sea—appeared in the world of letters and won its attention after Irving had become famous. We have wits, and humorists, and amusing essay-ists, authors of some of the airiest and most graceful compositions of the present century, and we owe them to the new impulse given to our literature in 1819. I look abroad on these stars of our literary fir-mament—some crowded together with their minute points of light in a galaxy—some standing apart in glorious constellations; I recognize Arcturus, and Orion, and Perseus, and the glittering jewels of the Southern Crown, and the Pleiades shedding sweet influences; but the Evening Star, the soft and serene light that glowed in their van, the precursor of them all, has sunk below the horizon. The spheres, meantime, perform their appointed courses; the same motion which lifted them up to the mid-sky bears them onward to their setting; and they, too, like their bright leader, must soon be carried by it below the earth.

From "Memoranda"

BY EVERT A. DUYCKINCK

This selection on the older Irving is from "Memoranda of the Literary Career of Washington Irving,*" a respectful survey of Irving's life and works, prepared by Evert A. Duyckinck (1816–1878), then a significant figure on the Knickerbocker scene as editor, literary critic, and patron of the arts and artists. The whole was the opening piece in *Irvingiana: A Memorial of Washington Irving,* an illustrated volume published in New York in 1860 by Charles B. Richardson. This was a compendium of thirty-one items, some journalism, some personal reminiscence, some contemporary scholarship. As Duyckinck's footnote indicates, some of his own pages appeared earlier in *The Cyclopedia of American Literature* (1855), edited by himself and his brother George L. Duyckinck (1823–1863), with whom in 1845–1853 he had also edited the important periodical *The Literary World.*

* A portion of this paper is made up from a previous sketch, published in "The Cyclopedia of American Literature."

His retirement at Sunnyside was all that his youthful fancy painted, and more than experience of the world could have promised. His age was not exempt from infirmities; but it was spared many of the sufferings common to mortality. And when he came to die, his soul passed to heaven the nearest way. His death, on the night of November 28, 1859, when he had just retired from his cheerful family circle, was instantaneous.

We now return to the concluding literary labor of the life we have thus traced to its close.

The preface to the first volume of the *Washington* bears date 1855. Two volumes were published in that year; a third in the following; a fourth in 1857; the fifth, and concluding portion, in 1859. It was the completion of a work to which, in his own words prefixed to the last volume, "the author had long looked forward as the crowning effort of his literary career." Continuing this retrospect, Mr. Irving relates that "the idea of writing a life of Washington entered at an early day into his mind. It was especially pressed upon his attention nearly thirty years ago, while he was in Europe, by a proposition of the late Mr. Archibald Constable, the eminent publisher of Edinburgh, and he resolved to undertake it as soon as he should return to the United States, and be within reach of the necessary documents." The purpose was never lost sight of, though the work was postponed. If there was any expiation due the delay, the author paid the penalty in the increasing difficulty of the theme. Thirty years ago less would have been demanded by the public in the performance of such a work. A thoroughly scientific school of historians had sprung up in the interval. The collection of facts by the historical societies and other agencies imposed new exactions in the weighing of evidence. Each addition to the vast Washington library brought additional care and responsibility. Researches of this nature may, indeed, be benefited by the judgment of age; but the labor would seem to require the strength and enthusiasm of youth.

The writer, no doubt, found the undertaking a very different one from that which presented itself to his mind, on his first conception of the idea in the presence of Mr. Constable. There were sterner requisitions, as we have said, to be met; and there was also a spectre of his own raising to be encountered, the shadow of his fame. But, whatever the struggle, it was manfully borne by the author, who sacrificed well-earned ease and leisure, with no other stimulus than the sense of duty, and with which we may associate the impulse of genius, performing a great part, if not the whole, of his allotted work after he had attained the age of threescore and ten. There are few more cheering instances of literary activity in the whole history of authorship. We have frequently thought, as our eye rested on the narrative, that the author needed all the encouragement to be derived from the conscientiousness and sense of duty of his great subject. There stood above the page the awful shade of Washington, with warning finger pointing the way his historian should follow. The monition was not unheeded. The history is such a one as Washington himself, were he privileged or condemned to revisit the scene of his earthly cares and anxieties, the country which he loved, the people for whom he gravely toiled, would, we think, calmly approve of.

The qualities of Washington in the book are its simple, straightforward manner; its dignity and reserve, associated with care and candor, its paramount truthfulness. It is scarcely possible that a work of the kind could be written with greater absence of display or personal pretension on the part of the writer. The labor of rejection must have been great, where the material was overwhelming. The forbearance and self-denial, the avoidance of the sin of surplusage, can be fully estimated only by one who has made the prevalent characteristics and vices of the literature of the day a study. There are eloquent, profound, learned works in abundance; but a well-written book is a great rarity. We are not aware that Mr. Irving goes out of his way to make a point, indulge in an unnecessary digression, or yield, in a single instance, to the temptation to description, which last must, at times, have sorely beset his pen. He never stops in his steady movement to attitudinize, to strike a position, arouse the attention of his reader with "Here we are!" like the mountebank in the ring, or violate in any manner the sober pace of history. Great men come and depart noiselessly on the plain republican stage, trumpeted by no rhetorical blare of adjectives; their acts only betray their presence. There are no set attempts, no efforts for effect. A half reflection inwrought with the progress of the sentence, a single epithet does all —and the whole is any thing but a barren recital. It is the charm of the writings of Washington himself, where we are impressed by the truthfulness and pleased by a certain native gracefulness—a plain thing like the clown's mistress, but his own. Little, winning idiomatic touches frequently appear in the composition; but it has also the higher merit of dramatic unity and steady progress. Washington is the central personage, never far distant, always inspiring and directing the scene: he appears firmly planted amidst the historical elements of his people and country.

Mr. Irving always received handsome sums for his copyrights. In 1850 it began to be doubted in England whether the copyright of a book by an American or alien could be held by a British publisher, and Irving's works were boldly taken from Murray, and issued in cheap editions by Bohn & Routledge. The legal question was carried into the Court of Chancery, and the plea was at least meditated by Mr. Murray, that Mr. Irving was not an alien, his father being a native of the Orkneys, and his mother of Falmouth. The absurdity of this pretence to citizenship—with which, of course, Mr. Irving had nothing to do—in behalf of an American who had held military rank in a war with Great Britain, was at once apparent. What stood in the way, it was asked, if he were a British subject, of taking him from Westminster Hall, as a rebel, to a court-martial, and ordering him to be shot!

A more pertinent plea was Mr. Murray's long previous undisputed enjoyment of the copyrights, and a statement of the sums he had paid for them. As given in the *London Athenæum of* August 24, 1850, they were as follows:

Sketch Book	£467	10*s.*
Bracebridge Hall	1,050	0
Tales of a Traveller	1,575	0
Life of Columbus	3,150	0
Companions of Columbus	525	0
Conquest of Granada	2,100	0
Tour on the Prairies	400	0
Abbotsford and Newstead	400	0
Legends of Spain	100	0
footing up the respectable sum of	9,767	10

Mr. Bentley also published a statement of the sums paid by him to Irving, in conjunction with his partner, Colburn. They were, for the copyright of the *Alhambra,* £1,050; for *Astoria,* £500; for *Captain Bonneville's Adventures,* £900.

Nor were his copyrights of late less remunerative in America. In a recent statement it is said, that within the last ten years—the period of the revised edition of his works—there have been sold twenty-two thousand sets of fifteen volumes each, exclusive of the *Life of Washington,* and *The Sketch Book;* while of the latter thirty-five thousand copies have been distributed, and of the *Washington* forty-two thousand sets of five volumes each—a total of five hundred and seventy-five thousand volumes disposed of by Mr. George P. Putnam, the publisher of the works since 1849. These various editions, it is said, have paid to the author seventy-five thousand dollars. They owe much to the good taste of the publisher, especially in the illustrated series.

Mr. Allibone, who, in his "Critical Dictionary" has infused a loving spirit into his comprehensive bibliographical details of the writings of Irving, pays a just tribute to his publisher, Mr. Putnam, —"a gentleman who, by his extensive circulation of sound literature for many years both in Europe and America, has honestly earned the title of a benefactor to the public mind." A letter from Mr. Irving to Mr. Putnam, expresses a still more intimate and cordial sentiment. "I take pleasure," he writes, "in expressing the great satisfaction I have derived throughout all our intercourse, from your amiable, obliging, and honorable conduct. Indeed, I never had dealings with any man, whether in the way of business or friendship, more perfectly free from any alloy."

Mr. Irving was throughout life fortunate in his friendships with artists, who were attracted by the man, no less than his picturesque books, for subjects for their pencil. His friend, the Academician Leslie, who had much in common with his genius, designed for Murray a series of ten plates to illustrate *The Sketch Book,* and *Knickerbocker's History of New York,* which were engraved by the best artists of the day. He also introduced a portrait of his friend in his Roger de Coverly picture. Allston, likewise, made illustrations for the *Knickerbocker.* Heath, the engraver, drew a humorous design of the march of the great Amsterdam army to the attack of Fort Casimir, from the original of which, preserved at Sunnyside, an engraving was published by Mr. Putnam. He also engraved a choice series of Illustrations of the *Sketch Book,* from designs by Westall. George Cruikshank also made several capital pictures for an edition of *Knickerbocker,* published in the "Family Library," and also quite a number of very felicitous designs, chiefly from *Salmagundi,* and the *Knicker-bocker,* which appeared in an elegant little volume, by Tegg, of London, entitled *The Beauties of Washington Irving.* Of the American designs, by Mr. Darley, much might be said, particularly of the two series of "Sleepy Hollow," and "Rip Van Winkle," issued by the American Art Union. They seize with a firm grasp, and an individuality of their own, the stronger and deeper elements of Mr. Irving's pathos and humor. They are full of grace and feeling, and are something more than interpreters of the author,—they are revelations of the artist's own mind.

Washington Irving was so lucky in his choice of subjects, and treated them so happily, that his name and fame are associated with some of the most enduring objects of interest about the world. At Stratford-upon-Avon, the traveller, sitting down at the cheerful fireside of mine host of the "Red Lion," may, if he will, wield "the sceptre of Geoffrey Crayon;" when the traditional poker with which that pleasant tourist stirred the fire, bearing that identical inscription, is put into his hands, with a well-thumbed copy of the *Sketch-Book,* in which it is all written down, as voucher. The incident happened to ourself, and we presume the custom will be perpetuated to a late posterity, with the memories of the "Red Lion Inn"—for inns in England have a long life. Next to the birthplace of Shakspeare, the fancy of the world nestles in the quaint galleries, pillared courts, and carved recesses of the Alhambra—the deserted home of a fallen race, dear to the imagination in a land of poetry. Washington Irving is firmly installed in the traditions of the place, and will doubtless, in time, become a myth, with King Chico and the rest. A traveller who recently visited the Alhambra was immediately taken possession of, upon his arrival at Granada, by a youth of the town, who produced his plenipotentiary powers over English-speaking strangers in the card [used as the illustration on page 71—*Ed.*]

The Irving traditions were rife in his mind. He pointed out Geoffrey Crayon's apartments, and narrated how he was accustomed to pass his evenings with Mateo, Tia Antonio, and Dolores, exciting their powers of story-telling, listening to their recitals, and reviving their flagging memory or invention by a good supper when the night wore on. It was pleasant to hear how good Geoffrey had given a marriage portion to that "little, plump, black-eyed Andalusian damsel Dolores."

Our traveller visited Mateo, of course, and found him a quiet, slow, soft-spoken, good-looking old man, such as his beneficent guest would be inclined to cotton to. He saw, in fact, Washington Irving firmly rooted in the pockets and affections of the tribe, a sort of family estate or heirloom handed down from father to son.

If these are slight, though agreeable incidents to travellers, home-keepers are not forgetful of these haunts of the imagination. They, too, remember what they owe to Irving; and they have other claims upon their sympathy in the biographies of Goldsmith, of Columbus, and Washington. It is something to be associated with these names, and leave behind all baser matter.

We might linger, too, upon the nationality of Irving's descriptions of American nature; of the fortunate turn his mind took to the great western regions of the American continent before they were invaded by the advancing pioneers of civilization: we might say much of the fancy and humor with which he has invested his native island and city: and no reader of his writings can forget his love of the noble river which flowed by his doorway, which had tempted his youthful imagination with its magic wonders—which had been fondly remembered by him in distant lands as he traced it in description—which was the solace of his age, and glowed, deeply dyed in the rays of the setting sun at his burial. "I thank God," he wrote in his later years, "that I was born on the banks of the Hudson. I fancy I can trace much of what is good and pleasant in my own heterogeneous compound to my early companionship with this glorious river. In the warmth of youthful enthusiasm. I used to clothe it with moral attributes, and, as it were, give it a soul. I delighted in its frank, bold, honest character; its noble sincerity, and perfect truth. Here was no specious, smiling surface, covering the shifting sandbar and perfidious rock, but a stream deep as it was broad, and bearing with honorable faith the bark that trusted to its waves. I gloried in its simple, quiet, majestic, epic flow, ever straight forward, or, if forced aside for once by opposing mountains, struggling bravely through them, and resuming its onward march. Behold, thought I, an emblem of a good man's course through life, ever simple, open, and direct; or if, overpowered by adverse circumstances, he deviate into error, it is but momentary—he soon resumes his onward and honorable career, and continues it to the end of his pilgrimage."

The finest description, perhaps, of the American climate ever written is from the pen of Irving. It occurs in an out-of-the-way sketch of the Catskills in the *Book of the Picturesque,* published a few years ago. "Here let me say a word in favor of those vicissitudes which are too often made the subject of exclusive repining. If they annoy us occasionally by changes from hot to cold, from wet to dry, they give us one of the most beautiful climates in the world. They give us the brilliant sunshine of the south of Europe with the fresh verdure of the north. They float our summer sky with clouds of gorgeous tints or fleecy whiteness, and send down cooling showers to refresh the panting earth and keep it green. Our seasons are all poetical; the phenomena of our heavens are full of sublimity and beauty. Winter with us has none of its proverbial gloom. It may have its howling winds, and thrilling frosts, and whirling snow-storms; but it has also its long intervals of cloudless sunshine, when the snow-clad earth gives redoubled brightness to the day; when at night the stars beam with intensest lustre, or the moon floods the whole landscape with her most limpid radiance—and then the joyous outbreak of our spring, bursting at once into leaf and blossom, redundant with vegetation, and vociferous with life!—and the splendors of our summer; its morning voluptuousness and evening glory; its airy palaces of sun-gilt clouds piled up in a deep azure sky; and its gusts of tempest of almost tropical grandeur, when the forked lightning and the bellowing thunder volley from the battlements of heaven and shake the sultry atmosphere—and the sublime melancholy of our autumn, magnificent in its decay, withering down the pomp and pride of a woodland country, yet reflecting back from its yellow forests the golden serenity of the sky—surely we may say that in our climate 'the heavens declare the glory of God, and the firmament showeth forth his handywork: day unto day uttereth speech; and night unto night showeth knowledge.' "

In estimating the genius of Irving, we can hardly attach too high a value to the refined qualities and genial humor which have made his writings favorites wherever the English language is read. The charm is in the proportion, the keeping, the happy vein which inspires happiness in return. It is the felicity of but few authors, out of the vast stock of English literature, to delight equally young and old. The tales of Irving are the favorite authors of childhood, and their good humor and amenity can please where most literature is weariness, in the sick-room of the convalescent. Every influence which breathes from these writings is good and generous. Their sentiment is always just and manly, without cant or affection; their humor is always within the bounds of propriety. They have a fresh inspiration of American nature, which is not the less nature for the art with which it is adorned. The color of personality attaches us throughout to the author, whose humor of character is always to be felt. This happy art of presenting rude and confused objects in an orderly pleasureable aspect, everywhere to be met with in the pages of Irving, is one of the most beneficent in literature. The philosopher Hume said a turn for humor was worth to him ten thousand a year, and it is this gift which the writings of Irving impart. To this quality is allied an active fancy and poetic imagination, many of the choicest passages of Irving being interpenetrated by this vivifying power. On one or two occasions only, we believe,—in some stanzas to the Passaic River, some delicate lines descriptive of a painting by Gilbert Stuart Newton, and a theatrical address once pronounced by Cooper at the Park Theatre, —has he ever put pen to verse: but he is an essential poet in prose, in many exquisite passages of vivid description from Westminster Abby and English rural scenery to the waste beauties of the great region beyond the Mississippi.

In composition, Mr. Irving's style flowed easily, though in common with most writers of original genius he had his favoring moods and seasons. Some of his best works were struck off at a heat. He took pleasure in writing when he could have his own way, and nurse a subject in his mind. The many hours passed at his desk in the absorbing pursuit of tracing his small, neat manuscript pages, were among his happiest. His principles of composition were few and simple. He recommended short and direct phrases, in writing, with as few long words as possible, avoiding the use of conjunctions and expletives. On looking over his books we find that he is much less indebted to the Latin element of the language, for the flow of his composition, than we had supposed. He would, doubtless, have concurred with the advice of Sydney Smith to a young author, to improve his style by striking out every other word.

He attributed his ease in writing, we have heard it stated, to the early training which he received at his first school, where this branch of education was much insisted upon. He would write out the compositions of many of his school-fellows, and adapt his style to that of the one whose task he had undertaken. This is the remark of one who knew him well. But whatever direction may thus have been given to his powers, we suspect that, as in the case of Oliver Goldsmith, a happy instinct was his chief guide, and that he found his way to his place in English literature, with but little aid from schoolmasters or preceptors. Good British authors were his professors; his college was the library where the learned doctors were the wits of Queen Anne and such kindly instructors as Sterne, Johnson, and above all, Goldsmith; but his university was the world.

"He read much as a boy," remarks our narrator, "and always had entertaining books in his desk for a stealthy perusal, when the master's eye was turned. He was not a very deep classical scholar, not having received a collegiate education, but his deficiencies in this respect were amply compensated by his thorough ease in the use of plain, terse English, in which he was excelled by none. In reading, his memory of facts was not good, but he would grasp the spirit of a narrative, and conjure up a coloring of his own, which indelibly impressed it upon his mind, and was used as occasion required."*

We have said that the university of Irving was the world. He was never a very bookish man in the restricted sense; he was oftener to be found in good company than in the library, in the fields and streets than in the study; yet he was not a man of action in crowds. His life was a happy compromise between literature and society. A meditative disposition threw him upon himself; he was not cramped by pedantry, nor was his mind volatilized or lost in the dissipations or business of the world.

It was early remarked by one of the most subtle and powerful critics whom America has produced, Mr. Dana, the author of that more deeply-graven "Sketch Book," *The Idle Man,* that "Irving's wit and humor do not appear to come of reading witty and humorous books; but from the world acting upon a mind of that cast, and putting those powers in motion."†

We have now concluded our brief sketch of the literary career of Washington Irving. It would be an injustice to his memory, and a reproach to ourselves, not to say a word of those sterling moral qualities which were the secret springs nurturing, in the image of Jeremy Taylor, the "fair spreading tree" of his reputation in his books. He

*MS. Notes by Mr. J. Carson Brevoort.
†North American Review for 1819. Article—"The Sketch Book."

was intimately and essentially, in small things and in great, an honest, honorable man. His judgment was sound, and his course always straightforward; so that he attained success without craft or chicanery, which were entirely foreign to his nature. A modest simplicity guided him in every thing. A beneficent deity had given him neither poverty nor riches, and had removed far from him vanity and lies. He had none of the frequent affections of literature. He valued reputation, but he was never seen stumbling in the awkward pursuit of praise. It came to him through life, and in abundant measure in age, when it was most welcome to cheer drooping spirits, and clothe with a warm mantle of charity and affection, the chill, declining years.

"Nothing amazed him," writes Mr. Brevoort to us, "so much as to be lionized, or made the centre of a group of listeners. To hear him talk, and to draw him out, it was necessary to have but few present. He preferred the society of such as had some refinement of taste; not humorous or witty, but with a disposition to take the pleasant side of any question; neither boisterous nor satirical. He never said any thing for effect, nor with a view to its being repeated or recorded. His remarks would drop from him as naturally as possible, and he never monopolized the conversation, but followed, instead of leading it."

His chief guides were his tastes and affections, with which his principles of duty and religion, his love of independence, and his patriotism, were inwrought. Let his pastor, and the villagers and children of his neighborhood, as on the day of his funeral, that memorable first of December, when nature seemed to sympathize with his departure from earth, bear witness to his unaffected piety.

From "Nil Nisi Bonum"

BY WILLIAM MAKEPEACE THACKERAY

Using a traditional Latin idiom for the title, this affectionate memoir of his American friend was included by William Makepeace Thackeray (1811–1863) in the first number of *Cornhill Magazine,* which the English novelist began to edit in 1860. Early in his text, it is clear he will be pairing remembrance of Washington Irving with that of Thomas Babington Macaulay, also recently deceased, but those latter remarks do not concern us here. Thackeray, already by 1860 author of all his major works, had renewed old acquaintance with Irving, at "Sunnyside," on a first trip to the United States in 1852. The tongue-in-cheek description of that "pretty little cabin," etc., is balanced by the felicitous sentence (p. 30, ll. 11–12), much repeated since, about the American's ambassadorial uniqueness.

Almost the last words which Sir Walter [Scott] spoke to Lockhart, his biographer, were, "Be a good man, my dear!" and with the last flicker of breath on his dying lips, he sighed a farewell to his family, and passed away blessing them.

Two men, famous, admired, beloved, have just left us, the Goldsmith and the Gibbon of our time.* Ere a few weeks are over, many a critic's pen will be at work, reviewing their lives, and passing judgment on their works. This is no review, or history, or criticism: only a word in testimony of respect and regard from a man of letters, who owes to his own professional labour the honour of becoming acquainted with these two eminent literary men. One was the first ambassador whom the New World of Letters sent to the Old. He was born almost with the republic; the *pater patriæ* had laid his hand on the child's head. He bore Washington's name: he came amongst us bringing the kindest sympathy, the most artless, smiling goodwill. His new country (which some people here might be disposed to regard rather superciliously) could send us, as he showed in his own person, a gentleman, who, though himself born in no very high sphere, was most finished, polished, easy, witty, quiet; and, socially, the equal of the most refined Europeans. If Irving's welcome in England was a kind one, was it not also gratefully remembered? If he ate our salt, did he not pay us with a thankful heart? Who can calculate the amount of friendliness and good feeling for our country which this writer's generous and untiring regard for us disseminated in his own? His books are read by millions† of his countrymen, whom he has taught to love England, and why to love her? It would have been easy to speak otherwise than he did: to inflame national rancours, which, at the time when he first became known as a public writer, war had just renewed: to cry down the old civilization at the expense of the new: to point out our faults, arrogance, short-comings, and give the republic to infer how much she was the parent state's superior. There are writers enough in the United States, honest and otherwise, who preach that kind of doctrine. But the good Irving, the peaceful, the friendly, had no place for bitterness in his heart, and no scheme but kindness. Received in England with extraordinary ten-

---

*Washington Irving died, November 28, 1859; Lord Macaulay died, December 28, 1859.

†See his *Life* in the most remarkable *Dictionary of Authors,* published lately at Philadelphia, by Mr. Alibone.

derness and friendship (Scott, Southey, Byron, a hundred others have borne witness to their liking for him), he was a messenger of goodwill and peace between his country and ours. "See, friends!" he seems to say, "these English are not so wicked, rapacious, callous, proud, as you have been taught to believe them. I went amongst them a humble man; won my way by my pen; and, when known, found every hand held out to me with kindliness and welcome. Scott is a great man, you acknowledge. Did not Scott's King of England give a gold medal to him, and another to me, your countryman, and a stranger?"

Tradition in the United States still fondly retains the history of the feasts and rejoicings which awaited Irving on his return to his native country from Europe. He had a national welcome; he stammered in his speeches, hid himself in confusion, and the people loved him all the better. He had worthily represented America in Europe. In that young community a man who brings home with him abundant European testimonials is still treated with respect (I have found American writers, of wide-world reputation, strangely solicitous about the opinions of quite obscure British critics, and elated or depressed by their judgments); and Irving went home medalled by the King, diplomatized by the University, crowned and honoured and admired. He had not in any way intrigued for his honours, he had fairly won them; and, in Irving's instance, as in others, the old country was glad and eager to pay them.

In America the love and regard for Irving was a national sentiment. Party wars are perpetually raging there, and are carried on by the press with a rancour and fierceness against individuals which exceed British, almost Irish, virulence. It seemed to me, during a year's travel in the country, as if no one ever aimed a blow at Irving. All men held their hand from that harmless, friendly peacemaker. I had the good fortune to see him at New York, Philadelphia, Baltimore, and Washington,* and remarked how in every place he was honoured and welcome. Every large city has its "Irving House." The country takes pride in the fame of its men of letters. The gate of his own charming little domain on the beautiful Hudson River was for

---

*At Washington, Mr. Irving came to a lecture given by the writer, which Mr. Filmore and General Pierce, the President and President Elect, were also kind enough to attend together. "Two Kings of Brentford smelling at one rose," says Irving, looking up with his good-humoured smile.

ever swinging before visitors who came to him. He shut out no one.†
I had seen many pictures of his house, and read descriptions of it, in
both of which it was treated with a not unusual American exaggeration. It was but a pretty little cabin of a place; the gentleman of the
press who took notes of the place, whilst his kind old host was sleeping, might have visited the whole house in a couple of minutes.

And how came it that this house was so small, when Mr. Irving's books were sold by hundreds of thousands nay, millions, when
his profits were known to be large, and the habits of life of the good
old bachelor were notoriously modest and simple? He had loved once
in his life. The lady he loved died; and he, whom all the world loved,
never sought to replace her. I can't say how much the thought of that
fidelity has touched me. Does not the very cheerfulness of his afterlife add to the pathos of that untold story? To grieve always was not
in his nature; or, when he had his sorrow, to bring all the world in to
condole with him and bemoan it. Deep and quiet he lays the love of
his heart, and buries it; and grass and flowers grow over the scarred
ground in due time.

Irving had such a small house and such narrow rooms, because
there was a great number of people to occupy them. He could only
afford to keep one old horse (which, lazy and aged as it was, managed once or twice to run away with that careless old horseman). He
could only afford to give plain sherry to that amiable British paragraphmonger from New York, who saw the patriarch asleep over his
modest, blameless cup, and fetched the public into his private chamber to look at him. Irving could only live very modestly, because the
wifeless, childless man had a number of children to whom he was as
a father. He had as many as nine nieces, I am told—I saw two of
these ladies at his house—with all of whom the dear old man had
shared the produce of his labour and genius.

†Mr. Irving described to me, with that humour and good humour which
he always kept, how, amongst other visitors, a member of the British press
who had carried his distinguished pen to America (where he employed it in
vilifying his own country) came to Sunnyside, introduced himself to Irving,
partook of his wine and luncheon, and in two days described Mr. Irving, his
house, his nieces, his meal, and his manner of dozing afterwards, in a New
York paper. On another occasion, Irving said, laughing, "Two persons came
to me, and one held me in conversation whilst the other miscreant took my
portrait!"

"Be a good man, my dear." One can't but think of these last words of the veteran Chief of Letters, who had tasted and tested the value of worldly success, admiration, prosperity. Was Irving not good, and, of his works, was not his life the best part? In his family, gentle, generous, good-humoured, affectionate, self-denying: in society, a delightful example of complete gentlemanhood; quite unspoiled by prosperity; never obsequious to the great (or, worse still, to the base and mean, as some public men are forced to be in his and other countries); eager to acknowledge every contemporary's merit; always kind and affable to the young members of his calling: in his professional bargains and mercantile dealings delicately honest and grateful; one of the most charming masters of our lighter language; the constant friend to us and our nation; to men of letters doubly dear, not for his wit and genius merely, but as an exemplar of goodness, probity, and pure life:—I don't know what sort of testimonial will be raised to him in his own country, where generous and enthusiastic acknowledgment of American merit is never wanting: but Irving was in our service as well as theirs; and as they have placed a stone at Greenwich yonder in memory of that gallant young Bellot, who shared the perils and fate of some of our Arctic seamen, I would like to hear of some memorial raised by English writers and friends of letters in affectionate remembrance of the dear and good Washington Irving.

"Preface" and
"Literary Statistics"

BY PIERRE MUNRO IRVING

Pierre Munro Irving (1803–1876) was the son of Washington Irving's older brother William and Julia Paulding Irving, sister of the novelist James Kirke Paulding. One of Washington's writing nephews, Pierre Munro was closest to his beloved uncle, even present at his death at Sunnyside. He served him, at one time or another, as research assistant, personal attorney and business agent, and finally as designated literary executor. Immediately following his uncle's death, Pierre set to work to create a substantial biography which, as it turned out, found its subject mid-Victorian brick and affectionately alchemized it into togaed marble. *The Life and Letters of Washington Irving,* published first in four volumes (1862–1864), and revised in 1869, was thereafter frequently reprinted as part of sets of the complete works. In 1883 an extra-illustrated, limited Memorial Edition appeared. The first excerpt printed here is the Preface to Volume I (1862). The second, Appendix C, "Literary Statistics," Volume IV (1864), on actual income, was not carried over to Pierre's 1869 revision.

The work, of which I now offer the first volume to the public with the most unfeigned diffidence, has been mainly compiled from papers committed to me by Mr. Irving, with the understanding that I was to construct a biography from them, should it be my fate to survive him. "Somebody will be writing my life when I am gone," said he to me some years before his death, and after having resisted repeated applications for an autobiography, "and I wish you to do it. You must promise me that you will."

Though deeply sensible of the confidence implied in such a request, my first impulse was to decline an office so responsible, and for which I felt myself so little qualified; but the request was repeated with an earnestness which showed the subject had seriously engaged his thoughts, and with the assurance that he would be able to place in my keeping materials which he would only confide to a relative, and which would of themselves go far to furnish a picture of his life from his first launch in the world. I yielded my scruples to this assurance; and not long after, he placed in my possession a mass of material, consisting of journals, note-books, diaries at scattered intervals, and a large collection of family letters with files of others from various correspondents, which, as he said, he had neither time nor spirit to examine or arrange. He afterwards procured for me his numerous letters to his friend, Henry Brevoort, which were furnished through the kindness of his son, Carson Brevoort, Esq.; and shortly before his death indicated to me others, both in this country and in Europe, which, if still in existence, might be of interest in a narrative of the shifting scenes of his life. Of these I have been able to obtain, since his death, the originals or copies of such as had been preserved; and to them have been added numerous letters, both of his early and later life, which have been contributed by various friends, to whom I here offer my acknowledgments.

In the delicate office of sifting, selecting, and arranging these different materials, extending through a period of nearly sixty years, it has been my aim to make the author, in every stage of his career, as far as possible, his own biographer, conscious that I shall in this way best fulfil the duty devolved upon me, and give to the world the truest picture of his life and character.

Sums realized by Mr. Irving for his
Copyrights in England.

Sketch Book,	Murray, Publisher,	£467	10s.
Bracebridge Hall,	"	1,050	00
Tales of a Traveller,	"	1,575	00
Life of Columbus,	"	3,150	00
Companions of Columbus,	"	525	00
Conquest of Granada,	"	2,100	00
Tour on the Prairies,	"	400	00
Abbotsford and Newstead,	"	400	00
Legends of Spain,	"	100	00
Alhambra,	Bentley, Publisher,	1,050	00
Astoria,	"	500	00
Bonneville's Adventures,	"	900	00
	Total,	£12,217	10s.

Sums realized in the United States, where there was no
absolute sale of the Copyright, as in England.

Life of Columbus, 1st edition,	$3,000 00
" " and Abridgment, 2d edition,	6,000 00
Conquest of Granada (for five years),	4,750 00
Companions of Columbus (3,000 copies),	1,500 00
Alhambra,	3,000 00
Tour on the Prairies,	2,400 00
Abbotsford and Newstead,	2,100 00
Legends of the Conquest of Spain,	1,500 00
Astoria,	4,000 00
Bonneville's Adventures,	3,000 00
Lease of Copyright, from 1828 to 1835, of Knickerbocker's New York, Sketch Book, Bracebridge Hall, and Tales of a Traveller,	4,200 00

Lease of Copyright of the same works, and Life of Columbus, Conquest of Granada, Companions of Columbus, and Alhambra, from 1835 to 1842,	8,050	00
Estimated receipts, prior to 1828, on History of New York, Sketch Book, Bracebridge Hall, and Tales of a Traveller,	19,500	00
Making a total on the American Copyrights of the above enumerated works, prior to 1843, of	$63,000	00

Hiatus from 1842 to 1848, in which the author's writings were out of print.

In the latter year, Mr. George P. Putnam became his Publisher.

Total of receipts from Mr. Putnam, from July, 1848, to Mr. Irving's decease, November 28, 1859, (besides stereotype and steel plates, amounting to about $17,000.)	$88,143	08
Payments made for Irving's Works by Mr. Putnam, from the author's decease to September 30, 1863, showing the continued demand,	34,237	03
	$122,380	11

Whole amount realized on his Works during his life,	$205,383	34
Since his death to September 30, 1863,	34,237	03
	$239,620	37

"In The Churchyard At Tarrytown"

BY HENRY WADSWORTH LONGFELLOW

By mid-nineteenth century Henry Wadsworth Longfellow (1807–1882) was acclaimed, here and abroad, as the American poet laureate. The following reverential poem would have been read in that light. It represented, too, a very personal tribute: for Longfellow, then a little-known academic traveling for professional enrichment, had first met and been befriended by Irving in Madrid in 1827. Shortly, the influence of the established author would be extended as well to Longfellow's prose pieces in the Irvingesque *Outre-Mer* (1833–1834). Exactly when the poet visited the Irving family plot in Tarrytown Cemetery is unclear, but the poem has been dated reliably 1876. It was first published in "A Book of Sonnets, Part Second" in *Kéramos and Other Poems* (1878).

In The Churchyard
At Tarrytown

Here lies the gentle humorist, who died
  In the bright Indian Summer of his
    fame!
  A simple stone, with but a date and
    name,
  Marks his secluded resting-place beside
The river that he loved and glorified.
  Here in the autumn of his days he came,
  But the dry leaves of life were all aflame
  With tints that brightened and were
    multiplied.
How sweet a life was his; how sweet a
    death!
  Living, to wing with mirth the weary
    hours,
  Or with romantic tales the heart to
    cheer;
Dying, to leave a memory like the breath
  Of summers full of sunshine and of
    showers,
  A grief and gladness in the atmosphere.

From "Last Years:

The Character of His Literature"

BY CHARLES D. WARNER

Charles Dudley Warner (1829–1900), an established figure in the decades of the Genteel Tradition, was a Massachusetts-born attorney who settled in Hartford, Connecticut. Also a busy editor, literary critic, and novelist, he is best remembered as collaborator of Mark Twain on *The Gilded Age* (1873). In 1892 he succeeded Howells in the "Editor's Easy Chair," etc., at *Harper's New Monthly Magazine,* and later became President of the National Academy of Arts and Letters. This selection is the body of Chapter X (some of which appeared earlier, in 1880, as Warner's contribution to the tripartite *Studies in Irving*), the final one in his *Washington Irving* (1881), a volume in the first American Men of Letters series, of which Warner was the general editor. The London *Literary World* reacted with, "It would hardly be possible to produce a fairer or more candid book of its kind."

I have outlined the life of Washington Irving in vain, if we have not already come to a tolerably clear conception of the character of the man and of his books. If I were exactly to follow his literary method I should do nothing more. The idiosyncrasies of the man are the strength and weakness of his works. I do not know any other author whose writings so perfectly reproduce his character, or whose character may be more certainly measured by his writings. His character is perfectly transparent: his predominant traits were humor and sentiment; his temperament was gay with a dash of melancholy; his inner life and his mental operations were the reverse of complex, and his literary method is simple. He *felt* his subject, and he expressed his conception not so much by direct statement or description as by almost imperceptible touches and shadings here and there, by a diffused tone and color, with very little show of analysis. Perhaps it is a sufficient definition to say that his method was the sympathetic. In the end the reader is put in possession of the luminous and complete idea upon which the author has been brooding, though he may not be able to say exactly how the impression has been conveyed to him; and I doubt if the author could have explained his sympathetic process. He certainly would have lacked precision in any philosophical or metaphysical theme, and when, in his letters, he touches upon politics there is a little vagueness of definition that indicates want of mental grip in that direction. But in the region of feeling his genius is sufficient to his purpose; either when that purpose is a highly creative one, as in the character and achievements of his Dutch heroes, or merely that of portraiture, as in the "Columbus" and the "Washington." The analysis of a nature so simple and a character so transparent as Irving's, who lived in the sunlight and had no envelope of mystery, has not the fascination that attaches to Hawthorne.

Although the direction of his work as a man of letters was largely determined by his early surroundings,—that is, by his birth in a land void of traditions, and into a society without much literary life, so that his intellectual food was of necessity a foreign literature that was at the moment becoming a little antiquated in the land of its birth, and his warm imagination was forced to revert to the past for that nourishment which his crude environment did not offer,—yet he was by nature a retrospective man. His face was set towards the past, not towards the future. He never caught the restlessness of this century, nor the prophetic light that shone in the faces of Coleridge, Shelley, and Keats; if he apprehended the stir of the new spirit he still, by mental affiliation, belonged rather to the age of Addison than to that of Macaulay. And his placid, retrospective, optimistic strain pleased a public that were excited and harrowed by the mocking and lamenting of Lord Byron, and singularly enough, pleased even the great pessimist himself.

His writings induce to reflection, to quiet musing, to tenderness for tradition; they amuse, they entertain, they call a check to the feverishness of modern life; but they are rarely stimulating or suggestive. They are better adapted, it must be owned, to please the many than the critical few, who demand more incisive treatment and a deeper consideration of the problems of life. And it is very fortunate that a writer who can reach the great public and entertain it can also elevate and refine its tastes, set before it high ideas, instruct it agreeably, and all this in a style that belongs to the best literature. It is a safe model for young readers; and for young readers there is very little in the overwhelming flood of to-day that is comparable to Irving's books, and, especially, it seems to me, because they were not written for children.

Irving's position in American literature, or in that of the English tongue, will only be determined by the slow settling of opinion, which no critic can foretell, and the operation of which no criticism seems able to explain. I venture to believe, however, that the verdict will not be in accord with much of the present prevalent criticism. The service that he rendered to American letters no critic disputes; nor is there any question of our national indebtedness to him for investing a crude and new land with the enduring charms of romance and tradition. In this respect, our obligation to him is that of Scotland to Scott and Burns; and it is an obligation due only, in all history, to here and there a fortunate creator to whose genius opportunity is kind. The Knickerbocker Legend and the romance with which Irving has invested the Hudson are a priceless legacy; and this would remain an imperishable possession in popular tradition if the literature creating it were destroyed. This sort of creation is unique in modern times. New York is the Knickerbocker city; its whole social life remains colored by his fiction; and the romantic background it owes to him in some measure supplies to it what great age has given to European cities. This creation is sufficient to secure for him an immortality, a length of earthly remembrance that all the rest of his writings together might not give.

Irving was always the literary man; he had the habits, the idiosyncrasies, of his small genus. I mean that he regarded life not from the philanthropic, the economic, the political, the philosophic, the metaphysic, the scientific, or the theologic, but purely from the literary point of view. He belongs to that small class of which Johnson and Goldsmith are perhaps as good types as any, and to which America has added very few. The literary point of view is taken by few in any generation; it may seem to the world of very little consequence in the pressure of all the complex interests of life, and it may even seem trivial amid the tremendous energies applied to immediate affairs; but it is the point of view that endures; if its creations do not mould human life, like the Roman law, they remain to charm and civilize, like the poems of Horace. You must not ask more of them than that. This attitude toward life is defensible on the highest grounds. A man with Irving's gifts has the right to take the position of an observer and describer, and not to be called on for a more active participation in affairs than he chooses to take. He is doing the world the highest service of which he is capable, and the most enduring it can receive from any man. It is not a question whether the work of the literary man is higher than that of the reformer or the statesman; it is a distinct work, and is justified by the result, even when the work is that of the humorist only. We recognize this in the case of the poet. Although Goethe has been reproached for his lack of sympathy with the liberalizing movement of his day (as if his novels were quieting social influences), it is felt by this generation that the author of "Faust" needs no apology that he did not spend his energies in the effervescing politics of the German states. I mean, that while we may like or dislike the man for his sympathy or want of sympathy, we concede to the author the right of his attitude; if Goethe had not assumed freedom from moral responsibility, I suppose that criticism of his aloofness would long ago have ceased. Irving did not lack sympathy with humanity in the concrete; it colored whatever he wrote. But he regarded the politics of his own country, the revolutions in France, the long struggle in Spain, without heat; and he held aloof from projects of agitation and reform, and maintained the attitude of an observer, regarding the life about him from the point of view of the literary artist, as he was justified in doing.

43

Irving had the defects of his peculiar genius, and these have no doubt helped to fix upon him the complimentary disparagement of "genial." He was not aggressive; in his nature he was wholly unpartisan, and full of lenient charity; and I suspect that his kindly regard of the world, although returned with kindly liking, cost him something of that respect for sturdiness and force which men feel for writers who flout them as fools in the main. Like Scott, he belonged to the idealists, and not to the realists, whom our generation affects. Both writers stimulate the longing for something better. Their creed was short: "Love God and honor the King." It is a very good one for a literary man, and might do for a Christian. The supernatural was still a reality in the age in which they wrote. Irving's faith in God and his love of humanity were very simple; I do not suppose he was much disturbed by the deep problems that have set us all adrift. In every age, whatever is astir, literature, theology, all intellectual activity, takes one and the same drift, and approximates in color. The bent of Irving's spirit was fixed in his youth, and he escaped the desperate realism of this generation, which has no outcome, and is likely to produce little that is noble.

I do not know how to account, on principles of culture which we recognize, for our author's style. His education was exceedingly defective, nor was his want of discipline supplied by subsequent desultory application. He seems to have been born with a rare sense of literary proportion and form; into this, as into a mould, were run his apparently lazy and really acute observations of life. That he thoroughly mastered such literature as he fancied there is abundant evidence; that his style was influenced by the purest English models is also apparent. But there remains a large margin for wonder how, with his want of training, he could have elaborated a style which is distinctively his own, and is as copious, felicitous in the choice of words, flowing, spontaneous, flexible, engaging, clear, and as little wearisome when read continuously in quantity as any in the English tongue. This is saying a greal deal, though it is not claiming for him the compactness, nor the robust vigor, nor the depth of thought, of many others masters in it. It is sometimes praised for its simplicity. It is certainly lucid, but its simplicity is not that of Benjamin Franklin's style; it is often ornate, not seldom somewhat diffuse, and always exceedingly melodious. It is noticeable for its metaphorical felicity. But it was not in the sympathetic nature of the author, to which I just re-

ferred, to come sharply to the point. It is much to have merited the
eulogy of Campbell that he had "added clarity to the English
tongue." This elegance and finish of style (which seems to have been
as natural to the man as his amiable manner) is sometimes made his
reproach, as if it were his sole merit, and as if he had concealed
under this charming form a want of substance. In literature form is
vital. But his case does not rest upon that. As an illustration his "Life
of Washington" may be put in evidence. Probably this work lost
something in incisiveness and brilliancy by being postponed till the
writer's old age. But whatever this loss, it is impossible for any biography to be less pretentious in style, or less ambitious in proclama-
tion. The only pretension of matter is in the early chapters, in which
a more than doubtful genealogy is elaborated, and in which it is
thought necessary to Washington's dignity to give a fictitious importance to his family and his childhood, and to accept the southern estimate of the hut in which he was born as a "mansion." In much of this
false estimate Irving was doubtless misled by the fables of Weems.
But while he has given us a dignified portrait of Washington, it is as
far as possible removed from that of the smileless prig which has
begun to weary even the popular fancy. The man he paints is flesh
and blood, presented, I believe, with substantial faithfulness to his
character; with a recognition of the defects of his education and the
deliberation of his mental operations; with at least a hint of that want
of breadth of culture and knowledge of the past, the possession of
which characterized many of his great associates; and with no con-
cealment that he had a dower of passions and a temper which only
vigorous self-watchfulness kept under. But he portrays, with an admiration not too highly colored, the magnificent patience, the courage
to bear misconstruction, the unfailing patriotism, the practical sagacity, the level balance of judgment combined with the wisest tolera-
tion, the dignity of mind, and the lofty moral nature which made him
the great man of his epoch. Irving's grasp of this character; his lucid
marshaling of the scattered, often wearisome and uninteresting details of our dragging, unpicturesque Revolutionary War; his just judgment of men; his even, almost judicial, moderation of tone; and his
admirable proportion of space to events, render the discussion of
style in reference to this work superfluous. Another writer might
have made a more brilliant performance: descriptions sparkling with
antitheses, characters projected into startling attitudes by the use of

45

epithets; a work more exciting and more piquant, that would have started a thousand controversies, and engaged the attention by daring conjectures and attempts to make a dramatic spectacle; a book interesting and notable, but false in philosophy and untrue in fact.

When the "Sketch-Book" appeared, an English critic said it should have been first published in England, for Irving was an English writer. The idea has been more than once echoed here. The truth is that while Irving was intensely American in feeling he was first of all a man of letters, and in that capacity he was cosmopolitan; he certainly was not insular. He had a rare accommodation of tone to his theme. Of England, whose traditions kindled his susceptible fancy, he wrote as Englishmen would like to write about it. In Spain he was saturated with the romantic story of the people and the fascination of the clime; and he was so true an interpreter of both as to earn from the Spaniards the title of "the poet Irving." I chanced once, in an inn at Frascati, to take up "The Tales of a Traveller," which I had not seen for many years. I expected to revive the somewhat faded humor and fancy of the past generation. But I found not only a sprightly humor and vivacity which are modern, but a truth to Italian local color that is very rare in any writer foreign to the soil. As to America, I do not know what can be more characteristically American than the Knickerbocker, the Hudson River tales, the sketches of life and adventure in the far West. But underneath all this diversity there is one constant quality,—the flavor of the author. Open by chance and read almost anywhere in his score of books,—it may be the "Tour on the Prairies," the familiar dream of the Alhambra, or the narratives of the brilliant exploits of New World explorers; surrender yourself to the flowing current of his transparent style, and you are conscious of a beguilement which is the crowning excellence of all lighter literature, for which we have no word but "charm."

The consensus of opinion about Irving in England and America for thirty years was very remarkable. He had a universal popularity rarely enjoyed by any writer. England returned him to America medalled by the king, honored by the university which is chary of its favors, followed by the applause of the whole English people. In English households, in drawing-rooms of the metropolis in political circles no less than among the literary coteries, in the best reviews, and in the popular newspapers the opinion of him was pretty much the same. And even in the lapse of time and the change of literary fash-

ion authors so unlike as Byron and Dickens were equally warm in admiration of him. To the English indorsement America added her own
enthusiasm, which was as universal. His readers were the million,
and all his readers were admirers. Even American statesmen, who
feed their minds on food we know not of, read Irving. It is true that
the uncritical opinion of New York was never exactly reechoed in the
cool recesses of Boston culture; but the magnates of the "North
American Review" gave him their meed of cordial praise. The country at large put him on a pinnacle. If you attempt to account for the
position he occupied by his character, which won the love of all men,
it must be remembered that the quality which won this, whatever its
value, pervades his books also.

And yet it must be said that the total impression left upon the
mind by the man and his works is not that of the greatest intellectual
force. I have no doubt that this was the impression he made upon his
ablest contemporaries. And this fact, when I consider the effect the
man produced, makes the study of him all the more interesting. As
an intellectual personality he makes no such impression, for instance,
as Carlyle, or a dozen other writers now living who could be named.
The incisive critical faculty was almost entirely wanting in him. He
had neither the power nor the disposition to cut his way transversely
across popular opinion and prejudice that Ruskin has, nor to draw
around him disciples equally well pleased to see him fiercely demol-
ish today what they had delighted to see him set up yesterday as
eternal. He evoked neither violent partisanship nor violent opposition. He was an extremely sensitive man, and if he had been capable
of creating a conflict he would only have been miserable in it. The
play of his mind depended upon the sunshine of approval. And all
this shows a certain want of intellectual virility.

A recent anonymous writer has said that most of the writing of
our day is characterized by an intellectual strain. I have no doubt that
this will appear to be the case to the next generation. It is a strain to
say something new even at the risk of paradox, or to say something
in a new way at the risk of obscurity. From this Irving was entirely
free. There is no visible straining to attract attention. His mood is
calm and unexaggerated. Even in some of his pathos, which is open
to the suspicion of being "literary," there is no literary exaggeration.
He seems always writing from an internal calm, which is the necessary condition of his production. If he wins at all by his style, by his

humor, by his portraiture of scenes or of character, it is by a gentle force, like that of the sun in spring. There are many men now living, or recently dead, intellectual prodigies, who have stimulated thought, upset opinions, created mental eras, to whom Irving stands hardly in as fair a relation as Goldsmith to Johnson. What verdict the next generation will put upon their achievements I do not know; but it is safe to say that their position and that of Irving as well will depend largely upon the affirmation or the reversal of their views of life and their judgments of character. I think the calm work of Irving will stand when much of the more startling and perhaps more brilliant intellectual achievement of this age has passed away.

And this leads me to speak of Irving's moral quality, which I cannot bring myself to exclude from a literary estimate, even in the face of the current gospel of art for art's sake. There is something that made Scott and Irving personally loved by the millions of their readers, who had only the dimmest ideas of their personality. This was some quality perceived in what they wrote. Each one can define it for himself; there it is, and I do not see why it is not as integral a part of the authors—an element in the estimate of their future position—as what we term their intellect, their knowledge, their skill, or their art. However you rate it, you cannot account for Irving's influence in the world without it. In his tender tribute to Irving, the great-hearted Thackeray, who saw as clearly as anybody the place of mere literary art in the sum total of life, quoted the dying words of Scott to Lockhart,—"Be a good man, my dear." We know well enough that the great author of "The Newcomes" and the great author of "The Heart of Midlothian" recognized the abiding value in literature of integrity, sincerity, purity, charity, faith. These are beneficences; and Irving's literature, walk round it and measure it by whatever critical instruments you will, is a beneficent literature. The author loved good women and little children and a pure life; he had faith in his fellow-men, a kindly sympathy with the lowest, without any subservience to the highest; he retained a belief in the possibility of chivalrous actions, and did not care to envelop them in a cynical suspicion; he was an author still capable of an enthusiasm. His books are wholesome, full of sweetness and charm, of humor without any sting, of amusement without any stain; and their more solid qualities are marred by neither pedantry nor pretension.

"Introductory" and "Programme"

BY THE WASHINGTON IRVING ASSOCIATION

The following unsigned "Introductory" statement opened the volume *Washington Irving,* published in New York by G. P. Putnam's Sons in 1884 for The Washington Irving Association, which had been founded in Tarrytown in March of 1883, to celebrate the Centenary of Irving's birth. The "Programme" is page 5 of the commemorative volume which describes the Tarrytown ceremonies held on April 3, 1883, with Judge Noah Davis (1830–1910), presiding justice of the General Term of the State Supreme Court, in the chair. Its proceedings were recorded thereafter in this slender but well designed and appropriately illustrated book. The language of the explanatory preface is perhaps inflated in places, from our point of view, and "Woolfort's" Roost is a misspelling, but the overall sincerity of purpose involved speaks for itself.

INTRODUCTORY

In this hurrying age anniversaries, whether of the birth of great men or of great events, are easily lost sight of. Indeed, the number of memorable anniversaries is small at best. Back in the history of the world stretches an endless procession of men who were great in some one at least of all the possible elements of greatness, whose very names even form a subject for dispute, while the years of their birth are unknown, or if known seldom or never recalled. So there are records of great deeds which have changed the maps of the world, yet which are almost lost in the morning mist or dimly seen in faint perspective, while nearly all are imbedded in the intensity and dominance of the present. Interest in men and events of the past, it scarcely need be said, is not so much proportioned to their importance at the particular time of their existence, as to the relation which they sustain to the living issues and nearer generation of to-day. And so it might be expected that while the two hundredth anniversary of the death of quaint Sir Thomas Browne might pass unnoticed, at least the one hundredth birthday of our own Washington Irving, of whom it may historically be more truly said than Halleck said of Cooper, that

> His name is with his country's woven;
> *First* in her fields, her pioneer of mind;—

it might naturally be expected that the birthday of Washington Irving would not be forgotten either by those his fellow-laborers in the field of literature or by his sometime fellow-countrymen—some his immediate personal friends, inhabitants of Tarrytown, where he lived, where he worshipped, and upon whose every hill, valley, and bosky hollow he had cast like a spell the witchery of his romance. Yet so it was, that the approaching anniversary seems to have wholly escaped attention until a newspaper slip announcing the near centenary of Irving's birth arrested the attention of three gentlemen living in Tarrytown. These gentlemen meeting one day—it was about the middle of March—the question naturally arose, "Why not do something to commemorate the event?" Sure enough, why not? The question was answered in part by an agreement to invite a few friends to meet as soon as practicable for consultation over the matter. Later,

Mr. T. J. Temple invited the gentlemen interested to meet at his house—an invitation which was promptly accepted, and subsequently made to include not only that but all subsequent meetings.

On Monday, the 19th of March, the first meeting was held. There were present on that occasion the following gentlemen, viz.: M. H. Bright, Gen. James F. Hall, James T. Law, David A. Rowe, Rev. J. Selden Spencer, T. J. Temple, and L. T. Yale. The gentlemen then and there assembled organized themselves into an Association to be known as "The Washington Irving Association," whose object was declared to be that of "appropriately commemorating the life and services to literature of Washington Irving by appropriately celebrating the centennial anniversary of his birth in the town where he lived and died." Additions were made by election, constituting the General Committee of the Association as follows:

The General Committee.

MARSHAL H. BRIGHT.	JOHN ROCKWELL.
WASHINGTON CHOATE.	JAMES RICHARDSON.
HARRY A. GRANT, JR.	DAVID A. ROWE.
JAMES F. HALL.	J. SELDEN SPENCER.
N. C. HUSTED.	THOS. J. TEMPLE.
D. W. JUDD.	STEPHEN H. THAYER.
JAMES T. LAW.	WILLIAM C. WILKINSON.
M. D. RAYMOND.	LUCIUS T. YALE.

The following officers were then elected:

REV. J. SELDEN SPENCER, *President.*
T. J. TEMPLE, *1st Vice-President.*
D. W. JUDD, *2d Vice-President.*
L. T. YALE, *Secretary.*
D. A. ROWE, *Treasurer.*

It was then formally resolved, "that this Association celebrate the one hundredth anniversary of the birth of Washington Irving, in Tarrytown, on Tuesday evening April 3, 1883." A committee on speakers was then appointed, viz.: Messrs. Jas. T. Law, S. H. Thayer, M. H. Bright, L. T. Yale.

The next meeting of the General Committee was held at Mr. Temple's residence, on Thursday evening, March 22d. All the Com-

mittee were present. The offer of the Trustees of the Second Re-
formed Church, tendering the use of that building, was received and
accepted with thanks. It was ascertained that more extended facilities
could not be had;—whatever celebration was had must take place in
a church, and arrangements must be perfected during the ensuing ten
days. The necessary additional committees were then appointed.

It was resolved, that membership in the Association be placed
at one dollar, and that all citizens of Westchester County in sympathy
with the objects of the Association be invited to join. It was further
resolved, "that Mr. Donald G. Mitchell be invited to deliver an address appropriate to the occasion." A resolution was also adopted,
inviting the Westchester County Historical Society to be present on
the occasion; and a like invitation was extended to the old friends
and acquaintances of Mr. Irving, in Tarrytown. The presence of the
Misses Irving was also especially invited. Mr. S. H. Thayer was invited to write a poem for the occasion, which, though on brief notice,
he consented to do.

The Committee met again on Friday, March 30th. It was voted
to request of the Misses Irving, the favor of having Sunnyside open to
the public on the 3d day of April. [The request was promptly
acceded to later by the ladies, and Sunnyside was open for several
days, very many from all parts of the country availing themselves of
the opportunity to visit "Woolfort's Roost," which remained the
same as it was on the day of Mr. Irving's death.] The various Committees then made their reports, and the list of speakers being submitted, the following programme was adopted:

THE WASHINGTON IRVING ASSOCIATION

PROGRAMME

THE WASHINGTON IRVING CENTENARY,

AT TARRYTOWN-ON-HUDSON.

TUESDAY EVENING, APRIL 3, 1883,

AT THE

SECOND REFORMED CHURCH.

THE HON. NOAH DAVIS WILL PRESIDE.

PROGRAMME.

1. PRELUDE . . ("Rip Van Winkle") . . . Miss HAWES.
2. SALUTATORY ADDRESS . . . . JAMES WOOD.
3. READING OF LETTERS, ETC. . . . Rev. WASHINGTON CHOATE.
4. PERSONAL REMINISCENCES . . . Rev. J. SELDEN SPENCER.
5. ADDRESS . . . . DONALD G. MITCHELL.
6. ADDRESS . . . . CHAS. DUDLEY WARNER.
7. SONG . . . . "The Lost Chord" . . . . Miss SEARS.
8. ADDRESS . . . . W. C. WILKINSON, D.D.
9. BENEDICTION . . . . . . Prof. T. S. DOOLITTLE, D.D.

COMMENCING AT EIGHT O'CLOCK.

Under the Auspices of the Washington Irving Association:

Rev. J. SELDEN SPENCER, President,
T. J. TEMPLE, 1st Vice-President,
D. W. JUDD, 2d Vice-President,
L. T. YALE, Secretary,
D. A. ROWE, Treasurer,
MARSHAL H. BRIGHT,
WASHINGTON CHOATE,
H. A. GRANT, JR.,

Gen. JAS. F. HALL,
N. C. HUSTED,
JAMES T. LAW,
JOHN ROCKWELL,
JAMES RICHARDSON,
M. D. RAYMOND,
STEPHEN H. THAYER,
W. C. WILKINSON,
} General Committee.

53

"Address"

BY DONALD G. MITCHELL

Donald G. Mitchell (1822–1908), Yale graduate, journalistic travel writer, literary critic and Irvingesque essayist and humorist, is best remembered, despite numerous other titles to his credit, as the pseudonymous "Ik (or Ike) Marvel," especially of *Reveries of a Bachelor* (1850). That, late in Washington Irving's life, Mitchell sat reverentially at the master's feet, is obvious in this selection, the principal address given in Tarrytown on the hundredth anniversary of Irving's birth. The activities of that celebration, April 3, 1883, the program for which is part of the preceding selection here, went to make up *Washington Irving* (1884), a centenary volume published, inevitably, by Putnam's, from which Mitchell's sentimental speech is taken.

You are met to-night to pay tribute to the memory of a man we all loved—born a hundred years ago.

Yet, we who put voice to your tribute are brought to pause at the very start: Who can say over again—in a way that shall make listeners—the praises of a balmy day in June?

Simply to recall him, however, is—I think—to honor him: for there is no memory of him however shadowy or vagrant which is not grateful to you,—to me and to all the reading world.

It is now wellnigh upon thirty-five years since I first met Mr. Irving: It was in a sunny parlor in one of the houses of that Colonnade Row which stands opposite the Astor Library in Lafayette Place, New York. I can recall vividly the trepidation which I carried to that meeting—so eager to encounter the man whom all honored and admired—so apprehensive lest a chilling dignity might disturb my ideal. And when that smiling, quiet, well-preserved gentleman (I could hardly believe him sixty-five) left his romp with some of his little kinsfolk, to give me a hearty shake of the hand, and thereafter to run on in lively, humorsome chat—stealing all trepidation out of me, by—I know not what—kindly magnetism of voice and manner, it was as if some one were playing counterfeit—as if the venerated author were yet to appear and displace this beaming, winning personality, with some awful dignity that should put me again into worshipful tremor.

But no: this was indeed Mr. Irving—hard as it was to adjust this gracious presence so full of benignity, with the author who had told the story of the Knickerbockers and of Columbus.

Another puzzle to me was—how this easy-going gentleman, with his winning mildness and quiet deliberation,—as if he never *could,* and never *did,* and never *would* knuckle down to hard taskwork,—should have reeled out those hundreds—nay, thousands of pages of graceful, well-ordered, sparkling English.

I could not understand how he did it. I do not think we ever altogether understand how the birds sing and sing; and yet, with feathers quite unruffled, and eyes always a-twinkle.

My next sight of Mr. Irving was hereabout, at his own home. By his kind invitation I had come up to pass a day with him at Sunnyside, and he had promised me a drive through Sleepy Hollow.

What a promise that was! No boy ever went to his Christmas holidays more joyously, I think, than I, to meet that engagement.

It was along this road, beside which we are assembled to-night, that we drove. He all alert and brisk, with the cool morning breeze blowing down upon us from the Haverstraw heights and across the wide sweep of river.

He called attention to the spot of poor André's capture—not forbearing that little touch of sympathy, which came to firmer yet not disloyal expression, afterward, in his story of Washington. A sweep of his whip-hand told me the trees under which Paulding and the rest chanced to be loitering on that memorable day.

We were whirling along the same road a short way farther northward, when I ventured to query about the memorable night-ride of Ichabod Crane and of the Headless Horseman.

Aye, it was thereabout that tragedy came off too.

"Down this bit of road the old horse 'Gunpowder' came thundering: there away—Brom Bones with his Pumpkin (I tell you this in confidence," he said) "was in waiting; and along here they went clattering neck and neck—Ichabod holding a good seat till Van Ripper's saddle-girths gave way, and then bumping and jouncing from side to side as he clung to mane or neck, [a little pantomime with the whip making it real] and so at last—away yonder—well, where you like, the poor pedagogue went sprawling to the ground—I hope in a soft place." And I think the rollicking humor of it was as much enjoyed by him that autumn morning, and that he felt in his bones just as relishy a smack of it all—as if Katrina Van Tassel had held her quilting frolic only on the yester-night.

Irving first came to know Tarrytown and Sleepy Hollow when a boy of fourteen or fifteen—he passing some holidays in these parts, I think, with his friend Paulding. To those days belong much of that idle sauntering along brook-sides hereabout—with fly-hooks and fish-rods, and memories of Walton, which get such delightful recognition in a certain paper of the "Sketch-Book."

Then, too, he with his companions came to know the old Dutch farmers of the region—whose home interiors found their way afterward into his books.

I think he pointed out also, with a significant twinkle of the eye, which the dullest boy would have understood, some orchards, with which he had early acquaintance; and specially, too, upon some hill-top (which I think I could find now), a farmery, famous for its cider-mill and the good cider made there; he, with the rest, testing it over and over in the old slow way with straws, but provoked once on a time to a fuller test, by turning the hogshead, so they might sip from the open bung; and then (whether out of mischief or mishandling, he did not absolutely declare to me) the big barrel got the better of them, and set off upon a lazy roll down the hill—going faster and faster—they, more and more frightened, and scudding away slant-wise over the fences—the yelling farmer appearing suddenly at the top of the slope, but too broad in the beam for any sharp race, and the hogshead between them plunging, and bounding, and giving out ghostly, guttural explosions of sound, and cider, at every turn.

You may judge if Mr. Irving did not put a nice touch to that story!

After this memorable autumn drive amongst the hills, I met with Mr. Irving frequently at his own home; and shall I be thought impertinent and indiscreet if I say that at times—rare times, it is true—I have seen this most amiable gentleman manifest a little of that restive choler which sometimes flamed up in William the Testy,—not long-lived, not deliberate,—but a little human blaze, of impatience at something gone awry in the dressing of a garden border, in the care of some stable-pet—that was all gone with the first blaze, but marked and indicated the sources of that wrathy and pious zest (with which he is not commonly credited) with which he loved to put a con-temptuous thrust of his sharper language into the bloat of upstart pride, and of conceit, and of insolent pretension.

The boy-mischief in him—which led him out from his old home in William Street, after hours, over the shedroof—lingered in him for a good while, I think, and lent not a little point to some of the keener pictures of the Knickerbocker history; and, if I do not mistake, there was now and then a quiet chuckle, as he told me of the foolish indig-nation with which some descendants of the old Dutch worthies had seen their ancestors put to a tender broil over the playful blaze of his humor.

Indeed there was a spontaneity and heartiness about that Knick-erbocker history, which I think he carried a strong liking for, all his life.

The "Sketch-Book," written years later, and when necessity en-forced writing, was done with a great audience in his eye; and he won it, and keeps it bravely. I know there is a disposition to speak of it rather patronizingly and apologetically—as if it were reminiscent—

Anglican—conventional—as if he would have done better if he had possessed our modern critical bias—or if he had been born in Boston —or born a philosopher outright: Well, perhaps so—perhaps so! But I love to think and believe that our dear old Mr. Irving was born just where he should have been born, and wrote in a way that it is hardly worth our while to try and mend for him.

I understand that a great many promising young people—without the fear of the critics before their eyes—keep on, persistently reading that old "Sketch-Book," with its "Broken Hearts," and "Wife" twining like a vine, and "Spectre Bridegroom," and all the rest.

And there are old people I know,—one I am sure of,—who never visit St. Paul's Church-yard without wanting to peep over Irving's shoulders into Mr. Newbury's shop, full of dear old toy-books; —who never go to Stratford-upon-Avon but there is a hunt—first of all—for the Red Horse Tavern and the poker which was Irving's sceptre;—never sail on summer afternoons past the wall of the blue Katskills, but there is a longing look-out for the stray cloud-caps, and an eager listening for the rumbling of the balls which thundered in the ears of poor Rip Van Winkle.

What, pray, if the hero of "Bracebridge Hall" be own cousin to Sir Roger de Coverley? Is that a relationship to be discarded? And could any other than the writer we honor carry on more wisely the record of the counsinship, or with so sure a hand and so deft a touch declare and establish our inheritance in the rural beatitudes of England?

It may be true that as we read some of those earlier books of his we shall come upon some truisms which in these fast-paced times may chafe us,—some rhetorical furbelows or broidery that belong to the wardrobes of the past,—some tears that flow too easily,—but scarce ever a page anywhere but, on a sudden, some shimmer of buoyant humor breaks through all the crevices of a sentence,—a humor not born of rhetoric or measurable by critics' rules,—but coming as the winds come, and playing up and down with a frolicsome, mischievous blaze, that warms, and piques, and delights us.

In the summer of 1852 I chanced to be quartered at the same hotel with him in Saratoga for a fortnight or more. He was then in his seventieth year—but still carrying himself easily up and down upon the corridors, and along the street, and through the grove at the spring.

I recall vividly the tremulous pride with which, in those far-off days, I was permitted to join in many of these walks. He in his dark suit—of such cut and fit as to make one forget utterly its fashion—and remember only the figure of the quiet gentleman, looking hardly middle-aged, with head thrown slightly to one side, and an eye always alert; not a fair young face dashing past us in its drapery of muslin, but his eye drank in all its freshness and beauty with the keen appetite and the grateful admiration of a boy; not a dowager brushed us, bedizened with finery, but he fastened the apparition in my memory with some piquant remark—as the pin of an entomologist fastens a gaudy fly.

Other times there was a playful nudge of the elbow, and a curious, meaning lift of the brow, to call attention to something of droll aspect—perhaps some threatened scrimmage amongst school-boys—may be, only a passing encounter between street dogs—for he had all the quick responsiveness to canine language which belonged to the author of "Rab and his Friends"; and I have known him to stay his walk for five minutes together in a boyish, eager intentness upon those premonitions of a dog encounter—watching the first inquisitive sniff—the reminiscent lift of the head—then the derogatory growl—the growl apprehensive—the renewed sniff—the pauses for reflection, then the milder and the discursive growls—as if either dog *could,* if he *would*—until one or the other, thinking more wisely of the matter, should turn tail, and trot quietly away.

I trust I do not seem to vulgarize the occasion in bringing to view these little traits which set before us the man: as I have already said, we cannot honor him more than by recalling him in his full personality.

Over and over in his shrugs, in a twinkle of his eye, in that arching of his brow which was curiously full of meaning, did I see, as I thought, the germ of some new chapter, such as crept into his sketch-books. Did I intimate as much:—"Ah," he would say, "that is game for youngsters; we old fellows are not nimble enough to give chase to sentiment."

He was engaged at that time upon his "Life of Washington"—going out, as I remember, on one of these Saratoga days, for a careful inspection of the field of Burgoyne's surrender.

59

I asked after the system of his note-making for history. "Ah," he said, "don't talk to me of system; I never had any; you must go to Bancroft for that: I have, it is true, my little budgets of notes—some tied one way, some another—and which, when I need, I think I come upon in my pigeon-holes by a sort of instinct. That is all there is of it."

There were some two or three beautiful dark-eyed women that summer at Saratoga, who were his special admiration, and of whose charms of feature he loved to discourse eloquently.

Those dark eyes led him back, doubtless, to the glad young days when he had known the beauties of Seville and Cordova. Indeed, there was no episode in his life of which he was more prone to talk, than of that which carried him in his Spanish studies to the delightful regions which lie south of the Gaudalquiver. Granada—the Alhambra—those names made the touchstone of his most gushing and eloquent talk.

Much as he loved and well as he painted the green fields of Warwickshire, and the hedges and the ivy-clad towers and the embowered lanes and the primroses and the hawthorn which set off the stories of "Bracebridge Hall," yet I think he was never stirred by these memories so much as by the sunny valleys which lay in Andalusia, and by the tinkling fountains and rosy walls that caught the sunshine in the palace courts of Granada.

I should say that the crowning literary enthusiasms of his life were those which grouped themselves—first about those early Dutch foregatherings amongst the Van Twillers and the Stuyvesants and the Van Tassels—and next and stronger, those others which grouped about the great Moorish captains of Granada.

In the first—that is to say, his Knickerbocker studies—the historic sense was active but not dominant, and his humor in its first lusty wantonness went careering through the files of the old magnates, like a boy at play; and the memory of the play abode with him, and had its keen awakenings all through his life; there was never a year, I suspect, when the wooden leg of the doughty Peter Stuyvesant did not come clattering spunkily, and bringing its own boisterous welcome, to his pleased recollection.

In the Spanish studies and amongst the Moors the historic sense was more dominant, the humor more in hand, and the magnificent ruins of this wrecked nation—which had brought its trail of light across Southern Europe from the far East—piqued all his sympathies, appealed to all his livelier fancies, and the spendors of court and camp lent a lustre to his pages which he greatly relished.

No English-speaking visitor can go to the Alhambra now, or henceforth ever will go thither, but the name of the author we honor to-night will come to his lip, and will lend, by some subtle magic, the master's silvery utterance to the dash of the fountains, to the soughing of the winds, to the chanting of the birds who sing in the ruinous courts of the Alhambra.

But I keep you too long:—[Cries of "No! no!—go on!"]—and yet I have said no word yet of that quality in him which will, I think, most of all, make Centenary like this follow upon Centenary.

'T is the kindness in him: 't is the simple goodheartedness of the man.

Did he ever wrong a neighbor? Did he ever say an unkind thing of you, or me, or any one? Can you cull me a sneer, that has hate in it, anywhere in his books? Can you tell me of a thrust of either words or silence, which has malignity in it?

Fashions of books may change—do change: a studious realism may put in disorder the quaint dressing of his thought; an elegant philosophy of indifference may pluck out the bowels from his books.

But—the fashion of his heart and of his abiding goodwill toward men will last—will last while the hills last.

And when you* and I, sir, and all of us are beyond the reach of the centennial calls, I think that old Anthony Van Corlear's trumpet will still boom along the banks of the Hudson, heralding a man and a master, who to exquisite graces of speech added purity of life, and to the most buoyant and playful of humors added a love for all mankind.

*Chief-Justice Davis presided over the assemblage, and brought to his duties a dignity, a sympathy, and a quiet humor which went far to make the occasion memorable.

From
"Editor's Easy Chair"

BY GEORGE W. CURTIS

The much-read "Editor's Easy Chair" from *Harper's New Monthly Magazine,* here supplies from Volume LXVI (December 1882–May 1883), two commentaries. Both are by George W. Curtis (1824–1892), a major Knickerbocker editor, journalist, literary critic, and orator, who is, as usual in these columns, writing on a topical subject. The first, an excerpt from March of 1883, begins with a transatlantic difference of opinion, on Irving's fame, with the popular *Daily News* of London. The second, an excerpt from April of the same year, addresses itself more directly to the hundredth anniversary, April 3, 1883, of Washington Irving's birth. Curtis later wrote the laudatory *Washington Irving, A Sketch,* published in a limited edition by the Grolier Club in 1891.

The London *Daily News* recently said something which recalls something that Sydney Smith said more than sixty years ago. The *News* asserts that Washington Irving was much more relished and admired in England than in his own country, and that "it is only recently that American critics on the lookout for a literature have elevated him to his proper and almost more than his proper place. This docility to English guidance in the case of their best or almost their best prose writer may perhaps be followed by a similar docility in the case of their best or almost their best poet, Poe, whom also England has preceded the United States in recognizing." This comically patronizing air is all the droller because the patron is a British worthy who gravely calls Poe almost the best American poet. The tone reminds us of Sydney Smith's amusing passage in his article upon America in 1818: "Literature the Americans have none—no native literature, we mean. It is all imported. They had a Franklin, indeed, and may afford to live for half a century on his fame. There is, or was, a Mr. Dwight, who wrote some poems, and his baptismal name was Timothy. There is also a small account of Virginia by Jefferson, and an epic poem by Mr. Joel Barlow, and some pieces of pleasantry by Mr. Irving. But why should the Americans write books, when a six weeks' passage brings them, in their own tongue, our sense, science, and genius in bales and hogsheads? Prairies, steamboats, gristmills, are their natural objects for centuries to come. Then, when they have got to the Pacific Ocean, epic poems, plays, pleasures of memory, and all the elegant gratifications of an ancient people who have tamed the wild earth and sat down to amuse themselves. This is the natural march of human affairs."

Sydney Smith was certainly correct in assuming that there was hardly an American literature when he wrote, and his remarks are very like a passage of Fisher Ames's, a few years earlier, in which he groans at the literary paucity and want of promise in his country. But the *News* is sadly at fault in supposing that Irving's countrymen did not recognize him and honor him. If there were no evidence disproving this assertion, the only reasonable presumption of its possible truth would be the fact that the countrymen of Irving were descendants of the people who showed little contemporaneous appreciation of Shakespeare. It is certainly creditable to the literary England which was busily idolizing Scott and Byron that it recognized also the charming genius of Irving, and that Leslie, the painter, could truly write of him, "Geoffrey Crayon is the most fashionable fellow of the day." Doubtless national pride had a part in the feeling; for Irving had the same imaginative enthusiasm for traditional and poetic England that Burke had for political England. No English writer has touched "old England" with such airy grace as Irving, as indeed no native Englishman was likely to feel its spell so deeply. To change a word in Marvell's noble lines,

> "He nothing common saw, or mean,
> Upon that memorable scene."

England's debt to Irving is peculiar, because only an American could have seen England as he described it. The English regard for him is very becoming and very natural, although it was due rather to his theme than to his treatment or to his genius. It would have shown extreme stolidity in any people to be dull to the work of an artist who painted their own most familiar scenes as no native had painted them, and gave them a grace which the mass of those people had hardly suspected or perceived.

But while the English appreciation of Irving is very creditable to England, English conceit must not go so far as to suppose that it was that appreciation which commended him to his own countrymen. At the time when Sydney Smith wrote the article from which we have quoted there was apparently an almost absolute literary sterility in this country. The professional critics of the critical journals were, as Professor Lounsbury states in his admirable *Life of Cooper,* in the series of "American Men of Letters," undoubtedly greatly affected by English opinion. But there was an American reading public independent of the few literary periodicals, as was shown when Cooper's *Spy* was published, at the very end of 1821—the year in which Bryant's first volume of poems and Dana's *Idle Man* appeared. Cooper had published his *Precaution,* a book which Professor Lounsbury is the only man who was ever known to have read. He was an unknown author. But the *Spy* was instantly successful. Some of the timid journals awaited the English opinion. Murray declined, upon Gifford's advice, to publish it. But a publisher was found, and England and Europe followed America in their approval. Cooper always truly said that it was to his countrymen alone that he owed his first success, and his biographer concedes that the success was determined before the opinion of Europe was known.

Nearly three years before, in May 1819, the first number of Irving's *Sketch-Book* was published. It contained "The Wife" and "Rip Van Winkle." The success was immediate, and most gratifying to the author, who was then thirty-six years old. In September, 1819, he wrote: "The manner in which the work has been received, and the eulogiums that have been passed upon it in the American papers and periodical works, have quite overwhelmed me. . . . I feel almost appalled by such success." The echo of the acclamation reached England. Murray at first declined to publish it, as he had declined Cooper's *Spy,* and Irving published it at his own risk. When England ascertained that the American judgment was correct, and that it was a charming work, Murray was willing to publish it.

The delightful genius which his country had recognized with joy it never ceased proudly and tenderly to honor. When in 1832 he returned to his native land, as his latest biographer, Mr. Warner, records, "America greeted her most famous literary man with a spontaneous outburst of love and admiration." It was in his own country that he had published his works. It was his own countrymen whose applause had apprised England of the charm of the new author; and it is extremely amusing to hear in 1882, from an English writer who thinks Poe to be almost the greatest of American poets, that it was our happy docility to English guidance which enabled us to recognize and honor "almost our best" prose writer.

Was it docility to the same beneficent guidance which enabled us to perceive the genius of Carlyle, whose works we first collected, and taught England to read and admire? Was it the same docility which enabled us to reveal to England one of her most philosophic observers in Herbert Spencer, and to offer to Darwin his most appreciative correspondents and interpreters in Chauncey Wright, John Fiske, and Professors Gray and Wyman? There are many offenses to be scored against us, but failure to know our own literary genius is not one of them. There is not one great literary fame in America that was not first recognized here. Not to one of them has docility to English literary opinion conducted us, as is often believed. Bryant and Cooper and Irving, Bancroft and Prescott and Motley, Emerson and Channing, Longfellow, Lowell, Whittier, and Holmes, are all men whom we were content to admire and love, without knowing or asking whether England had heard of them, or what she thought of them. "The greatness" of Poe, according to the London *News,* England has preceded us in recognizing. That is an assertion which we are not disposed to dispute. But Walter Scott was not more immediately popular and beloved in England than Washington Irving in America; and American guidance led England to Scott quite as much as English guidance drew America to Irving.

*   *   *

It is a hundred years ago, on the 3d of April, that Washington Irving was born in the city of New York, and he is still its most famous son. The only New-Yorker who could dispute this claim is John Jay. But universal and honorable as is Jay's renown in his own country, the name of Irving is more familiar to the English-speaking race. It is the synonym of a sweet literary grace and harmless gayety of humor which retain their charm in the midst of new tastes and among powerful rivals. Irving no longer shares with Bryant and Cooper the glory of being the sole or chief representatives of American literature, but he is still and forever its kindly patriarch, the modest author who first modestly answered the truculent question, Who reads an American book? by offering to the world an American book which it was delighted to read.

That intrinsically modest air never disappeared either from the works or the character of the benign writer. In the height of his renown there was no kind of presumption or conceit in his simple and generous heart. Some time after his return from his long absence in Europe, and before Putnam became his publisher, he found some disinclination upon the part of publishers to issue new editions of his books, and he expressed with entire good-humor his belief that he had had his day; and meeting some years afterward, in Mr. Putnam's office, one of the youngest of literary beginners, he said, with a humorous twinkle in the eye and with the husky whispering voice which gave a proper flavor to every pleasantry, "We old fellows had the advantage of you young men, for we wrote without rivals."

Every literary man of Irving's time, whether old or young, had nothing but affectionate praise of his artless urbanity and exhaustless good-nature. These qualities are delightfully reflected in Thackeray's stories of him in the Roundabout Paper upon Irving and Macaulay —"the Goldsmith and the Gibbon of our time." He came to one of my lectures in Washington, Thackeray says, and the retiring President, Mr. Fillmore, and his successor, Mr. Pierce, were present— "Two kings of Brentford smelling at one rose," said Irving, with his good-humored smile. In his little bower of a home at Sunnyside he was always accessible. One English newspaper man came and introduced himself, and partook of luncheon with the family, and while the host fell into the little doze which was his habit, the wary Englishman took a swift inventory of everything in the house, and served up the description to the British public, including the nap of his entertainer. At another time Irving said, "Two persons came to me, and one held me in conversation while the other miscreant took my portrait."

Thackeray tells these little stories with admiring sympathy. His manly heart always grew tender over his fellow-authors who had no acrid drop in their sweet humor. Irving was the earliest of American satirists, but there is no sting in the laughter that he moves. He was the first of our humorists, but his humor is pure lymph. It is unmixed with malice, and although, as Warner states, even his friend Gulian Verplanck resented a little the fun of Knickerbocker, and some scions of the old Dutch stock of fair Mannahatta assumed to be indignant with his resistlessly droll portraiture of the fathers of New Amsterdam, Irving's own limpid good-nature dissolved the hard feeling, and left only the best understanding.

Sir Walter Scott, who recognized at once the power and the humor of *Knickerbocker's History,* felt its kindred with the great works of a similar genius in English literature—a stroke of Swift, a touch of Sterne. But a recent paper upon American literature in *Blackwood* holds that it is ludicrous to compare the mild humor of *Rip Van Winkle* with the "robustious fun" of Swift.* This is a curious "derangement of epitaphs." Swift has wit, and satiric power, and

* See *Blackwood's Edinburgh Magazine* (January, 1883) for the anonymous "American Literature In England," pp. 136–161. On p. 140, rebutting our C. D. Warner's ideas in *Century Illustrated Monthly Magazine* (November, 1882), brief reference is made to Irving's humor, in "Rip van Winkle," as too "mild" to compare with the "robust fun of Gulliver." [*Ed.*]

burning invective, and ribaldry, and caustic, scornful humor; but fun, in any just sense, he has not. The airy grace and imaginative play of *Rip Van Winkle* are wholly beyond the reach of Swift. It is certainly true, as *Blackwood* remarks, that Shakespeare, Milton, Dryden, Addison, Pope, and "so many more" will not be replaced by "Mr. Washington Irving and Mr. Lowell." But it is equally true that the "Rape of the Lock" and the "Absalom and Achitophel" will not displace *Knickerbocker's History* and the *Biglow Papers*. Since Swift the *Blackwood* critic can not find in English literature political satire more trenchant, humorous, and effective than the *Biglow Papers,* and nothing in Swift more original.

Irving and the other chief American writers are not rivals of their associates in the literature of the language; they are worthy comrades. Pope and Dryden are not the peers of Shakespeare and Milton, but they are nevertheless Pope and Dryden, and their place is secure. The brows of Irving and Cooper, of Emerson and Hawthorne, do not crave the laurels of any other master. The perturbed spirit of *Blackwood* may rest in the confident assurance that no generous and intelligent student of our literature admires Gibbon less because he admires Macaulay, or Bacon, because he delights in Emerson, or denies the sting of Gulliver because he owns the charm of Knickerbocker. It is with good fame as with true love,

> "That to divide is not to take away."

Knickerbocker's History was the work of a young man of twenty-six, who lived fifty years afterward with a constantly increasing fame, making many and admirable contributions to literature. But nothing that followed surpassed the joyous brilliancy and gay felicity of the earliest work. Appearing in the midst of the sober effusions of our Puritan literature, and of a grave and energetic life still engrossed with the subjugation of a continent and the establishment of a new nation, *Knickerbocker's History* was a remarkable work. To pass the vague and venerable traditions of the austere and heroic founders of the city through the alembic of a youth's hilarious creative humor, and turn them out in forms resistlessly grotesque, but with their identity unimpaired, was a stroke as daring as it was successful. The audacious Goth of the legend who plucked the Roman senator by the beard was not a more ruthless iconoclast than this son of New Amsterdam, who drew his civil ancestors from venerable obscurity by flooding them with the cheerful light of a blameless fun.

The skill and power with which this is done can be best appreciated by those who are most familiar with the history which the gleeful genius burlesques. Irving follows the actual story closely, and the characters that he develops faithfully, although with smiling caricature, are historical. Indeed, the fidelity is so absolute that the fiction is welded with the fact. The days of Dutch ascendency in New York are inextricably associated with this ludicrous narrative. The Wouter van Twiller, the Wilhelmus Kieft, the Peter Stuyvesant, who are familiarly and popularly known, are the figures drawn by Diedrich Knickerbocker. In a comical despair the historian Grahame, whose colonial history is still among the best, says of Knickerbocker, "If Sancho Panza had been a real Governor misrepresented by the wit of Cervantes, his future historian would have found it no easy matter to bespeak a grave attention to the annals of his administration."

Irving's position in literature is assured, although literary fashions will change, and critics will stoutly and ingeniously maintain their varying views of the quality and character of his genius. Horace Binney Wallace, one of his most careful American critics, denies him both imagination and humor, and finds him to be at once an extreme realist and caricaturist. Others hold him to be slenderly equipped for a long contest with the envious obscurity that forever threatens renown. Undoubtedly he is less read by this generation than by his own. But this is true of his chief contemporaries, Scott and Byron. Irving's exquisite literary art, the freshness and gayety and originality of *Knickerbocker,* the charming legends of the Hudson, the idyllic England of the *Sketch-Book* and *Bracebridge Hall,* the picturesque and poetic narrative of the *Columbus,* all touched by the nameless grace of a gentle, humane, refined, and healthy genius, secure to him as to Goldsmith a long and affectionate remembrance. His own aspiration, in the words which Willis oddly selected for the motto of his second volume, *Fugitive Poetry,* published in 1827, has been amply fulfilled: "If, however, I can by lucky chance, in these days of evil, rub out one wrinkle from the brow of care, or beguile the heavy heart of one moment of sadness if I can, now and then, penetrate the gathering film of misanthropy, prompt a benevolent view of human nature, and make my reader more in good-humor with his fellow-beings and himself—surely, surely, I shall not then have written entirely in vain."

The portrait of Irving which adorns this number of the Magazine is taken from the picture painted by his friend Stuart Newton,* ten years after the publication of the *Knickerbocker,* when Irving was thirty-six years old. It belonged to John Murray, the publisher, and shows the Irving of the *Sketch-Book* and the *Columbus,* the Irving of the sunny hour when Byron wrote to Moore that the American author's books were his delight, and the ever-generous Scott pleasantly told him, as Warner recalls,

> "Your name is up, and may go
> From Toledo to Madrid."

Irving's name has gone farther, and his native city may well reflect, on the centenary of his birth, upon the odd caprice of fortune which has made her most illustrious son the least representative of her character and interests.

* This oil on canvas, 1820, hangs in the Dining Room at Sunnyside. [*Ed.*]

The mid-19th century business card (enlarged) of the enterprising son of Irving's own guide and storyteller in the Alhambra, earlier in 1828 and 1829. It symbolizes the continuing tradition of Irving's links to this historic site, the city of Granada, and Spain itself. This was first printed* by Evert A. Duyckinck in 1860 in "Memoranda," the memorial piece he contributed to *Irvingiana* (N.Y., 1860).

* See Part I, p. 23, of the present volume.

Part II

THE LONG SUNSET

(1890–1920)

Irving's name stands as the first landmark in American letters. No other American writer has won the same sort of recognition abroad or esteem at home as became his in early life. And he has lost very little ground, so far as we can judge by the appeal to figures. The copyright on his works ran out long since, and a great many editions of Irving, cheap and costly, complete and incomplete, have been issued from many sources. Yet his original publishers are now selling, year by year, more of his books than ever before. There is little doubt that his work is still widely read, and read not because it is prescribed but because it gives pleasure; not as the product of a "standard author," but as the expression of a rich and engaging personality, which has written itself like an indorsement across the face of a young nation's literature.

Henry W. Boynton
Washington Irving
(Boston, 1901)

"Rip Van Winkle's Lilac"

BY HERMAN MELVILLE

Herman Melville (1819–1891), whose fame is now legendary, was an all-but-forgotten man when across the year 1890, and in retirement, he tentatively assembled the contents of a volume of miscellaneous poems to be called "Weeds and Wildings." He died before this project could be completed, and the verses involved had only posthumous publication, in the Constable edition in 1924.* "Rip Van Winkle's Lilac," which begins with a pleasant apostrophe to Irving, combined a prose essay (its possible symbolism variously interpreted since) on Rip and the lilac, as victims of old age and of Dame Van Winkle's wrath, with extended couplets under the same title, which include Melville's valedictory compliments to his Knickerbocker predecessor. This selection is reprinted from *Collected Poems of Herman Melville,* ed. Howard P. Vincent (1947).

* This 16 volume (London) edition, reprinted by Russell & Russell (New York 1963), included "Weeds and Wildings" in the final volume, *Poems.* There "Rip Van Winkle's Lilac" was identified as "From A Manuscript Dated February 13, 1890." [*Ed.*]

TO A HAPPY SHADE

Under the golden maples where thou now reclinest, sharing fame's Indian Summer with those mellowing Immortals who as men were not only excellent in their works but pleasant and love-worthy in their lives; little troublest thou thyself, O Washington Irving, as to who peradventure may be poaching in that literary manner which thou leftest behind. Still less is it thou, happy Shade, that wilt charge with presumption the endeavor to render something tributary to the story of that child of thy heart—Rip Van Winkle. For aught I, or anybody, knows to the contrary, thy vision may now be such that it may even reach here where I write, and thy spirit be pleased to behold me inspired by whom but thyself.

RIP VAN WINKLE

Riverward emerging toward sunset in leafy June from a dark upper clove or gorge of the Kattskills, dazed with his long sleep in an innermost hollow of those mountains, the good-hearted good-for-nothing comes to an upland pasture. Hearing his limping footfall in the loneliness, the simpletons of young steers, there left to themselves for the summer, abruptly lifting their heads from the herbage, stand as stupified with astonishment while he passes.

In further descent he comes to a few raggedly cultivated fields detached and apart; but no house as yet, and presently strikes a wood-chopper's winding road lonesomely skirting the pastoral uplands, a road for the most part unfenced, and in summer so little travelled that the faint wheel-tracks were traceable but on forming long, parallel depressions in the natural turf. This slant descending way the dazed one dimly recalls as joining another less wild and leading homeward. Even so it proved. For anon he comes to the junction. There he pauses in startled recognition of a view only visible in perfection at that point; a view deeply stamped in his memory, he having been repeatedly arrested by it when going on his hunting or birding expeditions. It was where, seen at the far end of a long vistaed close the head of one distant blue summit peered over the shoulder of a range not so blue as less lofty and remote. To Rip's present frame of mind, by no means normal, that summit seemed like a man standing on tiptoes in a crowd to get a better look at some extraordinary object. Inquisitively it seemed to scrutinise him across the green solitudes, as much as to say "Who, I wonder, art thou? And where, pray, didst thou come from?" This freak of his disturbed imagination was not without pain to poor Rip. That mountain, so well remembered on his part, *him* had it forgotten? quite forgotten him, and in a day? But the evening now drawing on revives him with the sweet smells it draws from the grasses and shrubs. Proceeding on his path he after a little becomes sensible of a prevailing fragrance wholly new to him, at least in that vicinity, a wafted deliciousness growing more and more pronounced as he nears his house, one standing all by itself and remote from others. Suddenly, at a turn of the road it comes into view. Hereupon, something that he misses there, and quite another thing that he sees, brings him amazed to a stand. Where, according to his hazy reminiscences, all had been without floral embellishment of any kind save a small plot of pinks and hollyhocks in the sunny rear of the house—a little garden tended by the Dame herself—lo, a Lilac of unusual girth and height stands in full flower hard by the open door, usurping, as it were, all but the very spot which he could only recall as occupied by an immemorial willow.

Now Rip's humble abode, a frame one, though indeed, as he remembered it, quite habitable, had in some particulars never been carried to entire completion; the builder and original proprietor, a certain honest woodman, while about to give it the last touches having been summoned away to join his progenitors in that paternal house where the Good Book assures us are many mansions. This sudden arrest of the work left the structure in a condition rather slatternly as to externals. Though a safe shelter enough from the elements, ill-fitted was it as a nuptial bower for the woodman's heir, none other than Rip, his next living kin; who, enheartened by his inheritance boldly took the grand venture of practical life—matrimony. Yes, the first occupants were Rip and his dame, then the bride. A winsome bride it was too, with attractiveness all her own; her dowry consisting of little more than a chest of clothes, some cooking utensils, a bed and spinning-wheel. A fair shape, cheeks of down, and black eyes were hers, eyes indeed with a rogueish twinkle at times, but apparently as little capable of snapping as two soft sable violets.

Well, after a few days occupying of the place, returning thereto at sunset from a romantic ramble among the low-whispering pines, Rip the while feelingly rehearsing to his beloved some memories of his indulgent mother now departed, she suddenly changed the subject. Pointing to the unfinished house, she amiably suggested to the bridegroom that he could readily do what was needful to putting it in trim; for was not her dear Rip a bit of a carpenter? But Rip, though rather taken at unawares, delicately pleaded something to the effect that the clattering hammer and rasping saw would be a rude disturbance to the serene charm of the honeymoon. Setting out a little orchard for future bearing, would suit the time better, and this he engaged shortly to do. "Sweetheart," he said in conclusion, with sly magnetism, twining an arm around her jimp waist, "Sweetheart, I will take up the saw and hammer in good time." That good time proved very dilatory; in fact, it never came. But, good or bad, time has a persistent, never-halting way of running on, and by so doing brings about wonderful changes and transformations. Ere very long the bride developed into the dame; the bridegroom into that commonplace entity, the married man. Moreover, some of those pleasing qualities which in the lover had won the inexperienced virgin's affections, turned out to be the points least desirable, as of least practical efficiency in a husband, one not born to fortune, and who therefor, to advance himself in the work-a-day world, must needs energetically elbow his way therein, quite regardless of the amenities while so doing; either this, or else resort to the sinuous wisdom of the serpent.

Enough. Alike with the unfinished house, and its tenants new to the complexities of the lock wedlock, things took their natural course. As to the house, never being treated to a protective coat of paint, since Rip's exchequer was always at low ebb, it soon contracted, signally upon its northern side, a gray weather-stain, supplying one topic for Dame Van Winkle's domestic reproaches; for these in the end came, though, in the present instance, they did not wholly originate in any hard utilitarian view of matters.

Women, more than men, disrelishing the idea of old age, are sensitive, even the humblest of them, to aught in any way unpleasantly suggestive of it. And the gray weather-stain not only gave the house the aspect of age, but worse; for in association with palpable evidences of its recentness as an erection, it imparted a look forlornly human, even the look of one grown old before his time. The roof quite as much as the clapboards contributed to make notable in it the absence of that spirit of youth which the sex, however hard the individual lot, inheriting more of the instinct of Paradise than ourselves, would fain recognise in everything. The shingles there, with the supports for the shingler—which temporary affairs had through Rip's re-missness been permanently left standing—these it took, but a few autumns to veneer with thin mosses, especially in that portion where the betrayed purpose expressed by the uncompleted abode had been lamented over by a huge willow—the object now missing—a willow of the weeping variety, under whose shade the house had originally been built. Broken bits of rotted twigs and a litter of discolored leaves were the tears continually wept by this ancient Jeremiah upon the evergreening roof of the house fatally arrested in course of completion.

No wonder that so untidy an old inhabitant had always been the object of Dame Van Winkle's dislike. And when Rip, no longer the bridegroom, in obedience to her imperative command, attacking it with an axe none the sharpest, and finding the needful energetic blows sorely jarring to the natural quiescence of his brain-pan, ig-nominiously gave it up, the indignant dame herself assaulted it. But the wenned trunk was of inordinate diameter, and, under the wens, of an obtuse soft toughness all but invincible to the dulled axe. In brief the venerable old tree long remained a monument of the nega-tive victory of a stub[b]orn inertia over spasmodic activity and an ineffectual implement.

But the scythe that advances forever and never needs whetting, sweeping that way at last, brought the veteran to the sod. Yes, during Rip's sylvan slumbers the knotty old inhabitant had been gathered to his fathers. Falling prone, and luckily away from the house, in time it made its own lowly monument; an ever-crumbling one, to be sure, yet, all the more for that, tenderly dressed by the Spring: an umber-lined mound of mellow punk, mossed in spots, with wild violets springing from it here and there, attesting the place of the departed, even the same place where it fell.

But, behold: shooting up above the low, dilapidated eaves, the Lilac now laughed where the inconsolable willow had wept. Lightly it dropt upon the green roof the pink little bells from its bunched blos-soms in place of the old willow's yellowed leaves. Seen from the wood, as Rip in his reappearance viewed it, in part it furnished a gay screen to the late abode, now a tenantless ruin, hog-backed at last by the settling of the ridge-pole in the middle, abandoned to leisurely decay, and to crown its lack of respectability, having a scandalous name as the nightly rendezvous of certain disreputable ghosts, including that of poor Rip himself. Nevertheless, for all this sad decay and disrepute, there must needs have been something of redeeming attractiveness in those deserted premises, as the following incident may show, the interest whereof may perchance serve to justify its insertion even at this critical point.

In the month of blossoms long after Rip's disappearance in the mountain forests, followed in time by the yet more mysterious evanishment of his dame under the sod of the lowlands, a certain meditative vagabondo, to wit, a young artist, in his summer wanderings after the Picturesque, was so taken by the pink Lilac relieved against the greenly ruinous home, that camping under his big umbrella before those admirable objects one fine afternoon he opened his box of colors, brushes, and so forth, and proceeded to make a study.

While thus quietly employed he arrested the attention of a gaunt hatchet-faced stony-eyed individual, with a gray sort of salted complexion like that of a died cod-fish, jogging by on a lank horse. The stranger alighted, and after satisfying his curiosity as to what the artist was about, expressed his surprise that such an object as a miserable old ruin should be thought worth painting. "Why," said he, "if you *must* idle it this way—can find nothing more useful to do, paint something respectable, or, better, something godly; paint our new tabernacle—there is it," pointing right ahead to a rectangular edifice stark on a bare hill-side, with an aspiring wooden steeple whereon the distant blue peaks of the Cattskills placidly looked down, peradventure mildly wondering whether any rivalry with them was intended. "Yes, paint *that* now," he continued; "just the time for it; it got its last coat only the other day. Ain't it white, though!"

A cadaver! shuddered the artist to himself, glancing at it, and instantly averting his eyes. More vividly than ever he felt the difference between dead planks or dead iron smeared over with white-lead; the difference between these and white marble, when new from the quarry sparkling with the minute mica in it, or, mellowed by ages, taking on another and more genial tone endearing it to that Pantheistic antiquity, the sense whereof is felt or latent in every one of us. In visionary flash he saw in their prime the perfect temples of Attica flushed with Apollo's rays on the hill-tops, or on the plain at eve disclosed in glimpses through the sacred groves around them. For the moment, in this paganish dream he quite lost himself.

"Why don't you speak?" irritably demanded the other; "won't you paint it?"

"It is sufficiently painted already, heaven knows," said the artist coming to himself with a discharging sigh, and now resignedly setting himself to work.

"You will stick to this wretched old ruin, then, will you?"

"Yes, and the Lilac."

"The Lilac? and black what-do-you-call-it—lichen, on the trunk, so old is it. It is half-rotten, and its flowers spring from the rottenness under it, just as the moss on those eaves does from the rotting shingles."

"Yes, decay is often a gardener," assented the other.

"What's that gibberish? I tell you this beggarly ruin is no more a fit object for a picture than the disreputable vagabond who once lived in it."

"Ah!" now first pricking his ears; "who was he? Tell me."

And straightway the hatchet-faced individual rehearsed, and in a sort of covertly admonitory tone, Rip's unheroic story up to the time of his mysterious disappearance. This, by the way, he imputed to a Providential visitation overtaking a lazy reprobate whose chief occupation had been to loaf up and down the country with a gun and game-bag, much like some others with a big umbrella and a box.

"Thank you, friend," said the sedate one, never removing his eyes from his work, "Thank you; but what should we poor devils of Bohemians do for the Picturesque, if Nature was in all things a precisian, each building like that church, and every man made in your image.—But, bless me, what am I doing? I must tone down the green here!"

"Providence will take you in hand one of these days, young man," in high dudgeon exclaimed the other; "Yes, it will give you a *toning down* as you call it. *Made in my image!* You wrest Holy Writ; I shake the dust off my feet and leave you for profane."

"Do," was the mildly acquiescent and somewhat saddish response; and the busy brush intermitted not, while the lean visitor, remounting his lank albino, went on his way.

But presently in an elevated turn of the hilly road man and horse, outlined against the vivid blue sky, obliquely crossed the Bohemian's sight, and the next moment as if swallowed by the grave disappeared in the descent.

"What is that verse in the Apocalypse," murmured the artist to
himself, now suspending the brush and ruminatingly turning his head
sideways, "the verse that prompted Benjamin West to his big canvas?
—*And I looked and beheld a pale horse, and his name that sat on
him was Death'.*—Well, I won't allegorise and be mystical, and all
that, nor even say that Death dwells not under the cemetery turf,
since rather it is Sleep inhabits there; no, only this much will I say,
that to-day have I seen him, even Death, seen him in the guise of a
living man on a living horse; that he dismounted and had speech with
me; and that though an unpleasant sort of person, and even a queer
threatener withal, yet, if one meets him, one must get along with him
as one can; for his ignorance is extreme. And what under heaven indeed should such a phantasm as Death know, for all that the Appearance tacitly claims to be somebody that knows much?"

Luck is a good deal in this world. Had the Bohemian, instead of
chancing that way when he did, come into the same season but a few
years later, the period of the present recital, who knows but that the
opportunity might have been furnished him of sketching tattered Rip
himself in his picturesque resurrection bewildered and at a stand before his own door, even as erewhile we left him.

Ere sighting the premises, Rip's doddering faculties had been
sufficiently nonplussed by various unaccountable appearances, such
as branch-roads which he could not recall, and fields rustling with
young grain where he seemed to remember waving woods; so that
now the absence of the old willow and its replacement by the lilac—a
perfect stranger, standing sentry at his own door, and, as it were,
challenging his right to further approach—these phenomena quite
confound him.

Recovering his senses a little, while yet with one hand against
his wrinkled brow remaining bodily transfixed, in wandering sort half
unconsciously he begins:

RIP VAN WINKLE'S LILAC

"Ay,—no!—My brain is addled yet;
With last night's flagons—full I forget.
But look.—Well, well, it so must be,
For there it *is,* and, sure, I see.
Yon Lilac is all right, no doubt,

Tho' never before, Rip—spied him out!
But where's the willow?—Dear, dear me!
This is the hill-side,—sure; the stream
Flows yon; and *that,* wife's house would seem
But for the silence. Well, may be,
For this one time—Ha! do I see
Those burdocks going in at door?
They only loitered round before!
No,—ay!—Bless me, it is the same!
But yonder Lilac! how now came—
Rip, where does Rip van Winkle live?
Lilac?—a lilac? Why, just there,
If my cracked memory don't deceive,
'Twas *I* set out a Lilac fair,
Yesterday morning, seems to me.
Yea, sure, that it might thrive and come
To plead for me with wife, tho' dumb.
I found it—dear me—well, well, well,
Squirrels and angels they can tell!
My head!—whose head?—Ah, Rip, (I'm Rip)
That lilac was a little slip,
And yonder lilac is a tree!"

But why rehearse in every section
The withered good-fellow's resurrection,
Happily told by happiest Irving
Never from genial verity swerving;
And, more to make the story rife,
By Jefferson acted true to life.
Me here it but behooves to tell
Of things that posthumously fell.

It came to pass as years went on
(An Indian file in stealthy flight
With purpose never man has known)
A villa brave transformed the sight
Of Rip's abode to nothing gone,
Himself remanded into night.
Each June the owner joyance found

In one prized tree that held its ground,
One tenant old where all was new,—
Rip's Lilac to its youth still true.
Despite its slant ungainly trunk
Atwist and black like strands in junk,
Annual yet it flowered aloft
In juvenile pink, complexion soft.

That owner hale, long past his May,
His children's children—every one
Like those Rip romped with in the sun—
Merrily plucked the clusters gay.

The place a stranger scented out
By Boniface told in vinous way—
"Follow the fragrance!" Truth to own
Such reaching wafture ne'er was blown
From common Lilac. Came about
That neighbors, unconcerned before
When bloomed the tree by lowly door,
Craved now one little slip to train;
Neighbor from neighbor begged again.
On every hand stem shot from slip,
Till, lo, that region now is dowered
Like the first Paradise embowered,
Thanks to the poor good-for-nothing Rip!

Some think those parts should bear his name;
But no—the blossoms take the fame.
Slant finger-posts by horsemen scanned
Point the green miles—*To Lilac Land.*

Go ride there down one charmful lane,
O reader mine, when June's at best,
A dream of Rip shall slack the rein,
For there his heart flowers out confessed.
And there you'll say,—O, hard ones, truce!
See, where man finds in man no use,
Boon Nature finds one—Heaven be blest!

Introduction to
The Alhambra, 1896

BY ELIZABETH ROBINS PENNELL

In 1896, in London and New York, Macmillan published a handsomely bound edition of *The Alhambra,* the Author's Revised Edition, somewhat abridged, but generously supplied with black-and-white illustrations done by the American artist Joseph Pennell (1857–1926). This art critic, teacher, and fertile creator of scenic drawings, was then an expatriate in England, an intimate of Whistler. The introduction, included here, to this unusually decorative edition of Irving's most popular Spanish book, was done by the artist's wife, Elizabeth Robins Pennell (1855–1936), herself an accomplished art editor, biographer, and literary journalist. Slight mistakes aside (the revised *Alhambra* appeared in 1851 not 1857), this remains a good example of the kind of impressionistic criticism this book attracted from the start of its long career as a favorite with travelers to Iberia.

It is not possible to forget Washington Irving in the Alhambra. With a single volume, the simple, gentle, kindly American man of letters became no less a figure in the Moor's Red Palace than Boabdil and Lindaraxa of whom he wrote. And yet, never perhaps did a book make so unconscious a bid for popularity. Irving visited Granada in 1828. He returned the following year, when the Governor's apartments in the Alhambra were lent to him as lodgings. There he spent several weeks, his love for the place growing with every day and hour. It was this affection, and no more complex motive, that prompted him to describe its courts and gardens and to record its legends. The work was the amusement of his leisure moments, filling the interval between the completion of one serious, and now all but unknown, history and the beginning of the next.

Not many other men just then could write about Spain or anything Spanish so naturally. For, in 1829, while, within the walls of Alhamar and Yusef, he was listening to the prattle of Mateo and Dolores, in Paris, Alfred de Musset was writing his *Contes d'Espagne,* and Victor Hugo was publishing a new edition of his *Orientales.* A year later and the battle of *Hernani* was to be fought at the *Comédie Française;* a few more, and Théophile Gautier would be on his way across the Pyrenees. Time had passed since Châteaubriand, the pioneer of romance, could dismiss the Alhambra with a word. Hugo, in turning all eyes to the East, had declared that Spain also was Oriental, and to his disciples the journey, dreamed or made, through the land where Irving travelled in single-minded enjoyment, was an excuse for the profession of their literary faith. Irving, whatever his accomplishments, was unencumbered with a mission and innocent of pose. There is no reason to believe that he had ever heard of the Romanticists, or the part Spain was playing in the revolution; though he had been in Paris when the storm was brewing; though he returned after the famous red waistcoat had been sported in the public's face. At any rate, like the original genius of to-day, he kept his knowledge to himself.

Literary work took Irving to Spain. Several years before, in 1818, he had watched the total wreck of his brother's business. This was the second event of importance in his hitherto mild and colourless existence. The first had been the death of the girl he was to marry, a loss which left him without interest or ambition. There was then no need for him to work, and his health was delicate. He travelled a little: an intelligent, sympathetic and observant tourist. He wrote a little, discovering that he was an author with *Knickerbocker*. But his writing was of the desultory sort until, when he was thirty-five years old, his brother's failure forced him to make literature his profession. It was after he had published his *Sketch-Book* and *Brace-bridge Hall* and *Old Christmas,* after their reception had been of the kind to satisfy even the present generation of writers who measure the excellence of work by the price paid for it, that some one suggested he should translate the journeys of Columbus, which Navarrete, a Spanish author, had in hand. Murray, it was thought, would give a handsome sum down for the translation. Murray himself, however, was not so sure: wanted, wise man, first to see a portion of the manuscript. This was just what could not be until Irving had begun his task. But already in Madrid, and assured of nothing, he found the *rôle* of translator less congenial than that of historian, and the Spanish work eventually resolved itself into his *Life of Columbus.* "Delving in the rich ore" of the old chronicles in the Jesuits' Library of St. Isidoro, there was one side issue in the history he was studying that enchanted him above all else. This was the Conquest of Granada, the brilliant episode which had fascinated him ever since, as a boy at play on the banks of the Hudson, his allegiance had been divided between the Spanish cavalier, in gold and silver armour, prancing over the Vega, and the Red Indian brandishing his tomahawk on the war-path. Now, occasionally, Columbus was forgotten that he might collect the materials for a new story of the Conquest to be told by himself. To consult further documents he started one spring (1828), when the almond trees were blossoming, for Andalusia; and Granada, of course, came into his journey. Thus chance brought him to the Alhambra, while (1829) the courtesy of the Governor and the kindness of old Tia Antonia put him in possession of the rooms of the beautiful Elizabeth of Parma, overlooking the oranges and fountains of the Garden of Lindaraxa.

The Alhambra reveals but half its charm to the casual visitor. I know, of my own experience, how far custom is from staling its infinite variety, how its beauty increases as day by day one watches the play of light and shadow on its walls, as day by day one yields to the indolent dreams for which it was built. There was one summer when, all through July and August, its halls and courts gave me shelter from the burning, blinding sunshine of Andalusia, and the weeks in passing strengthened the spell that held me there. For Gautier, the place borrowed new loveliness from the one night he slept in the Court of Lions. But by day and night alike, it belonged to Irving; he saw it before it had degenerated into a disgracefully managed museum and annex to a *bric-à-brac* shop for the tourist; and he had heard all its stories, or had had time to invent them, before he was called away by his appointment to some useless and unnecessary diplomatic post at the American Legation in London.

The book was not published until more than two years later (1832). Irving, though a hack in a manner, had too much self-respect to rush into print on the slightest provocation. Colburn and Bentley were his English publishers, their edition preceding by a few months the American, brought out by Lea and Carey of Philadelphia. The same year saw two further issues in Paris, one by Galignani, and the other in Baudry's Foreign Library, as well as a French translation from the house of Fournier. The success of *The Alhambra* was immediate. De Musset and Victor Hugo had left the great public in France as indifferent as ever to the land beyond the Pyrenees. Irving raised a storm of popular applause in England and America, where, of a sudden, he made Spain, which the Romanticists would have snatched as their spoils, the prey of the *"bourgeois"* they despised. Nor was it the general public only that applauded. There were few literary men in England who did not welcome the book with delight.

I think to-day, without suspicion of disloyalty, one may wonder a little at this success. Certainly, in its first edition, *The Alhambra* is crude and stilted, though, to compare it with the pompous trash which Roscoe published three years afterward, as text for the drawings of David Roberts, is to see in it a masterpiece. Irving, more critical than his readers, knew it needed revision. "It is generally labour lost," he said once in a letter to Alexander Everett, "to attempt to improve a book that has already made its impression on the public." Nevertheless, *The Alhambra* was all but re-written in 1857, when he was preparing a complete edition of his works for Putnam, the New York publisher, and it gained enormously in the process. It was not so much by the addition of new chapters, or the re-arrangement of the old; but rather by the changes made in the actual text—the light touch of local colour here, and there the rounding of a period, the developing of an incident. For example "The Journey," so gay and vivacious in the final version, was, at first, but a bare statement of facts, with no space for the little adventures by the way: the rest at the old mill near Seville; the glimpses of Archidona, Antiquero, Osuna, names that lend picturesque value to the ride; the talk and story-telling in the inn at Loxa. Another change, less commendable, is the omission from the late editions of the dedication to Wilkie. It was a pleasant tribute to the British painter, who, with several of his fellows—Lewis and Roberts—was carried away by that wave of Orientalism which sent the French Marilhat and Decamps, Fromentin and Delacroix to the East, and had not yet spent its force in the time of Regnault. The dedication was well-written, kindly, appreciative: an amiable reminder of the rambles the two men had taken together in Toledo and Seville, and the interest they had shared in the beauty left by the Moor to mark his passage through the land both were learning to love. As a memorial to the friendship between author and artist, it could less well have been spared than any one of the historical chapters that go to swell the volume.

Even in the revised edition it would be easy to belittle Irving's achievement, now that it is the fashion to disparage him as author. Certainly, *The Alhambra* has none of the splendid melodrama of Borrow's *Bible in Spain,* none of the picturesqueness of Gautier's record. It is very far from being that "something in the Haroun Alraschid style," with dash of Arabian spice, which Wilkie had urged him to make it. Nor are its faults wholly negative. It has its moments of dulness. It abounds in repetitions. Certain adjectives recur with a pertinacity that irritates. The Vega is blooming, the battle is bloody, the Moorish maiden is beauteous far more than once too often. Worse still, descriptions are duplicated, practically the same passage reappearing again and again, as if for the sake of padding, or else as the mere babble of the easy writer. Indeed, many of the purely historical chapters have been crowded in so obviously because they happened to be at hand, and he without better means to dispose of them, and then scattered discreetly, that there is less hesitation in omitting them altogether from the present edition. An edited *Tom Jones,* a bowdlerized Shakespeare may be an absurdity. But to drop certain chapters from *The Alhambra* is simply to anticipate the reader in the act of skipping. There is no loss, since all important facts and descriptions are given more graphically and entertainingly elsewhere in the book.*

Perhaps it may seem injudicious to introduce a new edition of so popular a work by pointing out its defects. But one can afford to be honest about Irving. *The Alhambra* might have more serious blemishes, and its charm would still survive triumphantly the test of the harshest criticism. For, whatever subtlety, whatever elegance Irving's style may lack, it is always distinguished by that something which, for want of a better name, is called charm—a quality always as difficult to define as Lowell thought when he found it in verse or in perfume. But there it is in all Washington Irving wrote: a clue to the lavish praise of his contemporaries—of Coleridge, who pronounced *The Conquest of Granada* a *chef d'œuvre,* and Campbell, who believed he had added clarity to the English tongue; of Byron and Scott and Southey; of Dickens, whose pockets were at one time filled with Irving's books worn to tatters; of Thackeray, who likened the American to Goldsmith, describing him as "one of the most charming masters of our lighter language."

Much of this power to please is due, no doubt, to the simplicity and sincerity of Irving's style at its best. Despite a tendency to diffuseness, despite a fancy for the ornate, when there is a story to be told, he can be as simple and straightforward as the child's "Once upon a time," with which he begins many a tale: appropriately, since the legends of the Alhambra are but stories for grown-up children. And there is no question of the sincerity of his love for everything savouring of romance. For that matter, it is seldom that he does not mean what he says and does not say it so truly with his whole heart, that you are convinced, where you distrust the emotion of De Amicis, pumping up tears of admiration before the wrong thing, or of Maurice Barrès seeing all Spain through a haze of blood, voluptuousness, and death. It was the strength of his feeling for the Alhambra that led Irving to write in its praise, not the desire to write that manufactured the feeling. Humour and sentiment some of his critics have thought

* These arbitrary omissions, nowhere listed by Pennell, number eleven: 1. The Jesuits' Library, 2. Alhamar, the Founder of the Alhambra, 3. Yusef Abul Hagig, the Finisher of the Alhambra, 4. The Truant, 5. The Abencerrages, 6. Public Fetes of Granada, 7. Local Traditions, 8. Relics and Genealogies, 9. Spanish Romance, 10. Legend of Don Munio Sancho De Hinojosa, 11. Poets and Poetry of Moslem Andalus [*Ed.*].

the predominant traits of his writing, as of his character. It is a foretunate combination: his sentiment, though it often threatens, seldom overflows into gush, kept within bounds as it is by the sense of humour that so rarely fails him. His power of observation was of still greater service. He could use his eyes. He could see things for himself. And he was quick to detect character. Occasionally one finds him slipping. In his landscape, the purple mountains of Alhama rise wherever he considers them most effective in the picture; and the snow considerately never melts from the slopes of the Sierra Nevada, which I have seen all brown at midsummer. He could look only through the magnifying glass of tradition at the hand and key on the Gate of Justice; symbols so gigantic in fiction, so insignificant in fact that one might miss them altogether, did not every book, paper, and paragraph, every cadging, swindling tout—I mean guide—in Granada bid one look for them. But these are minor discrepancies. In essentials, his observation never played him false. There may not be a single passage to equal in force and brilliance Gautier's wonderful description of the bull-fight at Malaga; but his impressions were so clear, his record of them so faithful, that the effect of his book remains, while the accomplishment of a finer artist in words may be remembered but vaguely. It is Irving who prepares one best for the stern grandeur and rugged solemnity of the country between Seville and Granada. The journey can now be made by rail. But to travel by road as he did—as we have done—is to know that his arid mountains and savage passes are no more exaggerated than the pleasant valleys and plains that lie between. For Spain is not all gaiety as most travellers would like to imagine it, as most painters have painted it, save Daumier in his pictures of Don Quixote among the barren hills of La Mancha. And if nothing in Granada and the Alhambra can be quite unexpected, it is because one has seen it all beforehand with Irving, from the high Tower of Comares and the windows of the Hall of Ambassadors, or else, following him through the baths and mosque and courts of the silent Palace, crossing the ravine to the cooler gardens of the Generalife, and climbing the Albaycin to the white church upon its summit.

There have been many changes in the Alhambra since Irving's day. The Court of Lions lost in loveliness when the roses with which he saw it filled were uprooted. The desertion he found had more picturesqueness than the present restoration and pretence of orderliness.

Irving was struck with the efforts which the then Commander, Don
Francisco de Serna, was making to keep the Palace in a state of repair and to arrest its too certain decay. Had the predecessors of De
Serna, he thought, discharged the duties of their station with equal
fidelity, the Alhambra might have been still almost as the Moor, or at
least Spanish royalty had left it. What would he say, one wonders, to
the Alhambra under its present management? Frank neglect is often
less an evil than sham zeal. The student, watched, badgered, op-
pressed by red-tapeism, has not gained by official vigilance; nor is the
Palace the more secure because responsibility has been transferred
from a pleasant gossiping old woman to half a dozen indolent guides.
The burnt roof in the ante-chamber to the Hall of Ambassadors
shows the carelessness of which the new officers can be guilty; the
matches and cigarette ends with which courts and halls are strewn
explain that so eloquent a warning has been in vain. And if the re-
storer has been let loose in the Alhambra, at the Generalife there is
an Italian proprietor, eager, it would seem, to initiate the somnolent
Spaniard into the brisker ways of Young Italy. Cypresses, old as Zo-
raïde, have already been cut down ruthlessly along that once unri-
valled avenue, and their destruction, one fears, is but the beginning
of the end.

But whatever changes the past sixty years have brought about in
Granada, the popularity of Irving's book has not weakened with
time. Not Ford, nor Murray, nor Hare has been able to replace it.
The tourist reads it within the walls it commemorates as conscientiously as the devout read Ruskin in Florence. It serves as text book
in the Court of Lions and the Garden of Lindaraxa. It is the student's
manual in the high *mirador* of the Sultanas and the court of the
mosque where Fortuny painted. In a Spanish translation it is pressed
upon you almost as you cross the threshold. Irving's rooms in the
Palace are always locked, that the guide may get an extra fee for
opening—as a special favour—an apartment which half the people
ask to see. As the streamers "Rip Van Winkle" and "Knickerbocker"
ply up and down the Hudson, so the Hotel Washington Irving rises
under the shadow of the Alhambra. Even the spirits and spooks that
haunt every grove and garden are all of his creation, as Spaniards
themselves will be quick to tell you; though who Irving—or, in their
familiar speech, "Vashington"—was, but very few of them could explain. And thus his name has become so closely associated with the

place that, just as Diedrich Knickerbocker will be remembered while New York stands, so Washington Irving cannot be forgotten so long as the Red Palace looks down upon the Vega and the tradition of the Moor lingers in Granada.

From "Washington Irving"

BY BARRETT WENDELL

Barrett Wendell (1855–1921), a turn-of-the-century academic leader, was after graduation from the College a member of the Harvard faculty from 1880 to 1917. There he early taught a course in our indigenous literature which, characteristically, combined the facts of history with the evolution of the American mind. Author of pioneering textbooks, and literary studies like *Cotton Mather: Puritan Priest* (1891), he also wrote his own essays, novels, and plays. His major work, *A Literary History of America* (1900), was a widely influential book despite, as later generations could plainly see, a fitfully anglophilic orientation. This is not obtrusive in his analysis of Irving's strengths and weaknesses in Chapter II, Book IV of that work, all but the conclusion of which is reprinted here.

The name of Washington Irving reminds us rather startlingly how short is the real history of American letters. Although he has been dead for a little more than forty years, many people still remember him personally; and when in 1842 he went as President Tyler's minister to Spain, he passed through an England where Queen Victoria had already been five years on the throne, and he presented his credentials to Queen Isabella II., who, although long exiled from her country, is still a not very old lady in Paris. Yet in one sense this Irving, who has not yet faded from living memory, may be called, more certainly than Brockden Brown, the first American man of letters. At least, he was the first whose work has remained popular; and the first, too, who was born after the Revolution had made native Americans no longer British subjects but citizens of the United States. His parents, to be sure, were foreign, his father Scotch, his mother English; but he himself was born in New York in 1783. He was not very strong; his early habits were rather desultory and his education irregular; he studied law and was admitted to the bar, but never practiced much; and at the age of twenty-one he was sent abroad for his health. There he remained two years.

His distinctly American character first becomes salient during this trip abroad, at that time an unusual experience. He was of simple origin; his family were in respectable trade. Born in England, he might have been as accomplished and agreeable as he ever became, but he could hardly have been received on equal terms by the polite society of Europe. Going abroad, as an American citizen, however, he took from the beginning a social position there which he maintained to the end. He was cordially received by people of rank, and incidentally had little to do with those of the station which would have been his had his family never emigrated to this side of the Atlantic. He was among the first, in short, of that distinguished body of Americans, of whom later examples are such men as Ticknor, Everett, Sumner, Motley, and Lowell, who have proved during the nineteenth century the social dignity of American letters.

In 1806, Irving returned home; the next year, in company with one or two kinsmen, he began writing a series of essays called the "Salmagundi Papers." Only his subsequent eminence has preserved from blameless oblivion these conventional survivals of the eighteenth century. About this time occurred an episode which deeply influenced his whole life: he fell in love with a young girl whose death at seventeen almost broke his heart. When she died he was at her bedside; and throughout his later life he could not bear to hear her name mentioned. The tender melancholy which one recognises all through his writings was probably due to this bereavement; and the intense simplicity and faithfulness of his pure and ideal love is characteristic not only of the man but of his country.

In 1809 he published his first considerable book,—the "Knickerbocker History of New York." Shortly thereafter he devoted himself to business; and in 1815 he went abroad in connection with his affairs. There, after a few years, commercial misfortune overtook him. In 1819 he brought out his "Sketch Book;" from that time forth he was a professional man of letters. He remained abroad until 1832, spending the years between 1826 and 1829 in Spain, and those between 1829 and 1832 as Secretary to the American Legation in London. Coming home, he resided for ten years at Tarrytown on the Hudson, in that house "Sunnyside" which has become associated with his name. From 1842 to 1846 he was Minister to Spain. He then finally returned home, crowning his literary work with his "Life of Washington," of which the last volume appeared in the year of his death, 1859.

Irving was the first American man of letters to attract wide attention abroad. The "Knickerbocker History" was favourably received by contemporary England; and the "Sketch Book" and "Bracebridge Hall," which followed it, were from the beginning what they have remained,—as popular in England as they have been in his native country. The same, on the whole, is true of his writings about Spain; and, to somewhat slighter degree, of his "Life of Goldsmith" and his "Life of Washington." The four general classes of work here mentioned followed one another in fairly distinct succession through his half-century of literary life. We may perhaps get our clearest notion of him by considering them in turn.

The "Knickerbocker History of New York" has properly lasted. The origin of this book resembles that of Fielding's "Joseph Andrews" some seventy years before, and of Dickens's "Pickwick Papers" some twenty-five years later. All three began as burlesques and ended as independent works of fiction, retaining of their origin little more trace than occasional extravagance. In 1807 one Dr. Samuel Latham Mitchill had published "A Picture of New York," said to be ridiculous, even among works of its time, for ponderous pretentiousness. The book had such success, however, that Irving and his brother were moved to write a parody of it. Before long Irving's brother tired of the work, which was left to Irving himself. As he wrote on, his style and purpose underwent a change. Instead of burlesquing Mitchill, he found himself composing a comic history of old New York, and incidentally introducing a good deal of personal and political satire, now as forgotten as that which lies neglected in "Gulliver's Travels." His style, which began in deliberately ponderous imitation of Dr. Mitchill's, passed almost insensibly into one of considerable freedom, evidently modelled on that of eighteenth-century England. Most of the book, then, reads like some skilful bit of English writing during the generation which preceded the American Revolution. The substance of the book, however, is distinctly different from what was then usual in England.

Assuming throughout the character of Diedrich Knickerbocker, an eccentric old bachelor who typifies the decaying Dutch families of New York, Irving mingles with many actual facts of colonial history all manner of unbridled extravagance. The governors and certain other of his personages are historical; the wars with New Englanders are historical wars; and historical, too, is the profound distaste for Yankee character which Washington Irving needed no assumed personality to feel. But throughout the book there mingles with these historical facts the wildest sort of sportive nonsense. Wouter Van Twiller, to take a casual example, was an authentic Dutch governor of New Amsterdam; and here is the way in which Irving writes about him:—

"In his council he presided with great state and solemnity. He sat in a huge chair of solid oak, hewn in the celebrated forest of the Hague, fabricated by an experienced timmerman of Amsterdam, and curiously carved about the arms and feet, into exact imitations of gigantic eagle's claws. Instead of a sceptre he swayed a long Turkish pipe, wrought with jasmin and amber, which had been presented to a stadtholder of Holland, at the conclusion of a treaty with one of the petty Barbary powers. In this stately chair would he sit, and this magnificent pipe would he smoke, shaking his right knee with constant motion, and fixing his eye for hours together upon a little print of Amsterdam, which hung in a black frame against the opposite wall of the council chamber. Nay, it has even been said that when any deliberation of extraordinary length and intricacy was on the carpet, the renowned Wouter would shut his eyes for full two hours at a time, that he might not be disturbed by external objects—and at such times the internal commotion of his mind was evinced by certain regular guttural sounds, which his admirers declared were merely the noise of conflict, made by his contending doubts and opinions."

More than possibly the chair here mentioned was some real chair which Irving had seen and in which an old Dutch governor might have sat. Conceivably the Turkish pipe may have been at least legendarily true. The rest of the passage is utter extravagance; yet you will be at a little pains to say just where fact passes nonsense.

Though this kind of humour is not unprecedented, one thing about it is worth attention. When we were considering the work of Franklin, we found in his letter to a London newspaper concerning the state of the American colonies a grave mixture of fact and nonsense, remarkably like the American humour of our later days. In Irving's "Knickerbocker History" one finds something very similar. The fun of the thing lies in frequent and often imperceptible lapses from sense to nonsense and back again. Something of the same kind, expressed in a far less gracious manner than Irving's, underlies Mark Twain's comic work and that of our latest journalistic humourist, Mr. Dooley. This deliberate confusion of sense and nonsense, in short, proves generally characteristic of American humour; and although the formal amenity of Irving's style often makes him seem rather an imitator of the eighteenth-century English writers than a native American, one can feel that if the "Knickerbocker History" and Franklin's letter could be reduced to algebraic formulæ, these formulæ would pretty nearly coincide both with one another and with that of the "Innocents Abroad." The temper of the "Knickerbocker History," may, accordingly, be regarded as freshly American. The style, meanwhile, is rather like that of Goldsmith. When the "Knickerbocker History" was published, Goldsmith had been dead for thirty-five years. In Irving, then, we find a man who used the traditional style of eighteenth-century England for a purpose foreign at once to the century and the country of its origin.

It was ten years before Irving again appeared as a serious man of letters. Then came the "Sketch Book," which contains his best-known stories,—"Rip Van Winkle" and "The Legend of Sleepy Hollow." The book is a collection of essays and short stories, written in a style more like Goldsmith's than ever. The year in which it appeared was that which gave to England the first two cantos of "Don Juan," Hazlitt's "Lectures on the Comic Writers," Leigh Hunt's "Indicator," Scott's "Bride of Lammermoor" and "Legend of Montrose," Shelley's "Cenci," and Wordsworth's "Peter Bell." There can be little doubt that in formal style the "Sketch Book" is more conscientious than any of these. Its prose, in fact, has hardly been surpassed, if indeed it has been equalled, in nineteenth-century England. This prose, however, is of that balanced, cool, rhythmical sort which in England flourished most during the midyears of the eighteenth century.

In the "Sketch Book," too, there are many papers and passages which might have come straight from some of the later eighteenth-century essayists. On the other hand, there are many passages, such as "Rip Van Winkle," which could hardly have appeared in Goldsmith's England. Though Goldsmith's England, of course, was becoming sentimental, it never got to that delight in a romantic past which characterised the period of which the dominant writer was Sir Walter Scott. By 1819, however, Scott had attained his highest development. In his work there was far more passion and meaning than in the romantic stories of Irving; in technical form, on the other hand, it is comparatively careless, nor on the whole is it more genuinely permeated with the romantic sentiment of the nineteenth century. The story of Rip Van Winkle, for example, is a legend which exists in various European forms. Whether Irving adopted it from such old German tales as that of the sleeping Barbarossa, or from some Spanish story such as he later told when he described the sleep of enchanted Moors, or whether in his time the legend itself had migrated to the Hudson Valley, makes no difference. He assumed that it belonged in the Catskills. He placed it, as a little earlier Brockden Brown placed his less significant romances, in a real background; and he infused into it the romantic spirit which was already characteristic of European letters, and soon to be almost more so of American. He enlivened the tale, meanwhile, with a subdued form of such humour as runs riot in the "Knickerbocker History;" and all this modern sentiment, he phrased as he had phrased his first book, in terms mod-

elled on the traditional style of a generation or two before. The peculiar trait of the "Sketch Book," in short, is its combination of fresh
romantic feeling with traditional Augustan style.

The passages of the "Sketch Book" which deal with England reveal so sympathetic a sense of old English tradition that some of
them, like those concerning Stratford and Westminster Abbey, have
become almost classical; just as Irving's later work, "Bracebridge
Hall," is now generally admitted to typify a pleasant phase of country
life in England almost as well as Sir Roger de Coverley typified another, a century earlier. There are papers in the "Sketch Book,"
however, which from our point of view are more significant. Take
those, for example, on "John Bull" and on "English Writers concerning [sic] America." Like the writing of Hopkinson at the time of the
American Revolution, these reveal a distinct sense on the part of an
able and cultivated American that the contemporary English differ
from our countrymen. The eye which observed John Bull in the aspect which follows, is foreign to England:—

"Though really a good-hearted, good-tempered old fellow at
bottom, yet he is singularly fond of being in the midst of conten-
tion. It is one of his peculiarities, however, that he only relishes
the beginning of an affray; he always goes into a fight with alac-
rity, but comes out of it grumbling even when victorious; and
though no one fights with more obstinacy to carry a contested
point, yet, when the battle is over, and he comes to the reconciliation, he is so much taken up with the mere shaking of hands,
that he is apt to let his antagonist pocket all that they have been
quarrelling about. It is not, therefore, fighting that he ought so
much to be on his guard against, as making friends. It is difficult
to cudgel him out of a farthing; but put him in a good humour,
and you may bargain him out of all the money in his pocket. He
is like a stout ship, which will weather the roughest storm unin-
jured, but roll its masts overboard in the succeeding calm.

"He is a little fond of playing the magnifico abroad; of pull-
ing out a long purse; flinging his money bravely about at boxing
matches, horse races, cock fights, and carrying a high head
among 'gentlemen of the fancy;' but immediately after one of
these fits of extravagance, he will be taken with violent qualms
of economy; talk desperately of being ruined and brought upon

the parish; and, in such moods, will not pay the smallest trades-man's bill, without violent altercation. He is in fact the most punctual and discontented paymaster in the world; drawing his coin out of his breeches pocket with infinite reluctance; paying to the uttermost farthing, but accompanying every guinea with a growl.

"With all his talk of economy, however, he is a bountiful pro-vider, and a hospitable housekeeper. His economy is of a whim-sical kind, its chief object being to devise how he may afford to be extravagant; for he will begrudge himself a beef-steak and pint of port one day, that he may roast an ox whole, broach a hogshead of ale, and treat all his neighbours on the next."

In "Bracebridge Hall" and the "Tales of a Traveller," works which followed the "Sketch Book," Irving did little more than con-tinue the sort of thing which he had done in the first. Perhaps his most noteworthy feat in all three books is that he made prominent in English literature a literary form in which for a long time to come Americans excelled native Englishmen,—the short story. During our century, of course, England has produced a great school of fiction; and except for Cooper and one or two living writers, America can hardly show full-grown novels so good even as those of Anthony Trollope, not to speak of the masterpieces of Dickens, Thackeray, and George Eliot. Certainly until the time of Robert Louis Steven-son, however, no English-speaking writer out of America had pro-duced many short stories of such merit as anybody can recognise in the work of Hawthorne and Poe and Irving. In this fact there is something akin to that other fact which we have just remarked,—the formal superiority of Irving's style to that of contemporary English-men. The English novel, whatever its merits, runs to interminable length, with a disregard of form unprecedented in other civilised lit-erature. A good short story, on the other hand, must generally have complete and finished form. Now, during the nineteenth century American men of letters have usually had a more conscious sense of form than their English contemporaries. The American conscience, in fact, always a bit overdeveloped, has sometimes seemed evident in our attempts at literary art. No one who lacks artistic conscience can write an effective short story; and it is doubtful whether any one troubled with much artistic conscience can write in less than a lifetime a three-volume novel. The artistic conscience revealed in the finish of Irving's style and in his mastery of the short story, then, may be called characteristic of his country.

"Astoria:
Its Author And The
'Sources Of His Inspiration' "

BY HIRAM M. CHITTENDEN

Astoria, Irving's 1836 account of John Jacob Astor's ill-fated Pacific Fur Company (1810–1813), was a rarity in its day, a conscientiously researched and professionally written far-western fur-trade chronicle. At first popular, like *The Adventures of Captain Bonneville* which followed it in 1837, *Astoria* then faded, especially after a European theory of more "scientific" history took hold in the later nineteenth century. In 1902 Hiram M. Chittenden (1858–1917), Captain, Corps of Engineers, U.S.A. (later Brigadier General), in his authoritative *A History of the American Fur Trade of the Far West,* rose to the defense of Irving's two pioneering books. This selection on *Astoria* and its critics, Chapter XIV of Volume I, is from a 1954 reprint, edited by Grace Lee Nute. The extended footnotes, however, are in the Chittenden original.

Astoria fortunate in her historian—Irving's accuracy impugned—Irving's interest in the fur trade—Alleged subservience to Mr. Astor—Irving charged with plagiarism—Irving's *Captain Bonneville*—Franchère's criticism of *Astoria*—Bancroft's treatment of Irving.

Astoria was as happy in finding an historian as she was unfortunate in working out her history. Irving's treatment of this subject has become classic. It has served a two-fold purpose—that of fixing in imperishable characters the history of a great enterprise, and that of preserving to posterity the most real and graphic picture now in existence of a phase of life which has entirely passed away. It is not the purpose here to offer anything in the way of criticism of this great work, but simply to notice one or two popular but erroneous notions concerning it.

The fashion among later writers upon western history has been to rate *Astoria* as a work whose classic standing in literature is due to the brilliancy of its author's style. If not directly, still constantly by innuendo, Mr. Irving's fidelity as an historian is impugned, and he is charged with having embellished his work at the expense of its accuracy. He has been accused by one writer of permitting his friendship for Mr. Astor to bias his judgment of men and events. Finally he has been charged, if not with plagiarism direct, at least with lavish use of the writings of others without due acknowledgment. It is these three matters that will here be given brief consideration.

Great in his calling is the architect or engineer who can design a work like the Brooklyn Bridge, in which every part is so related to every other that there is nothing useless or superfluous in its construction and that the highest result of which the material is capable is realized. But far greater is he who can do not only this, but can add the touches of artistic genius by covering up the cold and severe outlines with the adornments of painting and sculpture, until the result, like St. Peter's of Rome, is a living picture of beauty. The work has lost nothing of its architectural form and proportions, and beneath the superficial beauty are still the same perfect adaptations of the parts to their various uses; but the whole effect is many fold more important, because it appeals to the hearts as well as to the judgments of men. And yet it is a prevalent notion that these two important qualities rarely coexist, and that excellence in either is ordinarily obtained at the expense of the other.

In making a somewhat exhaustive study of the authorities relating to the Astorian enterprise it was expected at the outset to find this popular idea of Irving's *Astoria* the correct one, and that when it came to removing the lustre of art there would be found a rather shaky framework in which would be many a defective member. The result has been exactly the reverse, and it has been a matter of growing astonishment throughout these studies to find with what detail the illustrious author had worked out his theme, and with what judicial fairness he had passed judgment upon actors and events. Not in the allurements of style alone, but in the essential respects of accuracy and comprehensive treatment, Irving's work stands immeasurably above all others upon the subject.

In that always troublesome matter of dates, for example, Irving has fewer errors than any other of the Astorian authors. Most of those in *Astoria* are evidently slips, and are self-corrective from the context.[1]

A matter in which we have taken great interest is the recovery of the routes of the overland Astorians. At the time of these journeys there was almost no geographical knowledge of the country traversed between the Missouri and the Columbia—not even names in most instances to describe natural features by. Even when Irving wrote there were only the crudest maps and very little in the way of geographical information yet collected. It would seem, in this situation, that any attempt to work out routes from the meagre data derived from journals of the expedition must be in a large degree a failure, and from no fault of the author. Yet in spite of all these difficulties it is possible to identify most of the localities very closely, and many of them exactly, from Irving's description. Pen pictures which would probably pass for the effusions of a versatile pen are found to be true to the localities even at the present day. There are indeed some gaps and omissions, but these are nothing in comparison with the remarkable feat of preserving so well the line of march in which not a single scientific observation as to course or direction was taken, and in a country of which no map had ever been made.

No mistake could be greater than to suppose that Irving took up this subject simply as one affording him a good theme for his ever-

---

[1]To the casual reader Irving may seem to skip over his chronology rather carelessly, by his "next mornings," "following days," etc. But whoever will take pains to fit in the proper dates will find that the author has not lost his chronology by these omissions, but has carried it along with fidelity. For example take the following from the narrative of the overland journey of the Astorians east: "On the 11th . . . the next day . . . At daybreak . . . Before daylight . . . the next morning . . . the following day . . . the next day, October 17th" etc.

ready pen, or that he neglected in any degree the weighty responsibility of the historian. The fur trade had commanded his attention from early life. He had visited Montreal and the nearer establishments of the Northwest Company, as well as our own prairies. All his life he had been thrown in contact with those who had spent much of their time in the wilderness. The doings of those engaged in the fur trade "have always been themes of charmed interest to me," he once wrote, "and I have felt anxious to get at the details of their adventurous expeditions." And again: "It is one object of our task, however, to present scenes of the rough life of the wilderness, and we are tempted to fix these few memorials of a transient state of things fast passing into oblivion." Such was the purpose—to "fix" the "details" of events—and this motive finds expression in the remarkable accuracy which runs through the entire work.

As to the charge of undue subservience to Mr. Astor's views, it is difficult to see upon what it is based unless it be the fact that these gentlemen were warm friends. No evidence of it can be found in the book itself, which, though full of admiration for Mr. Astor's enterprise, is no more so than the subject deserves. Irving's treatment of the leading members of the company is eminently fair, and errs, if at all, on the side of generous indulgence. How could he treat more considerately than he has the action of Mr. Hunt or the conduct of Captain Thorn? McDougal might indeed wince under the lash of Irving's pen, but he could scarcely complain that the punishment was greater than the crime.

An oft repeated charge against Irving is that he made use of other authorities without due acknowledgment—and of *Franchère's Narrative* in particular. This is always a serious charge, and particularly reprehensible in an eminent author who filches from the works of obscure writers. Let us see what are the facts. At the time of the publication of *Astoria*, there were four published works which treated of portions of the enterprise. These were the works of Brackenridge and Bradbury, which related only the journey from St. Louis to the Aricara villages; and those of Franchère and Cox, which treated of the general history of the enterprise. What reference does Irving make to these works, and what is his own statement concerning the "sources of his inspiration"? He says: "All the papers relative to the enterprise were accordingly submitted to my inspection. Among them were journals and letters narrating expeditions by land

and sea, and journeys to and fro across the Rocky mountains by routes before untraveled, together with documents illustrative of savage and colonial life on the borders of the Pacific. With such materials in hand I undertook the work." Again he refers to the journals as the authorities "on which I chiefly depended." He explicitly states, however, that these were not all; that he derived information from other sources, and he tells us what those sources were. He adds: "I have, therefore, availed myself occasionally of collateral lights supplied by the published journals of other travelers who had visited the scenes described: such as Messrs. Lewis and Clark, Bradbury, Brackenridge, Long, Franchère, and Ross Cox, and make a general acknowledgment of aid received from these quarters." Not only does he thus discharge with the strictest fidelity his obligation to these authorities, but throughout the text, when he makes direct citation, he states the fact in a foot note.

As a matter of fact Irving follows none of his authorities closely, never to the extent of adopting their language. It is indeed difficult to trace his indebtedness, if there was any, and this fact alone negatives any possibility of extensive borrowing. If he did borrow, he so completely worked the matter over in his own incomparable style, that it was to all intents and purposes new matter.

The estimate that we have here given of *Astoria* applies as well to *Captain Bonneville,* a work equally remarkable for its accuracy of detail and its comprehensive treatment of a wide range of subjects. These two works are the classics of the American fur trade, unapproached and unapproachable in their particular field. They are the full fruition of Mr. Irving's desire to "fix these few memorials of a transient state of things fast passing into oblivion."[2]

---

[2]Although a few writers have seen fit to refer disparagingly to *Astoria* as an historical authority, there are only two who need be considered here— Franchère, whose *Narrative* is the earliest history of Astoria, and Bancroft whose treatment is the latest.

Gabriel Franchère, who is the most reliable authority on the history of Astoria except Irving, took occasion in the English edition of his work, to criticise *Astoria* somewhat severely; but nowhere does he complain that Irving borrowed from him without credit. The burden of his complaint is that Irving gave publicity to the choleric opinions of Captain Thorn touching the young Canadians who sailed in the *Tonquin*. It was indeed too rich a feast to be rejected by the genial author, and the world will always thank him for having made the most of it. Franchère, who was one of the "engravers of tombstones" and writers of journals who so moved the contempt of Captain Thorn, seems to have taken Irving seriously as endorsing the Captain's opinions, whereas he only reports them. This sensitiveness at the humorist's treatment of the young clerks is the only thing of consequence that Franchère has to urge against Irving—a complaint with so little foundation that his editor felt called upon to present a note of apology.

Hubert Howe Bancroft has endeavored to appropriate to himself the historical field of the trans-Mississippi country, and his efforts in this direction have borne fruit in thirty-eight massive volumes. He was compelled to rely mainly on co-laborers whose heterogeneous productions have been consolidated under his own direction and all placed in the first person indicative of personal responsibility. The work is unquestionably a great one in the breadth of subject covered and in the extensive list of authorities quoted, and it will always be a valuable reference work to the student. It is not a work of historical accuracy in its details. Such accuracy was not to be expected; for it would have been beyond the compass of human genius to have covered so vast a field in so short a time and have covered it well. It is not to be wondered at that it abounds in errors—wrong dates, confusion of persons, events and places, erroneous reliance upon authorities, and the like—which make it unsafe as a guide for him who would proceed carefully. These defects are inseparable from the immensity of the task and are not to have weight against the great value of the work as a whole.

No such indulgence, however, can be extended to Mr. Bancroft's discussion of certain historic questions, for pressure of work can not explain his implacable prejudices and his itching desire to put forth theories which shall subvert popular ideals or overthrow accepted conclusions. Particularly, whenever it is a question of an American view as against a Spanish, British, or Indian view, Mr. Bancroft, if the circumstances will possibly admit it, ranges himself against his own countrymen.

In no instance is this peculiar trait more flagrantly in evidence than in his treatment of Astoria, its founder and its historian. His persistent bias of judgment and his bitter prejudice, which place him in an attitude of constant hostility toward Astor and Irving, and lead him repeatedly into sheer falsifications and downright slander, are wholly without rational explanation. It will be alike idle and wearisome to examine in detail the several pages of close print in which Mr. Bancroft exploits his hatred of these two historic characters; but a few examples illustrate the tenor of the whole.

Referring to the articles of agreement of the Pacific Fur Company Mr. Bancroft, in his efforts to clear McDougal, says: "In their agreement with Astor they [the partners] reserved the right to close the business should their interests seem so to dictate. Whatever loss might arise from the enterprise fell on each in proportion to their share." This is not so. The association was not to be dissolved until it should prove unprofitable, and the loss for the first five years was not to be borne by the partners in proportion to their share, but by Mr. Astor alone.

"Had this scheme," says Mr. Bancroft, "been based on self-sacrifice, on pecuniary loss for the public good, or the promulgation of some great principle, the current of unqualified sycophancy, sentimentality, and maudlin praise which runs through *Astoria* might be more bearable." Since when has Mr. Bancroft known of a commercial enterprise being organized on the basis of "pecuniary loss for the public good"? Commercial undertakings are not conducted in that way. It is no criticism of Mr. Astor's projects to say that their sole purpose and aim were money-making. All great projects of discovery and colonization have been founded in commerce. It has been the genius of commerce, rather than that of arms, that has carried the flag of England around the world. The first motive in the foreign policy of all governments is the protection and fostering of the commercial enterprises of their subjects wherever they may be. It may, however, be truly said of the Astorian enterprise that it *did* involve the "promulgation of a great principle"—the cause of American empire on the Pacific coast—and it did involve enormous pecuniary loss in an enterprise that was fraught with the highest possibility for the public good. In respect to the vicious attack upon Irving contained in this paragraph, the candid reader will not find in *Astoria* a single sentence that will lend even the color of justification to it.

Mr. Bancroft says of Irving and Franchère: "There are whole pages in *Astoria* abstracted almost literally from Franchère. Pretending to draw all his information from private sources, the author makes no allusion to the source to which he is most indebted, not even mentioning Franchère's name once in his whole work." It is quite evident that Mr. Bancroft had never read carefully either Irving or Franchère or he would have avoided the pitiful blunders contained in this paragraph. The reader is referred to Irving's own statement of his authorities just given, and to his acknowledgment of aid from Franchère, Cox and others.

Again Bancroft says: "In telling this story [of Reed's massacre] Irving takes whole sentences from Ross and Cox without a sign of an acknowledgment; these works, however, were little read in America in Irving's day." The work of Ross was not published until *thirteen years after Astoria!* Irving does not take a sentence verbatim from Cox and moreover acknowledges his debt to that author for such information as was derived from him. His reference to Cox's work was a better introduction to the American reading public than the young author could have secured in any other way, and Mr. Bancroft's slur that Irving attempted to conceal his reliance upon Cox because of that author's obscurity is excusable only on the ground of ignorance.

Finally as a climax to his exhibition of spleen Mr. Bancroft says: "Up to this time the imputation that he [Irving] had received money from Mr. Astor for writing *Astoria* I believed to be utterly false and unworthy of consideration. But . . . I am otherwise unable to account for this unusual warp of judgment." Mr. Bancroft should produce his facts. To Irving living he would hardly make this accusation without proof in hand. It is not the part of courage at this late day, to placard the infamous slander upon the tombstone of one of America's most gifted and beloved authors. It is needless to say that the whole idea is a climax of absurdity. The work itself refutes the charge. Moreover, was Irving so simple as to suppose that he would escape detection at the bar of history if he departed knowingly from the facts? In the fulness of his reputation is it likely that he would tarnish his great name for any "money" that Mr. Astor might give him? Mr. Bancroft in this affair stands in no higher character than that of libeler and slanderer and his performance is a disgrace to American history.

A searching criticism of Mr. Bancroft's treatment of the Astorian enterprise was published in 1885 in the March number of the *Magazine of American History*. It is from the pen of Peter Koch of Bozeman, Montana.

I regret to note in some of the late Doctor Coues'* recent works an inclination to sanction these popular errors concerning Irving's works on the fur trade; and I deem it only just to say, as an inference from my correspondence with him, that these impressions were rather the result of reading hostile authors like Bancroft than from mature investigation. As his attention was called through specific examples to the general accuracy and originality of these works, he materially modified his earlier opinion of them.

* Elliott Coues (1842–1899) was a physician and ornithologist, who turned editor of key Western Americana [*Ed.*].

From "Washington Irving"

BY WILLIAM B. CAIRNS

William B. Cairns (1867–1932) was one of the shapers of American literature studies early in this century. After a Wisconsin doctorate in 1897 which has been called our first in this field, he remained on the faculty there until his death. Much of his career consisted of innovative successes such as the monograph, "British Criticisms of American Writings, 1780–1815" (1918), and its successor for 1815–1833, published in 1922. A member of the initial editorial board of *American Literature,* his greatest influence was through the careful, and admittedly conservative *A History of American Literature* (1912), a standard long before revision in 1930. This selection, from the unchanged Chapter III, Section I, on "Knickerbocker Writers," shows Cairns to be cautious but clear about Irving's place in literary history.

THREE WORKS COMPARED

Of the three works published between 1819 and 1824 the *Sketch Book* takes highest rank. It is fresher, more spontaneous, and more varied than the others. A few of the sketches are almost universally known. The popularity of "Rip Van Winkle" may have been increased by the wonderful dramatic interpretation of Joseph Jefferson; but the "Legend of Sleepy Hollow," in the broader vein of *Knickerbocker,* is almost equally a favorite. Even the English sketches, many of them on unpromising subjects and tinged with a sentimentality now wholly out of fashion, charm by their clearness and beauty of expression. In *Bracebridge Hall* the style is even smoother, but somewhat less vital and expressive. There is less narrative than the plan of the work seems to call for, and the many descriptions of persons and scenes, strung on so slight a thread of story, become a little monotonous. Only the sketch of "The Stout Gentlemen" approaches "Rip Van Winkle" and "The Legend of Sleepy Hollow" in popularity. The *Tales of a Traveller* has greater variety than *Bracebridge Hall,* but is inferior in almost every way. Irving was not thoroughly familiar with the spirit of the Continental countries in which many of his scenes were laid. His acquaintance with the cruder forms of German romanticism seems to have had a particularly unfortunate effect upon his work. He rarely succeeded in a story of action, and in this collection he attempted many lively tales. Buckthorne is a less pleasing character than most of his literary creations. Moreover, his taste seems to have failed him as it rarely did. "The Story of the Young Robber" fortunately finds no parallel in his other writings.

IRVING IN SEARCH OF A SUBJECT

Irving's difficulties in preparing the *Tales of a Traveller* doubtless showed him that he had worked out the vein opened in the *Sketch Book.* If not he must have been warned by the reviews, English and American. These, while mostly friendly, were not lavish in their praises, and many of them made unfavorable comparison with the earlier volumes. So it came about that Irving found himself, at the age of forty-two, a literary man with an established reputation looking for a remunerative literary job. He declined liberal offers of editorships because he disliked to be tied down to routine work. He refused to contribute to the London "Quarterly Review" because it was unfavorable to America. While still uncertain what to do he went over to Bordeaux "to see the vintage." Here he lingered until he received from Alexander H. Everett, then United States minister to Spain, the suggestion that he translate Navarette's *Voyages of Columbus,* soon to appear at Madrid.

THE SPANISH WRITINGS

On reaching the Spanish capital he found Navarette's work too scrappy to suit his purpose, and he resolved to write an independent life of Columbus. Accordingly he remained at Madrid, working on manuscripts in the government archives and on other original sources. Following a habit of his, he laid aside the *Life of Columbus* to write the first draft of the *Conquest of Granada,* and the former was not finished until 1827 and not published until 1828. He now travelled about Spain, visited the Alhambra, and settled down for about a year at Seville. Here he prepared a second edition of the *Columbus,* and put the *Conquest of Granada* into shape. In 1829 he made another visit to the Alhambra, and it is chiefly the experiences of this second trip that are narrated in the work of that name. The *Legends of the Conquest of Spain* are said to have been finished at this time, but they were not published until later. In 1829 Irving was appointed secretary of legation at London. Here he put in shape the *Voyages of the Companions of Columbus and the Alhambra.*

CHARACTERISTICS OF THE SPANISH WORKS

The Spanish subjects to which Irving was led by the chance suggestion of Everett were admirably suited to his taste. The two chief characteristics seen in the *Sketch Book* were love of the picturesque and genuine patriotism. Spain could gratify the first of these, and Columbus had a connection with America. Irving's fitness for writing biography and history was, however, not remarkable. He was careful, conscientious, and though desultory in his methods, by no means afraid of hard work. He investigated thoroughly many authorities. But he had neither the training nor the temperament of an ideal biographer. Even in the languages that he must use he was mostly self-taught. He had an eye for the picturesque rather than for that which was intrinsically important. The result was that in the *Life of Columbus* he produced a work readable, accurate in statement of unquestioned fact, and as judicial as he knew how to make it, but not, as the great biography must be, the final word on the subject. In the *Conquest of Granada* he made the mistake of trying to tell history in the guise of fiction. The work purports to be extracts from the chronicle of an imaginary monk, Fray Antonio Agapida. Irving intended Fray Antonio to personify the churchman's intense hatred of the Moors, as Carlyle signified a certain temper of mind by Dry-as-Dust. The device was an unfortunate one. The monk is always felt to be a dummy, and his presence tends to discredit the whole work. Irving saw this as soon as the book was published. In a review that, according to the custom of the time, he was asked to write for the "Quarterly" his one object was to maintain that the narrative is veritable history. In the *Alhambra* he was again free to mingle his observations and the results of his imagination without the historian's strict subserviency to facts. This collection of descriptions and tales is called with some justice a Spanish Sketch Book; but it is somewhat thinner and less virile than the earlier work. It seems, too, a little more artificial, as if the author had planned some of his experiences in the old Moorish palace for the "copy" that might be made of them. With the passing of the popular fondness for sentiment it has probably suffered more than the *Sketch Book.*

WRITINGS ON AMERICAN SUBJECTS

The *Alhambra* was published just as Irving returned to America in 1832. He had been absent about half a generation, during which time he had achieved an international reputation, and his native country had experienced great changes. He had always protested his loyalty to America, but had said that he found less distraction from work and more inspiration in the old world. Although there had been much newspaper criticism of his course in remaining abroad, his reception on his return was enthusiastic, and there was a general demand that he write on American themes. It may have been in response to this demand that he took an extensive trip through the new West, going with a government party as far as the Arkansas river, and returning by way of New Orleans and Washington. The literary result of this journey was *A Tour on the Prairies,* published with other material as the *Crayon Miscellany* in 1835.

ASTORIA

Even before the *Miscellany* appeared Irving had received from John Jacob Astor a request to write the history of that merchant's business ventures on the Pacific coast. The circumstances attending the preparation of *Astoria* were once the subject of much controversy, now of interest only as showing how jealously the country watched its literary men. The unquestioned facts are that John Jacob Astor offered to pay Irving for writing the history; that at the suggestion of the latter his nephew, Pierre M. Irving, was employed on the work at a liberal salary paid by Astor; and that the book appeared as *Astoria,* by Washington Irving. It was charged that Pierre M. Irving did most of the work, and that Washington Irving sold his name to Astor for a large sum. Pierre M. Irving maintains, and there is no good reason for doubting his word, that his own labors were mostly clerical, and that his uncle received no remuneration except from the sale of the book in the usual way.

ADVENTURES OF CAPTAIN BONNEVILLE

The third of Irving's writings with a western American theme was more purely a commercial venture. While engaged on *Astoria* he met Captain Bonneville, an adventurer who had spent some time in the West, and had prepared an account of his experiences. Irving bought his manuscript for $1,000, touched it up somewhat—very slightly, if his preface is to be believed—and issued it in 1837 as *The Adventures of Captain Bonneville.* The speculation was a good one, for Nephew Pierre proudly tells us that the sale of the work brought $7,500.

These American works add little to the fame of Irving. The subjects were not such as he was best fitted to treat, and he was directed to them more by patriotism and popular demand than by any real interest. The *Tour on the Prairies* and the best parts of *Astoria* are of the grade of good magazine work, to be read, enjoyed, and forgotten.

LATER BIOGRAPHIES

Irving next planned to continue his studies of Spanish achievement in a history of the conquest of Mexico; but he procrastinated until he found that Prescott was working upon the same subject, and then generously relinquished the field to the younger man. He began a life of Washington, but it was interrupted by his appointment as Minister to Spain in 1842, and by other writings. The first volume appeared in 1855, and the last just before his death in 1859. Meanwhile he had published a short *Life of Goldsmith* and *Mahomet and his Successors,* both in 1849. *Wolfert's Roost,* a collection of stories part of which had been written for magazines, appeared in 1855. Some sweepings of his portfolio were issued after his death as *Spanish Papers.*

Many of the short sketches in the later volumes were good, though none equal the best of his earlier days. Of the later biographies, the *Goldsmith* is the best and the *Mahomet* the poorest. Irving was fitted by temperament to understand Goldsmith, and he had neither the temperament nor the training for an adequate study of Mahomet. The *Life of Washington* was a respectable treatment of a difficult theme. Irving undertook it from motives of patriotism, but it was not the kind of subject that he really enjoyed. He complained of the "want of feature" even in the Revolutionary war. The present neglect of the work is due, however, not to its lack of picturesqueness, but to the fact that it represents a kind of biography now out of fashion. In the early years of the century the veneration of Washington was carried to ridiculous extremes. Even conservative magazines printed his name only in capitals; and the introduction of the Commander-in-Chief, even in disguise, in Cooper's *Spy* was condemned as sacrilege. Irving belonged to the time when these traditions prevailed; and his ancestry, his training, even his name, predisposed him to take an exalted view of his hero. It should be remembered to his credit that, artificial as the Washington he pictured seems to us, the portrait is more lifelike than any drawn by his predecessors.

GENERAL CHARACTERISTICS OF IRVING

Irving lived until a change in literary taste had taken place. Just after his death there was a reaction against his works, and a generation fed on Transcendentalism and reform felt that they were thin and unprofitable. Since that time there has been no enthusiastic Irving revival, yet he has slowly increased and seems to be still increasing in popular favor. In a study of American literature he is important, if for no other reason, because of his historical position. He was the first American to win international fame solely as an author. He was one of the first Americans to write without a didactic purpose. He was the last and the greatest of the American Addisonians. The intrinsic merit of his writings, however, warrants his fame. This merit is of style rather than of content, though the two are inseparable. And in style his writings are surprisingly uniform. Unlike Charles Brockden Brown and many other men who have depended on authorship for support, he did not divide his time between hackwork and more purely literary efforts. Virtually everything that he wrote appears in his collected works; and there are few pages of which he need have felt ashamed or which the reader with leisure will not find fairly interesting. Still, his fame has come to rest mainly on the *Knickerbocker History,* the three works of the *Sketch Book* group, and the more imaginative of the Spanish writings; and in these may be seen his chief excellences. The adjective most frequently applied by contemporaries to both the man and his writings was "genial." With geniality were combined a certain old-fashioned quality and a masculine delicacy of taste. It is easy to enumerate many things that he could not do, yet he appeals as do few other American authors to the reader who is in the proper mood.

"Irving"

BY GEORGE HAVEN PUTNAM

In 1917 the Macmillan Company published, here and abroad, the first modern history of American achievements in letters, produced by a team effort. Scores of writers, headed by William P. Trent of Columbia, trained professionals and gifted amateurs together, produced three volumes, in a wide-ranging plan based on Britain's *The Cambridge History of English Literature* and "our encyclopedic Duyckinck." The whole, though uneven in execution, became a standard and is still on occasion reprinted. The chapter on Irving, IV of Book II, Volume I, here reprinted in full, was contributed by George Haven Putnam (1844–1930), son and successor of Irving's last publisher, and himself a man of letters. Having as a boy known Irving, he was able to add a personal touch.

Washington Irving was born in William Street, New York City, 3 April, 1783. As this was the year in which the colonies finally achieved the independence for which they had been fighting for seven years, Irving may be regarded as the first author produced in the new republic.

The writer recalls that he visited Sunnyside with his father a year or two before the death of Irving and heard him narrate, doubtless not for the first time, how, when he was a youngster a year old, his nurse had held him up in her arms while Washington was passing by on horseback, in order that the General might place his hand on the head of the child who bore his name. "My nurse told me afterwards," said Irving, "that the General lifted me in his arms up to the pommel of his saddle and bestowed upon me a formal blessing." The listening boy looked, with reverential awe, at the head that had been touched by the first president, but when later he told his father about Irving's words, the father said: "You did not see the spot that Washington touched." "And why not?" was the natural question. "You goose," came the retort, "do you not know that Mr. Irving wears a wig?"

Washington Irving was prevented by poor health from following his two elder brothers to Columbia College. His formal training was limited to a course of a few years in the public schools of the day. He had always, however, encouraged in himself a taste for reading and an interest in human affairs so that his education went on steadily from year to year. His father, a Scotchman by birth, had built up an importing business and ranked well among the leading merchants of the city. The family comprised in all five sons and two daughters. The relations to each other of these brothers and sisters were always closely sympathetic, and throughout the record of Irving's career the reader is impressed with the loyal service rendered, first, by the elder brothers to the younger, and later, when the family property had disappeared and the earnings of the youngster had become the mainstay of the family, by Washington himself to his seniors, and to his nieces.

In 1804, Irving, who had just attained his majority, made his first journey to Europe. His father had died some years earlier, and the direction of the family affairs was in the hands of the eldest brother William. The trip seems to have re-established Washington's health, which had been a cause of anxiety to his brothers. After a voyage of forty-two days he landed in Bordeaux, whence he journeyed to Paris. He then travelled by way of Marseilles to Genoa, from which point he went by stage-coach through some of the picturesque regions in Italy. It was on these trips that he secured his first impressions of the Italian hill country and of the life of the country folk, impressions that were utilized later in the *Tales of a Traveller*. From Naples, crossing to Palermo, he went by stage to Messina, and he was there in 1805 when the vessels of Nelson passed through the straits in their search for the combined French and Spanish fleet under Villeneuve, a search which culminated in the great victory at Trafalgar.

Journeying in Europe during those years of war and of national upheaval was a dangerous matter. Irving was stopped more than once, and on one occasion was arrested at some place in France on the charge of being an English spy. He seems to have borne the troublesome interruptions with a full measure of equanimity, and he used each delay to good purpose as an opportunity for a more leisurely study of the environment and of the persons with whom he came into touch. He returned to New York early on 1806, shortly after Europe had been shaken by the battle of Austerlitz.[1]

Irving was admitted to the bar in November, 1806, having previously served as attorney's clerk, first with Brockholst Livingston and later with Josiah Ogden Hoffman. The law failed, however, to exercise for him any fascination, and his practice did not become important. He had the opportunity of being associated as a junior with the counsel who had charge of the defence of Aaron Burr in the famous trial held in Richmond in June, 1807. The writer remembers the twinkle in the old gentleman's eye when he said in reply to some question about his legal experiences, "I was one of the counsel for Burr, and Burr was acquitted." In letters written from Richmond at the time, he was frank enough, however, to admit that he had not been called upon for any important service. During Irving's brief professional association with Hoffman, he was accepted as an intimate in

---

[1]During these journeys he took notes, wrote them out in a full journal, portions of which are shortly to be published, and utilized his material in elaborate letters to his relations. [See Introduction, pp. *xxxi–xxxii—Ed.*]

the Hoffman family circle, and it was Hoffman's daughter Matilda who was the heroine in the only romance of the author's life. He became engaged to Matilda when he was barely of age, but the betrothal lasted only a few months, as she died suddenly at the age of seventeen. At the time of Irving's death it was found that he was still wearing on his breast a locket containing her miniature and a lock of hair that had been given to him half a century before.

The first literary undertaking to which Irving's pen was devoted apart from a few ephemeral sketches for one of the daily papers, was a serial publication issued at irregular intervals during 1807-08, under the title of *Salmagundi*. In this work, Irving had the collaboration of his brother William and his friend James K. Paulding. The *Salmagundi papers,* reissued later in book form, possess, in addition to their interest as humorous literature, historical value as pictures of social life in New York during the first decade of the nineteenth century.

The famous *History of New-York* was published in 1809. The mystery surrounding the disappearance of old Diedrich Knickerbocker, to whom was assigned the authorship, was preserved for a number of months. The first announcement of the book stated that the manuscript had been found by the landlord of the Columbian Hotel in New York among the effects of a departed lodger, and had been sold to the printer in order to offset the lodger's indebtedness. Before the manuscript was disposed of, Seth Handaside, the landlord, inserted in New York and Philadelphia papers an advertisement describing Mr. Knickerbocker and asking for information about him. When acknowledgment of the authorship of the book was finally made by Irving, it was difficult for his fellow New Yorkers to believe that this unsuccessful young lawyer and attractive "man about town" could have produced a work giving evidence of such maturity and literary power. He had secured an excellent position in New York society, a society which in the earlier years of the century was still largely made up of the old Dutch families. In the "veracious chronicle" of Mr. Knickerbocker free use was made of the names of these historic families, and it is related that not a few of the young author's Dutch friends found it difficult to accord forgiveness for the liberty that had been taken with their honourable ancestors in making them the heroes of rollicking episodes.

After a brief editorial experience in charge of a Philadelphia magazine called the *Analectic,* to which he contributed some essays later included in *The Sketch Book,* Irving enjoyed for a few months the excitement of military service. He was appointed a colonel on the staff of Governor Tompkins, and during the campaign of 1814 was charged with responsibilities in connection with the defence of the northern line of New York.

In 1810, Irving had been taken into partnership with his two brothers, Peter and Ebenezer, who were carrying on business as general merchants and importers; and on the declaration of peace in 1814 he was sent by his firm to serve as its representative in Liverpool. If the business plans of that year had proved successful, it is possible that Irving might for the rest of his life have remained absorbed in commercial undertakings, but in 1818 the firm was overtaken by disaster and the young lawyer-merchant (never much of a lawyer and by no means important as a merchant) found himself adrift in England with small funds and with no assured occupation or prospects. He had already come into friendly relations with a number of the leading authors of the day, a group which included Scott, Moore, Southey, and Jeffrey. Scott had in fact sought him out very promptly, having years earlier been fascinated by the originality and the humour shown in *The History of New-York.*

After a couple of years of desultory travelling and writing, Irving completed a series of papers which were published in New York in 1819–20 and in London in 1820, under the title of *The Sketch Book.* It is by this volume that he is today best known among readers on both sides of the Atlantic. The book has been translated into almost every European tongue, and for many years it served, and still serves, in France, in Germany, and in Italy as a model of English style and as a text-book from which students are taught their English. In this latter rôle, it took, to a considerable extent, the place of *The Spectator.*

The publication by Murray of *The Sketch Book,* and two years later of *Bracebridge Hall,* brought Irving at once into repute in literary circles not only in Great Britain, but on the Continent. In 1826, after a year or two chiefly spent in travelling in France, Germany, and Italy, he was appointed by Alexander Everett, at that time Minister to Spain, attaché to the Legation at Madrid, and this first sojourn in Spain had an important influence in shaping the direction of Irving's future literary work. In July, 1827, he brought to completion his biography of Columbus, later followed by the account of the *Companions of Columbus* (1831). The *Columbus* was published in London and in Philadelphia in 1828 and secured at once cordial and general appreciation. Southey wrote from London: "This work places Irving in the front rank of modern biographers"; and Edward Everett said that "through the Columbus, Irving is securing the position of founder of the American school of polite learning." Irving continued absorbed and fascinated with the examination of the Spanish chronicles. He made long sojourns in Granada, living for a great part of the time within the precincts of the Alhambra, and later he spent a year or more in Seville. He occupied himself collecting material for the completion of *The Conquest of Granada,* published in 1829, and for the *Legends of the Alhambra,* published in 1832.

In 1828, Irving declined an offer of one hundred guineas to write an article for *The Quarterly Review,* of which his friend Murray was the publisher, on the ground, as he wrote, "that the Review [then under the editorship of Gifford] has been so persistently hostile to our country that I cannot draw a pen in its service." This episode may count as a fair rejoinder to certain of the home critics who were then accusing Irving (as half a century later Lowell was, in like manner, accused) of having become so much absorbed in his English sympathies as to have lost his patriotism.

In 1829, Irving was made a member of the Royal Academy of History in Madrid, and having in the same year been appointed Secretary of Legation by Louis McLane, he again took up his residence in London. Here, in 1830, the Royal Society of Literature voted to him as a recognition of his "service to history and to literature" one of its gold medals. The other medal of that year was given to Hallam for his *History of the Middle Ages.* A little later Oxford honoured Irving with the degree of Doctor of Laws. The ceremony of the installation was a serious experience for a man of his shy and retiring habits. As he sat in the Senate Hall, the students saluted him with cries of "Here comes old Knickerbocker." "How about Ichabod Crane?" "Has Rip Van Winkle waked up yet?" and "Who discovered Columbus?"

In 1832, Irving returned to New York, having been absent from his country for seventeen years. His fellow citizens welcomed him, not a little to his own discomfiture, with a banquet given in the City

Hall, where the orator of the evening addressed him as the "Dutch Herodotus." Later in the year, he made a journey through the territory of the Southwest, an account of which he published under the title of *A Tour on the Prairies* (1835). His description of St. Louis as a frontier post and of the great wilderness extending to the west of the Mississippi still makes interesting reading. Returning from his journey by way of New Orleans, he visited Columbia, South Carolina, where he was the guest of Governor Hamilton. The Governor, who had just transmitted to the legislature the edict of nullification, insisted that the author must repeat his visit to the state. "Certainly," responded the guest, "I will come with the first troops."

In 1834, Irving declined a Democratic nomination for Congress, and in 1838 he put to one side the Tammany nomination for mayor of New York and also an offer from President Van Buren to make him Secretary of the Navy. In 1842, he accepted from President Tyler the appointment of Minister to Spain. The suggestion had come to the President from Daniel Webster, at that time Secretary of Sate. The succeeding five years were in large part devoted to the collection of material relating to the history and the legends of Spain during the Moorish occupation.

On his return to New York in 1846, he met with a serious disappointment. His books were out of print, at least in the United States, and his Philadelphia publishers assured him that, as there was no longer any public demand for his writings, it would be an unprofitable venture to put new editions upon the market. They explained that the public taste had changed, and that a new style of authorship was now in vogue. The books had in fact been out of print since 1845, but at that time Irving, still absent in Spain, had concluded that the plan for revised editions might await his return. To be told now by publishers of experience that *The Sketch Book, Knickerbocker, Columbus,* and the other books, notwithstanding their original prestige, had had their day and were not wanted by the new generation, was a serious shock to Irving not only on the ground of the blow to his confidence in himself as an author, but because his savings were inconsiderable, and he needed the continued income that he had hoped to secure from his pen.

His personal wants were few, but he had always used his resources generously among his large circle of relatives, and having neither wife nor child he had made a home at Sunnyside for an aged brother Ebenezer, and at one time for no less than five nieces. Some western land investments, which in later years became profitable, were at this time liabilities instead of resources, and his immediate financial prospects were discouraging. He had taken a desk in the office of his brother John Treat Irving, and to John he now spoke, possibly half jestingly, of the necessity of resuming the practice of the law. He was at this time sixty-five years of age, and as it was forty years since he had touched a law book, it is hardly likely that he could have made himself of much value as a counsellor.

One morning early in 1848, he came into the office in a joyful frame of mind. He tossed a letter over to his brother saying: "John, here is a fool of a publisher willing to give me $2000 a year to go on scribbling." The "fool of a publisher" was the later George P. Putnam, who had recently returned from London where he had for eight years been engaged in the attempt to induce the English public to buy American books. Mr. Putnam now proposed to issue a uniform revised edition of all of Irving's writings, with which should be associated the books that he might later bring to completion, and to pay to the author a royalty on each copy sold, guaranteeing against such royalty for a term of three years a sum increasing with each year. It may be mentioned as evidence of the accuracy of the publisher's judgment that the payments during the years in which this guaranty continued were always substantially in excess of the amounts contracted for.

In 1849, the London publisher Bohn began to print unauthorized editions of the various books of Irving. A series of litigations ensued, as a result of which the authorized publishers, Murray and Bentley, discouraged with a long fight and with the great expense incurred in securing protection under the existing copyright regulations, accepted the offer of the pirate for the use, at a purely nominal price, of their publishing rights, and Irving's works came thus to be included in Bohn's Library Series. Copyright in Great Britain, as in the United States, was in 1850 in a very unsatisfactory condition, and it was not easy to ascertain from the provisions of the British statute just what rights could be maintained by alien authors. So far as American authors were concerned, this uncertainty continued until, through the enactment of the statute of 1891, an international copyright relation was secured.

As one result of the transfer to Bohn of the control of the English editions of Irving's earlier volumes, the author found that he could not depend upon any material English receipts for his later works. For the right to publish the English edition of the *Life of Washington* (a work comprised in five volumes) Bentley paid the sum of £50, which was a sad reduction from the £3000 that Murray had given him for the *Columbus*.

In December, 1852, Irving wrote to his American publisher a letter of thanks, which is notable as an expression both of the sense of fairness and of the modest nature of the man. That this expression of friendship was not a mere empty courtesy, he had opportunity of making clear a few years later. In 1857, partly because of the mismanagement of his financial partner and partly because of the general financial disasters of the year, Mr. Putnam was compelled to make an assignment of his business. Irving received propositions from a number of other publishers for the transfer of his books, the commercial value of which was now fully appreciated. From some of these propositions he could have secured more satisfactory returns than were coming to him under the existing arrangement. He declined them all, however, writing to his publisher to the effect that as long as a Putnam remained in the publishing business, he proposed to retain for his books the Putnam imprint. He purchased from the assignee the plates and the publishing agreements; he held these plates for a year or more until Mr. Putnam was in a position to resume the control of the publication, and he then restored them to his publisher. He waived the larger proceeds to which, as the owner of the plates, he would have been entitled, and insisted that the old publishing arrangements should be resumed. Such an episode is interesting in the long and somewhat troubled history of the relations of authors with publishers and it may be considered equally creditable to both parties.

The final, and in some respects the greatest of Irving's productions, the *Life of Washington,* was completed on his seventy-sixth birthday, 1859, and a month or two later he had the pleasure of holding in his hands the printed volume. His death came on 29 November, of the same year, and he was laid to rest in the beautiful little graveyard of the Sleepy Hollow Church. The writer has in his memory a picture of the great weather-beaten walls of the quaint little church with the background of forest trees and the surroundings of the moss-covered graves. Beyond on the roadside could be seen the grey walls of the mill, in front of which Ichabod Crane had clattered past, pursued by the headless horseman. The roadside and the neighbouring fields were crowded with vehicles, large and small, which had gathered from all parts of the countryside. It was evident from the words and from the faces of those that had come together that the man whose life was closed had not only made for himself a place in the literature of the world, but had been accepted as a personal friend by the neighbours of his home.

Washington Irving occupied an exceptional position among the literary workers of his country. It was his good fortune to begin his writing at a time when the patriotic sentiment of the nation was taking shape, and when the citizens were giving their thoughts to the constructive work that was being done by their selected leaders in framing the foundations of the new state. It was given to Irving to make clear to his countrymen that Americans were competent not merely to organize a state, but to produce literature. He was himself a clear-headed and devoted patriot, but he was able to free himself from the local feeling of antagonism toward the ancient enemy Great Britain, and from the prejudice against other nations, always based upon ignorance, that is so often confused with patriotism. Irving's early memories and his early reading had to do with the events and with the productions of colonial days. Addison and Goldsmith are the two English writers with whose works his productions, or at least those relating to English subjects, have been most frequently compared. His biography of Goldsmith shows the keenest personal sympathy with the sweetness of nature and the literary ideals of his subject. Irving's works came, therefore, to be a connecting link between the literature of England (or the English-inspired literature of the colonies) and the literary creations that were entitled to the name American, and they expressed the character, the method of thought, the ideals, and the aspiration of English folk on this side of the Atlantic.

The greatest intellectual accomplishment to be credited to New York during the first years of the republic was the production of *The Federalist*. It is fair to claim, however, that with Irving and with those writers immediately associated with his work during the first quarter of the nineteenth century, began the real literature of the country. Partly by temperament and by character, and partly, of course, as a result of the opportunities that came to him after a close

personal knowledge of England, with a large understanding of things
Continental, Irving, while in his convictions a sturdy American, became in his sympathies a cosmopolitan. His first noteworthy production, *The History of New-York,* is so distinctive in its imagination
and humour that it is difficult to class. It is purely local in the sense
that the characters and the allusions all have to do with the Dutch occupation of Manhattan Island and the Hudson River region, but, as
was evidenced by the cordial appreciation given to the book on the
other side of the Atlantic, the humour of Mr. Knickerbocker was accepted as a contribution to the liteature of the world.

In the production of *The Sketch Book,* Irving was able not only
to enhance his fame by a charming contribution to literature, but to
render a special service to two countries, England and America. The
book came into print at a time when the bitterness of the war which
closed in 1841 was still fresh in the minds of both contestants. It was
a time when it was the fashion in America to use Great Britain as a
bugaboo, as a synonym for all that was to be abominated in political
theories and in political action. The word "British" was associated in
the minds of most Americans with an attempt at domination, while in
England, on the other hand, references to the little Yankee nation
were no more friendly, and things American were persistently de-
cried and sneered at.

It was of enormous value that at such a period, first in the list of
patriotic Americans who through sympathetic knowledge of England
have come to serve as connecting links between the two countries,
Irving should have been a resident in England and should have absorbed so thoroughly the spirit of the best that there was in English
life. It was in part because men honoured in Great Britain, writers
like Scott, Southey, Rogers, Roscoe, Moore, men of affairs like Richard Bentley, John Murray, and many others, came not only to respect, but to have affectionate regard for, the American author, and it
was in part because the books written by this man showed such sympathetic appreciation of things and of men English, that England was
brought to a better understanding of the possibilities of America. If
there could come from the States a man recognized as one of nature's
gentlemen, and to be accepted as a companion of the best in the
land, a man whose writings on things English won the highest approval of the most authoritative critics, it was evident that there were
possibilities in this new English-speaking state. If one American could

secure friendships in Great Britain, if one American could make a noteworthy contribution to the literature of the English tongue, the way was thrown open to other Americans to strengthen and widen the ties and the relations between the two countries. An American critic who might have been tempted to criticize some of the papers in *The Sketch Book* as unduly English in their sympathies and as indicating a surrender by the author of his American principles, was estopped from any such folly by the fact that the same volume contained those immortal legends of the Hudson, *Rip Van Winkle* and *The Legend of Sleepy Hollow*. In these stories, poems in prose, the author utilized, as the pathway and inspiration for his imagination, the great river of which he was so fond. If Irving's descriptions of rural England were to give fresh interest to American readers in the old home of their forefathers, the skill with which he had utilized the traditional legends of the Catskill Mountains and had woven fanciful stories along the roadway of Sleepy Hollow made clear to readers on the other side of the Atlantic that imagination and literary style were not restricted to Europe.

The work begun in *The Sketch Book* was continued in *Bracebridge Hall*. Here also we have that combination (possibly paralleled in no other work of literature) of things English and things American. Squire Bracebridge is, of course, a lineal descendant of Sir Roger de Coverley. It is not necessary, however, because Irving was keenly sympathetic with Addison's mode of thought, to speak of Irving's hero as an imitation. England has produced more than one squire, and Bracebridge and the family of the Hall were the creations of the American observer. The English home of the early nineteenth century is presented in a picture that is none the less artistic because it can be accepted as trustworthy and exact. In this volume we have also a characteristic American study, *Dolph Heyliger,* a fresh romance of Irving's beloved Hudson River.

The *Tales of a Traveller,* the scenes of which were laid partly in Italy, show the versatility of the author in bringing his imagination into harmony with varied surroundings. Whether the subject be in England, in France, or in Italy, whether he is writing of the Alhambra or of the Hudson, Irving always succeeds in coming into the closest sympathy with his environment. He has the artist's touch in the ability to reproduce the atmosphere in which the scenes of his stories are placed.

The *Life of Columbus* may be considered as presenting Irving's first attempt at history, but it was an attempt that secured for him at once a place in the first rank among historians. In this biography, Irving gave ample evidence of his power of reconstituting the figures of the past. He impresses upon the reader the personality of the great discoverer, the idealist, the man who was so absorbed in his own belief that he was able to impress this upon the skeptics about him. We have before us a vivid picture of the Spanish Court from which, after patient effort, Columbus secured the grudging support for his expedition, and we come to know each member of the little crew through whose service the great task was brought to accomplishment. Irving makes clear that the opposition of the clerics and the apathy of King Ferdinand were at last overcome only through the sympathetic support given to the project by Queen Isabella.

In the *Conquest of Granada,* the narrative is given in a humorous form, but it represents the result of very thorough historic research. By the device of presenting the record through the personality of the mythical priestly chronicler, Fray Agapida, blindly devoted to the cause of the Church, Irving is able to emphasize less invidiously than if the statements were made direct, the bitterness, the barbarism, and the prejudices of the so-called Christianity of the Spaniards. Through the utterances of Agapida, we come to realize the narrowness of Ferdinand and the priestly arrogance of Ferdinand's advisers. The admiration of the reader goes out to the fierce patriotism of the great Moorish leader, El Zagal, and his sympathies are enlisted for the pathetic career of Boabdil, the last monarch of Granada. *Granada* was Irving's favorite production, and he found himself frankly disappointed that (possibly on the ground of the humorous form given to the narrative) the book failed to secure full acceptance as history and was not considered by the author's admirers to take rank with his more popular work.

The *Alhambra,* which has been called the "Spanish Sketch Book," is a beautiful expression of the thoughts and dreams of the author as he muses amid the ruins of the Palace of the Moors. The reader feels that in recording the great struggle which terminated in 1492 with the triumph of Spain, Irving's sympathies are not with the conquering Christians but with the defeated Moslems.

The *Life of Mahomet* and the supplementary volume on the successors of Mahomet followed in 1849–50. The biographies consti-

tute good narrative and give further examples of the author's exceptional power of characterization. If they fail to reach the high standard of the *Columbus,* it is doubtless because Irving possessed no
such close familiarity with the environment of his subjects. In Spain
he had made long sojourns and had become imbued with the atmosphere of the Spanish legends and ideals. He knew his Italy, in like
manner, from personal observation and from sympathetic relations
with the peasants no less than the scholars, but Arabia was to him a
distant land.

The writing of *Columbus* prepared the way for Irving's chief
historical achievement. The *Life of Washington* is not only a biography presenting with wonderful precision and completeness the nature
and career of a great American, but a study, and the first study of
importance, of the evolution of the republic. Irving had given thought
and planning to the biography for years before he was able to put a
pen to the work. As early as 1832 he had confided to some of his
nearer friends his ambition to associate his name with that of Washington and to devote such literary and historical ability as he possessed to the creation of a literary monument to the Father of the
Republic. The work had, of necessity, been postponed during his
long sojourn in England and the later residence in Spain, but he
never permitted himself to put the plan to one side. As soon as the
sales of the new Putnam edition of the earlier works and of the later
volumes that he had been able to add to these freed him from financial care, he began the collection of material for the great history. He
had already travelled over much of the country with which the career
of his hero was connected. He knew by the observations of an intelligent traveller the regions of New England, New Jersey, Western
Pennsylvania, and Virginia, while with the territory of New York he
had from his youth been familiar. The Hudson River, which had heretofore served as the pathway for Irving's dreams of romance, was
now to be studied historically as the scene of some of the most critical of the campaigns of the Revolution. Since the date of Irving's
work, later historians have had the advantage of fuller material, particularly that secured from the correspondence in the homes of Revolutionary leaders, North and South, but no later historian has found
occasion for any corrections of importance, either in the details of
Irving's narrative, or in his analysis of the characters of the men
through whom the great contest was carried on. Irving possessed one

qualification which is lacking in the make-up of not a few conscientious and able historians. His strain of romance and his power of imagination enabled him to picture to himself and to make vivid the scenes described, and the nature, the purpose, and the manner of thought of each character introduced. The reader is brought into personal association with the force and dignity of the great leader; with the assumption, the vanity, the exaggerated opinion of his powers and ability of Charles Lee; with the sturdy patriotism, the simple-hearted nature, persistence, and pluck of the pioneer fighter Israel Putnam; with the skill, leadership, and unselfishness of Philip Schuyler; with the pettiness and bumptiousness of Gates; with the grace, fascination, and loyalty of Lafayette; and with the varied attainments and brilliant qualities of that wonderful youth Alexander Hamilton. We are not simply reading descriptions, we are looking at living pictures, and the historic narrative has the quality of a vitascope.

The production of this great history constituted a fitting culmination to the literary labours of its author. When Irving penned the last word of the fifth volume of the *Washington,* he was within a few months of his death. The work on this volume had in fact been a strain upon his vitality, and there were times when he needed to exert his will power to the utmost in order to complete the task allotted to himself for the day. He said pathetically from time to time to his nephew and loyal aid Pierre and to his friend Putnam, "I do not know whether I may be spared to complete this history, but I shall do my best." In this his final work, the shaping of the fifth volume, he did his best.

It may fairly be contended for this American author, whose work dates almost from the beginning of the Republic, that his writings possess vitality and continued importance for the readers of this later century. His historical works have, as indicated, a distinctive character. They are trustworthy and dignified history, while they possess the literary charm and grace of the work of a true man of letters. For the world at large, Irving will, however, doubtless best be known by his works of imagination, and the students in the gallery in Oxford who chaffed "Diedrich Knickerbocker" as he was receiving his degree were probably right in selecting as the characteristic and abiding production of the author his *Rip Van Winkle.*

This imaginary gathering of 44 literary worthies is in an engraving, by A. H. Ritchie, of an oil painting "Authors of The United States" by the American artist Thomas Hicks (1823–90). The original canvas is unlocatable as yet. Hicks copyrighted the engraving in 1866. It is here much reduced from its initial size, c. 40″ x 28″. A later "Key," to another such engraving, by Abbie Crane, identified Irving, seated at center table right, as No. 1. The bearded Bryant opposite is No. 2, and Cooper, standing between them, is No. 3.

PART III

SLOW AWAKENING

(1920–1945)

This basis of classicism, which in a way he had been forced upon, was, as we see it now, tremendously important to the young writer: it came first, it came in his impressionable years; he never wholly left it. It gave him stability while others went to extremes, it compelled restraint, it rendered impossible anything save beauty of style and perfect clearness, and it made him observant of men and manners and times.

But the eighteenth century was dead: even while Irving was writing his Oldstyle papers the reaction against all it had stood for had become a revolution. Already had come what Carlyle was terming "the sickliest of recorded ages, when British literature lay all puking and sprawling in Werterism [sic], Byronism, and other sentimentalism, tearful or spasmodic (fruit of internal wind)." That the impressionable young New-Yorker sooner or later should have been affected was inevitable. How the new forces laid hold upon him and modified his classicism is a problem tremendously important, for it is at this point, where in him the Addisonian Arctic current was cut across by the Gulf Stream of romanticism, that there was born the American short story, a new genre, something distinctively and unquestionably our own in the world of letters.

Fred Lewis Pattee
*The Development of the American
Short Story* (New York, 1923)

From "Washington Irving"

BY FRED LEWIS PATTEE

Fred Lewis Pattee (1863–1950), a long-lived contributor to studies
of American literature, after education at Dartmouth joined the faculty of Pennsylvania State College, where he would remain as an in-
spirational teacher, and sometime chairman, for thirty-four years.
Thereafter he taught at Rollins College until 1941. As early as 1896
he wrote *A History of American Literature,* beginning a career in literary historiography that reached even beyond *The First Century of
American Literature* (1935). This selection comprises the summariz-
ing final sections VII and VIII from the long Chapter I on Irving
as a mixed blessing as a pioneer in this genre, in Pattee's *The Development of the American Short Story* (1923).

Excluding such rambling character sketches as "The Wife" and the "Widow and Her Son" in *The Sketch Book,* and such abandoned fragments as "Buckthorne" and "Ralph Ringwood" in his later collections, Irving wrote something like forty-eight narrative pieces that, in a general way, we may call short stories. Roughly we may classify them under four heads: first, sentimental tales in the conventional manner of the time, like "The Pride of the Village," "Annette Delabre," and "The Widow's Ordeal"; second, seven Knickerbocker tales—"Rip Van Winkle," "The Legend of Sleepy Hollow," "Dolph Heyliger," "The Devil and Tom Walker," "Wolfert Weber," "The Adventure of the Black Fisherman," and "Guests from Gibbet Island"; third, other tales touched by German romance, like "The Spectre Bridegroom" and Parts I and III of *Tales of a Traveller;* and, fourth, Arabesque tales and sketches of Spanish romance, like those in *The Alhambra, Legends of the Conquest of Spain,* and *Wolfert's Roost.*

Arranged in chronological order, the tales reveal an evolution that is most instructive. The *Salmagundi* papers are of the eighteenth century: only one of them by any stretch may be called a short story. "My Aunt" is a whimsical ancedote, "My Uncle John" is an Addisonian sketch of character and manners, but "The Little Man in Black" has elements in it that are new: it is the transition link between the *Spectator* sketches of the book and the Germanized "Rip Van Winkle" that was to follow ten years later. So redolent of the eighteenth century is it that John Neal could declare it a direct imitation of Goldsmith's "Man in Black" in No. 26 of *The Citizen of the World,* yet it is not a study of manners or of character, and it is not an apologue—it has no moral. It is a graphic picture—the man is alive and he is presented not to make the reader think, but to make him feel. It has dialogue, characterization, but no development of character, and it has verisimilitude. The author's whole object is to entertain: to surprise, indeed, the reader. The little man is the first shadow of the coming Knickerbocker, and the first shadow also of the coming of the romantic into its author's work. In the story there is first a mystery, then a seeming solution, then a surprise-ending almost of the modern type: the little man is no other than a descendant of the erudite Linkum Fidelius who has been so whimsically and so ponderously quoted through the volume just as the Little Man in Black runs through *The Citizen of the World* to be revealed at the end. A stupendous tome, the labor of a lifetime, has been left in the hands of the author and the source of his learned quotations is now plain. The reader is left with the impression that the tale was told with no other purpose than to set the stage for this surprise.

The Sketch Book, which came a decade later, after Scott and romanticism had come into Irving's life, marks the boundary line between the new and the old. The first critic clearly to recognize that a new literary form had arisen was Prescott, the historian, who under the title "Essay Writing" made, in *The North American Review* as early as 1822, his remarkable analysis:

> *The Sketch Book* certainly forms an epoch in the history of this kind of literature; for, although of the same generic character with the British essayists, it has many important specific peculiarities. The former were written . . . with a direct moral tendency, to expose and to reform the ignorance and the follies of the age. *The Sketch Book,* on the other hand, has no direct moral purpose, but is founded on sentiment and deep feeling. . . . In one word, the principal object of the British essayists was to instruct, so they have for the most part given a picture of common life, in simple language; while the principal object of *The Sketch Book,* being to delight, scenes only of exquisite emotion are selected, and painted in the most exquisite, but artificial language.

Irving touched the eighteenth-century apologue with emotion, stripped it of its obvious moral, and reduced it from the general to the particular. Addison saw the type, Irving the individual; Addison aimed at the head, Irving at the heart; Addison lighted his work with flashes of wit, Irving suffused his with the mellow glow of humor.

From *The Sketch Book* the progress of Irving into the full stream of romantic fiction was rapid, until, indeed, his *Alhambra* sketches are all picture, all emotion, sentiment, entertainment. Save in their restraint, their beauty of style, their clearness and simplicity, there is little in all of his later tales to remind us that their author had once been completely under the spell of the eighteenth century.

For the short story as we know it to-day Irving performed perhaps nine distinctive services:

1. He made short fiction popular. He was peculiarly endowed
for writing the shortened form and he used it exclusively. After the
sensational triumph of *The Sketch Book,* a success that stirred
greatly the imagination of the younger seekers for literary recognition, sketches and tales became the literary fashion in America, and
in such volume did they come that vehicles for their dissemination
became imperative. The annual, the gift book, and lady's books like
Godey's and *Graham's,* and the various popular magazines that
sprang up in the 'thirties and 'forties—nurseries for the short story
—were thus indirectly the fruit of Irving's success as a sketch writer.
He set the bells ringing.

2. He was the first prominent writer to strip the prose tale of its
moral and didactic elements and to make of it a literary form solely
for entertainment. Knowing the fashions of his day, he was constantly
apologizing for his lack of didactic basis. "I have preferred address-
ing myself to the feeling and fancy of the reader more than to his
judgment," he wrote Brevoort in 1819. "My writings, therefore, may
appear light and trifling to our country of philosophers and politicians." His apology in the introduction to *Bracebridge Hall* is facetious and characteristic. No more clever explanation is to be found in
English literature. The suggestion that there might be a moral to his
tales aroused his mirth. "I was once," his biographer tells us, "reading aloud in his presence a very flattering review of his works, which
had been sent him by the critic in 1848, and smiled when I came to
the sentence 'His most comical pieces have always a serious end in
view.' 'You laugh,' said he, with that air of whimsical significance
so natural to him, 'but it is true. I have kept that to myself hitherto,
but that man has found me out. He has detected the moral of *The
Stout Gentleman.'* "

3. He added to the short tale richness of atmosphere and unity
of tone.

4. He added definite locality, actual American scenery and people. Though only seven of his forty-eight tales are native in setting,
these seven have been from the first his best loved and most influential work. They were the result of no accident. Deliberately he set out

to create for his native land that rich atmosphere which poetry and romance had thrown over the older lands of Europe, or, to quote his own words, "To clothe home scenes and places and familiar names with those imaginative and whimsical associations so seldom met with in our new country, but which lie like charms and spells about the cities of the Old World." He was the pioneer, therefore, in that new school that demanded an *American* literature, an art that would work in native materials in an original manner.

5. He was the first writer of fiction to recognize that the shorter form of narrative could be made something new and different, but that to do it required a peculiar nicety of execution and patient workmanship. To quote his own words:

> There is a constant activity of thought and a nicety of execution required in writings of the kind, more than the world appears to imagine. It is comparatively easy to swell a story to any size when you have once the scheme and the characters in your mind; the mere interest of the story, too, carries the reader on through pages and pages of careless writing, and the author may often be dull for half a volume at a time, if he has some striking scene at the end of it; but in these shorter writings every page must have its merit. The author must be continually piquant; woe to him if he makes an awkward sentence or writes a stupid page; the critics are sure to pounce upon it. Yet if he succeed, the very variety and piquancy of his writings—nay, their very brevity, make them frequently referred to, and when the mere interest of the story is exhausted he begins to get credit for his touches of pathos or humor; his points of wit or turns of language.

6. He added humor to the short story and lightness of touch, and made it human and appealing. A pervasive humor it was, of the eighteenth-century type rather than of the pungent American type that was to be added by Aldrich and his generation, but nevertheless something new and something attractive.

7. He was original: he pitched the short story in a key that was as new to his generation as O. Henry's was to his. He constantly avoided, as he expressed it, the "commonplace of the day": "I choose to take a line of writing peculiar to myself, rather than to fall

into the manner or school of any other writer." And again, "It is true other writers have crowded into the same branch of literature, and I now begin to find myself elbowed by men who have followed my footsteps; but at any rate I have had the merit of adopting a line for myself, instead of following others."

8. Though his backgrounds may often be hazy, though the complaint of the early *Blackwood's* critic that there is "no reality about his Yorkshire halls" has a basis of truth, his characters are always definite individuals and not types or symbols. Rip Van Winkle and Ichabod Crane are more vividly real as human personages to-day than is George Washington, their contemporary. Even "Mountjoy," a complete failure as a short story, has a character in it that is most decidedly alive, that is, indeed, a study in adolescence worthy even of a Henry James.

9. And finally, he endowed the short story with a style that was finished and beautiful, one that threw its influence over large areas of the later product. To many critics this was Irving's chief contribution to American literature, and to some New Englanders at least it was his only contribution. To Emerson, Irving was "only a word-catcher." Perhaps he was, and yet it is by no means a calamity that our pioneer short-story writer should have begun with a literary style that has been the despair of all of his followers. It would have been well if many others who have practiced the art, especially some in recent days, could have learned Irving's secret of a distinctive and beautiful style.

But in many respects Irving was a detriment to the development of the short story. So far as modern technique is concerned he retarded its growth for a generation. He became from the first a model followed by all: unquestionably he was in America the most influential literary figure of the nineteenth century. To him as much as even to Scott may be traced the origin of that wave of sentimentalism and unrestrained romance that surged through the annuals and the popular magazines for three decades. Longfellow received his first inspiration from *The Sketch Book*. His *Outre-Mer,* and many other books of the early period issued in parts, like Dana's *Idle Man,* came as direct results of Irving's work. Bryant wrote tales of the *Sketch Book* type; the young Whittier planned a novel which was to be in style "about halfway between the abruptness of Laurence Sterne and the smooth gracefulness of Washington Irving," and even Thoreau began his literary life with a "meditative description" in the manner of Irving. Everywhere in the midcentury the softness and sentiment of this first great leader, as notably in Mitchell's *Reveries of a Bachelor,* and *Dream Life,* and Curtis's *Lotus Eating, Prue and I,* and the "Easy Chair" papers. One may skip a generation and still be in the presence of the great romancer: Harte, the leader of the new school of short story writers after the war, began by writing legends modeled after the legends of the Hudson. Poe was powerless in the 'thirties and 'forties in his attempts to change the technique of the form. His careful analysis was either unread by his generation or else unheeded because it was a revolt from Irving.

Of form as we know it to-day the tales of Irving, even the best of them, have little. He had begun as an eighteenth-century essayist, and according to Dr. Johnson an essay is "a loose sally of the mind; an irregular, undigested piece; not a regular or orderly composition"; he had ended as a romanticist, and romanticism may be defined as lawlessness. His genius was not dramatic. He delighted to saunter through his piece, sketching as he went, and chatting genially about his characters. "Rip Van Winkle" has six pages of material before there is any movement. The well-known stage version of the tale has little in it of Irving's material. "The theme was interesting, but not dramatic." Jefferson tells us in his Autobiography: "The silver Hudson stretches out before you as you read, the quaint red roofs and queer gables of the old Dutch cottages stand out against the mist upon the mountains; but all this is descriptive. The character of Rip does not speak ten lines. What could be done dramatically with so simple a sketch?" A study of what the dramatist added to the tale and what he left out will reveal how far it falls short of modern short-story requirements. There is lacking sprightly dialogue, movement unimpeded by description or exposition, additional characters with more collisions and more contrasts, and finally a swift culmination involving all the *dramatis personæ.*

To Irving plot seemed unessential. He had evolved with deliberation a form of his own that fitted him perfectly. In a letter to Brevoort he explains its characteristics:

For my part, I consider a story merely as a frame on which to stretch my materials. It is the play of thought, and sentiment, and language; the weaving in of characters, lightly, yet expressively delineated; the familiar and faithful exhibition of scenes in common life; and the half-concealed vein of humor that is often playing through the whole—these are among what I aim at, and upon which I felicitate myself in proportion as I think I succeed.

Of "The Legend of Sleepy Hollow" he could say: "The story is a mere whimsical band to connect descriptions of scenery, customs, manners, etc."

But there is a more serious indictment. *Blackwood's* mentioned it as early as 1824. About all of Irving's writings, the reviewer had complained, there is a languorous softness that relegates them almost to the realm of feebleness, and he added, "Nobody has ever taken a strong hold of the English mind whose own mind has not had for one of its first characteristics manliness." Expressed in modern phraseology, it means that Irving lacked robustness, masculinity, "red-bloodedness." He was gentle to the verge of squeamishness. Mrs. Foster, who knew him intimately in Dresden, noted that "he looks upon life as a picture, but to catch its beauties, its lights—not its defects and shadows. On the former he loved to dwell. He had wonderful knack at shutting his eyes to the sinister side of anything." Beyond a doubt this lack of robustness in Irving must be reckoned with as one cause of the general effeminacy and timid softness that characterized so much of American fiction during the greater part of the century.

But criticism of Irving's defects is thankless labor. It is best to overlook his faults and be profoundly thankful for him, for with him began American literature. He brought with him wholesomeness and distinction of style and careful workmanship; he introduced to us the form that has become our most distinctive literary product; and, in the words of his earliest critic, Dana, he took our crude American materials and turned them "all to beauty like clouds shone on by the moon."

BIBLIOGRAPHY

A Chronology of Irving's Short Stories

1807. *Salmagundi.*
    1. The Little Man in Black. November, 1807.
1819–20. *The Sketch Book.*

2. Rip Van Winkle. May, 1819.
3. The Spectre Bridegroom. November, 1819.
4. The Pride of the Village. March, 1820.
5. The Legend of Sleepy Hollow. March, 1820.

1822. *Bracebridge Hall.*
6. The Stout Gentleman. September, 1821.
7. The Student of Salamanca.
8. Annette Delarbre.
9. Dolph Heyliger.

1824. *Tales of a Traveller.*
10. The Hunting Dinner.
11. The Adventure of My Uncle.
12. The Adventure of My Aunt.
13. The Bold Dragoon. February, 1824.
14. The Adventure of the German Student.
15. Adventure of the Mysterious Stranger.
16. The Story of the Young Italian.
17. The Inn at Terracina.
18. The Adventure of the Little Antiquary.
19. The Belated Travellers.
20. The Painter's Adventure.
21. The Devil and Tom Walker.
22. Wolfert Weber, or Golden Dreams.
23. Adventure of the Black Fisherman.

1832. *The Alhambra.*
24. Adventure of the Mason.
25. Legend of the Arabian Astrologer.
26. Legend of Prince Ahmeid [*sic*] Al Kamel.
27. Legend of the Moor's Legacy. 1829.
28. Legend of the Three Beautiful Princesses.
29. Legend of the Rose of the Alhambra.
30. The Governor and the Notary.
31. Governor Manco and the Soldier.
32. The Legend of the Two Discreet Statues.

1835. *Legends of the Conquest of Spain.*
33. The Legend of Don Roderick. 1829.
34. Legend of the Subjugation of Spain. 1829.
35. Legend of Count Julian and His Family. 1829.
36. The Widow's Ordeal. *Cunningham's Annual.* 1829.

1839–41. *Knickerbocker's Magazine.*
37. Mountjoy. 1839.
38. Adelantado of the Seven Cities. 1839.
39. Legend of Don Munio. 1839.
40. Guests from Gibbet Island. 1839.
41. Pelayo and the Merchant's Daughter. 1840.
42. The Grand Prior of Minorca. 1840.
43. Legend of the Engulfed Convent. 1840.
44. Abderahman. 1840.
45. The Taking of the Veil. 1840.
46. The Count Van Horn. 1840.
47. Don Juan: a Spectral Research, 1841.
48. The Abencerrage. *Wolfert's Roost.* 1855.*

*Forty-eight is a debatable number. Charles Neider, in his popularized *The Complete Tales of Washington Irving* (1975), scrapes the barrel for sixty-two stories. [*Ed.*]

From "The Closing Years"

BY GEORGE S. HELLMAN

George S. Hellman (1878–1958), after distinguished student years at Columbia, moved on to become art critic, collector, and dealer, literary journalist, novelist, and poet. He helped J. Pierpont Morgan acquire objects of art now in the Morgan Library, and was president of the New Gallery (1925–1929). His publications include articles in prominent magazines, book reviews for *The New York Times,* and *Lanes of Memory* (1927). Early attracted to Irving, in 1915 he edited *Letters of Washington Irving to Henry Brevoort,* followed in 1916 by *Letters of Henry Brevoort to Washington Irving.* In 1929 his collection of Irvingiana was given to the New York Public Library. Reprinted here is the final section of the last chapter, XVII, from Hellman's openly supportive biography, *Washington Irving, Esquire* (1925).

The summer of 1853 (after a brief visit to George Washington Lewis's home in the Shenandoah Valley for the study of manuscrips relating to Washington) Irving spent in part at Berkley Springs, where his chief amusement was bowling; in part at Saratoga; and in part on the St. Lawrence River, among the Thousand Islands, and thence to Niagara Falls. Arriving in New York late in September, he went to the Irving House, intending to stay there over night. The clerk, not recognizing him, told the visitor that there was little chance of getting a room; whereupon Irving recalled the advice that his niece Sarah Storrow gave him in Europe, and wrote out his name not as "W. Irving," but at full length in the hotel register. The quiet, modest stranger was the great man after whom the hostelry had been called! He was led at once to a "sumptuous apartment," where "everyone was enormously attentive," including the chambermaid. "If she had been pretty, I absolutely should have kissed her," wrote Irving, "and henceforth I abjure all modesty with hotelkeepers and will get as much for my name as it will fetch."

A few months later the little village south of Tarrytown, at the petition of all its inhabitants and by order of the Postmaster General, changed its name from Dearman to Irvington, in honour of its best loved townsman. This was but one in a long list of personal tributes during the closing years of his life. They varied from gifts for his garden, in the way of cuttings of figs and grapes, and gifts for his house, as the table for his study that Putnam sent him (and on which, it is pleasant to recall, some of the notes for this biography were written); to dedications of books by writers young and old; and to such more official tribute as the vote of the Board of Visitors in session at the United States Military Academy at West Point to pay in a body a call of homage on "so distinguished an American." But this visit, with his inevitable modesty and shyness, Irving refused, pleading ill health as an excuse. And though he was always accepting invitations to be the guest of honour at the "Irving Literary Union," a society formed by a group of young New York fellows in 1852, somehow or other he never turned up, although he wrote when the society was first formed: "As my long and desultory career is drawing to a close, I regard such demonstrations on the part of my young fellowmen as a soothing assurance that with all my shortcomings and however imperfectly I may have performed my part, I have not lived entirely in vain."

To old friends, however, his door was always open, and he would, from time to time, go on brief visits to Gouverneur Kemble, to James K. Paulding, to John P. Kennedy, and once to the home of Nathaniel Parker Willis, that now almost forgotten writer who was the prototype of later semi-literary journalists, and who, in his early years, had met many of the well-known English men and women among whom Irving had been such a favourite. The name of Thomas Moore, who had died after his mental faculties had broken down, came up in a talk between Irving and Willis, and Irving, with his old loyalty for old friends, insisted on the high-mindedness and liberality and generosity of the Irish poet. During this same talk Irving accepted with good nature Willis's teasing remarks concerning Irving's Beau Brummeldom during the London days, when Thomas Moore "insisted on being introduced to Irving's tailor."

Irving delighted in reminiscences. His conversation and his letters of later life are full of them. In 1851, on hearing from the schoolmaster, Jesse Merwin (Ichabod Crane's prototype, so it is said), whom he had met long ago at the Kinderhook home of Judge Van Ness, Irving recalls a fishing expedition in which Merwin, Congressman Van Alen and he had taken part. "Do you remember our piratical prank when we made up for our lack of luck in fishing by plundering John Moore's canoe of its fish when we found it adrift? And do you remember how John Moore came splashing along the marsh on the opposite border of the lake, roaring at us; and how we finished our frolic by driving off and leaving the Congressman to John Moore's mercy, tickling ourselves with the idea of his being scalped at least? Ah! well-a-day, friend Merwin, these were the days of our youth and folly!" Irving adds that this same John Moore, and the anecdotes Merwin had told of the old fisherman, gave him the idea of the vagabond character of Dirck Schuyler in "Knickerbocker's History" on which Irving was then engaged.

The "days of youth and folly" were, in the domain of memory, most happily renewed for Irving as he sympathetically watched the doings of the young people at Sunnyside. In a letter to Sarah Storrow he writes concerning two grandnieces, Hattie, and "sweet little Nellie" (daughters of Pierre Paris Irving), who, with their young friends, are sailing by moonlight on the Hudson. "It puts me in mind of the water parties in former days in *The Dream*, with the Hoffmans, Brevoorts, etc., when the old chorus used to be chanted,

We wont go home till morning,
Till daylight doth appear."

With Sarah Storrow also, he reminisces concerning the days in France. The coup d'étât which set Louis Napoleon on the imperial throne brings up thoughts of the strangeness of destiny. "Louis Napoleon and Eugenie Montijo, Emperor and Empress of France! one of whom I have had as a guest in my cottage on the Hudson, the other of whom when a child I have had on my knee at Granada!" Strange indeed that the granddaughter of a minor American official—Kirkpatrick, Consul at Malaga—was now the consort of an emperor.

Irving's memory as an old man must have been unusually good for it carried him back almost to infancy. Once when he spoke of children who did not believe in Santa Claus as "too wise to be happy," he added that when he was a child his belief continued until "they ['they,' no doubt, being his elder brothers] put snow balls in my stocking." He remembers following Genet down Wall Street. The ten year old Washington, walking behind the first Minister from the French Republic, envied "a little boy who had a feather stuck in the side of his hat." In a letter to Mrs. Storrow in 1856, he recalls and explains why he never visited Florence during his travels in Italy in 1805. "A malignant fever had led a cordon of troops to be drawn around Tuscany." But though he regrets having failed to see Venice, he does not, we are amused to note, explain that this omission was due to the desire of Cabell and himself to get as quickly as possible to the gaieties of Paris. Doubtless the old gentleman did not wish the children of the Storrow family to know too much concerning their once rather gay uncle; and perhaps Sarah Storrow was already aware of the circumstance. A more interesting bit of information in the same letter has to do with the Duchess of Duras, at whose castle Washington and Peter had received such delightful hospitality. The Duchess, Irving states he had later learned, "had hoped I might be excited to write something about the old chateau in the style of Bracebridge Hall; and it would indeed have been a fine subject."

Recollections of Scotland—"Scott stumping along in brown pantaloons, greenish frock coat, white hat and stick, and mumbling to himself in gruff tones some bit of old minstrelry"; of Spain, with Irving's first intense zest in bull fights that later he seldom attended—"the cruelty in my nature had been worn out"; of England, and of the performances at Covent Garden where Mrs. Siddons, Kemble and Cooke thrilled their audiences; of the Rhine country, and the dungeon under the old castle at Baden-Baden, where the "Vehm Gericht," the "mysterious and tremendous association that once held such sway over Germany," had its secret sessions;—of all these and much besides Irving reminisces in letters or in talks; but the most precious of his European recollections (as shown in a letter written in July, 1856, when he was seventy-three years old) have to do with the Dresden days. In writing to the Englishwoman—the English girl that he had loved—he refers to the miniature copy of the head of Herodotus she painted at Dresden and which he still treasures: "Farewell, my dear Mrs. Fuller," the letter ends; "if any of those of your family whom I ever knew and valued are at hand, assure them that I ever retain them in cordial remembrance; and believe me, ever, my dear Emily Foster, your affectionate friend, Washington Irving."

The past was renewed for Irving also by reminiscences penned by correspondents on both sides of the ocean. Notable among such letters are those of Preston concerning their early travels together; and of Robert C. Winthrop of Boston, who brought up Spain when he wrote to Irving of the sketch that David Wilkie had made of Irving when he was studying the archives at Cordova, a picture that now formed the frontispiece of the Wilkie volume dedicated to Lord Lansdowne. Then, too, there is the letter from Charles Dickens wherein Irving reads a pathetic story of Samuel Rogers in his advanced age. His memory gone, the old banker-poet was seated at breakfast between Mrs. Proctor and Mrs. Carlyle and both these brilliant women were eager to entertain the old man. But when Jane Carlyle had done her brilliant best, "Who is *she?*" asked Rogers. So Mrs. Proctor told him and spoke at length of the writings of Carlyle himself. "All of which," writes Dickens to Irving, "he heard staring in the dreariest silence, and then said, indignantly as before: 'And who are *you?*'"

Rogers, Newton and Moore, with dimmed or extinguished faculties, these old friends of his had passed away. In 1848, Henry Brevoort, the best of all Irving's friends, had died. Death itself Irving did not in the least fear. He was "always ready to lay down this remnant of existence," thankful that his "erratic and precarious career has been drawn to so serene a close." The thought of possibly becoming a charge on his relatives, of not going down "with all sails set," was the sole fear, as it was indeed the fact, of the final months. Towards the very end asthma and insomnia brought about a state of nervousness which frequently made him afraid to be alone at night, and sometimes he would reach a stage of excitement where he would become "horror-ridden" by some fantasy of the mind. But all in all (despite depression and nervousness) unselfishness, kindliness and humour continued to give forth their warmth even at the end of the path.

And to the end also Irving kept up his enjoyment of art and literature, and of music and the drama. To the pages of Shakespeare he had frequent recourse. As late as the autumn of 1858 he went to New York to see young Joseph Jefferson take the part of Goldfinch in Holcroft's comedy of "The Road to Ruin." Young Jefferson, who was later to become for our own generation so lovable a Rip Van Winkle, had, as a boy, appeared in that play, in support of the elder Hackett, Jefferson's father also being on the program. James Henry Hackett was the original Rip Van Winkle, and in a letter to me by his son, Mr. James K. Hackett, there is, among many interesting paragraphs, the following: "Washington Irving was a warm personal friend of my father, as were also most of the prominent literary men and men of culture of his time; and while I cannot put my hands upon the letter this moment, nor perhaps without great searching and trouble, there is among my papers a letter from Washington Irving to my father in which he says—this is not a quotation but the pith:— 'My dear Hackett: I am astounded and surprised and amazed that you could have made such a wonderful play out of such scanty material as my sketch of Rip Van Winkle'; and he also said that my father was, to his mind, the embodiment of the character which he drew." The elder Hackett had made his début in London, at Covent Garden, in 1827, and it was shortly thereafter that his Rip Van Winkle secured for this American actor high recognition in Great Britain. Ninety-three years later, in "Macbeth," the younger Hackett made *his* début in London. "This," as he writes, "seems incredible, but it is true."

The thirteen years that intervened between Irving's return from the post he had resigned as Minister to Spain and his death in 1859, have been called a period largely idyllic. The joys of friendship, of family life, of his country place; the pleasure of opera and plays; of authorship and of reading; mild horseback rides, until too many falls ended these; occasional games of whist, chess and backgammon; correspondence whose chief charm lay in the reminiscences there involved; playing with children; a little church-going towards the end; —these attest the quiet tenor of the life that along paths of simplicity and in surroundings of natural beauty approached its gentle termination. In the sphere of public events there is nothing more important to record than Irving's participation, with William Cullen Bryant and Daniel Webster, in the trio that presided at the exercises in commemoration of James Fenimore Cooper. In civic celebrations perhaps the most important episode was associated with the laying of the Atlantic cable in 1858, which, as Irving wrote, "caused a day to be set apart for everyone throughout the union to go crazy on the subject." However valuable an influence he may have been, and was, in affecting the American world of letters, the former diplomat played no part in political events or in social movements during this period. In Woman's Rights, free trade, temperance societies, States Rights, and the abolition of slavery he seemed curiously uninterested. The year of his return from Spain, the Wilmot Proviso, with its plan to exclude slavery in the territory acquired in the war with Mexico, had, although it met with defeat, started anew those embers which the Clay Compromise of 1850 could not extinguish and which (when South Carolina seceded from the Union) were to burst forth into flames of civil war so very soon after Irving's death. Throughout that critical period when Daniel Webster, as a matter of principle, was trying, at all costs, to preserve the Union, and John Brown, equally as a matter of principle, was intent, at all costs, on freeing the slaves, the most generally, the most generously loved of American writers employed neither his pen nor voice in the sphere of public controversy. That he was an old man eager to enjoy repose, is not the explanation; nor that Preston, the Senator from South Carolina, and Henry Clay, the Senator from Kentucky, and men of all parties had been his friends from youth; nor that he did not love the Union; nor that he was not opposed to any system of human slavery. The cause of Washington Irving's abstention from the controversy which shook the foundations of this country is too deep for any surface explanation. He had, as a young man, become even at the risk of the severance of friendships, even at the cost of being misinterpreted by indignant fellow-countrymen, firmly convinced that an author best serves the world by adhering to the employment of those talents as an author which are peculiarly his natural gifts. A Washington Irving who would take sides in public argument with Calhoun or with Garrison, or, somewhere between the two, with Clay or Webster, was, in Irving's opinion, less serviceable than a Washington Irving who would portray for the American people and for all peoples the illuminating life of George Washington, or the endearing qualities of Oliver Goldsmith. Of course if his had been a different nature, with the inherited traditions of a Whittier, a Lowell, a Higginson, he must have entered the arena. But with his temperament, and with the philosophy of life that he had with much bravery maintained, there was neither the intellectual nor the moral urge to cause him to deviate from his point of view. He believed in self-development, but not greatly in the reform of others; in the sunshine of Nazareth rather than in the lightning of Sinai. He was the patriarchal embodiment of good-will towards men, and it is much to be questioned whether his value to America would have been greater had he, in those pre-Civil War days, swerved from that beneficent symbolization. Some comments that he had made in connection with George Washington's Will, freeing his slaves, had called forth from a Southern newspaper a casual gibe. But, by and large, Washington Irving was loved in all the states of the Union. Indeed, it is not too much to say that of all Americans during their lifetime he was the most unqualifiedly endeared to his countrymen. Benjamin Franklin may have been his peer in this regard, but neither the immensely popular Henry Clay, nor the intensely admired Daniel Webster, nor Washington, nor Lincoln, was loved in such unpartisan manner.

The glorious sunset, by whose beauty Irving had been captured only a few hours before he died in the night of November 28th, 1859, glows forth with double significance as the mellow radiance before the impending dark. Irving's rôle, as man, as writer, as statesman, was to meliorate, to reconcile, to give pleasure, to refine. We may leave to the literary historian the evaluation of his achievement purely from the point of view of belles lettres; to the recorder of unusual facts we may suggest in passing that no other man has given a nickname to a great city, a nickname to its inhabitants, so that even to-day, as in the day of *Salmagundi,* we New Yorkers are "Gothamites" (Gotham being that English town whose wise men could be depended upon to speak nonsense) and New York is "Father Knickerbocker." But in concluding, we must with emphasis recur to the thought that it was Irving, more than any other man, who brought into accord the English-speaking peoples; that it was Irving who through his legends and his descriptions developed in his countrymen local sentiment and pride in the natural grandeur of their land. A fate not wholly kind to this kind and winning gentleman showed a fitting courtesy in bringing him to his simple grave at Sleepy Hollow before his brothers of the North and of the South faced one another, with vindictive eyes, on the however imperative, yet intellectually humiliating and ever tragical, field of war.

"Washington Irving"

BY ROYAL CORTISSOZ

Though Irving was elected to the Hall of Fame for Great Americans
at the first balloting in 1900 (See Introduction, p. *xxix*), according to
protocol his induction could not be finalized until details of a formal
ceremony were arranged, including the gift of an appropriate bust.
This all took place at the then Bronx campus of New York University, on May 5, 1927, when six electees were installed, including
Audubon and Franklin. The bronze bust of Irving by Edward Mc-
Cartan, donated by the Hispanic Society of America, was unveiled
by Alexander Duer Irving, a great-grandnephew. Among the top-
hatted guests was Don Alejandro Padilla y Bell, the Spanish Ambassador, who spoke briefly. Also, the succinct address below was
given by Royal Cortissoz (1869–1948), critic and author, who
beginning in 1891 was art editor, and later literary editor, of the
New York Herald Tribune. Biographer of Augustus St. Gaudens
(1907) and Whitlaw Reid (1921), and author of *American Artists*
(1923), Cortissoz was a member of the American Academy of Arts
and Letters. His remarks are a predictable lapidary inscription.

He who would speak briefly in tribute to Washington Irving must choose his path of approach, for there is more than one leading to appreciation of his character and genius. He was an imaginative author. He was a traveller. He was an historian. He was a diplomat. He was, too, in social life an uncommonly endearing man, and it would be possible for the eulogist to celebrate just his personal traits alone. Since I cannot touch upon all the phases of my subject I venture to choose the one which most interests me.

I would speak of Washington Irving strictly as the man of letters. As a man of letters born in the eighteenth century and living well past the middle of the nineteenth he achieved a special distinction. There is a clue to it in a saying of his own: "It is by the constant collision of mind that authors strike out the sparks of genius, and kindle up with glorious conceptions." So he went through life, foregathering with the brightest spirits of his time and enjoying "the constant collision of mind." It meant for him the constant play of his own mind. He dealt all the time in impressions and ideas, developing the art of writing out of the art of living. Human sympathy energizes his pen and though he loved books he was never a merely bookish author.

What is it that keeps alive his pages on this city? It is not the organizing power of the scholar, though Irving had scholarship. It is his sympathy, it is his humor, it is the wholesome naturalness with which he tells his story. Irving had a most beguiling style, lucid and supple, but this master of literature was never content to be purely "literary." Behind his grace, the grace of a man who knew his literary manners as he knew the technique of living, there is a warmth that springs from the heart. He who lived so much in the past lived intensely in the present and he so lives in *our* present because the figures of history were to him living men and women.

Besides this everlasting human sympathy of his, that so vividly animates his writings, there was a strain in him that it is well to recall in our prosaic age—a strain of generous romance. You feel it in his Knickerbocker History. You feel it in what he wrote of Granada and the Alhambra. You feel it, too, in so tender and humorous and pathetic a tale as that of Rip Van Winkle. He rose instinctively to a romantic theme, rose to its magic and its beauty. There is much beauty in the work of Washington Irving. It touches the mind to fine issues.

To him we owe a golden thread in modern literature. That is one reason, only one, why we must rejoice in today's commemoration of his fame.

"Washington Irving"

BY VERNON LOUIS PARRINGTON

Vernon Louis Parrington (1871–1929) as biographer, critic, historian, and teacher was a seminal figure in post–World War I American studies. Nurtured on middle-western Populism, after graduating from Harvard in 1893 he taught for a decade at the University of Oklahoma, and then moved to the English Department of the University of Washington in 1909. He was Professor there from 1912 until his untimely death. Parrington contributed to, among others, *The Cambridge History of American Literature* (1917), *The Reinterpretation of American Literature* (1928), and the 14th edition of the *Encyclopedia Britannica* (1928). His three-volume *Main Currents in American Thought* (1927–1930) was a bold endeavor to organize our intellectual history in one sequential narrative. His stance there was, admittedly, "liberal rather than conservative, Jeffersonian rather than Federalist," and his unsympathetic treatment of Irving, reprinted here complete from Chapter III, "Two Knickerbocker Romantics," of Book II, Volume Two, shows this bias. The other "Romantic" was James Kirke Paulding.

Fortunately the stolid New York of earlier days was not to pass away without bequeathing to posterity some fragments of its chronicles. In the midst of a pleasant society of smallclothes and tie-wigs, of feudalism and Federalism, appeared young Washington Irving at the precise moment when Sansculottism was beginning to make a stir in the land, and gentlemen were putting away their knee-breeches to don a republican dress—a decline in taste to which he would not easily reconcile himself. A boyish wit from the eighteenth century, a genial loiterer in the twilight of the old, he found himself out of humor with the ambitions that were making over the little city he loved. The present seemed to him not so amusing as the past, nor so picturesque. That he had any business with the world of trade and speculation he could not believe. Its concerns were not his. Its new Wall Street counted for less in his eyes than the pipe of old Diedrich Knickerbocker. Its decadent Federalism that was clinging to the wreck of its hopes, and its roistering Democracy that wore greasy clothes, spoke with an Irish accent, and was marshaled to the polls by Tammany Hall, were of less consequence to him than the black bottle that brought such curious adventures to Rip Van Winkle. The wit and romance he took pleasure in were of another sort than the kind his generation was getting drunk on—more insubstantial, less heady, picturesque rather than profitable. So Irving gently detached himself from contemporary America, and detached he remained to the end of a loitering life, untroubled by material ambitions, enjoying the abundance of good things that fell in his way, mingling with prosperous folk and liking everybody—men as diverse as John Jacob Astor and Martin Van Buren and John P. Kennedy—and unconsciously taking the color of his environment, careful to turn into limpid prose such romantic tales as he came upon and achieving thereby both reputation and profit—a pleasant blameless way of living, certainly, yet curiously unrepresentative of the America in which chance had set him and which was to claim him as its first man of letters.

An incorrigible *flâneur,* Irving's business in life was to loaf and invite the picturesque. A confirmed rambler in pleasant places, in the many lands he visited he was a lover of the past rather than the present, seeking to recreate the golden days of the Alhambra or live over the adventurous mood of the fur trader. The immediate and the actual was an unsatisfying diet for his dreams. There was in him nothing of the calm aloofness of the intellectual that stands apart to clarify its critical estimate, and none of the reforming zeal of the Puritan that is at peace only in the thick of a moral crusade. The duty of saving the world was not laid on his untroubled soul. No man of his generation was less of a rebel than Irving, and he went his way unconcerned at things that quite upset Fenimore Cooper's peace of mind. In his early days, to be sure, he broke with the ambitious middle class—if gently drawing away can be called breaking—because he could not bring himself to like its ways and the devastation those ways were entailing on the leisurely world he loved. Revolutions seemed to him somewhat vulgar affairs. The French Revolution had brought destruction on too many lovely things, and the industrial revolution was taking too heavy a toll of the picturesque, to please him. He thought it a pity that steam should drive the clipper ship from the seas and put an end to snug posting in the tally-ho. Progress might be bought at too dear a price. The bluff squire with his hounds, the great hall with its ancient yuletide customs, the patriarchal relations between master and man, seemed to him more worth while than the things progress was substituting for them; so he turned away from the new and gently ingratiated himself into the past in order to gather up such fragments of the picturesque as progress had not yet destroyed.

But only for a time. His dislike of capitalism rested on no more substantial basis than its substitution of vulgar trousers for gentlemanly smallclothes. It was too new to have achieved dignity or the charm of assured position. When that time should come and masters of finance should stand before the world as generous dispensers of patronage, when the development of business should have produced its new barons, Irving's dislike would lessen and he would associate with the new capitalism on the same easy terms that he associated with the old feudalism. In the meantime he stood apart, unconcerned with praise or blame. The industrial revolution might work itself out as it would. The seventeen years he spent abroad on his great pilgrimage were black years for England. Wretchedness and poverty were all about him if he chose to see. The "condition of England" question was rising out of the factory smoke to challenge the conscience of England. But he did not choose to see and his conscience was untroubled. As he idled about the countryside or visited the hospitable manor houses, his eye was caught by the grace of medieval spires rising from parish churches rather than by the condition of the proletariat. He saw no children working in the coalpits, for he did not choose to visit the collieries. He sympathized vaguely with the new social movements than getting under way, but it was not in his nature to be partisan to a cause. He may not have been a Tory but he had lived so long with Tories and enjoyed so frankly the charm of upper-class society, that his outlook was unconsciously determined by such intimate contacts. While Secretary to the Legation at London in the reform years from 1829 to 1831, he was aware of the tremendous stir all about him, but his infrequent references to the Reform Bill in his letters turned usually on its disastrous effects on the publishing business. Only once during his long residence abroad does he seem to have felt deeply the significance of the current revolutionary unrest, and the mood that swept him away from his habitual indifference bears the marks of a sudden awakening. Writing from London on March 1, 1831, he said:

> We are in the beginning of an eventful week. . . . However, *the great cause of all the world* will go on. What a stirring moment it is to live in. I never took such intense interest in the newspapers. It seems to me as if life were breaking out anew with me, or that I were entering upon quite a new and almost unknown career of existence, and I rejoice to find my sensibilities, which were waning as to many objects of past interest, reviving with all their freshness and vivacity at the scenes and prospects opening around me. I trust, my dear Brevoort, we shall both be spared to see a great part of this grand though terrible drama that is about to be acted. There will doubtless be scenes of horror and suffering, but what splendid triumphs must take place over these vile systems of falsehood in every relation of human affairs, that have been woven over the human mind, and for so long a time have held it down in despicable thraldom. (Pierre M. Irving, *Life and Letters of Washington Irving,* Vol. II, p. 199.)

Irving lacked a month of being forty-nine when he wrote this confession of interest in matters political. It marks the first appearance of liberalism in his thinking, and the last—somewhat vague to be sure, unduly bottomed on romantic expectations, yet significant in so placid a life and explanatory of his course, when a year later he returned to America to knit up once more the raveled threads of his interests. It was as an incipient liberal that he came back to a land then in the first flush of the Jacksonian victory, eager to discover a romantic charm in the vast changes that had come during the seventeen years he had been abroad. He plunged into the business of rediscovery with enthusiasm. He was in want of new literary materials, and as he took his bearings, his creative interest was stirred to write on American themes. He went to Washington and for three months listened to the great debate on Nullification. He talked with business men and politicians, with those who were prosperous and prominent, and he drifted easily with the tide of liberalism. To be sure he could scarcely be called a Jacksonian. Parties and causes did not greatly interest him even then. An intelligent man, indeed, could hardly be less concerned about political principles. Thirty years before, as a clever young man about town, he had gone with the dominant Federalism of the times, and had amused himself with political ambitions. His brother Peter was editor of the Lewisite paper the *Chronicle,* but Josiah Ogden Hoffman, with whose firm Irving was connected during his desultory incursion into the law and to whose daughter Matilda he was betrothed, was an old Loyalist and ardent Hamiltonian. His wife, to whom Irving was warmly attached, was a daughter of John Fenno, Hamilton's editor. Under such tutelage it was natural for Irving to poke good-natured fun at President Jefferson's red velvet breeches in *Salmagundi;* but his venture into practical politics proving little to his taste, he quickly gave over such ambitions. In a letter to a clever young lady of Republican sympathies, he thus announced his abandonment of political hopes:

> I am as deep in mud and politics as ever a modern gentleman would wish to be; and I drank beer with the multitude; and I talked hand-bill fashion with the demagogues; and I shook hands with the mob, whom my heart abhorreth. . . . Truly this saving one's country is a nauseous piece of business, and if patriotism is such a dirty virtue,—prythee, no more of it. (*Life and Letters,* Vol. I, Chap. XI.)

Years now separated him from that youthful experience. His long absence from his native land had completely alienated him from the fierce partisanship of contemporary America and he could view matters political with calm detachment. Inclined to make the best of

any government *de facto,* he found it easy on his return to accept
Jacksonianism, and he soon discovered a genuine liking for Old
Hickory. "The more I see of this old cock of the woods," he wrote
from Washington, "the more I relish his game qualities" (*ibid.,* Vol.
II, p. 255). No doubt his early friend Paulding had much to do with
his ready acceptance of the new order, although he had come in close
contact with Martin Van Buren at the London legation and was
drawn to him. "He is one of the gentlest and most amiable men I
have ever met with," he wrote to his brother, "with an affectionate
disposition that attaches itself to those around him, and wins their
kindness in return" (*ibid.,* Vol. II, p. 220). Although distrustful of
some of the "elbow counsellors" of the Democracy he found little
cause for criticism and soon came to be regarded as one with them.
The Jacksonians were eager to make political capital out of his literary reputation, and he was urged by Tammany Hall to stand for Congress and later to accept a mayoralty candidacy. In 1837, probably
through the intervention of Paulding, he was offered a post in Van
Buren's cabinet. These partisan offers he had the good sense to decline, but when in 1842 he was tendered the post of Minister to
Spain he gladly seized the opportunity to revisit a land he loved. His
nephew is explicit in his statement that the offer came wholly unsolicited, but Fenimore Cooper was of another opinion.[1] Very likely
Cooper was misinformed, but whatever the truth the appointment
was a godsend to Irving. His affairs were in a bad way. The popularity of his writings was on the wane, the panic had caught him with
much of his capital invested in unprofitable land speculations, and
the "Roost" at Tarrytown was a heavy drain, although he wrote
whimsically, "I beat all the gentlemen farmers in my neighborhood,
for I can manage to raise my vegetables and fruits at very little more
than twice the market price" (*Life and Letters,* Vol. II, p. 320).
Only a severe nature like Cooper, sorely wounded by the angry reception of his own honest criticism, would cavil at an appointment so
honorable to the government.

[1]Writing to his wife a month afterwards, Cooper said: "By the way, Mrs.
Willing has let out the secret of Irving's appointment. He wrote to Webster to
remember him *if any good thing offered.* So that instead of not asking for the
office, he asked for anything that was good. There has been more humbug
practised concerning this man than concerning any other now living" (Cooper,
Correspondence of James Fenimore-Cooper, Vol. II, p. 469).

A friendly nature, Irving discovered friendliness wherever he went. His own generosity appealed to the generosity of others, and he found it easy in consequence to take a kindly view of men and parties. He was harassed by none of Cooper's quick suspicions and rigid principles, and it must be added he had none of Cooper's intuitive penetration into the secret springs of human action that made the latter so acute a critic of contemporary America. The sharp contrast in moods in which the two men returned to America from their travels, the one harshly critical of middle-class economics and frontier leveling, the other responding naïvely to the enthusiasm for speculative expansion and eager to exploit the romance of the westward movement, sufficiently reveals the difference between them. The one was a dogmatic Puritan with the dictatorial ways of the quarter-deck, the other was a play-boy of letters temperamentally incapable of critical analysis. There was not a grain of realism in Irving's nature. His cheerful optimism was little more than the optimism of the prosperous. Wholly ignorant of economics, he never comprehended the significance of the revolutions in process all about him, and this *naïveté* blinded him to the motive of John Jacob Astor in financing Astoria, as it blinded him to all the major forces of the times. He was easily brought to see the romance of the great struggle between rival companies for mastery of the fur trade, but he did not comprehend how the glamour he threw about the venture must inevitably strengthen his patron's investment in imperialism. Gullible as a child, he discovered nothing more significant in the great struggle between agrarianism and capitalism for control of government than the ungenerous suspicions and novel theories it bred. For the outstanding liberals of New York he had scant sympathy. William Leggett, Horace Greeley, Albert Brisbane, William Cullen Bryant, influenced his views far less than did the masters of Wall Street; and from the courageous movement of Locofocoism he drew back in distrust. The one letter in which he elaborated such political convictions as he had come to hold, is an interesting document that deserves quotation.

As far as I know my own mind, I am thoroughly a republican, and attached, from complete conviction, to the institutions of my country; but I am a republican without gall, and have no bitterness in my creed. I have no relish for puritans either in religion or politics, who are for pushing principles to an extreme, and for overturning everything that stands in the way of their own zealous career. I have, therefore, felt a strong distaste for some of those locofoco luminaries who of late have been urging strong and sweeping measures, subversive of the interests of great classes of the community. Their doctrines may be excellent in theory, but, if enforced in violent and uncompromising opposition to all our habitudes, may produce the most distressing effects. The best of remedies must be cautiously applied, and suited to the taste and constitution of the patient. . . . Ours is a government of compromise. We have several great and distinct interests bound up together, which, if not separately consulted and severally accommodated, may harass and impair each other. . . . I always distrust the soundness of political councils that are accompanied by acrimonious and disparaging attacks upon any great class of our fellow-citizens. Such are those urged to the disadvantage of the great trading and financial classes of our country. You yourself know . . . how important these classes are to the prosperous conduct of the complicated affairs of this immense empire. You yourself know, in spite of all the common-place cant and obloquy that has been cast upon them by political spouters and scribblers, what general good faith and fair dealing prevails throughout these classes. Knaves and swindlers there are doubtless among them, as there are among all great classes of men; but I declare that I looked with admiration at the manner in which the great body of our commercial and financial men have struggled on through the tremendous trials which have of late overwhelmed them, and have endeavored, at every pecuniary sacrifice, to fulfill their engagements. (*Life and Letters,* Vol. II, pp. 312–313.)

This persuasive presentation of the philosophy of compromise, with its implicit defense of capitalism, marks Irving's drift back to the middle class with which he had long before broken. In the six years since his return he had watched the country react to the great panic, and he went with it in its veering towards the Whiggery of Henry Clay. The fragile bonds of his attachment to the Democracy were becoming tenuous; other attachments were insensibly drawing him towards the more congenial representatives of wealth. He had all his life associated with the Tory classes and it was easy for him to transfer his loyalty to the American Tories. Under such influences began a slow *rapprochement cordial* towards the new philosophy of progress. He was seized with the common mania of speculation and made some unfortunate investments in wild lands and railways that seriously hampered him later, and he commercialized his literary reputation by such moneymaking ventures as *Astoria* and the *Adventures of Captain Bonneville*. He discovered a new romance in the great business of exploitation, and found the hand of God in the profits of unearned increment. In the letter above quoted from, he justified the ways of speculation thus:

> There are moral as well as physical phenomena incident to every state of things, which may at first appear evils, but which are devised by an all-seeing Providence for some beneficent purpose. Such is the spirit of speculative enterprise which now and then rises to an extravagant height, and sweeps throughout the land. . . . The late land speculations, so much deprecated, though ruinous to many engaged in them, have forced agriculture and civilization into the depths of the wilderness; have laid open the recesses of primeval forests; made us acquainted with the most available points of our immense interior; have cast the germs of future towns and cities and busy marts in the heart of savage solitudes, and studded our vast rivers and internal seas with ports that will soon give activity to a vast internal commerce. Millions of acres which might otherwise have remained idle and impracticable wastes, have been brought under the dominion of the plough, and hundreds of thousands of industrious yeomen have been carried into the rich but remote depths of our immense empire, to multiply and spread out in every direction, and give solidity and strength to our confederacy. All this has in a great measure been effected by the extravagant schemes of land speculators. I am, therefore, inclined to look upon them with a more indulgent eye than they are considered by those violent politicians who are prescribing violent checks and counter measures, and seem to have something vindictive in their policy. (*Life and Letters,* Vol. II, p. 314.)

Thus did Irving become completely domesticated in the new world that Rip Van Winkle had found so disconcerting when he came upon it out of the quiet colonial past. The rediscovery of America proved to be an agreeable business, and profitable in a professional way. His enthusiasms, which in 1831 he felt were "waning as to many objects of past interest," were stimulated by the vast stir of the country, and the spirit of romance once more ran briskly in his veins. The better part of a year he rambled widely about the country, in order, as he said, to get at home "upon American themes." He visited Boston and the White Mountains, then West to Ohio and St. Louis, then with an Indian commissioner he penetrated the southwest prairies as far as the wild Pawnee country beyond the South Canadian River, then to New Orleans and Charleston, finally settling down in Washington to immerse himself in politics. From there he passed over the Potomac for an extended trip through the Old Dominion, returning to New York where he spent some time with Astor at Hell Gate, finally in 1835 settling at Tarrytown which was to be his home to the last. He had definitely determined on his new field of work. His imagination had been stirred by his visit to the prairies; the romance of the westward expansion was beginning to find expression in the works of Timothy Flint and James Hall; the public interest was ripe and John Jacob Astor was at hand to encourage him. Thus stimulated Irving proposed to make the field of western romance his own, with the result that he published in quick succession *A Tour of* [sic] *the Prairies, Astoria,* and *The Adventures of Captain Bonneville.*

On the whole the new venture did not prosper. The spirit of the West was not to be captured by one whose heart was in Spain. In *A Tour of the Prairies* there is a certain homely simplicity and straightforwardness that spring from a plain recital of undramatic experience; and in *Astoria* there is an unembellished narrative of appalling hardship and heroic endurance, with none of the tawdry romantics that mar the work of Flint and Hall. Yet neither is creatively imaginative, neither stirs one with a sense of high drama. The atmosphere of Snake River could not be created in the quiet study at the "Roost"; it needed the pen of a realist to capture the romance of those bitter wanderings in mountain and sagebrush. It is journeyman work, and on every page one is conscious of the professional man of letters faithfully doing this day's allotment. It is much the same with his *Life of Washington.* In this last great undertaking Irving no longer writes with gusto. The golden days of Diedrich Knickerbocker and

Rip Van Winkle are long since gone; the magic is departed from his pen; and a somewhat tired old gentleman is struggling to fulfill his contract with his publisher. It was a mistake to venture on the work, despite the fact that he had long been planning it. His historical equipment was inadequate. He might make a pretty story out of Washington's early life and his days with the army, but he was far too ignorant of politics, too credulous in judging his materials, to interpret justly the fierce party struggles that seethed about the President. Quite unconsciously in this last work he returned to the political prejudices of his youth, and wrote an account of Washington's administrations deeply colored by his Federalist sources.

The most distinguished of our early romantics, Irving in the end was immolated on the altar of romanticism. The pursuit of the picturesque lured him away into sterile wastes, and when the will-o'-the-wisp was gone he was left empty. A born humorist, the gayety of whose spirits overflowed the brim, he was lacking in a brooding intellectuality, and instead of coming upon irony at the bottom of the cup —as the greater humorists have come upon it after life has had its way with them—he found there only sentiment and the dreamy poetic. As the purple haze on the horizon of his mind was dissipated by a sobering experience, he tried to substitute an adventitious glamour; as romance faded, sentiment supplied its place. So long as youth and high spirits endured, his inkwell was a never-failing source of gayety, but as the sparkle subsided he over-sweetened his wine. This suffices to account for the fact that all his better work was done early; and this explains why the Knickerbocker *History* remains the most genial and vital of his volumes. The gayety of youth bubbles and effervesces in those magic pages, defying time to do its worst. The critic may charge the later Irving with many and heavy shortcomings, but the romantic smoke-clouds that ascend from Wouter Van Twiller's pipe cannot be dissipated by the winds of criticism.

From "Washington Irving"

BY HENRY SEIDEL CANBY

Henry Seidel Canby (1878–1961), whose education at Yale was climaxed by a Ph.D. in 1905, achieved distinction as biographer, editor, literary critic, and teacher, the last for some two decades as a lecturer at Yale, 1922–1941. In 1924 he helped found the *Saturday Review of Literature,* serving as editor to 1936 and then chairman of the editorial board until 1958. He was widely influential too as chairman, from 1926 to 1958, of the board of judges of the Book-of-the-Month Club. His publications include *The Short Story* (1902), *Walt Whitman: An American* (1943), and *Turn West, Turn East: Mark Twain and Henry James* (1951). Here reprinted are sections 4, 5, and 6 of Chapter Two, from Canby's *Classic Americans* (1931), which may have overemphasized Federalism as a formative influence on the young Irving, but nevertheless became thereafter a catalyst for more serious scrutiny of the latter's political, economic, and social ideas.

4.

If any outside influence is to account for Washington Irving's really remarkable success with only a humorous temperament and a sensitive soul to go on, then that influence will be found in American Federalism. For Irving, so far as his instrument permitted, represented the Federalist spirit in American literature, and this relationship is the key to much that is otherwise puzzling in a man at the same time so gentle and so famous. Not that Irving was ever interested in politics. He loathed them consistently through a long life in which he owed more to politics than most men, he was disgusted with his single electioneering experience as a Federalist,* found Republicans and Federalists equally agreeable and equally absurd when he met them socially, and made some of his closest friends in New York among that faction of the Republican party which, though aristocratic in feeling, yet used the masses for its own advantage against the Federalists, the faction of Judge Van Ness and Aaron Burr; nor can his attacks upon Jefferson and his supporters in "Salmagundi" and the Knickerbocker "History" be regarded as purely political. Jefferson to him was a fanatical hustler and bustler who would give authority to greasy mechanics. He was a disturbing factor in the settled, easy world that Irving loved, an antiromantic like the full-feeding, big-bottomed Dutch that Irving made fun of with a little less animus.

And yet, if Federalism as an ideal of living was to find literary expression, it was bound in that age of the romantic movement to have its Irving. For Federalism was essentially an aristocratic ideal struggling to adapt itself to the conditions of a republic and the equalities of a new country. The men who made the Constitution were neither dreamers like Irving nor prophets like Jefferson. They proposed, as has been many times made clear, to achieve a stable government by enlisting the monied interests in its defense. Privilege, in theory at least, had been abolished by the Revolution, but money remained, and not merely the provisions of the Constitution but the assumption of State debts and the redemption of depreciated currency were calculated to make speculators and capitalists friends of the existing order. Against the rising wave of democracy the Federalists set the barrier of class interests, and before it began to give way

*See Pierre Irving, *op. cit.*, Letter to Mary Fairlee, of May 2, 1807, when "my forlorn brethren," the Federalists, were defeated.

in 1800 (when Irving was seventeen) they had organized a government that, in its emphasis upon property, has remained the same ever
since. On the other side was Jefferson, a landholder always short
(like all landholders) of ready money, a practical idealist, as doubtful as the Federalists of democracy, but determined that in this new
government the man who produced, whether laborer or landowner,
should have political power, and be able to protect himself from mili-
tarists, speculators, bureaucrats, and all the parasites belonging to the
capitalist system of a plutocracy. He was, if you please, an intellectual aristocrat, but more intellectual than aristocratic. The rise of
democratic opportunism that swept away both Federalist and Republican in Jackson's days would have appalled him. But he looked
backward toward the dangers of monarchy, not forward to the inevitable result of his policy of opportunity for the common man in
America. He was determined to save the fruits of the Revolution, the
Federalists were resolved to check the upheaval that accompanied it
before the pleasant world they had made should be overwhelmed.
Not again, with the exception of the decade of the Civil War, have
such strong and diverse political and social emotions been aroused in
America.

Irving was not interested in the political aims of either party. In
his letters and occasional writings he calls a plague on both their
houses every time an election stirs the muddy minds of the populace.
His New York did not take politics seriously except as a means of
aggrandizement. Indeed, the modern Tammany Hall was already implicit in the factions of the Republican party headed by Burr and
Clinton, and a young wit and beau, pretending to read law in a
worldly little seaport where polite affiliations were almost as much
European as American, could not be expected to sympathize either
with ward politics, or with the moral intensities of a Dwight who believed that God had given America into the government of respectable church members, or with that Virginia idealism which proposed
to erect a newfangled state utterly different from anything in the romances of Sir Walter Scott. In the England of Coleridge, Shelley,
Byron, Wordsworth—to cite literary names merely—he was to see
nothing but the picturesque, and the relics of Moorish Spain were to
mean far more to him than Germany in its golden age. The ideas,
great and small, of the formative period of the United States naturally passed over his head.

Indeed, when he does defend the American system he is a little absurd. In 1831, attacking European monarchies, he speaks of "these vile systems of falsehood . . . that have been woven on the human mind and . . . held it down in despicable thralldom."* All Americans were republican, in principle at least, after 1800! But an urbane New Yorker could scarcely be expected to side with a political party that existed to give tradesmen and farmers their rights, or to be vitally interested in the economic ideals of the Federalists, when he hated making money and could not keep it. It was not merely old age that led him to end the "Life of Washington" at the moment when a heroic life of glory became involved in questions of domestic politics and a great career was used by partisans for their not very creditable purposes. Politics, for Irving, were New York politics, which meant a squabble between the ins and the outs.

And yet Irving, in spite of his indifference to party, was more Federalist than the Federalists, more Federalist essentially than the Hartford wits, who adumbrated in their vast poems a government by moral didacticism that was New Englandism rather than aristocracy. He was keenly aware of the deeper struggle of which the brawls of politicians and the ideology of statesmen were only symptoms. Like Talleyrand, he felt the old world slipping, and to him, an American, it was fresh and infinitely desirable, not stale and doomed. He felt, with the sensitiveness of a dreamer, the raucousness of a trading, manufacturing, exploiting society. Sprung from trade himself, and hating it, spending his youth in an illusion of a gay gentleman's world of the arts and conversation in a commercial town, he did not rationalize his desires, yet clearly lived and wrote them. "Salmagundi," like the "Spectator," and still more curiously like the "columns" of modern New York papers, is an onslaught upon manners, an attempt to give detachment, gaiety, civility, to a sodden town. Diedrich Knickerbocker's "History of New York" in its purely Dutch aspects is a satire upon a thoroughly bourgeois civilization, in its attacks upon the Yankees a satire on the ideals of traders and business men. The life of the gentleman, as the eighteenth century understood that word, is

---

*Letter to Brevoort, March 31, 1831. Philip Hone in his "Diary" for May 24, 1833, says that Irving on his return after seventeen years abroad "came out a Jackson man," with "warmth and enthusiasm," evidently a part of the same reaction, although not unaffected by Jackson's concurrence in 1829 in his appointment abroad.

praised and chronicled through a long series of Irving's books, in which tradesmen, demagogues, innovators, upstarts (like the village poet in "The Sketch Book"), are the butts of ridicule, and feudal squires, however eccentric, noble adventurers like Columbus, heroes of lost causes, such as Boabdil, are the pets of his imagination. Half of Irving's heart is in "Rip Van Winkle," where the picturesque Rip and his cronies, so full of humor and honest if stupid happiness, are set in contrast to the shabby pretentiousness of the village twenty years later. And the other half is in "Bracebridge Hall" and "The Alhambra," for in each is a life tinged with the melancholy of departing, yet rich in loyalty, solidity, and human worth instead of human rights.

The struggle between the new and the old world, however confused in its apparent issues, was uppermost in the American mind of the early eighteen hundreds. The West, removed in space and time, did not, it is true, count heavily in the contest, for it was scarcely America, yet the influence of that vast region so rapidly filling up with the rebel and the discontented who had lost the sense of respect for their betters, was already beginning.* More immediate in men's minds were the dangers from the common people who were determined not to stay common. Immorality, as has been noted before, had increased in the social demoralization that followed the long years of the Revolution. There was that sharp increase in acquisitiveness to be expected in a people diverted for almost a generation from the free pursuit of their private business. There was the example of France in turbulent democracy, and the opposite influence of aristocratic England, curiously dear to the aristocracy of the new world. Indeed the America of the early eighteen hundreds was alive in all its parts, perhaps more so than the standardized and accomplished America of the twentieth century. Pathetic, from this point of view, is the young Irving's illusion that he and the few like him could create and keep a milieu of taste in hustling young New York, but strong the pressure, far stronger than if he had lived in contemporary Europe, to do something, be something, that expressed his loves and his hates. Hence the sense of futility that is mentioned again and again in Irving's letters and implied in his prefaces from early manhood on. What could he do? I will not say, What could he do that was needed?

*Reflections of this are to be found in the Knickerbocker "History," with its descriptions of the upland Dutch.

for such a question, so familiar in New England, and later in a puritanized West, was not likely to be raised in New York! But what could he do that he wanted? The answer was to write, to write like an aristocrat, like a gentleman, like a Federalist.

For Federalism, as even the sinuous Walcott and the vehement Ames and certainly as Hamilton understood it, was much more than a political and economic system. It was a government by the best, the ideal to which all philosophic statesmen have aspired. It was, more specifically, an aristocracy, not of birth or of privilege, but of achievement, with the entrance door always open but a censor of manners, of morals, of capability, at the threshold.* The idea was never better expressed than in the provisions made by the New Haven colony (later the heart of Federalism) for the settlement of the wild lands in the parish of Mt. Carmel.† Land and the authority that went with it were to be taken up in quantity only by such as had means and character for its proper development with due reference to the religious nurture, the education, and the prosperity of those who were to inhabit it. To him who hath shall be given, provided that he deserves what he has, was the motto of Federalism. This was an ideal well worth fighting for—we may well regret that we have lost it through the greed and the tyranny of Federalist politicians and capitalists, and the rise of a democratic spirit that was oblivious to such subtleties and would not be denied.

It was to this intangible spirit of Federalism that Irving owed allegiance, a spirit deeper than economic theory, deeper than the struggle for power, a spirit which outlived the party that professed to represent it, so that it is still possible to call a man or a book Federalist in the United States. Irving shared the Federalist respect for the tried, its distrust of the new, its hatred of the vulgar, of "the beast," as Hamilton called the crowd. He was Anglophile as the Federalists were, and for the same reason. England, even in wartime, meant "the good old times" for Federalism. But Irving's feeling for England was magnified by his love for English literature, which was the basis of

---

*Josiah Quincy said that it took a half century after the Declaration of Independence "to reach a vital belief that the people and not gentlemen are to govern this country." (Quoted by Max Farrand in "The Development of the United States.") This vital belief was reached only over the dead body of the Federalist party.

†"The Old Mount Carmel Parish," by George Sherwood Dickerman.

his education. What reading he did later in the literature of France, Spain, and Germany only served to turn his already active romanticism toward such veneration of the old as would fifit him more than ever to play his part as the spokesman of Federalist culture. Indeed, if George Washington was an English country gentleman, with a difference, Irving was an English man of letters, with a difference, who turned in disgust from the sprawlings for food and water of the gigantic infant, his country, and in protest against the crude and new sought to write as elegantly as he could. Yearning for civilized urbanity in a continent designed to be great in quite another fashion, he perfected a style, and only then ceased to feel beaten, discouraged, and futile.

Irving as the arch-Federalist of American literature is much more interesting than Irving as a custodian of the romantic movement in America. In the latter function he had many colleagues, some, like Hawthorne, Poe, and Emerson, far more powerful, both intellectually and emotionally, than himself. It is true that the romantic haze that still hangs over the noble estuary of the Hudson rose from his pen, and the romantic past of that least romantic of American cities, New York, is his contriving. True, too, that he made Europe picturesque for Americans. England was not picturesque to Richard Mather, or to Benjamin Franklin, but Irving imbued it with all that the rest of us have ever since felt of romantic veneration. Yet, although as a maker of glamour he was a pupil of Walter Scott, his inspiration was not all literary. He spoke for the nostalgia of the Federalists, for the decorum, the stability, of colonial days, for the richness of living of the mother country. He was a divided soul, like that stout old rebel, John Adams, with his agonies over the proper ritual for the first Federal government. He belongs with the Philadelphia society that was so gay and exclusive at the Binghams' when Congress met in Philadelphia. He explains the truckling to English visitors, the imitation in town house and countryseat of life in Britain, the intense sensitiveness to British criticism, which he voiced himself in "English Writers on America"—all of which betrayed a passionate reverence for the old land. The best of all this, and very little of the worst, is in Irving. As a romantic among the greater romantics of Europe he is humble and usually derivative, but as an American and as a Federalist he speaks in his own right, and had a motive to speak well.

5.

To read Irving's works again with these facts in mind is to form a new estimate of the man as a writer. When he was young and heady, when, fresh from his first and idle ramblings over Europe in 1806, the Federalist conception of an aristocratic America caught his imagination (rebel as he was from a hardware store), there was more edge than sentiment in his romance. Though he said in his Preface of 1848 that his desire in the Knickerbocker "History" had been "to clothe home scenes and places with imaginative and whimsical associations, which live like charms about the cities of the old world," yet that really remarkable book was as much contemporary satire as whimsical chronicle of the picturesque old times. Does anyone read it from beginning to end? Certainly there is infrequent reference to the opening burlesque of world history in the manner of Sterne and Swift, adorned, like their work, with mock erudition, but far less excellent. It is only when the Dutch come to New Amsterdam that the book takes life, and why? Because these stupid Dutch with their sluggish bourgeoisity, their absurd parodies of courage, the "happy equality" of their intellects, their lack of fire, energy, grace, are perfect symbols of that sodden materialism which Irving found ridiculous in others and hated for himself. In spite of its comforts, which he did not disdain, it was the very opposite of all qualities of romance.* Because, again, the shrewd, invading Yankees of the "History," with the "duty to go right" constantly sounding in their ears and making hypocrites of them, with their ungainly manners and their shady tricks, represent the trading class and trading manners triumphant and odious.† And what a chance to take pot shots at absurd great ones of the opposition! If under the pseudonym of Wouter the Doubter,

*His youthful impression of the Dutch when he visited Holland on his first trip abroad is not forgotten in the Knickerbocker "History." They were unromantic traders, in sharp contrast to the French with their imperial fervor and to his venerated England. He writes to Peter Irving on October 20, 1805, of the "monotonous uniformity prevailing over the whole country," which reminds one of the "happy equality" of the stolid New Amsterdamers.

†Note, for his general attitude, his letter to Brevoort apropos of the War of 1812 (January 12, 1813)—"If this war continues and a regular be raised instead of depending on volunteers and militia, I believe we shall have the Commissions sought . . . by young gentlemen of education and good breeding, and our army will be infinitely more respectable and infinitely more successful."

the apoplectic little John Adams escaped with a few digs that his
enemies in New York could not have missed, he at least was a Federalist. But William the Testy, who undertakes to conquer by procla-
mation and arms his ramparts with windmills, was no merciful portrait of Jefferson of the embargo and the wars waged by words
against England and France, while the drunken meetings and windy
discontent of the Dutch democracy, and their panic at the arrival of
the British fleet, reflect with perfect clarity what gentlemen like Irving
thought of his democratic clubs and his propaganda for the rights of
man. Indeed, if the "History" is, as I believe, the meatiest of Irving's
books, and excelled in style only by a few of the best of his later
sketches, the reason is that never again did he have so much of his
own observation, his own prejudice and rooted dislike, to add to the
documents he drew upon. Never again were his spirits so high, never
again was he so close in experience as well as in imagination to his
subject. When, later, he began to conceive of his task as the romantic
rendering of the European scene for Federalist consumption,* the
reverence of the new world for the old or his concern with what to
him was picturesque in England, Scotland, or Spain suppressed the
satiric vein, or rather, his own detachment from the scenes he described reduced irony and humor to a consideration of general, and
often very abstract, human nature. Instead of Jefferson and the commercial New Yorker one gets Spanish rascals and English eccentrics.
When he returned to his symbolic Dutch, as he did from time to time
throughout his career, he was always fresh and humorous.

The Knickerbocker "History," erudite, polished, suave, anti-
bourgeois, a satire upon the unromantic, an attack upon democracy,
a challenge to all ideologues, pedants, moralists, fanatics, a lampoon
on besotted commercialism, stands at the head of Federalist literature. Poe and Lowell could understand it, though not each other;
Whitman could not.

In later years, when Irving worked *con amore* it was not upon
the continuous writing necessary for a complete book, but in bursts
of energy upon the occasional sketches which he felt rightly to best
represent his genius. His histories are admirable for style, but they
are not literature, though often more literature than history. Indeed,
Irving if he had lived in the twentieth century would have been a

*See Irving to Brevoort, March 10, 1821.

magazine writer, if not a columnist. His best work, after "Knicker-bocker," consisted of essays and short stories, produced when time and mood were propitious and collected when the market was ready. Yet "The Sketch Book," which in 1819 won him international fame, is not a good book. It was arranged with the tact of an American who sought British recognition as eagerly as the British novelist today seeks an American sale,* but its texture lacks the homogeneity of ei-ther "The Alhambra" or the Dutch part of the Knickerbocker "His-tory." As a book it displays, in its two Introductions, first Irving the humorist, then Irving the man of sentiment who "traversed England a grown-up child." It contains Irving at his humorous best in "Rip Van Winkle" and "The Legend of Sleepy Hollow," Irving at his shrewdest in "John Bull," at his manliest in "English Writers on America,"† at the full stretch of his romantic veneration in the series of papers on English life, of which the famous "Westminster Abbey" is the most rhetorical and the less known "Country Church," "Rural Life in England," and the "Bracebridge Hall" sketches are far the best. But it is padded also with perfunctory Indian sketches, and with stories in the worst romantic taste of the time, full of false pathos and strained sentiment. "The Sketch Book" is a miscellany, a travel book, sweet-ened to the taste of the times by romantic sugarplums, and rising to literature only when Irving was more Federalist than romanticist, or more story-teller and essayist than an adorner of sentiment by style.

There was of course some truth, and a good deal of insight, in the romanticizing of jolly old England that makes up so much of "The Sketch Book." And it is Irving, not Dickens, who is chiefly responsi-ble for the glamour that ever since his day has hung about Christmas in the old hall, the stagecoach, the waits, the loyal tenantry, and all the paraphernalia of merry England. It is only romantic truth, as can readily be ascertained by reading in order from "The Sketch Book" and from the contemporary pages of Jane Austen. Nevertheless, the literary symbolism that he found for the picturesque as he saw it at Abbotsford and Newstead Abbey took such hold on his readers on both sides of the water that it became to them history, and is as vivid

*I am aware that Pierre Irving thinks that he had only an American mar-ket in mind, but do not believe it.

†An essay that says all that has been resaid a dozen times since on Eng-lish condescension, in spite of its typically Federalist inference that all Amer-icans were once English.

in the imagination of the American tourist as manor houses and crumbling castles to his eye. With such an England, Irving was quite sure to please both the Federalist at home and John Bull in his romantic mood, and it had much to do with the book's success.

Without the two Dutch stories, however, "The Sketch Book" would not have worn so well. They are perfect examples of what Irving best loved to do, and naturally he did them well. "Rip Van Winkle" and "The Legend of Sleepy Hollow" are history of that legendary character which he fed upon—history that preserves, with little care for too minute reality, the memories of a period. "The Alhambra" is full of such stories, whose plots are old tales, whose characters are fireside companions, the scenes in those golden ages before hustle and bustle were invented, the subjects such as to arouse that humorous irony which was Irving's reaction to wiseacres, busybodies, scolds, gluttons, fanatics, the whole imbued in the mist of romance. He himself, in "The Sketch Book," was Rip, gentle, pleasure-loving, inadaptable to the crudities of business and family support. He loved the rascal because he was as Irving might have been without brothers and friends. Dame Rip was the urge of hustling, unsubtle America that threatened to drive him away from the pleasant loafing that he loved into a mode of life he most philosophically disapproved of. The Catskills were those hills of romantic dreaming in which he wandered seeking the future—and the harsh disillusion of the bustling ugly village of twenty years afterward, where no one knew Rip, or wanted him, was no bad similitude of the future in those depressing years from 1816 to 1819 when the failure of his brother's business roused in his imagination the spectre of a return, *auctor ignotus,* to job-hunting in New York. No such symbolism, I suppose, was in Irving's consciousness, but he wrote these humorous idylls of picturesque living from his heart, and told them superbly in a prose so pure and harmonious as to speak of a master at his best.

Reviewers and readers, however, praised "The Sketch Book" and Irving most often, not for the narrative, but for the style, the source of which I have already put in question. The sense for style in 1819–20 had not yet been sicklied by the welter of romanticism. Houses were still being built with that easy mastery of form and proportion which was the gift of the eighteenth century, and if the crisp outlines of English prose were blurring under the pen of a Walter Scott, and if the quaintness of Charles Lamb and the profuseness of

De Quincey were beginning to be preferred to the cool clarity of Goldsmith, the conception of measure, harmony, restraint, was to last as long as good architecture. Indeed, it is perhaps not altogether a coincidence that Irving and good architecture died in the same decade in America. A delightful temperament, a pleasing play of sentiment and humor upon fortunate themes, and a triumph of style—this was the current estimate of "The Sketch Book." And it remains our estimate, except that the "sob stories," as they would be called in the modern vernacular, can no longer be regarded as fortunate.

The rest of Irving that really matters is implicit in the books I have already discussed. "The Alhambra," that romance of history mellowed in a style that is too pure and clear to permit of turgid extravagance, is of course another "Sketch Book," with the single theme of a lost and beautiful civilization. The earlier "Tales of a Traveller" are less admirable because, paradoxically, they are more original. Here Irving trusted too much to invention, and when he left legend and history and scenes that he knew by deep experience he fell almost invariably into mawkishness or into rhetorical display. Irving could write well on any theme, but rhetoric alone never turned a bad theme into literature. "Bracebridge Hall," written because of the success of his earlier narratives of the romantic last stand of English feudal life, was also a miscellany, successful this time because the book flowed from the romantic reverence that was Irving's second rich reaction to life. "A Tour of [sic] the Prairies," a work that deserves more reputation, was conceived as another "Sketch Book," with included stories, and, like "The Alhambra," with a single romantic theme—the march of the Rangers through the Indian country. But here Irving was too close to his subject. The Indian stories were not in his vein, the companions of his voyage did not project their shadows against historic backgrounds. There is a camp scene, firelight flickering on wild faces, psalm-singing, alarms, rough humor of the frontier, which is Irving at his best, but he could not sustain it. The material that Cooper found so rich was, for him, too thin. Edward Everett, reviewing the book in *The North American Review,* thanked Mr. Irving for "turning these poor barbarian *steppes* into classical land." That was the trouble: they would not turn, ought not to be turned, and Everett was ridiculous in thinking that they could be turned into the kind of romance that Irving practised. Nor were they poor either to the right imagination, as Cooper showed in his admirable "Prairie," but Irving was not the man. He was, after all, a bookish writer, and the life he best interpreted was seen through books or under their influence. For the frontier he had no books with the flavor of history and hence no perspective.

6.

Some of the current estimates of Irving must be altered after such an analysis. He did little to illumine American life and character although so much to enrich the American romantic imagination. He endowed the Hudson Valley with a past of legend and fable borrowed from the old world, but his Dutch are quite false, except as satire, his Yankees no more true than Yankee Doodle, his New Amsterdam a land of Cocaigne, which has bequeathed to posterity an idea that New Netherlands was the comic relief of colonial history.

He was not a great romantic, if Scott and Byron and Shelley be taken as models of romanticism. His gentle melancholy is more akin to Collins, and his humor to Goldsmith. In truth, where Irving was most eighteenth century in manner he has best survived, for his humor, his sense for the quaint, and his admirable feeling for proportion are more valuable than his attempts at pathos, terror, and grandeur in the style of the Teutonized romance of his own period. Revolt, that great theme of his English contemporaries, never moved him, for, like his fellow Federalists, he had had enough of rebellion. In pure romance he is never excellent except in that minor category where the light of fancy is made to play over the vanishing scene—there he is superb.

Yet many a more pretentious author of his age has died utterly, while Irving, in spite of his modern detractors, lives. Stylists do not die if they are fortunate enough to find even a few themes that summon all their powers. The romanticist in Irving powerfully influenced a century of American writers ("The Sketch Book" was Longfellow's first school of literature) and usually to their hurt. They sucked sentiment from him and left the humor behind. But equally strong, and much more fortunate, has been the ideal of excellence set up by his style. Every American writer who has cherished the Federalist hope of urbanity and a counsel of perfection in the midst of democratic leveling may claim Irving as his spiritual father.

The textbooks call him the first ambassador of the new world to the old. That is to look at him through English eyes and is in fact a repetition of his first authentic praising, which came from abroad. He proved that the barbarous American could write as the captains of 1812 had proved that Americans could fight on the sea, he tickled John Bull's romantic rib, but his true ambassadorship (and his real importance) was all the other way, and his oft-repeated arguments for his residence abroad show that he knew what he was about. Call him rather an American Marco Polo, bringing home the romance of other countries, bearing their gifts of suavity, detachment, ease, and beauty to a raw country dependent upon its vulgar strength, stronger in brains than in manners, yet not devoid of a craving for civility. He was in this always a good republican, but a better Federalist.

In 1860 William Cullen Bryant published "A Discourse on the Life, Character, and Genius of Washington Irving," which he had previously delivered at a meeting in commemoration of the dead author. Bryant also was a Federalist in spirit, a Federalist in American literature whose very respectable poetical talents were diverted into a lifetime of struggle as editor of Alexander Hamilton's *Evening Post,* which long after the death of the Federalist party kept its ideals alive. In his early promise, in his absorption by a commercial, political régime, in the decline of his writing, and the lessening reputation, as time goes on, of even his best, he is a picture of what Irving might have been had he come home to an office or an editorship. Irving, Bryant said, was the first to make Americans believe in the possibility of financial success for a native author. Our American fiction, poetry, history, so he maintained, should be dated from the publication of "The Sketch Book" in 1819–20. Undoubtedly, as the literary criticism of the time pathetically indicates, the United States was suffering from an inferiority complex, made more grievous by the competition of English books, which could be pirated and sold at a price that the native product naturally could not touch. And undoubtedly Irving's triumph over handicaps* and his recognition abroad spurred on Cooper, Prescott, Parkman, Hawthorne, and his many other successors. He may be said to have indicated the possibility of a literature not merely didactic or utilitarian in America.

*There was a complaint of the $.75 price set upon the first number of "The Sketch Book."

And yet it is more noteworthy, I think, that he gave it dignity. In 1832, Irving, then in London, addressed to Samuel Rogers a Preface to the Poems of Bryant, which he thereby introduced to English readers. What he admired, what he expected Rogers to admire, in Bryant was the "purity of moral, and elevation and refinement of thought, and a terseness and elegance of diction" that belong to "the best school of English poetry." Irving might well have written, for his own epitaph, that his writing belonged to the best school of English prose, that his style also was terse and elegant, that the "persuasive grace," which he maintained was shed over Bryant's descriptions, was his in larger measure, and that he too was "imbued" with the "buoyant aspiration incident to a youthful, a free, and a rising country." He praised, as so often happens, those qualities in the work of another which were most certainly his own. They were precisely what England expected of America, still regarded as a colony, and what the American who wished reunion with the culture and grace of the old country most desired. This was not the American ambition that burned in Jefferson, or John Adams, or Daniel Boone, nor certainly the American desires of an Aaron Burr or an Andrew Jackson, but it was a voice of America. Great American themes, native to our development, were later to find both prose and verse; they are not in Irving. He was the type of that American, always commoner than Europe believes, whose nostalgia in the midst of prosperity, strenuosity, and progress is genuine and enduring. Federalist that he was, he longed for types of character and achievement alien to the United States of his own days, and was blind to romance of a far different order, which, with axes and rifles and hopes for the common man instead of banners and swords, was a living presence in the forests of his own land, forests that he loved only because they were solitary and vast. Cooper and Parkman succeeded where Irving trod halfheartedly because his heart was elsewhere.

And yet his theme is as genuine as theirs and he was more perfect in the voicing of his romantic melancholy than Cooper in his romance of the pioneer. The America of the early eighteen hundreds was profoundly different from Europe, in spite of an external resemblance in all that concerned culture and the ordinary practice of living. Its economic outlook was different, its spiritual and ethical emphasis was different. It was committed to a different theory of the future. Nevertheless, it was bound to Europe by the strongest ties. The social history of America is a history of straining at the bounds, straining toward the West. At the points of juncture and of binding—the seaports most of all—a profound tension of the spirit resulted. Every man looked two ways, and wished to go in two directions. There was that genuine emotional lesion which gives rise to literature. One sees it in Crèvecœur, in some of the discourses of Franklin, but the medium was imperfect. Irving, the first to make his pen a perfect instrument, took the side of regret. He wrote like a European, but with the desires, the mentality, the outlook (already defined), of an American. His style is English, but made in America, for an American need.

And because in order to speak for Federalist America he learned to write with a vanishing grace and a suavity not again to be attained on this side of the Atlantic, his future is more secure than that of his successors in the historical vein, Motley and Prescott and Parkman, better historians than he, who transcended the "Washington" and the "Columbus," but could not write an "Alhambra." Cooper, crabbed republican aristocrat, came nearer the ruling passions of his country, but his loosely held romance of the frontier has already suffered from its slovenly diction and uneven texture. Hawthorne's didactic obsession stiffens the sombre beauty of his work, but Irving's lighter craft is well trimmed for the shifting gales of fame. He had a style, he had a temperament, he had an eye for the humors, he was born a New Yorker, he could say, as New Englanders would not say, as Philadelphians and Virginians and Carolinians could not say effectively: While we create a new society in a new republic, let us not forget the mellowness of the age we have left behind us overseas, let us not forget the graces of life, let us not forget to be gentlemen. And if this was all he said, it was put admirably, in a time of need, and with apposite and succinct example. He made Spain glamorous, England picturesque, and his own land conscious of values not to be found in industry, morals, or politics. A slight achievement beside Wordsworth's, a modest ambition by comparison with Byron's, but enough. Not a great man, not even a great author, though a good chronicler, an excellent story-teller, a skillful essayist, an adept in romantic coloring; not in accord with progress in America but the most winning spokesman for the Federalist hope; a musician with few themes, and the minor ones the best, and many played perfectly—that is Washington Irving.

Introduction
to *Washington Irving —*
A Bibliography

BY WILLIAM R. LANGFELD AND PHILIP C. BLACKBURN

The first descriptive bibliography of Washington Irving's works was completed by William R. Langfeld (1882–1941) and Philip C. Blackburn (1907–?). Their *Washington Irving—A Bibliography* was published by the New York Public Library in 1933 after the contents, later revised, appeared in its *Bulletin*. Langfeld, a Philadelphia collector and gentleman scholar, had previously compiled *The Poems of Washington Irving* (1931). Blackburn, earlier a New York Public Library librarian, went on to assist Robert E. Spiller with a similar bibliography of Cooper. This selection, the preface by Langfeld and Blackburn, is given in its entirety in order to illustrate one painstaking, if technical, approach to its subject, an approach understandably unfamiliar to many readers. In the Bibliographical Society of America's ongoing *Bibliography of American Literature,* the information on Irving first editions, etc., in Volume 5 (1969) edited by Jacob Blanck, supersedes Langfeld-Blackburn in places.

IRVING AND THE COLLECTOR

Recent years have witnessed a vast expansion of interest in book collecting. The reading public has multiplied in numbers and advanced in knowledge and discrimination. It is inevitable that a certain proportion of this growing body of readers should be lured by the beguilement of first editions.

The most logical field for an American collector is that of American literature. The worthies of his own land are nearest his heart, their works are more accessible, and most items may be obtained at moderate prices. Many of these authors have been the subject of exhaustive bibliographies. In the case of Washington Irving there appears to be none that is extensive and thoroughgoing in its scope.

Irving is particularly deserving of study. Historically, he is practically the Father of American literature. No American writer has been longer in vogue or more highly regarded over a period of years both in this country and abroad. The constant republication of his works here and in England is evidence of the high esteem in which he has long been held. His personality has an engaging charm; he possesses undeniable literary merits; his wit, his urbanity, his touches of quaint eighteenth-century style, his scholarship, the plots of his tales—all have a distinct appeal. To the bibliographer, the variations in the editions of his books, the occasional "points," the existence of little known items offer an absorbing study.

ASSOCIATION WITH THE NEW YORK PUBLIC LIBRARY

The name of Washington Irving is closely associated with The New York Public Library—both historically and by the notable collection of Irvingiana that has been brought together in its Reference Department. Named by John Jacob Astor, in the third codicil (1839) of his will, as a trustee of the library to be created under his bequest, Irving consulted in 1840 with Astor and Joseph Green Cogswell (also designated in the will as a trustee, and in 1849 chosen as the first superintendent of the Astor Library), as to plans for the organization and book collection of the proposed library. On February 18, 1849, he was chosen by the trustees as the first president of the Astor Library—an office he held until his death ten years later. The

Astor Library, later to be combined with the Lenox Library and the Tilden Trust to make The New York Public Library, owed much during this formative period to Irving's knowledge of men and affairs, as well as of books.

The New York Public Library had long owned some important Irving manuscripts. In 1925, the collection of Irvingiana assembled by the late Isaac N. Seligman was presented to the Library, in his memory, by Mrs. Seligman. At the same time, Mrs. Seligman's nephew, Mr. George S. Hellman, presented certain Irving manuscripts and portraits, which were placed on exhibition with the Seligman collection. Mr. Hellman, in 1929, added the remaining portion of his collection to that already given—this gift being made in honor of his mother, Mrs. Frances Hellman. The Seligman-Hellman collections, with other Irving material from the Library's collection, are kept on permanent exhibition in the Fifth Avenue entrance hall of the Library's Central Building. Catalogues of the Seligman and Hellman collections were printed in the *Bulletin* in February, 1926, and April, 1929, respectively, and were later reprinted in separate form.

THE BIBLIOGRAPHY—ITS MECHANISM

The data of this list have been obtained from many sources. The collations of all first editions have been made from copies in the collection of the compiler, with few exceptions. Information as to the first English editions has been secured in some cases from English book-dealers, or other persons in England, and where such is the case it has been mentioned; catalogues of the Bibliothèque Nationale, British Museum, Library of Congress, and The New York Public Library have been searched.

Capitals and italics have been indicated, but not black letter. Where pages are irregular in size, being untrimmed, the largest size is given. Title-pages and collations of the first American edition of each book are given immediately under the book title; those of first English editions follow all matter concerning American editions.

FLYLEAVES

The problem of flyleaves has always vexed bibliographers, who looked at them; dealers, who sold them; and collectors, who bought them. The present is no exception; the extreme proponents of both viewpoints have represented to us that, (a) *any* blank leaf before or after the printed matter should be counted; and, (b) *none at all* should be reckoned with. Agreeably to the tradition, neither school of practice has been followed; the result may be satisfactory to none. For the purposes of this bibliography, we have counted as flyleaves, any unprinted leaves, other than the free half of the end- (or lining-) paper, either before or after the printed matter of the book itself. The exception to this is that if an extra sheet is pasted to the free half of the end-paper, it is not counted. Thus there may be two blank leaves, but no flyleaves, as was frequently the case; the first American edition of *Columbus* is an example. Advertisements cannot generally be regarded as part of the book itself, but are rather something extraneous or foreign, associated with the casing process. This is true even of printed wrappers bearing advertisements. It is therefore possible to have several pages of advertisements before a front flyleaf or after a back one. (A notable exception is the first American edition of *Abbotsford and Newstead Abbey,* q. v.) It is realized that this allows room for the vagaries of the binders, but we call your attention to the fact that, since at times the status of a blank leaf cannot be determined without ripping the book apart, in no instance is the number of flyleaves considered a necessary 'point' in identifying an edition or issue.

If it seems to some that the allowance of flyleaves for a given title is somewhat parsimonious, we say that we have preferred to err on the side of strictness than to require an unobtainable quantity of blank paper. Responsible dealers and careful collectors will naturally concern themselves with sound copies of books. A collector obviously does not rejoice in a copy which bears the scars of mutilation and removed sheets. Flyleaves should indicate a sound copy, but bibliographically they tell nothing more than the fact that either the binder or printer was a generous man.

Similarly, the matter of advertisements at times threatens to become a fetish. When three copies of a first issue of a book vary only in the number of advertisements, an earlier date on them is likely to prove attractive, but it is not reliable. Publishers' advertisements were inserted so wholly willy-nilly that their importance hovers around the vanishing-point. Where we have found advertisements, we have noted them, but here again, as with flyleaves, they are more ornamental than useful.

Any such standard as the one arbitrarily laid down here, will be confounded with exceptions. We cannot formulate any rule which would cover the cases of freak ways of binding. In the second volume of the first American edition of *The Alhambra,* for instance, the blank half of page 235–236 (which would be called p. 237–238) is used as the end-paper for the back cover, and two blank sheets from the first signature are sewn between this end-paper and the last page of text. Such cases are, we are grateful to say, rare.

No effort has been made to dissect the body of the text. That is, in a number of cases there are sub-titles following blank pages through the text. These unnumbered pages have not been listed, since they are not, as a rule, of bibliographic interest.

There has been no attempt to include all works of critical, biographical, or reminiscent interest, except full biographies and a few volumes of particular concern, since such books are constantly appearing. If a list were to be fully inclusive it would necessarily embrace every history of American literature and every literary and historical work on the period 1800 to 1860 in America. A list of such critical books or essays is given in the *Cambridge History of American Literature.* It is full, but not, however, complete.

It is apparent that Irving is an author whose works are particularly adapted to illustration and tempting to illustrators. His popularity, his availability as a classic for gift-book purposes, the romance and whimsicality of his characters—have made a strong appeal to many artists. Irving's tremendous and lasting popularity is perhaps in no way better demonstrated than by the great number of illustrated editions of his books which have appeared and are still appearing frequently. Most of the prominent artists of the last century in this field have illustrated one or more of Irving's books. It is worthy of note also that perhaps more of these illustrated editions have been published in England than in America. Where it is reasonably certain that the book noted is the first publication with the particular illustrations mentioned, it is listed as a first edition; otherwise the date given is merely that of the volume to which reference was found. The list of illustrated editions has been compiled from the author's collection, from other private libraries, and from catalogues of libraries and book dealers. Whenever possible, publisher, page size and number of pages have been given. Additional publications are, of course, constantly being issued.

The bibliography of the plays on which Irving collaborated with Payne has been derived from published letters of Irving and Payne, biographies of both authors, and standard literary histories. In several cases the fact or extent of Irving's participation could not be definitely established.

It did not prove practicable to compare all manuscripts viewed with each of Irving's published works. It is therefore possible that some errors may appear in the manuscript lists. A few pages described as unpublished may prove to be merely unidentified portions of a published work. In stating the number of pages, particularly of long manuscripts, there may be variances from computations by others, as in several instances portions of two pages were mounted as one, extra unnumbered pages inserted, some leaves written on both sides while the body of the manuscript was written on one side only, etc. Different methods of counting would give different results. The principal object in mentioning these manuscripts is to locate, identify, and describe complete manuscripts, as well as important (and some unimportant) portions. When the pagination of the printed page is given, it is that of the first edition.

Copies have been located sufficiently to indicate where they are to be found. This is not a census of first editions; no effort has been made to list all holdings. In the case of manuscripts, all such material that has come to our attention has been included; likewise copies of unusual interest have been cited.

All editions have been mentioned which contain new material or offer any variations from the text of the first edition, and certain others, such as Paris editions of the same year. The collection of the compiler contains many additional volumes, including copies of all the revised 1848 [etc.] set, most of the Paris editions, and others.

ACKNOWLEDGMENTS

The preparation of this list has been a pleasure, because of a lifelong interest in the works of Irving in the one case, and a great interest in whichever Muse rules Bibliography in the other. Not the least of the pleasure has been the courteous and helpful assistance received from many sources and the agreeable contacts with others of like interests. Among the many persons who have generously given of their time and information, special thanks are due to

Mr. Whitman Bennett; Mr. Barnet J. Beyer; Mr. Albert A. Bieber; Dr. William G. Braislin; Dr. Maurice Chazin; Mr. James H. Drake; Mr. George S. Hellman; Mr. Kennard McClees; Mr. Boies Penrose, 2nd; Mr. Carl H. Pforzheimer; Mr. Alfred L. Rose; Dr. A. S. W. Rosenbach; Mr. Alwin J. Scheuer; Mr. Charles Sessler (Miss Mabel Zahn); Dr. Robert E. Spiller; Mr. Leon C. Sunstein; Mr. Arthur Swann; the Rev. Dr. Roderick Terry; Dr. Stanley T. Williams; Mr. Carroll A. Wilson; Mr. Owen D. Young.

We are grateful also for assistance from England: from Mr. Reginald Atkinson; the British Museum; Mr. Stephen Hunt of Southborough; Maggs Brothers; and Mr. F. D. Webster of Tunbridge Wells, who supplied many useful facts about English editions.

American institutions have been kind, and our indebtedness includes certain of their officials: The American Antiquarian Society (Mr. R. W. G. Vail); Columbia University Library; The Free Library of Philadelphia; the Henry E. Huntington Library and Art Gallery; The Library Company of Philadelphia, including its Ridgway Branch; The Library of Congress; The Mercantile Library of Philadelphia; The New York Historical Society; The Pierpont Morgan Library; Yale University Library; University of Pennsylvania Library.

Introduction to
The Life of Washington Irving

BY STANLEY T. WILLIAMS

Stanley T. Williams (1888–1956), whose academic life was centered at Yale, after a Ph.D. there in 1915, joined the English faculty, becoming Colgate Professor of English in 1933 and department chairman 1939–1945. Soon attracted to the burgeoning studies in American literature, he authored in 1926 *The American Spirit in Letters.* By this time also, he had developed the special interest in Irving which would be climaxed in 1935 by a monumental two-volume biography, *The Life of Washington Irving.* In preparation for this he had traveled widely, labored as scholar-detective in many special collections, and edited a number of Irving's journals and letters. The selection here, the introduction to *The Life,* offered a clear focus on this historic author, at a time when, in the troubled 1930s, the waters of criticism were often being muddied by current proletarian perspectives on the past. In 1948 Williams updated these authoritative interpretations in his Irving chapter in *The Literary History of the United States* [See Introduction, p. *xxxvi*].

The reader, after glancing through the pages of this long book, will, perhaps, wonder momentarily about the need for so detailed a portrait of the first American man of letters, Washington Irving. Out of the past he emerges as a talented writer, hardly more; as the author of two or three enduring sketches or tales; as a man singularly lovable, commanding the affections of his countrymen during his lifetime and after his death. How else, in the usual broad outlines, should his portrait be? But is it possible to add subtler, more delicate tints to the conventional image, showing him hated as well as loved, writing desperately for bread instead of dwelling serenely in the Alhambra or at Sunnyside? I think so. It is unlikely that the old painting of Geoffrey Crayon will fall from the wall; my investigation reaffirms some of Irving's best-known characteristics. Yet it is my hope that the familiar memory of a rare spirit may be enriched by better perspective, more finish, more understanding, more finality of knowledge. At any rate, this is my purpose in attempting a definitive biography of Irving.

Other interests have encouraged me to complete a manuscript commenced ten years ago. One of these has been to inquire into a problem which puzzled that acute critic of the literature of his epoch Edgar Allan Poe, and which still arises in the minds of modern readers of Irving, namely, the contrast between this essayist's actual intellectual equipment and his enormous popularity in his own day. "It is a theme," declared Poe, "upon which I would like very much to write. . . . A nice distinction might be drawn between his just and surreptitious reputation—between what is due to the pioneer solely, and what to the writer."* Indeed, as I continued my study of the age in which Irving lived, the question became not at all the measuring of his literary work by the immemorial touchstones of the past, tested by which he is often trivial, or by the standards of to-day, by which he has been outmoded, but a study of his career and writings in fusion with the literary criteria of his own time. For through such an approach he becomes a clarifying mirror of some aspects of culture in America during the first half of the nineteenth century. To understand Irving's hold upon his generation is to understand a dominating tendency of American literature prior to the Civil War, which, begin-

* See, in the present work, II, 101-102.

ning only two years after Irving's death, helped to destroy the cult of elegance and made comprehensible the voices of a Whitman or a Clemens. Hence, in this biography, the emphasis upon Irving's contemporary reputation; it reveals the literary principles of the age for which he wrote.

Yet my study of literary standards in an era which consistently intermingled the aims of art, morality, politics, and business, involved me at once in the study of Irving as a public figure. For his fame as a man of letters was inseparably joined with his rôles of journalist, politician, diplomat. It may be said, I think, that no writer before 1850, with the exceptions of Poe and Hawthorne, became eminent among Americans without their approval of his opinions on subjects far dearer to them than what Irving called "the gentlemanlike exercise of the pen." Was the literary man a Democrat or a Whig? Was he a successful man of affairs, perceiving that literature, among men who were building a republic, should be avocational? Did his books inculcate sound nationalism, sound politics, sound morality? The delay in the recognition of Hawthorne and Poe may be attributed partly to their heterodoxy under such catechisms; and the prolonged obloquy suffered by the patriot and social critic Cooper may be ascribed to his violent expression of his honest convictions concerning America. Admiration at the world-famous "Leatherstocking Tales" could not survive, among Cooper's contemporaries, the resentment aroused by *A Letter to My Countrymen*. But Irving's answers to these questions satisfied the vast majority of Americans. "You have," wrote John Pendleton Kennedy, "convinced our wise ones at home, that a man may sometimes write a volume, without losing his character."* When Irving was not orthodox, he was tactfully silent, and praise of him as an author was never drowned out, as in the case of Cooper, by abuse of him as a critic of his own people. His writings epitomized his compatriots' *bourgeois* culture and flattered their aspirations to be gentlemen, to write according to English models, to make money, to exploit the West, to found traditions, to be respected abroad. And always behind this attitude, which so sickened Cooper, was the drama of Irving's life, externally remote from the artistic aims which in his best moments begged him to have done with all this: reporter at the trial

Horseshoe Robinson, Philadelphia, 1835, Dedication to Irving.

of Aaron Burr, Secretary of the American Legation in London, agent of Jackson and Van Buren, tenderfoot explorer of the frontier, Minister to Spain. This story my biography endeavors to tell.

The story, moreover, apart from its illumination of Irving's character and writings, is not commonplace. The brothers in the Orkneys, one of whom was a sailor, the other a tailor, did not foresee that this member of their family was, in the next generation, to return to Europe to be presented at the courts of Frederick Augustus I, Queen Victoria, and Isabella II. In spite of his protests concerning his maladjustment to the world of men, Irving had his part in the events of his time. Few careers of American men of letters are more varied in background; few offer so many glimpses behind the scenes into the literary, social, and political worlds of five different nations. If Irving himself wearies us, mild-mannered, urbane, indecisive, discreetly ambitious, imitatively romantic, affectionate, and, at times, timid and dependent, the picturesque settings in which he moved, and which he repeatedly changed to satisfy his volatile temperament, do not. Historians of the nineteenth century may learn a good deal from following Irving down Broadway on the day when he saw Washington, to remember him "perfectly"; into the Paris of 1805, with its gossip of Napoleon; into the Philadelphia of 1807; to Sacketts Harbor, in the War of 1812; or to the frontier post of St. Louis. For the Paris newspapers, in 1824, he wrote an article on the death of Louis XVIII; he was in Alexander Everett's counsel in Madrid in the days of Ferdinand VII; he directed the American Legation in London during England's turbulent struggles for the Reform Bill; he betrayed, so his enemies said, President Van Buren, and helped to elect Harrison; he managed American policies in Spain toward Cuba, and—but the reader, if patient, may, I hope, see for himself how Irving's weakness, in respect to our curiosity about the past, becomes his strength. Never deeply creative, never the leader in events nor wisely critical of these, he was a sharp-eyed observer. Few significant episodes of contemporary life escaped his pen, and if we tire of him as a minor actor, we do not forget the stage which he described so vividly.

In recounting this story of Irving's life, I have had constantly in mind those students and scholars of American literature and American history who hope by factual investigation to lay the foundations of a criticism of American thought, for which, in my judgment, the materials are not yet fully discovered and ordered. Such a criticism must be based not merely upon imaginative interpretation of the past, but upon those tedious researches, well described by Diedrich Knickerbocker, which underlie the best criticism in older countries than America. If the biography errs upon this side, I can only plead my honest belief that out of such preparation will be born eventually America's best self-criticism. Thus some facts, inconsequential, perhaps, except in a full-length portrait of Irving, have been included in these volumes in the hope that they may aid critics and historians in their reconstruction of our past since the Revolution.

Yet this groundwork, such as the analysis of the sources and content of Irving's forgotten books or of his debts to the literatures of Germany and Spain, has, for the most part, been relegated to notes and appendices. Over these, all save the scholar and the antiquarian will, I fear, pass hastily. Yet I have thought of other readers than the student of American literature, and as I finish my long task, I still feel, as at its beginning, that the narrative of Washington Irving will remain, for nearly everyone, invested with interest. Whether the reader was introduced to Irving by "Rip Van Winkle" in childhood, by the classroom lecturer, by the condescensions of modern criticism, or merely by Irving's associations at every turn with American traditions, still he will think, I believe, this story of the first American man of letters worth retelling in detail. For Irving's career, in contrast to his writings, had that volume and variety which entitle him to be remembered, through a full biography, as a famous American; this, despite his modesty, his caution, and the slenderness of his talents, he was. Lacking force and concentration, his life experience, nevertheless, ranged freely over that past to which we now look back with mingled feelings of superiority and longing. Irving, as Poe said, pioneered in the democracy—in literature, history, travel, politics, and diplomacy. These adventures and the man himself I have tried to describe for all readers, completely and truly.

"A Master of the Obsolete: Washington Irving in the Shadows"

from THE TIMES LITERARY SUPPLEMENT

The "Literary Supplement" (*TLS*) of *The Times* of London has for generations reigned all but supreme as a weekly book-review magazine, with stimulating comment and correspondence. Until quite recently its contributors (other than letter writers) were by tradition anonymous. On March 21, 1936, it devoted this extensive unsigned front-page review to Stanley T. Williams's two-volume biography of Irving (1935). Seemingly from a British source, though *TLS* uses American contributors too, this review was, beginning with the leader, negative *in extenso* about Irving, though positive about Williams. The review was accompanied by an illustration, a much-reduced engraving after Gilbert Stuart Newton's 1820 portrait of his friend Irving.

"Geoffrey Crayon is very good," said Byron, echoing popular opinion. Jeffrey placed the "Sketches" among "the best classical writings
of our country," a compliment which in that day, when an indigenous
literature was unthinkable, delighted American citizens with artistic
leanings. Scott, Lockhart, Gifford- and other lawgivers agreed. Two
hemispheres acclaimed him. American culture had been emancipated
by Washington Irving as political America by George Washington,
from whom came the baptismal name, and yet it could remain classical and polite. A nation's literature had begun. There were traditions
in her mountains, her villages and in her sleepy hollows, traditions
and legends that could be compared with Europe's—indeed, as later
rebels so unkindly pointed out, they were Europe's. And they could
be memorialized, not in raw defiance of the approved masters, not in
the uncouth tongue of an aborigine, but in the style of an English
gentleman, one who was no thought-ridden poet like Wordsworth
and other upstart insurrectionists, but a gentleman of feeling who remembered the writings of Addison and Steele and Goldsmith—and
remembered them remarkably well. For half a century, though
doubters arose, America conceded Irving as her first classic, an immortal beyond questioning, the "Goldsmith of the Age." But even in
the 1820's some English grumblers wondered what the fuss was
about. There was that brow-drawn fellow Hazlitt, who linked Crayon
and Elia in one mischievous essay in order to bring the American
down the heavier. He ran a corrosive pen through the graceful Irving, which remains embedded to this day. Even the friendly Rogers
muttered "Addison and water."

"Authors, like coins, grow dear as they grow old," said Pope.
Not at all. Perhaps Irving was born too old. He was outdated from
the start. The honours due to him are the honours due to one of the
originators of imaginative literature in the United States. Yet a re-
reading of his work brings curious questionings. How is it that a vital
literature originated in anything so unoriginal as Irving's imitations
of writers already outmoded? What quality was it that so captivated
even the sophisticated English public? Decaying customs and dead
habits were his subjects, and a memory for the obsolete in writing
formed his style. He was indeed a master of the obsolete in style
and substance. His knowledge of the use of a disused technique and

his acquaintance with discarded ideas are astonishing and almost deserve fame. His manner is drained of volition, and he seems void of responsibility. He knew no high ecstasies or profound griefs. His sole theme is that man has but little time to live. Mutability has seldom worn a dress so banal. A monument of past glory produced a sob; sometimes a whimper. A new Goldsmith! said the critics. Goldsmith directed an eye of intellect at the manners and experiences of his day. He worked in the literary fashion and was not isolated from the popular taste; but he had fresh purposes of his own to turn them to. Nearly everything that Irving acquired—style, subject, outlook—is secondhand and improverished. His interests are homely; he takes us into his confidence though he has little to confide; pours into our ears a copious but thin flow of emotions. His mind runs on anecdotage and quotation. He interweaves his feelings with the landscape, utterly unabashed by their subjective quality and their insignificance. He could assimilate but not recreate. Herman Melville, who dealt with the mysteries of life, could be expected to react against literature as a plaything; in his championship of Hawthorne, he makes a deadly comparison which recalls the strictures of Hazlitt. He saw Irving only as a popular and amiable copyist, one who was not even a fine failure. For it is better to fail in originality than to succeed in imitation.

The fact remains that for nearly half a century Irving was popular. It is difficult to explain. It is best to take stock of what he accomplished by following more or less the course of his career. There could be no better illustration of the style being the man. We see that his verbal decorations were part of his character, his reverence for the past and the pretty an expression of his sadness and good nature. All the facts are now available, all. Professor Williams, in the thorough American way, has explored two continents in Irving's footsteps, and has written almost a day by day record. He has studied the revealing notebooks and journals kept by Irving, and produces much unknown material. His careful references and explanations take up a considerable part of the volumes, and will prove of great service to the student of letters. Professor Williams would not agree entirely with the attitude to Irving's work indicated above; but he is no blind worshipper.

Irving was born in New York in 1783, the year peace was declared; and his mother said: "Washington's work is ended and the child shall be named after him"—a preluding phrase to the sentimental life. The condition of the country was chaotic, and most of its institutions were engendered while Irving played with his toys and read romances; yet his impression of childhood was that "everything was fairyland." The fairyland complex was abiding. His nurse, who must have been one of the elves of his destiny, pressed the infant on the attention of Washington in a shop. "Here's a bairn that's called after ye." The great man laid his hand on the child's head, and his blessing secured a biographer. The young Irving found romances more to his mind than lessons, and he left school with little more knowledge than how to compose sentences which would not shame the authors of the light literature he read so intelligently. He haunted the pier-heads, where he listened to gossip of the outer world; or wandered in the woods, where his meditations with nature meant squirrel shooting. Addison and Goldsmith came early in his way. His mind went on expeditions from the pages of "The World Displayed," and it was here he met Columbus and heard of Mexico and Peru. But Europe, as he tells us in the "Sketch Book," "held forth all the charms of storied and poetical association." There were the "quaint peculiarities of ancient and local custom." The "quaint" overcame him early and late. His native land might be full of youthful promise, but Europe was rich in the accumulated treasures of age. He longed, he tells us, to "wander over the scenes of renowned achievement—to tread as it were in the footsteps of antiquity—to loiter about the ruined castle—to meditate in the falling tower." His fate in literature is that he fulfilled that longing. He could seldom look a present reality in the face; and his meditations on past "grandeurs" rarely had the impress of actuality. When he took up the study of law his preconceptions were Irvingesque: he would "overwhelm the guilty—uphold the innocent—I would scarcely have changed my anticipation for the fame of Cicero." But legal activities became servitude. It was all very well for Cicero, but it was too much like task-work for Irving. It gave little time for indulgence in those reveries which he mistook for thought.

"The Letters of Jonathan Oldstyle" was his first publication. Twenty years later it startled even its author with its puerilities. But the critics tempted him on. *Blackwood* found in these letters, after the "Sketch Book" and "Bracebridge Hall" had brought him fame, a "happy, sly humour," a "grave pleasantry (wherein he resembles Goldsmith so much)," and pronounced that they would "outlive the fashion of this day, and set him apart, after all, from every writer in our language." Irving was to be killed by kindness. At the age of twenty-one he came to Europe in search of health and stayed for two years. His notebooks and journal accuse him. They show him in search of confirmation of what Sterne had seen and thought, or Addison or Goldsmith. Professor Williams traces in these manuscripts "the increasing power of his style. He was learning to write with ease and some distinction." In hours of idleness, we learn, he "devoted himself not to meditation, but to his flute." Goldsmith, also, played a flute. Any incidents which could feed the moods of sensibility and romance were packed into the notebooks for future reference. He gathered rosebuds everywhere, as can be seen in his letters: "Genoa figured conspicuously in the time of the Crusades and still bears the red cross." "I am once more venturing my life and fortunes on the 'vasty deep,' speeding away to Sicily, that island of fable and romance." "I haste to those 'poetic fields' where fiction has shed its charms o'er every scene."

Returning to New York, he impressed his family by the elegance he had acquired, legal studies were renewed, but he fancied himself now as a writer and a man about town. He, his brother William and Paulding began the ridicule of their town's foibles in "Salmagundi." Addison's *Spectator* and Goldsmith's *Citizen* had done something in the world; why not the opinions of Launcelot Langstaff? History proves that the pitiful imitation, the weak burlesque and facetiousness were highly acceptable to the New York readers of that day, who were told how to "instruct the young, reform the old, correct the town and castigate the age." The papers were collected in a volume, which will hardly bear looking at to-day, yet for long it was spoken of as a starting point of a national literature. "Salmagundi," which derided the foibles of the town, had a lustier and bolder offspring, "A History of New York," in which Diedrich Knickerbocker satirized the whole history of the town. Even to-day one can applaud the assiduity of Irving's researches and the readiness of his references to Cervantes, Smollett, Fielding, Sterne and Swift; but it was a confused huddle of odds and ends, and a sad mix up of the real and the spurious.

Irving was now an American celebrity: "I was noticed, caressed, and for a time, elated." The public was prepared for a greater effort. In 1815 he was in Europe again with his note books, and remained for seventeen years. In Liverpool he "stepped upon the land" of his forefathers. He was soon at Stratford-on-Avon experiencing "indescribable emotions"; and in attempting the "indescribable" he was not afraid to tell his readers that "the long interval during which Shakespeare's writings lay in comparative neglect has shed its shadow over his history." Under "the wizard influence of Shakespeare" he walked all day "in a complete delusion. I had surveyed the landscape through the prism of poetry, which tinged every object with the hues of the rainbow." He and a friend spent "days of chivalry" in Wales emulating "the deeds and adventures of Don Quixote." And there were living wizards in this romantic land. Thomas Campbell gave him a letter of introduction to Scott, who had written to him as master to pupil. Irving spent four blissful days at Abbotsford, where he had a great spirit to share his interest in ancient retainers, castles and abbeys. This was life. Jeffrey was friendly. Coleridge he called upon, but he was not impressed. Wordsworth it was not worth while to visit; of Elia and Hazlitt he was contemptuous; but he was honoured with the intimacy of really great poets such as Moore and Rogers.

The temptation to irony is checked for a while. During this English tour in search of sentiment, eld and decay, he suffered a blow by the bankruptcy of the family business, of which brother Peter was managing the Liverpool branch. In the act of composition Irving was bound by verbal conventions and the spell of fancies; but he met an emergency in his life bravely. He took a course of book-keeping to disentangle Peter's muddles. He fought stubbornly with the job. Suffering the bankruptcy like a personal disgrace, he became neurasthenic. Still, he continued to make voluminous notes, and he sought an anodyne from sorrow in the study of German folklore. Other men of his time, wrestling with ideas beyond the borders of the day's routine, were also looking to Germany. But the philosophers did not disturb Irving, who was not troubled by any impulse to unravel the universe. Legends and castles and haunted forests filled the landscape of his dreams. There would he find inspiration for the literature of escape. And he did. "Rip Van Winkle," his best achievement, had its origin in "Peter Klaus."

He was still in England when the "Sketch Book of Geoffrey Crayon, Gent.," was published. It is his most finished work and was greeted with applause. The gentle author was received everywhere —in literary circles, in fashionable society, generally conducted thither like a tame lion by Moore. The "Sketch Book" may be taken as the epitome of his work—and in a sense of his life. As fearless in declaring himself as in writing a platitude, he explained that he hoped in this work to escape "from the commonplace realities of the present and lose myself among the shadowy grandeurs of the past." He had travelled, he confessed, pencil in hand and had brought home a portfolio filled with sketches. They showed him making a momentous passage from the new world to the old, "musing for hours together on the tranquil bosom of a summer's sea," with "finny herds" roaming "its fathomless valleys"; admiring the "refreshing verdure" of English rural life; our churches, castles, parks and particularly the "moral feeling" that pervades them—with never a hint that the world had moved since Goldsmith's day, that industrialism was disturbing the "calm and settled security" that spoke to him so "deeply and touchingly."

All descriptive epithets are counters, he never breaks into an original phrase; but he did have a gift for keeping a careful balance in the tone and rhythm of his sentences. That and his sentimentality was the secret of his popularity; as to-day they may explain why he has few to admire him. In Westminster Abbey he works up the right mood for "solemn contemplation" by intoning clichés in every device of cadence of which he was capable. But after Sir Thomas Browne's harmonies on mutability what a tinkle of words is this over "the congregated bones of the great men of past times who have filled history with their deeds and the earth with their renown." There is something to be said on the credit side. The "Sketch Book" does contain a story which may survive those "dilapidations of time" which Irving never ceased to lament. The plagiarism from a German source for "Rip Van Winkle" is a less important matter than some writers have pretended. Irving made the legend his own in the Catskill Mountains; and a re-reading brings again a childish thrill at the sight of the weird brotherhood of Dutchmen whose game of bowls sent the echoes rumbling through the ravine like peals of thunder. England praised and America was triumphant. "Bracebridge Hall" was Irving's next effort. A few questions had been raised in the meanwhile, and Irving saw the need of another conquest. He thought his new work less callow. Acute critics recognized at once that it was more watery; Miss Edgeworth found that too much care and cost had been bestowed on petty objects—a valid objection to most of his work. But in general it was acclaimed.

With "Bracebridge Hall" the reservoir of England was exhausted. He had done all he could with her enchanted castles, the hospitable inns, her squires and ladies, her buxom chambermaids, her country stiles, her Christmas customs. A new poetry was beginning, philosophical questions were reopening, a revolutionary age warned of vast changes. Irving cared nothing for these things. Since he must have material, he would dip into the wells of German folk lore, or go to Granada, where he could conjure up Moors and Spanish heroes, as he had pictured old Dutchmen in the Catskills. He had used up all the English archaisms he had learned. "The Germans," he wrote to his sister, "are full of old customs and usages which are obsolete in other parts of the world." After Waterloo a new Germany was stirring; but Irving wanted pixies in a setting of great forests, baronial halls and "quaintness." He found things which put him in mind "of the Emperor and his army shut up in the enchanted mountain— which mountain I have absolutely seen with my own eyes." Wandering in a Vienna garden, he planned to collect "tales of various countries made up from legends." In Dresden he was fêted as a famous man, petted at court, and found enough sentiment and supernatural in the city to satisfy the greediest romantic.

It all resulted in the banalities of "Tales of a Traveller," a book which will not bear examination: it falls to pieces at a glance. Some critics formerly complacent now declaimed against his lack of invention. He was even accused of indecency, though a modern reader would be hard put to it to find a trace. The sensitive author was puzzled and hurt. He brooded over the injustice. Lady Harvey bravely advised him to take a pattern from the Duke of Wellington, who laughed at Press attacks. But Irving had never faced Napoleon; Hazlitt was terrible enough. His thoughts turned to Spain. There was healing magic in her history. His notebooks record much luscious self-pity, but he studied the language and was for long immersed in Spanish literature. An appointment to the Embassy at Madrid lasted for seven years,* and meant four more books. As his writings grew, so they declined in character. He had rich material for his "Life and Voyages of Columbus" and the exacting task of the historian should have left no room for Irving's "whim-whams." What he made of it was a mellow romance, in which pageantry is the note and Columbus a novelist's hero. Murray paid three thousand guineas for the work and came to regret the bargain. "The Conquest of Granada" was written in the same spirit; he revelled in the "magic glow which poetry and legend have shed over this romantic place." The inevitable adjective and the stage scenery were fully employed: battlements frowned, trumpets brayed, steeds neighed, Moors "looked down upon glistening cavaliers struggling and stumbling among the rocks." Even the enduring Professor Williams admits that the reader succumbs long before the Moors. This effusion brought in two thousand guineas, and again Murray groaned. In order to write "The Alhambra" he took up his abode, of course, in the haunted wing of a castle and lived as "in the midst of an Arabian tale." In that mood his history became another sort of "Sketch Book"—Irving's tender impressions of the picturesque and languorous past. Sometimes, it is true, his feeling in this work does manage to communicate itself and his writing to take on some colour; but as history, these Spanish books are negligible.

The Spanish sojourn was ended by an elevation in diplomacy. Irving became secretary to his country's Legation in London. He was not now the only American writer known to England; Cooper and others were sharing the honours; but he was still the foremost, and his name was known throughout Europe, "a standard writer among British men of genius," said *Fraser's*. The Royal Society of Literature awarded medals in 1832 [1830, *Ed.*] to Irving and Henry Hallam. A rapturous New York welcomed the wanderer home in 1832, but for long he looked at his hobbledehoy country with the eyes of an aristocratic European. He did not see, as did Cooper (whose attitude to Irving was always bellicose), the material of a vigorous native literature; he was interested in the bewildering national strife,

*This is misleading. Irving was a temporary attaché in Madrid, 1826–1829, and U.S. Minister there, 1842–46. [*Ed.*]

but surprised chiefly that there should exist in the same world such contrasts to the scenes of civilization he had enjoyed. Why, asked Emerson, in his journal four years after Irving's return,

> Is there no genius in the fine arts in this country? In sculpture Greenough is picturesque; in painting, Allston; in poetry, Bryant; in eloquence, Channing; in architecture, —; in fiction, Irving, Cooper; in all, feminine, no character.

These questions were being asked by the new generation. Irving could not have answered, because the questions themselves would be unintelligible to him. He was, and he remained, as unaware of what Poe and Cooper and Hawthorne were doing as he had been of the work of Wordsworth and Shelley and Keats; indeed, those English poets seemed to write in a kind of savagery. A mind awake to affairs might have found subjects for satire in the scramble for success in money and politics. Irving's idea of a national theme was his mild "Tour on the Prairies," his "Astoria," with its laudation of the commercial spirit, and other pot-boilers. He had "sensed the common man's interest in the West," as his biographer says, but had no vision of America's destiny. Even the tolerant Longfellow shook his head —"old remnants—odds and ends—about Granada and Sleepy Hollow. What a pity!" His literary work was nearly ended. A preposterous Life of Mahomet and a ponderous biography of George Washington, who had blessed him, were to occupy the closing years, and he toiled at the Washington bravely; but before that there were some years of aggrandisement as Minister to Spain, where he was received with respect, although in commending him to the Madrid authorities the Spanish Minister to the United States had written:—

> He knows our language well, which has served him to advantage in taking notes and translating Spanish works, in order to offer them later in his own country as originals. . . . Nevertheless, this little blemish does not lessen his great reputation as a man of letters.

Irving made an excellent Minister, and his good nature made him liked in Spain as everywhere else. Yet, in the midst of the Regency troubles and later, after the accession of Isabella II, he seems to have thought of history never in terms of peoples but only as a drama of personalities. It was a kind of make-belief by which the blessed past projected itself into the prosaic present. "Shadows," he said, "have proved my substance; from them I have derived my most exquisite enjoyments." It could be his epitaph.

THE LIFE OF WASHINGTON IRVING. By Stanley T. Williams. In Two Volumes. New York: Oxford University Press. London: Milford. 50s, the two volumes.

"Farewell To Spain"

BY CLAUDE G. BOWERS

Claude G. Bowers (1878–1958) had a long, active career as journalist, popular historian, and diplomat. An influential writer for the New York *World,* 1923–1931, and a Democratic Party orator, he turned his energies as well to formal history, in works like *The Tragic Era* (1929) and *Thomas Jefferson,* 3 vols. (1945). U. S. Ambassador to Spain, 1933–1939, and to Chile, 1939–1953, he wrote reminiscences of both posts. In 1940, capitalizing on experience, both professional and personal, Bowers produced *The Spanish Adventures of Washington Irving,* adding to familiar tales of the romantic author a largely realistic account of Irving's labors as U. S. Minister to Spain. Selected here is the final Chapter 14, a salute to a conscientious predecessor and still-influential hispanophile.

Irving now had but a few months more in Spain, but events moved rapidly and with the flourish of drama. On March 11, immediately after his return to Madrid, we find him writing the Marquis of Mira-flores, the Premier, asking for an appointment to pay his respects to the Queen and Maria Christina. Eight days later he was acknowledging the note of the Duke of Valencia announcing his appointment as the successor of Miraflores, and eighteen days after that, he was congratulating Don Xavier Isturiz on his appointment as the successor of Valencia. Narvaez had suffered a momentary eclipse, but Irving wrote Buchanan that the Miraflores Government had 'never had a vigorous existence,' but had been suffered to carry on temporarily while intrigues in the palace and conferences among the politicians arranged matters on a compromise. Then the Miraflores Cabinet 'was suddenly despatched by a kind of *coup d'état.*' Narvaez returned to power with a Ministry of his own choosing, and for the moment he seemed again on the crest of the wave. And Narvaez acted like a dictator.

'The first measures of his government are significant,' Irving wrote Buchanan. 'The sessions of the Cortes are suspended indefinitely. A manifesto has been published by the Cabinet Ministers from which it appears that they intend to carry on the Government by decrees; thus giving, as they say, a "rapid impulse to those public measures which have been impeded for years by the stormy discussions of the legislative chambers." ' The Ministers added that should they 'occasionally transgress the limits of their constitutional faculties' they would finally give an account of their acts to the Cortes and trust their exoneration to the exigencies of circumstances. 'Meanwhile,' they continued, the Ministers would depend on 'a numerous, well-disciplined, and loyal army,' on the good sense and prudence of the nation, and 'on the energy inspired by a generous enterprise, as exciting in its causes as it is holy in its ends.' And with that, the Government, with a heavy hand, broke the back of the freedom of the press.

But Irving had an inspiration that Narvaez would not last. His all but dictatorial power had momentarily 'struck a degree of awe into the community.' The opposition press ceased publication. Meandering through the streets and to the Puerta del Sol, the center of all gossip and much intrigue, Irving listened to the whisperings of the people. He heard some say that the purpose of it all was to force the Trapani marriage on the nation—or Isabella, who scarcely counted. No, said others deep in their throats, the purpose is to put in operation 'the most profligate schemes of finance to retrieve the immense losses which Narvaez and the Duke of Rianzares are said to have sustained in recent gamblings with the funds.' Not at all, interjected another gossip, the whole play is to prepare the way for the final elimination of Narvaez. Had he not lost much of his prestige with the army as well as with the people? Had he not multiplied his enemies, civil and military? Had he not become odious to a great part of the Moderate Party? These, of course, clacked the gossips, would co-operate with the Progresistas in casting him down from his eminence, just as they had toppled Espartero from his seat. Of course, said others, the Trapani marriage would be his Waterloo.

But as Irving snooped about, he heard the explanations of Narvaez's friends. He merely had in mind measures of great public utility and wished to lose no time. He thought Spain behind the age and behind her own institutions, and the faction and corruption in the Cortes made progress impossible. Destroy the Constitution? Not at all—perish the thought! He would merely act 'independently of it'— nothing more. All this gossip Irving sent on to Washington, along with Narvaez's purported statement:

> Give me a few months to carry my plans into effect, unembarrassed by the Cortes and the press, and I will engage to clear away some of the most important evils which are pressing upon my country. I will then report what I have done to the Cortes and will say, 'If I have done wrong, punish me. Order me to the scaffold if you think fit. I will go there.'

In higher circles, Irving heard much speculation as to Narvaez's relations with Maria Christina. The two had never cared for one another, and merely their common benefit had drawn them together. Now that Narvaez knew how odious the Queen Mother had made herself because of her urging of the Trapani marriage, Irving wondered if he might not defy her and take the popular side.

But within three weeks Irving was informing Washington that Narvaez had fallen and had been banished. Irving wrote that he had reasons to believe 'that his fall had for some time been meditated in the secret councils of the palace.' His program did not meet with the approval of Maria Christina, that grand mistress of intrigue. The breach between them widened. Narvaez was defiant, and, to her, offensive. 'His intentions may have been patriotic,' thought Irving, 'but he overrated his means of carrying them into effect, or rather he underrated the influences against him. He was too confident of himself and in that fiery spirit which had borne him on to power.' At one of his first Cabinet councils he had committed the unpardonable sin by saying bluntly that the army would not tolerate the Trapani match.

And then came a violent scene in the Council of Ministers in which Narvaez's position was embarrassing. It grew out of a proposed law regulating the stock exchange and prohibiting speculations in the funds. Many thought the law had been aimed at Narvaez's speculations in the funds and that he would have it rescinded. But his enemies in the Cabinet, who were the partisans of Maria Christina, deliberately forced the fighting by insisting on the law's stringent enforcement. 'The consequence,' Irving heard, 'was violent altercations in which Narvaez gave way to his stormy temper, and at times lost all guard over his language. Some of these took place in the presence of the young Queen, who, it is said, conducted herself on these occasions with a dignity and discretion beyond her years.'

Then Isabella, who hitherto had been grateful for the loyalty of Narvaez to her interests, turned against him. The occasion was the reorganization of a portion of the Ministry. She agreed that some should go. But whoever Narvaez proposed for the succession she promptly vetoed. Urged to give her reasons, Isabella sounded the death-knell of Narvaez in her reply that they were 'enemies of [her] mother.'

Thus, with the realization that Maria Christina was a menace to him in the palace, he made a more serious blunder. In an unguarded or rash moment he proposed to Isabella that it would be excellent for her mother to leave the court and find residence in the provinces. The Queen resented the suggestion and Narvaez's fate was sealed. He tendered his resignation, and, to his surprise, it was accepted. Isturiz hastily formed the rudiments of a Ministry composed of the adherents of Maria Christina, and Narvaez was out.

Then for the moment it was the turn of the palace to tremble. In one of the stormy scenes in the Council Narvaez had referred to the palace intrigues against him, and with Andalusian heat and eloquence had boasted of his popularity with the army and implied that if thrown out he would turn it against the throne. Irving did not take these boasts seriously, but the palace did. It wanted Narvaez not only remote from the capital but from the provinces as well. Military measures instantly were taken to defend the city, and Narvaez unctuously was offered the post of Ambassador in Naples. Proudly he declined.

Meanwhile, the palace heard of mutinous murmurings in the army, and of threats to march upon the royal residence and demand the expulsion of Maria Christina. Panic seized the courtiers about the palace. Isabella by royal command ordered Narvaez to leave Madrid and Spain at once and repair to Naples to await further orders. Then there was turmoil in the town and Irving reported that 'this harsh mandate, equally pusillanimous and impolitic, was regarded with disgust even by the adherents to the court.' Narvaez's popularity revived. He was a political martyr and victim. That day his house was packed by personages of all parties and he was a national hero. Irving thought some of the callers were 'actuated by a generous sympathy, others by the idea that his disgrace might be but temporary, while still others merely wished to express their hostility to the court.' 'Nothing was heard,' reported Irving, 'but exclamations against the royal ingratitude toward so loyal a subject and one who had rendered such vast service to the throne.'

In the midst of the tumult and the shouting Narvaez conducted himself with a quiet dignity as he made his preparations for departure, professing his loyal devotion to the Queen. The popular reaction to the harsh order gave pause to the palace, which now wished to modify its criticized decree. It was much too late. Narvaez was in the act of entering his carriage when a member of the Cabinet appeared unctuously to offer a royal document constituting him Ambassador to Naples. Narvaez returned to his house and sat down at his writing desk to pen a proud reply. Since his presence in Spain was considered detrimental to the country, he had not hesitated a moment in making preparations for departure. But he begged the Queen for permission to decline serving a government which regarded him as an encumbrance. Smilingly offering the letter to the Minister, he entered his carriage and turned toward France.

At Bayonne, he had an amusing encounter. In the last few days of his power his protégé and choice for the hand of Isabella, Don Enrique, the Duke of Seville, was suspected of having plans to place himself at the head of a Galician insurrection at Coruña. Narvaez took military measures to suppress the insurrection, and Isabella ordered the Prince instantly to leave the kingdom for some point in France and not return, else he would be deprived of all the honors and considerations of a royal Prince of Spain. He obeyed at once, and chose Bayonne as his place of residence. Arraying himself in full uniform, Narvaez paid the Prince a call of respect. Madrid smiled at the comedy or tragedy.

Irving was pessimistic over the prospect of an adequate successor to Narvaez. 'The terror of his name and the vigor and promptness of his measures have daunted opposition, kept down insurrection, and contributed to carry on a discordant government for nearly three years,' he wrote. 'In this respect I see no one within the precincts of the court likely to supply his place.'

Never during his tenure was Irving so much engaged in official business of large import as during the brief period between his resignation and the arrival of his successor. In April he was much concerned over a report in the *Heraldo,* a Ministerial paper, concerning the ideas of some prominent Spanish politicians, urged on by France, for concerted action in erecting a monarchy in Mexico with one of the Princes of Spain upon the throne. The throne was to be upheld by the joint action of Spain, France, and England.

Irving would have liked to talk bluntly about it with his friend Valdivieso, the Mexican Minister, with whom he had made the memorable drive to Aranjuez for the meeting of the Queens. But Valdivieso had been almost two years absent from his post. He had gone to Rome and then to Mexico, but for some months he had been dividing his time between Paris and London. Irving wondered if he were engaged in negotiations on this project, and wrote his suspicions to Buchanan.

If Washington knew anything about it, it gave no sign. Indeed, Irving began to feel that his existence had been forgotten. His letter of resignation of December had brought no reply by July 11, when his patience was exhausted. In angry mood, he wrote brusquely to Buchanan. Not only had he been denied the courtesy of a reply to his resignation, but he had not received a line from the State Department for nine months. But for the newspapers he would not have known that his successor had been selected. Assuming that he was not in favor, he wrote modestly enough and yet with some spirit in defense of his mission. He could find no instructions that had been neglected.

True, one of the foremost of these had not been carried out. He had secured no commercial treaty. He explained:

> Finding at an early period of my mission that important reforms to the system of trade were in preparation, and that England and Belgium were pressing for commercial treaties with great prospect of success, I thought it a favorable moment to open a negotiation on the subject. Hastily availing myself therefore of such statistics as I could command, relative to our trade with Spain, I addressed a note of some length to the Spanish Government, and at the same time wrote home to my government for further instructions in the matter. A change in the Spanish Cabinet and in the course of Spanish policy destroyed the temporary hope I had conceived; neither did I ever receive from my own government any encouragement to renew the attempt.

From the Spanish Government he had received courteous and friendly treatment, but he noted a growing distrust and uneasiness regarding the movements of the United States in the Gulf of Mexico and our ultimate designs on Cuba. These suspicions had been accentuated by the 'incessant calumnies of the British press.' An ardent friend of England, and numbering Englishmen among his closest, dearest friends, he had been embittered by the British propaganda throughout Europe which was endeavoring to debase the national name. 'I had noticed for some time past slanderous articles copied from the English journals into the Madrid *Gazette,* in which all our acts and intentions in regard to the Oregon question and the disputes with Mexico were crassly misrepresented and we were charged with a grasping and unprincipled avidity of empire.' This had alarmed him, since the Madrid *Gazette* was 'exclusively a court paper edited by persons about the Government.' Irving had gone directly to Isturiz and pointedly asked if these slanders were 'actually believed and countenanced by the Cabinet.' The Minister had assured him that he had not even noticed the articles, that the *Gazette* was not used politically by the Government but merely for the publication of official acts. However, he would 'take care to have such offensive articles excluded for the future.'

All this Irving sent to Buchanan, whose silence had become offensive. Again explaining the reason for his prolonged sojourn in

England and referring to his previous explanation, to which no reply had been received, he concluded his letter with a stinger: 'If this silence is meant to intimate that the explanation has not been satisfactory, I can only say that I had rather the rebuke had been fully and frankly expressed than left to mere surmise.'

Within a week, Irving was to have more occasion for indignation. A dispatch of May 14 announcing the declaration of war against Mexico did not reach him until July 13. Through the European press, he had known for some time that a state of war existed and that the United States had blockaded the Mexican ports. He understood that official notice had been sent American Ministers in other countries for transmission to the governments to which they were accredited. But he had been in darkness all the while. Time and again he had been embarrassed in talking with Isturiz, who spoke of the war and manifested a keen interest. 'I had to confess myself without official instructions,' he wrote indignantly to Buchanan, 'as to the causes which led to it and the temper and spirit with which it would probably be carried on.'

He was saddened by the war and ascribed it to the bad advice given the Mexican Government. Had Slidell been received, Irving had no doubt that an amicable settlement would have been possible. He thought some European powers that had given Mexico the impression they would support her would betray her. And for days he was worried about General Taylor's fate, and lived in dread of some humiliating defeat that would prolong the war by forcing his country to continue the fighting until the disgrace should be wiped out. He wrote:

> When I read therefore the account of the gallant manner in which Taylor and his little army had acquitted themselves, and the generous manner in which they had treated their vanquished enemies, the tears absolutely started into my eyes. . . . I sincerely hope this brilliant victory will be followed up by magnanimous feeling on the part of our government, and that the war may be brought to a speedy close on fair and honorable terms.[1]

[1]Irving, *Life,* III, 111.

On the receipt of notice, Irving called on Isturiz. The Minister expressed much regret over the war and hoped that an honorable peace could be speedily effected. He assured Irving that Spain would maintain a strict neutrality, and that he would issue orders to the authorities in Cuba and Puerto Rico to exert their utmost vigilance in preventing any attempts to fit out privateers in the islands against the United States. In reporting the conversation to Buchanan, Irving wrote:

> The opening of this war has been propitious. Should it be carried on in the same spirit and temper in which it has been commenced and brought to a speedy triumphant and magnanimous close, the present year will add a page to our national history of which every American patriot may well be proud.

In compliance with the request of Isturiz that Irving present him with a formal note covering the conversation, he set forth the cause and purpose of the war. Considering the source, this strong statement in justification of the war that still is the subject of controversy deserves more notice than it ever has received. Beginning with an explanation and apology for the delay in communicating such 'important intelligence . . . to Her Majesty's Government,' he launched vigorously into his statement.

'Whatever may be said of the ambitious designs and the aggressive policy of the United States with regard to Mexico,' he said, 'I feel authorized to assure Your Excellency that we have engaged in this war with extreme reluctance. It is our interest and it has ever been our inclination that Mexico should be a powerful republic, and that our relations with her should be of the most friendly character.' But a succession of revolutions, and the character of some of the heads of her government, had 'brought her to the brink of ruin.' The United States had hoped for 'a stable government, sufficiently powerful and pacific to prevent and punish aggressions upon her neighbors.' But for years we had been subjected 'to a series of wrongs and insults.' True, 'she pledged her public faith in solemn treaties to redress, but the treaties have been disregarded and the wrongs complained of have been reiterated.' Our commerce had been all but 'annihilated by the outrages and distortions practiced by her authorities upon our merchants, while all attempts to obtain indemnity have been fruitless.' Despite all this, we had acted with forbearance and patience. 'Ultimately the Mexican Government chose to consider the annexation of Texas . . . as a violation of her rights, though that republic was an independent power, owing no allegiance to Mexico, constituting no part of her territory or rightful jurisdiction, and although its independence had been acknowledged by the most powerful and enlightened nations of Europe.'

At length, Irving wrote, Mexico broke off diplomatic relations and announced her determination to wage war. 'As a matter of self-preservation, we prepared to repel the threatened aggression.' Even then efforts were renewed to persuade her to an amicable agreement. 'Having received informal assurances from the Mexican Government that it was willing to renew diplomatic intercourse and would receive a Minister from the United States, we waived all ceremony as to the manner of reviving our relations, assuming the initiative and sending an Envoy Extraordinary and Minister Plenipotentiary to Mexico, clothed with full powers to adjust and definitely settle all pending difficulties between the two countries.' And how was he received? He was courteously welcomed at Vera Cruz, but before he could reach the capital a military revolution took place and General Paredes took possession of the Government by force of arms. 'Our envoy was refused reception and credence, notwithstanding that he came under the plighted faith of the Mexican Government. No attempt was made to ascertain what propositions he was empowered to offer; no propositions were suggested on the part of Mexico. His passports were given him and the door of peace was in a manner shut in his face.'

Thereafter, Irving wrote, nothing but threats of war were heard. Troops were marched in the direction of Texas. Our army was ordered to the frontier but with instructions to 'abstain from all aggressive acts toward Mexico or Mexican citizens.' And the result? 'The public papers have informed Your Excellency of the results. After the armies had remained encamped on the opposite bank of the Rio del Norte, which we claim as the boundary of Texas, the Mexican troops crossed the river, surprised and killed some of our soldiers, and took others prisoners.' Thereupon by practical unanimity Congress declared a state of war.

Such, said Irving, is the story. 'It has been forced upon us by the conduct of Mexico, who has either mistaken our forbearance for pusillanimity or has been urged on by evil counsels to take advantage of a crisis when we appeared to be on the point of hostilities with England on the Oregon question.' Now the war would be prosecuted with vigor both by land and sea but 'we shall bear the olive branch in one hand and the sword in the other, and whenever she will accept the former the latter will be sheathed.'

With refreshing frankness he passed on to the purpose of the blockade. 'The object is to deprive Mexico of the revenues derived from customs and in the hope of speedily compelling her to offer or accept reasonable terms, and to induce foreign nations, who now enjoy a monopoly on her commerce, to exert their influence with her government in effecting a fair and honorable peace. The liberal mode in which this blockade has hitherto been conducted by the officers of our navy has been acknowledged in the English journals.' Referring to the possible danger of privateers' being fitted out in Cuban and Puerto Rican waters to prey upon the commerce of the United States, Irving asked that instructions be sent to the authorities in both islands. 'I feel confident,' he concluded, 'that the good faith manifested toward us on all other occasions by the Spanish Government will continue throughout the present conflict in which we unwillingly are involved, and that it will discountenance anything calculated to add to the evils of a war which it is the desire of the United States to conduct and terminate with as little injury as possible to the general interest of the civilized world.'[1] Having written this, his final and perhaps his most interesting dispatch, Irving laid his pen aside and turned from his desk.

Irving's successor reached Madrid on July 23, and Irving was busy packing. Members of the Ministry and his colleagues of the diplomatic corps were sorry to see him go. During the next few days he was occupied in making his farewell calls: on the de Bressons, within whose Embassy he had passed merry evenings; on Bulwer, whose irony and dry humor and languid manner he would miss; on Prince Carini, whose charming wife he had found so interesting; on the Albuquerques, with whom he had from the beginning enjoyed an intimate friendship. And then he went to the palace for his last audience with the Queen, whose real well-wisher he had been, and whose vicissitudes and dangers had often moved him. "I could not but feel a

---

[1] MS. Archives, United States Embassy, Madrid, July 17, 1846.

little sensitive in visiting the royal palace for the last time, and passing through its vast apartments but partially lighted up,' he wrote his sister. He was received in an inner cabinet by Isabella, attended by Isturiz and several ladies- and gentleman-in-waiting. His speech in taking leave was brief. He said:

> For my own part, I can assure Your Majesty that I shall carry with me into private life the same ardent desire for the welfare of Spain, and the same deep interest in the fortunes and happiness of its youthful sovereign, which have actuated me during my official career; and I now take leave of Your Majesty, wishing you, from the bottom of my heart, a long and happy life and a reign which may form a glorious epoch in the history of this country.

The youthful sovereign, expressing her regret at his departure, also touched the personal note. She replied:

> You may take with you into private life the intimate conviction that your frank and loyal conduct has contributed to draw closer the amicable relations which exist between North America and the Spanish nation, and that your distinguished personal merits have gained in my heart the appreciation which you merit by more than one title.

And for the last time Irving passed from the presence of Isabella, to whom he had presented his credentials in the presence of her nurse.

That evening at six o'clock in the carriage of Weismuller of the House of Rothschild, to whom he had offered the refuge of the Legation on a perilous occasion, Irving drove out from the sunny streets of Madrid en route for France. The middle of August found him in London, and early in September he embarked on the *Cambria* for Boston.

It has been written with reason that Spain always calls one back, but Irving was never to see its plains and mountains again. But in the quiet of his closet at Sunnyside on the Hudson he was to remember it with a deep affection to the end of his days. In his meditations he was to revisit it in spirit and to recall his intensive labors in the house of

Rich; his joyous hours with the d'Oubrils romping on the floor with the children; chatting with the lively Antoinette; his merry parties with Dal Borgo; his mornings in the studio of Wilkie; his meanderings among the countless treasurers of Toledo; his journeys to the Escorial. He was to relive in memory the thrilling days in Seville and the Sunday picnics at Guadalajara; his nocturnal rambles on the Alameda; his dinners at Mrs. Stalker's; his summer with Hall in the walled-in house near the city; his driftings down the river; his countless hours in the cool library of the cathedral; and the festival of Corpus Christi. Never was he to forget his summer in the country on the outskirts of the Port of Saint Mary, and least of all his memorable life at the Alhambra and his friend the Duke of Gor, whose palace always gave him hearty welcome. As history unrolled and clouds descended on the reign of Isabella, he was always to recall her as a winsome, innocent child with preternatural poise, and to hear from afar her merry laughter at her first ball at Narvaez's. When he read the story of an imperial wedding in the Tuileries he was to recall the tiny baby he had danced upon his knee in the castle of the Count of Teba near Granada, and the baby, later a dashing belle who cast a spell on all who saw her at the balls of the Madrid of the forties. Again he was to rise at dawn to jolt over the road to Aranjuez to the meeting of the Queens, and to follow the court to Barcelona and marvel at the lordly manner in which Dal Borgo lavished coins in the villages on the way. And often he ascended in recollection the grand marble staircase to undergo the torture of interminable standing before the throne, and to push through the festive crowds of the capital with the sprightly Countess de Bresson. The Albuquerques, the Carinis, and Bulwer would sit in fancy at his table at Sunnyside. He would review again with Espartero the troops in the Prado, and see Narvaez riding through the city gates to exile.

Never was he to forget or cease to love the expansive plains shut in by mountains in their purple haze, the rugged, awe-inspiring mountain passes, the rich fields of Andalusia, the picturesque age-old villages drowsing in the sun, the witchery of a Spanish night, the geniality of the Spanish people, and the beauty, charm, and glory that is Spain.

From "William Dunlap and His Circle"

BY VAN WYCK BROOKS

Van Wyck Brooks (1886–1963), a major twentieth-century literary critic and historian, was educated at Harvard, then taught English at Stanford University (1911–1913). A vocal figure during the rebellious 1920s, he was sometime associate editor of *Seven Arts* and then of *Freeman*. In time he became a member of the American Philosophical Society, of the American Academy of Arts and Letters, and Fellow of the Royal Society of Literature. In 1946 Brooks was awarded the Gold Medal of the National Institute of Arts and Letters. In 1937 his *The Flowering of New England* was both a Pulitzer Prize and National Book Award winner. That, the first volume published in his "Makers and Finders: A History of the Writer in America, 1800–1915," was followed in 1944 by *The World of Washington Irving,* from Chapter VII of which, "William Dunlap and His Circle," this lively sketch of the young Irving is taken.

Dunlap and Brown were often together, and Dunlap painted a miniature of this ill-fated, melancholy man of genius, the first American writer who had made a profession of letters and never turned aside from the path he had chosen. Later Dunlap wrote his life, while the two had been early thrown together when Brown appeared in New York in 1793, voyaging up the Hudson and visiting Connecticut, the Shaker village at Lebanon, New Haven and Hartford. Aside from the theatre, they had many common interests, especially William Godwin and William Bartram, and Brown spent summers with Dunlap at Perth Amboy, where he placed the lonely and desolate mansion of Ormond. There he read aloud to Dunlap the opening chapters of *Wieland,* the hero of which was of German extraction and related to Wieland the poet. But Brown outgrew his novel-writing, as the "Hartford wits" outgrew their poetry, and later became a writer of political pamphlets. He died in 1810, a victim of consumption, before he had outlived his fortieth year.

One of Dunlap's younger friends, whom Brockden Brown also knew, was a writer who had begun to attract attention with a series of newspaper articles signed "Jonathan Oldstyle." These papers appeared in 1802 in the New York *Morning Chronicle* when the author, Washington Irving, was not yet twenty, and there was so little American writing of a literary kind that they were at once reprinted in other journals. A few were mild comments on life in New York, as pale as the moon in the morning, but others discussed theatrical matters in a way that interested Dunlap, who was doing his best to mature and develop the stage. Irving satirized the conditions that Dunlap was fighting against, the bombast and buffoonery, the foolish music, the rudeness of the audiences in the New York theatre, and Dunlap saw in Irving a valuable ally; while the young man made friends in other quarters. Brockden Brown called upon him and asked him to contribute to his new monthly magazine, and he also met Joseph Dennie. Aaron Burr cut out the papers and sent them off to Theodosia, saying they were "very good for so young a man." Irving, already a hanger-on at stage-doors, knew all the actors in New York, for he had a passion for the stage and had even written a play himself. He had known Dunlap's theatre from his earliest childhood, —it stood just round the corner from his father's house. He had contrived, as a little boy, to go there again and again, with his older friend James K. Paulding, hastening home to prayers at the end of the play. Then, climbing out of his bedroom window and scrambling over the roof, he had gone back in time for the after-piece.

Irving, the son of a Scottish merchant who had settled in New York some time before the Revolution, was one of a large and flourishing family that lived in William Street, with a garden full of apricot and plum trees. He had been named after Washington when the British evacuated the city and the general's work was ended, as his mother said; and he had grown up in a Federalist household that was also strictly Calvinist, though more and more unexacting as the years advanced. He was a law-student and a very attractive young man, good-looking, sweet-tempered, affectionate, humorous and gay, a favourite of his older brothers, who had prospered in various ways and liked to make things easy and pleasant for him. Peter, a doctor, was editor of the *Morning Chronicle,* in which the "Jonathan Oldstyle" papers appeared, and William, the oldest brother, was a thriving merchant whose wife was the sister of Paulding, Irving's friend. The family trade was hardware, wine and sugar. All the brothers had literary interests, and William, a rhymester and *bon viveur,* was an essayist of no small talent, urbane and amusing. They were all men of the world, in the New York fashion, as all were Episcopalians, sooner or later, and their Federalism too was mellow and vague. William was a democrat, and, while Washington was a Hamiltonian, it was not so much from conviction as from atmosphere and habit. He was singularly untroubled by thoughts of his own in speculative, religious and political matters, although he had antiquarian tastes and a liking for old customs and was therefore, in a sense, a natural Tory. While two of his brothers had gone to Columbia, he had left school at sixteen, with a good reading knowledge of Cicero and Livy; but he had already developed the leanings that marked his writing later and some of his peculiar later interests. His favourite author was Oliver Goldsmith, who was Paulding's favourite also, and whose softly flowing rhythms passed into his mind, and he loved books of voyages and travels, tales of Columbus and Cortes and especially almost everything that spoke of Europe. He had grown up on Newberry's picture-books and old English magazines and prints and constantly heard of England from his father and mother, and on sunny days he haunted the wharves, watching the ships sail down the bay, and often longed to go to sea himself.

While Irving was moody and had occasional fits of depression, he was high-spirited, impressionable and naturally happy. As a young New Yorker, he shrewdly observed the ways of the town, for he was in temperament urban and always remained so. But he liked to wander and dream on the banks of the Hudson, and, visiting at Tarrytown, where his friend Paulding's family lived, he explored the old Dutch farms and pastoral valleys. In the Sleepy Hollow church, the minister still preached in Dutch, and Dutch had been the language of the Paulding household, and the general feeling was anti-British, as in few circles in New York, for the old rivalry of the races had been maintained there. Paulding's father, a sea-captain, had been ruined by the Tories, and Paulding never outgrew his dislike of the English, while Irving loved the English tradition and was merely amused by the Dutch, although he was charmed and fascinated by the old Dutch legends. He liked to hear of Paulding's grandfather reading his big Dutch Bible, with its silver corners and silver clasps. Together the friends went squirrel-hunting along the Saw-mill river,—called in those days the Neperan,—and up the Pocantico, which wound through Sleepy Hollow, shrouded in groves and dotted with prosperous farms. The rough rambling roads were lined with elms and walnuts and gardens full of hollyhocks and roses, and the cosy low-eaved cottages teemed with broad-built urchins, as numerous as the sleek porkers and the snowy geese. The hum of the spinning-wheel resounded from the vine-choked windows, while the walls were overgrown with elder and moss, and old hats were nailed on the trees for the housekeeping wrens. For Irving this was a haunted region, and he heard all sorts of stories there that he was to retell in later years, the story of Hulda the witch, for instance, and the woman of the cliffs, who was seen on the top of the rocks when a storm was rising. People heard strange cries at night round the great tree where André was taken, and there was the wooden bridge where the headless horseman passed along the hollow with rushing speed. He was the ghost of a Hessian trooper, hurrying back to the churchyard, and he frightened people who encountered him at midnight. He sprang into the treetops with a clap of thunder and vanished in a flash of fire. There was another legend about the wizard chieftain who laid the Sachem of Sing-Sing and his warriors to sleep among the recesses of the valley, where they remained asleep to the present day, with their bows and war-clubs beside them. Sometimes a ploughman, shouting to his oxen on a quiet day, was surprised to hear faint sounds from the hillsides in reply, the voices of the spell-bound warriors half starting from their rocky couches, grasping their weapons but sinking to slumber again. The gravestones by the mossy old church were over-hung with elms, and the English in the small log schoolhouse was taught with a thickness of the tongue, instead of what might have been expected, a twang of the nose. Little old-fashioned stone mansions still stood here and there, made up of gable-ends and angles and corners, and Irving felt that he was living in the midst of history and romance. What spot could be richer in themes for a writer of stories? He often rowed his boat to the willows over the little brook that ran through the Sunnyside glen and dreamed away the summer afternoons. Years later he returned to make his home there.

Meanwhile, on journeys up the Hudson, taking his gun and his flute,—which Alexander Anderson had taught him to play,—Irving grew familiar not only with the river but also with the wilderness above and beyond it. He knew Saratoga and Ballston Spa, little resorts in the forest, where the old traders' stores were converted into ballrooms, and with a group of friends he went to Montreal, where his crony Henry Brevoort was engaged in the fur-trade. Brevoort, an agent of John Jacob Astor, collected pelts in the West and brought them back to Albany by canoe and packhorse, to be shipped on sloops to New York, and he was in Montreal in 1803. Astor had not yet founded his colony of Astoria, at the mouth of the Columbia river on the Pacific, but he dreamed of a great commercial empire beyond the Rocky Mountains and was already taking steps to build it. He had tramped with a pack on his back through the northern forests, toiling up the rivers in his own canoe, trading knives, beads and hatchets with the Indians for pelts, and he had a string of agencies and trading-posts in the western woods and was soon to be the most famous of American merchants. It was Alexander Henry who had started Astor's career in the West by telling him the secrets of the fur-trade, and Henry, the New Jersey adventurer, who was one of the lords of the trade, was also in Montreal when Irving arrived there. Henry was soon to publish his *Travels and Adventures in Canada,* the classic story of the fur-trade,—worthy of Defoe,—a lasting picture of life in the woods and the ways of the Indians and trappers that recalled the days of the French and Indian war. Captured by the Chippewas and rescued by the Ottawas, Henry witnessed massacres and had wild adventures at old Machilimacinac and Sioux Saint-

Marie, and he was a naturalist who observed the habits of mink and beaver with a wonderful eye for detail as for character also. The book could scarcely have been more actual if Defoe had imagined the whole story. No one knew better than Henry the voyageurs and the *coureurs de bois,* the revellers and toilers of the fur-trade, the swashbuckling troubadours who had been so dextrous with oar and paddle and whose feats of hazardous errantry had passed into legend.* Irving met and dined with the great partners and chiefs of the trade and shared the baronial wassailing of these veteran magnates, the "mighty Northwesters" who had appeared at Mackinaw with dirks, feathers in their hats and swelling chests. Enthralled by these swaggering heroes and Sinbads of the wilderness, Irving listened to their stories, perfect themes, he felt, for poetry and romance; and the grand enterprises of the great fur companies were of charmed interest to him for the rest of his life.

Before Irving was twenty-three, he had also spent two years in Europe. His brothers were troubled about his health, for he seemed to be consumptive, and they thought a leisurely tour would be excellent for this. They were only further troubled because he liked good company more than his opportunities for self-improvement. He had small interest in sight-seeing, but he studied Italian and French, while he followed a careful plan in keeping a journal, for he was determined to learn to write, with accuracy and ease, and to put down only what he saw. He began to make character-sketches of odd types along the way,—he always excelled especially in descriptive writing, —and he had, meanwhile, many adventures. He was captured by Mediterranean pirates, who were impressed and let him go when they found that he had a letter to the governor of Malta, and, between larks in Sicily and balls in Paris, he travelled through Italian mountains that were infested with robbers. He was introduced into great houses at Naples, Florence and Rome, where he met Madame

---

*Parkman drew from Henry's book when he wrote *The Conspiracy of Pontiac.* Thoreau recalled it (in *A Week on the Concord*) as "a sort of classic among books of American travel . . . There is a naturalness, an unpretending and cold life in this traveller, as in a Canadian winter . . . He has truth and moderation worthy of the father of history, which belong only to an intimate experience . . . [The book] reads like the argument to a great poem, on the primitive state of the country and its inhabitants, and the reader imagines what in each case, with the invocation of the Muse, might be sung, and leaves off with suspended interest, as if the full account were to follow."

de Staël, Canova and Humboldt, and he visited the tomb of Laura and the fountain of Vaucluse in the spirit of the true romantic pilgrim. In Paris he saw much of the New York artist John Vanderlyn, who made a charming portrait of him, and he was intimate in Rome with Washington Allston. They went the rounds of the museums, and Allston praised his pencil-sketches and urged him to remain and become a painter; for Irving had studied in New York with a drawing-master. Irving, who was going home to take up law again, seriously thought for a few wild days of this, and he never forgot these weeks in Rome, with Allston as his cicerone, strolling through Italian palaces and terraced gardens. Irving was always drawn to painters, his closest friends in England later, and he had a real talent for drawing, as his sketches showed. His writing was pictorial and sympathetic to men of the brush, and his pen-name "Geoffrey Crayon" was chosen with reason.

Back in New York, with health restored, a young man of fashion, Irving resumed his interest in theatrical matters. He had seen Mrs. Siddons and Talma in London and Paris, while he studied the Elizabethan drama, and soon, already well-known as an author, when the New Park Theatre was opened, he was asked to write a poem for its dedication. When John Howard Payne's first play was produced in 1806, he and Payne struck up a lifelong friendship. Payne, who was eight years the younger, had appeared in New York the year before and was editing the *Thespian Mirror,* a journal of the theatre, although he was not yet fifteen, a romantic-looking boy over whom Irving watched with fatherly interest. This prodigy, whose infancy had been spent at East Hampton, Long Island, had been taken to Boston at five by his father, a teacher, and, infant that he still was, he had worked on a magazine for children that was edited by Samuel Woodworth, who was learning his trade as a printer. This was the Woodworth who later wrote *The Old Oaken Bucket,* a song that was almost as famous as Payne's *Home, Sweet Home.* The half-Jewish Payne was in love with the stage, an ambition that horrified his father, who made off with his Shakespeare, Congreve and Beaumont and Fletcher and hid them among the cobwebs of the family attic. Payne ran away to New York, where Woodworth presently followed him, and began to write dramatic criticism, and he was already regarded as a person of importance. He was everybody's prodigy, a universal pet, and his friends felt sure that he would be spoiled and ruined. They thought he needed discipline and shipped him off to Union College, which was ruled with a very stiff rod by Eliphalet Nott. Brockden Brown went with him on a Hudson sloop, and they stopped four times on the voyage and took long walks among the hills, delighting in each other's conversation. Payne kept a journal and wrote verses that Brown soon after published and that caused a sensation in Albany when the friends arrived there; for Payne charmed everyone, and possibly even Dr. Nott, who was determined to check his "frantic sallies." But Payne was irreclaimable, as the doctor found, and within a few years he was touring the country in triumph, appearing in every theatre from Boston to Charleston. He made his debut in Providence, reciting Collins's *Ode to the Passions,* the test of perfect elocution, and he brought down the house in Boston, where he outshone the David Poes, who were quite unable to get engagements as long as Payne remained in the town. This was in 1809, the winter in which Mrs. Poe became the mother of Edgar Allan, the poet. A charming little English actress who had married a well-born Maryland boy, Mrs. Poe was a favourite in Boston as in Charleston, especially perhaps as a dancer and singer, though she also played serious parts. Her "romps and sentimental characters" were generally applauded. But Payne, as Romeo, to whom she played Juliet, won all the laurels in Boston in 1809, and, hearing that she was in great distress, he gave a benefit for her. Payne, soon called the "American Roscius,"—a reference to the old Roman actor,—was particularly famous as Norval in a tragedy called *Douglas,* and it was in this role that he made his appearance in England, the first American actor who was ever to appear there. Before this he had become a favourite of George Frederick Cooke, Dunlap's friend in New York, the English actor, the old baccanalian veteran of the sock and buskin who drank himself into a grave beside Trinity Church. Dunlap grieved over Cooke, who appeared in New York in 1810, after ruining his reputation by drink in England, and whose arrival caused as much excitement as if St. Paul's cathedral had crossed the ocean. He lived at the Tontine Coffee-house,—"busier with his bottle than his book, full of wine, life and whim," as Dunlap said,—by turns humorous, pettish, good-natured, truculent and winning, and abounding in romance and rodomontade. He bragged of his imaginary exploits,—he had driven Putnam from Bunker Hill and once he had almost captured Washington. Dunlap loved him and wrote his life and a novel with Cooke as a principal character.* Cooke and Payne played in *King Lear* together, with Cooke as Lear and Payne as Edgar, and Cooke thought Payne a "polite and sensible youth."

Irving, whom nothing escaped in the theatre, was to see much of Payne later, when they even worked together in Paris and London; and he showed Payne how to excite curiosity without wearing his welcome out, caressed and surrounded as he was with applause and friends. Meanwhile, Irving rejoiced in the growth of New York, where magazines, books and plays were multiplying and everyone was reading Scott, Thomas Moore and Thomas Campbell, whose brother was living in the town. Moore, who had visited the country in 1804, had written a number of impudent verses about it; but he was popular nevertheless, while all the Americans were grateful to Campbell, the author of *Gertrude of Wyoming*. There were few American spots that had local associations bestowed on them by history and literature, and this poet had given a classical charm to the Pennsylvania valley that had witnessed a terrible massacre in the Revolution. Campbell was the only British poet of renown who had written a serious poem on an American subject, and his father had lived for a while in Virginia, and his uncle had kept an academy there,—John Marshall was one of this Scottish parson's pupils. One of the poet's other brothers had settled in Virginia, where he had married a daughter of Patrick Henry. So Campbell seemed almost half an American himself; and Irving presently brought out an American edition of his poems and wrote a memoir of the author. Fitz-Greene Halleck, a few years later, when he had become a New York poet, journeyed to the valley of Wyoming to see it for himself.

As for Irving's work as a lawyer, he did not take this seriously, —he was said to have had but one client, whom he left in the lurch; but his brothers were glad to keep him going and even made him a nominal partner, so that he might have the leisure to follow his tastes. He made long visits at Hell Gate and in country-houses up the

---

*Dunlap's *Life of Cooke* was an amusing book, full of anecdotes and good round writing. His novel, *Memoirs of a Water-Drinker,* was lively and vivid in spots but hasty and disorderly, like all of Dunlap's writings. It contained good pictures of the old Park Theatre and its life of the dressing-room and green-room, and abounded in talk about actors and acting, Garrick, Mrs. Siddons, Kemble, etc. Much of the conversation also dealt with portrait-painting, discussing colour and keeping, tint and touch and "why this eye does not sparkle like that."

Hudson and joined in convivial suppers in the New York taverns, Dyde's in Park Row and a porter-house in John Street, where the floors were sprinkled with sand from Coney Island. Through the open windows one heard the street-cries.* There clever young men could almost feel that they were in Fleet Street or Covent Garden, for most of their thoughts as writers had a colour of London. Irving's favourite promenade was the Battery and Bowling Green, where the poplars stood like so many brooms on end, and he liked to read there, under the trees, and sometimes in the portico of St. Paul's chapel. He would join a party of friends in a walk to Cato's, four or five miles from the City Hall,—one followed the Bowery out the Boston Post Road,—where Mrs. Cato Alexander, the famous Negro cook, kept her little tavern with the signpost and the horse-shed. Not to know Cato's was not to know the New York world, and nothing compared with the iced punch there after a walk in the summer sun.

Irving was born for the pleasures of a town, but on Saturdays and Sundays, with William and Paulding and Gouverneur Kemble, he drove to "Cockloft Hall" on the outskirts of Newark. They travelled on the stage-coach and had merry times in the big old mansion,—an American version of Irving's "Bracebridge Hall,"—with a summer-house facing a fish-pond and groves of chestnuts, elms and oaks and punch-bowls almost as large as the mahogany tables. They played leapfrog on the lawn and talked over their plans for writing; and they made this old house famous in their *Salmagundi,* in which Paulding and William and Washington Irving appeared as a club of eccentrics, Anthony Evergreen, Langstaff and William Wizard. Published in a yellow cover, this occasional magazine was modelled on *The Spectator* and *The Citizen of the World,* which still seemed new and exciting in little New York; and the three authors met for discussion in the back parlour of Longworth, the publisher, for whom the paper proved a profitable venture. Eight hundred copies were sold in a single day. Longworth, who called his bookshop the "Sentimental Epicure's Ordinary," had a flair for elegance in his printing; and he adopted eccentricities that were repeated a century later and printed "philadelphia" and "new york" without capital letters. *Salmagundi* had a great vogue as a mildly satirical series of comments on life in

*Here's your fine clams,
  As white as snow!
  On Rockaway these clams do grow, etc.

231

the town which the authors first called "Gotham." It was full of the human bric-a-brac that had long since lost its freshness in England, the beaux, belles and coxcombs of an earlier day, though this still seemed novel in New York as in the South; but it pictured fairly, though somewhat archly, the fashions, the gossip, the scenes of the town, where every clever girl was described as the tenth muse or the fourth grace. It burlesqued the political discussions that were almost a mania in parlour and tavern, it had much to say of the theatre that was shrewd and good, and it satirized the foibles of "the most enlightened people,"—as they had no doubt they were,—"under the sun."

A few years later, Paulding, whose glory it was to have worked with Irving, brought out a second series of *Salmagundi*. The stone that Irving rejected was the head of his corner. But Irving's *History of New York* grew out of *Salmagundi,* little as he thought of this in after days. He had been surprised to find how few of his fellow-citizens were aware that the town had been called New Amsterdam. They had never heard of its early Dutch governors, nor did they care a straw for their own Dutch forbears. New York had a history extending back into the regions of doubt and fable, yet this was regarded with indifference and even with scorn, and he wished to provide the town with local tales and pleasantries that might season its civic festivities as rallying-points of home-feeling. How few American scenes and places possessed the familiar associations that lived like spells about the old-world cities, binding to their homes the hearts of the natives. So it was that he conceived the history of Dietrich [*sic*] Knickerbocker, the doting antiquarian of old New York, the short brisk-looking gentleman, dressed in a rusty black coat, with olive velvet breeches and a small cocked hat. This good old worthy's few grey hairs were clubbed and plaited behind, and he wore square silver shoe-buckles, and he carried a pair of saddle-bags under his arm. He had the air of a country schoolmaster, and his history was the whole business of a dedicated life. Dr. Samuel Latham Mitchell [*sic*], with whom Dunlap had taken a walking-trip in England in 1786, had written and published *A Picture of New York,* a guide-book full of pedantic lore and innocent pomposity that revealed an excessive pride of place and race. There were other American historians, among them Cotton Mather, with much of the vainglorious pedantry that Irving burlesqued when he made the story of New York the final fruit of history and began with the creation of the world. He recalled the proud days of the burgher-aristocracy, the Van Dycks, the Van Wycks, the Ten Eycks, the Schermerhorns and the Schuylers who had loomed out in all their grandeur in the train of Peter Stuyvesant, "brimful of wrath and cabbage," to repel the invaders.

This masterpiece of learned spoofing offended some of the old New Yorkers who felt that the names of their ancestors were taken in vain, and, in fact, for generations there were New Yorkers of Dutch descent who refused to make their peace with Washington Irving.* But who could quarrel seriously with such a ripe expression of a mind that was so well-furnished and so good-natured? It was in this book that Irving's talent declared itself, the first high literary talent the country had known.

*At the time, Gulian C. Verplanck, the leading New Yorker of Dutch descent, expressed this general resentment. Later, Walt Whitman described the book as "shallow burlesque, full of clown's wit." Still later, Hendrik Willem van Loon often spoke of Washington Irving with a somewhat disgusted annoyance.

The "Washington Irving Memorial," including a bust of Irving flanked by Rip Van Winkle and Boabdil, King of Granada, stands at Sunnyside Lane and Broadway (U. S. Route 9) in Irvington, N.Y. One of the last works of the distinguished American sculptor Daniel Chester French (1850–1931), it was dedicated June 27, 1927, after being commissioned by the local "Washington Irving Memorial Association."

PART IV

A NEW DAY

(1945–1975)

Lacking the sustaining qualities of a great imagination, his sensitive versatility made him an ideal moderator of differences between past and present, Europe and America. Because his undoubted genius fitted so exactly the role he was called upon to play, he became the first purely cultural ambassador from the New World to the Old, the first American man of letters to gain international fame.

Robert E. Spiller
The Cycle of American Literature
(New York, 1956)

"Washington Irving"

BY MARCUS F. CUNLIFFE

Marcus F. Cunliffe has since 1965 been Professor of American Studies at the University of Sussex. After military service, he returned to Oxford for B.Litt. and M.A. degrees, and then from 1947 to 1949 studied at Yale on a Commonwealth Fellowship. Thereafter he taught American History at Manchester University. A Fellow of the Royal Historical Society, he was during 1958–1963 Chairman of the British Association of American Studies. A sometime visiting faculty member at Harvard and the City University of New York, his books include *George Washington: Man and Monument* (1958) and *The Nation Takes Shape, 1789–1837* (1959). This selection, a compressed and contemporary transatlantic view of Irving, is from Chapter Three, "Independence—The First Fruits," of Cunliffe's *The Literature of the United States* (1954), a Pelican Book.

Washington Irving was—closely followed by James Fenimore Cooper—the first man of letters from the United States to win an international reputation. The reputation of the third author discussed in this chapter, Edgar Allan Poe, could likewise be described as international, though during his own life-time his fame was far surpassed by that of Irving and Cooper. The case of Poe is somewhat special, yet he, like the others, reveals some of the complexities of being an American.

As for Irving:

> He is not a learned man, and can write but meagrely and at secondhand on learned subjects; but he has a quick convertible talent that seizes lightly on the points of knowledge necessary to the illustration of a theme . . . his gifted pen transmutes every thing into gold, and his own genial nature reflects its sunshine through his pages.

This is Irving's appraisal of Oliver Goldsmith, but it could well have been written of Irving himself by his contemporaries, in Europe and at home, who so often called him the 'American Goldsmith' or spoke of him as a latter-day Addison or Steele. Most of those who met Irving liked him; Scott, Moore, and a score of others testified to his personal charm, and agreed that his literary style matched his personality. As with Charles Lamb, something of his appeal was bound to evaporate when he died. When he was alive, not everyone rated him highly. To one satirist he was 'Dame Irving'; another writer defined him as 'Addison and water'; Maria Edgeworth said of his *Bracebridge Hall* that 'the workmanship surpasses the work. There is too much care and cost bestowed on petty objects.' The present-day reader is more likely to agree with Irving's critics than with his admirers. But it is worth our while to examine why he had such stature in his own day.

Poe offers a clue, in observing that

> Irving is much overrated, and a nice distinction might be drawn between his just and his surreptitious and adventitious reputation—between what is due to the pioneer solely, and what to the writer.

It is the word *pioneer* that arrests us. What has a man like Irving, with 'his tame propriety and faultlessness of style' (to quote Poe again), to do with pioneering? His prose, while less archaic than some critics have maintained, has no new note in it: though this statement will be qualified later. Why, then, *pioneer*? We can begin to answer the question with a sentence by Irving's biographer, Stanley T. Williams: 'Here was an American with a feather in his hand instead of on his head:'[1] a product of the New World who, emerging from a family in trade and from the callow literary circles of New York, managed to entertain the entire civilized world: an author who could please both his own countrymen and the English—both exacting in their different ways. How he did so can be studied in the volume that brought him his renown.

The Sketch Book of Geoffrey Crayon, Gent., including 'The Author's Account of Himself' and 'L'Envoy', consists of thirty-four sketches. The great majority depict English scenes: 'The Inn Kitchen', 'Westminster Abbey', and so on. Cottages are thatched, churches ivied, forlocks tugged. Two essays only might be thought 'controversial'. One was a portrait of 'John Bull', the other about 'English Writers on America'. John Bull has his weaknesses, says Irving: 'he will contrive to argue every fault into a merit, and will frankly convict himself of being the honestest fellow in existence'. But Irving's amiable varnish shines over the subject; John Bull is, after all, we learn, 'a sterling-hearted old blade'. As for the English writers (and their reviewers) whose accounts of America had stirred up so much trouble, Irving managed to make his reprimands acceptable by suggesting that instead of the gentlemen of England, who are such fair-minded observers, 'it has been left to the broken-down tradesman, the scheming adventurer, the wandering mechanic, the Manchester and Birmingham agent, to be her oracles respecting America'. It is not a very good essay, but it is a quite astonishingly tactful one.

Of the few pieces in the *Sketch Book* that deal with America, one on 'Traits of Indian Character' is a conventional glimpse of the noble savage, who after the day's hunting 'wraps himself in the spoils of the bear, the panther, and the buffalo, and sleeps among the thunders of the cataract'. Another piece, the most famous and enduring in

---

[1]*The Life of Washington Irving* (2 v., New York, 1935), i. 211.

the whole book, tells the tale of Rip Van Winkle, the Dutchman be-witched in the Catskill Mountains, who after a twenty-year sleep makes his way back to his native village: an old man whose former cronies are all dead. Thanks to Irving, the New World was now be-ginning to pass on its myths and legends to the Old. Or so his con-temporaries believed. In fact, as Irving not too loudly hinted, he had borrowed the story from a German tale, translating some of its para-graphs so literally as to lay himself under the charge of plagiarism. And though he preserved the original, Spanish setting in some of his other and later stories, similar objections were made: he had, it was said, simply moved his material from one language to another, and added some incidental ornament.

But the charge did not much harm Irving's place in popular es-teem. How did he win his place, and merit the description of *pio-neer*? The first, and indispensable step, was to go to Europe. The sec-ond was to secure approval by European readers, without forfeiting his right to be considered an American. This was an extremely diffi-cult problem, to which Irving came as near to a solution as was possi-ble. He also indicated for subsequent Americans the necessary ap-proaches to the problem. To begin with, style: it must be above all refined. For all practical purposes, Irving saw, America had no style of its own. British models must therefore be followed. Irving sur-passed his models by evolving a fluent yet dignified prose that made a successful passage from the eighteenth to the nineteenth century. Next, subject: if he had merely given himself over to describing Eu-rope, his countrymen would have rejected him. As it was, they re-minded him continually during his seventeen-year absence of his ob-ligation to come back home again. However, he did more than merely describe the contemporary scene. He dug into folklore. Oth-ers were at work in the same vein; Scott, his friend and hero, had put the balladry of the Border to good use, and Scott perhaps encouraged him to study German folk-literature. From German stories he passed to those of Spain. They were rich sources, and Irving explored them eagerly. His own land was deficient in such material; therefore he, like Ticknor and Everett and Longfellow, was driven to seek it in Europe. As later Americans searched diligently for old paintings and manuscripts, these pioneers hunted the neglected folk-past of the Old World.

Also, Irving lacked a creative gift; he needed plots readymade. Temperamentally, like Hawthorne, he preferred a plot out of the past; though, more superficial than Hawthorne, he sought for something colourful, whimsical, a little melancholy: something that hinted, not too sternly, at change and alteration. If America was born in broad daylight, Irving brought it an imported twilight, to the best of his ability. In *Bracebridge Hall,* to take one example, he concocted an American version ('The Storm-Ship') of the *Flying Dutchman* legend. It would be wrong to imply that Irving had any clear notion of inventing, single-handed, a set of American traditions. Rather, he tried to please simultaneously audiences on either side of the Atlantic. He was born just early enough to escape the oppressive claims of nationality, and he was too equable to fret over the demands that were laid on him. When American material was of value, he used it. He journeyed out into the Indian country, and wrote *A Tour on the Prairie* [*sic*] about his trip; he became interested in the development of the American West, and compiled a competent account in *Astoria* (1836). But he was no frontiersman, and was too much the cosmopolitan to become one; while his enemies suggested that *Astoria* was proof of nothing but Irving's pleasure in the patronage of the millionaire fur-trader John Jacob Astor.

In fact, as Emerson saw, Irving and his American contemporaries were 'picturesque': a deeper power eluded them. His pioneering was a matter of setting the example for others to follow. He suggested lines of approach: he translated and adapted. He soothed native pride by becoming a great author. At the end, grinding out the enormous biography of George Washington, he was still a capable craftsman; however pedestrian the treatment, there was always the easy rhythm of the sentences, and the mild occasional relief of a pleasantry. Though his glory was beginning to tarnish, he had at any rate held out longer than most of his colleagues, men like Bryant and Fitz-Greene Halleck, who had either gone silent or turned into bores.

But did Irving set the wrong example? Yes, if one visualizes the relationship between American and Europe as a cops-and-robbers (or rather, snobs-and-patriots) melodrama, in which the hero (in terms of literature) is the man who stays at home and nurtures his American vocabulary, like a primeval Mencken, while the villain slips off to Europe to acquire an English accent and a mastery of

French menus. We may allow that Irving was something of a snob:
or, as he put it, a *Gent*. One of his favourite targets was the 'pale and
bilious' taproom agitator, scheming to overturn John Bull's household, or Peter Stuyvesant's New York. Nor could he applaud the
equivalent in literature. He confided to his diary in 1817:

> There is an endeavour among some of the writers of the day
> (who fortunately have not any great weight) to introduce into
> poetry all the common colloquial phrases and vulgar idioms—In
> their rage for simplicity they would be coarse and common-
> place. Now the Language of poetry cannot be too pure and
> choice.

Granted that he is speaking of poetry, not of prose, does not this
exhibit place him among the villains?

Surely not, if we admit another and more substantial piece of
contrary evidence, the *History of New York,* written eight years earlier. It is an uneven book, half fact, half fancy; yet it has a cocksure,
irreverent quality that makes everything Irving wrote afterwards
seem by comparison sadly insipid. How was America peopled? Gro-
tius, says Knickerbocker-Irving, supposed it was 'by a strolling company of Norwegians', while 'Juffredus Petri' ascribed it 'to a skating
party from Friesland'. The tone is that of Mark Twain; and so is this:

> And now the rosy blush of morn began to mantle in the east,
> and soon the rising sun, emerging from amidst golden and pur-
> ple clouds, shed his blithesome rays on the tin weathercocks of
> Communipaw.

True, there are only isolated paragraphs that have just the Twain fla-
vour; yet it is there, in 1809, sixty years before the publication of *Innocents Abroad*, in which 'native' American prose made a triumphant appearance. It is true also that Knickerbocker's burlesque saga
is a young man's squib. But added years and personal worries are not
enough to explain why Irving abandoned Knickerbocker and Salmagundi for Geoffrey Crayon, and in fresh editions of the *History* steadily pruned away what he now held to be its vulgarities. Nor is residence in Europe the explanation: that is to confuse cause and effect.

The reason is simple: 1809 was not 1869. American prose could not survive until conditions were more favourable. More recent writers than Irving have been unable to accept the idea that a serious style could grow out of a burlesque intention. Is Irving so much to blame in judging his *History* a dead end, when it was only a false start?

"The Soviet Controversy over Pushkin and Washington Irving"

BY JOHN C. FISKE

John C. Fiske, after undergraduate and graduate studies at Harvard, took his doctorate at Columbia. After teaching at Iowa State College, his association with The Human Relations Area Files, Inc., an affiliate of Yale, involved co-authorship of *USSR, its people, its society, its culture* (1960). Since 1974 he has been Professor Emeritus of Foreign Languages and Literature at the University of Iowa, where he had taught French studies on the graduate faculty. This discussion of an *Alhambra* tale, as an influence on Pushkin become politically controversial in our time, includes the role of the famous twentieth-century Russian poet Anna Akhmatova. It is reprinted from *Comparative Literature*, Vol. VII (1955), 25–31.

Washington Irving is not today a figure widely known to Soviet readers. There have been few translations of his works in the last thirty-five years, and critics have awarded to him far less attention, favorable or otherwise, than to Cooper, Poe, Whitman, Mark Twain, or a large number of more recent American writers. What interest there has been is shown in the occasional translations of a few of his short stories, especially "Rip Van Winkle," and in the controversy arising from the discovery, in 1933, that Pushkin had undoubtedly borrowed from Irving the subject of "The Golden Cockerel."[1]

Irving was translated into Russian as early as 1825,[2] and by 1830 was widely known to the Russian reading public. In that year *Moskovskij vestnik,* introducing a translation of excerpts from *The Conquest of Granada,* referred to Irving as "one of the most distinguished writers in the United States, notable not so much for the depth and originality of his views as for the richness of his imagination and for a style always pure and colorful." Irving was popular among the Decembrists, and, on the other side of the political fence, the government-sponsored journalist N. Greč spoke of him as his favorite author.

That this interest in Irving should be shared by Pushkin was natural enough. N. A. Polevoj, as early as 1831, noted a relationship between Knickerbocker and Belkin,[3] and Pushkin himself once quoted Irving with regard to the "noble savage" in literature.[4] But it was only a century later that Soviet critics were to unearth evidence of the full extent of Irving's connection with Russia's most honored writer.

Interest in Irving, in Russia as in America, died down after the middle of the nineteenth century; by 1917 he was not a sufficiently

[1]The material for this study was gathered under a graduate student fellowship at the Russian Research Center at Harvard University, to which the author makes grateful acknowledgement.
[2]Translation of "The Art of Making Books," by N. A. Polevoj, *Moskovskij telegraf,* 1825. Cited by M. P. Alekseev, in the article, "K istorii sela Gorjukhina," *Puškin, stat'i i materialy* (Odessa, 1926), II, 70–87. Alekseev is also the source for other references in this paragraph.
[3]In "Literaturnye pribavlenija k russkomu invalidu," *Moskovskij telegraf,* 1831; cited by A. Akhmatova, in "Poslednjaja skazka Puškina," *Zvezda* (Leningrad, 1933), No. 1, pp. 161–176.
[4]*Polnoe sobranie sočinenij* (Moscow, 1949), XII, 105.

prominent figure in the Russian public eye to merit the attention of revolutionary critics. It was only in 1926 that there opened up the line of speculation that came to link Irving's name with that of Pushkin himself. In that year, in a collection of articles on Pushkin, published in Odessa, there was included a study by M. P. Alekseev "On 'The History of The Village of Gorjukhino'."[5] In the course of his discussion of this unfinished work of Pushkin's Alekseev mentions various Western parallels for the little parody, and finally remarks (p. 77):

> However, all of western analogies which might be recalled in this connection, there is one which merits closer examination. I refer to Washington Irving's *History of New York*, a work which won considerable fame in the early years of the nineteenth century, and with which Pushkin was in all probability acquainted.

For ten pages Alekseev goes on with a detailed account of Irving's story, its similarity in original purpose, manner of treatment, and later development to that of Pushkin, and the general resemblance between the characters of Belkin and Knickerbocker. He also cites the large number of translations of Irving in the 1820s and 1830s, as well as various other evidence of Irving's popularity in that period.

Alekseev's discussion is well documented, and he has certainly established some remarkable similarities. He notes that both authors have done much to depict the character of the narrator in the course of the story, and that much of the humor of both "histories" rests on the eccentricities of Belkin and Knickerbocker, who maintain throughout the rather pompous air of serious historians, despite the ridiculous triviality of the matters of which they treat. He notes that both narrators are constantly trying to show their learning by reference to imaginary authorities, and that the appearance and voices of the two are, though not at all points similar, at least similarly described. Finally, he remarks that both stories tend to develop into satirical portraits of contemporary society.

That these details establish a resemblance between the two works one may well admit; but such devices are by no means limited

[5]Alekseev, *op. cit.*

to these two. Many of them are familiar currency of British and French eighteenth-century writing, and one might well be able to establish comparable similarities to the works of such writers as Montesquieu, Voltaire, Swift, Defoe, or in the nineteenth century, Walter Scott. Quite possibly Pushkin had read the Knickerbocker *History;* but to infer that one work exerted a direct influence over the other is a dangerous course too often followed. Certainly a great wealth of external evidence would be necessary to support such a thesis.

A more conservative approach to the subject is exhibited in an article in the collection, *Pushkin in World Literature,*[6] published in the same year. The article is devoted largely to a comparison of Pushkin's and Scott's devices of mystification through a thoroughly characterized narrator. Irving is mentioned several times, both for his direct connection with Scott and for his employment of similar mystifications. The American's appearance in Russian translation in 1827 is also mentioned, but without the drawing of any inferences.

In 1933 the poet Anna Akhmatova, who had read Alekseev's article and probed further into the possible relationship between Irving and Pushkin, came up with a very interesting discovery.[7] Comparing Irving's "Legend of The Arabian Astrologer" in *The Alhambra* and Pushkin's "Skazka o zolotom petuške" (Tale of the Golden Cockerel), she found a resemblance that could scarcely be explained as pure coincidence. She could discover no evidence of a common source; and indeed the element of parody in Irving's story, which is done in what that author calls his "Haroun al Rashid style," is in itself a strong indication that the tale is largely, if not entirely, Irving's own invention.[8]

Irving's story, which was published in 1832, is ascribed to Mateo Ximenes, ostensible narrator of many of the tales. It tells of one Aben Habuz, king of Granada, who, wishing to retire after a long career of depredations, finds himself beset by enemies on all

[6]D. Jakubovič, "Predislovic k 'Povestjam Belkina' i povestvovatel'nye priemy Waltera Scotta," in *Puškin v mirovoj literature, Sbornik statej* (Moscow, 1926), pp. 160–187.

[7]A. Akhmatova, "Poslednjaja skazka Puškina," *Zvezda* (1933), No. 1, pp. 161–176.

[8]Irving himself tells of a similar legend, which he ascribes to the Moorish historian Al Makkari; Washington Irving, *Representative Selections* (New York, 1934), p. 388, note 75.

sides. To him there comes one Ibrahim, full of the lore of Egypt, who tells of a certain brass cock and ram, who used to warn an ancient king of danger. For Aben Habuz the astrologer offers to make a similar device, a bronze horseman who shall point toward approaching danger. Such a horseman is placed on a tower of the king's palace; and within the tower are placed toy armies, which will come to life to represent approaching armies and can be easily knocked down by the king, thus causing destruction of the armies they represent. The talisman works most effectively, and Habuz enjoys the defeat of his enemies without even the effort of sending armies out to meet them. Ibrahim, who at first sought only a cave as his reward, constantly increases his demand for various luxuries; and Aben Habuz somewhat grudgingly fulfills all his requests.

At last there comes a time when the bronze horseman points, but the armies fail to move. Scouts are sent out, but these find nothing but a beautiful Christian princess, whom they bring home to Habuz. The astrologer warns the king that the maiden may be a sorceress and asks to be given custody of her. This request Habuz refuses. Ibrahim retires in dudgeon to his cave, and the monarch saps his treasury for the entertainment of his beloved until his own people rise up against him. Habuz quells the rebellion, then seeks a way to retire with his princess to some secluded retreat. Ibrahim offers him a fabulous garden, demanding in return the first beast, with its burden, that shall pass through the gate of that garden. This beast, of course, proves to be the palfrey carrying the princess. When the king seeks to withdraw his promise, Ibrahim, the princess, and the garden all disappear, the talisman ceases to work, and Habuz, again beset by enemies, soon goes to a weary grave.

The tale is as leisurely as most of Irving's writings. It captures, in parody, much of the flavor of *The Arabian Nights,* poking fun at the peaceful though bloodthirsty old king and at the two old greybeards who fall out in rivalry over the charms of the Christian princess. Pushin's tale, on the other hand, reduced to the clipped tetrameter usual in his *skazki* (fairy tales), does away entirely with the Moorish background and with much of the detail of Irving's story. Tsar Dadon, the central figure, is king of a vague and unidentifiable land; the astrologer is similarly vague in origin, characterized only by his *saračinskaja sapka* (Saracen cap), mentioned once in the course of the tale. The princess is called *šamakhanskaja,* an epithet which puzzles even Russian scholars. The talisman has become a golden cockerel, who flies from his pinnacle and destroys Dadon when Dadon kills the astrologer for demanding the princess as his sole gift. The fabulous garden, the cave, and the toy soldiers are absent from Pushkin's tale. Additions consist chiefly in the incident of the tsar's two sons, who go out to fight and are mysteriously killed on the occasion when the princess is discovered. There are also a few slyly derogatory remarks about kings in general, which were pounced upon by the censors of Nicholas I.

The differences I have listed are sufficient to show that there can be no question of plagiarism on the part of Pushkin. His tale, complete with moral couplet at the end, is an entirely different work of art. But it is equally obvious that Irving's prose provided the source material for Pushkin's verse. The king, the astrologer, the talisman, the mysterious foreign princess as the source of discord, the broken promise, and the vanishing of the maiden, all are repeated in Pushkin's tale. Furthermore, Akhmatova discovered that Pushkin owned a French translation of *The Alhambra,* which he had apparently acquired shortly before he started to work on "The Golden Cockerel." As a final and most convincing piece of evidence, Akhmatova calls attention to a Pushkin fragment of 1833, the year before the publication of "The Golden Cockerel," which very closely reproduces Irving's description of the astrologer's little model armies.[9] Akhmatova notes further that an early Russian review of *The Alhambra* calls special attention to "The Arabian Astrologer"; and that Prince D. I. Dolgorukov, or Dolgorukij, who was a good friend of Irving in Spain and checked some of his manuscripts, was also an acquaintance of Pushkin.

Akhmatova's article is not limited to a study of similarities and differences between the two stories. She suggests that Pushkin's tale may have been intended as a veiled reference to his relations with Nicholas I, who, Pushkin believed, had broken promises to him. Pushkin would thus be represented by the astrologer, who in "The Golden Cockerel" is less demanding than in Irving's legend, and is

[9]This fragment appears in *Polnoe sobranie sočinenij,* ed. J. G. Oksman and M. A. Cjavlovskij (Moscow-Leningrad, 1936), II, 116.

killed by the guilty king, while Irving's astrologer suffers no such fate. Akhmatova also thinks that Pushkin's simplifications have gone so far that characters and motivations are not sufficiently developed, and that Pushkin's work is thus in some ways inferior to Irving's.

In 1936, in the collection of Pushkin's works published in commemoration of the centennial of the poet's death,[10] the fragment about the toy armies is printed, I believe for the first time; and in the notes to "The Golden Cockerel" (II, 564), Akhmatova's article is acknowledged and the resemblances and differences between the two stories are discussed at some length. The editors consider that Akhmatova's suggestions as to the political and autobiographical intent of Pushkin's tale would require further documentation, and take exception to her idea that Irving's work is in any way superior. There is no need to put this down to Soviet chauvinism. Matters of relative merit are always open to argument; and the idea that Pushkin is without fault or flaw is common to many Russians, regardless of political stamp.

B. Tomasevškij, who in the same year edited a one-volume edition of Pushkin's works,[11] also acknowledged Irving's legend as the source of Pushkin's tale, but stressed the extent to which Pushkin had departed from the original. And in 1938 the folklorist M. K. Azadovskij,[12] discussing the sources of Pushkin's tales, states that Akhmatova has "irrefutably established" that "The Golden Cockerel" was taken from Irving's tale, though he insists that Pushkin's version is "more dramatic and complex." Much the same view is taken by the French Slavicist André Mazon, who, in an article in 1939,[13] went on to seek other foreign sources for those parts of "The Golden Cockerel" that were not obviously taken from Irving.

[10]*Polnoe sobranie sočinenij* (see note 9).

[11]*Sočinenija*, ed. B. Tomaševskij (Leningrad, 1936), p. 845.

[12]M. K. Azadovskij, "Istočniki 'skazok' Pushkina" in his *Literatura i folklor* (Leningrad, 1938), pp. 65–105. This may be a reprint of Azadovskij's article with the same title in *Puskin. Vremennik Puškinskoj kommissii*, No. 1 (1935), pp. 134–163.

[13]André Mazon, "Le Conte du Coq d'or: Pouchkine, Klinger et Irving," in *Mélanges en l'honneur de Jules Legras* (Paris, 1939).

After 1939 there appears to have been little mention, in the always voluminous literature on Pushkin, of Akhmatova's discovery; one writer, however, calls attention to the fact that one of Pushkin's enemies in 1830 referred to the poet in veiled terms as a producer of "imitations of Walter Scott and Washington Irving."[14]

It was not until 1947 that Akhmatova's discovery came under attack. In that year there appeared in *The Literary Gazette* an article by V. Sidel'nikov entitled: "Against Distortion and Servility in Soviet Folklore Study."[15] This article is part of the campaign for *partipnost'* (roughly, party-consciousness) and against "cosmopolitanism" that was born out of the Zhdanov speech of August 1946. The particular interest of the article, so far as Irving is concerned, is the condemnation of Akhmatova's study of fourteen years earlier. Akhmatova, one of the Acmeist poets of the preceding generation, had within the last decade come out of a sort of literary retirement, only to have her verse savagely attacked by Zhdanov in 1946. Thenceforth she was fair game for any critic. But Sidel'nikov's article is not limited to a personal condemnation. He makes no attempt to refute her discovery but he inveighs against her for suggesting that Pushkin's work was in any way inferior to Irving's, and demands rhetorically whether there could be a clearer example of servility before the foreign. He adds: "The pseudo-scientific, fundamentally vicious 'theory' of Akhmatova was repeated on all sides by the Leningrad folklorist Azadovskij." And, in the course of a general attack on Azadovskij for attempting to tie Pushkin's tales more closely to Western than to Russian tradition, the critic remarks sarcastically that "The Tale of the Golden Cockerel' turns out to be a reworking of a story of Irving's." The American correspondent Robert Magidoff[16] tells us in this connection

---

[14]G. Gippius, "Puškin v bor'be s Bulgarinym v 1830–1831 gg.," *Puškin. Vremennik Puškinskoj kommissii* (Moscow-Leningrad, 1941), VI, 235–255. The remark which Gippius quotes he places in *Syn Otečestva*, No. 16 (Apr. 19, 1830). The exact quotation reads: "Drugoj prijatel' moj, takze dvorjanin prosviščem Rjapuskin, prevoskhodjaščij prodrazanijami W. Scotta i W. Irvinga."

[15]V. Sidel'nikov, "Protiv izvraščenija i nizkopoklonstva v sovetskoj folkloristike," *Literaturnaja gazeta*, (June 29, 1947). Sidel'nikov was himself a former contributor to Azadovskij's *Sovetskij folklor*.

[16]R. Magidoff, *In Anger and Pity* (New York, 1949), p. 152.

that the late Ju. M. Sokolov, elder folklorist whose student Sidel'nikov had been, was also attacked for the same reason.

A *History of American Literature,*[17] published in the same year as Sidel'nikov's article, contains a chapter on Irving by A. A. Elistratova. In the course of placing Irving in relation to world literature, she mentions his friendship with Prince Dolgorukov, as well as Pushkin's apparent interest in his works. In this latter connection Elistratova remarks that " 'The Tale of the Golden Cockerel' might be shown to have a relationship with 'The Legend of the Arabian Astrologer' in Irving's *Alhambra.*" But she adds that "In Pushkin's hands, however, the plot of Irving's story receives a completely new ironic subtlety." Here she is apparently accepting Akhmatova's theory that Pushkin's tale was aimed at Nicholas I.

The note of caution in Elistratova's remarks is fairly obvious; but it is doubtful if any recognition whatever of the connection between Irving and Pushkin would satisfy such critics as Sidel'nikov. In February 1948 the *History of American Literature* received a very sharp attack from one A. Tarasenkov.[18] His article does not specifically mention the chapter on Irving; but Elistratova's reference to the Irving-Pushkin connection was very probably one of the "mass of errors" which Tarasenkov accuses the editor of committing. Elistratova is herself included in a distinguished list of what Tarasenkov calls "grovelers before the West."

Such attacks may be considered to have a strong political backing; and subsequent treatment of the matter shows that other Soviet literary scholars heeded the warning. A sesquicentennial edition of Pushkin's works, published in 1949,[19] though in other respects very thoroughly annotated, makes no mention of Irving in connection with "The Golden Cockerel" or "The Village of Gorjukhino"; and the fragment which Akhmatova brought to light is entirely omitted.

Thus, apparently, the "Golden Cockerel controversy" has been brought to an end. Any suggestion that revered Russian writings may

---

[17]*Istorija amerikanskoj literatury* (title page gives English title also), ed. A. I. Starcer (Moscow-Leningrad, 1947).

[18]A. Tarasenkov, "Kosmopolity ot literaturovedenija," *Novyi Mir* (Moscow, 1948), No. 2, pp. 124–137. The relevant section (IV) is on pp. 131–132

[19]*Polnoe sobranie sočinenij* (Moscow, 1949).

derive from foreign sources is a sign of "decadent cosmopolitanism" and "groveling before the West."*

*There is, however, no quarrel about Pushkin's own influence through "The Golden Cockerel" on *Le Coq d'or* by Rimsky-Korsakov (1844–1908), a fairy-tale opera first performed in Moscow in 1909. On the Irving-Pushkin connection, see also Carl R. Proffer, "Washington Irving in Russia: Pushkin, Gogol, Marlinsky,' *Comparative Literature*, XX (1969), 329–342, and Frank L. Ingram, "Pushkin's 'Skazka o zolotom petuške' and Washington Irving's 'The Legend of the Arabian Astrologer,' " *Russian Language Journal*, LXXXIV, 3–18. [*Ed.*]

From "Washington Irving"

BY STANLEY T. WILLIAMS

Stanley T. Williams (1888–1956) was, at the time of his death, retired from his longtime position as Sterling Professor of American Literature at Yale, where he had made a distinguished career as scholar and teacher in that field in particular, among other things as director of graduate studies in American Literature. In 1935, his *Life of Washington Irving* (see p. 194, Part III above) firmly established him as an authoritative figure in studies of Irving, the man and the artist. In time, like his subject, the biographer too became an experienced and enthusiastic hispanophile, with one result being the two full volumes of *The Spanish Background of American Literature* (1955.) This selection, a well-informed literary overview of Irving-and-Spain, is the conclusion of Chapter One, Volume II of that detailed work.

Alone among the Hispanophiles whom we are now studying in detail, Irving went to the Peninsula with the specific purpose of writing. His life story after 1825 has shown his deepening understanding of the country and also his sustained use for more than thirty years of materials collected in Spain. Out of his study and observation there he constructed some sixteen tales or sketches, his subsidiary but substantial book, *The Voyages of the Companions of Columbus,* and three major volumes.[161] Altogether on Spain Irving wrote some three thousand pages and approximately one million words, amounting to about one third of his total writings. Although he is still known as the traditional interpreter in American literature of old England, he devoted far more space and effort to his books on Spain. Nor are these inferior. The *Columbus* and the *Granada* are the equals of *Bracebridge Hall* and *Tales of a Traveller,* and, except for one or two classic tales such as "Rip Van Winkle" or "The Legend of Sleepy Hollow," they include some of his best writing. Apart from these, *The Alhambra* is the peer of *The Sketch Book.* To understand Irving we must recognize the importance of his writings on Spain.

The most interesting of these, both in its origins and in its consequences for Irving's reputation, was that book of mingled history and romance which he called *The Life and Voyages of Christopher Columbus.* This began as a translation of Navarrete's documents and ended as a popular narrative of the explorer's achievements. In synthesizing this complicated body of material on Columbus into a tranquil romance Irving was neither the scholar which a few extravagant admirers proclaimed him nor the mere paraphraser of Navarrete which his enemies asserted him to be.[162] From the days when he had studied Cervantes for *Salmagundi* or obscure Dutch historians for *A History of New York* he had loved to play with the apparatus of scholarship: prefaces, footnotes, appendices.[163] Whatever may be said of his amateurishness or of his somewhat easygoing use of others' labors, there can be no doubt of his honest investigation of primary sources or of his patience in regard to small details. Nor can we question his desire to tell the truth in his long and splendid story:

> There are [he wrote Storrow] so many points in dispute, and so many of a scientific nature into which I have been obliged to enter with great study and examination. I have fagged night and day for a great part of the time, and every now and then some

further document, throwing a different light on some obscure part of the work has obliged me to rewrite what I had supposed finished.[164]

In any real sense of the word, this was not, however laborious, scholarship. Practically everything necessary for his smooth narrative Irving had already at hand in the published documents of Navarrete. His work was primarily rearrangement of these materials, the metabolism of known facts into his own story. Probably the only truly original parts of his history were connected with these "points in dispute." This work of verification took him to the manuscripts, but these had almost always been scoured previously by Navarrete. It is, indeed, impossible to think of the *Columbus* as coming into existence at all except for Navarrete's researches. Irving's "collation," as he called it, was actually, with the exception of a few minor details, a reassembling of materials made available by the Spanish scholar. So Irving told the story again, always with reference to the standard sources, such as Herrera, Oviedo, or Andrés Bernáldez (Cura de Los Palacios). He was a superb compiler, with an extraordinary art for supplementing his narrative with bits of knowledge from odd and out-of-the-way places, such as the library of the Duke of Veragua or the manuscripts of Don Antonio de Uguina. Often he summarized his collected data with skill, and sometimes he translated from his originals with surprising literalness. His book was an ingenious patchwork; it was both biography and history.

The reception of the *Columbus*, in 1828 and later, was uneven in character. Among various charges, that of plagiarism was inevitable, and this attained in some quarters an ugly insistence.[165] No one has ever been able to validate the differing rumors: that Navarrete was hurt by the popularity of Irving's work and that he never forgave the American for his borrowings,[166] or, on the other hand, that he was grateful for this dissemination of his fame. No book of Irving's has, through the years, been so variously judged, from the denunciation in the *Southern Literary Messenger* to the praise from Menéndez y Pelayo, who at the fourth centenary of the explorer declared of the *Columbus* that "without ceasing to be one of the most agreeable, readable books which can be found [it was] at the same time a serious historical work, in which the author, holding back the luxuriance of his pen [had] had the good taste not to add any fabulous accessories to a reality which is through itself more poetic than fiction."[167] The history was popular in Spain. We know of nine editions available before 1893,[168] and in the Biblioteca Colombina we find proof of its wide influence in translations into German, Dutch, Spanish, Swedish, and Hungarian. Some historians, for example, Prescott, possibly out of friendship for Irving, kept their reservations on its faults to themselves, but Henry Harrisse, although he praised the book, pointed out the unfortunate absence of "the why and wherefore of events."[169]

This last seems to the modern reader the book's catastrophic fault. Indeed, in this particular the *Columbus* is not history at all. It is a story, on a subject as romantic as those elected by Prescott, related by one of the great stylists of the nineteenth century. Irving was, says Don Enrique Gil, the "skilful colorist [*colorista*] of Columbus's great enterprise."[170] The pleasant narrative is vitiated by sentimentality, moralizing, and infinite repetition. About the entire book still remains something ornamental and theatrical. Nevertheless, the story, held in a firm, if intricate, structure of eighteen books and 123 brief chapters, always moves forward. If it sometimes bores the present-day reader, it created in its own time a new image of the heroic navigator. If different from the actual Genoese, the Columbus of Irving's narrative is, like King Boabdil, a vivid character in fictionized history. With an astute perception of the universal interest in Columbus, Irving made him for the first time a human being, a personage in American literature. Out of this conception, which rendered the dim, uncertain figure real, were to emerge tales, poems, and plays. Irving crystallized one abiding interest of the age in this graceful pseudo history of the discovery of America.

In the examination of Irving's life during his first stay in Spain we observed his gradual apostasy from scholarship in antiquarian materials. He was tempted away from the severe labor of composing the *Columbus* to the more congenial legends of early Spain and to the collections of anecdotes about the Moors and the palace of the Alhambra. Possibly, then, we may perceive in the book's concluding chapters, on the death and on the character of Columbus, an illustration of this relaxation. Perhaps they are transitional to his foolish compromise of history and fiction, *The Conquest of Granada*.[171] This book of eight hundred pages he offered as a record but in "an entertaining and popular form, without sacrificing the intrinsic truth of history." He kept the chronology, the footnotes, and other machinery but submitted the story to his reader "coloured and tinted." In addition, he introduced, strange indeed in a history, a fictitious monk, Fray Antonio Agapida, through whose eyes we see the endless battles, sieges, and duels near Ronda, Cordova, and Granada.[172] The plan, to speak frankly, was preposterous. Though Prescott placed it in the "narrative class of history," *The Conquest of Granada* was a kind of freak romance with a disconcerting alloy of truth.

Why did Irving not renounce entirely the bondage of historical method, for which his talents were unsuited? Why did he not tell his tale freely as if it was one of the stories bequeathed him by Mateo? Instead he weighted his narrative by at least thirty Spanish works, most of which he had studied during the composition of the *Columbus*.[173] To eight or nine of these, which he knew so well, among them Mariana, Garibay y Zamalloa, Andrés Bernáldez, or Pulgar, he referred at every turn. In *The Conquest of Granada* he summarized, paraphrased, or translated. One reviewer put it aptly: "Mr. Irving, in fact, seems to have been afraid of his subject; he shrinks from appearing boldly and gravely in so serious a field; he shelters himself under the pasteboard shield of some fictitious historian; and like the discreet Bottom, while roaring like any nightingale, assures the ladies that he is only in jest."[174] Some of the Spanish translations, which were almost as numerous as those of the *Columbus,* drained off portions of the history and so unwittingly revealed what Irving might have accomplished had he left the story, nearly as exciting to Americans as that of Columbus, wholly within the realms of romance.

If we forget, in reading *The Conquest of Granada,* the would-be historian and listen only to the romancer, we find at times his natural powers at their best, as in his account of Boabdil's return to captivity or of his farewell to Granada ("El último suspiro del moro") or of the final assault on the city ("El día de toma"). When Irving's prose flowed directly from his pleasure in an incident or character he wrote well. In particular, Boabdil, who on the monument in Tarrytown stands shoulder to shoulder with Diedrich Knickerbocker* and Rip Van Winkle, comes to life in this book, at least to a kind of dream life. "El Chico" was an old love of Irving's. He had handled his coat of mail in the Arsenal in Madrid, and in the Generalife he had stared

---

*Williams here makes a rare mistake. Diedrich Knickerbocker is not on this monument. See illustration, p. 234. [Ed.]

long at the portrait of this king, a kind of Spanish Richard II, with his "mild, handsome face, a fair complexion, and yellow hair."[175] Boabdil, like another Spanish hero in our fiction whom Irving would have understood, Benito Cereno,[176] was unfit for rule, as Irving himself in some ways was unfit for the ways of men, even for the writing of history. Boabdil was a man after his own heart. He could delineate this type of human being. The Moorish king lives again as a hero of romance in this strange, composite book, *The Conquest of Granada.*

In some respects Boabdil is also the hero of *The Alhambra,* in which he reappears, amplified by Irving's supplementary studies in Luis del Mármol Carvajal. The fair-haired king reminds us of the historical past of Spain; at least twelve of the book's forty-one sections contain material which Irving collected in the libraries of Madrid. After making this concession to its historical character, we can hail *The Alhambra* as the most distinguished literary work on Spain written by an American before 1850. Behind it lay two of the most indelible experiences of Irving's life: his residence in the palace and his friendship with Fernán Caballero. As to the former, both characters and incidents became part of the book. Irving was entirely honest in telling his friend Allibone: "The account of my midnight rambles about the old palace is literally true . . . Every thing in the work relating to myself and to the actual inhabitants of the Alhambra is unexaggerated fact; it was only in the legends that I indulged in *romancing.*"[177] This autobiographical element brings Irving back again, in this sheaf of graceful essays and stories on Spain, to his old role, renounced since *Bracebridge Hall,* of the observer of picturesque ways of life. For this point of view his stay in the Alhambra with Mateo and Dolores was indispensable.

This intimate knowledge of the Spanish peasant was, unless we prefer the pretty fairy tales of princesses and buried gold, the charm of this new *Sketch Book.* But Irving's knowledge had another source. His months in the palace were a sequel, almost a consequence, of his counsel from Fernán Caballero. From her he had received confirmation of his own belief, exemplified in *The Sketch Book,* that the function of the essay was to convey "impresiones de la vida ordinaria."[178] By her he was more than ever convinced that the aim of a novelist or short-story writer should be "poetizar la realidad sin alterarla."[179] Possibly in their discussions of the *artículo de costumbres,* whose principles were so congenial to him, they had talked of its beginnings about 1820 in the *Cartas del pobrecito holgazán* of Sebastián de Miñano.

In any case, in writing of Dolores or Mateo, Irving had not forgotten the Spanish novelist. His own version of her ideas appears in his preface: "Care was taken," he says, "to maintain local coloring and verisimilitude; so that the whole might present a faithful and living picture."[180] In this way Fernán Caballero helped to establish him in his philosophy of the essay. The Spanish translations (*Cuentos de la Alhambra*), of which at least nineteen became available between 1833 and 1933,[181] seemed to re-emphasize the application of Irving's art to this "vida ordinaria." These light essays of his became part of a general European pattern.

The Alhambra, in echoing the *artículo de costumbres,* not only linked the American with the European essay of manners but introduced into the beginnings of our literature across the Atlantic a note of exoticism. This quality mellowed a little the somewhat neutral character of our belles-lettres. For this exoticism, as well as for its "impressions of common life," *The Alhambra* was so popular in England that David Wilkie congratulated Irving on becoming "the founder of a school."[182] In Spain there was praise for "su profundo conocimiento . . . de las costumbres populares granadinas"[183] and also for the book's Oriental temper. Mario Méndez Bejarano, the literary historian, remarked that "the soul of Granada is more apparent in the beautiful pages of Irving than in the stories of Chateaubriand, the poems of Zorrilla, or in any of those writers who have celebrated its charms."[184] Irving had learned of this "soul of Granada" from his "historiographic squire," Mateo. The Notebook of 1829 shows emphatically the wealth of lore bestowed on him by these peasants. It describes a white phantom in an enormous white hat haunting the palace, an Arabian chemist, and Pedro the Cruel in disguise. These and other legends were garnered into the Notebook. In this fashion Irving communicated "Alhambraism" to American literature.[185]

Irving's seven years in Spain, as well as his several thousand pages of history and fiction inspired by this country, make his interpretation peculiar to himself. No other major American writer of the nineteenth century became through residence and use of materials so deeply identified with any one Continental nation. Lowell lived in Spain but wrote relatively little about the country. Prescott wrote of it voluminously but never set foot on its soil. In spite of Irving's ventures into scholarship his interpretation was essentially poetic. Without powers, like Bryant's or Longfellow's, to translate Spanish poetry, his adaptations of Moorish legends and ancient Spanish lore were, nevertheless, those of the poet. What Longfellow attempted in *Outre-Mer,* Irving achieved in *The Alhambra.* Master and disciple —for in regard to romantic Europe this was their relationship—complemented each other. Each gave to the hordes of uncritical American readers curious about the Continent glimpses of an unknown Spain, Irving in prose, Longfellow primarily in poetry. From his earliest days when he read Pérez de Hita until his final posthumous volume, *Spanish Papers,*[186] Irving's temper, save for the brief interval as a young satirist and imitator of Cervantes, was that of "the poet Irving."

At the same time this conception of Irving, the Irving whose *Alhambra* attracted thousands of Americans to the palace,[187] demands qualification. The actual living in Spain for seven years, the intimacy with peasant and nobleman, the companionship with Spanish statesmen, permitted him to speak of contemporary Spain with knowledge and with realistic understanding of the country's strength and weakness. The portrait of Espartero in the dispatches is different from that drawn for the nieces in "the romance of the palace." The characterizations of the dwellers in the Alhambra have a truth worthy of Fernán Caballero. This writing reveals his comprehension of deeply rooted traits of Spanish character. It is interesting that he should have received from the father, one of the German "Romantiker," confirmation of a special attitude and from the daughter reaffirmation concerning another. As a matter of fact, something a little whimsical tempers all of Irving's sentimentalization of Spain. He knew the country too well to be completely deluded by its romance. If in the *Columbus* there are such absurdities as the blackhearted villain Roldán, the mermaids, or the seas of milk and in *The Alhambra* the three preposterous princesses, still the creator of Dame Van Winkle and Ichabod Crane did not himself regard these marvels too seriously. His interpretation of Spanish legends, and of all phases of Spain, was often shrewdly humorous—and altogether it was just.

[161]*The Life and Voyages of Christopher Columbus, The Conquest of Granada,* and *The Alhambra.*
(Williams specifies general reference to Irving's Author's Revised Edition in the "Geoffrey Crayon Edition ([New York, 1888–93])".)

[162]See S. T. W., *2,* 300–2.
(Stanley T. Williams, *The Life of Washington Irving,* 2 vols. [New York: Oxford, 1935]).

[163]See Williams and McDowell, pp. xliii–lii.
(*Diedrich Knickerbocker's A History of New York,* ed. S. T. Williams and Tremaine McDowell [New York: Harcourt, Brace & Co., 1927]).

[164]Irving to T. W. Storrow, Madrid, Feb. 26, 1827 (H.) [Harvard].

[165]See S. T. Wallis, "Navarrete on Spain," *So. Lit. Mess.,* 7 (March 1841), 231–9; and "Mr. Washington Irving, Mr. Navarrete, and the Knickerbocker," *ibid.,* 8 (Nov., 1842), 725–35. This controversy still retained some life about thirty-five years ago. See "Reparaciones de la historia de España, Fernández Navarrete y Wáshington Irving," *Boletin de la Real Academia de la Historia,* 73 (agosto-octubre, 1918), 258–81. This is apparently a translation of the article in the *So. Lit. Mess.* See the reply to the *So. Lit. Mess.* in *Knick., 20* (Aug., 1842), 194–8.

[166]See J. C. Brevoort, "Spanish American Documents, Printed or Inedited," *Mag. Am. Hist., 3* (March, 1879), 176.

[167]*Estudios de crítica literaria,* 2ª ser. (Madrid, 1895), pp. 270–2.

[168]Williams and Edge, pp. 82–3.
(S. T. Williams and Mary A. Edge, comp. *A Bibliography of the Writings of Washington Irving* [New York: Oxford, 1936]).

[169]See S. T. W., *2,* 303. For Prescott's admiration of Irving as a writer and for his misgivings regarding him as a scholar, see below, p. 318, n. 93, and p. 40. The two attitudes are suggested in a letter to A. H. Everett, written early in 1827, when Prescott first feared Irving's rivalry: "The freshness of part of my subject is to be taken off, I find by Mr. Irving. But as the world will be so much a gainer by it, how can I repine? I could wish, however, as in the case of Scott that a genius so rarely qualified to excel in fiction should not trammel itself with the vulgar material of fact." Prescott to A. H. Everett, 1827 (M.H.S.) [Massachusetts Historical Society].

[170]See J. De L. Ferguson, *American Literature in Spain* (New York, Columbia University Press, 1916), pp. 22–3.

[171]For the various letters and documents in which Irving states his purposes in *The Conquest of Granada,* see S. T. W., *1,* 344–6.

[172]Years later Irving regretted his use of this device. See *ibid., 1,* 347. The account in his introduction is suggestive: "The manuscript of the worthy Fray Antonio will be adopted wherever it exists entire; but will be filled up, extended, illustrated, and corroborated, by citations from various authors, both

Spanish and Arabian, who have treated of the subject. Those who may wish to know how far the work is indebted to the chronicle of Fray Antonio Agapida, may readily satisfy their curiosity by referring to his manuscript fragments, carefully preserved in the library of the Escurial." *A Chronicle of the Conquest of Granada* (Philadelphia, 1829), *1*, x.

[173]See S. T. W., *2*, 309-10. For a recent study of this book, see L. M. Hoffman, "Irving's Use of Spanish Sources in *The Conquest of Granada*," *Hisp.*, *28* (Nov., 1945), 483-98.

[174]Mo. R. [3d] Ser., *11* (July, 1829), 431.

[175]*A Chronicle of the Conquest of Granada, 2,* 306. (Quotation from the Philadelphia edition, 2 vols. [Carey, Lea & Carey: 1829]).

[176]Melville's story of the ineffectual sea captain appeared in *Putnam's Monthly Magazine* in 1855, four years before Irving's death. See above, *1*, [Vol 1] 116-7. Early in 1846 Irving knew Melville and read in manuscript parts of *Typee*. (S. T. W., *The Spanish Background of American Literature,* 2 vols. [New Haven: Yale, 1955]).

[177]Irving to S. A. Allibone, Sunnyside, Nov. 2, 1857. S. A. Allibone, *A Critical Dictionary of English Literature and British and American Authors* (Philadelphia, 1859-71), *1*, 943.

[178]See S. T. W., *1*, 499-500.

[179]"Carta á mi lector de las Batuecas" in *Clemencia, novela de costumbres* (Madrid, Hijos de M. Guijarro, 1902), *1*, xxxii.

[180]*The Alhambra,* p. 11.

[181]See Williams and Edge, pp. 33-4. Of the many reviews, one of the longest and most appreciative was that by A. H. Everett, who continued to be a sponsor for Irving's Spanish studies. See *NAR, 35* (Oct., 1832), 265-82.

[182]David Wilkie to Irving, London, Oct. 23, 1833 (Y.) [Yale].

[183]*Cuentos de la Alhambra,* tr. J. Ventura Traveset (Valencia [1893?]), Prólogo del traductor, p. vii.

[184]*Historia literaria, ensayo* (Madrid, 1902), *1*, 495.

[185]See M. A. Buchanan, "Alhambraism," *HR, 3* (Oct., 1935) 269-74. For the influence of "Alhambraism" on American architecture, see above, *1*, 302.

[186]See S. T. W., *2*, 323.

[187]Many articles and books comment on Irving's associations with the palace. E.g., W. H. Bidwell, "Reminiscences of the Alhambra," *Ecl. M., 46* (March, 1859), 434-6; Henry Coppée, "A Glimpse of the Alhambra," *Appletons', 6* (Dec. 16, 1871), 683-6; G. P. Lathrop, "Spanish Vistas," *Harper, 65* (Aug., 1882), 390; G. E. Vincent, "Memories of Spain," *Chaut., 15* (Aug., 1892), 540; H. C. Chatfield-Taylor, "Granada and the Alhambra," *Cosmopol., 21* (Sept., 1896), 452.

Introductory Essay
to
A Tour on the Prairies

BY JOHN FRANCIS MCDERMOTT

John Francis McDermott, after graduate studies at Washington University, taught English and Cultural History there from 1924, before moving in 1963 to Southern Illinois University, where since 1971 he has been Adjunct Research Professor of Humanities. A Guggenheim fellow, 1954–1955, he was a library research associate of the American Philosophical Society, 1958–1963. Among his numerous publications, many on early middle-western history, are *Caleb Bingham, River Portraitist* (1959) and the compilation, *Research Opportunities in American Cultural History* (1961). This "Introductory Essay" from his 1956 edition of Irving's *A Tour on the Prairies,* reflective of recent interest in Western Americana, is perhaps best read in conjunction with McDermott's scholarly edition of *The Western Journals of Washington Irving* (1944).

I

A Tour on the Prairies is first of all a voyage of personal discovery. Washington Irving's excursion into the wild lands beyond the frontier was not a pathfinding exploration such as Lewis and Clark made, nor a business enterprise such as Wilson Price Hunt or Josiah Gregg undertook, nor a military survey like that of Frémont, nor a search for beasts or birds or plants like Bradbury's or Nuttall's or Audubon's. Irving's was a voyage of discovery made by a man who had been long absent from his home and who wanted now to see and feel and smell and hear his own country, who ardently desired to realize it for himself. His book was the personal record of "a month's foray beyond the outposts of human habitation . . . a simple narrative of every day occurrences; such as happen to every one who travels the prairies." He had "no wonders to describe, nor any moving accidents by flood or field to narrate;"—and story, "none to tell, sir."[1]

Out of a brief round over the Oklahoma prairies, on a military mission of no importance, during which the party saw not one hostile Indian, nor gathered any significant information about terrain, nor marked a road, nor accomplished anything except to wear out a few horses and to run short of food—out of this unpromising material Washington Irving made a travel book that was immediately taken up by the reading public, as Stanley T. Williams, his chief biographer, has remarked with some astonishment, even though it was "unscientific [and] unenriched by new data."[2] Its perennial popularity owes much to the suavity, the urbanity, the geniality, the grace of expression which his critics have commonly allowed Irving, for the man could write as few of his contemporaries could. But the book is more than a literary exercise. Its true worth and its enduring fascination lie in the brilliantly drawn pictures of frontier life that flow from the pencil of a great genre artist.

It was a chance meeting on a Lake Erie steamboat late in Au-

---

[1] Author's Introduction. All quotations not otherwise acknowledged are from *A Tour on the Prairies*, as reprinted here.

[2] *The Life of Washington Irving* (New York, Oxford University Press, 1935), II, 80–81.

gust, 1832, that sent Irving southwest over the prairies.[3] Returning
from a seventeen-year residence in Europe, eager to know what his
native land had become, he was ripe for a suggestion which would
open new vistas in his life. When Henry L. Ellsworth, newly-appointed
commissioner to treat with the western Indians, invited him to go
out to Fort Gibson as secretary *pro tem* to the commission, Irving
fired up with enthusiasm. "The offer was too tempting to be resisted,"
he wrote to his brother Peter. "I should have an opportunity of seeing the remnants of those great Indian Tribes, which are now about
to disappear as independent nations, or to be amalgamated under
some new form of government. I should see those fine countries of
the 'far west,' while still in a state of pristine wildness, and behold
herds of buffaloes scouring their native prairies, before they are driven
beyond the reach of a civilized tourist."[4]

Putting aside other plans, Irving and his traveling companions
Latrobe and Pourtalès landed with Ellsworth at Ashtabula, crossed
Ohio to Cincinnati, passed by steamboat to St. Louis, and thence by
horseback via Independence to the Arkansas. Arrived at the south-
western outpost, Fort Gibson, Irving felt he was now "completely

[3] Irving had left New York early in August for Saratoga, where he met
once more his traveling friends Latrobe and Pourtalès. With them he visited
Trenton Springs not far from Utica and then Niagara Falls. At Buffalo, New
York, they boarded a steamer for Detroit, the Europeans intending to return
by way of Montreal and Quebec, Irving proposing to cross Ohio and thence
home by river. But they met Henry Leavitt Ellsworth on the boat. "After
some acquaintance we discoursed upon the nature of my mission [Ellsworth
wrote from Fort Gibson, December 5, 1832], and discovering a desire to accompany me, I invited them all to go with me even to the Buffalo range,
promising them the protection of the Government, and my individual exertions
to make their excursion pleasant." (Stanley T. Williams and Barbara D. Simison, "A Journey through Oklahoma in 1832: A Letter from Henry L. Ellsworth to Professor Benjamin Silliman," *Mississippi Valley Historical Review*,
Vol. XXIX, No. 3 [December, 1942], 387–93.) The four travelers reached
Cincinnati on September 1, St. Louis on September 13, and Fort Gibson on
October 8. For a full account of Irving's western travels, of Ellsworth's mis-
sion, and of Captain Bean's Rangers, see *The Western Journals of Washington
Irving*, edited by John Francis McDermott (Norman, University of Oklahoma
Press, 1944), 3–40.

[4] Washington City, December 18, 1832. Originally published in the London *Athenaeum* (1833), 137–38; reprinted in the New York *Commercial Advertiser*, and copied from the latter by the *Arkansas Gazette*, June 26, 1833.

launched in savage life" and was "extremely excited and interested by this wild country, and the wild scenes and people" by which he was surrounded.[5] He was delighted to set out with Ellsworth and a company of Rangers on a foray "beyond human habitation." His notebooks, his letters, his narrative repeatedly display his eager participation in the new life. The expedition reaching the Red Fork of the Arkansas (the Cimarron), a stream too broad and deep for fording, Irving was charmingly pleased by the boat their man Beatte constructed from a buffalo hide. When it had been half filled with saddles, saddlebags, and other luggage and placed in the water, Irving stepped in "as cautiously as possible, and sat down on the top of the luggage, the margin of the hide sinking to within a hand's breadth of the water's edge. Rifles, fowling-pieces, and other articles of small bulk, were then handed in, until I protested against receiving any more freight. We then launched forth upon the stream, the bark being towed as before. It was with a sensation half serious, half comic, that I found myself thus afloat, on the skin of a buffalo, in the midst of a wild river, surrounded by wilderness, and towed along by a half savage, whooping and yelling like a devil incarnate."

In camp the next day, having traveled by this time more than one hundred miles from Fort Gibson, he summed up in his journal the pleasures and satisfactions of his excursion:

Delightful mode of life—exercise on horseback all the fore part of the day—diversified by hunting incidents—then about 3 o'clock encamping in some beautiful place with full appetite for repose, lying on the grass under green trees—in genial weather with a blue, cloudless sky—then so sweet sleeping at night in the open air, & when awake seeing the moon and stars through the tree tops—such zest for the hardy, simple, but savory meats, the product of the chase—venison roasted on spits or broiled on the coals—turkeys just from the thicket—honey from the tree—coffee—or delightful prairie tea. The weather is in its perfection—golden sunshine—not oppressive but animating—skies without a cloud—or if there be clouds, of feathery texture and lovely tints—air pure, bland, exhilarating—an atmosphere of perfect transparency—and the whole country having the

[5]Irving to his sister, Mrs. Paris; Fort Gibson, October 9, 1832. Pierre M. Irving, *The Life and Letters of Washington Irving* (4 vols., London, Richard Bentley, 1862–64), III, 23.

mellow tint of autumn. How exciting to think that we are breaking thro a country hitherto untrodden by white man, except perchance the solitary trapper—a glorious world spread around us without an inhabitant.[6]

In *A Tour on the Prairies,* then, we have the zestful response of a man to his first experience beyond the Western Frontier. But Irving has a great deal more to offer than a readable account of personal experience. His book is a document, for in it he has preserved a segment of society. Its scenes and activities are original and unique because, perceiving them as an artist, he captured life rather than merely recorded information. The historian searching for facts who finds none in the *Tour* is gravely limited in his concept of the word. Facts are not limited to scientific, military, topographical, ethnological, or commercial data: whatever "fixes" a scene of human activity or a person is a fact. Irving's intention, as much as his skill, differs from that of other travelers. He had no scientific training or interest; consequently, he gathered no scientific information. He was not a soldier or a pathfinder or a businessman and did not concern himself with the affairs of such persons. He was, in his own word, a tourist —a visitor traveling for his own information, seeking to find out for himself what this frontier country and its people were like. He had no purpose but to observe human behavior. He made his own discoveries—and these discoveries are facts as valuable in the long run as the finding of an undescribed plant or the charting of a river or the locating of a new pass through the mountains. Any intelligent traveler may collect information: only an artist of true skill can capture in sketches the living world about him.

The "occurrences that happen to every man who travels the prairies" are set down in the *Tour* with an intimate detail, a sense of values, an understanding of behavior, a pictorial vividness seldom found in the journals of men concerned with scientific or military or commercial purposes. Traveling with Irving, we learn the difficulty of fording deep streams on horseback, of working through mile after mile of tangled undergrowth ("forests of cast iron") like the Cross Timbers. With him we are jogging comfortably on when a thunderstorm breaks and the rain comes "rattling upon us in torrents, and

[6]October 16; *The Western Journals of Washington Irving,* 130–31. This work will hereafter be referred to as *Western Journals.*

spattered up like steam along the ground; the whole landscape was suddenly wrapped in gloom that gave a vivid effect to the intense sheets of lightning, while the thunder seemed to burst over our very heads, and was reverberated by the groves and forests that checkered and skirted the prairie. Man and beast were so pelted, drenched, and confounded, that the line was thrown in complete confusion; some of the horses were so frightened as to be almost unmanageable, and our scattered cavalcade looked like a tempest-tossed fleet, driven hither and thither, at the mercy of wind and wave."

We see horses worn out and abandoned. We live on the country, and we learn what it is, with our small supply of flour exhausted, to find no game better than a few birds that we scorned when venison and buffalo were aplenty. In the immensity of the prairie we too come to understand that there is "something inexpressibly lonely. . . . The loneliness of a forest seems nothing to it. There the view is shut in by trees, and the imagination is left free to picture some livelier scene beyond. But here we have an immense extent of landscape without a sign of human existence. We have the consciousness of being far, far beyond the bounds of human habitation; we feel as if moving in the midst of a desert world. . . . The silence of the waste . . . now and then broken by the cry of a distant flock of pelicans, stalking like spectres about a shallow pool . . . the sinister croaking of a raven in the air . . . [a wolf whining] with tones that gave a dreariness to the surrounding solitude."

Nowhere else do we get to know a military company as we do these Rangers. Irving was not an army officer to be concerned with the effectiveness of his unit or the impression that the world might get of his professional aptitude. He was free to "ramble among the natural actions of men,"[7] and he brought together a lively record of a most casual and unmilitary outfit, representative enough of short-term volunteers in that day. A "raw, undisciplined band, levied among the wild youngsters of the frontier," who had signed up "for the sake of roving adventure," they were without a tradition of military service, without training, without uniforms or commissary, with-

---

[7]His own phrase as reported by Ellsworth, *Washington Irving on the Prairie or a Narrative of a Tour of the Southwest in the Year 1832* (New York, American Book Company, 1937), 71. Ellsworth's work will hereafter be referred to as *Narrative*.

out consciousness of rank. "Many of them were the neighbors of their officers and accustomed to regard them with the familiarity of equals and companions. None of them had any idea of the restraint and decorum of a camp, or ambition to acquire a name for exactness in a profession in which they had no intention of continuing." Restless, rough, good-natured, adventurous, wasteful, stuffed with curious lore, they possibly did not know that they were sitting for their portrait, but they could not have cared less.

Peals of laughter, ribald jokes, lugubrious psalms, mockery of comrades resounded at the evening campfires. Stories of their hunting adventures, gossip of their neighborhoods, and secondhand tales about the Indians filled the idle hours. The day's ride over the prairie took little out of them: they were at any moment leaping, wrestling, shooting at a mark, indulging in horseplay. One morning, "scarcely had the first gray streak of dawn appeared, when a youngster at one of the distant lodges, shaking off his sleep, crowed in imitation of a cock, with a loud, clear note and prolonged cadence." Another "rooster" answered immediately, and in a moment, "the chant was echoed from lodge to lodge, and followed by the cackling of hens, quacking of ducks, gabbling of turkeys, and grunting of swine."

The Rangers were eternally trading: "In the course of our expedition, there was scarce a horse, rifle, powderhorn, or blanket, that did not change owners several times." Carelessly destructive and appallingly wasteful they were: "our late bustling encampment [Irving wrote one day] had a forlorn and desolate appearance. The surrounding forest had been in many places trampled into a quagmire. Trees felled and partly hewn in pieces, and scattered in huge fragments; tent-poles stripped of their covering; smouldering fires, with great morsels of roasted venison and buffalo meat, standing in wooden spits before them, hacked and slashed by the knives of hungry hunters; while around were strewed the hides, the horns, the antlers and bones of buffaloes and deer, with uncooked joints, and unplucked turkeys, left behind with reckless improvidence and wastefulness which young hunters are apt to indulge when in a neighborhood where game abounds. In the meantime a score or two of turkey-buzzards, or vultures, were already on the wing, wheeling their magnificent flight high in air, and preparing for a descent upon the camp as soon as it should be abandoned."

"The Indian of poetical fiction," Irving underscored, "is like the shepherd of pastoral romance, a mere personification of imaginary attributes." Uninfluenced by personal concerns, Irving found the Indian not the solemn, stoical hero or the sullen vermin that most travelers reported him, but a human being lively and humorous. Repeatedly Irving noticed the "excitability and boisterous merriment" of the Osages at their games and more than once had seen a group "sitting around a fire until a late hour of the night, engaged in the most animated and lively conversation; and at times making the woods resound with peals of laughter."

Taciturn he found the Indians "when in company of white men, whose good-will they distrust, and whose language they do not understand," and so would the white man be, he said, under like circumstances. But among themselves, "there cannot be greater gossips. Half their time is taken up in talking over their adventures in war and hunting, and in telling whimsical stories. They are great mimics and buffoons, also, and entertain themselves excessively at the expense of the whites with whom they have associated, and who have supposed them impressed with profound respect for their grandeur and dignity. They are curious observers, noting every thing in silence, but with a keen and watchful eye; occasionally exchanging a glance or a grunt with each other, when any thing particularly strikes them: but reserving all comments until they are alone. Then it is that they give full scope to criticism, satire, mimicry, and mirth."

On one occasion their skill at improvising was demonstrated for Irving. Three Osages joined their evening campfire and after supper began a chant, which, the interpreter told the tourists, "related to ourselves, our appearance, our treatment of them, and all they knew of our plans. In one part they spoke of the young Count, whose animated character and eagerness for Indian enterprise had struck their fancy, and they indulged in some waggery about him and the young Indian beauties, that produced great merriment among our half-breeds."

Indian humor found expression in other ways. With straight faces the tall Osages (famous as walkers) explained the desperate valor of their once-deadly foes the Delawares: "Look at the Delawares—dey got short leg—no can run—must stand and fight a great heap." There was something too of dry satire in Osage reaction to speeches by the Commissioner. The expedition coming on a village empty of warriors, Mr. Ellsworth seriously called together the women and children and old men and "made a speech from on horseback; informing his hearers of the purport of his mission, to promote a general peace among the tribes of the West, and urging them to lay aside all warlike and bloodthirsty notions, and not to make any wanton attacks upon the Pawnees." The speech, interpreted by Beatte, "seemed to have a most pacifying effect upon the multitude, who promised faithfully that, as far as in them lay, the peace should not be disturbed."

Late in the excursion they met a war party of seven Osage hunters who hoped to carry off some Pawnee scalps or horses before returning to their village. The Commissioner "now remembered his mission as pacificator, and made a speech, exhorting them to abstain from all offensive acts against the Pawnees; informing them of the plan of their father at Washington, to put an end to all war among his red children; and assuring them that he was sent to the frontier to establish a universal peace. He told them, therefore, to return quietly to their homes, with the certainty that the Pawnees would no longer molest them, but would soon regard them as brothers." To such solemn and well-intentioned but somewhat naïve remarks the Indians listened "with their customary silence and decorum; after which, exchanging a few words among themselves, they bade us farewell." Because he fancied he saw a smile lurking on Beatte's face, Irving asked him privately what the Indians had said to each other after the speech. The interpreter replied that the leader had observed that "as their great father intended so soon to put an end to all warfare, it behooved them to make the most of the little time that was left them. So they had departed, with redoubled zeal, to pursue their project of horse-stealing!"

It is not merely in the life he gave to the trials and difficulties and commonplaces of prairie travel or the military informality of the Rangers or his interpretation of Indians as real people that the excellence of the *Tour* lies. Most notable of all is Irving's skill as a genre artist. He had feeling as a landscapist and produced views that would qualify him for the Hudson River school,[8] but his forte was

[8]Many examples could be cited; I quote a passage at the crossing of the Red Fork: "The river scenery at this place was beautifully diversified, presenting long, shining reaches, bordered by willows and cotton-wood trees; rich bottoms, with lofty forests; among which towered enormous plane trees, and the distance was closed in by high embowered promontories."

genre, the portrayal of scenes of everyday life, as it had been since his earliest years. The masterful handling of composition and color, the superb drawing, the simplicity and variety of details, the commonplace character yet unique quality of his subjects, the clarity of vision, the unity of tone and the feeling for action, and the objective realism with which he saw life combine to produce a remarkable picture of life in far western America. Few of his fellows of the brush could attain his effects. It is no wonder that he still charms us.

Very early in the narrative we are vividly aware that he saw life with a painter's eye. Eager to begin his tour, Irving rode over from Fort Gibson to Chouteau's post on the Verdigris, from which they were to set out. In the background he saw "a few log houses on the banks of the river." An escort of a dozen rangers was waiting for the Commissioner: some "on horseback, some on foot, some seated on the trunks of fallen trees, some shooting at a mark." A motley crew they were, dressed in "frock-coats made of green blankets . . . [or] leathern hunting-shirts" and "marvellously ill-cut garments, much the worse for wear, and evidently put on for rugged service."

His quick eye moved on to a group of Osages, stately fellows, stern and simple in garb and aspect. No ornaments. Their only dress blankets, leggings, and moccasins. Heads bare, hair cropped close, except for a bristly ridge on the top like the crest of a helmet with a long scalp lock hanging behind. Blankets wrapped about their loins, leaving bust and arms bare—noble bronze figures, the finest looking Indians in the West. In contrast, there was a band of gayly-dressed Creeks "in calico hunting-shirts of various brilliant colors, decorated with bright fringes, and belted with broad girdles, embroidered with beads." Leggings of dressed deerskin or of green and scarlet cloth, embroidered knee bands and tassels. Moccasins fancifully ornamented. Gaudy handkerchiefs around their heads. Elsewhere he saw "a sprinkling of trappers, hunters, half-breeds, creoles, negroes of every hue."

The picture is not yet rich enough. Observe the special studies that fill spaces left in this superb canvas. Movement everywhere. A blacksmith's shed with "a strapping negro . . . shoeing a horse" and two half-bloods "fabricating iron spoons in which to melt lead for bullets." Near by, "an old trapper, in leathern hunting frock and moccasons, had placed his rifle against a work-bench, while he superintended the operation, and gossiped about his hunting exploits."

Dogs are "lounging in and out of the shop, or sleeping in the sun-shine." Watching the horseshoeing is "a little cur, with head cocked to one side, and one ear erect . . . with that curiosity common to little dogs . . . as if studying the art, or waiting his turn to be shod." Here is no prettifying, no seeking of glamor, no indulgence in the mere picturesque, no romantic dreaming about an imaginary world. This is life itself on the frontier. Not until a decade later in George Caleb Bingham does America produce a painter to stand with Irving in the portrayal of western scene and character.

Occasionally Irving slipped into the sentimental, into well-tried literary reference, into mere picture making, but what prolific artist has not? Banditti and Moorish towers and Don Quixote and Gil Blas we could readily do without, but they fill few pages in his abundant portfolio. Rather, it is crowded with vigorous, quickly and surely drawn sketches of American frontier life, the frontiersmen, the Indi-ans, the Rangers. Turn back to the crossing of the Red Fork at the moment when the artist has climbed out of the bullboat. With him we watch the "raft of logs and branches, on which the Captain and his prime companion, the Doctor were ferrying their effects across the stream; and . . . a long line of rangers on horseback, fording the stream obliquely, along a series of sand-bars, about a mile and a half distant."

See the Rangers in camp, all "bustle and repose." Some of the men were "busy round the fires, jerking and roasting venison and bear's meat, to be packed up as a future supply. Some were stretch-ing and dressing the skins of the animals they had killed; others were washing their clothes in the brook, and hanging them on the bushes to dry; while many were lying on the grass, and lazily gossiping in the shade. Every now and then a hunter would return, on horseback or on foot, laden with game, or empty handed. Those who brought home any spoil, deposited it at the captain's fire, and then filed off to their respective messes."

They break camp of a morning: "Horses driven in from the purlieus of the camp; rangers riding about among rocks and bushes in quest of others that had strayed to a distance; the bustle of packing up camp equipage, and the clamor after kettles and frying-pans bor-rowed by one mess from another, mixed up with oaths and exclama-tions at restive horses, or others that had wandered away to graze after being packed." The bugle sounds, and the troop rides off in irregular file, disappearing through the open forest. "The rear-guard remained under the trees in the lower part of the dell, some on horse-back, with their rifles on their shoulders; others seated by the fire or lying on the ground, gossiping in a low, lazy tone of voice, their horses unsaddled, standing and dozing around: while one of the rangers, profiting by this interval of leisure, was shaving himself before a pocket mirror stuck against the trunk of a tree."

Look at the portrait-sketches. The young Count, "caracoling his horse, and dashing about in the buoyancy of youthful spirits," has given himself over completely to the adventure of the frontier. There he is, clad in "a gay Indian hunting frock of dressed deer skin, setting well to the shape, dyed of a beautiful purple, and fancifully embroidered with silks of various colors; as if it had been the work of some Indian beauty, to decorate a favorite chief. With this he wore leathern pantaloons and moccasons, a foraging cap, and a double-barrelled gun slung by a bandoleer athwart his back." The perfect frontier dandy.

In contrast, observe Pierre Beatte, man of the frontier, guide and interpreter, "lounging about, in an old hunting frock and metasses or leggings, of deer skin, soiled and greased, and almost japanned by constant use." Perhaps thirty-six years of age, square and strongly built, he had features "not unlike those of Napoleon, but sharpened up, with high Indian cheek bones. Perhaps the dusky greenish hue of his complexion, aided his resemblance to an old bronze bust I had seen of the Emperor. He had, however, a sullen, saturnine expression, set off by a slouched woolen hat, and elf locks that hung about his ears. . . . He was cold and laconic; made no promises or professions; stated the terms he required for the services of himself and his horse, which we thought rather high, but showed no disposition to abate them, nor any anxiety to secure our employ."

One final scene. Weary and hungry, Irving and his horse crept on the last stage of their journey homeward. Suddenly before him was a farmhouse, "a low tenement of logs, overshadowed by great forest trees . . . a stable and barn, and granaries teeming with abundance, while legions of grunting swine, gobbling turkeys, cackling hens and strutting roosters, swarmed about the farm-yard." Irving glanced into the cabin. "There sat the Captain of the Rangers and his officers, round a three-legged table, crowned by a broad and smoking dish of boiled beef and turnips." Irving sprang off his horse. A fat, good-humored negress met him at the door. "In a twinkling, she lugged from the fire a huge iron pot. . . . Placing a brown earthen dish on the floor, she inclined the corpulent cauldron on one side, and out leaped sundry great morsels of beef, with a regiment of turnips tumbling after them, and a rich cascade of broth overflowing the whole. This she handed me with an ivory smile that extended from ear to ear; apologizing for our humble fare, and the humble style in which it was served up. Humble fare! humble style! Boiled beef and turnips, and an earthen dish to eat them from! To think of apologizing for such a treat to a half-starved man from the prairies; and then such magnificent slices of bread and butter!"

In such vivid portrayal of the common life on the frontier is the genius of Irving and the enduring interest of his *Tour on the Prairies.*

II

On his excursion to the West, Irving continued his lifelong habit of keeping notebooks. "His mode of recording events," Ellsworth observed, "is not to confide much to the memory, but to sketch in a little book every occurence worthy of remembrance and especially *dates & facts.*"[9] Although he must have filled at least ten notebooks during those four months, only five are extant. These cover his route from Cincinnati to St. Louis, September 3–14; from Independence, Missouri, to Cabin Creek some seventy miles north of Fort Gibson, September 26–October 6; from Cabin Creek to a point on the Red Fork (Cimarron) reached two days after crossing the Arkansas, October 6–17; from a camp on the Little River to Fort Gibson, October 31–November 10; from Fort Gibson to Stack Island in the Mississippi, about 120 miles below the Arkansas, November 11–17.[10] As far as the *Tour* is concerned, the important lacuna is the journal covering thirteen days of the prairie excursion, a portion to which he devoted Chapters XVI–XXXII inclusive in the published account. The

[9]Ellsworth, *Narrative,* 71.

[10]The extant notebooks are all included in my edition of *Western Journals,* published in 1944 by the University of Oklahoma Press. About eight years ago, however, a journal for the overland travel from Ashtabula to Cincinnati was in the possession of Walter Hill, an antiquarian bookseller of Chicago; since his death, its whereabouts remain unknown.

Tour and the *Western Journals* then are complementary, not identical works.

Although as a professional literary man all was grist to Irving's mill, he had while traveling no immediate and definite plans for a book about the West. Public pressure, however, was great. The tour was made, Irving said in his preface, "for the gratification of my curiosity, [but] it has been supposed that I did it for the purpose of writing a book." The newspapers everywhere played up these expectations. The editor of the Columbia *Missouri Intelligencer,* on September 29, 1832 (he had met the travelers ten days earlier on their way to the southwest prairies), declared that Irving "will no doubt acquire a valuable fund of materials in his progress, for interesting works or Sketches, which, ere long, we may have the gratification of perusing."[11] At the close of the tour when Irving arrived in Little Rock, the *Arkansas Gazette* (November 21, 1832) held that "Should he favor the world with a description [of the prairies] from his glowing pen, which is more than probable, it will excite emotions of unmingled delight in the bosom of thousands, and unfold innumerable beauties in nature, which, to the majority of travellers, remain unnoticed and unknown." The editor of that paper, on January 30, 1833, commenting on the extensiveness of Irving's western trip, predicted "the result . . . will be in every way gratifying. The ardent patriotism of the author of Columbus will prompt him to inspire his countrymen with some of his own laudable curiosity about the land we live in; and his pen, invigorated by themes so novel to the rest of the world and so grateful to himself, will trace his impressions with a freshness and force that will rival its happiest exercise in any of his works." The New York *Commercial Advertiser,* early in 1833 (republishing from the London *Athenaeum* his letter of December 18, 1832, to his brother Peter), earnestly hoped that it would not be long "before we have something more than a *sketch* of this interesting tour; although we believe he has as yet written nothing upon the subject for the press."[12]

Irving had always "had a repugnance, amounting almost to disability, to write in the face of expectation." Nevertheless, he presently

[11] I owe this reference to Floyd C. Shoemaker, secretary of the State Historical Society of Missouri.
[12] See note 4.

faced the job, "plucked a few leaves" out of his notebooks, and by November 24, 1834, had completed the narrative of his excursion. A copy of the manuscript he sent off to Colonel Thomas Aspinwall in London before January 8, 1835, and the English edition was brought out by Murray in March. On April 11, he was able to tell Peter, "My 'Tour on the Prairies' has just been published" in Philadelphia. By November 10, Carey, Lea and Blanchard's American edition was in its eighth thousand.[13] Since that time the "little narrative" that Irving let go to press with such hesitancy has passed through more than thirty editions in English and twenty in translation.[14] Certainly it is well established as a minor American classic.

[13]Pierre M. Irving, *Life and Letters of Washington Irving,* III, 43–46; Washington Irving to Henry Carey, New York, April 8, 1835 (New York Public Library). Pierre M. Irving said his uncle received $2,400 in all from American sales and £400 for the English rights. Williams (*Life of Washington Irving,* II, 74) gives the latter figure as £600.

[14]Stanley T. Williams and Mary Allen Edge, *A Bibliography of the Writings of Washington Irving* (New York, Oxford University Press, 1936).

"In England"

BY WALTER A. REICHART

Walter A. Reichart, Austrian-born, was educated at the University of Michigan and is now Professor Emeritus of that school, where he long served on the graduate faculty for German studies, with his special interest the playwright Gerhart Hauptmann. Dr. Reichart was a member of the executive board of the Rackham School of Graduate Studies beginning in 1950, and during 1951 served as president of the American Association of Teachers of German. He is a founding member of the Editorial Board for *The Complete Works of Washington Irving,* and for this project edited Volume III (1818–1827) of the "Journals and Notebooks," published in 1970. Reprinted here is the entire first chapter of his *Washington Irving and Germany* (1957), which thoroughly investigates the antecedents in German Romantic literature of, among others, favorite tales such as "Rip" and the "Legend".

In the summer of 1822 Washington Irving left London for the Continent in the hope of effecting a cure for a cutaneous complaint that had troubled him for almost a year. In February of that year he had been considering the baths at Aix-la-Chapelle,[1] but the final work of preparing the manuscript of *Bracebridge Hall* and seeing it through the press had demanded his presence in London. These obligations fulfilled, he could set out upon the journey to that yet unexplored realm of romantic Germany that had beckoned to him ever since he had heard of Thomas Campbell's travels in Germany and had witnessed Walter Scott's enthusiasm for German literature, an enthusiasm shared by English readers for more than two decades.

The publication of *The Sketch Book* had made Irving "the most fashionable fellow of the day"[2] in England, and literary men as well as Hyde Park society eagerly sought his company. Irving, gratified and flattered, readily accepted such a welcome. His fondness for society and literary gossip, already a characteristic of his New York days, had increased with the years. Though he was dazed by such unexpected fame and adulation, he was no more astonished than his hosts, who had to acknowledge that here was an American who could write like an Englishman. Irving was welcomed to John Murray's drawing room and soon felt at home in the circle of prominent men of letters who met there regularly. He relished the intimate friendship of Francis Jeffrey and Walter Scott, he enjoyed the company of the genial Thomas Moore and the witty Sydney Smith, and he was dazzled by the brilliant company at Holland House. Gradually, however, the gaiety of the social whirl with its irregular hours and demands upon his time and energy began to tire him; he actually longed for a quiet interlude of travel and study to refresh his mind and body. On June 1, 1822, he wrote to his friend Brevoort:

> . . . I am nearly killed with kindness, for I have not a moment to myself and am so fatigued with company and dinners and evening parties, that I find it impossible to regain a perfect state of health but am still troubled with lameness & inflammation in the ancles, the lingering of my tedious malady. I shall however, soon leave this scene of bustle & dissipation and go to a watering place on the continent (Aix la Chapelle) where I hope thoroughly to reinstate my health. Within these two months past I have given myself up to society more than I have at any time

since I have been in Europe, having for the last four or five years been very much shut up & at home. I was determined this spring to give myself a holiday & make use of the opportunity presented me of seeing fashionable life. I have done this to a considerable degree, though I have suffered much draw back on account of the indifferent state of my health.

The success of my writings has given me ready access to all kinds of society—and I have been the round of routs, dinners, operas, balls, & blue stocking coteries. I have been much pleased with those parties in which rank & fashion and talent are blended; and where you find the most distinguished people of the day in various departments of literature, art & science brought into familiar communion with leading statesmen and ancient nobility.[3]

The choice of Irving's destination was not accidental. He had been dissatisfied with the progress of his convalescence and with the advice of his London physician,[4] so he was willing to attempt his own cure. Having heard of famous watering places in Germany, he decided to combine the advantages of such treatment with the pleasures of foreign travel. His curiosity and impatience to see the land whose literature had already served as a source for some of his most popular tales in *The Sketch Book* determined his itinerary. *Bracebridge Hall,* despite its good reception in England, showed clearly that Irving was exhausting his English environment and needed new scenes and new anecdotes that could be metamorphosed into respectable literary sketches. He was ready for one of those romantic interludes of travel that recurred regularly in Irving's life and usually preceded a period of composition. He was hoping to explore Germany—a little hurriedly, perhaps, since he expected to return to Paris in autumn[5]— in order to relish her medievalism and to read enough of her folklore to spur his imagination and to enable him to produce a "German Sketch Book."

Irving liked to travel after completing a volume of sketches, as, contrary to the widely held view, writing was always an exhausting process for him.[6] His *Journals,* with their minute details concerning the laborious composition and revision of his work, constantly reflect Irving's eager efforts to overcome the limitations of a mediocre mind. The task of writing worried him and left his nerves on edge.

It was neither a scholar's zeal nor intellectual curiosity, therefore, that took Irving inside the German borders, as was the case o
his countrymen George Ticknor, Edward Everett, George Bancrof
and Henry Wadsworth Longfellow, who studied at Göttingen i
order to understand German life, literature, and civilization.[7] Irvin
was thirty-nine years old, hardly an age to set out upon his *Wande
jahre;* he was not eager or young enough to be receptive to the varie
influences of foreign travel and study. Eighteen years earlier Irvin
had seen Europe for the first time with the buoyant exuberance o
youth, excited by the landscapes and the exotic customs; even the
he had not made a great effort to acquire new ideas or to extend h
mental horizon, and now his thought patterns were set. Outwardl
Irving seemed satisfied with his world and was prone to contempla
every foreign scene with almost an air of English condescension.[8]

Before proceeding to Irving's actual experiences in Germany,
may be well to recall his earliest contacts with German culture and t
establish the degree of his familiarity with the language in order t
explain his eager anticipation of travel in Germany. His childhoo
and youth had given him only a desultory education with no systen
atic training in foreign languages. He had still heard Dutch spoken i
church and market place so that he had acquired a smattering, bu
aside from some routine Latin, which helped him somewhat in late
years with his French, Spanish, and Italian studies, he had had n
real experience with a foreign tongue in his school days.[9] Not unt
after his arrival in England in 1815 was Irving tempted to begin th
study of German—once he had really become aware of the recent in
fluence of this foreign literature on English letters.

Irving's early enthusiasm for the theatre, which made him
"hanger-on" at stage doors and in the greenrooms even in London
score of years later,[10] may well have brought him into contact wit
German drama in English translation on the New York stage. Wi
liam Dunlap, who had assumed the management of the Park Stre
Theatre in 1798, had translated a number of original dramas from th
German: his version of Zschokke's *Aballino, der grosse Bandit* wa
first performed in 1801 and maintained its popularity for years. Kotz
ebue, whose vogue was world-wide, led all foreign productions i
America, and Schiller's *Die Räuber* was performed at intervals an
reprinted four times.[11] More definitely established is the likelihood o
Irving's acquaintance with some magazine articles that touched upo

German literature and philosophy. If he read the *Literary Magazine and American Register* or the *Port Folio* or any other American magazines between 1806 and 1813 he could not fail to see constant references to the work of Klopstock, Wieland, and Goethe, and to articles containing general observations about German life.[12] Moreover, established as "the most eminent New York man of letters,"[13] Irving was persuaded late in 1812 to assume the editorship of *Analectic Magazine,* formerly *Select Reviews,* a monthly which furnished American readers with a selection of foreign materials. Irving was more than a nominal editor and contributed at least eleven articles during the following two years.[14] Hence he must have read and even selected some of the copy, which included a number of significant items bearing upon German literature.

In the November, 1813, issue appeared an "account of C. M. Wieland," a glowing and sentimental tribute upon the occasion of the poet's death, which characterized him as "equally eminent as a poet and a prose writer, as a moralist and a philosopher, as a translator and an author of the most brilliant originality and invention."[15] Such unrestrained praise reflected the popularity of Wieland in England after the middle of the eighteenth century, rivaled only by that of Gessner.[16] William Sotheby's translation of *Oberon* had appeared in 1798 and was reprinted in America in 1810 from the third London edition.[17] Only a few years later Irving made this entry in his notebook: "light tales in the manner of Wieland,"[18] a reminder, perhaps, to try to emulate the facile pen of this popular author. After a preliminary notice of the publication of Mme de Staël's *De L'Allemagne,* also in the November, 1813, issue, the *Analectic Magazine* of April, 1814, reprinted from the *Edinburgh Review* a twenty-four page discussion of it. This article must have aroused Irving's interest and supplied him with much literary information. The review traced the growing importance of German literature in the eighteenth century and its reception in England, and made the observation that Germany "possesses a greater number of laborious scholars and of useful books than any other country."[19] What could have proved more enticing to Washington Irving? Though there is no definite proof that Irving read *De L'Allemagne,* it seems likely in view of its international reputation. If he did not have access to the American edition he probably came to know the work during his English residence after 1815.[20] Irving's fondness for literary associations could not have allowed him to forget that he had made the personal acquaintance of Mme de Staël at the house of (Karl) Wilhelm von Humboldt on his first journey to Europe. Obviously it had been a red-letter day for Irving, and in his journal he made the following entries:

[March 30, 1805.] We also presented a letter of introduction from Mr. Degen of Naples to the Baron Humbolt [*sic*], minister for the Court of Prussia at Rome. He recieved [*sic*] us very politely and we passed half an hour with him in an agreeable & interesting manner. He is brother to the celebrated Humboldt who has made such an extensive tour in America—and informs us that he expects his brother in Rome in a few days when he will make us acquainted with him. The Baron is said to be a very literary man and bears an amiable character in other respects.

[April 4.] In the evening we visited the Prussian Minister Baron Humbolt. We found there Madam De Sta[ë]l the celebrated authoress of Delphine &c. She is a woman of great strength of mind & understanding by all accounts—we were in company with her but a few minutes.

[April 7.] In the evening we accompanied the Baron de Humboldt to the conversazione of the Marquis [*blank*], Minister imperial at the Court of Rome. Here we found a crowded assembly, . . . consisting of the first nobility of Rome and several foreigners of distinction. The company was very brilliant, as usual they mingled together for an hour or so conversing together till the assembly was formed . . .

[April 10.] In the evening we were to a private conversazione at the Baron De Humboldts.[21]

Whether Irving met the famous scientist Alexander von Humboldt at this time is not certain, but he came to know him later in Paris[22] and could say upon hearing of his death, "I met Humboldt often in society in Paris. A very amiable man. A great deal of bonhommie."[23] Irving's nephew recorded concerning Mme de Staël that "*Delphine* was the only one of her productions which Mr. Irving had then read"

284

and that he seemed, "by what he once stated to me, to have been somewhat astounded at the amazing flow of her conversation, and the question upon question with which she plied him."[24] It is unthinkable that Wilhelm von Humboldt, who had lived in Jena as a close friend of Goethe and Schiller, would fail to speak to Mme de Staël, who had just visited Weimar in 1803, of his own experiences there, and surely Irving must have listened carefully. The announcement of the publication of *De L'Allemagne* must have awakened fond memories in Irving and have led him to an early perusal of this important estimate of German culture.

The first tangible evidence of Irving's awareness of the prevailing enthusiasm for German literature is revealed in a biographical sketch which he wrote in 1810 as an introduction to an American edition of Thomas Campbell's poetical works. With the factual details furnished by Campbell's brother Archibald, who was living in New York, Irving made a polite attempt at a critical estimate.[25] He praised "the exquisite little poems" in sentimental platitudes and superficial verbiage but without a semblance of analysis or incisive criticism. Campbell's interest in German letters Irving accepted as characteristic of the age: "About this time the passion for German literature raged in all its violence in Great Britain, and the literary world was completely infatuated by the brilliant absurdities of the German muse . . . The universal enthusiasm with which this new species of literature was admired, awakened in the inquiring mind of our author a desire of studying it at the fountain head." This passion for German literature, which eventually gripped Irving as it had gripped Campbell, sent them both to Germany. Irving quoted further without comment a revealing passage from Campbell's own reactions as recorded in one of his letters from Germany:

My time at Hamburgh was chiefly employed in reading German; and, I am almost ashamed to confess it, for *twelve successive weeks* in the study of Kant's philosophy. I had heard so much of it in Germany, its language was so new to me, and the possibility of its application to so many purposes, in the different theories of science and Belles Lettres, was so constantly maintained, that I began to suspect Kant might be another Bacon, and blamed myself for not perceiving his merit. Distrusting my own imperfect acquaintance with German, I took a disciple of

Kant's for a guide through his philosophy, but found, even with
all his fair play, nothing to reward my labors. His metaphysics
are mere innovations upon the received meaning of words, and
the coinage of new ones, and convey no more instruction than
the writings of Duns Scotus and Thomas Aquinas. In Belles
Lettres, the German language opens a richer field than in their
philosophy. I cannot conceive a more perfect Poet than their favourite Wieland.[26]

Such second-hand information was supplemented in the summer
of 1817 when Irving was living in England and visited Thomas
Campbell at Sydenham. Campbell had first gone to Germany in
1800, hoping "to see Schiller and Goethe—the banks of Rhine—and
the mistress of Werter."[27] Actually, at Hamburg he saw Klopstock
(who impressed Campbell greatly and inspired a poem), found the
material for his best-known lyric "Hohenlinden," and formed a lifelong friendship with August Wilhelm Schlegel. Campbell returned to
Germany again in 1814 and in 1820, visited Heidelberg, and traveled
along the Rhine and down the Danube to Vienna, an itinerary not
unlike the one that Irving was to follow.

Most important among Irving's literary associations in Great
Britain was his staunch friendship with Walter Scott. In 1813 Henry
Brevoort had delighted Scott with a copy of Knickerbocker's *History
of New York*,[28] and when, in August, 1817, Irving was traveling
through Scotland, the land of his forefathers, and he appeared at Abbotsford with a letter of introduction from Thomas Campbell, "the
glorious old minstrel himself came limping to the gate,"[29] took him
by the hand, and promptly made him a member of the household.
Already familiar with much of Scott's work, Irving came now completely under the influence of Scott's romanticism and was definitely
directed toward German letters. In a sense, however, the Gothic
romances of Walpole and Mrs. Radcliffe, the grotesque tales of M.
G. Lewis, and even the writings of his own countryman, Charles
Brockden Brown, had prepared him for the new fashion in literature.
The style of Goldsmith and Sterne, of Addison and Steele, in short
the literary tradition of the eighteenth century under whose tutelage
he developed, had left their mark upon his writing, but the library of
Abbotsford impressed Irving with the untapped resources of German
romance and medieval lore. Scott himself had been struck by the

German fever that had spread through England two decades earlier;[30] he had plunged into the study of German so that by 1794 a certain facility in reading the language was his and he was able to begin to translate Bürger's "Lenore," a ballad that became the rage in England and appeared in five translations in 1796.[31] Scott completed it and "Der wilde Jäger" and published both poems anonymously under the titles "William and Helen," and "The Chase."[32] In 1798 he translated Goethe's *Götz von Berlichingen,* the historical drama which influenced the direction of his own literary development.[33]

When Irving arrived at Abbotsford, Scott was at the beginning of his great creative period, and the identity of the "Great Unknown" was still something of a mystery to the public. He was writing the drama *The Doom of Devorgoil,* in which "the story of the ghostly barber" admittedly is based upon the legend "Stumme Liebe," by Musäus.[34] *The House of Aspen,* written immediately after translating *Götz* though not published until 1827, and the novel *Anne of Geierstein* include the motif of the Vehmgericht, which Goethe's drama had used and which was the subject of Veit Weber's *Die heilige Vehme,* a volume which both Scott and Irving came to own. The vast library at Abbotsford, "well stored with books of romantic fiction in various languages, many of them rare and antiquated,"[35] caught Irving's interest. German literature was well represented, and here Irving probably examined for the first time editions of Goethe, Schiller, Wieland, Bürger, Tieck, Fouqué, and Musäus. Scott's interest in history, legends, and wondrous tales explains the abundance of medieval historical accounts, tales of magic and necromancy, folklore, and fairy stories that he continued to acquire even in later years (as indicated by the dates of publication), when his enthusiasm for German literature was waning. More than three hundred German titles are listed in Scott's library, and the majority of these volumes were on his shelves when Irving visited him.[36] The period of his own German studies already lay behind Scott, but it is fair to assume that he encouraged Irving in his new German interests. Washington Irving's acquisition of the poems of Bürger, a folklore collection of Büsching, some volumes of Goethe, tales and legends collected by Gottschalck, the Grimm brothers, Wieland, Musäus, and Tieck, his purchase of the dramas of Müllner and Schiller, and even of seven volumes of *Sagen der Vorzeit* by Veit Weber, an author to whom Scott acknowledged his own indebtedness in the foreword to *The House of Aspen,* can hardly be coincidental.[37] At Abbotsford Irving's eyes were opened to the vast possibilities in such sources. Scott's conversation strengthened Irving's resolve to write, to study the fascinating history of folklore, and to direct his narrative talent toward themes of the romantic and the miraculous. He had found a sympathetic mentor whose wise talk of legend and writing Irving kept turning over in his mind. No one else had ever spoken to him so understandingly of his lifelong interests.[38]

The trip through Scotland completed, Irving returned to Liverpool and to the office of the family firm of P. and E. Irving, which was tottering on the brink of bankruptcy. Business affairs had grown steadily worse since the autumn of 1815, when Washington Irving, hoping to avert complete disaster, had first participated actively in the management of the firm. Finally, bankruptcy proceedings offered the only way to wind up the tangled financial affairs. In the face of such humiliation and in the vague hope of making himself independent through his pen, Irving began his serious study of German. "At this time he had shut himself up from society, and was studying German, day and night, in the double hope that it would be of service to him, and tend to keep off uncomfortable thoughts; and I have heard him say," noted his nephew, "that while waiting for the examination [in bankruptcy court] he was walking up and down the room, conning over the German verbs."[39] Irving himself wrote: "For months I studied Germany day & night by way of driving off horrid thoughts."[40] He set to work learning the declensions of the German adjective. *Guter Wein, gute Milch, gutes Bier* served as paradigms, and a full page of declensional endings are recorded in his notebook.[41] Rabenhorst's *Pocket Dictionary of the German and English Languages* (1814), Schiller's *Don Carlos* in an English translation (1798) and *Die Räuber* (1816), and Wieland's *Die Abentheuer des Don Sylvio von Rosalva* (1772), which he purchased in Liverpool, are still preserved at Sunnyside and testify to Irving's serious purpose.

The last-mentioned novel reflects a change in technique that had a strong appeal for Irving. Walpole's genre, the Gothic novel emphasizing supernatural elements, had gained ground so rapidly that tales of horror and terror soon became commonplace. Clara Reeve then varied the formula a little and introduced what Walpole called the "tame ghost." She managed at the end of a work to explain away all apparitions, unearthly voices, mystifications, and occult experiences as misapprehensions or coincidences, though often the explanations were as difficult to accept as the mysterious occurrences. Wieland's narrative, also veering from the straight ghost story, with wit and a spirit of enlightenment, struck a satirical note. The subtitle of the English translation (1773), "Reason Triumphant Over Fancy; Exemplified in the Singular Adventures of Don Sylvio de Rosalva. A History in Which Every Marvellous Event Occurs Naturally," emphasized this aspect. Such a description would attract Irving, whose own predilection for the rational explanation of *diablerie* was to be the touchstone of his most successful tales. *Don Quixote* had made fun of the antiquated romance of knighthood and adventurous chivalry; *Don Sylvio* was a satire upon the fairy tales, superstitions, and sentimentalism so popular in Wieland's day.

Never before had Irving worked so hard. The leisurely dabbling in literature which had produced his earlier work, a distillate of satire and good-natured humor reflecting the conscious sophistication of a growing urban center, lay behind him. His brothers' failure provided the necessary economic pressure to advance his literary apprenticeship, and Scott gave him confidence in a firm determination to support himself by his writings. In August, 1817, some nine sketches lay unfinished in his porfolio,[42] but it was almost a full year before he could rid himself of all feelings of despondency and lethargy in order to write his masterpiece, "Rip Van Winkle." This interval was filled with long hours of study to acquire a working knowledge of German. Only his unpublished Notebook gives further hints of this preoccupation and lists a few additional German phrases like *Das schwartze Pferd, Das deutsche Schifferhaus, Auchs bequemes Lager & Mittagessen*,[43] and some book titles, among which Wagener's *Die Gespenster,* Laun's *Erzählungen* (with a price of seven shillings indicated), and Lafontaine's *Kleine Romane* represent German material. Whether these volumes were acquired to advance his reading skill cannot be ascertained, but the entry of a cost price supports this assumption, as any expenditure—even the price of two shillings and six pence for the little red morocco volume that served as the Notebook of 1818—is recorded in it. More easily established is the fact that such reading left no tangible evidence in his own compositions and probably served only as exercise material. But Irving was reading with a purpose and kept his eyes open for any bits of lore that might furnish bone and sinew for a tale. How much Irving was reading about Germany in English publications lies in the realm of conjecture, but some notations in his Notebook of 1818 are significant. The cryptic phrase "light tales in the manner of Wieland," written at a time when Irving had probably read, at least in translation, some of this affable but discursive raconteur, does not necessarily promise great familiarity with the work of this author—Irving's transcription reveals his struggle with the name—but looks more like a reminder to himself to cultivate a similar vein of writing. In the earlier part of this Notebook Irving had made extracts from Riesbeck's *Travels through Germany* that have some bearing on the story of "Rip Van Winkle." (Actually, Riesbeck's work contained enough praise of Wieland to warrant Irving's favorable notation.[44]) By far the most striking extracts are those from the fourteenth travel letter of Riesbeck, dealing with the romantic environs of Salzburg. Here Irving may have found the lodestar that directed him toward "Rip Van Winkle." He carefully copied almost verbatim—though sometimes shortened or paraphrased—the essence of such lore as might serve him later as material for a tale. In the following quotation, entirely from his Notebook, the phrases in parentheses were supplied by Irving to give context and meaning to his citations; the text in italics (mine) is particularly pertinent for the source of the story of "Rip Van Winkle":

Watzman (Mountain in Bavaria where it is said) the Emperor Charles the Great and all his army are confined until Doomsday, (near Saltzburg—a) *cleft of the mountain from whence you hear a dull rumbling like a distant thunder*—probably the mountain has some lake in its bosom.

On a certain day of the year about midnight the Emperor is to be seen with his whole train of ministers & generals going in procession to the cathedral of Saltzburg.—

From the cleft whence the spirit of the great Charles issues to walk by night, the stream precipitates itself with a loud noise and falls in a variety of cascades down the deep and narrow gully which it seems to have dug itself in the hard marble.

I am a lover of mountain scenes. The pulse of nature beats strongly here. Everything discovers more life & energy and emphatically speaks an almighty power at work. The stream which without knowing the path it must pursue, meanders thro the plain, works thro the mountain & grows impetuously in its course, the motions of the clouds, the revolutions of the sky and the peals of thunder are all more strong & animated.

The vallies in the fair season of the year are filled with finer perfumes of flowers & herb than those of the plains. Nature is here more varied & picturesque, (man more vigorous, fanciful, imaginative, meditative).

Wizards whose white beards have grown—ten or 20 times around the table on which they sit sleeping in the mountain— and of hermits a thousand years old who have led stray goat- hunters through subterranean passages and shown them fairy palaces of gold and precious stones.[45]

The bulk of *The Sketch Book,* in which "Rip Van Winkle" first appeared, consists of literary essays in the manner of eighteenth-cen- tury English authors and reflects the style in which Irving had schooled himself, but there is also a new note of romanticism. This concession to the age by the very impressionable New Yorker is at- tributable to a number of influences and literary contacts, not the least of which was his growing acquaintance with German literature. His urbane manner, the dignity and grace of his descriptive writing —humorous yet tinged with a faint touch of good-natured irony or a nostalgic longing for the passing romance of English country life— endeared him at once to readers on both sides of the Atlantic. Ir- ving's success was immediate, first in America and a little later in England: abroad because of the gracious and flattering attitude of an American toward the mother country, at home because of a natural pride in the international success of a native son and also because of the vogue for a genteel and somewhat romanticized approach to life. Today most of the essays are forgotten. They read like pages from the memory books of an ancient past. A few like "Westminster Abbey," "Stratford-on-Avon," or "The Mutability of Literature" have not lost their charm. They can be read with full enjoyment and seem hardly touched by the passage of time; but the artificiality, the dullness and pedantry of "Rural Funerals," of "Roscoe," of "The Pride of the Village" reveal Irving's most serious shortcomings. He was not a great or original talent; he was able to embellish rather than to create. Hence he sought to relieve the monotony of the literary essays filled with bookish lore, assembled at the Athenaeum in Liverpool or at the British Museum in London, with fictional narratives. Irving had neither great inner resources nor a stock of learning to draw on, and was dependent upon literature not only to furnish the necessary stimulation for writing, but actually to yield the materials that could be molded into finished literary products.

Obvious proof of Irving's fortuitous reading as a momentous factor in the composition of *The Sketch Book* is revealed in the numerous quotations, often from almost forgotten Elizabethans, traceable to thirty-seven English writers.[46] Such a study of books, reflected in his notes, included the reading of much contemporary writing, particularly the new literature by Byron, Scott, and Moore.[47] Equally significant were the numerous publications translated or adapted from the popular literature of Germany. Available were *Tales of Wonder, Tales of Terror,* and *The German Museum, or Monthly Repository of the Literature of Germany, the North & the Continent in General* (1800–1801), which attempted to give the British a survey of what was newest in the German language, and translated many tales of Wieland and Musäus.[48]

Irving was well aware of what was being printed, reprinted, and imitated concerning German literature in English books and magazines, but he was also making laborious efforts to find in this foreign literature original stories that might be suitable for his purpose. The opportunities were great and fortune smiled on Irving. His German studies had not been in vain. He found legends and folklore that gave substance to his work and furnished the plots for his best known short stories, a genre acknowledged as an American contribution to literature. "Rip Van Winkle" and "The Legend of Sleepy Hollow" set the pattern for a type of fiction so successful and popular in its appeal that Irving utilized it in his later collections of tales in place of the more conventional literary sketch. However, he never surpassed—in fact never equaled—his initial achievement. These two stories, hailed more than twenty years later as "perhaps the finest pieces of original fictitious writing that this century has produced next to the works of Scott,"[49] have kept *The Sketch Book* alive. Such praise was not uncommon throughout the nineteenth century, and their popularity even today has suffered little when compared to the fate of the bulk of the essays, whose faded charm and bookish flavor are only too apparent. In these two stories Irving achieved something of immortality.

What enhanced the appeal of these stories was their acceptance as original, indigenous literature, reflecting the spirit of early American life. His depiction of the intimate details of the domestic scene, realistically portrayed against an American background, of the local color and atmosphere, done with whimsical humor—elements always characterized as typically native—gave Irving a deserved reputation as the first American man of letters. In England the immediate reaction to the publication of *The Sketch Book* was one of hearty approbation; the laudatory appraisals revealed amazement at "the work of an American, entirely bred and trained in that country . . . , written throughout with the greatest care and accuracy, and worked up to great purity and beauty of diction, on the model of the most elegant and polished of our native writers."[50] Not until after the publication of *Bracebridge Hall* and *Tales of a Traveller* was Irving subjected to frequent criticism for a lack of originality in his writing and for a dependence upon literary materials which he refurbished before publishing as his own. Some inquiring voices were raised and even Irving's most successful story, "Rip Van Winkle," did not completely escape criticism. General legends of enchanted sleep were sometimes mentioned,[51] as were the story of Epimenides as told by Diogenes Laertius,[52] the account of the haunted glen of Thomas the Rhymer, to which Scott had called Irving's attention—"a fine old story, said he, and might be wrought up into a capital tale"[53]—and, most important of all, the Kyffhäuser stories of the Harz Mountains. In reference to these last stories, which are of special significance for this study, Irving found it necessary to defend his position in a footnote at the end of the essay "The Historian," in *Bracebridge Hall*:

> I find that the tale of Rip Van Winkle, given in the Sketch Book, has been discovered by divers writers in magazines, to have been founded on a little German tradition, and the matter has been revealed to the world as if it were a foul instance of plagiarism marvelously brought to light. In a note which follows that tale, I had alluded to the superstition on which it is founded, and I thought a mere allusion was sufficient, as the tradition was so notorious as to be inserted in almost every collection of German legends. I had seen it myself in three. I could

hardly have hoped, therefore, in the present age, when every ghost and goblin story is ransacked, that the origin of the tale would escape discovery. In fact, I had considered popular traditions of the kind as fair foundations for authors of fiction to build upon, and made use of the one in question accordingly. I am not disposed to contest the matter, however, and indeed consider myself so completely overpaid by the public for my trivial performances, that I am content to submit to any deductions, which, in their afterthoughts, they may think proper to make.[54]

Irving had made no claim to originality and had, as he said, indicated his source for "Rip Van Winkle" at the end of his narrative. Here he stated succinctly, before indulging in his customary Knickerbocker flourish of substantiating the veracity of the tale by vowing that he himself even talked with old Rip Van Winkle, that "The foregoing tale, one would suspect, had been suggested to Mr. Knickerbocker by a little German superstition about the Emperor Frederick *der Rothbart,* and the Kypphäuser mountain."[55]

Such similarities in plot were recognized in Irving's own day without much investigation. In 1822 an anonymous author contributed to the American magazine the *Port Folio* a complete translation of "Peter Klaus" and in a brief note identified Büsching as Irving's source and recounted the basic Kyffhäuser legend.[56] In time, the matter was so completely lost sight of that no investigator has referred to it since.

In 1868 Bayard Taylor and in 1883 J. B. Thompson named "Peter Klaus" as Irving's source without, however, revealing and emphasizing the full extent of such indebtedness.[57] The first scholarly investigation was made in Germany (1901) by Professor Sprenger,[58] who printed the text of "Peter Klaus" from Grässe's *Sagenbuch des preussischen Staats,* fully aware that this story was first printed in Otmar's *Volkssagen*[59] in 1800 and is a composite of a series of Kyffhäuser legends. (For that reason, presumably, the Brothers Grimm who included eighteen items from Otmar's twenty-four in their famous *Deutsche Sagen* (1816) did not include "Peter Klaus";[60] it lacked the simplicity of genuine folklore and reflected the technique of a professional narrator.) Sprenger collated the texts of "Rip Van Winkle" and "Peter Klaus" and showed such similarities of phrase and idiom that he clearly established Irving's dependence upon this German source. He listed further German legends of lost herds, mysterious games of nine-pins, and prolonged periods of supernatural sleep which Irving might have known, but erred in believing that Irving's travels through the Harz region took place before the writing of "Rip Van Winkle." Sprenger's article remained practically unknown because it was printed in an annual school report of a German *Gymnasium,* but was discovered by Professor Pochmann in 1930, when he was making a broader study of the German sources in *The Sketch Book.*[61]

Irving had found the story of a simple herdsman who followed his straying goats into a subterranean cave, where he was pressed into service as pin boy in a mysterious game of nine-pins. The man partook of the fragrant wine that was available, and when he awoke he was alone in the meadow, his dog and his herd were gone. Somewhat puzzled and with a feeling of strangeness in an environment that should have been familiar, he returned to his village. Everything had changed: his beard had grown a foot, people whom he had never seen before stared at him, his own hut was dilapidated, and his wife and children had disappeared. Strangers questioned him, but finally he recognized a woman, a former neighbor suddenly grown old and senile. When a young woman with two small children appeared, whose resemblance to his wife startled him, he asked her name and her father's. Then followed the recognition and his sudden realization that he had been gone twenty years.

Irving did more, however, than merely expand the story to four times its original length. With his unique style he provided a picturesque setting of a small Dutch community in the Catskill Mountains. The goatherd of the legend became the good-natured, indolent Rip Van Winkle, beloved by all in the village, a special favorite among the children to whom he was a willing companion and playmate, but hopelessly henpecked at home. His only refuge from the tart temper and the sharp tongue of Dame Van Winkle was the woods, into which he strolled, gun in hand and his faithful dog Wolf at his side, whenever flight from the wrath of his spouse became advisable. Under such circumstances Rip fell into the company of odd-looking personages who, instead of being knights of the Kyffhäuser, were cronies of Hendrick Hudson and lineal descendants of Irving's Knickerbocker clan. The rest of the story followed naturally within the

framework of such a milieu. Rip Van Winkle's return home, his bewilderment at the political changes, his confusion at having lost his
identity and at finding the precise counterpart of his youth standing
before him reveal masterly touches of the narrator's technique. The
final recognition of his son and daughter is skillfully motivated by the
appearance of a young mother whose infant becomes frightened by
his disheveled appearance. She tries to reassure her offspring with a
"hush, Rip, hush you little fool; the old man won't hurt you," and in
a flash he senses the situation. And when he hears that his termagant
wife had burst a blood-vessel in a fit of passion, he can contain himself no longer, and embraces his daughter and her child. "I am your
father!" cried he,—"Young Rip Van Winkle once—old Rip Van
Winkle now!—Does nobody know poor Rip Van Winkle?"

Having accepted Irving's dependence upon Otmar, Pochmann
was somewhat puzzled by the curious reference in the author's note
to "the Emperor Frederick *der Rothbart,* and the Kypphäuser mountain." It seemed a misleading suggestion to direct the reader "to 'Der
verzauberte Kaiser'—which incidentally, is the legend that immediately follows 'Peter Klaus' in Otmar's collection,"[62] but has no immediate bearing upon the plot of "Rip Van Winkle." It is merely the
legend of the great Emperor, his red beard growing through the stone
table, sleeping in his subterranean castle. This version does not even
include the popular motif of the Emperor rousing himself every
hundred years to ask whether ravens still fly on the mountain and,
after an affirmative reply, relapsing into sleep for another century,
awaiting a call to deliver his people from their enemies.

In all essential points "Rip Van Winkle" is the story of Otmar's
"Peter Klaus," but Irving did not use Otmar as his source. He depended upon Büsching's[63] collection of German folklore. This volume of *Volks-Sagen, Märchen und Legenden,* still among the books
at Sunnyside, contains eight main geographic categories subdivided
into eighty-four groups of legends and fairy tales, whereas Otmar
printed only twenty-four separate stories. Both Otmar and Büsching
group "Peter Klaus" and the Kyffhäuser stories among "legends of
the Harz," a designation that Irving used in reference to "Rip Van
Winkle" in a notation among his manuscripts.[64] But only Büsching's
arrangement and sequence of legends explains Irving's notations:
Under section VII, "Sagen und Mährchen vom Harz" (pp. 303–70)
there is a collection of six stories as item 69, entitled "Der Kyff-

häuser." The fourth of these, "Der Ziegenhirt," is the story of "Peter Klaus," the sixth is "Der verzauberte Kaiser," which is again subdivided into four separate stories of Emperor Frederick. Hence it was perfectly logical and proper for Irving to refer to his source for "Rip Van Winkle" as the "little German superstition about the Emperor Frederick *der Rothbart,* and the Kypphäuser mountain." These stories both belong to the same cycle of legends and he had found the Emperor Frederick stories grouped together with the "Peter Klaus" story. His sincere protest against any innuendoes of plagiarism was justified by his awareness of the prevalence of this traditional legendary material. He had seen it in three different collections; precisely which the three were cannot be established, but Otmar, Büsching, an anonymous volume of *Volkssagen* (Eisenach, 1795), Gustav's *Volkssagen* (1806), and Behrens' *Hercynia curiosa* (1712) contain some phases of the Kyffhäuser legends.

The only remaining problem, which can be discussed but hardly solved, pertains to the extent of Irving's knowledge of German at the time he composed "Rip Van Winkle." William Roscoe's translation of "Peter Klaus" was still eight years off.[65] With his limited training in foreign languages, once Irving had determined to learn German it demanded will power and determination to cling to his purpose, but on May 19, 1818, he could write:

> I have been some time past engaged in the study of the German language, and have got so far as to be able to read and *splutter* a little. It is a severe task, and has required hard study; but the rich mine of German literature holds forth abundant reward.[66]

In view of his difficulties with German during his travels on the Continent three years later, some doubt is justified about his familiarity with the idiom, but his claim at this time is modest enough. Excluding the possibility that Irving received some assistance in the matter of translating (he knew the Roscoe family in Liverpool and had probably seen Scott's own copy of Büsching at Abbotsford, or had found a ready-made translation in an out-of-the-way magazine, no longer available), it is fair to assume that his studies had progressed sufficiently far by the summer of 1818, when he was writing "Rip Van Winkle," that with the aid of a dictionary he could make a tolerable translation of simple material. And "Peter Klaus" is written in plain, unadorned, straightforward German. Its vocabulary is simple, the sentence structure easy, the narrative brief and without bombast or syntactical difficulties: the sort of task that might be set today for a freshman in college German. Normally, translating might have been a dull and monotonous chore for Irving, but this time he had both purpose and determination. His brothers had lost only their money in the failure of their business enterprise, but he had lost more. The dark clouds that settled over his usually happy temperament smothered his creative talents. His ability to work gone, his prospects as a writer were dim. His German studies, prosaic and uninspiring in themselves, served at least as an intellectual exercise and filled this barren period. Eventually Washington Irving was aroused from this lethargy and stimulated artistically by Henry Van Wart, who recalled their happy youth in the Sleepy Hollow area with "the oddest characters of the valley, the ridiculous legends and customs, habits, and sayings" of those quaint Dutchmen.[67] Irving's imagination was fired, and suddenly boyhood memories and German legends coalesced. His efforts at language study bore fruit as he fused personal recollections and folklore materials into the story of Rip Van Winkle, his finest tale.

The writing of "The Legend of Sleepy Hollow" followed the pattern of "Rip Van Winkle," and it is also indebted to German literature for much of its plot. Irving had sketched the outline for the story while visiting his sister at Birmingham in the fall of 1818, after hearing his brother-in-law's recollections of his early days at Tarrytown on the Hudson and the story of one Brom Bones, a wild blade who boasted of having once met the devil on a return from a nocturanal frolic.[68] The rest of the descriptive setting followed easily. As in "Rip Van Winkle," it is a romantic and sequestered region, this time along the Hudson, with its inhabitants predominantly descendants of early Dutch settlers. This prosperous rural community, in which Mynheer Van Tassel's comfortable home was situated, was set apart from all other communities of the sort by an abundance of haunted spots and twilight superstitions. In fact it boasted of a very special apparition, the galloping ghost of a Hessian trooper whose head had been carried away by a cannonball during the Revolution—the Headless Horseman of Sleepy Hollow. The happy domestic scene at Baltus Van Tassel's, the contemplated quilting frolic, the schoolhouse of Ichabod Crane, and his luckless wooing of the beautiful Katrina gave the story an American setting so genuine and realistic as to place it, with "Rip Van Winkle," into almost every collection of American short stories; yet the climactic episode of Ichabod Crane's encounter with the Headless Horseman—a typical Knickerbocker caper—is taken directly from a German source. The comic relief that clears the atmosphere of terror and fear, that explains the weird and supernatural events as a simple mad-cap prank, distinguishes this tale from a more serious effort like Burns's "Tam O' Shanter." This parallel has been drawn before and there are external similarities: the haunted church, the romantic pursuit that terminates in or near a stream with a bridge over which, according to the belief of both Tam and Ichabod, fiends may not cross.[69] These similarities, however, do not touch the crux of the source problem. In all likelihood Irving was familiar with the poem of Burns and in a general sense may have drawn upon it, as he no doubt also was aware of the legend of the ruthless huntsman of Bürger's ballad, "Der wilde Jäger," which Scott had translated. But the fantastic adventure at midnight, the headless horseman who threw his detached head at Ichabod's skull, the unexpected denouement that implicates a disguised rival, and the hurled pumpkin, in short, the climax of Ichabod's unhappy adventure, were borrowed by Irving from the fifth of the "Legenden von Rübezahl" in the collection of *Volksmärchen* by Musäus.

Pochmann, in his previously mentioned article,[61] gave convincing citations from the German source, but was unaware of an English translation available to Irving. In 1791 two volumes of *Popular Tales of the Germans,* containing about half the stories in Musäus, had been published anonymously (though the translation is now ascribed to William Beckford, the author of *Vathek*). The second volume included five chapters of Rübezahl legends under the title "Elfin Freaks; or, the seven legends of Number-Nip."[70] This was the first and perhaps the most significant collection of German romances and tales to appear just before popular taste in England created an insatiable demand for German translations or for imitations of this kind of story, encompassing the gruesome, the uncanny, the fantastic, and the horrible. An absurd musical adaptation of the first "Number-Nip" story, presented at the Covent Garden Theatre, October 6, 1819, attests to the popularity of these legends.[71] Irving, the inveterate patron of the theatre, was in London at that time and may have seen it. John Miller, who was Irving's first publisher in England, distributed it. No evidence points toward any translation of Musäus other than the anonymous one available to Irving at this time despite the reference of Walter Scott to works of Musäus, "of which Beddoes made two volumes."[72]

In transferring the episodes in "The Legend of Sleepy Hollow" from the Riesengebirge of Silesia to his own native haunts along the Hudson, Irving repeated the procedure he had used in writing "Rip Van Winkle." He used a setting similar to the original to provide the necessary background of haunted woods, superstitious fears, and spectral apparitions, but converted the adventure of a simple-minded and credulous coachman into a real American tale of local color and native humor.[73] The hair-raising experience of the coachman had served Musäus only as introductory material for one of his fairy tales, tales that delighted eighteenth-century readers because they maintained a kindly though skeptical attitude toward the fanciful qualities of folk legends. He elaborated a mock-serious appraisal of the severed head:

> The examination of the head was committed to the physician. However, without subjecting it to his anatomical knife, he instantly recognized it for an huge hollowed out gourd filled with sand and stones, and worked up into a very grotesque figure, by the addition of a wooden nose, and a long flax beard.[74]

Irving emphasized the nocturnal adventure and concluded the story with a sly Knickerbocker touch. The disillusioning discovery of the shattered pumpkin and Brom Bones's knowing laugh at all references to the unhappy Ichabod reveal Irving's human understanding.

Among the other writings in *The Sketch Book,* the numerous sketches of English life afford a curious blend of fact and fiction. Irving was realizing the dreams of his childhood in observing at first hand historic scenes in the land of his fathers, but he ignored the wretched poverty engendered by the increasing conflict between new industrialism and an established agrarian economy and fixed his mind's eye on the subdued elegance and glamour of the historical past, or on things like the patriarchal setting of a squire's country hall. Here he found England, or at least the England that he sought. He had come to Europe "to escape from the commonplace realities of the present, and lose myself among the shadowy grandeurs of the past,"[75] and he remained faithful to his purpose. The Old World was for him completely a world of romance and enchantment.

"The Spectre Bridegroom," the third of *The Sketch Book* stories indebted to German sources, differs in its setting as well as in its spirit from "Rip Van Winkle" and "The Legend of Sleepy Hollow." Here is a tale based entirely upon literary sources. The background of the story, the romantic scenery of the Odenwald in Germany, the names of places and characters lay completely outside of Irving's experience. Hence it was impossible to give intimate and lifelike portrayals of persons or scenes. Irving had not yet reached the borders of Germany and depended solely upon his imagination or his booklore for the creation of his setting. Therefore he avoided descriptive details and was content to create the impression of familiarity with the environment through a casual use of German phrases. The designation of the great family of Katzenellenbogen (a name that Irving explained with pretended seriousness in a footnote), judicious references to the tender ballads of the *Minnelieder* or the chivalric wonders of the *Heldenbuch*, actual preference for German terms like *Rhein-wein* and *Ferne-wein,* and even the somewhat ill-chosen appellation of *Saus und Braus* to characterize the reception of the distinguished guest, are examples of an effort to create atmosphere. It might be argued that the effort seems studied and forced, that this foreign phrase, conveying the meaning of "riotous living," is inappropriate to characterize the good fellowship and hospitality which are implied here. But the impression created, and certainly borne out by the concluding episodes of the story, argues that Irving was slyly and humorously satirizing not only the romantic and supernatural trappings dear to him and his contemporaries, but also the solemn and ponderous style of the German stories of the time.

The climax of the story is reached in the sudden realization of the wedding company that the pale and gloomy bridegroom, who already had caused annoyance and consternation by his delayed arrival, was leaving without his bride, gravely and precipitously, immediately after the banquet:

> "I must away to Wurtzburg [*sic*] *cathedral*—" "Ay," said the baron, plucking up spirit, "but not until tomorrow—tomorrow you shall take your bride there."
>
> "No! no!" replied the stranger, with tenfold solemnity, "my

engagement is with no bride—the worms! the worms expect me!
I am a dead man—I have been slain by robbers—my body lies
at Wurtzburg—at midnight I am to be buried—the grave is
waiting for me—I must keep my appointment!"

He sprang on his black charger, dashed over the draw-
bridge, and the clattering of his horse's hoofs was lost in the
whistling of the night.

The baron returned to the hall in the utmost consternation,
and related what had passed. The ladies fainted outright, others
sickened at the idea of having banqueted with a spectre. It was
the opinion of some, that this might be the wild huntsman, famous in German legend.[76]

The consternation of the company was surpassed only by the indignation of the baron and the dismay of the bride, widowed even
before she was married; but the return of the ghostly lover two nights
later and the disappearance of the bride the succeeding night, presumably abducted by the goblin and borne away to his tomb, wrung
the full measure of grief and terror from the hearts of the great family of Katzenellenbogen. Preparations for the pursuit of the spectre
bridegroom were being made when the lovers returned and the mystery was solved. The handsome cavalier, suspected of being a spectral apparition, revealed his identity as Sir Herman Von Starkenfaust.
He had originally come to the castle with grievous news: his friend,
whose marriage was to be celebrated, was dead, killed by robbers.
The betrothal had been arranged by the two families and the young
people had not yet met. Sir Herman fell in love with his friend's betrothed at sight, but fearing the hostility of her family, failed to clarify a confused situation. After his unseemly departure from the wedding festivities as a ghost, he returned to woo and win the fair bride.
Fear and laments turned to joy as the old count embraced a substantial son-in-law instead of a wood-demon who promised perchance a
troop of goblin grandchildren. Everyone was happy except one of the
aunts who "was particularly mortified at having her marvelous story
marred, and that the only spectre she had ever seen should turn out a
counterfeit."[77]

In "The Legend of Sleepy Hollow" Irving had explained away
the mystery that had inspired fear and terror in Ichabod Crane in
terms of natural phenomena and had made sly thrusts at the extrava-

gances of the narrative. In "The Spectre Bridegroom" he went a step further. Instead of a facetious twist at the end of the story, which gives a burlesque touch to a Gothic theme, Irving unfolded in mock seriousness an entire story. His whimsical humor and Knickerbocker flourishes constantly reassure the reader, despite an atmosphere of ominous foreboding. Actually what he had written was a parody upon the famous German ballad "Lenore." This poem of August Bürger, first printed in 1773 in the *Göttinger Musenalmanach* for 1774, took England by storm in the nineties and fired Scott's imagination. His translation, or more accurately, adaptation, "William and Helen," was obviously known to Irving. He probably had read some of the other versions also. His reference in "The Spectre Bridegroom" to "the history of the goblin horseman that carried away the fair Leonora; a dreadful story, which has since been put into excellent verse, and is read and believed by all the world,"[78] implies as much since only Stanley, Spencer, and Beresford used the spelling "Leonora."[79] The atmosphere of this dramatic ballad and its haunting melody assured its immediate success in a romantic and sentimental age. "Lenore" relates a folk legend of a brave soldier who falls in battle while his sweetheart vainly awaits his return. Her bitter grief and constant tears allow him no peace; such impious lamentation summons the spirit of her lover from his grave. He returns at night, claims his love, lifts her on his horse, and gallops away. The midnight hour reveals him as a skeleton.

Irving utilized the theme, but in his affable manner avoided any serious implications. The betrothal in his tale had been arranged by the parents. The appearance of Herman Von Starkenfaust in place of the expected but unkown lover proved soul-satisfying. There was no real grief, only consternation and dismay at the sudden disappearance of the ghostlike lover. Such temporary distress was quickly dissipated by the revelation of the true facts, and the playful and romantic mood, interrupted momentarily, could be resumed. The deft touch of a masterly narrator good-naturedly ridiculed the popular love of the grotesque and the supernatural.

In Irving's ghost stories the literary device of the humorous flourish which suddenly reveals the absurdity of the earlier mystification, is almost his trademark. It is also characteristically American. The New World lacked the ancient customs and traditions of Europe, where genuine and long-acclaimed ghosts were a part of the local heritage. Neither castle ruins nor prison vaults were available in America and once the primeval forests were cleared and the frontier pushed back, where was the necessary setting for acceptable tales of horror? The synthetic atmosphere which Irving effectively created had to be sustained by the narrative itself. Irving never intended to write fairy tales or stories of the supernatural, but used the spectral apparatus of these genres to make the reader the dupe of his genial wit.

The extent of Irving's contact with German materials before 1819 and their influence on *The Sketch Book* were virtually unknown when the book appeared, and such direct borrowing was an interesting but not the determining factor in its success. Its favorable reception depended upon the charm of the author's style, the purity and melody of his prose, as well as upon the content. Paradoxically, the stories based on German sources reveal more robust characterization of flesh and blood persons than many of the sketches based on Irving's observations and experiences in England. Irving did not create out of an inner abundance, but needed substance for the spinning of yarns, in which he was a master. Though he was delighted with the variety and richness of German inventions, he was careful to avoid the grotesque absurdities accepted at this time as the hallmark of German fiction. The elegance and ironic didacticism of Musäus, who could express in a playful or even jesting tone sound principles of human behavior, were closer to Irving's own spirit than the historical romances of Veit Weber or the overwrought terror of Grosse. Unfortunately, many of the ephemeral publications of the first two decades of nineteenth-century England have disappeared and only a small proportion of these once popular stories is available for examination. Here and there references to them can be found in collections of folklore still extant, even when not mentioned in Morgan's bibliographical compilation.[80] Irving recorded the price of a volume of Laun's *Erzählungen* in his "Notebook of 1818," at the very time that he was trying to master the German language. How much Irving knew about this prolific and popular Dresden author cannot be demonstrated, but Laun was acknowledged in England as "the historian of ghost-stories, which have really occurred but which have subsequently been capable of rational explanation," and three or four of his stories were published in English by Ackermann about this time.[81] Direct borrowing from German sources has been established in the three best-known stories of *The Sketch Book,* but the more intangible and elusive influence of Irving's wide and varied reading during his residence in England can only be surmised. His determined effort to read German and his eagerness to visit the regions where the folklore originated are perhaps the most acceptable tokens of his awareness of such sources.

The success of *The Sketch Book,* so complete in America, was not immediately duplicated in England. Irving had difficulties in finding a publisher, but once the book appeared, England too succumbed to its musical prose, its quiet humor, and its charming elegance. Murray, after having seen the printed numbers from America, refused at first to undertake its publication: "I do not see that scope in the nature of it which would enable me to make those satisfactory accounts between us, without which I really feel no satisfaction in engaging";[82] Irving was forced to seek help elsewhere. His determination to publish a British edition was intensified by the prospect of an unauthorized republication, a common practice at the time because of inadequate copyright protection. He turned to Scott and inquired whether Mr. Constable might be inclined to become his London publisher. The sincere encouragement of Scott's reply, his generous offer of the editorship of an Edinburgh periodical, and his "earnest recommendation to Constable to enter into the negotiation" came too late to save Irving from another disappointment. Irving "had determined to look to no leading bookseller for a launch, but to throw my work before the public at my own risk, and let it sink or swim according to its merits," a procedure that Scott warned against in another letter as "certainly not the very best way to publish."

The failure of Irving's publisher, J. Miller, after the first volume was put to press and "getting into fair circulation," had dashed any hopes of the successful distribution of *The Sketch Book* in England, when the intercession of Scott, now Sir Walter, saved the day. He prevailed upon Murray to take over. So the "Prince of Booksellers,"[83] as Irving called Murray a few years later, became his publisher, and the prestige of this firm and the support of friendly critics launched Irving's success abroad. Whereas *Salmagundi* amused and delighted only a small coterie of kindred spirits in New York and *A History of New York* gave Irving prestige at home as a distinguished American writer, *The Sketch Book* made Irving famous in England as well as in America. In fact his fame and popularity spread rapidly to the

Continent so that three years later French and German translations of his works greeted his eyes in the bookshops of Paris, Leipzig, and Dresden.

After a year's sojourn in France, Irving, intending to strengthen his reputation as a writer, began another series of sketches that eventually constituted *Bracebridge Hall*. It was a less spontaneous effort than *The Sketch Book*. Irving wrote incessantly without too clear a concept or a specific plan in mind, and finished the work only under the constant prodding of an impatient publisher. Thomas Moore, who was enjoying his enforced residence in Paris and knew all distinguished British visitors who crowded that metropolis after travel on the Continent had become possible again, had given Irving two practical suggestions: the idea for "the description of the booksellers' dinner,"[84] which furnished the underlying idea of "Buckthorne," a story that was expanded, rewritten, and finally included in *Tales of a Traveller,* and the hint to take "the characters in his 'Christmas Essay,' Master Simon, etc. etc., for the purpose of making a slight thread of a story on which to string his remarks and sketches of human feelings."[85] Irving avidly seized upon this suggestion for the skeletal structure of the new volume in order to give continuity to his sketches "of English house-keeping in something like the genuine old style."[86] Yet he found it difficult to keep such a long story alive without introducing separate narratives, somewhat in the manner of his most successful tales of *The Sketch Book*. Hence he resorted to the device of storytelling, "a good old-fashioned fireside amusement," as the Squire of the Hall termed it, in order to fill the two volumes expected by Murray.

Irving even attempted to recapture some of the grotesque humor and quaint background of the early Dutch settlements in New York by introducing a manuscript tale from the papers of the late Mr. Diedrich Knickerbocker, "Dolph Heyliger." Here Irving may have drawn again upon some German sources for part of his plot. A volume of English sketches hardly afforded many opportunities for utilizing legendary materials, ghosts and goblins, or ghoulish superstitions. Only one general reference occurs, a reference to "the wild huntsman, the favorite goblin in German tales,"[87] who had figured so prominently in "The Spectre Bridegroom." "Dolph Heyliger" boasts of a mysterious and learned Dr. Knipperhaus, who "had a secret belief in ghosts, having passed the early part of his life in a country where they particularly abound; and indeed the story went, that, when a boy he had once seen the devil upon the Harz Mountains in Germany,"[88] and actually owned a haunted farmhouse a few miles from town. There are references to "pistols loaded with silver bullets," reminiscent of the legend of *Der Freischütz*, and to "a spectre without a head."[89] The real kernel of the somewhat tedious and drawn-out story is the search for the buried treasure, which Dolph finally locates in the old well near the haunted house. To gain this prize Dolph had received on three successive nights a visitation from a ghostly Dutchman, had taken a journey up the Hudson under the influence of this apparition, was knocked overboard in a storm, and finally saw the phantom in a dream point out near the haunted house the well that held the treasure. This parallels rather closely the story of the man who shaved and is shaved by a ghost: The ghost directs him to someone who relates a dream in which he recognizes the location of a treasure in his father's garden. All this and a love story of the silent lover are related by Musäus in "Stumme Liebe," included in the collection of *Volksmärchen der Deutschen*.

The question of whether Irving might have read this hundred-page story in the original German, with all the elegance and stylistic locutions that Musäus delighted in, can be answered negatively. Even after his protracted residence in Germany Irving called upon his friends to read and translate this author for him.[90] "Stumme Liebe" was not included in *Popular Tales of the Germans* (1791) and was assumed unavailable in English translation ("The Spectre Barber") until 1823, when it appeared in the volume of *Popular Tales and Romances of the Northern Nations*—obviously too late for Irving's purpose. However, an examination of many tawdry and worthless collections of horror stories, ephemeral successes in England at this time, disclosed a volume of *Tales of the Dead*[91] which includes "The Spectre Barber" in a shortened and somewhat mutilated version. The essential elements of the plot are here, and it is easier to assume that Irving knew this source than to credit him with reading the original in German or even in French, where the title was the precise translation, "L'Amour Muet," hardly likely to attract a devotee of spectral research.

This collection of *Tales of the Dead* held much interest for Irving and his contemporaries. According to the "Advertisement" of the English edition, "the first four tales in this collection, and the last, are imitated from a small French work, which professes to be translated from the German."[92] Of these not only "The Spectre Barber" but "The Death Bride" and "The Family Portraits" bear some resemblance to stories of Washington Irving. The last of these will be discussed in connection with *Tales of a Traveller.* "The Death Bride" shows similarities to "The Spectre Bridegroom" in title and content, but it is the bride who assumes the form of a ghost. What lends real weight to the argument that Irving had read *Tales of the Dead* in England is the fact that the preface refers to Wagener's *Die Gespenster. Kurze Erzählungen aus dem Reiche der Wahrheit,* which "endeavors to explain apparitions by attributing them to natural causes."[93] This title was recorded by Irving in his Notebook of 1818 and must have attracted his attention particularly, as he favored natural explanations for his ghostly narratives. The notation was obviously for the future, one of the many isolated titles scattered throughout his journals and notebooks, recorded for use when his German studies had advanced.

The collection of *Tales of the Dead* must have been easily accessible, and Irving was not alone in his enthusiasm for such stories. Curiously enough, this identical volume in its French original[94] was read breathlessly by Byron, the Shelleys, and Polidori on June 18, 1816, at the Maison Chapuis on the shore of Lake Geneva,[95] and stimulated Mary Wollstonecraft Shelley to write her *Frankenstein.* She described this occasion and testified to the profound impression these stories made:

> But it proved a wet, uncongenial summer, and incessant rain often confined us for days to the house. Some volumes of ghost stories, translated from the German into French, fell into our hands. There was the story of the Inconstant Lover, who, when he thought to clasp the bride to whom he had pledged his vows, found himself in the arms of the pale ghost of her whom he had deserted. There was the tale of the sinful founder of his race, whose miserable doom it was to bestow the kiss of death on all the younger sons of his fated house, just when they reached the age of promise. His gigantic shadowy form, clothed, like the ghost of Hamlet, in complete armour, but with the beaver up, was seen at midnight, by the moon's fitful beams, to advance slowly along the gloomy avenue. The shape was lost beneath the

shadow of the castle walls; but soon a gate swung back, a step was heard, the door of the chamber opened, and he advanced to the couch of the blooming youths, cradled in healthy sleep. Eternal sorrow sat upon his face as he bent down and kissed the forehead of the boys, who from that hour withered like flowers snapt upon the stalk. I have not seen these stories since then, but their incidents are as fresh in mind as if I had read them yesterday. "We will each write a ghost story," said Byron; and his proposition was acceded to.[96]

Today the volume seems dull and long-winded, but our taste has changed, and today *Bracebridge Hall* also seems lifeless. With one or two exceptions the characters are pale, shadowy figures that flit across the pages without coming to life. Irving's easy, good-natured humor becomes rather pedestrian and a little forced as it is spread over the many pages of a languishing narrative. There is no brilliance or sparkling wit, but much garrulity. Irving's contemporary critics were kinder. To be sure some reviewers recognized that Irving lived in the past rather than the present; one declared that "the great blemish of the work *Bracebridge Hall,* indeed is, that it is drawn not from life, but from musty volumes";[97] another that "no such beings exist now a days";[98] another that "the characters seem to dawdle and hang about without a purpose, while the title of the chapter is being fulfilled."[99] But "the quiet, gentle enthusiasm inspired by the modest English landscape in a genuine lover of nature"[100] and "the singular sweetness of the composition, and the mildness of the sentiments,"[101] to quote the influential Jeffrey, endeared the work to the English public. The British themselves were sentimental in their affection for their landscape, and of course Irving had the benefit of a friendly press. The beauty of his language and the cadence of his prose, the gentleness and urbanity of his own person achieved a tribute to the charm of English countryside and to the dignity of the traditions that remained forever Irving's delight. His own words are the best testimony:

> Having been born and brought up in a new country, yet educated from early infancy in the literature of an old one, my mind was early filled with historical and poetical associations, connected with places, and manners, and customs of Europe, but

which could rarely be applied to those of my own country. To a mind thus peculiarly prepared, the most ordinary objects and scenes, on arriving in Europe, are full of strange matter and interesting novelty. England is as classic ground to an American, as Italy is to an Englishman; and old London teems with as much historical association as mighty Rome. . . .

I thought I never could be sated with the sweetness and freshness of a country so completely carpeted with verdure; where every air breathed of the balmy pasture, and the honeysuckle hedge. I was continually coming upon some little document of poetry in the blossomed hawthorn, the daisy, the cowslip, the primrose, or some other simple object that has received a supernatural value from the muse. The first time that I heard the song of the nightingale, I was intoxicated more by the delicious crowd of remembered associations than by the melody of its notes; and I shall never forget the thrill of ecstasy with which I first saw the lark rise, almost from beneath my feet, and wing its musical flight up into the morning sky.[102]

[1]*Washington Irving and the Storrows. Letters from England and the Continent 1821–1828*, ed. S. T. Williams (Cambridge, Mass., 1933), p. 15.

[2]C. R. Leslie, *Autobiographical Recollections* (Boston, 1860), p. 230.

[3]*Letters of Washington Irving to Henry Brevoort,* ed. G. S. Hellman (New York, 1918), pp. 385f.

[4]P. M. Irving, *The Life and Letters of Washington Irving* (New York, 1863), II, 79. (Cited as *Life and Letters*.)

[5]*Ibid.,* p. 90.

[6]E.g., this frank statement in a letter to Brevoort *(op. cit.,* p. 356): "I have, by patient & persevering labour of my most uncertain pen, & by catching the gleams of sunshine in my cloudy mind, managed to open to myself an avenue to some degree of profit & reputation. I value it the more highly because it is entirely independent and self created; and I must use my best endeavours to turn it to account."

[7]See the various sketches in O. W. Long, *Literary Pioneers* (Cambridge, Mass., 1935).

[8]A full realization of his shortcomings was clearly indicated by his urgent plea to Bancroft in Paris in 1821 "to lay aside all cares, and only be bent on laying a stock of knowledge for future application . . . scramble to it; get at it as you can; but be sure to get at it . . . The time will soon come, when it will be too late for these things." M. A. De Wolfe Howe, *The Life and Letters of George Bancroft* (New York, 1908), I, 107.

[9]S. T. Williams, *The Life of Washington Irving* (New York, 1935), I, 15. (Cited as *The Life.*)

[10]*Ibid.*, p. 37.

[11]F. H. Wilkens, *Early Influence of German Literature in America* (Philadelphia, 1900), pp. 12–31.

[12]See S. H. Goodnight, "German Literature in American Magazines prior to 1846," *Bulletin of University of Wisconsin, Philology and Literature Series,* IV (1908), 115–23.

[13]*The Life,* I, 136.

[14]*Ibid.*, p. 138.

[15]*Analectic Magazine,* II (Nov., 1813), 419.

[16]V. A. Stockley, *German Literature as Known in England 1750–1830* (London, 1929), p. 77.

[17]Wilkens, *op. cit.,* pp. 92–93.

[18]Irving's Notebook of 1818 (unpubl.; in New York Public Library).

[19]*Analectic Magazine,* III (Apr., 1814), 297ff. Among the many names and titles mentioned are the following: Hagedorn, Weiss, Gellert, Bodmer, Klopstock, Wieland, Lessing, Werner, Gerstenberg, Illinger [Klinger], Tieck, Oechlenschläger [*sic*], J. P. Richter, William and Frederic Schlegel, Goethe, Schiller; *Robbers, Leonora, Oberon, Wallenstein, Nathan, Iphigenia in Tauris, Goetz of Berlichenzen* [*sic*], *Niebelungen, Mary Stuart, Joan of Arc, William Tell, Torquato Tasso,* and *Faust.*

[20]The English ed. of three volumes (London: J. Murray, 1813) was followed by an American one: *Germany* by the Baroness Staël-Holstein. Translated from the French. (New York: Eastburn, Kirk & Co., 1814).

[21]*Notes and Journal of Travel in Europe 1804–1805,* ed. W. P. Trent (New York, 1921), III, 38, 59, 65, 68.

[22]See *Journal of Washington Irving (1823–1824),* ed. S. T. Williams (Cambridge, Mass., 1931), pp. 63, 163; and *The Journals of Washington Irving* (from July, 1815, to July, 1842), eds. W. P. Trent and G. S. Hellman (Boston, 1919), II, 145, 150.

[23]*Life and Letters,* IV, 285.

[24]*Ibid.*, I, 136–37.

[25]See letter of Washington Irving to Harper and Brothers:

"My acquaintance with Campbell commenced in, I think, 1810, through his brother, Archibald, a most amiable, modest, and intelligent man, but more of a mathematician than a poet. He resided at that time in New York, and had received from his brother a manuscript copy of 'O'Connor's Child; or, The Flower of Love Lies Bleeding,' for which he was desirous of finding a purchaser among the American publishers. I negotiated the matter for him with a publishing house in Philadelphia, which offered a certain sum for the poem, provided I would write a biographical sketch of the author to be prefixed to a volume containing all his poetical works. To secure a good price for the poet, I wrote the sketch, being furnished with facts by his brother; it was done, however, in great haste, when I was 'not in the vein' and, of course, was very slight and imperfect. It served, however, to put me at once on a friendly footing with Campbell, so that, when I met him for the first time a few years subsequently in England, he received me as an old friend." In William Beattie, *Life and Letters of Thomas Campbell* (New York, 1855), I, xi–xii. Reprinted at the end of "Thomas Campbell" in *The Works of Washington Irving,* Hudson ed. (New York, 1882), XVII, 166–67. (Cited as *Works.*)

[26]*The Poetical Works of Thomas Campbell* (Baltimore, 1810), pp. xix–xxii. When Irving revised this biographical sketch into the essay "Thomas Campbell" and printed it in the *Analectic Magazine* two years later, he eliminated these naive, absurdly uncritical comments on German philosophy and restricted himself to a brief noncommittal reference to Campbell's German contacts. See *Analectic Magazine,* V (Mar., 1815), 234–50. The essay was reprinted first with other biographical sketches in *Spanish Papers* (New York, 1866). Also see *Works,* XVII, 141–65. The reference to German philosophy in Campbell's letter was printed later by his biographer (See Beattie, *op. cit.,* I, 283).

[27]Beattie, *op. cit.,* I, 233. See also D. B. Shumway, "Thomas Campbell and Germany," in *Schelling Anniversary Papers* (New York, 1923), pp. 233–61.

[28]*Life and Letters,* I, 240.

[29]Irving to his brother Peter. *Ibid.,* p. 381.

[30]James Skene, *Memories of Sir Walter Scott,* ed. Basil Thomson (London, 1909), p. 3: ". . . in his quest for a supply to feed the craving for German romance that seized him, Sir Walter learned that I had recently returned from a several years' residence at school in Germany, and that I had brought a collection of the best authors along with me, which he, of course, became desirous to obtain access to . . . However, the objects of his research were there before him in a goodly range of German volumes, comprehending the works of most of the German authors then in repute."

[31]F. W. Stokoe, *German Influence in the English Romantic Period, 1788–1818, with Special Reference to Scott, Coleridge, Shelley and Byron* (Cambridge, Eng., 1926), pp. 48, 65. For a comprehensive survey of Scott's literary and personal relations with Germany see John Koch, "Sir Walter

Scotts Beziehungen zu Deutschland," *Germanisch-Romanische Monatsschrift,* XV (1927), 36–46, 117–41.

[32]*Two Ballads, from the German of Gottfried Augustus Bürger.* (Edinburgh, 1796). The second ed. of 1807 gave Scott's name.

[33]See [R. P. Gillies], "Recollections of Sir Walter Scott," *Fraser's Magazine,* XII (Sept., 1835), 265: " . . . *Goetz of Berlichingen* had more influence in disposing his mind for the course which he afterwards pursued than any other production, either foreign or domestic, which fell his way."

[34]Scott acknowledged his source in his preface (*The Poetical Works of Sir Walter Scott, Bart.,* XII (1834), p. 117): "The story of the Ghostly Barber is told in many countries; but the best narrative founded on the passage, is the tale called Stummé Liebé [*sic*], among the legends of Musaeus."

[35]Irving in his essay "Abbotsford," *Works,* VIII, 281.

[36]See *Catalogue of the Library at Abbotsford* (Edinburgh, 1838), particularly pp. 38–55.

[37]See Catalogue of Washington Irving's German books at Sunnyside, Appendix, pp. 199–202. [This long list not included here. *Ed.*]

[38]*The Life,* I, 162.

[39]P. M. Irving in *Life and Letters,* I, 395f.

[40]Manuscript fragment at Yale University, printed in *The Life,* II, 260.

[41]Notebook of 1818.

[42]*The Life,* I, 168.

[43]Notebook of 1818. The German phrases sound like designations of inns that he recorded while reading.

[44]J. K. Riesbeck, *Travels through Germany,* tr. P. H. Maty (London, 1787), II, 208f.: "Wieland, is, without a doubt, the first of all the German writers. No writer, Lessing alone excepted, unites so much study with so much genius as he does. He has not only formed and fixed his taste on a thorough acquaintance with the beauties of the ancient writers, but possesses also all the literature of France, Italy, and England. His works are not like the rhapsodies of the modern German poetasters, but have the true smack of art. Even the most fugitive trifles that fall from his playful and humorous pen, bespeak a workman who is thorough master of his business, and has a manner of his own. . . . None of the German writers know so well how to please the public as Wieland does. He is most fruitful in the invention of trifles, in order to make his journal, which is good as any other we have, sell."

[45]Notebook of 1818. Quoted from Riesbeck, *op. cit.,* I, 140–42; 160f. The legend of the sleeping monarch or *Kaisersage,* here referring to Charlemagne, is generally related to Frederick Barbarossa, Frederick II, Otto I, or Otto II, and at times even to Charles V.

[46]Ferdinand Künzig, *Washington Irving und seine Beziehungen zur englischen Literatur des 18. Jahrhunderts* (Heidelberg, 1911), pp. 10–12.

[47]*The Life*, I, 179.

[48]Stockley, *op. cit.*, pp. 324–28.

[49]*Chambers's Cyclopaedia of English Literature*, quoted in *Life and Letters*, I, 418.

[50]Francis Jeffrey, in *Edinburgh Review*, XXXIV (Aug., 1820), 160, a sixteen-page review that reprinted almost half of "Rip Van Winkle."

[51]Legends of enchanted sleep are common enough in all European literatures and are found even in Oriental lore. The Japanese version of Rip Van Winkle is of Chinese origin and tells of Lu-wen, a pious woodcutter who lost his way and watched two lovely ladies play checkers. Returning to his village as a wrinkled old man, he finds only his descendants in the seventh generation. A stranger in their midst, he returns to the mountain to find solace in the company of those spirits. In W. E. Griffis, *The Mikado's Empire* (New York, 1895), 8th ed., pp. 502f.

[52]*Blackwood's Edinburgh Magazine*, IX (May, 1821), 225.

[53]"Abbotsford," *Works*, VIII, 298.

[54]Printed in the London ed. (1822), II, 230, from which it was translated for the German ed., Washington Irving's *Sämmtliche Werke* (Frankfurt, 1826–37), XVII, 94–95. This note is missing in the first American edition of 1822, but a revised edition of the same year (in New York Public Library) prints the note in Vol. II, p. 187.

[55]*Works*, XIX, 74. The spellings Kypphäuser or Kipphäuser occur around 1800 as variants of the usual Kyffhäuser.

[56]"Peter Klaus. The Legend of the Goatherd. Rip Van Winkle," *Port Folio, and New York Monthly Magazine*, XIV (Aug. 1822), 144–47.

[57]B. Taylor, "By-Ways of Europe," *Atlantic Monthly*, XXI (May, 1868), 623; J. B. Thompson, "The Genesis of the Rip Van Winkle Legend, *Harper's New Monthly Magazine*, LXVII (Sept. 1883), 617–22.

[58]R. Sprenger, "Über die Quelle von W. Irvings Rip Van Winkle," *Programm des mit Realabteilungen in Tertia und Sekunda verbundenen Progymnasiums zu Northeim, Nr. 344* (Northeim, 1901), 3–14.

[59][J. C. C. Nachtigal] *Volcks-Sagen nacherzählt von Otmar* (Bremen, 1800), pp. 153–58.

[60]F. L. Pattee in *The Development of the American Short Story* (New York, 1923), p. 11, n. 1, speaks of "Grimm's tale 'Peter Klaus, the Goatherd'," but is definitely in error.

In the foreword to *Deutsche Sagen* (Berlin, 1818), pp. xviif, the Brothers Grimm paid tribute to Otmar: "In Absicht auf Treue und Frische verdient Otmar's Sagen [Sammlung] der Harzsagen so viel Lob, dass dieses den Tadel der hin und wieder aufgesetzen unnöthigen Bräme und Stielverzierung zudeckt. Viele sind aber auch selbst den Worten nach untadelhaft und man darf ihnen trauen." Proof of their recognition of Otmar's importance as a collector of folklore is found in the credit line of their legends, numbered (Vol. I) 153–56, 190, 201, 215, 228, 304, 305, 311, 312, 320, 326, 328, 355; (Vol. II) 575 and 583.

[61]H. A. Pochmann, "Irving's German Sources in *The Sketch Book*," *Studies in Philology*, XXVII (1930), 477–507.

[62]*Ibid.*, p. 496.

[63]J. G. Büsching, *Volks-Sagen, Märchen und Legenden* (Leipzig, 1812), pp. 327–31.

[64]Unpublished MS which was in the possession of the late Dr. Roderick Terry. See *The Life*, I, 183, n. 93.

[65]William Roscoe, *The German Novelists* (London, 1826), II, 55–60.

[66]*Letters of Irving to Brevoort*, pp. 286f.

[67]E. Burritt, "Birthplace of Rip Van Winkle" *Packard's Monthly*, n. s., I (Nov., 1869), 333.

[68]*Life and Letters*, I, 448.

[69]O. S. Coad, "The Gothic Element in American Literature," *Journal of English and Germanic Philology*, XXIV (1925), 84.

[70]J. K. A. Musäus, *Volksmährchen der Deutschen* (Gotha, 1782–87); a new edition stylistically revised by C. M. Wieland (Gotha, 1804–5) became very popular. Recently E. L. Brooks has also called attention to the Beckford translation. See "A Note on Irving's Sources," American Literature, XXV (May, 1953), 229f.

[71][William Coleman] *The Gnome-King; or, the Giant Mountains,* a dramatic legend in two acts (London, 1819).

[72]Scott wrote to his friend Daniel Terry (Jan. 9, 1823) in reply to a query from a bookseller: "Unquestionably I know many interesting works of the kind he mentions, which might be translated from the German:—almost all those of Musaeus, of which Beddoes made two volumes, and which are admirably written; many of La Motte Fouqué; several from the collection bearing the assumed name of Beit [sic] Weber." In J. G. Lockhart, *Memoirs of Sir Walter Scott* (London, 1900), IV, 78.

Dr. Thomas Beddoes, father of the poet, "was master of the French, Italian, Spanish and German languages; with the polite and the scientific authors in the last, in particular, he was equally conversant, and his library contained a rich collection of works of both descriptions." J. E. Stock, *Memoirs of the Life of Thomas Beddoes, M.D. with an analytical account of his writings* (London, 1811), p. 409. No reference to such a translation is made by Stock. Professor H. W. Donner, whose authoritative works on Thomas Beddoes, the poet, have utilized all manuscript materials available, has kindly checked this matter for me and found no evidence of such a translation.

As Beckford's work was published anonymously and as Dr. Beddoes was known to be keenly interested in foreign literature, he may have been looked upon as the possible translator, unless Scott, writing thirty years after the appearance of these volumes, simply confused the somewhat similar names.

[79]The following parallel passages from Musäus and then Irving reveal the actual borrowing:

"All the stories of Number-Nip, which he had formerly devoured with such eager attention, came rushing at once into his mind, now he was traversing the stage where these adventures had happened, and he could have wished with all his soul never to have heard a syllable about the matter. . . . From time to time he cast a timid look on every side: often sweeping, with his half closed eyes, the two-and-thirty points of the compass in less than a minute's time. When he espied any suspicious appearance, a cold shudder ran down his back, and his hair grew stiff like bristles.

"Peeping up cautiously he saw, to his utter confusion, stalking on about a stone's throw before the coach, a jet-black figure, of a size exceeding that of man, crowned with a broad Spanish tippet; but what was the most suspicious circumstance in its whole appearance, was its being without an head. If the coach halted, the figure also halted; and when the postilion drove on, it proceeded also . . . It was now plain to be seen that John's eye had taken a false measure—the man on foot had an head as well as other people, only he did not wear it, according to the usual fashion, between his shoulders, but carried it under his arm, just as if it had been a lap-dog. . . . John . . . began, in the anguish of his heart, the salutation appointed to be addressed to all good spirits, *Angels and Ministers* . . . but, before he could speak it out, the monster took his head from under his arm, and hurled it at John: it struck him right on the forehead, and the blow was so severe that he tumbled headlong from the box over the forewheel, and at the same time the postilion was stretched in the dust by a severe stroke with a club." *Popular Tales of the Germans* (London, 1791), II, 143–51.

"All the stories of ghosts and goblins that he had heard in the afternoon, now came crowding upon his recollection. The night grew darker and darker; the stars seemed to sink deeper in the sky, and driving clouds occasionally hid them from his sight. He had never felt so lonely and dismal. He was, moreover, approaching the very place where many of the scenes of the ghost stories had been laid . . . As Ichabod approached this fearful tree, he began to whistle. . . . Suddenly he heard a groan—his teeth chattered and his knees smote against the saddle . . . he beheld something huge, misshapen, black and towering. It stirred not, but seemed gathered up in the gloom, like some gigantic monster ready to spring upong the traveller.

"The hair of the affrighted pedagogue rose upon his head with terror . . .

"He appeared to be a horseman of large dimensions, and mounted on a black horse of powerful frame. . . . Ichabod, who had no relish for this strange midnight companion, and bethought himself of the adventure of Brom

Bones with the Galloping Hessian, now quickened his steed, in hopes of leaving him behind. The stranger, however, quickened his horse to an equal pace. Ichabod pulled up, and fell into a walk, thinking to lag behind—the other did the same. . . . On mounting a rising ground, which brought the figure of his fellow-traveller in relief against the sky, gigantic in height, and muffled in a cloak, Ichabod was horror-struck, on perceiving that he was headless!—but his horror was still more increased, on observing that the head, which should have rested on his shoulders, was carried before him on the pommel of the saddle: his terror rose to desperation. . . . Just then he saw the goblin rising in his stirrups, and in the very act of hurling his head at him. Ichabod endeavored to dodge the horrible missile, but too late. It encountered his cranium with a tremendous crash—he was tumbled headlong into the dust, and Gunpowder, the black steed, and the goblin rider, passed by like a whirlwind." *Works*, XIX, 510–16.

[74]*Popular Tales of the Germans*, II, 165.

[75]"The Author's Account of Himself," *Works*, XIX, 17.

[76]*Ibid.*, pp. 230–31.

[77]*Ibid.*, p. 237.

[78]*Ibid.*, p. 229.

[79]For a full treatment, see A. Brandl, "Lenore in England," in Erich Schmidt, *Charakteristiken* (Berlin, 1886), pp. 244–48.

[80]B. Q. Morgan, *A Critical Bibliography of German Literature in English Translation 1481–1927* (Stanford University, 1938).

[81]*Popular Tales and Romances of the Northern Nations.* (London, 1823), p. xi.

[82]"Preface to the Revised Edition," *The Sketch Book, Works*, XIX, 6.

[83]*Ibid.*, pp. 11ff.

[84]*Memoirs, Journal and Correspondence of Thomas Moore*, ed. Lord John Russell (London, 1853), III, 252f.

[85]*Ibid.*, p. 211.

[86]*Bracebridge Hall, Works*, IV, 19.

[87]*Ibid.*, p. 410.

[88]*Ibid.*, p. 468.

[89]*Ibid.*, p. 480.

[90]*Life and Letters*, IV, 369.

[91]*Tales of the Dead.* Principally translated from the French [by Mrs. Sarah Utterson] (London, 1813).

[92]*Ibid.*, p. ii.

[93]*Ibid.*, pp. vif.

317

[94]*Fantasmagoriana, ou recueil d'histoires d'apparitions de spectres, revenans, fantômes etc.; traduit de l'Allemand, par un amateur* [J. B. B. Eyriès] (Paris, 1812), 2 vols.

[95]Edward Dowden, *The Life of Percy Bysshe Shelley* (London, 1886), II, 33: "During a few days of uncongenial weather, which confined them to the house, some volumes of ghost stories, *Fantasmagoriana* . . . a collection translated into French from the German—fell into their hands, and its perusal probably excited and overstrained Shelley's imagination."

[96]Mrs. Julian Marshall, *The Life and Letters of Mary Wollstonecraft Shelley* (London, 1889), I, 139f.

[97]*Blackwood's Edinburgh Magazine,* XI (June, 1822), 689.

[98]*Gentleman's Magazine,* LXXXXII (July, 1822), 54.

[99]*London Magazine,* VI (Nov., 1822), 438.

[100]*Eclectic Review,* XIX (Mar., 1823), 236.

[101]*Edinburgh Review,* XXXVII (Nov., 1822), 338.

[102]*Bracebridge Hall, Works,* IV, 10ff.

From
"Author and Publisher"

BY WILLIAM CHARVAT

William Charvat (1905–1966), after a Ph.D. from the University of Pennsylvania in 1933 and teaching there and at New York University, joined the faculty of Ohio State in 1944, to remain until his too early death. He was research fellow at the Huntington Library in 1943, a Guggenheim fellow in 1943–1944, and contributed "Literature as Business" to the *Literary History of the United States* (1948). Professor Charvat's publications included *American Critical Thought, 1810–1835* (1936) and works on W. H. Prescott, and the publishing house of Ticknor and Fields. He was deeply involved in the opening field of scholarship on the economics of authorship. It is from his key work there, *Literary Publishing in America, 1790–1850* (1959), that this part of Chapter 2 is taken, a factual discussion concerning among others Irving as writer-and-businessman.

The first era of successful professional authorship in America began in the years 1819 to 1821 with the publication of Irving's *Sketch Book* and James Fenimore Cooper's *The Spy*. The twenty years that followed were notable for a tremendous expansion of the national economy. Except for minor recessions in the late twenties and in 1834 and 1837, which the book trade duly reflected,[1] it was, to use Irving's phrase, a time of "unexampled prosperity." Equally unexampled in the history of the profession were Irving's income of $23,500 in the year 1829—all from books—and Cooper's average of $6,500 a year in the 1820's. No first-rate author of the brilliant fifties—the years of the American renaissance—came even close to such affluence. The reasons are many; for the major ones we must look into the book trade economy and the changes in it between 1820 and 1850.

On December 19, 1819, Mathew Carey of Philadelphia—publisher, bookseller, and chief jobber for the southern states, sent what was probably, in America, a record-breaking order for a purely literary work. It was for four hundred copies of the fifth number of *The Sketch Book:* "Send 150 by Swiftsure Stage and the remainder by Mercantile Line." Number five was a slim pamphlet which sold for what was also probably a record-breaking price—seventy-five cents. The order was the climax of a controversy. It was sent to Ebenezer Irving in New York (Washington was in England) rather than to the printer because the Irvings had paid for the manufacture of *The Sketch Book* and therefore were in complete control of sales and discount policy. Orders for the first American classic had been coming in to Carey from bookstores throughout the South and Middle States, but he had been unwilling to fill them. A Philadelphia rival, Moses Thomas, had had a monopoly on all sales in the area, and Carey had had to pay him sixty-five and one-half cents (a discount of one-sixth) for a book which he himself had to sell to country booksellers for sixty cents. But because Thomas was close to insolvency, Carey had managed to break his monopoly by appealing to C. S. Van Winkle, the New York printer of the work, who interceded with Ebenezer. As a result, Carey was given the usual one-fourth discount, four-fifths of which he gave up on those copies which he sold to his retailers. It was a small profit for a wholesaler, but he had to supply the booksellers' demand, for many of them bought their entire stock of books from him.

Reconstructing the account from such correspondence as survives,[2] one finds that the score on *Sketch Book No. 5* was somewhat as follows:

Printing	26½ cents	35 per cent
Discount	18¾ "	25 " "
(Retailer 20%		
Wholesaler 5%)		
Profit (for Irving)	30 "	40 " "

The set of seven pamphlets which constituted the work cost the retail buyer $5.37½—an enormous price in America, where Scott's novels were selling for two dollars. In setting such high prices Irving was following British practice, and that he succeeded in it—just this once—is a not wholly comprehensible historical accident. There were protests (especially in thrifty New England) against the price of *The Sketch Book* and what was then considered its luxurious format, but an estimated five thousand American readers were willing to buy it, and Irving's profit for two years was, incredibly, over nine thousand dollars. But his publishing methods contained the seeds of their own destruction.

The economic history of *The Sketch Book* reveals all the elements of the early American writer's publishing problem: the retail price of books, the cost of manufacture, the discount to the trade, and the division of profit between author and publisher. The basic pattern, which seems to have been borrowed from England, allowed one-third of the retail price for manufacturing costs, one-third for trade discount, and one-third for profit, which theoretically was divided equally between author and publisher. (Note that the author's share of this profit was the equivalent of a sixteen and two-thirds per cent royalty.)

But, from the start, American facts upset the British formula. In the first place, British publishers kept competition under control through "courtesy of the trade" and other more coercive devices; kept retail prices high through collusion, even to the extent of destroying "remainders" rather than dumping them at low prices; had a closely predictable sale for every type of book; and, in general, enjoyed all the advantages of a geographically small and homogeneous market. As a result, they were able to keep retail prices at a high and stable level that was impossible in our primitive American conditions. By 1821, many new British novels (usually issued in three volumes) were selling for thirty-one and a half shillings, or about $7.30 in American money. The same novels sold for two dollars in American reprints. One can see why no American writer could hope to achieve Scott's income (for a period) of ten thousand pounds a year.

In the second place, in the early twenties American publishers were not accustomed to paying anything at all to native writers, nor did they, except on rare, and usually unfortunate occasions, print native literary works at their own risk. Hence, when Irving and Cooper found that they could produce literature of commercial value, they followed the established custom and financed their own works; and because they held the purse strings they decreed the discounts that were to be allowed. There was, of course, no obligation to divide profits equally with the so-called publisher, who simply acted as wholesale distributor. As a result, what we think of as the normal arrangement between author and publisher was often reversed: instead of being paid royalties by publishers, authors, in effect, paid publishers a royalty. The publisher got his pay either in the form of a commission which he charged for distributing the work, or from the difference between the whole discount he was allowed—say, one-third—and the smaller discount which he allowed the retailer.

But though the author could, under these conditions, make a profit of forty per cent or more, the system worked against him in some ways. When a publisher reprinted a foreign work at his own risk, he divided what would have been the author's profit with his retailers in the form of high discounts, which encouraged the retailers to push sales. But the small discount which the retailer received on a copyrighted native work was no inducement to salesmanship. Hence American books had a relatively smaller circulation than foreign ones partly because the retailer had smaller incentive to sell them. Even when the publishing economy became more mature, the retailer's natural prejudice against native works continued. As late as 1848, Ticknor & Fields wrote a Cincinnati dealer that their discount on a certain list was one-third—except for Longfellow's works, which discounted at twenty-five to twenty-eight per cent because "the copyright [we pay] is unusually high." The same firm offered only twenty-five per cent on *The Scarlet Letter*.[3]

The difficulties of early American authorship are often attributed to American prejudice against American literature. But equally important was the lack of adequate risk capital in the publishing industry. Its members lived on such a narrow margin that not many had a life of more than a few years. Carey's was the only eighteenth century firm that lived on long into the nineteenth (its capital of a quarter of a million dollars in 1834 was uniquely high),[4] and of those firms established before 1820, only the Harpers prospered beyond mid-century. The panic of 1837 was particularly disastrous, but even the slightest recession brought on a rash of bankruptcies, reorganizations, or assignments of assets. Few authors escaped losses in one or more of these failures.

This lack of capital resulted in a number of different arrangements by which the writer took the whole or some of the risk of publication, sometimes to his own advantage, sometimes to the advantage of the publisher. He took the entire risk when he paid the cost of manufacture, paid a commission to a distributor, and allowed the retailer to receive the work on consignment. This was the normal fate of the untried author, like Bryant with his early poems, and R. H. Dana, Sr., with *The Idle Man* (one of several attempts to emulate Irving's success with *The Sketch Book*).

A safer variation of this method was that of Irving and Cooper before they took their business to Carey. These two paid for manufacture, but sold whole editions to jobbers who took the risk of unsold copies.

Still better was the method adopted by Prescott and other historians in the thirties, and Longfellow and Lowell in the forties. Here the author paid only for the stereotype plates and retained ownership. Sometimes he leased them to a publisher for a stated period, but normally he was paid a relatively high royalty, at the time of issue, for each edition printed from his plates. The difference between the normal ten per cent and Longfellow's twenty per cent gave him a high return for his investment in plates, because his works were often reprinted.

Seemingly fair, but frequently pernicious, was the half-profits system. The publisher made no payments until his risk of manufacturing costs was covered, and he often yielded to the temptation of padding the actual costs of production, or added a commission charge for his services. This was the Harpers' favorite method with novelists in the 1830's,[5] and Herman Melville was its victim for over thirty years. He owned the plates of his first book, *Typee,* but for all others he was on the half-profits system; and on *Pierre,* the publisher actually exempted the first 1190 copies from royalty. Moreover, Melville always borrowed in advance against a new book, and was charged interest for these advances, so that he was in debt to the Harpers for almost his entire career.[6]

At the other extreme was an arrangement which few authors but Irving and Cooper could make, and they only with the house of Carey. Carey purchased the right to publish their works for a term of years, for a stated sum; they took no risk and made no investment themselves, and were paid whether a work sold or not. Even in modern times there is no equivalent to this arrangement, except when really large advances are made against future royalties. In originating this system, Carey anticipated the later arrangement (which was carried over into the twentieth century) whereby established authors got contracts and payments for works before they were completed or even written.

This variety of ways of sharing or assuming the risks of publication resulted in professional fortunes that ranged from feast to famine, depending upon whether a writer had no capital, like Poe, Hawthorne, and Melville, or enough to dictate terms to his publisher, like Cooper, Irving, Longfellow, and Prescott.

Many changes in publishing conditions took place between 1820 and 1850. At the time of *The Sketch Book,* relations between retailers, printers, publishers, and jobbers were extremely complex. Almost all publishers were retailers; many printers were also publishers and sometimes also retailers; all jobbers were retailers; no jobber could deal profitably in the books of all publishers; and no publisher could reach directly all markets in the country. Currency and credit were so unstable that the mere process of paying and getting paid was difficult. The result was a system of distribution so complicated that the publishers were almost as confused as the historian who tries to read their surviving records and correspondence. It is no wonder that when Richardson & Lord of Boston formed a partnership in 1820, their articles of agreement stated their intention of engaging in the "art, trade, and mystery of bookselling."[7]

The basis of the system was a loose inter-city structure of tie-ins between particular booksellers. A large publisher had agreements with one or more firms in every other large city. These firms were called "correspondents" and acted as bankers, post office, retailers, co-publishers, and sometimes jobbers for their principals. The correspondent was a co-publisher when he co-operated in the issue of a book under the multiple-imprint system, whereby a firm split the risk on a book which it had contracted to distribute. Suppose, as in the case of *Sketch Book No. 1*, a first edition of two thousand copies was published simultaneously in four cities—New York, Philadelphia, Boston, and Baltimore. The printer and quasi-publisher, C. S. Van Winkle of New York, arranged with his correspondents in the other three cities to take, say, five hundred copies each, at a twenty-five per cent discount, the names of all four firms appearing on the cover as a multiple-imprint. Each of the correspondents took charge of publicity for the work in his region. Probably no returns of unsold copies were allowed: the correspondents shared the risk with Van Winkle. But their risk was mitigated by their regional monopoly: no copy could be bought in New England, for example, except from the Boston correspondent, who split his discount with the retailers who bought from him.

If the work was a book rather than a pamphlet, the publishers usually sent sheets (or folded "gatherings") to his correspondents, who had them bound up locally. This fact explains why so many first editions of the time survive in a number of different bindings. Somewhat later, it happened occasionally that a publisher ordered one or more extra sets of stereotype plates. He would sell a set of these to a bookseller, say in Cincinnati, who would print a new title page bearing his own imprint and that of the original publisher. This, again, was a way of dividing risk, for extra sets of plates, inexpensively cast from the same forms as the first set, were sold at a considerable profit, or were paid for by a charge for each copy printed therefrom.

The multiple imprint system was probably at its peak in 1820; certainly so far as literary works were concerned, it was on the decline from then on. By 1850, most publishers had enough capital to manufacture their books at their own risk; and distribution had so improved, with the spread of railroads, that many booksellers in the interior did their buying directly from publishers.

Necessary in its time, the multiple imprint system was doomed. Its vices were regional monopoly and an unprofitable division of discounts. A potential purchaser in Boston might know, through advertisements, that *The Sketch Book* was available in the correspondent's shop, but if he lived on the other side of the town he might not bother to make the trip. The Boston correspondent was willing to supply the work to, and split his discount with, a bookseller in Salem; but in Boston he was likely to prefer to monopolize the retail sale and keep the whole discount himself—if he was sure his whole stock would sell. This practice was fine for the correspondent, but bad for the purchaser—and for the author.

The same objections applied to the "exchange" system. Periodically, the publisher printed a list of his publications, sent it to his correspondents in other cities, and received their lists in return. Each ordered from the other as many books as he could use. No cash changed hands until the end of the year, when the books were balanced and the debtor paid the creditor. In 1822, Carey's correspondent in New York was Wiley & Halstead; in Boston, Wells & Lilly. Apparently (the facts are not entirely clear) in Philadelphia, some of Wiley's titles could be bought only at Carey's; and in New York, some of Carey's only at Wiley's. However, the larger publishers sold some books—especially the less popular or the more doubtful ones —to non-correspondents as well. These were either purchased outright on credit, or taken "on sale" or "commission," the retailer returning unsold copies at the end of a stated period. About the latter, there was constant bickering because sometimes, for example, a Boston book, sent to Louisville on commission, was returned at the end of the year in shopworn condition, when the popularity of the work had passed.

For a period in the early twenties, New York and Philadelphia publishers competed through their correspondents for the first sales of new books in the smaller towns of New York, Pennsylvania, and New Jersey. Carey complained bitterly about a clever co-operative move among New York booksellers to corner the small-town market for themselves. When one of the New York firms published a new and popular British novel, it divided up the whole edition among half-a-dozen of the booksellers of the city. All the firms then supplied the correspondents in Pennsylvania and other smaller towns before they sold in quantity to a large Philadelphia jobber like Carey. When Carey tried to buy a large quantity at a big discount, he was forced to take small lots from six New York firms at small discounts. "It is the case with almost every book published in New York for a considerable time," he wrote Wiley & Halstead in 1820.[8] The result was that he was squeezed from two directions: he could not get a discount large enough to make jobbing profitable, and he found some small towns supplied before he could get to them.

Such schemes were profitable for the New Yorkers, but they were not good for the trade. Even the allotment of territories to specific booksellers operated unfairly. Ebenezer Irving gave the Charleston rights to *The Sketch Book* to a bookseller named Mills, and refused Carey's order to ship a number of copies direct to his own correspondent in Charleston. Thus Carey, a legitimate jobber, with correspondents who depended on him, was unable to supply them with a popular work.

Obviously the methods of book distribution were inadequate; and certainly publishing did not mix well with jobbing and retailing. The most prosperous, stable, and long-lived publishing houses avoided the confusion. Carey gave up his retail business in 1830, and probably his jobbing for other publishers at the same time. One reason why his rich and powerful neighbor to the north, the house of Harper, became the oldest general publisher in America was that, from its founding in 1817, it restricted itself to printing and publishing.

Discounts were at the core of the American writer's problem. In 1820, in both England and America, the average discount to the trade was one-third, though the range was from twenty-five per cent to forty per cent—even fifty per cent, depending on quantity. These rates, however, applied only to books on which little or no royalty was paid. In the twenties, works for which American writers were paid rarely discounted for more than twenty-five per cent, many for less. In 1821–22, twenty-five per cent was the regular discount for Irving's *Sketch Book,* and Cooper's *The Spy.* Two documents from the beginning and end of the twenties show what this situation meant in the competition. On May 5, 1820, Moses Thomas wrote Carey, "I will take 50 [Scott's] *Monastery* at 40pc. and pay for them in Salmagundi [Paulding's second series] at 25pc. The terms on which I get the *Sketch Book* are such that I cannot include that."[9] (On the *Sketch Book* he offered only one-sixth.) In 1829, Carey printed a list of his prices to the trade: Scott's, Disraeli's, and Moore's works were discounted at from fifty per cent to sixty-six and two-thirds per cent. Cooper's oldest works were offered at fifty per cent, a later one at forty per cent, and two new ones at twenty-five per cent. In Boston the situation was even worse. A twenty per cent discount on American works was common, and in the early forties Emerson decreed discounts as small as ten per cent on some of his books.

In the years when Irving and Cooper showed that a literary profession in America was possible, the publishing industry was unprepared for it. The popularity of *The Sketch Book* and *The Spy* made the more alert firms lift their heads and sniff the wind for commercially desirable literary works. Venturesome small fry like Van Winkle, and Wiley & Halstead in New York, were literary-minded and popular with authors, but they lacked capital, and their business methods were often slovenly. Year after year, publishing firms went out of business, or formed new combinations and died again—unable to keep up with the bewildering changes in the American economy. In 1815, when Bradford & Inskeep, the Philadelphia publishers of *The History of New York,* went bankrupt, dragging Moses Thomas down with them, Irving wrote that Thomas was "not to be censured in the affair otherwise than for having conducted his business in the same diffuse, sprawling manner in which all our principal booksellers dash forward into difficulty. . . . These failures I am afraid will sensibly affect the interests of literature and deter all those from the exercise of the pen who would take it up as a means of profit."[10] Some publishers grew stronger as time went by, but twenty-four years later, Samuel Ward, reporting to Longfellow on the unreliability of Samuel Colman of New York, made a typical judgment: "The whole race of booksellers among us are a pack of inefficient felons. With little means and, if possible, less credit, they undertake what they fail to perform."[11]

It is no wonder, then, that in the early twenties our successful authors used publishers only as agents and directed the business of manufacture and distribution themselves in order to protect their profits.

[1]Publisher-author correspondence shows that literary economics has been in close accord with the economy of the nation. The literary historian can make use of the charts on the business cycle from the eighteenth century to the present in Leonard P. Ayres, *The Chief Cause of This and Other Depressions* (Cleveland Trust Co., 1935).

[2]My figures on *Sketch Book* sales and profits are conjectural because the records are not complete. These estimates are based on all available printed sources, as well as on a mass of scattered manuscript material, much of it in the Carey archive in the Historical Society of Pennsylvania.

[3]Data from the MS, "Letter Books of Ticknor & Fields" (Harvard College Library). See also W. S. Tryon and William Charvat (eds.), *The Cost Books of Ticknor and Fields and Their Predecessors, 1832–1858* (New York, 1949).

[4]Carey & Lea to Cooper, Feb. 20, 1834 (MS, Yale University Library).

[5]Harper and Brothers to J. P. Kennedy, Nov. 2, 1835: "We usually share profits . . . equally. We publish for Miss Sedgwick, for Messrs. Paulding, Simms, Slidell, etc., upon these terms." (MS, Kennedy Papers, Peabody Institute Library).

[6]Melville's royalty accountings from the Harpers are in the Harvard College Library.

[7]Aug. 11, 1820 (MS, American Antiquarian Society).

[8]Oct. 3, 1820 (MS, Historical Society of Pennsylvania).

[9]May 5, 1820 (MS, Historical Society of Pennsylvania).

[10]Jan. 17, 1815 (MS, New York Public Library).

[11]Nov. 18, 1839. Maude Howe Elliott, *Uncle Sam Ward and His Circle* (New York, 1938), p. 256.

"Rip, Ichabod, and the American Imagination"

BY TERENCE MARTIN

Terence Martin, after a doctoral degree in English from Ohio State University, in 1954 joined the faculty of Indiana University, where he is now a Professor. He has been both a lecturer and a visiting professor in American literature at the University of Dijon, and was in 1963–1964 an American Council of Learned Societies study fellow. Among his publications are *The Instructed Vision* (1961) and *Nathaniel Hawthorne* (1965). This article, which is chiefly concerned with key examples of Irving's imagination reacting to the, for him, present and past realities of American life, is taken from *American Literature,* Vol. XXX (1959), 137–149.

To place the work of Washington Irving in its cultural matrix—and to view it as literature within that matrix—is to gain a particular insight into the working of the creative imagination in a particular period in our past. As literature, as, thus, a unique *kind* of cultural expression, Irving's tales and sketches allow us to see the manner in which attitudes, assumptions, and values were imaged in and by the creative act. We come to know better the interrelationship of the tales and the culture out of which they come by catching ideas going into a kind of dramatic action given its particular definition by the distinctive and formal quality of literary expression.

I

Let us first recall briefly several aspects of Irving's society. Obviously, Irving's America (as R.W.B. Lewis has reminded us in *The American Adam*) was a new nation which saw itself, fresh and innocent, as emancipated from history; concomitantly, this new nation desired to elicit confidence from within and without by assuming an immediate adulthood in the family of nations. The United States was thus a new but self-consciously adult nation: "The old people in a new world, the new people made out of the old," as Gertrude Stein remarks; "an old race though a young nation," observed Charles Astor Bristed in 1850.[1] Because hope for the future entailed and fed on responsibility and stability in the present, a belief both in progress and practical conservatism sustained this anomalous self-image.

The conservative impulse of America generated by the desire for immediate adulthood quite naturally had its effect on the working of the creative imagination; the writer, as we know, worked in the context of a pervading mistrust of the imagination. Especially in the adverse criticism of fiction and the novel, which came from pulpits, commencement addresses, and at times from writers themselves, do we sense the suspicion of the imagination which the writer might at once confront and share. One example of this kind of criticism may serve to illustrate the seriousness of the problem and to set the terms of our argument. In 1810 the Reverend James Gray, a trustee of the

---

[1]Gertrude Stein, *The Making of Americans* (New York, 1934), p. 3; [Charles Astor Bristed], *Pieces of a Broken-Down Critic* (4 vols. in one; Baden-Baden, 1858), III, 27.

Philadelphia Academy for Young Ladies, delivered an address on "Female Education" to a large convocation of students and friends. After soberly examining the effects of novel reading, Gray returns a powerful indictment against fiction. More generous and more penetrating than most of his contemporary critics, he concedes that during the "very transient" period of childhood one might legitimately take an interest in fiction, for "the mind is then itself the region of fiction, of hopes and fears, of plans and projects, far beyond the narrow limits of sober reality." Childhood is the time for "ghosts, goblins, and enchanted castles," for the indulgence of fancy. But when one matures he must put away the things of the child and call for "more substantial food"; men and women, states Gray, "demand fact and doctrine" as the natural course of things. The adult must assume his place in the actual, and practical, world.[2]

Such an argument constitutes an American version of the theory that poetry and art belong properly to primitive, that is, culturally childish, societies, a theory given much attention by the Anglo-European eighteenth century. Thomas Blackwell, John Robert Scott, and Hugh Blair—among others—had articulated this idea in England and Scotland, and William Hazlitt would employ it later in his essay "Why the Arts are Not Progressive."[3] These men saw great art as of the stuff of primitive society; one sign of a society's maturity was that it no longer offered conditions conducive to the creation of great art. The major function of this aesthetic primitivism in eighteenth-century England was to explain why no great art was being created and to celebrate the progress away from primitivism. In America the idea had a similar function, with a larger insistence on the concomitant fact of cultural adulthood. But a more specifically American use of the idea was the attempt to insist on personal adulthood by equating the imaginative and the childish. Childhood, says Gray, is the time for imaginative indulgence; adulthood brings with it a demand for fact and doctrine. That he sees progression here is clear; the adult perforce grows away from "the region of fiction" to a higher and better reality. Likewise, a childish (primitive) society might legitimately

[2]*The Port Folio,* n.s., IV, 94–97 (July, 1810).

[3]See John Robert Scott, *Dissertation on the Progress of the Fine Arts,* with an Introduction by Roy Harvey Pearce (Augustan Reprint Society, No. 45, 1954).

take an interest in things imaginative; such a society, however, was precisely what America wanted not to be. And the proof and the price of cultural adulthood was the willing renunciation or at least containment of the imaginative order. Gray admits that he is as "liberal" on the matter as he can afford to be: he is concessive toward childhood, but he celebrates adulthood; he is concessive toward fancy, but he celebrates fact and doctrine; he is concessive toward the youthful mind as the region of fiction, but he celebrates the adult demand for "more substantial food." In the terms of Gray's argument, representative rather than original, only a culturally childish America could provide the proper nourishment for fiction.

Gray's consideration of fiction and responsibility explains more fully why America wished to assume an immediate adult status—there was simply no time for childhood. As a writer in the *Edinburgh Review* put it in 1829: "No ghost . . . was ever seen in North America. They do not walk in broad day; and the night of ignorance and superstition which favours their appearance was long past" before the United States came into being.[4] Conservative, self-consciously adult, America had no place for ghosts and hobgoblins; as a new nation it did not feel that it could afford to indulge its imagination. The exigencies of the adult (better) world were all too apparent.

But if America did not want to be very young, neither of course did it want to be very old. As a nation which lacked a past, which was beginning history again in a better way, America had to shrug off as it were the implications of history; antiquity, mystery, evil—all products of the process of history—were not a substantial part of the American vision. From one point of view (shared by Emerson, Thoreau, Whitman, and others) this was a good thing: getting rid of the past meant living more fully in the promise of the present. From another point of view, however, the lack of a past had its lamentable side: the result was a cultural thinness and bleakness which left little for the writer to work with. Henry James's disconcerting catalogue of what America lacked in Hawthorne's time is well known.[5] But Hawthorne, too, experienced cultural deficiencies which he applauded as a citizen and lamented as a writer. Imaginatively cramped by the lack of a "poetic or fairy precinct" in America, he explains, in his preface

[4]*Edinburgh Review*, L, 127 (Oct., 1829).
[5]Henry James, *Hawthorne* (New York, 1880), pp. 42–43.

to *The Marble Faun*, the difficulty of writing in the "broad and simple daylight" that "happily" prevails in the United States, with no shadow, antiquity, or mystery to mitigate the necessary insistence on actualities.

For Hawthorne, romance and poetry implied an atmosphere of ruin. That he could not write romance easily about America is significant, measuring his hope in an America free from the consequences of historic process. Romance would not thus seem to belong by nature to America. But with the primitive condition and what it appeared to offer effectively and unequivocally ruled out by the desiderata of American society, a number of our early writers (Charles Brockden Brown, Irving, Poe, and Hawthorne among them) did attempt to create an art based at least implicitly on an aesthetic of age or shadow. They pretended shadow, ruin, decay as prerequisites of imaginative creation; at times they wrote as if America were very old. In view of the American self-image it was a massive pretense. But it produced a significant body of fiction which reflected the tension between what America wanted to be and what these writers had to pretend it to be.

II

The work of Washington Irving reflects significantly the quality of this tension between imaginative endeavor and cultural tendency. In *Bracebridge Hall* (1822), Irving tells us that he had experienced England with "the delightful freshness of a child," but that he was "a grown-up child." He admits in *The Sketch-Book* (1819–1820) that the scenic splendor of America has failed to stimulate him imaginatively; in Europe are "all the charms of storied and poetical association." America is filled with youthful promise, but Europe is rich "in the accumulated treasures of age." He longs for a meditative antiquity, for the "shadowy grandeurs of the past," in place of the "commonplace realities of the present." Irving's most profoundly felt imaginative need was to escape from such "commonplace realities," from—in Hawthorne's phrase—the American insistence on actualities. In *Bracebridge Hall* he lamented that America "unfortunately cannot boast of a single ruin." Yet in Europe he failed to get in touch with the essentials of any older culture and remained, as Stanley Williams terms him, "a young man with slender knowledge of the past," one who loved "scraps of culture."[6] The very vagueness of Irving's conception of the past served his artistic temperament; he required for imaginative creation, not the actuality but the "shadowy grandeurs" of the past.

Although (and because) they are known to all, "Rip Van Winkle" and "The Legend of Sleepy Hollow" will repay a close analysis and reveal Irving's mode of literary creation in such a culture. Early in his tale of Rip, Irving speaks of the "magical hues and shapes" of the Kaatskill mountains; next he calls them "fairy mountains." The terms "magical" and "fairy," apparently incidental, adjectively subordinate, invite the reader away from the "commonplace realities of the present" to a region of greater imaginative latitude. In beginning his account of Rip's famous adventure, Irving constructs his scene so as literally to remove it from "broad and simple daylight." Rip gazes into a wild and lonely mountain glen which is "scarcely lighted by the reflected rays of the setting sun." Out of this shadowy glen, the American equivalent for the "shadowy grandeurs" of the past, Rip hears a voice calling his name and meets a "strange" figure in antique Dutch dress. In silence and wonder Rip helps the man carry a keg of liquor up a wild mountain: "there was something strange and incomprehensible about the unknown, that inspired awe and checked familiarity." The reader is now, with Rip, in a realm of the strange and unknown that inspires awe and checks familiarity. Only after such careful preparation, after guiding us away from the commonplace practicality of everyday life, does Irving introduce, in four brief paragraphs, the purely marvelous element of the story—the company playing ninepins. At the end of these paragraphs Rip falls into a sleep; when he awakens—on a "bright sunny morning," with the "birds hopping and twittering among the bushes"—we are back in the world of actuality. Rip returns to the village to find not only the people but "the very character of the people" changed.

Irving has taken Rip out of the context of everyday reality, but then has deliberately put him back in it. The tale, in its beginning and end, has historical location. And when Rip returns at the end of the tale he finds a metamorphosed community, no longer even the same country. The image of George Washington—the father of a new

---

[6]Stanley T. Williams, *The Life of Washington Irving* (New York, 1935), I, 44.

country—has replaced that of George III on the sign at the inn, and Rip has no way of orienting himself in terms of this new father image. Irving has had Rip sleep through the American Revolution, through what we might call the birth pangs of our country, and return to a "busy, bustling, disputatious," self-consciously adult United States of America. There his uncompetitive spirit, his predisposition to idleness, his inclination to imaginative indulgence are badly out of place; he is no more at home than he was with Dame Van Winkle, who prefigured the bustling, disputatious tone of this new world, though she at least knew him. Irving does not exact the full penalty from Rip; he allows him to settle in a corner of this world, but with a function extremely limited and marginal. Nonetheless, the tale dramatizes Rip's loss of identity, and, by inference, the loss of identity of the imaginative function. Rip's miraculous sleep has left him ignorant of the American Revolution—the magical, the marvelous, the imaginative, and the indolent have had no place in the founding of the new republic. And when these qualities return in the person of an antique but childlike man, there arises a sense of embarrassment overcome only when he is known to be harmless, one who will not interfere.

In "The Legend of Sleepy Hollow" Irving goes to even greater lengths in creating a never-never land to contain his tale: "a drowsy, dramy influence" hangs over the land and pervades the atmosphere; the people have trances and visions and entertain marvelous beliefs. Haunted spots and "twilight superstitions" abound in the neighborhood. All of this of course prepares for the bold reference to the Headless Horseman. And, as if to urge a spirit of enchantment upon his readers, Irving states that even visitors to Sleepy Hollow become bewitched: inhaling the "witching influence" of the air, they begin to "grow imaginative, to dream dreams, and see apparitions." The quotation holds the key to Irving's method of literary creation: the wide-awake reader, dwelling in the "broad and simple daylight" of the actual world, is invited to enter Irving's sleepy region (Gray's "region of fiction"), to dream there under the bewitching influence of fictional apparitions.

Irving's introduction of Ichabod Crane defines a particular problem of the early American writer. "In this by-place of nature," he writes, "there abode, in a remote period of American history, that is to say, some thirty years since, a worthy wight of the name of Ichabod Crane." The archaic substantive *wight* serves to emphasize the incongruity of the introduction; only in the America of the time could a remote period of history be defined as thirty years. That Irving could speak ironically about the poverty of the past in America did not make it less a fact for him to deal with. Without a large, commonly shared, and hence more than personal past to work with and out of, the writer himself had to contain and be the measure of antiquity.

Ichabod Crane personifies the protagonist as comic figure. "His appetite for the marvelous, and his powers of digesting it, were . . . extraordinary; and both had been increased by his residence in this spellbound region. No tale was too gross or monstrous for his capacious swallow." Throughout the tale Irving plays on the idea of Ichabod's tremendous appetite and his "capacious swallow." But not only does this appetite pertain to the marvelous: Ichabod is a "huge feeder"; he contemplates with longing the largesse of the Van Tassel farm; the very prospect of winning the hand of Katrina comes to him in terms of a superabundance of food. In a manifold sense he yearns to swallow the world and thereby realize an oral heaven. By fitting the notion of gullibility into the dominant metaphor of Ichabod's oral preoccupation, Irving emphasizes the childlike quality of his protagonist. Ichabod can swallow and digest anything; therefore he is always and increasingly gullible. But growing up involves learning what not to swallow, in every sense of the word. Ichabod has failed utterly to learn this first lesson in the practical knowledge of survival precisely because of his extreme addiction to the imagination. Irving couples the oral stage and imaginative indulgence; both signify childhood. There is, moreover, a price to be paid for continuing in childhood. In our natural laughter at the story, we often forget that Ichabod goes down to defeat because he is overimaginative. For he loses all chance for the double prize of Katrina and the wealth of the Van Tassel farm when, terrified by his excessive imagination, he is literally run out of the region by Brom Bones impersonating the Headless Horseman. Brom Bones—the scoffer at superstition, who boasts that he has ridden a winning race against the Headless Horseman—triumphs, marries Katrina, and is the victor of the tale. It is a victory for common sense and hard-headed practicality over imaginative indulgence.

In each of these tales Irving has created his setting as a writer of romance; he overcomes the difficulty of creating imaginatively in the "broad and simple daylight" of his America by positing shadow, mystery, superstition. He writes, in short, as if his settings had antiquity, as if America had a past. Into each tale, however, he introduces a childlike protagonist, whom we may recognize as primitive if we allow for the fact that Irving would share the disbelief in contemporary primitivism and would create such a character out of that disbelief. Rip Van Winkle, with his "insuperable aversion to all kinds of profitable labor," delights in playing with children, and they in turn love him; he is a favorite among the village wives; not a dog in the neighborhood will bark at him. Ichabod Crane spends much time telling ghost stories with the old Dutch wives of Sleepy Hollow; he is the "playmate" of his larger students. In bringing each of these protagonists to a kind of defeat, Irving is echoing James Gray's pronouncement that America must be mature, must call for "substantial food." Rip and Ichabod lose out because they fail to see the necessity of demanding "fact and doctrine," which are at once the prerequisite for and the evidence of personal and cultural maturity. They are would-be heroes, but would-be heroes of the imagination, who cannot withstand or successfully come to terms with the terror that is the lot of such a hero, the terror implicit in Rip's loss of identity, explicit in Ichabod's flight. They defeat themselves. It would appear that for Irving there is no place, or a very limited place, for the hero of the imagination in the culture of early America. A nation of Rips and Ichabods, Americans might reason, would soon be no nation at all.

Not even the settings can endure in these tales. It is as if Irving must admit that this is not a real past, that he will not persist in playing with the imagination. In "Rip Van Winkle" the village is transformed from "drowsy tranquility" to a bustling disputatiousness. There are no more shadows in Rip's world. In Sleepy Hollow, to be sure, the people remain unchanged. But we have been shown who is master there: it is Brom Bones (whose true name, Brom Van Brunt, also suggests the kind of strength Irving wants him to have), perhaps the first American bully, who can play upon fear and superstition to get what he wants. His apparent audacity in impersonating a ghost shows how fully in control Brom Bones is. For this impersonation is audacious only if we see it from the point of view of the villagers of Sleepy Hollow. To Brom Bones, to the only authentic American in the tale, it must literally be child's play. Irving has thus shown his American readers images of themselves in the changed village of

"Rip Van Winkle" and in the character of Brom Bones. The manner of each tale suggests that Irving did not find these images entirely flattering, albeit necessary, and, indeed, readers have never found them attractive. Instinctively we sympathize with Rip and Ichabod; we laugh at them and in doing so at what there is of them in us; at the same time, we regret their failure. But what we regret is only what we had to give up to become what we are.

Irving's most characteristic fiction involves variations on the basic pattern of victory for the practical and defeat for the impractical and visionary. In "The Spectre Bridegroom," Herman Von Starkenfaust's bold decision to impersonate a dead lover wins for him a beautiful wife. The "very manly" aunt in "The Adventure of My Aunt" exposes a robber by her refusal to be frightened when the eyes of a picture on the wall begin to move, while the unfortunate Young Italian of "The Adventure of the Mysterious Stranger" confesses that he has always been "a visionary, imaginary being." At the end of the Italian Banditti section of *Tales of a Traveler,* it is the Englishman, vexatious, hardheaded, insensitive, blind to chivalric courtesy, who saves the lovely Venetian Lady from the bandits whom he alone has scorned. "Dolph Heyliger" shows us how Dolph's daring to sleep in a haunted house ultimately leads him to wealth and a beautiful girl. For the grown-up person, for the practical and bold, the prize is wealth and beauty; for the childish, visionary, imaginary being, the price is the same wealth and beauty. Brom Bones, Herman Von Starkenfaust, and Dolph Heyliger are all recognizably related by a success that comes from their control of the imagination. The others, those duped by their imaginations, share the brotherhood of failure.

Even the symbolic structure of a sketch may tell us about the functioning of the imagination in Irving's work and thus about the relationship of such characters as Rip and Ichabod to the culture out of which they come. A miraculous conversation between a narrator and a book makes up the substance of "The Mutability of Literature." Irving's introduction of the conversation is significant. He postulates certain half-dreaming moods of mind in which we seek solitude, so that we may "indulge our reveries and build our air-castles undisturbed." In such a mood the narrator of the sketch is loitering around the clositers of Westminster Abbey, when the noise of boys playing football breaks in upon his reverie. Instinctively, he seeks to retreat "still deeper into the solitudes of the pile." He applies for admission to the library and is shown "through a portal rich with the crumbling sculpture of former ages" which opens "upon a gloomy passage"; just within the passage there is "a small door on the left," double-locked, "opened with some difficulty, as if seldom used." The narrator and a guide ascend "a dark narrow staircase, and, passing through a second door," enter the library. It is here that a book bound in parchment strikes up a conversation on the mutability of literature.

The trip to the library has of course a literal necessity: Irving must find an old book to converse with, and what better place to find such a book than in the library of Westminster Abbey. But the carefully wrought details of getting to the library suggest as well a symbolic significance: these details mark not only a retreat from the glare and noise and distraction of the outer world, but also, if we may adopt a given symbology as a heuristic device, a symbolic journey back to the womb—in this case the womb of the mother country—a psychic regression into the very antithesis of the adult world of "broad and simple daylight." Here the marvelous can be cultivated, the imagination can function unembarrassed. In the adult world, we remember, the world of fact and doctrine, the imagination has little function; thus Irving stages a retreat from the noise of actual children and symbolically regresses to an earlier psychological-historical period of existence in order to achieve imaginative freedom.

Irving's choice and treatment of historical subjects is likewise significant for our analysis. In Christopher Columbus, William L. Hedges points out, Irving had "a full-fledged legendary hero," both mythic and real.[7] The subject of the biography takes us back to a time when Europe was the known and America the unknown. When Columbus's ships set out, writes Irving, "they seemed literally to have taken leave of the world." "Before them was chaos, mystery, and peril." Columbus, as we know, is the hero of the piece, who meets the challenges of the unknown rationally and scientifically. Their imaginations stimulated by the unknown before them, the sailors are often in terror and despair. Columbus, however, is a man of a different stamp: "Columbus tasked his science and ingenuity for reasons with which to allay their terror"; "Columbus endeavored to

---

[7] William L. Hedges, "Irving's *Columbus*: The Problem of Romantic Biography," *The Americas*, XIII, 134 (Oct., 1956). Mr. Hedges sees this biography as history transforming itself into fiction.

dispel these gloomy presages"; "Columbus continued with admirable patience to reason with these fancies." The sailors lose faith in the outcome of the voyage and desire to turn back; Columbus, however, maintains his faith in what he knows rationally must be true, assuages their fears as best he can, and is ultimately responsible for the success of the venture. Science, ingenuity, and reason have triumphed over superstition, fear, and fancy, and the result has been the discovery of a New World.

Irving's selection of George Washington rather than Queen Isabella for extended biographic treatment marks a final decision to do what he could with the American past. Yet the "essentially historic" nature of the work indicates a concession to the insistence of his culture on actualities. He conceives of Washington as a man who "had very little private life," who was "eminently a public character. All his actions and concerns almost from boyhood were connected with the history of his country." Irving sees Washington as a man whose life, molded by "fact and doctrine," epitomized adult, public existence.

Unable to achieve a satisfactory mode of imaginative expression from the stuff of the "commonplace realities of the present," Irving turned, as we have seen, to techniques which would give him the requisite imaginative latitude. He pretended both childishness and antiquity for America, then, in effect, stood back and saw these things fail before an always triumphant broad daylight which existed to celebrate the absence of childishness and antiquity. He handled his materials urbanely, with a diffused humor stemming largely from his use of the mock-heroic ("sportively Gothic," Henry A. Pochmann calls some of his early tales[8]); this allowed him to maintain a stylistic, mannered, and gentlemanly distance from the resolution of his tales.

In Westminster Abbey Irving contemplated the tomb of a Crusader, in whose exploits he saw "the connecting link between fact and fiction; between the history and the fairy tale." No such connecting link existed for the artist in America; Captain Bonneville would not do, at least for Irving, who could see him only conventionally as one who challenged the romantic unknown.[9] Irving constantly harkened

[8]*Washington Irving*, American Writers Series (New York, etc., 1934), p. lxvi.
[9]See Williams, *Life*, I, 34.

back to what were for him prototypical men and situations. His treatment of one colored his treatment of any other, for to him imaginative creation rose out of the potential tension in basically one type of situation. The typical locus of creation in Irving's work is that in which a protagonist confronts the mysterious and unknown: if the protagonist lacks vision and reason he becomes a comic figure and goes down to some kind of defeat—for example, Ichabod Crane; if he possesses vision and reason he triumphs over the unknown and qualifies as an authentic hero—for example, Christopher Columbus. But Ichabod, of course, is a product of Irving's imagination, while Columbus is a historical figure. Irving's imaginatively created protagonists are childish, primitive images of what America could not assimilate into the national self-image; his historical protagonists, on the other hand, are images of exactly what made America what it wanted to be. Between the two types of protagonist there could be no valid traffic: Irving could not historicize Rip and Ichabod nor could he fictionalize Christopher Columbus and George Washington. The reality of history was a recognizable factor in the development of America. It was not to be confused with the reality of the imagination, which had no part in the discovery of the New World or in the birth of the new country.

That Irving did deal with both types of protagonist might suggest that he was seeking to transcend the limitations of his society in some tentative way in the interests of literary art. Although he could not bring the would-be hero of age, he could and did modulate the failure of his principal creations Rip and Ichabod after a moment of insight into the nature of terror—Ichabod, we recall, evidently reforms, grows up, and succeeds in another locale. The fact of their failure is nonetheless laden with meaning, signifying the inadequacy of imaginative endeavor, defining reality as the actuality of history and the present day. "Rip Van Winkle" and "The Legend of Sleepy Hollow" show us meaning in action (if I may so emend a text of Ezra Pound's),[10] meaning created, structured, dramatized. And if we know the tales better because of the culture, we know the culture immeasurably better because we have the tales.

[10]"The history of a culture is the history of ideas going into action," *Guide to Kulchur* (London, 1938), p. 44.

"Prefigurations:
'The Legend of Sleepy Hollow' "

BY DANIEL HOFFMAN

Daniel Hoffman, after teaching posts at Columbia, where he completed his graduate work, Rutgers, and Swarthmore, and a visiting professorship in American literature and history at the University of Dijon, has been since 1966 a Professor of English at the University of Pennsylvania. Distinguished both as poet and literary critic, he has had numerous honors, including an award in 1967 from the National Institute of Arts and Letters. His scholarly books include *The Poetry of Stephen Crane* (1957) and *Poe, Poe, Poe, Poe, Poe, Poe, Poe* (1972). This city slicker-versus-shrewder yokel selection is Section 4 of Part I of Hoffman's *Form and Fable in American Fiction* (1961). There it was slightly revised from its first appearance as "Irving's Use of American Folklore in 'The Legend of Sleepy Hollow'," in *PMLA*, Vol. LXVIII (1953), 425–435.

ONE

The first important literary statement of the themes of native folk character and superstition was made, fittingly enough, in the first literary work by an American to win world-wide acclaim. When *The Sketch Book of Geoffrey Crayon, Gent.* appeared in London in 1819, its author became the first of a long series of expatriate Americans who found their native roots all the more poignant for viewing them from a distance.

Washington Irving was fortunate, granted his special though restricted gifts, to be alive and in England at that moment in the history of literature. He sought out, and was taken up by, Sir Walter Scott, who was showing how the sentiment of nostalgia for the past could infuse fiction and become its informing principle. In his novels Scott projected that sense of historical continuity which formed a curious undercurrent of sensibility even before the Romantic movement began. Little though the Augustans attended the medieval or more recent past, there were important eighteenth-century successors to such early antiquarian works as Sir Thomas Browne's collection of *Vulgar Errors* (1648) and Samuel Pepys' collection of broadside ballads. Bishop Percy's *Reliques of Ancient English Poetry* (1765) and John Brand's *Observations on the Popular Antiquities of Great Britain* (1795) laid the groundwork for the two directions British folklore study has followed ever since. Scott took his prominent place in both with his ballad collection, *The Minstrelsy of the Scottish Border* (1802) and his comprehensive *Letters on Demonology and Witchcraft* (1830). Much more influential, however, than these formal studies in introducing a whole generation of readers—and authors— to such materials was his use of folklore in his own fiction. One of Scott's earliest and most popular disciples along this line was a young American *littérateur,* the London representative of P. E. Irving & Co., New York dealers in hardware.

Washington Irving was already something of an antiquary. His early *Knickerbocker's History of New York* reveals him to be enchanted with the very past he satirized. In *The Sketch Book* Irving used several themes to which he would again and again recur: the Gothic tale in the German manner of 'The Spectre Bridegroom,' the antiquarian nostalgia of the four sketches on English Christmas customs, the character sketch of 'The Village Angler.' The two selections destined for most enduring fame, however, were careful reconstructions of the scenes of Irving's own boyhood in the Dutch communities of the Hudson Valley. One of these retells a German folktale in this American setting, in which Rip Van Winkle sleeps away his twenty years after a heady game of bowls with the ghostly crew of the Half-Moon. In the other tale, 'The Legend of Sleepy Hollow,' Irving brought into belles-lettres for the first time the comic mythology and folk beliefs of his native region. In Ichabod Crane and Brom Bones he dramatized that clash of regional characters—the Yankee versus the Backwoodsman—which would soon become a major theme in our literature, as well as a continuing motif in a century and a half of folktales, and in our national history.

It is surprising that the extent to which Irving drew upon native folklore has scarcely been acknowledged. The chief reason for this seems to be Henry A. Pochmann's convincing demonstration, in 1930, of the extent of Irving's indebtedness to his German contemporaries. Stanley T. Williams, in his definitive biography, gives us a further exploration of Irving's methods of composition.[1] When we see the extent to which Irving depended on other men's books, often translating without acknowledgment, we can understand why recent critics are reluctant to grant him credit for originality in interpreting American themes.

The foremost students of American humor have strangely overlooked 'The Legend of Sleepy Hollow.' Walter Blair does call it 'a characteristic piece of American humor,' but his remark is relegated to a footnote. And Constance Rourke, writing with her usual felicity,

---

[1] Irving's use of folk traditions of piracy is noted by W. H. Bonner, *Pirate Laureate: The Life & Legends of Captain Kidd* (New Brunswick, N. J., 1947), pp. 151–65; Leonard Beach discusses Irving's use of American themes and recognizes Ichabod as 'Irving's judgment of Puritanism': 'Washington Irving,' *University of Kansas City Review,* XIV (1948), 259–66. Pochmann notes 'Irving's German Sources in The Sketch Book,' *Studies in Philology,* XXVII (July 1930), 477–507; see also 'Irving's German Tour and Its Influence on His Tales,' *PMLA,* XLV (Dec. 1930), 1150–87. Pochmann shows, with parallel texts, that in 'Rip Van Winkle' Irving translated and expanded the story of Peter Klaus, a German goatherd who fell asleep for years, which he found in the *Volkssagen* of Othmar; and in 'The Legend of Sleepy Hollow,' he demonstrates Irving's indebtedness to the Rübezahl legends in *Volksmärchen der Deutschen,* by Musaeus. See also Williams, *The Life of Washington Irving* (New York, 1935), I, 177–86.

remarks that 'in the Knickerbocker History and in Rip Van Winkle Irving created a comic mythology as though comic myth-making were a native habit, formed early . . . But his Dutch people were of the past, joining only at a distance with current portrayals of native character,'[2] Why did Miss Rourke not mention 'Sleepy Hollow'? I do not know; but I hope to show that in Ichabod and Brom Bones, Irving gave us portrayals of *current* native character projected backwards in time, rather than merely historical types unrooted in contemporary folklore.

There are of course good reasons why Brom and Ichabod have not been so recognized. For one thing, Irving's style is hardly what we expect in a folk document. For another, the Hudson Valley Dutch have long been thought an alien people by the Anglo-Saxons who conquered, surrounded, and outnumbered them. But the third and principal reason is Irving's own treatment of his Dutch materials. Almost everywhere *except* in 'The Legend of Sleepy Hollow' he deliberately altered the traditional characteristics of the Dutch for the purposes of his own fiction. As a consequence of Irving's popularity and of widespread ignorance of what the Dutch were really like, his caricatures were widely accepted as portraits of the Dutch-Americans. Paulding, writing *The Dutchman's Fireside* twenty-two years after the *Knickerbocker History,* imitated his friend in attributing chuckleheadedness and indolence to the brothers Vancour. In Cooper's *Satanstoe* (1845), however, we get a more realistic picture of the Dutch; his Guert Ten Eyck amply fulfills the historian Janvier's description: the Dutch 'were tough and they were sturdy, and they were as plucky as men could be.'[3] Only in 'The Legend of Sleepy Hollow' did Irving give a Dutchman these attributes; everywhere else he made them fat, foolish, pompous, and pleasure-loving. Here his usual Dutchman does appear (Van Tassel), but only in the background.

---

[2]Blair, *Native American Humor,* p. 16, n. 3. Basing his judgment of Irving as a native humorist on the *Knickerbocker's History of New York,* Blair considers Irving as primarily 'a disciple of neoclassicism,' and concludes (p. 14) that 'he employed a technique which, admirable though it was, differed from that of typical American humor.' Rourke, *American Humor,* p. 77.

[3]Thomas A. Janvier, *The Dutch Founding of New York* (New York, 1903), p. 4; Janvier takes issue with Irving's characterization of the Dutch on pp. 1–3, 9, 14, 46, 105, and 131–2.

Brom Bones is his realistic Dutch frontiersman, who meets and bests a Yankee in the traditional conflict of our native folk humor. Why did Irving choose this theme, so different from his usual preoccupations?

When we admit his dependence upon books, we must look at the kinds of authors on whom he depended. Othmar and Musaeus were collectors and redactors of folktales and märchen. Irving knew personally a third folklorist, Dr. Karl Böttiger, 'who undoubtedly was able to give him expert advice on his folklore studies.'[4] Wherever Irving went he collected popular sayings and beliefs; he was prepossessed by a sense of the past, and recognized the power—and the usefulness to a creative artist—of popular antiquities. Brom and Ichabod had their beginnings in local characters he had known as a boy;[5] what made them take their singular form, however, was the direction in which Irving's imagination impelled them. And that direction was toward the fabulous. The fabulous was Irving's milieu.

In a reminiscence twenty years after *The Sketch Book*, Irving revealed that Diedrich Knickerbocker had learned the legend of Sleepy Hollow from an old Negro who gave him 'that invaluable kind of information, never to be acquired from books,' and from 'the precious revelations of the good dame at the spinning wheel.'[6] Of Musaeus' *Volksmärchen* he says nothing. But he may well indeed have heard such stories in the old Dutch chimney corners. H. W. Thompson recounts similar motifs in York State folklore: nightly visitations by a shrieking woman 'tied to the tail of a giant horse with fiery eyes'; and 'a curious phantom . . . uttering unearthly laughter, lights shining from her finger tips.' There were revenants aplenty in Catskills. Still another important part of Dutch folk culture was the lusty practical jok-

[4]Pochmann, 'Irving's German Tour,' *PMLA*, XLV, 1153–4.

[5]Brom Bones was identified by Pierre M. Irving as a wag of Tarrytown who 'boasted of once having met the devil . . . and run a race with him for a bowl of milk' (*Life and Letters of Washington Irving*, London, 1892, I, 282). See Williams, *Life*, I, 429, n. 90, for a similar account; on p. 430, n. 91, he names Brom Van Allstyne of Kinderhook as the original of Irving's character. Ichabod Crane, Williams finds (p. 109), was modelled upon 'Jesse Merwin, the homespun wit' and village schoolmaster, as well as upon Fielding's Partridge and the schoolmaster in Goldsmith's *Deserted Village*.

[6]'Sleepy Hollow,' in *Biographies and Miscellanies*, ed. Pierre M. Irving (New York, 1866), pp. 514–16.

ing[7] which Cooper used in some of the most spirited pages in *Satanstoe*. Both aspects of Dutch folk life—the villagers' superstitions and their humor—are immortalized in 'The Legend of Sleepy Hollow.'

TWO

Irving sets his story in a folk society: 'It is in such little retired Dutch villages . . . that population, manners, and customs remain fixed; while the great torrent of migration and improvement, which is making such incessant changes in other parts of this restless country, sweeps by them unobserved.' And again: 'The neighborhood is rich in legendary lore . . . Local tales and superstitions thrive best in these sheltered long-settled retreats.' Into this community comes Ichabod Crane, 'a native of Connecticut, a State which supplied the Union with pioneers for the mind as well as for the forest.' Ichabod is Irving's Connecticut Yankee, the fictional ancestor of Mark Twain's Hartford mechanic. But his nearer descendants are Sam Slick, Jack Downing, Hosea Biglow. Before any of these was born in print Ichabod had already been a country teacher, a singing master, a sometime farmer; later he is to undergo still further metamorphoses which link him still more closely to these heroes of popular legend and literature. Like Ben Franklin, like Hawthorne's Holgrave, like the schoolmaster in *Snow-Bound* and Melville's marvelous Confidence Man, he was a jack of all trades. Metamorphosis is always magical, but now, in an egalitarian society, the magic is the power of self-reliance, not of Satan.

Ichabod's native shrewdness and perseverance are somewhat compromised by his credulity. 'No tale was too gross or monstrous for his capacious swallow.' Ichabod devoutly believed in all the remarkable prodigies retailed in Cotton Mather's *History of New England Witchcraft* (that is, the *Magnalia Christi Americana*). There he found spectral ships manned by ghostly women, heretics giving birth to monsters, revenants pursuing the innocent with invisible instruments of torture. But of all the ghostly tales in the valley, the one

---

[7]Thompson, *Body Boots & Britches* (Philadelphia, 1939), pp. 119–21; Carl Carmer, *The Hudson* (New York and Toronto, 1939), p. 35, lists some typical pranks.

Ichabod Crane most liked to hear was that of the Headless Horseman.

Meanwhile, we remember, Ichabod falls in love with Katrina Van Tassel; more exactly, seeing her father's prosperous farm, he envisages 'every roasting pig running about with a pudding in his belly, and an apple in his mouth.' Considerations of this sort lead Ichabod into a most interesting reverie: he imagines 'the blooming Katrina, with a whole family of children, mounted on the top of a wagon loaded with household trumpery, with pots and kettles dangling beneath; and beheld himself bestriding a pacing mare, with a colt at her heels, setting out for Kentucky, Tennessee, or Lord knows where.' Here we have Ichabod Boone—Connecticut's pioneer of the wilderness as well of the mind. Traditionally the American frontiersman has resented the mercantile civilizer; in a thousand folktales the shaggy woodsman frightens the Yankee clear out of the district.

Ichabod's fatuous dream of pioneering prepares the way for his rival's entrance: 'a burly, roaring, roistering blade . . . Brom Van Brunt, the hero of the country round, which rang with his feats of strength and hardihood.' He had 'a mingled air of fun and arrogance,' and was 'always ready for either a fight or a frolic; but had more mischief than ill-will in his composition.' Famous for horsemanship, 'foremost at all races and cockfights' was Brom; 'and when any madcap prank, or rustic brawl, occurred in the vicinity, [the neighbors] always shook their heads, and warranted Brom Bones was at the bottom of it.'

Making allowances for Irving's smoothly flowing style, what we have here described is a Catskill Mike Fink, a Ring-Tailed Roarer from Kinderhook. While Irving was writing these lines in London, the real Mike Fink was somewhere west of Pittsburgh, shooting the heel off a nigger to make his foot fit the shoe, scalping Indians for the pure hell of it, roistering in towns along the Ohio. In Brom Bones's good-natured mischief there is a tinge of Mike Fink's brutality, if not of his sadism. That other favorite frontiersman, Davy Crockett, had not by 1819 become a national figure; yet the type—the swaggering frontier braggart, the prodigious hunter and strong man, the daredevil, the mischief-maker—was already well established in oral tradition. Irving's depiction of Brom Bones certainly gave these characteristics new clarity as they are combined for the first time in a fictional portrait of the *genus* frontiersman.

349

Irving now pits his rival suitors against each other. Ichabod, the Yankee, 'had a happy mixture of pliability and perseverance in his nature.' Although he is caricatured unmercifully, he is not entirely unworthy of our grudging admiration; a thoroughly self-reliant citizen, he adapts his strategy to meet the case. 'To have taken the field openly against his rival would have been madness,' so Ichabod insinuates himself into Katrina's notice while masquerading as her singing-master. Here he outwits Big Brom in the contest, perennially fresh in American comic lore, between wit and strength. But Ichabod forces Brom Bones to draw upon his own resources—the rough fancy of the frontiersman—as well as upon brute strength. This proves a dangerous combination for the scholar.

At Van Tassel's quilting frolic, when the old Negro tunes the fiddle and rosins the bow, Ichabod finds his métier, fair grounds whereon he can excel Brom Bones. The ungainly form of the pedagogue achieves animation if not grace, for he is from Down East in Connecticut and is sufficiently sophisticated to know how to dance with a lady. Brom, the bumpkin, 'sorely smitten with love and jealousy, sat brooding by himself in one corner.'

The dancing over, talk now turns to the recently concluded Revolutionary War. Old soldiers' exploits become more heroic at each telling, as Irving skillfully moves us from the reality of the dance to mildly comic exaggerations of heroic truth, then to the supernatural itself. We are near Sleepy Hollow, and 'there was a contagion in the very air that blew from that haunted region.' The mythology of war blends with that of the otherworld, lending credence to the supernatural, as we learn that 'mourning cries and wailings [were] heard and seen about the great tree where the unfortunate Major André was taken'; and we hear of 'the woman in white, that haunted the dark glen at Raven Rock,' who 'was often heard to shriek on winter nights before a storm, having perished there in the snow.' But the presiding spirit at this haunted conference was the Headless Horseman, who tethers his horse in the graveyard, haunts the church, and chases travellers. Brom Bones has met him. Riding his horse, Daredevil, Brom challenged the ghost to race for a bowl of punch—'and should have won it too, for Daredevil beat the goblin horse all hollow, but, just as they came to the church-bridge, the Hessian bolted, and vanished in a flash of fire.'

Here is the bravado of the American hero, so confident of his own powers that he will risk everything for nothing, as Sam Patch did when he jumped Niagara just to prove that 'Some things can be done as well as others.' Such reckless daring makes the Faustus legend seem native in this land; Irving tried his hand at that in 'The Devil and Tom Walker' a generation before Hawthorne gave the devil's compact more sombre treatment, a century before Stephen Vincent Benét outdid him in this comic mode.

But Ichabod reasserts the dominance of evil over American self-reliance: he quotes Mather on witches, and describes the ghosts he has seen himself. The homely Puritan cannot accept the bravado of the backwoods Natural Man; Ichabod and Brom inhabit different worlds although they live in the same village. When Ichabod bids Katrina good night, he is chagrined to find that his hopes for a prosperous match have somehow gone awry. Perhaps, having observed her rival swains' reactions to supernatural perils, she has decided not to be a Puritan's bride, however nimbly he may dance the quadrille. Ichabod steals away heavy at heart.

Now, in the best-known part of the story, comes Irving's debt to Musaeus. But the stylistic control of the atmosphere shows Irving's own talent at its best, while the conclusion of the story is of signal importance in the literary development of an American myth. The darkness deepens; all the tales of ghosts and witches crowd into Ichabod's brain. Now he crosses the stream where André was captured, a haunted brook. Ichabod is appalled to find he no longer rides alone. A silent horseman plashes beside him. Coming out of the valley, Ichabod gets a look at his companion and discovers, in terror, that he carries his head in his hands! Crane rushes toward the church-bridge, where the Hessian, pursuing Brom, had disappeared. Reaching the bridge, Ichabod turns 'to see if his pursuer should vanish, according to rule'—a fine pedantic touch!—but sees instead 'the goblin rising in his stirrups . . . hurling his head at him. Ichabod endeavored to dodge the horrible missile, but too late.' He falls from his horse, 'and the black steed, and the goblin rider, passed by like a whirlwind.'

Ichabod was never seen again in Sleepy Hollow. His landlord burns his copy of Mather's *Witchcraft* and determines to keep his own children from school, 'observing that he never knew of any good come of this same reading and writing.'

THREE

Here in this York State valley, Irving's Dutch braggart concocts the perfect backwoodsman's revenge on the Yankee.[8] This first statement of the theme is among the most memorable it has ever received in our literature; it is with us yet and ever has been, in Davy Crockett outwitting peddlers, in a thousand dime novels and popular magazines in which the yokel gets the best of the city slicker.[9]

The rustic hero may be naïve and honest, with only his common sense to help him make his way in the world; so he appears as Jack Downing, as Hosea Biglow, as Robin in Hawthorne's *My Kinsman, Major Molineux,* as Huckleberry Finn. Or he may be a swashbuckling braggart, half horse, half alligator. like all the ring-tailed roarers and Thorpe's Big Bear of Arkansas. No matter; in either form he represents the American élan, the pioneer, the Natural Man rebelling against the burden of guilt of the ages. It was he who cut the cords that bound him to the English throne, to all king-ridden Europe. Naked he stands in the wilderness, bereft of the past, confident that all human history begins—with *him.*

Who is his adversary? Perhaps an insufferable fop from the city to the East—traditions, culture, lineage, class distinctions always come from the East in American mythology: from New England, from Europe. Perhaps he is a shrewd, narrow-nosed Yankee peddler. No matter; in either form he stands for that ancient heritage of useless learning and inherited guilt against which the American, in each succeeding generation, must rebel.

Such are the roles in this ever-recurring fable of the American

---

[8]The perfection of Irving's 'Legend' becomes even more apparent by comparison with 'Cobus Yerks,' Paulding's imitation of 'Sleepy Hollow.' Instead of Yankee vs. backwoodsman, we find a stupid, superstitious Dutchman frightened by a ghostly dog, otherwise Tim Canty, a merry Englishman. Now the story is reduced to its supernatural motif only; the richness which Irving's 'Legend of Sleepy Hollow' holds for us, its reverberations on the themes of national and regional character, are entirely lacking in Paulding's caricature. *Tales of The Good Woman,* ed. W. I. Paulding (New York, 1867), pp. 285–99.

[9]Mark Twain's first newspaper sketch was a version of this motif, called 'The Dandy Frightening the Squatter,' reprinted in *Tall Tales of the Southwest,* ed. F. J. Meine (New York, 1930), pp. 447–8; discussed by Bernard DeVoto in *Mark Twain's America* (Boston, 1932), pp. 90–91.

destiny. Washington Irving, whose birth coincided with that of the Republic, formulated a theme of its national literature with his dramatization of the Republic's dominant myth. Even Henry James is in his debt.

But what of Ichabod Crane? Did the pumpkin kill him? Of course not! Our folk heroes never die. Wearing the magic cloak of metamorphosis, they stave off death forever by simply changing their occupations. The ungainly pedagogue is no more—long live the New York City lawyer! For that is what Ichabod becomes after he makes his way from Sleepy Hollow. And onward and upward he goes: from the bar into politics, from his office to the press, thence to the bench. Far be it from Washington Irving to analyze or criticize the great American myth; where he finds a mythology of humor, he improves it on its own grounds. Responding instinctively to his fabulous materials, he makes Ichabod unforgettable in a stunning caricature. Brom, who is much more like life, is not so memorable, even though Americans always love a winner.

Yet Ichabod is not utimately the loser in this legend. All he has lost is a farm girl's love and a measure of self-respect; the former was no real passion, the latter can be repaired. Ichabod Crane is a sorry symbol of learning, of culture, of sophistication, of a decayed religious faith, of an outworn order in the world. His very name suggests decrepitude: 'And she named him Ichabod, saying, The glory is departed from Israel' (I Sam. iv. 21). But Ichabod Crane is no Israelite; although an anachronism in all other respects, he is yet an American. And therefore he is immortal. Back to the city he goes, to find success.

Brom Bones stays in the village and gets the girl. He deserved her more than Ichabod did, for while the scholar danced and counted his stuffed pigs, Brom experienced two human emotions: jealousy and love.

Ichabod also knew two emotions, and two only. His were fear and ambition. He is not the loser, because he leads a full and prosperous life, experiencing to the brim the two emotions which give meaning to his existence: fear, in Sleepy Hollow, and ambition, in New York City. For it is the same ambition which led him to court Katrina Van Tassel that takes him later to the bar and the polls, to the editor's chair and the judge's bench. Ambition of this magnitude requires for its satisfaction a culture sufficiently complex to be capable of corruption. It cannot be gratified in the folk society of Sleepy Hollow Village, where the good people are as pure as the air.

Fear and ambition are Ichabod's, but not love. That is because Ichabod Crane is not wholly human. A sterile intellectual, his head aswim with worthless anachronisms, his heart set on material gain, Ichabod is gracelessly devoid of the natural human affections. He is the bumpkin's caricature of what life in the seat of a corrupt civilization can make of a man.

When one compares 'The Legend of Sleepy Hollow' to the bulk of Irving's work it seems anomalous that he could have mustered the imaginative power to enrich us so greatly, for most of Irving's writing betrays a lack of creative energy, a paucity of invention. Irving, after all, was never able successfully to transcend the limited aims of a 'sketch,' and he continued to rework his old themes in new disguises,[10] telling a tale now set in old Dutch New York, now in Germany, now in England, now in Spain. *Bracebridge Hall, Tales of a Traveller,* most of *Wolfert's Roost* and *The Sketch Book* itself make tedious reading today. They show all too plainly Irving's faults: his dependence upon secondary sources, and the restricted range of emotional experience from which he was able to create fiction. But in the characters of Ichabod and Brom Bones, Irving found archetypal figures already half-created by the popular imagination. Among all of Irving's characters only Rip Van Winkle has as great a power to move us; and Rip, too, is what the highly developed but narrow gift of a storyteller whose milieu was the fabulous has made of a character from folklore. Although the original Peter Klaus was German, the

[10]Much later Irving was to return to the frontier materials he used for Brom Bones in 'The Early Experiences of Ralph Ringwood,' a fictionalized biography of Governor Duval of Florida (*Wolfert's Roost,* New York, 1865. pp. 294–341). Some of the supernatural lore from 'The Legend of Sleepy Hollow' turns up here too, notably an apparition of a horse as a devil (pp. 298–9). Of his late frontier sketches Beach notes, 'Strange that Irving should have come so close to Longstreet's and Craddock's property! Strange too that he should not have known what to make of it' ('Washington Irving,' *University of Kansas City Review,* XIV, 266). Perhaps the key to this puzzle is that Ralph Ringwood, a Kentuckian, meets only Westerners and hence there is no opportunity for Irving to give this sketch the dramatic power which the conflict of regional characters made possible in 'The Legend of Sleepy Hollow.' In view of the popularity, as well as the artistic success, of the earlier sketch, it is indeed surprising that Irving should have followed it with so poor an effort.

354

themes of Rip Van Winkle are universal: the pathos of change, the barely-averted tragedy of loss of personal identity. And, as Louis Le-Fevre has pointed out,[11] Rip is indeed close to an aspect of the American national character—that yearning for escape from work and responsibility which is exemplified by a host of gadgets and the daydream dramas of contemporary popular culture. Irving's Knicker-bocker Dutchmen were, as Miss Rourke observed, remote caricatures resurrected from a distant past. But when Irving dramatized the homely comic figures he found in native American folk traditions, his Ichabod and Brom pass so readily into the reader's own imagination that they seem to be persons we have always known. 'The Legend of Sleepy Hollow' sketches the conflict of cultures which the rest of our literature has adumbrated ever since. One could predict *that* from Irving's story; both Ichabod Crane and Brom Bones lived lustily ever after. They are rivals yet.

[11]'Paul Bunyan and Rip Van Winkle,' *Yale Review,* XXXVI (Autumn 1946), 667–6.

"The Work"

BY EDWARD WAGENKNECHT

Edward Wagenknecht, initially a University of Washington Ph.D., was thereafter on the faculty of the universities of Chicago and Washington and the Illinois Institute of Technology. In 1947 he joined the English Department of Boston University, where he became Professor Emeritus in 1965. His sizeable list of publications includes a *Cavalcade* of both the English and the American novel. For the Oxford University Press he has done a series of artist-and-man "portraits" of American authors, including Hawthorne, Longfellow, Poe, and Irving, which is the source of the present selection. It is Section III of Wagenknecht's well-balanced *Washington Irving: Moderation Displayed* (1962), the Preface of which considers our author's winning personality "considerably more complicated than it is generally supposed to have been."

No American writer has been more succesful than Irving in creating a legend. Henry Seidel Canby may pedantically object that "his Dutch are quite false, except as satire, his Yankees no more true than Yankee Doodle, his New Amsterdam a land of Cocaigne." But since it is Irving's version, not the historians', that survives in the popular imagination, what difference does this make?

The vitality of legend is ever greater than that of fact, but it does not always make for the survival of its creator as a personality. And "Rip Van Winkle" might well have been expected to survive as a fragment of universal human experience—and of humanity's endless dream of being delivered from the tyranny of time—without permitting the personality of its author to get in the way. With Irving it has not worked out that way.

It may well be, however, that contemporary readers do not quite realize how great Irving's fame was in his own time. Hotels, steamboats, public squares, wagons, and cigars were named after him, as well as a spring in Oklahoma and a cliff in New Jersey. The town of Dearman near his home changed its name to Irvington.

James Grant Wilson found that Niagara Falls and Washington Irving were the two American topics that excited the most interest among Britons. H. G. Wells's father learned about the life of the English landed gentry by reading Irving. When he died, New York closed down to honor him as if he had been some leading politician; his funeral procession contained 150 carriages, some 500 "citizens and strangers" on foot, and enough clergy to bury a bishop; the floor of the church sank slightly from the unaccustomed weight of those who crowded into it, while nearly 1000 more waited outside.

This, it may be said, is the kind of fame reserved for movie stars and sports celebrities today—and worth nothing. Be that as it may. From one point of view, all fame is worth nothing, but there is no genuine fame that leaves this element out. Moreover, Irving's réclame was not confined to this sort of thing. There was the flood of formal honors with which he was overwhelmed: the academic degrees, the gold medal from the Royal Society of Literature, the membership in the Real Academia de la Historia, the Smithsonian Institution, and elsewhere. More importantly there was the lofty position accorded him in the literary world. It would be absurd to pretend that no Americans knew in 1859 that their country had already produced greater writers than Irving. It was even widely felt that in some

respects his kind of literature was now "old hat" and that leadership
had passed on to another "school" of younger and more vital writers. For all that, his was the first name that came to mind in connection with American letters, and he was universally recognized as having exercised considerable influence not only in English-speaking
countries but on the Continent as well. In Spain he became a legend.
As Melville said [see p. 83, Part II, above], the lilac he planted
was a little slip,

And yonder lilac is a tree!

Melville is not the only writer whose homage to Irving may
somewhat surprise a less susceptible generation. Look at Dickens's
homage. Look at the way Scott accepted him. And what are we to
make of Byron, who wept over "The Broken Heart" and called Irving's praise of *Don Juan* "feather in my (fool's) cap"?? Crotchety
Carlyle's reaction to *Bracebridge Hall* was not very favorable, yet
when the news came of Irving's death, he wrote, "It was a dream of
mine that we two should be friends!"

But this is history. History too is the extrinsic importance Irving
acquired through becoming the first American writer to achieve a
lasting vogue both here and abroad, and who initiated the long task
of disabusing European readers of their prejudice against American
books, "the first Ambassador," as Hellman said, "whom the New
World of Letters sent to the Old." But what remains today as living
literature?

"Rip Van Winkle," "The Legend of Sleepy Hollow," "The
Devil and Tom Walker," "The Stout Gentleman," and a few more
tales, plus the best of the essays in *The Sketch Book,* outstandingly
those which, like "Westminster Abbey," sound the note of mutability
which he never failed to strike with practiced hand—this much all
would grant. There would be general agreement, too, upon the
beauty of his style; whether or not you are interested in what he is
saying, you can hardly fail to be pleased by his way of saying it.
Canby, to be sure, finds the style "a patina upon the metal of his
thought rather than the flexible soul of the thought itself," but this
does not cancel out either the finish or the charm. And, for all his
elegance, he was not verbose. "Had I more time," he once wrote
Storrow about a manuscript submitted to him, "I should have taken

the liberty occasionally of shaking some superfluous words out of the sentences, which weaken them."

The sentence quoted is not a model of construction; it may, therefore, conveniently illustrate the point that Irving's stylistic accomplishments are not wholly, or perhaps even basically, a mechanical matter. His editors tried to take care of his rackety spelling, but they were not able to do anything with the incurable addiction to the dangling modifier which sometimes turned him into an unconscious humorist. "Alas!" he cries in *Columbus,* "while writing that letter, his noble benefactress was a corpse!" And in *Mahomet* faulty syntax even drives the Deity into evil ways: "Having fallen into blind idolatry, God sent a prophet of the name of Saleh, to restore them to the right way." In his journals he writes of Dante's "L'Inferno," and misspells the names of intimate friends.[1]

Jonathan Oldstyle and *Salmagundi* may by common consent be passed over; they presaged a rather extraordinary number of themes afterwards developed, but they are not in themselves extraordinary supporters of reputation. *Knickerbocker's History* is another matter. Probably not many of us today nearly kill ourselves laughing at it as Fanny Kemble said she did, or even make our sides sore as Scott did his. But as a sustained imaginative effort it is still Irving's greatest book:

> I wrote the History of New York [wrote Irving in 1843], with the slightest materials. A complete history had been in course of preparation by Mr. _____[2] and only knowing some of the ludicrous points of our city's history I could not imagine what would be found interesting enough for a volume on the subject and thought therefore of getting up Knickerbocker's idea of it. I offended many good families by bringing their names into it in ludicrous points of view and several persons never forgave me for it. It was a youthful folly.

The histories of colonial America supplied him with materials for Books II–VII, but William Smith's *History of New-York from the First Discovery to the Year 1732* (London, 1757) was practically all he had for the founding of New Netherlands and the actual history of the colony, and the only contemporary work he employed was Ebenezer Hazard's *Historical Collections Consisting of State Papers, and*

Other Authentic Documents . . . (Philadelphia, 1794). "In order to populate his town of New Amsterdam," writes Robert S. Osborne, who gives an excellent account of all these matters, "Irving simply took a Dutch community of his own time [and transferred it in time (*Ed.*)] back into the first decade[s (*Ed.*)] of the seventeenth century."*

The first section (which may be Peter Irving's) contains an amusing digest of all the absurd ideas concerning the origin of the world and of pre-history that were—or were not—ever entertained among men. The author gets good fun out of the elaborate prolegomena employed by historians and their naïve attempts to settle questions on which no decisive evidence exists one way or the other by assuming that the reasonable thing must have happened. There are burlesque etymologies, and while a surprisingly large amount of the documentation is accurate, some of it refers to books which never existed. Probably no other book in American literature has a longer list of sources;³ of these, Cervantes, Fielding, Sterne, and Swift are the most important.

Part of the fun is Knickerbocker's pretense of complete accuracy:

> But the chief merit on which I value myself, and found my hopes for future regard, is that faithful veracity with which I have compiled this invaluable little work; carefully winnowing away the chaff of hypothesis, and discarding the tares of fable, which are too apt to spring up and choke the seeds of truth and wholesome knowledge. . . . I have scrupulously discarded many a pithy tale and marvelous adventure, whereby the drowsy ear of summer indolence might be enthralled; jealously maintaining that fidelity, gravity, and dignity, which should ever distinguish the historian.

He records the legend that Peter Stuyvesant once shot Beelzebub with a silver bullet, but he will not vouch for the truth of this. "Perish the man who would let fall a drop to discolor the pure stream of history!" There is even one editorial footnote in which D. K. is

---

*See Osborne's *"A Study of Washington Irving's Development as a Man of Letters to 1825."* Unpublished doctoral dissertation, Univ. of North Carolina, 1947. p. 185. [*Ed.*]

criticized because, "in his scrupulous search after truth," he is "sometimes too fastidious in regard to facts which border a little on the marvelous."

Yet it is also true that D. K. claims to be an artist-historian. He admits that he introduced a storm into one of his chapters "to give a little bustle and life to this tranquil part of my work, and to keep my drowsy readers from falling asleep—and partly to serve as an overture to the tempestuous times which are about to assail the pacific province of Nieuw-Nederlandts." And while he cannot save the life of a favorite hero, or absolutely contradict the event of a battle, as a romancer might do, he can occasionally permit one whom he admires to "bestow on his enemy a sturdy back stroke sufficient to fell a giant; though, in honest truth, he may never have done any thing of the kind."

Knickerbocker's History is not a completely accurate book; neither Irving nor anybody else could have made it that with the materials available—but it is much more accurate than we have a right to require of a burlesque history. He cuts the number of Dutch governors down to three, making Wouter Van Twiller the third instead of the fifth; then in Book V he carelessly speaks of him as having surpassed "all who preceded him." He ridicules the Dutch for their eating, drinking, and smoking; for their phlegmatic temperament and their passion for scrubbing. But he does not save all his shafts for them—their Swedish and Yankee neighbors are, on occasion, handled quite as roughly—and it would be an insensitive reader indeed who should fail to recognize that in his pages Peter Stuyvesant, though at times a figure of fun, is also an heroic figure and almost a tragic one.[4]

It is not required of the author of a burlesque that he should be altogether consistent. Irving makes fun of Peter Stuyvesant for his fire-eating tendencies, but he also ridicules the pacifism of the second governor William Kieft, whom he describes with one eye on Thomas Jefferson. Irving's knowledge of history was not great, but he was quite sophisticated enough in his attitude toward it. He knew that complete accuracy is not possible in historical writing, and that history and fiction cannot be completely separated from each other; a good many contemporary conflicts of opinion concerning the nature of history are reflected in his pages. Diedrich Knickerbocker "explores the nature of history as *Dox Quixote* had explored the nature of fiction, revealing the complexity of the problem without finally solving it," and a good many of the jokes are on the reader.[5]

As we have already seen, the common view that Irving was neo-classical up to *The Sketch Book* and romantic thereafter is much too simple to be maintained; it is true, however, that, once having begun to do his writing in a foreign land, he was less encouraged to develop that side of his talent which inclined him toward social and political satire. Publishing as he did on both sides of the Atlantic, he must appeal to two reading publics. When he wrote down what he observed in English villages, for example, he was as realistic as he could have been in America; he "added greatly to . . . [his] stock of knowledge, by noting down . . . habits and customs." Had he been merely a lover of fine scenery, he tells us, there would have been no need to leave his own country. "But Europe held forth the charms of stories and poetical associations."

Realism and romanticism can be much more easily separated in theory than in practice; there cannot have been many works of literature that were wholly one or the other. It is quite natural that there should be differences of opinion about these matters in Irving. Thus McDermott finds him reducing even the people he knew on his Western journey to literary types—"Irving is not a traveler reporting what he sees; he is ever the self-conscious literary man, the feature-story writer who, by the ready use of his imagination, makes a little fact go a long way"—while Nathalia Wright is so much impressed by his tendency to tie himself down to actual localities, even in such highly romantic stories as the banditti yarns in *Tales of a Traveller,* that she is willing to credit him with beginning a tradition in the American novel about Italy, "the chief characteristic of which, in contrast to the Gothic tradition, was an essential realism of background." Nobody can doubt that *The Sketch Book* has its romantic elements, but we can think of it as all romantic only by concentrating wholly upon "Rip Van Winkle," "The Legend of Sleepy Hollow," and "The Spectre Bridegroom" and ignoring everything else.[6]

All three of these stories have been derived from German sources, but the first two—the great ones—have been ingeniously transplanted to the Hudson River country. "When I first wrote the Legend of Rip Van Winkle," so Irving remembered it in 1843, "my thoughts had been for some time turned towards giving a color of romance and tradition to interesting points of our national scenery which is so generally deficient in our country." He succeeded so well that translators have always had trouble with the story.[7]

Irving's "Rip Van Winkle" is four times the length of Otmar's "Peter Klaus." He changes Otmar's knights to the ghosts of Henrik Hudson and his crew; he localizes; he characterizes Rip in his own manner, builds up his domestic background, and tells what happened after his return. If this is not a legitimate way to create literature, then Chaucer and Shakespeare will have to be cast into the outer darkness. As Longfellow once remarked, a modern writer cannot strike a spade into Parnassus anywhere without disturbing the bones of a dead poet.[8]

The sleep-motive in "Rip Van Winkle" has roots which run very deep in world literature. There is the classical story about Epimenides, who retired into a cave to escape the heat of the day when he should have been watching his flock, and slept there for fifty-seven years.[9] Otmar himself tells of Frederick Barbarossa, who sleeps in the Kyffhäuser, from which he will return to succor his people in their need. Once a pair of lovers visited the Emperor to borrow crockery for their wedding feast, but when they got home again they found they had been away 200 years.

Scott told Irving the story of Thomas Rhymer, who was carried off by the Fairy Queen, and at Inverness he may have seen the Hill of the Fairies and heard the story of the two fiddlers of Strathspey, who were lured into this hill and detained for 100 years. They recognized nothing and were recognized by nobody upon their emergence, and they crumbled to dust when the Scriptures were read in church.[10]

After the three stories, the part of *The Sketch Book* that is most read today comprises the several papers describing English Christmas celebrations. It should be remembered that this is pre-*Christmas Carol* material, though of course Addison had already described Sir Roger de Coverley's Christmas in *The Spectator*. But there are twenty-six papers altogether in *The Sketch Book* which concern English themes, and all but six of them have their scene outside of London. Irving catches the atmosphere of English rural life and the English Sunday as well as he catches the Christmas spirit. There is an essay about King James I of Scotland, the author of *The King's Quair*, and there are two papers about Shakespeare, one describing a visit to Stratford, and the other on Falstaff and the Boar's Head Tavern. There is also an essay on "The Mutability of Literature," which is developed fancifully and imaginatively. The same melancholy which the thought of time's triumph over everything that is mortal calls forth here appears again in the famous paper on "Westminster Abbey": "The coffin of Edward the Confessor has been broken open, and his remains despoiled of their funeral ornaments; the sceptre has been stolen from the hand of the imperious Elizabeth, and the effigy of Henry the Fifth is headless." And I suppose no reader of *The Sketch Book* ever forgets the passage in which Irving muses over the neighboring tombs of "the haughty Elizabeth" and "her victim, the lovely and unfortunate Mary." Despite his penchant for the picturesque, Irving's English papers are not mere antiquarianism: he was also seeking to understand the British character, as the essay on "John Bull" shows. "The Wife," "The Widow and Her Son," and "The Pride of the Village" have too much eighteenth-century sentimentalism to interest modern readers very deeply, but they are all based on realistic, not legendary, materials, and the incidents on which "The Wife" rests involved two of Irving's friends.

Of *Bracebridge Hall* Osborne has remarked [Osborne, p. 319, *op. cit.*] that as Irving "had built *A History of New York* out of parts of *Salmagundi,* so he built *Bracebridge Hall* out of parts of *The Sketch Book.*" But Osborne knows better than anybody else, and has clearly demonstrated, that *Bracebridge Hall* itself also descends not only from *Salmagundi* but even from *Jonathan Oldstyle*. Except for the four stories included (Irving finds a place for them on the pretext that they were told at the Hall), the book is considerably more unified than its predecessor. It is an attractive picture of English rural life, viewed from the upper-class standpoint, but the author does not neglect rural superstitions and May Day customs; this side of the volume is further developed through the device of bringing in a band of gypsies. It is clear that the old folk beliefs appealed to Irving by reason of their picturesqueness, and that he would like to accept them, but his usual balance and common sense do not desert him; he knows, for example, that in their time the May Day games were considerably less innocent than those who cherish them merely because they are old would like to believe.

As for the stories: "The Stout Gentleman" contains one of the most artful uses of anti-climax in literature. "Dolph Heyliger," a story of old New York, involves a doctor's idle apprentice and a search for buried treasure, and is one of the best of Irving's longer tales. "The Student of Salamanca" is pleasant enough reading about love, alchemy, intrigue, and the Inquisition.[11] "Annette Delarbre," the least substantial of the four, is another nineteenth-century tale about the tender-hearted maiden who could not distinguish between fidelity and fixation. Among them all, only *Evangeline* survives.

Irving himself thought *Tales of a Traveller* his best book, and his judgment was not absurd, for this was the only volume he had devoted entirely to fiction, and he was developing a new theory of narrative form[12] which might have come to more than it did if further experiments had not been discouraged by the savage press which the book received. Poe, Longfellow, and Stevenson all loved it; perhaps Irving might find comfort here against not only the insensitiveness of contemporary reviewers but even the deplorably unimaginative tendency of many modern writers to echo them. It is true of course that the book lacks unity—but then it is called *Tales of a Traveller*— being divided into four parts: "Strange Stories by a Nervous Gentleman," "Buckthorne and His Friends," "The Italian Banditti," and "The Money-Diggers."

I do not understand Williams's judgment that "both the ghost stories and the robber tales designed for a public in love with German romantics and Gothic prestidigitators, are obsolete, as dead as the fashions which begot them." Most of the literature of the past is, in that sense, as dead as the fashions which begot it, but surely it ought to be possible for a scholar to read it and judge it in the light of the standards which prevailed when it was written. Williams continues: "we yawn over the machinery of haunted châteaux, sinister storms, mysterious footsteps, and hidden panels. Spirits sigh in the darkness; portraits wink; furniture dances; and brooding, sensitive heroes woo melancholy maidens—in vain."

There is no law against yawning, but it can hardly take the place of literary evaluation, and if we cannot enjoy these things, the loss is ours, for it means that one whole large area of Romantic literature is closed to us. "The Adventure of My Uncle" and "The Adventure of My Aunt," though "primitives" among ghost stories, do not, I think, lack the supernatural thrill, and of course it is not fair to judge any such tale by the standards which have evolved through the intensive development to which this type of literature has been subjected since Irving's time. But I do not see how anybody can snap his fingers at "The Bold Dragoon," whose merit was recognized by Anne Carroll

Moore, when she gave it the place of honor in her collection, *The Bold Dragoon and Other Ghostly Tales,* by Washington Irving, which was delightfully illustrated by James Daugherty, and published by Alfred A. Knopf, in "New Amsterdam," as the title-page has it, in 1930. And nobody has ever been able to find a source for the horrible French Revolutionary tale, "Adventure of the German Student," which very much resembles one of Marjorie Bowen's supernatural stories. Here we have a dream which anticipates experience, quite in the modern manner, and an ending in a madhouse, which suggests the great German film, *The Cabinet of Dr. Caligari.* And here at least Irving's refusal to commit himself has less in common with the silly, shallow rationalism of Mrs. Radcliffe than with Hawthorne's skillful, subtle, and deliberate ambiguity.

"Buckthorne and His Friends," Irving's longest and most varied narrative, has perhaps been sufficiently discussed elsewhere in this volume. "The Italian Banditti" is made up of conventional romantic materials of the kind one might expect to encounter under that title, not particularly distinctive perhaps but thoroughly enjoyable; the plots seem to be Irving's own. "The Money Diggers" is American material again, centered on the ideas of digging for pirate gold or gaining wealth through diabolical means. "The Devil and Tom Walker" is, of course, the finest narrative in this part of the book— and in the book in general—but "Wolfert Webber; or Golden Dreams" is still well worth reading.

The Alhambra, as has already been said, combines *Arabian Nights* material, in the stories told, with honest, straightforward description of the place as it was in Irving's time, and of the people he encountered there. As he himself says, "Every thing in the work relating to myself and the actual inhabitants of the Alhambra is unexaggerated fact; it was only in the legends that I indulged in *romancing.*" As romancing it was very good.

The rest of Irving's work was repetition and addenda, or else it was factual and historical writing. Though not widely or intensively read today, it still commands considerable respect.

That Irving was not a great historian goes without saying. He read enormously, and great libraries thrilled him as a voluptuary might be thrilled by a houris' paradise; he was even capable of hard, grueling work when necessary, but basically he did not malign himself when he wrote:

I have wandered through different countries, and witnessed many of the shifting scenes of life. I cannot say that I have studied them with the eye of a philosopher; but rather with the sauntering gaze with which humble lovers of the picturesque stroll from the window of one printshop to another; caught sometimes by the delineations of beauty, sometimes by the distortions of caricature, and sometimes by the loveliness of landscape.

"That work was written so rapidly," he writes cavalierly of his life of Goldsmith, "with the printer's devil at my heels that I should not be surprised if many errors were detected in it. I had no time to refer to authorities that were not immediately at hand." He refused to "join in the severe censures that have been passed upon Sparks for the verbal corrections and alterations he has permitted himself to make even in some of Washington's letters." He even told Ik Marvel that he had no system—"you must go to Bancroft for that: I have, it is true, my little budget of notes—some tied one way, some another, and which, when I need, I think I come upon in my pigeonholes by a sort of instinct. That is all there is to it."

"He had no taste for research," writes one distinguished modern student of historiography, "and confronted with the graver tasks of the historian he fails. In the lighter sphere of anecdote and romance he is supreme."[13] Alexander H. Everett anticipated this view in Irving's own time when he credited him with "the merit of plain and elegant narrative," but added that he did not "aspire to the higher palm of just and deep thought in the investigation of causes and effects, that constitutes the distinction of the real historian." Irving's burlesque of scholarship and the scholarly method in "The Art of Book-Making" and "The Boar's Head Tavern, Eastcheap" is very interesting in view of his own mining and sapping for books yet to come. He well knew that even when he wrote history he functioned as a man of letters. In 1837 it was suggested to him that he write a biography of Robert Fulton. Irving admitted that the subject was a good one,

but, somehow or other, I do not feel in the vein to undertake it; and unless a thing "jumps with my humour" I can make nothing of it—I wish, however, you could suggest some task to fill up intervals between such moods—the editing of any standard author or authors, or any other of those tasks which require judgment, taste and literary research, rather than fancy or invention. I need at this moment all the pecuniary aid that my pen can command.

It is interesting to note that the plan he conceived for his work on the conquest of Mexico was wider than the one Prescott finally used.[14] And Prescott himself, in his enthusiastic article about *The Conquest of Granada,* though clearly understanding and stating everything that Irving could not or would not do, also realized and paid tribute to his special gifts. "But all these particulars, however pertinent to philosophical history, would have been entirely out of keeping in Mr. Irving's, and might have produced a disagreeable discordance in the general harmony of his plan."

After *Knickerbocker, Granada* was the work most imaginatively handled. There he had exempted himself from the demands of strict fidelity by creating a ·burlesque: here he attributed the work to a mythical Fray Antonio Agapida; if the good friar is bigoted or credulous, Washington Irving's withers are unwrung. He recognized the work as "something of an experiment, and all experiments in literature or in anything else are doubtful." And he tells Colonel Aspinwall, "I have made a work out of the old chronicles, embellished as much as I am able, by the imagination, and adapted to the romantic taste of the day. Something that was to be between a history and a romance." The interesting thing is that both here and in *Knickerbocker* he was much more modest in taking advantage of the opportunities he had made for himself than he might have been expected to be. Substantially he was quite just[15] when he wrote Prince Dolgorouki of the *Granada:*

I have introduced nothing that is not founded on historical authority, but I have used a little freedom of pencil in the coloring, grouping, &c—and have brought out characters and incidents in stronger relief than they are to be met with in the old histories. . . . I really believe the work will contain a fuller and more characteristic amount of that remarkable war than is to be found elsewhere.

It is quite inadequate, then, to attempt to differentiate between Irving and more "serious" historians by describing his work as "narrative history." As Hedges says, it is "in a literary class almost by itself—which means, practically, it is in no class." Yet it shows the effect of most of the thinking of its time in the world of literary and historical theory. Irving was not uninterested in ideas or in generalizations, and he certainly was not less inclined than other historians to discern pattern in history or to see his characters as types or embodiments of forces larger than themselves.

Technically most of Irving's works in this field were biography rather than history. Because it lay farthest out of his range the *Mahomet* is the thinnest of these; the richest, in a sense, is the Goldsmith, not because Irving did independent research on the subject but rather because his own temperamental affinity for Goldsmith enabled him to make literature out of what John Forster and others had discovered. But the real tests of his skill and his methods came with the prodigious works on Columbus and George Washington.

The *Washington* began when the President placed his hand in blessing upon a six-year-old's brow. *The Life and Voyages of Columbus* may be said to have begun when that same boy pored over the geographical narratives in *The World Displayed:* "The early volumes treated of the voyages of Columbus and the conquests of Mexico and Peru. They were more delightful to me than a fairy tale, and the plates by which they were illustrated are indelibly stamped on my recollections."

As we have seen, the work grew out of—or took the place of—his plan to translate Navarrete's collection of documents, and though Irving thought it unnecessary to check Navarrete's work—"wherever I found a document published by him, I was sure of its correctness, and did not trouble myself to examine the original"—he would have resented the implication that he had relied entirely upon the Spaniard. As he described his plan in prospect to T. W. Storrow in 1826:

> I shall form my narrative from a careful comparison and collation of the works of Las Casas and Columbus' son Ferdinando, both founded on Columbus' Journal—and shall at the same time make use of Oviedo, who lived in Columbus' time and in fact all the old Spanish writers. I have various works relative to the subject in Italian, French, &c. I am in fact surrounded by

works of the kind. I shall endeavor to make it the most complete and authentic account of Columbus and his voyages extant and, by diligent investigation of the materials around me, to settle various points in dispute. It will require great attention and study & hard work, but I feel stimulated to it, and encouraged by the singular facilities which are thrown in my way. I want to do something that I must "take off my coat to." . . . My brother will be of much assistance to me in my researches and in the examination and collation of facts and dates, about which I mean to be scrupulously attentive and accurate, as I know I shall be expected to be careless in such particulars and to be apt to indulge in the imagination. I mean to look into every thing myself, to make myself master of my subject and to endeavor to produce a work which shall bear examination as to candor and authenticity.

When he had finished, it seemed to him that he had been faithful to this ideal:

I have woven into my work many curious particulars not hitherto known concerning Columbus, and I think I have thrown light upon some parts of his character which have not been brought out by his former biographers. I have labored hard to make the work complete and accurate as to all the information extant relative to the subject, which I have sought to execute in such a manner as would render it agreeable to the general reader.

Impartial judges have sometimes spoken nearly as sympathetically. Thus Bancroft gave *Columbus* "all kinds of merit—research, critical judgment, interest in the narrative, picturesque description and golden style." Nor is the distinguished Menèndez y Pelayo the only Spanish authority who has praised it warmly. Henry Harisse called it "a history written with judgment and impartiality, which leaves far behind it all descriptions of the discovery of the New World published before or since." Edward G. Bourne thought well of it, and though John Fiske charged and proved that Irving was sometimes guilty of misplaced eulogy and of attributing modern knowledge to the men of the past, he still felt respect and a warm regard for the work. "We have learned a great deal more about Columbus than Irving knew," writes Edward H. O'Neill, "but Irving has seldom been found wrong."

Yet, Irving's *Columbus* was less an independent piece of investigation than he claimed—and probably believed. He simply did not have the time or the knowledge or the training to make such an investigation; he probably did not even have the knowledge he would have needed to state the problem fairly. In assuming that Navarrete did not need his attestation, he was quite correct, and he could have added nothing substantial to Navarrete's labors if he had tried. His final claim must rest upon his having turned the story of Columbus into a work of art.

McCarter finds Irving's Columbus "the romantic hero of the nineteenth-century adventure-novel"; he cannot, he thinks, have been very unfamiliar to readers of Scott. Hedges is substantially in accord when he declares that, in *Columbus* and its successors, Irving "was to give almost free rein to the impulse to view history aesthetically, to organize it into a series of re-enactments of archetypal mythic dramas."

Such statements may be read disparagingly, but it is not necessary to read them thus. As Theodore Roosevelt perceived and proclaimed, imagination does not tend to distortion in the writing of history unless it is a distorted imagination. All historians select materials and make assumptions, and though many of Irving's superiors as research workers have certainly viewed history less aesthetically than he did, this does not in itself prove that they viewed it more accurately. Irving's uncritical state of mind has been well indicated by Hedges, as well as the fundamental reasonableness of his bent. He accepts what he has been told except when he runs into conflicts; then he tries to mediate between conflicting evidences, striking a balance between them, and generally assuming that the truth lies somewhere near that middle of the road in which his feet felt most at home. But though he "sins against literal accuracy," he often needs only to insert a "probably" or two to satisfy most historians, and though his annotation is somewhat sloppy, most of it is probably substantially accurate. In the end, Hedges defends *Columbus* against most of Stanley Williams's criticisms. It "does exactly what it was supposed to—utilizes the materials Navarrete had published and the manuscript histories in Rich's library. Thus it was, when it appeared,

new and original, at least in one sense." Irving dramatized and high-
lighted and interpreted his hero on his own terms, and communicated
his essence to the reader in a style which was the unmistakable expression of the writer's own personality. He expressed his own sense
of values through him. His work might be done again and done better, but until another Washington Irving should be born into the
world, nobody else could do what he had done. He had taken one of
the momentous events of human history into the cosmos of his own
mind and spirit.

As early as 1825 Archibald Constable asked Irving to write a
life of Washington. On August 19 Irving wrote Constable from Paris
and declined: "After the various works . . . which have appeared on
the subject it would be very difficult to treat it anew in a manner to
challenge public attention or to satisfy public expectation if much excited." He also objected that "it would require a great deal of reading
and research, and that too of a troublesome and irksome kind among
public documents and state papers; for Washington's life was more
important as a Statesman than as a General." And he concluded: "I
feel myself incapable of executing my idea of the task. It is one that I
dare not attempt lightly. I stand in too great awe of it."

Ultimately, it would seem, the awe was overcome, and in his
Preface to his first volume he outlined his formula for success:

> My work is founded on the correspondence of Washington,
> which, in fact, affords the amplest and surest groundwork for his
> biography. This I have consulted as it exists in manuscript in the
> archives of the Department of State, to which I have had full
> and frequent access. I have also made frequent use of "Washing-
> ton's Writings," as published by Mr. Sparks; a careful collation
> of many of them with the originals having convinced me of the
> general correctness of the collection, and of the safety with
> which it may be relied upon for historical purposes; and I am
> happy to bear this testimony to the essential accuracy of one
> whom I consider among the greatest benefactors to our national
> literature; and to whose writings and researches I acknowledge
> myself largely indebted throughout my work.

He tells us specifically where he got his information about
Major André, Nelly Custis, and that tragic bride of darkness, Jane

McCrea. There is a letter to Benjamin Silliman accepting the latter's offer to let him see Jonathan Trumbull's diary and offering to "defray the expense of having a copy made of it." On the other hand, when F. C. Yarnell wrote, offering to lend him a narrative of André's capture, he replied (after more than three months' silence), that he "had already disposed of the subject" and "had diligently consulted every authority I could find relating to it. I have endeavored to treat the matter as candidly and dispassionately as possible; which is not a very easy task where there is so much to touch and interest the feelings."

Irving returned to his use of Washington's own writings in an explanatory note at the end of Volume IV—"for never did man leave a more truthful mirror of his heart and mind, and a more thorough exponent of his conduct, than he has left in his copious correspondence"—and he also apologized for his inclusion of even those Revolutionary War campaigns in which Washington did not participate— "for his spirit pervaded and directed the whole, and a general knowledge of the whole is necessary to appreciate the sagacity, forecast, enduring fortitude, and comprehensive wisdom with which he conducted it." In a private letter of 1856, he explained himself more fully to Henry T. Tuckerman:

You have discerned what I aimed at, "the careful avoidance of rhetoric, the calm, patient and faithful narrative of facts." My great labor has been to arrange these facts in the most lucid order and place them in the most favorable light; and without exaggeration or embellishment; trusting to their own characteristic value for effect. Rhetoric does very well under the saddle but is not to be trusted in harness; being apt to pull facts out of place or upset them. My horse *Gentleman Dick* was very rhetorical and sheered off finely, but he was apt to run away with me and came near breaking my neck.

I have availed myself of the license of biography to step down occasionally from the elevated walk of history and relate familiar things in a familiar way; seeking to show the prevalent patterns, and feelings and humors of the day, and even to depict the heroes of Seventy Six as they really were, men in cocked hats, regimental coats and breeches; and not classic warriors in shining armor and flowing mantles with brows bound with laurel and truncheons in their hands.

But he also told F. S. Cozzens that he

had a great deal of trouble to keep the different parts together, giving a little touch here and a little touch there, so that one part should not lag behind the other nor one part be more conspicuous than the other. I felt like old Lablache when he was performing in a rehearsal of his orchestra . . . bringing out a violin here, a clarinet there, now suppressing a trombone, now calling upon the flutes, and every now and then bringing out the big bass drum. So I have to keep my different instruments in play, not too low in one passage nor too loud in another, and now and then bringing in the great bass drum.

The orchestral comparison is interesting, and it shows that Irving was as much the artist-historian when he was Irving as when he was Diedrich Knickerbocker. But he goes on to add that he wanted a style simple enough for a child to read. "I want the action to shine through the style. No style, indeed; no encumbrance of ornament. . . ."

Irving also said that he had been collecting material for *Washington* for twenty years before he wrote the work, and that to write it seemed a kind of duty. "Yet his character suggested the idea of a statue; however you might admire it, you could not embrace it. But as I became better acquainted with the real life of the man, his constant untiring benevolence, I loved him more and more." This was precisely what Prescott praised his biography for: "You have done with Washington just as I thought you would, and, instead of a cold, marble statue of a demigod, you have made him a being of flesh and blood, like ourselves—one with whom we can have sympathy." Later he added generously that he himself had never understood Washington's character until Irving had written about him. Bancroft, too, was generous: "The narrative is beautifully told, in your own happy diction and style, felicitous always; never redundant; graceful and elegant."

Modern detractors of Irving, like modern detractors of Longfellow, have generally been distressed over the fact that he was neither

Herman Melville nor Ernest Hemingway. This much is undeniable, but why it should occasion so much distress is not quite clear. That he was a "genteel" writer admits of no doubt, but in his time "genteel" was not a dirty word. When he was seventy-five years old, he wrote a letter to a young relative not yet out of his teens, in which he described the personal qualities he admired:

> I have always valued in you what I considered to be an honorable nature; a conscientiousness in regard to duties; an open truthfulness; an absence of all low propensities and sensual indulgences; a reverence for sacred things; a respect for others; a freedom from selfishness, and a prompt decision to oblige; and, with all these, a gayety of spirit, flowing, I believe, from an uncorrupted heart, that gladdens everything around you.

His own possession of all these qualities was far above the average. And he valued their manifestation of themselves in books as well as in men.

It was not his function either to scale the heights or sound the depths of life; neither did he ever pretend to be able to do so. Though he was never so indifferent to either ideas or social evils as his critics would have us believe, he consistently inhabited a middle region which he surveyed and described with a winning, companionable charm. If you must have death in the afternoon and an orgy at night, he has nothing for you. And if life is flat and meaningless to you except in moments of rare spiritual ecstasy, he has nothing for you either. Between the heights and the depths, however, there still lies a very wide and attractive area. The reading public which dwells there may be smug, and it may be dull, but it does not need to be kicked every few minutes to stay awake, and it is possible that the tides of life run higher and stronger here than in many other publics, and that it will survive longer. This is the area that Irving inhabits, and whatever other shortcomings it may have, there can be no question that it embraces a good deal of what we generally mean to indicate when we speak of civilization.

¹Irving's standards in all matters of usage were very conservative, as see his letter to M. D. Phillips, Feb. 17, 1852, in the Berg Collection: "I certainly do not make Webster's Dictionary my standard of orthography though I regret to say I often find myself inadvertently falling into some of the vitiations which the industrious circulation of his work has made so prevalent in our country. From the same cause also I find it almost impossible to have a work printed in this country free from some of his arbitrary modifications, which are pronounced provincialisms by all foreign scholars critical of the English language."

²This passage is quoted from Irving's own memorandum in "Notes made in Madrid, Jan. 10–23, 1843," in the Sterling Library at Yale. The blank space is his.

³These are well summed up by Williams and Tremaine McDowell in the introduction to their reprint of the first edition (ABC, 1927): "Passages reminiscent of Sterne jostle others from Cotton Mather. Sometimes a character speaks and acts in the idiom of Cervantes, or there is phrasing, perhaps half unconscious, which recalls . . . [Irving's] severe training in the Bible. Fielding is here, as are Swift and Rabelais, the New England historians, and the Jesuit fathers. It is not ostentatious learning, but a boyish pleasure of playing with words. Allusions tumble after one another throughout the book, occasionally badly assimilated or badly adapted, but all touched with the curiosity of the young writer's eager mind. . . . Interspersed are echoes from Shakespeare . . . the plays of Ben Jonson and John Dryden or the *Hudibras* of Samuel Butler. Irving can allude to Aesop . . . to Homer, Hobbes, Bacon, Sidney, Tom Paine, or Sheridan's Pizarro. . . . He quotes from Hesiod, and he draws parallels from English, Greek, Roman, and Italian legend. . . . He was deep not merely in Cervantes, Rabelais, and Ariosto, but in Arthurian legend and in out-of-the-way tales of knighthood."

⁴See C. G. Laird, "Tragedy and Irony in *Knickerbocker's History*," AL, XII (1940), 157–72.

⁵See W. L. Hedges's Harvard dissertation, "The Fiction of History,"* for the most learned discussion of Irving as an historian that I have encountered. It is also the discussion which makes Irving himself appear, in this aspect, the most sophisticated.

⁶And, of course, one would have to ignore the stylistic elements even in the works cited. Osborne has now shown that "five of the seven numbers of the *Sketch Book* were written to conform to a set and established pattern. Each issue was to contain one humorous writing, one pathetic writing, and one serious writing—usually concerned with relations between England and America. If the issue contained a fourth number, that added writing might be on any subject, but generally it took the form of nature description. . . . The humorous writings were generally in the tradition of the eighteenth century

*"The Fiction of History: Washington Irving Against a Romantic Transition." Unpublished doctoral dissertation, Harvard, 1953. [*Ed.*]

and remind one of Goldsmith's writing or even of the writings of Sterne, Fielding, and Smollett. The pathetic writing was in the Romantic tradition, and 'The Widow and Her Son' and 'The Pride of the Village' remind one strikingly of such romantic writings as Wordsworth's *The Excursion*. . . . In some of the writings, as in 'The Legend of Sleepy Hollow,' there was a fortunate mingling of the Augustan style with romantic plot, and these works have proved extremely fortunate and have lasted well in the popular taste. Irving had had from his earliest writings a slight taste for what is generally considered romantic . . . and when this vein of Romanticism was introduced into his Augustan technique, his full powers were brought into his writing and the writings produced were those which have contributed most to his permanent fame."

[7]See Williams, "The First Version of the Writings of Washington Irving in Spanish," *MP*, XXVIII (1930), 185–201. Daniel G. Hoffman, "Irving's Use of American Folklore in 'The Legend of Sleepy Hollow,'" *PMLA*, LXVIII (1953), 425–33, comments, "Although the original Peter Klaus was German, the themes of Rip Van Winkle are universal: the pathos of change, the barely-averted tragedy of loss of personal identity." I cannot, however, agree with Osborne (p. 287) that the "primary purpose" of "Rip Van Winkle" was "to illustrate the transformation wrought by democracy" in the community in which Rip lives. The machinery of the story is supernatural, but it derives its power from the theme of mutability plus the common human longing to escape problems by, in some form, throwing off the tyranny of time. Surely any sociological interest it may have is secondary. The changes which take place in Rip's village during his absence are important so far as the story is concerned merely because they help the reader to feel the lapse of time and contribute to Rip's isolation in his final phase.

[8]See H. A. Pochmann, "Irving's German Sources in *The Sketch Book*," *SP*, XXVII (1930), 477–507; E. L. Brooks, "A Note on Irving's Sources," *AL*, XXV (1953), 229–30; and "A Note on the Source of 'Rip Van Winkle,'" *AL*, XXV (1954), 495–9; John T. Krumpelman, "Revealing the Source of Irving's 'Rip Van Winkle,' *Monatshefte*, XLVII (1955), 361–2; Walter A. Reichart, "Concerning the Source of Irving's 'Rip Van Winkle,'" *Monatshefte*, XLVIII (1956), 94–5; see, also, the discussions in Reichart's *Washington Irving in Germany* (which plausibly explains why Irving apparently cited the wrong story as his source), and Williams, *Life*, I, 181–91.

[9]Tieman de Vries, *Dutch History, Art, and Literature for Americans* (Grand Rapids, Michigan: Eerdmans-Sevensma Co., 1912) describes Erasmus's use of the story of Epimenides in his *Epistles* and absurdly accuses Irving of plagiarizing from Erasmus, with much hand wringing over his wickedness in maligning the Dutch.

[10]William E. Griffis, *The Mikado's Empire* (H, 1896) summarizes an ancient Chinese story in which Rip's part is played by "a pious woodcutter," Lu-wen, who pursues a fox upon the holy mountain Tendai, and emerges into a clearing where two lovely ladies are playing checkers. He does not sleep but

only stands watching them for a few minutes. When he turns to go, his limbs feel stiff, his ax-handle falls to pieces, and when he stoops to pick it up he finds his face covered with a long white beard. He returns to his village, where he finds everything as strange as Rip did. Finally an old woman identifies herself as "a descendant of the seventh generation of a man named Lu-wen. The old man groaned aloud, and, turning his back on all, retraced his weary steps to the mountain again. He was never heard of more, and it is believed he entered into the company of the immortal hermits and spirits of the mountain." For a "Rip Van Winkle" situation in a Spanish setting, see Irving's "The Adalantado of the Seven Cities," in *Wolfert's Roost.*

[11]In the same memorandum cited above (n. 2), Irving says that he originally placed the scene of this story in Italy. The alchemist came partly from an old bookworm described by Isaac D'Israeli. His speculations on alchemy "were the result of an extensive course of reading in books on alchymy and the philosphers stone etc., in which I got very much interested and therefore handled the subject familiarly."

[12]See McCarter, "The Literary, Political, and Social Theories of Washington Irving," p. 170.*

[13]G. P. Gooch, *History and Historians in the Nineteenth Century* (Longmans, Green, 1913).

[14]See Pierre M. Irving, *Life,* Volume III, Chapter VI.

[15]See Louise M. Hoffman, "Irving's Use of Spanish Sources in *The Conquest of Granada,*" *Hispania,* XXVIII (1945), 493–8.

*Unpublished doctoral dissertation by Pete Kyle McCarter, Wisconsin, 1939. [*Ed.*]

"Irving
and the
Gothic Tradition"

BY JOHN CLENDENNING

John Clendenning, whose teaching career has been a concentration on American Literature and Civilization, after a Ph.D. from the University of Iowa, has taught in the California State University system since 1960. He is at present Professor and Chairman of the English Department at the Northridge campus. He has held an American Council of Learned Societies student fellowship, and in 1971–1972 was a Guggenheim fellow. This colorful discussion of Irving as an early and "sportive" gothicist appeared in *The Bucknell Review,* Vol. XII (1964), 90–98; it had been presented as a paper in an earlier and somewhat different form at the annual meeting of the Modern Language Association at Chicago in December, 1963.

Although we may scoff at the thrills, tricks, and flights of gothic fiction, its durable influence cannot be ignored. How this popular genre, despite its medieval twaddle and its supernatural bombast, was appropriated by our most serious writers remains an enigma, though some critics have argued convincingly that the genre was, in some ways, serious from the outset. Whatever the case, everyone will agree that the gothic element which survived in the novels of Henry James was distinctly different from the heavy machinery of *The Monk*. To identify this difference, let me risk a generalization: James learned to subjectify all that Lewis had to objectify; in James unvarnished horror may occur in full sunlight, whereas the grimness of *The Monk* exists only behind the abbey's closed door. The gothicists' traditional "machinery" was necessarily tangible, because it produced a terror which always fascinated them. But when Isabel Archer Osmond sits before her fireplace, her anguish produces the images which are identifiably gothic in origin. She sees herself in "a dark, narrow alley with a dead wall at the end"; she is locked behind a closed door; she is "draped . . . in pictured tapestries . . . shut up with an odor of mould and decay." Lewis was admittedly an interesting psychologist, having accurately described phenomena which today we call suppression, sublimation, projection, and so forth, and yet he could not treat human motivation without a chiller-thriller cause. On the other hand, we admire James because he preserved the gothicists' imagery but treated it as a psychic result, not the factual cause of terror. It was a major accomplishment of the modern novelist to have seen the images of the gothic world as distorted perceptions of reality.

Washington Irving was about half-way between modern fiction and the cult of Mrs. Radcliffe. When he began producing his major works—*The Sketch Book* (1819–20), *Bracebridge Hall* (1822), and *Tales of a Traveller* (1824)—the popularity of gothic novels was falling apart, and a period of reaction, represented chiefly by Jane Austen's *Northanger Abbey* (1818), was under way. That Irving probably sensed this decline of gothicism and the dangers of aping its style is indicated by these remarks to his brother in 1823:

> There are such quantities of the legendary and romantic tales now littering from the presses, both in England and in Germany, that one must take care not to fall into the commonplace of the day. Scott's manner must likewise be avoided. In short, I must

strike out some way of my own, suited to my own way of thinking and writing.[1]

Instead, therefore, of continuing an exhausted tradition, Irving hoped to find some original use for gothic material. To be sure, he did not always succeed, but at his best he became a skillful parodist and a highly suggestive psychologist.

When Irving failed, and his failures were frequent, he merely imitated the "littering" sensationalism at its worst. "The Story of the Young Robber," a sentimental bandit tale commonly associated with gothic fiction, will serve as an example. Here we have the inane plot of a young Italian who falls madly in love with a girl, appropriately named Rosetta, but has his hopes spoiled when he learns that the girl's father has arranged a more lucrative marriage. Unable to control his rage, the young man murders his rival and joins a band of robbers, who eventually kidnap Rosetta and attempt to sell her back for ransom. Unfortunately, the father rather curiously decides that, since the robbers have probably raped his daughter, she may as well be left to die. And die she must. But hoping to make her death painless, the young bandit volunteers to murder her himself, an act which is described with the cheap sentiment typical of the whole tale: "So perished this unfortunate." Everything is false—the bizarre actions, the feigned passions, the histrionic prose. The story exists on the most superficial of surfaces. Never do we enter the world of motives; never is the description a sign of the unwilling killer's agony.

But as innovator of the so-called "sportive" gothic, Irving was a master. Although the term "sportive" is too vague, it is generally assumed to describe a tale which employs an abundance of "machinery" assembled in a light-hearted tone, as is characteristic of "The Legend of Sleepy Hollow." So pervasive is this tone that the mystery and terror common to most gothic tales are permitted to flourish only in the ironic sense that melodrama is used to promote humor and satire. How Irving managed to employ the machinery without its usual tone is not easy to determine. Certainly his zestful narrator, whom he had used earlier in his *Knickerbocker History* and who was conspicuously missing in "The Story of the Young Robber," provides the

[1]Pierre M. Irving, *The Life and Letters of Washington Irving*, II (New York, 1864), 166.

basic ingredient for the humorous tone. The structure of "Sleepy Hollow" also guards against gothic terror, for though the headless Hessian dominates the last pages of the story, he is preceded by amusing details that never lose their influence on the narrative. Finally, the central characters themselves resist a melodramatic treatment. The original gothic hero (a fair representative being Irving's Italian robber) claimed only an ideal existence, whereas Ichabod Crane, the prototypic Yankee schoolmaster who wants only food, comfort, and a plump Dutch wife, brings to the story such a weight of actuality that a world of haunted forests seems, by contrast, absurd.

This local-color element is, on the simplest level, what Irving made the story's central interest: the Connecticut Yankee meets the New York Dutch. The same element, however, by itself so superficial, gives way to an exploration of the role of imagination and the artistic process. Ichabod, we are told, was "an odd mixture of small shrewdness and simple credulity." Having the wit of a Yankee peddler, he is careful to win the affection and confidence of the village. But having also the superstitions of a Puritan, he trembles in fear. One quality enables him to deal with the world as he wishes; the other eventually causes him to leave town at midnight, fearful for his life, never to return. But the "odd mixture" is really two applications of the same thing; for what chiefly characterizes Ichabod's mind is his rich imagination, a mind which dreamingly arranges the pieces of his experience—sometimes giving vivid impressions of himself luxuriating in food, wealth, and women, and giving also clues for realizing them. Thus the New England pedagogue manages, until the end of the story to stay a few steps ahead of the intellectually lethargic Dutch. And when Ichabod is defeated, Brom Bones is not the real victor; he merely stimulated the Yankee's self-destructive imagination. Thus the capacity that enables Ichabod to see the world as it may be—a "sumptuous promise of luxurious winter fare"—is the same irresistible curse which makes ghosts and goblins as palpable as pigeon pies. The story can, then, be understood as an allegory of the artistic process itself, for the literary artist must imaginatively create legends for the world's sleepy hollows. But the limits on the imagination—limits that Irving failed utterly to observe in his "Italian Robber"—demand that the artistically created world coexist with actuality. Permit the imagination to be wholly separated from human experience—as gothic fiction constantly separates them—and the art is destroyed. This problem is, of course, familiar to every student of American literature; our writers, particularly the New Englanders, have repeatedly felt a tension, whether as identified by Emerson between experience and reality, or as seen by Henry James between art and life. Thoreau, Hawthorne, Dickinson, Robinson, Frost, Cummings, Stevens—all of these Yankee artists felt the tension. Frost wanted to climb his birch tree of imagination *toward* the ideal, but he feared it, prayed that the tree would set him down again to earth, the right place for love. Ichabod's fate was not so kind; he is indeed snatched away not to return, for he rambled too exclusively in the world of pure imagination, and was lost. Thus, the gothic material in "Sleepy Hollow" serves a vital function. Constantly juxtaposed with the actual world, it represents the extreme form in literary art of the imagination disassociated from life. Hence, if Irving has given us a "sportive" gothic, he has not done so uncritically.

But "sportive" gothicism is not parody, though Irving's critics have tended to confuse them. "Sleepy Hollow" is only allegorically an attack on gothicism; parody reveals the excesses of a genre by imitating it. This distinction should be clear enough if we examine a genuine parody of gothic fiction, "The Spectre Bridegroom."

Unlike the other *Sketch Book* tales, this story has the stereotypic setting of medieval Germany, complete with the satiric names, Baron Von Landshort, Herman Von Starkenfaust, and Katzenellenbogen. For his plot, Irving chose the impossibly obvious formula of the supernatural *expliqué,* popularized by Mrs. Radcliffe and imitated extensively in America: the hero pretends to be the ghost of the murdered bridegroom in order to win the affections of the heroine and the confidence of her family. The major element, however, which makes "The Spectre Bridegroom" a travesty is not the artificial structure, the grotesque setting, or the ridiculous names, but rather the minds of the characters. Irving presents a society which, craving the supernatural, is ideally prepared to find it. The daughter's literary fare consists exclusively in "church legends" and "the chivalric wonders of the Heldenbuch." Her morbid imagination is clearly indicated by the agonized expressions of the saints she embroiders, who "looked like so many souls in purgatory." Other members of the family seem equally drawn to gothic themes. The baron's greatness seems to consist chiefly in his ability to tell ghost stories. "He was much given to the marvellous and a firm believer in all those supernatural tales with which every mountain and valley in Germany abounds." Indeed, young Starkenfaust got his idea of posing as a spectre from one of the baron's stories, and the family's commitment to the supernatural explanation was their own idea. Like Catherine Morland in *Northanger Abbey,* the Katzenellenbogens attempt to interpret their experience in terms of German legends. In fact, the poor relation who suggests the truth—that the spectre may be some evasive young cavalier—draws upon himself the "indignation of the whole company." And when the hoax is finally revealed, one of the aunts is "particularly mortified at having her marvellous story marred. . . ." The most important facet of this parody, therefore, is Irving's interest in the psychology of gothicism. Turning the eternal gothic theme inward, he treated the supernatural world as an expression of an excessively morbid imagination.

If "The Spectre Bridegroom" is a delightful though serious parody of the gothic tale—particularly of the Radcliffian supernatural *expliqué*—Irving designed other stories to render it quite as ridiculous, but in an exactly opposite manner. Instead of resolving the supernatural in natural terms, his heroes sometimes—as in "The Bold Dragoon," for example—disguise their very embarrassing natural activities under a gothic mask. Here is our saucy-eyed dragoon, a bold fellow indeed, weaseling his way into an already-filled inn by blarneying the landlord and charming the women, notably "the hostess's daughter, a plump Flanders lass." Then after rousing the entire house by crashing to the floor in the middle of the night, he tells a perfectly incredible story about a "weazen-faced" ghost of a bagpiper, dancing furniture, and a midnight caper with a clothes-press. Though doubts are suggested, these are easily silenced by the dragoon's ever-threatening sword and shillelah and by the even more preposterous corroboration of the daughter, who, we are told, was already with the dragoon when the rest of the house appeared. Apparently, therefore, we have an inverted form of the explained supernatural tale; Irving has given us what we may, in fact, call the *inverted* gothic story—not unlike Chaucer's "Miller's Tale"—in which the lusty dragoon escapes recrimination for his midnight peccadillo with the landlord's daughter by throwing up an absurd haze of supernaturalism.

Although this form has failed to survive in modern fiction, it was one of Irving's favorites. In "Dolph Heyliger," for instance, we have a similarly inverted gothic tale, in which the picaresque hero returns with his life's fortune and a ghost story to explain how he got it. Doubts of Dolph's honesty are never uttered, not of course because his character is spotless but because it is noted that he is "the ablest drawer of a long-bow in the whole province."

If we consider "Rip Van Winkle" in the context of "Dolph Heyliger" and "The Bold Dragoon," it appears that this most famous of Irving's stories also employs the techniques of inverted gothicism. Like Dolph, Rip disappears, only to return later with a supernatural account of his absence. And like the dragoon's story, Rip's tale is "authenticated" in a fashion which is as irrational as the story itself; crucial testimony is given by Peter, "the most ancient inhabitant of the village, and well versed in all the wonderful events and traditions of the neighborhood." The gullible narrator, old Diedrich Knickerbocker, who relates the story without a flicker of doubt, believes Rip's account because (1) stranger stories have been told, (2) Rip was "venerable," "rational," and "consistent," and (3) the story had been recorded by an illiterate country justice. Indeed, the whole community refused even to consider what they should have suspected from the first: that Rip had finally become exasperated with his "termagant wife," took his dog and gun, and deserted. He was, long before his disappearance, a great teller of ghost stories and a notorious malingerer—exactly the sort of man who would ramble for twenty years, then return with a bit of gothic nonsense designed to amuse the town and avoid its scorn. The final paragraph of the story seems to point directly toward this conclusion. Old Knickerbocker admits that Rip had several versions of his account: "He was observed, at first, to vary on some points every time he told it. . . ." Only later did Rip settle down to the story as we have it related. Those few who doubt it suspect that Rip has lost his faculties. The others—men, women, children—have the story memorized. Some even literally believe that thunder is the sound of "Hendrick Hudson and his crew . . . at their game of ninepins. . . ." We have, then, a society willingly trying to turn life into a gothic legend; as such, "Rip Van Winkle" is a brilliant satire on the gothic mind.

But what should we make of Rip? Only he escapes Irving's satire, for he unites both Starkenfaust and Ichabod: the poseur in one sense, the artist in another. Like Irving himself, and like countless writers in America, Rip's problem is that of a vocation. What is a creature of the imagination to do in a world whose values are represented by Dame Van Winkle? Art in such a world is, as Hawthorne complained in his sketch "The Custom-House," driven to become a mere escape. Thus, the youthful Rip spends his days "telling endless sleepy stories about nothing." Finally, "reduced almost to despair," he is driven to an actual escape: he rambles off, a sad counterpart to Odysseus, not to return for twenty years, a ragged old man, greeted by his dog with a snarl. Yet one quality in him has not been destroyed by age; his imagination is even richer than before, and he had "arrived at that happy age when a man can be idle with impunity. . . ." Perhaps that was what brought him home, the hope that his world could finally accommodate him. It does: Rip becomes an honored village patriarch and chronicler. Unlike Ichabod, therefore, Rip is not defeated by his gothic imagination, because, for him, it was never dissociated from life. Even if the village skeptics are right, and they may be, in believing that old Van Winkle is edging toward senility, he is granted "an old man's frenzy," which Yeats hoped for and which he recognized in King Lear and William Blake. Imagination alone, whether inspired by frenzy or plain cunning, makes Rip's life significant. Thus, in "Rip Van Winkle," Irving accomplished a judgment of the extremes of the gothic mind and a frail reconciliation between it and the role of the artist.

In most of these modifications of the gothic tradition, Irving's "psychology" played an important part. The too richly imaginative Ichabod Crane, with Puritan superstitions whirling in his brain, was able to manufacture his own midnight goblin, whether or not the external world of fact could give evidence of it. An imitation spectre bridegroom captured the credulity of nearly all the Katzenellenbogens nourished as they were on the gothic thrills of German legends. This emphasis on the subjective rather than the objective, which was, as I have indicated, the really significant use of gothic motifs in the nineteenth and twentieth centuries, was brought to an intriguing climax in "The Adventure of the German Student." At the outset of the story we learn that young Gottfried Wolfgang, a student of German philosophy who literally believes that he is dwelling among "spiritual essences," had been sent by his family to Paris to regain his mental stability. Unfortunately, his monastic life at the Sorbonne, together with the sobering effect of the reign of terror, cancels "the splendors and gayeties of Paris." In the extremity of his isolation. Gottfried has a recurring dream of a woman, "a female face of transcendent beauty."

Occupied constantly with thoughts of this dream-woman, he comes one evening upon the guillotine at the Place de Grève, where he meets her, exactly the woman of his dreams. They talk; he brings her home; they make love. The next morning, on rising to greet his bride, he finds her dead. A closer examination reveals that she has been decapitated; in fact, she is the very woman who had been guillotined the day before. This knowledge is too much for Gottfried who screams, "I am lost forever," just before he suffers a mental breakdown. We are left, as we are often left in Irving's stories with two possible explanations: either Gottfried met the transcendent lady truly incarnated, a ghost who became a corpse in the morning, or the woman was a corpse from the beginning. If the psychic condition of Gottfried who, we are told, related the story to the narrator in a madhouse, is significant, then the second version has the greater validity. Viewed in this way, the tale is a story of a madman having sexual intercourse with a decapitated cadaver, thinking she is the transcendent lover of his wildest dreams. No doubt the whole plan is too fantastically sensational. But this is not the sensationalism of "The Young Robber" or indeed of the usual gothic novel. For the factual events are not those that create the terror of the story, nor can the avowal of supernaturalism account for its effectiveness; the acute terror of "The German Student" results from the derangement and the delusions that give a horribly false view of the world. Irving has, therefore, given us one of the first examples of psychological gothicism, in which the crude supernatural motif is dismissed and the gothic tale becomes genuinely a study of grim terror and anguish.

I do not pretend that Irving was a great artist; he was not. But as a parodist, he mirthfully helped to destroy all that was crude in gothic fiction. More importantly, one cannot deny that he anticipated the advanced gothic fiction of Poe and Hawthorne. Then following admittedly in their wakes, we have French symbolism and Henry James—two fundamental forces behind twentieth-century fiction. We should not be surprised, therefore, to find traces of Irving's "sportive" gothic in the works of William Faulkner or his subjectified "machinery" in the midnight novels.

"Washington Irving and the Conservative Imagination"

BY ALLEN GUTTMANN

Allen Guttmann, whose major career concentration, like his University of Minnesota doctorate to begin with, has been in American Studies, is a Professor at Amherst College, where he has taught since 1959. He has been a Fulbright lecturer and professor in German universities, an officer of the American Studies Association, and a member of the editorial board of *American Literature*. His numerous publications include *The Wound in the Heart* (1962) and *The Jewish Writer in America* (1971). He is co-editing *The Life of George Washington* for *The Complete Works of Washington Irving*. This incisive article, parts of which were later absorbed into Chapter II of Guttmann's *The Conservative Tradition in America* (1967), is a reassessment for literary purposes of Irving's adult political and socio-economic values. It first appeared, as printed here, in *American Literature,* Vol. XXVI (1964), 165–173.

388

As long ago as 1931, Henry S. Canby characterized Washington Irving as "the arch-Federalist of American literature."[1] Henry A. Pochmann, repeating Canby's phrase, agreed that Irving was "more Federalist than the Federalists."[2] Stanley T. Williams's two-volume *Life of Washington Irving* (1935) provided much information on young Irving's predominantly Federalist environment and much evidence to substantiate earlier judgments of the anti-Jeffersonian satire in *Salmagundi* and in *Knickerbocker's History*. More recent opinion, concentrated on the mythic and folkloric aspects of Irving, has contributed little to a reassessment of Irving's politics. No one has taken up Williams's hint that Irving was made "of the very stuff of Tories."

The fact is that Irving's Federalism was always *faute de mieux*. The egalitarianism of Jefferson was fair game for Diedrich Knickerbocker, but Irving's *persona* was also a ruthless hunter of the stolid bourgeoisie of mercantile New Amsterdam. And the bourgeoisie was very much at home within the Federalist Party. Hamilton believed in strong government to check the democratic impulses of the people, but even Hamilton was in his economic policies an agent of change, the prophet of the transformation of property into the stocks, bonds, and certificates of the modern corporation. Hamilton, Adams, and the literati of Boston's *Monthly Anthology* might have snorted at Jeffersonian tendencies, but they themselves were far closer intellectually to Jefferson than to Edmund Burke and the tradition of English Conservatism. If Irving lost interest in the quarrels of Hamilton and Jefferson, it was at least in part because he discovered an aristocratic society based on continuity rather than on revolution, on landed property rather than on national banks, funded debts, and capitalistic enterprise.

In England and Scotland Irving found what America lacked even under the Federalist administrations of Washington and Adams —a Conservative society with a sense of the past. Writing to Sir Walter Scott shortly after his famous visit to Abbotsford, Irving revealed the sources of his political commitments. Although convinced that Republicanism was the "best form of government for my own country, yet I feel my poetical associations vividly aroused by the old in-

[1] *Classic Americans: A Study of Eminent American Writers from Irving to Whitman* (New York, 1931), p. 86.
[2] *Washington Irving: Representative Selections* (New York, 1934), p. xlv.

stititutions of this country, and should feel as sorry to see them injured or subverted as I would be to see Windsor Castle or Westminster Abbey demolished to make way for brick tenements."³ The metaphors are central. While Major L'Enfant and Benjamin Latrobe labored to lay out and construct public structures for the new nation, the old world already gloried in the castles, the churches, the country houses that were the visible symbols of its past and of its determination to resist the world of brick tenement and iron factory. Never a political theorist, Irving was nonetheless the first American writer successfully to articulate the prodigal's discovery of what Hawthorne came to call "Our Old Home."

Irving found in Europe the ruins of a civilization that deserved better than it received. With due allowance for a tendency to sentimentalize, with account taken for the distance gained by use of his narrator (Geoffrey Crayon), we see him, in 1819, responding as a true Conservative to the European past. England's "every mouldering stone was a chronicle. I longed . . . to tread . . . in the footsteps of antiquity—to loiter about the ruined castle,—to meditate on the falling tower,—to escape . . . from the common-place realities of the present, and lose myself among the shadowy grandeurs of the past."⁴

If Irving's mood were consistently nostaglic, he might be dismissed as a sentimentalist, but, like James Fenimore Cooper, he responded to more than antiquity and hoary ruin. English society provided also "perpetual volume of reference, wherein are recorded sound deductions from ages of experience . . ." (*Sketch-Book,* p. 89). Where could one turn for "sound deductions"? In the letter to Scott, Irving instanced Windsor Castle and Westminster Abbey as symbols of State and Church, and in Westminster Abbey his awe was appropriately religious: "It seems as if the awful nature of the place presses down upon the soul and hushes the beholder into noiseless reverence" (*Sketch-Book,* p. 241). But the traveler from America had little hope of access to royal or ecclesiastical rulers. Where else might one turn? To the "real" England, to the countryside dominated by the estates of the aristocracy and squirarchy. "The great charm . . .

---

³Quoted in Pierre M. Irving, *Life and Letters of Washington Irving,* 4 Vols. (New York, 1862–1863), I, 441.

⁴*The Sketch-Book of Geoffrey Crayon, Gent.,* XIX, 17. All references are to the Hudson Edition (New York, 1882–1887).

of English scenery is the moral feeling that seems to pervade it. It is associated in the mind with ideas of order, of quiet, of sober well-established principles, of hoary usage and reverend custom" (*Sketch-Book*, p. 98). Irving's sense of the countryside as locus of order and tradition is like Edmund Burke's; in a letter to Will Weddell (January 31, 1792), Burke defined the Whig Party as the one "connected with the solid, permanent, long-possessed property of the country; a party which, by a temper derived from that species of property, and affording a security to it, was attached to the ancient usages of the kingdom; a party, therefore, essentially constructed upon a ground-plot of stability and independence. . . ." It is no accident that three of the chapters of *The Sketch-Book* and almost all of *Bracebridge Hall* are set upon the "groundplot" of the solid, permanent, and long-possessed ancestral estate.

Irving had already, in *Salmagundi*, erected Cockloft Hall as a Tory citadel in egalitarian New York. "As the Cocklofts are remarkable for their attachment to everything that has remained long in the family, they are bigoted toward their old edifice, and . . . would sooner have it crumble about their ears than abandon it."[5] Bracebridge Hall is modeled after Cockloft Hall as well as Abbotsford, and the values ironically held in democratic New York become worthy of serious consideration when found solidly in place on English soil. When the crotchety old Cocklofts condemned the customs of the young Republic, they seemed themselves anachronisms more notable for ill-temper than for insight; when Geoffrey Crayon discovers Bracebridge Hall, he speaks for an Irving ready to acknowledge himself attracted to values and institutions whose antiquity proved their viability.

Bracebridge Hall, in Yorkshire, is the scene of the amours of Julia Templeton, a ward of the squire, and Guy Bracebridge, the squire's second son. The plot is trivial. The narrative interest is most intense when Julia, recovering from a fall, hears the story of "The Student of Salamanca." Fortunately, narrative interest is not the only kind. Before Julia and Guy wed, the reader has been introduced into the intricacies of family ties among the gentry, to the daily routine of life among the upper classes, to horsemanship and hawking—in

[5]*Salmagundi; or, The Whim-Whams and Opinions of Lancelot Langstaff, Esq., and Others*, XVIII, 150.

short, to the orderly world of settled society as Irving found it in England, as Irving attempted to recreate it at Sunnyside, as Cooper hoped to rebuild it at Coopertown.

But even English society is threatened by disorder. The threat is a double one. The neighborhood is, first, menaced by the arrival of Mr. Faddy, a "substantial manufacturer" who has remodeled an old country seat until "it looks not unlike his own manufactory."[6] Mr. Faddy, like Dickens's Mr. Gradgrind, urges the squire to prohibit the celebration of May Day. When Mr. Faddy departs, the squire, who is "at the bottom of these May-day revels," denounces manufacturers as a class: "What's to become of merry old England, when its manor-houses are all turned into manufactories, and its sturdy peasantry into pin-makers and stocking weavers" . . . (p. 302)? What will happen when England becomes "a region of fire; reeking with coal-pits, and furnaces, and smelting-houses, vomiting forth flames and smoke" (p. 302)? The Industrial Revolution has also brought radical readers of Cobbett, men equally impatient with traditional society *and* with Mr. Faddy's utilitarianism. On Geoffrey Crayon's first visit to the hall, the squire told him the nation had altered. Peasants had "broken asunder from the higher class" and had begun "to read newspapers, listen to alehouse politicans, and talk of reform" (*Sketch-Book*, p. 305). When Geoffrey Crayon returns, the squire's fears have become reality. In the village taproom is an agitator, a newspaper-reader who has shocked the villagers "by talking lightly of the Squire and his family; and hinting that it would be better the park should be cut up into small farms and kitchen-gardens, or feed good mutton instead of worthless deer" (*Bracebridge Hall*, p. 339). Happily, one of the villagers is present to defend the good old ways with "half a dozen maxims, which he advances on all occasions" (p. 340). The lower-class threat is turned aside and the middle-class threat fails to stop the May day fête, but Irving has nonetheless suggested what Cooper was soon to insist upon: the hierarchical society of the eighteenth century was doomed by democratic revolution. Irving and Cooper lived to see, in 1832, the passage of the Reform Bill and the triumphant re-election of King Andrew the First.

Judged by its plot, *Bracebridge Hall* deserves much of the abuse

---

[6]*Bracebridge Hall, or The Humorists: A Medley,* V, 299.

it has received, but there is more to the book than romance and political implication. The mansion and its grounds are, in Irving's phrase, a "fertile subject for study," and they give the book a solidity like that which Cooper achieved with the same symbol of the ancestral mansion in *his* novels devoted to the virtues of a landed aristocracy in control of an established society.[7] Bracebridge Hall, like John Pendleton Kennedy's Swallow Barn (which was modeled on Irving's hall), is a country mansion, but those who wish to discern the primitive in the tended groves will be disappointed. Irving could, in a fit of enthusiasm, hymn "the glorious independence of man in a savage state," but his second thoughts led him always to conclude that the "Indian of poetical fiction is, like the shepherd of pastoral romance, a mere personification of imaginary attributes."[8] The "sacred groves" that stirred his imagination were neither Bryant's sylvan temples nor Natty Bumppo's prairie; his groves surround homes and are valuable not as reservoirs of natural value but as reminders of "the ever-interesting story of human existence." It is their "moral associations" and their relation to history that attract Irving's attention. Alluding to the estate lauded by Ben Jonson in "To Penshurst," Irving asks, "Who can walk, with soul unmoved, among the stately groves . . . where the gallant, the amiable, the elegant Sir Philip Sidney passed his boyhood . . .?" (*Bracebridge Hall,* pp. 107–108).

Irving was by no means unaware of this relation between political principle and landed property. The squire asserts that "the boasted imitation of nature in modern gardening [has] sprung up with modern republican notions, but [does] not suit a monarchical government; it smacked of the levelling system . . ." (*Sketch-Book,* p. 277). Geoffrey Crayon smiles at this "introduction of politics into gardening," but all the context buttresses the squire's conviction that a stand against change must be taken on a wide front or not at all.

It should be clear from the argument above that Irving's letter to Scott contains architectural metaphors which Irving did not use carelessly. With this in mind, we may respond to Irving's half-comic, half-pathetic, letter to Mrs. John Pendleton Kennedy, written near

---

[7]Allen Guttmann, "Images of Value and the Sense of the Past," *New England Quarterly,* XXXV, 3–26 (March, 1962).

[8]*The Crayon Miscellany,* IX, 9, 53. *Astoria* is largely an account of the hardships of Western exploration.

the end of his life, and reverting to the central metaphor as Irving's imagination undoes the Industrial and the Democratic Revolutions:

> I should like nothing better than to have plenty of money to squander on stone and mortar, and to build chateaux . . . , but I would first blow up all the cotton mills . . . and make picturesque ruins of them; and I would utterly destroy the railroad; and all the cotton lords should live in baronial castles . . . and the cotton spinners should be virtuous peasantry of both sexes. . . . (*Life and Letters*, IV, 167)

And his last words were these: "I am getting ready to go; I am shutting up my doors and windows."

The Sketch-Book and *Bracebridge Hall* represent a movement from Federalism to a variety of Burkean Conservatism instinctively rather than rationally held; these two books also contain the social tensions dramatized in Cooper's best work. His interest for the present generation is precisely his ability to respond both to the necessity for an order and hierarchical society *and* to the vision of the American Adam on the virgin land. Although Irving never moved as far in the direction of primitivism as Cooper did, he too, with less intensity, set the antisocial frontier hero against the institutions of society. *The Sketch-Book* contains "Rip Van Winkle" and "The Legend of Sleepy Hollow" as well as Bracebridge Hall. Significantly, these tales are told by Diedrich Knickerbocker rather than by Geoffrey Crayon, perhaps because the latter had become too closely associated with Europe to speak out very strongly for America.

Irving's sympathy for Rip is so clear that none needs dispute it. Less obvious is his very severe qualification of the world Rip returns to. In place of his friends, Rip finds the politician: "a lean bilious-looking fellow, with his pockets full of handbills, was haranguing vehemently about the rights of citizens—elections—members of congress—liberty—Bunker's Hill—heroes of seventy-six—and other words, which were a perfect Babylonish jargon to the bewildered Van Winkle" (p. 67). Not all the irony is directed against dismayed Rip when he says, "I am a poor quiet man, a native of the place, and a loyal subject of the king, God bless him!" (p. 68). Introduced to his son Rip, the old man is confused by change:

"I'm not myself—I'm somebody else—that's me yonder. . . . I was myself last night, but I fell asleep on the mountains, and they've changed my gun, and every thing's changed, and I'm changed, and I can't tell what's my name, or who I am!" (p. 70)

It would be nonsense to claim that Irving felt the American Revolution a change for the worse, but it would also be nonsense not to see the tale as a gentle reminder that revolution, as Burke insisted, disrupts "the unchangeable constancy" of society's "decay, failure, renovation, and progression" through the orderly sequence of generations of men.[9] Moreover, if one accepts Philip Young's account of the tale as an archetype of separation from the world, discovery, and return, the tale is a cautionary one of the evasion of responsibility. Rip has avoided "all the obligations of maturity: occupation, domestic and financial responsibility, and political position, duty to society in time of war."[10]

The resolution in "Rip Van Winkle" is, with many reservations, on the side of the new; "The Legend of Sleepy Hollow" is much more clearly and outspokenly a prefiguration of the tradition of Mark Twain and the frontier humorists of the middle nineteenth century. Moving from the English countryside to the American, Irving in the first paragraphs of the story alludes to the "ancient Dutch navigators" of the Tappan Zee, as the Hudson was first known, and to the "original Dutch settlers" of Sleepy Hollow. The peace and plenty of the valley are disturbed by two intruders, one real and one mythical, Ichabod Crane of Connecticut and the ghost of a Hessian trooper. Before the tale is over, the first is repelled by a Dutchman in the guise of the second.

Ichabod Crane and Brom Bones compete for Katrina Van Tassel, whose virtues are those of the settled landscape itself; she is a "blooming lass of fresh eighteen, plump as a partridge; ripe and melting and rosy cheeked as one of her father's peaches . . ." (p. 486).

[9]Burke, *Reflections on the Revolution in France, Works,* 12 Vols. (Boston, 1865), III, 275.

[10]"Fallen from Time: The Mythic Rip Van Winkle," *Kenyon Review,* XXII, 547–573 (Autumn, 1960); see also Terence Martin, "Rip, Ichabod, and the American Imagination," *American Literature,* XXXI, 137–149 (May, 1959).

With her go her father's bounty of troops of porkers, squadrons of geese, fleets of ducks, and regiments of turkeys. The competition is for affluence, and the basic flaw in Ichabod's candidacy is his inablity to accept God's plenty (and Van Tassel's) for what it is; Ichabod, like the archetypal capitalist, imagines not enjoyment but profit: "his heart yearned after the damsel who was to inherit these domains, and his imagination expanded with the idea, how they might be readily turned into cash, and the money invested in immense tracts of wild land, and shingle palaces in the wilderness" (pp. 488–489).

Gangly, spindle-necked, glassy-eyed, snipe-nosed, book-learned Ichabod fights with the only weapons he has—the arts of civilized life. From his strongholds in school and church he sallies forth quixotically "like a knight-errant in quest of adventures"; leaving his unfinished verses behind, he advances "under cover of his character as a singing-master" (p. 493). The climax of the struggle for Katrina comes when Ichabod, crane-like, dances for the favor of his mistress.

Brom Bones is, of course, everything Ichabod is not. He is the "burly, roaring, roystering" hero of the country round, "which rang with his feats of strength and hardihood" (p. 491). A rider and a fighter, he approaches Katrina with "the gentle caresses and endearments of a bear, yet it was whispered that she did not altogether discourage his hopes" (p. 492). In Daniel Hoffman's slightly exaggerated analysis, he becomes a "Catskill Mike Fink, a Ring-Tailed Roarer from Kinderhook."[11]

Ichabod's wise reluctance to fight with his fists leaves uncouth Brom at a disadvantage. But when Baltus Van Tassel begins to gossip about the past, Brom sees his chance and, as everyone knows, surprises Ichabod that night as he makes his way home. The scene of the surprise is the neighborhood of Major André's tree. Ichabod is startled, as André had been, and quite literally brought down from his high-horse by a pumpkin-head. The Dutch of Sleepy Hollow have won their comic war for cultural independence. The schoolhouse falls into decay while the erstwhile schoolmaster goes off on a middle-class career as lawyer, judge, and politican. Meanwhile, Brom Bones conducts "the blooming Katrina in triumph to the altar" (p. 518). It

[11]*Form and Fable in American Fiction* (New York, 1961), p. 89.

was Irving, not Longstreet or Mark Twain, who first hit upon the characteristic pattern of American humor.[12]

Unfortunately for Irving's reputation today, the conflicts masterfully dramatized in the tales were never embodied in a longer, more substantial work. It was for Cooper to bring Natty Bumppo and Marmaduke Temple into direct opposition and to make the struggle between the Littlepages and the Newcomes the dramatic center of a trilogy of novels. Nevertheless, Irving stands with Cooper in that both men were divided between the attractions of the new and the steady appeal of the old. Both were committed *explicitly* to an ordered and hierarchical agrarian society; both were betrayed by their own best work into an implicit celebration of American democrats. Natty and Chingachgook, Rip and Brom, are American heroes who would have been as unwelcome in the council rooms of the Federalist Party as in the chambers of Bracebridge Hall.

---

[12]"Dolph Heyliger," also attributed to Diedrich Knickerbocker, is a much weaker tale, inserted into *Bracebridge Hall,* which repeats the pattern of "The Legend of Sleepy Hollow." The boisterous ne'er-do-well surprises the learned and the well-to-do, unearths a buried treasure, and becomes the leader of the community.

"New York and New England: Irving's Criticism of American Society"

BY DONALD A. RINGE

Donald A. Ringe, a General Education Board fellow while completing a Harvard Ph.D., after teaching at Tulane and the University of Michigan, has been Professor of English at the University of Kentucky since 1965. Concentrating on American Literature studies, his publications have included books on *James Fenimore Cooper* (1962), *Charles Brockden Brown* (1966), and *The Pictorial Mode: Space and Time in the Art of Bryant, Irving and Cooper* (1971). The following article, which underlines a very American regional conflict as an important element in Irving's conscious art as a satirist, appeared in *American Literature,* Vol. XXXVIII (1967), 455–467.

398

Although Washington Irving's best-known tales, "Rip Van Winkle" and "The Legend of Sleepy Hollow," have been interpreted from a number of points of view, critics have missed a significant dimension in the stories by failing to take into account a fundamental regional conflict—the mutual hostility between New York and New England —that appears not only in these two tales, but in other of Irving's works as well.[1] That the New York-New England conflict is basic to "The Legend of Sleepy Hollow" is obvious enough: Ichabod Crane is clearly a Connecticut Yankee invading—and threatening—a New York Dutch society. Less easily recognized, however, is that the same invasion seems to have occurred by the end of "Rip Van Winkle." The inn of Nicholas Vedder has been supplanted by the Union Hotel of one Jonathan Doolittle, a name identified elsewhere in Irving's works as that of a Yankee;[2] "Bunker's Hill" is one of the rallying cries of the "lean, bilious-looking fellow" who harangues the crowd; and Dame Van Winkle has been defeated at last by the one type of person, presumably, that she cannot overcome, the Yankee peddler (XIX, 66–67, 71).

In other of Irving's works, moreover, the same antagonism appears. A number of chapters in *Knickerbocker's History of New York* present the antipathy between Dutch and Yankee at considerable length, as, to a lesser degree, do such tales and sketches as "Wol-

[1]Although Daniel G. Hoffman treats Ichabod Crane as a typical Yankee, he does not discuss the specific regional conflict. See "Irving's Use of American Folklore in 'The Legend of Sleepy Hollow,'" *PMLA*, LXVIII, 425–435 (June, 1953), reprinted with minor alterations in *Form and Fable in American Fiction* (New York, 1961), pp. 83–96. Sara Puryear Rodes, in "Washington Irving's Use of Traditional Folklore," *New York Folklore Quarterly*, XIII, 3–15 (Spring, 1957), mentions the conflict in passing (p. 8).

[2]The name appears in a list of Yankees in the first three editions of *Knickerbocker's History of New York* (New York, 1809), I, 220; (New York, 1812), I, 227; (Philadelphia, 1819), I, 253. It may conveniently be found in the modern reprint of the 1809 edition edited by Stanley T. Williams and Tremaine McDowell (New York, 1927), p. 199; or in that of the 1812 edition edited by Edwin T. Bowden (New York, 1964), p. 181. The name is omitted in the corresponding list of Yankees in the 1848 revision as reprinted in the Hudson edition of Irving's *Works* (New York, 1902). See XI, 260. All subsequent citations of Irving's works are to volume and page numbers in the Hudson edition. (I am indebted to Mr. Lewis M. Stark, Rare Book Division, New York Public Library, for information concerning the third edition, and to Professor Bowden for information concerning his edition of the book.)

fert's Roost," "Communipaw," and "Conspiracy of the Cocked Hats,"—all first published in the *Knickerbocker* in 1839. Wherever the conflict appears in Irving's works, it is always presented in much the same terms and usually serves a satiric end. It may thus be considered a significant element in any interpretation of his major writings.

I

Irving was not alone in depicting the regional conflict. So widespread, indeed, is the use of the material in the works of James Fenimore Cooper and, to a much more limited extent, James Kirke Paulding, that a brief discussion of its basic elements is necessary if Irving's stories are to be seen in the proper context. To be sure, not all of the writers use the material in precisely the same way. Paulding, like Irving, expresses the conflict in some of his works in terms of Yankee settlers encroaching upon the New York Dutch,[3] whereas Cooper presents the antagonism in a broader context that includes the New York English as well.[4] They all agree, however, on the nature of the regional antipathy, and Irving and Cooper in particular make it the vehicle for some serious social criticism.

The satire, of course, is not directed solely against the Yankees,

[3]See the briefly developed incidents in *The Diverting History of John Bull and Brother Jonathan* (New York, 1835), pp. 83–84, and *The Dutchman's Fireside* (New York, 1837), I, 145–146. This is the edition of Paulding's works published in fourteen volumes (New York, 1834–1837). Since the copy I have used, however, binds two volumes in one with separate pagination for each, and since I also cite a work not included in this set, I have found it convenient to refer to title and page numbers in all citations of Paulding's works. Brief mention of the New York-New England conflict may also be found in *The Book of St. Nicholas* (New York, 1836), pp. 89, 104, and *The Puritan and His Daughter* (New York, 1849), II, 128, 244.

[4]For a discussion of Cooper's use of the conflict in his novels, see Warren S. Walker, *James Fenimore Cooper: An Introduction and Interpretation* (New York, 1962), pp. 102–115. For Cooper's own treatment of the conflict, see his historical aside in *Wyandotté* (New York, 1859), pp. 368–369. All subsequent citations of Cooper's novels are to page numbers in the Darley-Townsend edition (New York, 1859–1861). Some additional discussion of the conflict may also be found in passing in *Satanstoe*, pp. 17–23.

who are sometimes praised for their admirable qualities,[5] nor are the New York characters always seen in a favorable light. Everyone will recall Irving's amusing picture of the ponderous Dutch burghers who eat, sleep, and blow clouds of tobacco smoke in *Knickerbocker's History of New York.* Through them, Irving projects an image of Dutch stolidity that appears as well in Cooper's portrayal of the slow-moving Dirck Follock in *Satanstoe* and the seemingly slow-witted Andries Coejemans in *The Chainbearer.* Although this image is somewhat controverted by such vigorous Dutch characters as Irving's Brom Bones and Dolph Heyliger and Cooper's Guert Ten Eyck, the defects of the Dutch character are not concealed by either writer.[6] Indeed, the New Yorkers are sometimes depicted as having a desire for money not very much different from that most frequently attributed to Yankees. Cooper, for example, includes a miserly Dutch moneylender, one Squire Van Tassel, in *Miles Wallingford,* and Irving allows his Wolfert Webber to succumb to dreams of gold, go searching for pirate treasure, and eventually grow rich by dividing his cabbage garden into building lots and renting them out to tenants.

By and large, however, the New York writers reserved their sharpest satiric thrusts for the New England character. Their task was not difficult. The image of the typical Yankee, tall and spare, had already been developed in American folklore,[7] and they had only to turn the easily recognized type to their own purposes. The result was not only Irving's Ichabod Crane, who reveals a number of typical New England traits, but also Cooper's Elnathan Todd in *The Pioneers,* and David Gamut in *The Last of the Mohicans,* whom critics have recognized as Crane's literary descendants.[8] All are awkward, ungainly men who fit the pattern of the gaunt New Englander. The New York writers, too, agree in satirizng the Yankee's propensity to

---

[5]Cooper, for one, attempts to be fair to the Yankees and presents their virtues as well as their faults. See especially his narrator's estimate of the New Englanders' practicality and interest in education in *The Chainbearer,* pp. 126–127. Cf. Paulding, *The Puritan and His Daughter,* II, 140–141, where the Puritans are commended for their respect for knowledge.

[6]Cf. Hoffman, p. 427.

[7]Constance Rourke, *American Humor: A Study of the National Character,* (Garden City, N. Y., 1953), pp. 15–36.

[8]Thomas Philbrick, "Cooper's *The Pioneers:* Origins and Structure," *PMLA,* LXXIX, 583 (Dec. 1964); Walker, pp. 105–106.

talk and to question his neighbors and acquaintances about their business. In *The Chainbearer,* Cooper observes through the character of his narrator that this particular trait has been "so generally admitted by writers and commentators on American character," that one can probably assume its truth (p. 98), and Irving and Paulding both present amusing pictures of the consternation caused among the taciturn Dutch by the voluble invaders from the east.[9]

The New York writers, however, do not end here, but direct their criticism against the far more serious traits of Yankee restlessness and desire for change. The American Arabs, as they are called by both Irving and Paulding,[10] are always on the move. In contrast to their more firmly rooted neighbors, the Yankees have, in Irving's words, "a certain rambling propensity, with which, like the sons of Ishmael, they seem to have been gifted by heaven, and which continually goads them on to shift their residence from place to place, so that a Yankee farmer is in a constant state of migration" (XI, 212). This view is projected by Cooper in the character of Aaron Thousandacres, the Vermont frontiersman in *The Chainbearer,* who tells us himself that he has squatted seventeen times and is ready to make his "eighteenth pitch" if circumstances require it (p. 257).

To their more conservative neighbors, the Yankees' desire to move, change, and improve posed a serious threat to the social order that New Yorkers were trying to establish and maintain. In Cooper's Littlepage novels, the stable order of society is threatened by Yankee settlers and Yankee principles, for both Aaron Thousandacres and the Newcome clan try to disrupt the Littlepage order.[11] New England speculators almost gain possession of a Dutch village in Irving's "Communipaw" and attempt to lay out streets and lots to turn the peaceful village into a bustling Yankee town before it is saved by a gallant Dutch family "just as some of the worthy burghers were on the point of capitulating" (XVII, 547). Indeed, Irving's "Conspiracy of the Cocked Hats" ends in just such a manner when an enterprising Yankee elopes with a Dutch heiress, divides her cabbage garden into

---

[9]Irving, *Works,* XI, 216; Paulding, *The Dutchman's Fireside,* I, 146.

[10]Irving, *Works,* XI, 212; Paulding, *The Dutchman's Fireside,* I, 145–146.

[11]Cooper's view of social change is discussed in my article, "Cooper's Littlepage Novels: Change and Stability in American Society," *American Literature,* XXXII, 280–290 (Nov., 1960).

town lots, and offers them for sale (XVII, 558–559). As Irving writes in *Knickerbocker's History of New York,* "it is not the nature of this most indefatigable of speculators to rest contented with any state of sublunary enjoyment: *improvement* is his darling passion" (XI, 213).

By far the most serious charge that New Yorkers level at their New England neighbors, however, is that their great concern is money. In American folklore, of course, the New England peddler is always a shrewd bargainer whose sharp practices empty the pockets of others into his own,[12] and Irving and Cooper draw upon this image in their presentation of the New England character. Irving describes the Yankees as experts in the "profitable hocus-pocus of trade" (XI, 344) and on one occasion has "a crafty man of Pyquag" bargain Peter Stuyvesant out of his horse, "leaving in place thereof a villanous [*sic*], foundered Narraganset pacer" (XI, 465). Cooper, moreover, depicts the Yankee peddler himself in the person of Harvey Birch in *The Spy,*[13] who masks his patriotic purposes behind the appearance of avarice. To be sure, Cooper allows this New Englander to act from unselfish motives. More often, however, he presents his Yankees as impelled by a desire for gain. Jason Newcome, in *The Chainbearer,* is willing to profit personally from timber cut illegally on Littlepage land, and Joel Strides, in *Wyandotté,* betrays the Willoughby family, whom he serves as overseer, in his desire to gain possession of their lands.

To oppose the material values they see in the Yankee desire for change, improvement, and profit, the New York writers affirm a stable society that places its emphasis on order, tradition, and the family values that accompany social stability. Although their New York characters are not averse to amassing wealth, by and large they seek their fortunes on the land. Once settled on the land, moreover, they tend to stay upon it. Some three generations of Littlepages and five of Wallingfords, in Cooper's novels, have held their family property, and Irving depicts Dutch farmers whose ancestors settled their land in the early days of the colony. The sense of permanence and social stability thus attained marks out the superiority of the New York

[12]See Rourke, pp. 15–17.

[13]For a discussion of Harvey Birch as a New England peddler, see Walker, pp. 104–105.

characters. They create a tradition impossible to be achieved by the restless Yankees and instill a sense of values in later generations that can only be maintained in this way.

Thus, in *Afloat and Ashore,* Cooper presents the Wallingford farm as a place of "peace, plenty, and happiness" (p. 116), a haven of security from the tempestuous seas of trade on which Miles Wallingford risks his life and fortune; and Paulding in *The Dutchman's Fireside,* places the Vancour home on the banks of the Hudson in a setting that bespeaks the same quiet and repose (I, 9–10). Irving, too, stresses the peace and security of New York farms and villages. Wolfert's Roost is built in "as quiet and sheltered a nook as the heart of man could require in which to take refuge from the cares and troubles of the world" (XVII, 497); Wolfert Webber's family mansion, "the seat of government" of his paternal acres, exudes "the air of long-settled ease and security" (XXI, 471); and the town of Albany in "Dolph Heyliger" is "quiet and orderly; everything [is] conducted calmly and leisurely; no hurry, no bustle, no struggling and scrambling for existence" (IV, 520). Farms and estates like Clawbonny and Ravensnest, in Cooper's novels, and villages like Communipaw, in Irving's tales, may thus be seen symbolically as bastions holding out against the pressure for change, improvement, and financial profit which Yankees most frequently represent.

II

To read "Rip Van Winkle" and "The Legend of Sleepy Hollow" in terms of this literary background is to perceive at once the significance of their social themes. The stories arise out of the same intellectual matrix that provided material for other works by Irving and his New York contemporaries, and both make penetrating comments on some of the more unpleasant aspects of American life. The issue is most clear-cut, of course, in "The Legend of Sleepy Hollow," where, in what seems to be almost a kind of wish fulfilment on Irving's part, New England goes down to defeat at the hands of the New York Dutch. In "Rip Van Winkle," on the other hand, the peaceful village society is swept away by the torrent of social change.

The theme of the former tale is developed in terms of the threat posed to a New York farm by the voracious Connecticut Yankee, Ichabod Crane. To prepare for the conflict that is to embody his basic theme, Irving invests both the farm and its environment with symbolic meaning. Even the general setting contributes to the major pattern of development, for Irving creates a number of images of isolated and circumscribed localities by means of which he suggests the values of peace and security that both the valley itself and the farm of Baltus Van Tassel are supposed to represent. The "small market-town or rural port" of Tarry Town nestles secure "in the bosom of one of those spacious coves which indent the eastern shore of the Hudson," while about two miles inland lies the "sequestered glen" of Sleepy Hollow. This "little valley, or rather lap of land, among high hills . . . is one of the quietest places in the whole world. A small brook glides through it, with just murmur enough to lull one to repose; and the occasional whistle of a quail, or tapping of a woodpecker, is almost the only sound that ever breaks in upon the uniform tranquillity" (XIX, 474–475).

This image of peace and security is strengthened by the contrasts that Irving develops as the story progresses. The valley is presented first as a possible retreat where one "might steal from the world and its distractions, and dream quietly away the remnant of a troubled life" (XIX, 475); it is later described as typical of such "retired Dutch valleys," those nooks of quiet water, bordering "a rapid stream; where we may see the straw and bubble riding quietly at anchor, or slowly revolving in their mimic harbor, undisturbed by the rush of the passing current." Indeed, Irving explicitly states that such pockets of order are to be praised, for in them "population, manners, and customs, remain fixed; while the great torrent of migration and improvement, which is making such incessant changes in other parts of this restless country, sweeps by them unobserved" (XIX, 477–478).

The farm of Baltus Van Tassel contributes to the image of a peaceful, self-contained society. "His stronghold," we are told, "was situated on the banks of the Hudson, in one of those green, sheltered, fertile nooks, in which the Dutch farmers are so fond of nestling"; a broad elm spreads its branches above it; and Baltus himself seldom allows "his eyes or his thoughts" to wander "beyond the boundaries of his own farm." Within this secure and protected haven, Van Tassel has flourished, and Irving goes to great lengths to describe the vast barn almost "bursting forth with the treasures of the farm" and the squadrons and regiments of pigs, geese, ducks, turkeys, and chickens that thrive there. Although Baltus Van Tassel is rich, he is not proud of his wealth. He is satisified, of course, yet he piques "himself upon the hearty abundance, rather than the style" he lives in (XIX, 486–488). Old Baltus is hospitable, too, for he shares his abundance with his neighbors by giving the quilting party that Ichabod Crane attends just before he is driven from Sleepy Hollow. The whole description of the farm as "snug, happy, and well-conditioned" (XIX, 486) is designed to illustrate the peace and security of the thriving Dutch community.

The major threat to the stability of this pleasant society is the New Englander, Ichabod Crane, a man of voracious appetite, who, "though lank," is said to have "the dilating powers of an anaconda" (XIX, 480). The description of Crane is developed through a number of such images. When seen from a distance on the hillside, he looks like "the genius of famine descending upon the earth" (XIX, 478–479), and "his devouring mind's eye" sees all the livestock on the farm as delicious dishes to satisfy his greedy appetite (XIX, 488). "His great green eyes"—clearly a symbol of envy—survey the flourishing fields that surround "the warm tenement of Van Tassel," and he hardly thinks of Katrina, old Baltus's blooming daughter, apart from the obvious wealth that the man who wins her will acquire. The conquest of his heart comes not when he sees the girl, but when he views the well-appointed house that she inhabits (XIX, 488–489). He does "ample justice to every dainty" served at the party and rolls his eyes over the "almost unimaginable luxury and splendor" (XIX, 502–503). In short, Ichabod Crane covets the wealth he sees spread before him, and he values it at least as much as he does the girl.

Yet, ironically, even should he gain what he most desires, he would not be content with it, for the very drive that makes him want to get on in the world "by hook and by crook" (XIX, 482) would leave him dissatisfied with what he had gained and would prevent him from enjoying it in the way that the contended, good-humored, and hospitable Baltus Van Tassel can. For Ichabod Crane is quick to see that the farm could be "turned into cash, and the money invested in immense tracts of wild land, and shingle palaces in the wilderness." The fever of speculation possesses him, so that even if he should win Katrina, he would very likely carry her off to the wilderness. With a wagon-load of household goods and "a whole family of children," he would be on the move for "Kentucky, Tennessee, or the Lord knows where" (XIX, 489). Thus, the threat that Ichabod Crane poses is something much more serious than his simply coming into possession of the Van Tassel farm. He would literally devour it, destroying in the process not only the wealth itself, but also the very conditions of stability and contentment that gave rise to it in the first place and that, once gone, might never be so productive of peace and security again.

Thus, the struggle that Irving comically portrays in "The Legend of Sleepy Hollow" has serious social implications. It raises the question of the value of change and progress if they must be bought at the price of the destruction of stability and order, and it pleads in effect for the values of the settler and conserver over those of the speculator and improver. In the story, of course, Irving gives the victory to the forces of stability, for Ichabod Crane is defeated twice: once by Katrina herself, who obviously will not have him, and again by Brom Bones, who uses Crane's own credulity to drive him from the countryside. And yet for all the humor of the situation, the story has its somber side, for Ichabod Crane loses only a battle, not the war. Defeated here, he departs for other fields to conquer. Moving "to a distant part of the country," he keeps school and studies law; turns lawyer, politician, and newspaper editor; and finally ends up "a justice of the Ten Pound Court" (XIX, 518). He joins, in other words, the torrent of change that sweeps by Sleepy Hollow and that leaves it only an eddy in the irresistible current of progress.

But if Sleepy Hollow escapes, at least for a time, the deluge of change, the village in "Rip Van Winkle" does not. Indeed, a major point in the story is the havoc wrought in just twenty years in the little Dutch village that had nestled at the foot of the Catskills since the time of Peter Stuyvesant. A symbol of rural peace and security, the village, when we first see it, blends into the landscape, the light smoke of domestic fires curling up through the trees that shade it. Even some of the original Dutch houses still stand, "built of small yellow bricks brought from Holland," their "latticed windows and gabled fronts" bespeaking their age and origin (XIX, 51–52); and the inn of Nicholas Vedder, "a patriarch of the village" (XIX, 57), serves as a stronghold of tranquillity within the secure community. By the time the story closes, however, everything has changed. The village is "larger and more populous"; new houses have been built and familiar ones have disappeared; the inn has given way to a Yankee hotel; and even the great tree that had sheltered it has been replaced by a liberty pole (XIX, 65–66). The people themselves are "busy, bustling, disputatious," much different from the phlegmatic burghers of the vanished past (XIX,67).

Rip Van Winkle's village has succumbed to the very onslaught which, in the form of Ichabod Crane, was turned away from Sleepy Hollow, and the effect is just what would have happened there had not Katrina Van Tassel and Brom Bones defeated the Connecticut schoolmaster. The quiet village has been destroyed in a social revolution that has a strong New England accent, and little of its earlier nature remains. Rip, of course, is the only character upon whom the change has its full effect, for only he has missed the invasion and gradual destruction of the community. One function he serves in the story, therefore, is to provide a measuring stick for change. It is through him that Irving drives home the theme that the Yankee desire for change, improvement, and progress can subvert a stable society in so short a period of time as the middle years of a man's brief life. Thus, at one level of meaning, Rip's sleep in the Catskills is simply a convenient way of bringing into sharp contrast the two competing ways of life.

There is, however, a great deal more to the story than that, for Rip himself also represents to some extent the view of life that is rapidly being supplanted. Hence, what happens to him in the story may be taken as a symbolic account of the fate of such a man in a society where only success matters. Rip Van Winkle is "a simple, good-natured fellow" and "a kind neighbor" (XIX, 52). Though described at one point as lazy (XIX, 69), he is nonetheless capable of performing heavy work, Irving tells us explicitly: "He would never refuse to assist a neighbor even in the roughest toil, and was a foremost man of all country frolics for husking Indian corn, or building stone-fences." He runs errands and does "little odd jobs" for the good women who ask him, and he is a great favorite with the wives, children, and dogs of the village (XIX, 53–54). Indeed, the one great flaw in Rip's nature is his "insuperable aversion to all kinds of profitable labor" (XIX, 53). In other words, Rip will do for neighborliness and good fellowship what he will not do for profit, an attitude which unfortunately causes his family to suffer. Yet whatever the errors that may be charged against him, Rip Van

Winkle is certainly more attractive as a human being than the covetous Ichabod Crane.

Rip, of course, cannot survive in a society that demands, in the form of a nagging wife, that he strive for success.[14] He retreats first to the tavern, then to the woods, and as he goes deeper and deeper into the Catskills, the reader perceives that he has indeed withdrawn from the struggle. He unconsciously scrambles to one of the highest parts of the mountains. Far away on one side lies the Hudson River and home; "on the other side he looked down into a deep mountain glen, wild, lonely, and shagged, the bottom filled with fragments from the impending cliffs, and scarcely lighted by the reflected rays of the setting sun" (XIX, 58–59). Rip, of course, following the phantom bowler who summons him twice as he is on the point of returning home, goes even deeper into the wilderness, passes through a ravine, and enters "a hollow, like a small amphitheatre, surrounded by perpendicular precipices, over the brinks of which impending trees shot their branches, so that you only caught glimpses of the azure sky and the bright evening cloud" (XIX, 60). Such a symbol of isolation reveals the solitary withdrawal from society that Rip has made.

But if Rip Van Winkle escapes the demands of a profit-oriented society, he pays a fearful price for his success. To be sure, Rip seems to have achieved his heart's desire. He finds himself with nothing to do in his daughter's home when he returns to society, for, having arrived at last "at that happy age when a man can be idle with impunity" (XIX, 73), he is free to spend his days as he will at the door of the inn. Yet Rip's escape from the workday world is not a happy one. To achieve it, he has had to surrender the major part of his mature life and become an alien in the community of which he had once been a valued part. Life has moved on without him. Death has taken a number of his old Dutch cronies, and one, Van Bummel, the schoolmaster, has gone on to a useful life in the service of his new country. Rip has played no role in the most important events of his times. He has missed, moreover, the growth of his children to maturity, and he remains essentially a child himself to the end of his

[14]Cf. the interpretation of Rip and Dame Van Winkle in Louis Le Fevre, "Paul Bunyan and Rip Van Winkle," *Yale Review,* XXXVI, 66–76 (Autumn, 1946), esp. p. 68.

days.[15] Thus, although Rip Van Winkle slips back into the groove of life, retrieves old friends, and makes new ones in the rising generation, Irving does not present his experience as an unmixed blessing. Read in these terms, "Rip Van Winkle" is a much more sober —and fundamentally more realistic—tale than "The Legend of Sleepy Hollow," for it admits that change is inevitable, and can only be evaded, if at all, by paying a terrible price. Yet both of these stories must be taken together if we are to understand Irving's criticism of American society. The symbolic weight he gives to the traditional, rural communities in both tales clearly indicates the value he places upon a stable society strongly oriented toward the security, hospitality, neighborliness, and good-fellowship of a long established community life. Two views of life, therefore, come face to face when New Yorker and Yankee meet, and Irving abhors the kind of society —disputatious, money oriented, and constantly changing—which, he believed, could result only from a New England victory.

That such a victory is inevitable seems also to be suggested by Irving's stories. Ichabod Crane is only deflected, not stopped, in his career; the torrent of change sweeps past the cultural island of Sleepy Hollow; and Rip Van Winkle's village has been altered beyond recognition. In these stories and elsewhere, Irving writes as if the country had already passed the point of no return in its espousal of those principles that he associates with the New England character. Like Cooper and Paulding,[16] he had serious reservations about the results of material progress. Thus, in "Conspiracy of the Cocked Hats," he describes "all turnpikes, railroads, and steamboats [as] those abominable inventions by which the usurping Yankees are strengthening themselves in the land, and subduing everything to utility and commonplace" (XVII, 551). The point, of course, is not that Irving believed time could be stopped or the course of history reversed. "Rip Van Winkle" is evidence that he did not. He does suggest, however, that important values are lost when men prefer change to stability

---

[15]Cf. Philip Young, who makes the point, in his "Fallen from Time: The Mythic Rip Van Winkle," *Kenyon Review*, XXII, 547–573 (Autumn, 1960), that Rip escapes his manhood and passes "from childhood to second childhood with next to nothing in between" (p. 570).

[16]Cooper, *Afloat and Ashore*, pp. 533–534; Paulding, *The Dutchman's Fireside*, I, 15–16; II, 125–128, 170; *The Puritan and His Daughter*, II, 134–135.

and are ready to sacrifice everything—even the homes of their fathers—to speculation in land and material progress.

The good-natured humor of Irving's style and the aura of myth and legend with which he invests his stories mask to a considerable degree the seriousness of his social theme. It is for this reason, perhaps, that Irving was able to escape the kind of criticism leveled against the more outspoken Cooper, who makes similar points in his novels, but, unfortunately for his reputation, makes them far more bluntly. Irving and Cooper, of course, are not often seen in this relation, partly because of Cooper's hostility toward Irving, for whom he had little respect.[17] Yet the evidence clearly suggests that Irving, like Cooper, was seriously concerned about the direction American life was taking and deeply regretted the material orientation of his countrymen. His distaste for the New Englander, though more discreetly revealed, was surely as real as that of the novelist, and his attachment to the order, stability, and security of New York society was no less strong. He did not, of course, leave as full and detailed a picture of New York life as did Cooper, but in "Rip Van Winkle" and "The Legend of Sleepy Hollow" he projected his theme with a symbolic force that, in its own way, is surely as effective.

[17]For a discussion of Cooper's attitude toward Irving—and of certain similarities in the thought of the two men—see James Grossman, *James Fenimore Cooper* (New York, 1949), pp. 165–167. Allen Guttmann also observes, in a different context, some similarities in Irving's and Cooper's social thought. See "Washington Irving and the Conservative Imagination," *American Literature*, XXXVI, 165–173 (May, 1964), esp. pp. 168, 170, 173.

From "The Writers' Friendships With American Artists"

BY JAMES T. CALLOW

James T. Callow took his doctorate, in American Culture, at Western Reserve University. Since 1954 he has taught at the University of Detroit, where in 1968 he was appointed Director of the Folklore Archive and in 1969 promoted to Professor. A member of the Bibliography Committee of the Modern Language Association's American Literature Group beginning in 1963, he was also a National Endowment for the Humanities research grantee, 1973–1975. This selection, which illuminates Irving's instinctive attraction to contemporary painters, is taken from Chapter II, "The Writers' Friendships with American Artists," of Callow's *Kindred Spirits: Knickerbocker Writers and American Artists, 1807–1855*, published in 1967.

Before analyzing the art-material in Knickerbocker literature, which is the purpose of the next chapters, we must examine the close personal ties between the artists and the authors; for in most cases these friendships not only prompted the Knickerbockers to write about the fine arts but also gave them enough familiarity with their subject to write with confidence and perception. In the previous chapter relatively large groups of friends were seen working together in clubs and other organizations; in this chapter we narrow our focus to pairs—to Irving and Allston, Cooper and Greenough, Bryant and Durand, and to some combinations of writer and artist which, though important, have been neglected for almost a century.

WASHINGTON IRVING

Washington Irving should be treated first, for he was the oldest of the major Knickerbockers. Moreover, his connection with the fine arts began early and lasted long.[1] In his pre-teens he received drawing instructions from Archibald Robertson, a Scottish immigrant, who later became a director of the American Academy. At this time Irving's interest was bolstered by his admiration for the artists John and Alexander Anderson, family friends, one of whom, John, was the unsuccessful suitor of Irving's sister Catherine. Stimulated by the sketch books of these men, Washington kept up his own drawing. This practice afforded him amusement on trips to the North in 1802–1803, and he continued it long after his first visit to Europe in 1804, the beginning of his extensive relationships with American painters studying and working overseas.[2]

[1]For an extensive study of this subject see Jules D. Prown, "Washington Irving's Interest in Art and His Influence upon American Painting." pp. 5–45. [Unpublished Master's thesis, Univ. of Delaware, 1956. (*Ed.*)]

[2]See Donald A. Shelley, "American Painting in Irving's Day," p. 19 [*American Collector.* XVI (October, 1947), 19–21, 50. (*Ed.*)]; William Dunlap, *A History of the Rise and Progress of the Arts of Design in the United States,* II, 79–88; Stanley T. Williams, *The Life of Washington Irving,* I, 17–18; Pierre M. Irving, *The Life and Letters of Washington Irving,* I, 42. For reproductions of Irving's drawings, see *The Journals of Washington Irving"* [ed. W. P. Trent and G. S. Hellman, 3 vols. Boston: The Bibliophile Society, 1919. (*Ed.*)].

IRVING AND ALLSTON

Of the painters who became Irving's friends after his arrival in Europe only one achieved a reputation close to his own. This was Washington Allston, remembered today, like Irving, as a leader in the development of romanticism. In Rome during the spring of 1805 Irving met Allston for the first time. He was immediately impressed with the young painter's genius, and an intimacy between them was nurtured by frequent visits to art galleries, where Allston taught Irving to concentrate on one masterpiece at a time.[3] Then but twenty-one years old and not yet settled in a career, Irving began to think of becoming a painter himself. "I mentioned the idea to Allston, and he caught at it with eagerness," Irving later recalled. "Nothing could be more feasible. We would take an apartment together. He would give me all the instruction and criticism in his power, and was sure I would succeed." But after a few days Irving declined the proposal, "doubts and fears" having turned him to "sterile reality";[4] for he saw, as Stanley Williams suggests, more potential in his notebooks, systematically filled with observations on the scenery, history, and character types of Europe, than in his charming but casual drawings.[5]

When Irving left Rome in April of 1805, Allston stayed on. They did not meet again until both had returned to America—and then they met but infrequently. Later, when they found themselves together in England, their friendship reached its greatest intensity. In his essay on Allston Irving described their relationship during this period, which began in 1815 with his arrival in London and ended three years later with Allston's departure for the United States: "I used to pass long evenings with him and [Charles R.] Leslie; indeed Allston, if any one would keep him company, would sit up until cock-crowing, and it was hard to break away from the charm of his conversation. He was an admirable story-teller; for a ghost-story none could surpass him."[6] Allston and Irving respected each other's abilities. Irving

---

[3]Washington Irving, "Washington Allston," in *Biographies and Miscellanies,* pp. 143–44 [ed. P. M. Irving, Knickerbocker Edition. Philadelphia: J. B. Lippincott & Co., 1873 (*Ed.*)]; Williams, I, 65, 165, 394; P. M. Irving, I, 108–111; Jared B. Flagg, *The Life and Letters of Washington Allston,* p. 61.

[4]Irving, *Biographies,* p. 145.

[5]Williams, I, 45–46.

[6]*Biographies,* p. 146. Also see P. M. Irving, I, 297.

waxed enthusiastic over Allston's work and was especially pleased with his illustrations for a new edition of Knickerbocker's *History of New York*. Allston himself always eagerly awaited Irving's comments on his paintings and once expressed disappointment that Irving could not furnish "hints" for his "Belshazzar's Feast." After 1818 when Allston returned to America to waste away his life on this ill-fated picture, their paths seldom crossed, and their friendship became little more than a pleasant memory. Irving mentioned only one meeting with Allston after that. The painter was then "in the gray evening of life, apparently much retired from the world."[7] He died in 1843, more than a decade before Irving, who during his own last days, upon hearing Allston's name mentioned, was "set . . . all glowing with tender, affectionate enthusiasm."[8]

LESLIE'S CIRCLE

Allston's departure for the United States had been the occasion for a deepening friendship between Irving and Charles R. Leslie, an American painter who lived in England nearly all of his life.[9] Upon first meeting Leslie in 1817, Irving had been "somewhat pleased, and more amused" with the young artist;[10] but their mutual love of painting, Allston, and England kindled their friendship into a lifelong fervency which such a mild beginning would hardly seem to foreshadow. Soon they were breakfasting with Walter Scott, attending the coronation of George IV, calling on Samuel Rogers, dining at the York Chop House, and taking enjoyable excursions to Greenwich and Richmond. As Leslie remarked: "The harmony that subsisted among us was uninterrupted."[11]

Another member of this circle was Gilbert Stuart Newton, also an American, and a relative of Gilbert Stuart.[12] Having come to Eng-

[7]W. Irving, *Biographies*, p. 150.

[8]William G. Dix's account of a call on Irving, given in P. M. Irving, III, 386. Also see III, 313; Williams, II, 237, 401.

[9]See P. M. Irving, I, 297, 379, II, 43; Prown, p. 138, n. 2; Charles R. Leslie, *Autobiographical Recollections* [ed. Tom Taylor. Boston: Ticknor & Fields, 1860 (*Ed.*)], pp. lii, 42.

[10]Quoted in P. M. Irving, I, 284.

[11]Leslie, p. 42.

[12]Dunlap, *Arts of Design*, III, 80–84; P. M. Irving, I, 298, 323, 340, 371–72, II, 42–43, 53–55, 195; Williams, I, 203, 498, II, 16; Prown, pp. 142–43, n. 16.

land after a period of halfhearted study in Italy, Newton was introduced to Irving by Leslie; and the three soon made a gay trio. Irving
stayed at Newton's apartment for a time, and Newton painted Ir-
ing's portrait, which the author's friends pronounced the best likeness
of him.

Irving followed every step of Newton's career, taking special delight in Newton's rapidity of execution and uncanny eye for color but
acknowledging his lack of skill in drawing. All these things Irving
wrote to Dunlap for publication, noting further that the current estimate of Newton as an arrogant and irascible puppy was not correct.
Dunlap was forced to conclude that any artist who was a friend of
Irving and Leslie must be blessed with "good sense" and "an amiable
disposition."[13] Furthermore, when Newton became a successful
genre painter, Irving could take part of the credit, for he had persuaded Newton to shun portraiture for this less remunerative branch
of art.

Other peripheral members of this circle were William Edward
West, an American who became famous for his portrait of Byron,
and David Wilkie, a Scottish painter. Irving and West spent a
great deal of time together in Paris and London, occasionally meeting
later in New York, Boston, and other parts of the eastern United
States.[14] Wilkie's connection with Irving seems more important, encompassing the years 1827 and 1828, when Irving was in Spain.[15]
Having just finished *The Life and Voyages of Columbus*, he was able
to luxuriate in the more enjoyable task of studying early Spanish art
with Wilkie. Irving regarded his friend as a kind of heaven-sent
teacher and once remarked, "I would not give an hour's conversation
with Wilkie, about paintings . . . for all the enthusiastic and rapturous
declamations of the common run of amateurs and artists."[16] Just how
extensive this Spanish experience was can be found in Irving's note-

---

[13]Dunlap, *Arts of Design*, III, 83.

[14]Williams, I, 283; P. M. Irving, II, 65; N. P. Dunn, "An Artist of the
Past: William Edward West and His Friends at Home and Abroad," [*Putnam's
Monthly*, II (September, 1907), 58–69 (*Ed.*)], pp. 661–62.

[15]The best treatment of this friendship is in Prown, pp. 23–32, 148–56.
Other references are in Williams, I, 283, 325, 335, 482, 485, 495; P. M. Irving, II, 90, 123, 195, III, 338.

[16]Quoted in Williams, I, 327.

book—filled with jottings about a tour to Toledo, the bull fights, excursions to museums, churches, and vaults, all undertaken by that inseparable trio of Irving, Wilkie, and Prince Dolgorouki, a Russian attaché. On the whole, it was a valuable experience, too. Irving learned about painting from an expert, and the expert in turn acquired a new facility and freedom in his art. No one would praise him more for this than his friend Irving who, in a sketch of the painter written probably for a Spanish newspaper, claimed that Wilkie excelled even the Flemish masters in style, taste, and imagination.[17]

There was a certain reciprocity in Irving's relationship with Leslie and his fellow painters, who have been accused by no less an able critic than James Thomas Flexner of exerting "a depressing influence" on Irving's work.[18] Dunlap once wrote: "Washington Irving . . . has told me . . . that while he was writing his 'Sketch Book,' he saw every step they [Leslie and Newton] made in their art, and they saw every line of his writing."[19] The same thing held true for some of Irving's other works in which the artist-influence is strong though not immediately apparent. For instance, Leslie advised Irving to omit "Buckthorne and His Friends" from *Bracebridge Hall;* he did so, substituting the "Student of Salamanca" in its place—"an ill-judged change, as he afterwards regarded it, but he was prone to yield too readily to the suggestions of others," wrote Pierre Irving.[20] Because Leslie had not seemed pleased with "Mountjoy," Irving threw the manuscript aside; and it remained unfinished until it was published as a fragment in a magazine.[21] And Irving's lamentable inferiority complex over what he thought to be the crudities in Knickerbocker's *History of New York,* stemmed at least partly from Leslie's comments: "I enjoyed very much the renewal of my acquaintance with my old friend 'Diedrich.' I have the highest respect for the old gentleman . . . , but I must say that in some of *his jokes* he goes near to be thought a little indelicate. . . . I really think he would not suffer by dispensing with them in the future."[22] Irving did dispense with them, and he

[17]The entire sketch is transcribed in Prown, pp. 114–17.
[18]James T. Flexner, *The Light of Distant Skies,* pp. 189–90.
[19]*Arts of Design,* III, 13.
[20]Williams, I, 204, 438, II, 289. The quotation is from P. M. Irving, I, 381.
[21]P. M. Irving, III, 268.
[22]Leslie, p. 227.

even traced these refinements to Allston's and Leslie's illustrations, which had set his mind on a new track.[23]

It is improbable that Leslie, Newton, Allston, and the other artists influenced Irving much beyond the matter of eliminating a few crude jokes. They have been accused of carrying "Irving away from the American themes that produced his most vital work into rhapsodies to English gentility."[24] Yet such observations deserve to be qualified. Irving's curiosity for things English and European had been developed before his intimacy with these painters, as is indicated in his prefaces to *The Sketch-Book* and *Bracebridge Hall*. Leslie, Allston, Newton, and Wilkie were only the means through which he expressed this interest, not the cause of it. Moreover, it is possible to demonstrate on the contrary that artist-influence could actually benefit Irving's work. Stanley Williams shows, for example, that the best stories in *Bracebridge Hall*—and this includes the famous "Stout Gentleman"—were derived from the association between Irving and Leslie.[25]

If Leslie over-advised Irving, he was paid back in kind; for Irving seldom hesitated to tell him what and how to paint. Yet for this service Leslie was ever grateful. "I not only owe to you some of the happiest social hours of my life," he wrote to Irving, "but you opened to me a new range of observation in my art, and a perception of qualities and characters of things which painters do not always imbibe from each other." [26] Irving in turn considered Leslie an excellent artist and on more than one occasion praised those powers which, according to Leslie, he had helped to mature.[27]

IRVING'S LIFELONG INTEREST IN ART

This intimacy between Irving and the Leslie circle, as well as acquaintance with other artists (listed in Appendix I) [not included here (*Ed.*)], constantly stimulated Irving's interest in art-matters. We are not surprised, therefore, to find him under the pseudonym of

[23]P. M. Irving, I, 270.
[24]Flexner, pp. 189–90.
[25]Williams, I, 204–205, II, 280.
[26]Quoted in P. M. Irving, I, 297.
[27]*Ibid.*, I, 298, II, 42, 175, 179, 223.

Geoffrey Crayon, or to discover him naming one of his works *The Sketch-Book;* helping William Dunlap to gather material for a history of American art;[28] recommending the painter William H. Powell for a government commission;[29] making frequent visits to cathedrals, castles, museums, mosques, and manor houses; planning the remodeling of his home at Sunnyside;[30] accepting special invitations to judge newly finished paintings;[31] and in general devoting his life to the fine arts in their various forms.

[28]See *Diary of William Dunlap,* III, 772, 776, 816, 819, 822.

[29]See photostatic copies of MS letters, Henry Brevoort to Irving, New York, May 26, 1844; Irving to The Library Committee of Congress, Sunnyside, Jan. 7, 1847, William H. Powell Miscellaneous Papers, NYPL; Prown, pp. 37, 159. For an anonymous expression of disappointment over the selection of Powell for the Rotunda commission, see "The Fine Arts," LW, I (Nov. 20, 1847), 159. Irving is excused for influencing this choice in "Editorial Notes—Fine Arts," *Putnam's Monthly Magazine,* III (Jan. 1854), 118.

[30]Washington Irving, "A Letter from Irving to His Architect," p. 47.

[31]P. M. Irving, III, 355. Durand, *A. B. Durand,* p. 174; Prown, pp. 39, 160, n. 32.

"Washington Irving: Amateur or Professional?"

BY HENRY A. POCHMANN

Henry A. Pochmann (1901–1973), Professor Emeritus at the University of Wisconsin at the time of his death, was long a senatorial figure in American Literature studies. After a Ph.D. and teaching at the University of North Carolina, he moved to Louisiana State University, then to Mississippi State University where he was Dean of the Graduate School (1935–1938). He became Professor in the English Department at Wisconsin, Madison, in 1938. A Rockefeller Fund fellow in 1936–1937, he was also a Huntington Library fellow in 1947. His long list of scholarly publications includes an "American Writers Series" *Washington Irving* (1934), and the prize-winning *German Culture in America, 1600–1900* (1957). He was the organizing General Editor of *The Complete Works of Washington Irving* in which he co-edited *Mahomet and His Successors* (1970). This Festschrift article, which carefully answers its own question, was contributed to *Essays on American Literature in Honor of Jay B. Hubbell,* ed. Clarence Gohdes (1967).

In recognition of Washington Irving's becoming the first American man of letters to win a wide international reputation, his grateful countrymen fastened upon him titles such as Inventor of the Modern Short Story, Ambassador of the New World to the Old, and Father of American Literature. Gratulatory admiration of this kind engendered a literary reputation that has suffered little diminution, comparable for example to Longfellow's or Holmes's. His fame and his honors, so the story goes, came unsought—the result of a happy conspiracy between fortuitous circumstances and innate talents; and with becoming modesty, he allowed them to rest lightly and gracefully on his slim shoulders.

Irving himself is as responsible as anyone for creating the atmosphere in which such a legend could grow. In his first writings he pictured himself as one of a knot of carefree young blades, who might have been known a generation earlier, in and about New York City, as bloods or macaroni whose primary concern, after wine-women-and-song, was literary dilettantism. In two series of periodical letters and essays appearing in 1802–1803 and 1807–1808 he represented himself as one of "the Nine Worthies," "the Lads of Kilkenny," or "the Ancient and Honorable Order of New York"—the others being his brothers William, Peter, and Ebenezer, Peter and Gouverneur Kemble, Henry Brevoort, Henry Ogden, and James Kirke Paulding. After exhausting the pleasures of the city, they often resorted to an old family mansion of the Kembles on the Passaic (Cockloft Hall in *Salmagundi*) for frolicsome entertainments befitting young bachelors with literary tastes. Sometimes they met for convivial suppers and literary powwows at a genteel public house known as Dyde's, and when their purse was low, contented themselves with "blackguard suppers" at a porterhouse on the corner of John and Nassau streets. Always they were in good spirits, and almost always their entertainment took a literary turn and concerned whatever social or political overtones the happenings of the day or the whims of the worthies suggested. So it was that the earlier series of letters by Jonathan Oldstyle, in which Irving masqueraded as a kind of nineteenth-century American reincarnation of Tatler-Spectator (of which he wearied after penning nine short epistles for his brother Peter's *Morning Chronicle*) developed into a joint production setting forth the opinions and whimwhams of the gay wags and making what they properly called a Salmagundi, a mixed dish, a medley, a potpourri of personal essays, poetical effusions, social satire, political innuendo, dramatic criticism, and editorial idiosyncrasy. Alternately grave and facetious, the youthful editors posed as "critics, amateurs, dilettanti, and cognoscenti," and proceeded merrily with cocksure insolence through twenty numbers, satirizing the ways of the fashionable world, inserting squibs on the theater, occasionally mixing a little political bastinade, waging war against "folly and stupidity," and teaching "parents . . . how to govern their children, girls how to get husbands, and old maids how to do without them." It was Addison and Steele transplanted from London to New York. It was all good-natured raillery, and all the more welcome as a change of fare from the heavy bombardment of polemics since the days of 1776. The essays were read in coffeehouses and gentlemen's clubs, and they made their way to many a proper belle's toilet table. Many of the "characters" were recognizable, and while some shunned being identified, others were secretly envied. The "fascinating [Mary] Fairlie" was obviously the original of Sophie Sparkle; there was no lack of young ladies who coveted her notoriety; and the superficial disguises under the names of Ding Dong, Ichabod Fungus, and Dick Paddle provoked no affairs of honor. But fatuous theatrical critics, taking a glance at themselves in the mirror of 'Sbidlikens, found it advisable to hold their peace; fashionable upstarts shrank before the portraits of the Giblets; the small beer of politicians soured at the portrait of Dabble; and the feathers of carpet soldiers wilted when they saw themselves paraded in the regiment of the Fag-Rags. *Salmagundi* made no great fortune for the three editors, but it became the talk and the mild terror of the town.

So it came to pass that Irving became less and less regular in his attendance at No. 3 Wall Street, where he had gingerly hung his shingle underneath that of his brother John. Instead of drawing up legal briefs, he was entertaining vague ideas of turning author. To be sure, the law had never been a serious vocation, but as the youngest of five sons of a substantial merchant (all the others already fairly launched in business, medicine, or the law) it behooved him to prepare for a profession. It was expected of him. So for a number of years he harried his inveterate enemies, the fathers of the law, in several lawyers' offices and was duly admitted to the bar "by the grace of God" and Josiah Ogden [*sic*], his latest mentor, who also served on his examining committee. It is said that at the conclusion of the examination, the other examiner said to Josiah Ogden [*sic*], "Well, Jo, I guess he knows a little law." "Make it stronger," said Jo, "damned little." But Irving knew very well that not much was expected of him as an attorney. He might take a turn at representing the brothers' business interests, or lobbying for them in Washington, but neither he nor they regarded his commissions or his returns as very weighty. It had already been decided among them that they could afford to indulge their youngest, favorite, and gifted brother to the extent of making him a nominal but profit-sharing partner and so leave him free to cultivate his talents. He would be a proper ornament, and so he was. He had already considered Washington Allston's advice that he turn painter, only to have "doubts and fears gradually cloud over that prospect"; turning now to the opposite extreme, he took a turn at practical politics by participating in a municipal campaign, but one such assay left him and his "forlorn brethren, the Federalists" intolerably beaten and discomfited. While he labored manfully, "talked handbill-fashion with the demagogues, and shook hands with the mob," "was sworn brother to a leash of drawers," and "drank with any tinker in his own language," in the end he had to conclude: "Truly, this saving one's country is a nauseous piece of business, and if patriotism is such a dirty virtue—prithee, no more of it." This does not mean that Irving foreswore for all time any crumbs that might fall into his hands (and several later did) at the dispensation of loaves and fishes in Albany or Washington. Nor did he forget (long after he had given up all ideas of turning painter) his facility at sketching with his pencil a scene for his notebooks when the descriptive power of his words failed him. Keeping a detailed journal early became a confirmed habit, and eventually an inestimable aid to his writing. Emerson called his own journals his "penny-savings bank"; Irving's diaries were in many cases his entire stock-in-trade.

Relieved of business cares by the largesse of his brothers and unconcerned about politics by his own preference, he was free to indulge his tastes and to meet the right people, for whom he had a natural affinity. In Washington he barely arrived before he put on his "pease blossoms and silk stockings" and sallied forth to one of the levees of Dolly Madison, with whom and "half the people in the assemblage" he was "hand in glove" within ten minutes. For the rest he spent his spare hours hobnobbing as agreeably with a knot of "Frenchmen & Democrats" as with his compatriots, the Federalists;

and he conducted the regular seasonal campaigns of "banquetry, re-
velling, dancing, and carousals" in Baltimore, Philadelphia, and
"Gotham."

Of a piece with his dilettante pursuit of the law was what he
called "the gentlemanly exercise of the pen." If there had been any
considerable returns from David Longworth, the printer of *Salmagundi,* and if there had been among their acquaintances any poor-
devil authors, he and his writing fraternity might have emulated
Byron who, during his expansive youthful years, showed "the same
blind contempt for pecuniary gains" and turned the profits of his
writings over to his more impecunious scribbling friends. There per-
sisted among them still something of the Renaissance gentleman's attitude toward the products of the pen as the fruits of idle hours, and
their monetary gains as beneath a gentleman's notice. When, therefore, "Duskie Davie" volunteered some unsolicited editorial suggestions and voiced objections to the length of the twentieth number of
Salmagundi, they summarily took their leave and turned to freer pur-
suits—Irving to another *jeu d'esprit,* a comic history of New York.

Begun with his brother Peter as an *œuvre de joie,* this first full-
length book of Irving's turned out quite otherwise before it was finished. Soon after it was fairly begun, the sudden death of Matilda
Hoffman threw a pall over the undertaking and a profound and unre-
lieved gloom over his spirit; but when Peter departed for England,
leaving him to go on alone, he rallied, radically revised the plan, and
set to a far more serious and prolonged stint of writing than he had
ever dreamed possible. After many delays and unanticipated complications, when the book was finally done and the first printing lined
his pockets with the tidy sum of three thousand dollars, the young
author of twenty-six had learned some serious lessons regarding literary craftsmanship—including the need for painstaking research, meticulous checking of sources, sticking to the plan in hand before giving way to will-o'-the-wisps and vagaries that beckoned invitingly, reliance upon his own resources, however meager they might be, and
above all, the necessity for keeping steadily at it, whatever the distractions. The result was a major contribution to the world's store of
wit and humor, and its success caused the erstwhile amateur littera-
teur to have some serious second thoughts then and later, when the
once abundant supply of funds from his family diminished. The success of *Knickerbocker* in 1809 confirmed his wish to embrace a writ-

ing career, but ten more years were to elapse before he was fully embarked on the road to professional authorship.

Until the War of 1812 began to cloud the horizon, Irving continued merrily as beau, reporter, essayist, satirist, detached politician, and occasional poet to sidestep every commitment that might have resulted in anything so time- and energy-consuming as another full-length book. He occasionally felt the "itching propensity to scribble which every man has who once appeared with any success in print," but did little for two years beyond editing the poems of Thomas Campbell, who then enjoyed in America a vogue nearly equal with that of Scott and Byron. His adulatory biographical sketch won him the friendship of Campell but served notice that he was unlikely to win many plaudits as a literary critic or that he had as yet arrived at any firm critical principles of his own. Beyond that, it affords the first indication of a mild interest in romantic modes and motifs, of which his writings hitherto had been virtually innocent—an interest that burgeoned a decade later in *The Sketch Book* and made him henceforth a traveler in search of more romantic and picturesque literary provender.

To supplement his irregular education, he immersed himself for varying periods of time in the well-stocked library of his friend Brevoort, or took a turn at lobbying for his brothers' firm in Washington. Next, he devoted upwards of a year to the "irksome business" of editing the *Analectic Magazine,* did a tour of duty as a colonel during the closing years of the War of 1812, and for the rest dutifully slaved in the Liverpool branch of the Irving business but failed to forestall the inevitable collapse of the firm. So ten years clicked by with monotonous regularity while he did little more than form resolutions to resume his interrupted literary career. In the end it was mainly the stimulation of new alliances formed with the reigning literati of London (during brief periods snatched from the grub and grime of the Liverpool counting house), the encouragement of Sir Walter Scott (whom he visited twice at Abbotsford), and the all-too-evident necessity for relying on his pen as the only remaining means to an independent livelihood that led to that rededication of which *The Sketch Book* was born. Begun haltingly and beset by trials of composition and by complications of publication, it proved a greater success even than *Knickerbocker,* and Irving the professional was fairly launched.

Never a tyro in the art of progress through favor, he still dallied with the idea of accepting "some situation of a moderate, unpretending kind," if his friends could swing it; but increasingly his letters and journals put the emphasis on "adding to my literary reputation by the assiduous operations of my pen," on a determination "to win solid credit with the public," "establishing a stock of copyright property," and amassing "a literary estate." So he put by proffered posts in Washington and consular posts elsewhere; he refused the flattering offer of Scott and his friends to edit, for a handsome salary, an anti-Jacobin journal to be founded. He rightly gauged his talents as wayward and his mind too untractable for any regularly recurring task. Indeed, much of Irving's success henceforth was owing to his properly appraising his capacities, or rather his incapacities, and wisely steering his fitful career away from whatever he had learned he could not do well. He knew by now that the only instrument given him was the lowly lyre—that if he would play at all, he must learn to play well on its few strings; that there was little likelihood of swapping the lyre for the harp, or of learning to play variations on an instrument beyond his capacity.

Irving's turn from a devil-may-care scribbler to a circumspect author took place about the time he wrote the stories and essays that form *The Sketch Book*—his first book written specifically for profit. This conversion was accompanied by a more guarded and decorous selection and handling of materials. Heretofore he had not scrupled to paint what the Dutch of New York denigrated as a coarse and libelous caricature of their forebears, or to relate with evident gusto the free love-life of some of the old Dutch worthies—all without the least compunction or remorse. But about the time he turned to writing for a livelihood, he became cautious. In 1818, while preparing a new edition of *Knickerbocker,* he took care to delete certain earthy Elizabethanisms and to remove both anti-British and anti-Catholic passages. He hoped the new *Knickerbocker* and the forthcoming *Sketch Book* might attract readers in Britain as well as in Catholic countries—as, indeed, they did beyond his expectations. But this did not prevent his continuing to record in his journals, for his own edification, any choice morsels he came upon in his travels. Pretty young women continued to elicit near ribald comments, as when he noticed with evident satisfaction meeting a fresh young Irishwoman whom "a man would feel no compunction in begetting children on" (*Journal,* April

8, 1824). Conversely, he made note of "the fierce virtue" of an ugly older woman "who arrogates great merit in preserving what nobody was ever tempted to steal" (*Journal,* Sept. 13, 1822). At Marseilles he recorded with relish how the bootblacks of the town, who knew no English beyond what they had picked up from American sailors, pursued him and his traveling companion, and in an effort to attract their attention and custom, cried, "Monsieur, monsieurs, God dam, God dam son de bish, son de bish." In Syracuse, where he was shown "no less than five thigh bones of St. John the Baptist, three arms of St. Stephen and four jaw bones of St. Peter," he observed in the privacy of his diary, "these disciples must have been an uncommon bony set of fellows." Two months later he was relieved when in Rome, at the church of St. Paul, he was shown "the preserved body of St. Paul." "I was happy to find his bones at length collected together for I had found them in my travels scattered through all the convents of churches I had visited." On another occasion he calculated that if all known fragments of the· Cross were collected, they would form "a tolerable stought [*sic*] ship of the line." Mark Twain made literary capital of all such titbits. Not Washington Irving! The sense of accommodaton which prompted him to regard discretion as the better part of wisdom begat the resolution that whenever he could not get a dinner to suit his taste, he would endeavor to get a taste to suit his dinner. He became circumspect, then hesitant, and finally timorous—lest he give offence in quarters where it might hurt. And when, after seventeen years of schooling in European decorum, he returned to his native land in 1832, his sense of propriety was shocked and outraged at what he saw of Jacksonian democracy in high places or of the free-and-easy manners of a frontier society. To his trusted friends he complained that Americans had obviously gone "masking mad" during his absence, but in his public statements he measured out his critical and patriotic sentiments guardedly: he complimented his fellow countrymen on the great strides forward of "progress" that he saw on every hand, and, as for Andrew Jackson, he confessed to "rather liking the old cock of the walk." Within a year, this erstwhile Federalist became known as "a Jackson man," and was probably not very much surprised when Old Hickory did not overlook him at the next division of the spoils.

Unconcerned as he had been about arrangements with publishers, or the exacting requirements of seeing his earlier writings through the press, he began, while the last numbers of *The Sketch Book* were being published, to attend to such details, either for himself or through the competence of Brevoort, and to begin negotiations that were obviously designed to entice John Murray to become his publisher. He managed the matter so well that while Murray had refused *The Sketch Book* in 1819, by May of the next year "the Prince of Booksellers" capitulated. For his part, Murray (said Irving) conducted himself "in a fair, open and liberal spirit," while Irving was at great pains to supply Murray with successive successes. At one point, when Irving sensed a lukewarmness on Murray's part toward a new manuscript, he outfoxed him by suggesting a figure well above what he expected, only to find Murray taking the bait. The reception of *Bracebridge Hall* was a disappointment; yet he played his cards so well that even *Tales of a Traveller* (the composition of which had caused him no end of grief so that he knew it was a mishmash) got him surprisingly good terms from Murray. "Your offer," he wrote to Murray on March 25, 1824, "of twelve hundred guineas without seeing the mss. is I confess a liberal one and made in your own gentlemanlike manner, but I would rather you see the mss. and make it fifteen hundred" (see also *Journal*, May 29, 1824). In the meantime he had traveled on the Continent, formed countless new alliances with great and little men and women, indulged in a variety of literary undertakings, and learned the ins and outs of the publishing business as it was conducted in Paris, as well as the complications brought on by the non-existence of a satisfactory international copyright law. His letters directing his agents or publishers were businesslike and specific, so much so that when it is remembered how nonchalant he had been about the tiresome details of publishing his earlier works (possibly in emulation of Byron's affectations in this regard), he strikes one as following now the older Byron's advice to authors to practice "the good old gentlemanly vice of avarice."

The adroit dealings by which he maneuvered his literary products through various publishers until he made the mutually profitable arrangement with George P. Putnam is a long story, too long to be detailed here, but it betokens a lively interest in, and capacity for, business. Equally important is the care he exercised during 1848–1850 in giving his books a complete and meticulous overhauling for the "Author's Revised Edition" by which he wished the world to know him. Although he complained often and long about slaving at revisions and reading proof in a hot city, while foregoing the comforts of his Sunnyside retreat, he stuck with it to safeguard and enhance his "literary capital." Even after this long chore was completed, he kept touching up individual volumes. *Knickerbocker,* having by then already undergone three complete revisions, was hauled out again for toning-up here and there, and *The Sketch Book* was subjected to a similar refurbishing. A recently discovered copy of an 1854 issue (printed from the 1848 plates) contains extensive revisions on the printed pages and forty-one new interleaves in Irving's handwriting. The precise identification of this volume and the edition for which these alterations were intended awaits exhausting collation with 1855 and 1857 impressions, but the evidence is enough to suggest that even while Irving was preoccupied with the five-volume *Washington,* he neglected no opportunity if so well-established a volume as *The Sketch Book* could be made to add another mite to his reputation and his income.

During his later years he sometimes allowed his real or fancied need for additional income to get the better of his aesthetic judgment. The compulsion to add "capital" led him to collect in volume form some of his earlier, more ephemeral periodical contributions that might better have been allowed to remain forgotten. It may also have blinded him to John Jacob Astor's motive in enlisting his pen to romanticizing Astoria. And there are other instances (related in detail by Stanley T. Williams in the second volume of his biography) that explain, though they do not entirely excuse, Cooper's saying that Irving always trimmed his sails to the prevailing winds: "What an instinct that man has for gold!" A more charitable man than Cooper might have observed that Irving's later potboiler writings represented simply the overanxious and perhaps ill-considered efforts of the oldest "pro" of the American writers' guild to sell what remained of his literary energy and ability to the best advantage in the popular market.

It may be doubted that when Irving wrote "Rip Van Winkle" and "The Legend of Sleepy Hollow" he was fully aware that he was inventing a new genre; but once it was done, he was not slow to realize what he had done or to understand the techniques of his storytelling art. Thenceforth, as he said, "I have preferred adopting a mode of sketches & short tales rather than long works, because I chose to take a line of writing peculiar to myself, rather than fall into the manner or school of any other writer. . . . I believe the works I have written will be oftener re-read than any novel of the size I could have written." And with true Irvingesque whimsicality he could point out that "if the tales I have furnished should prove to be bad, at least they will be found short."[1]

If in his stories about Rip and Ichabod, he wrote better than he knew, he was not slow to make an astute assessment of the short story's potentialities. By 1824 he recognized the sterility of the then current American novel as an art form, and said as much. In Cooper's case, for example, the format required that it be "In Two Volumes," and it did not matter much whether he strung together a series of short narratives or strung out a short narrative to make two volumes duodecimo. Hawthorne and Melville had not yet demonstrated what could be done in the genre by adapting it to the "romance," as they preferred to call their longer narratives. At any rate, by the end of 1824 Irving knew what he was about, and, possibly with an eye on Cooper, he said, "It is comparatively easy to swell a story to any size when you have once the scheme & the characters in your mind; the mere interest of the story too carries the reader on through pages & pages of careless writing and the author may often be dull for half a volume at a time, if he has some striking scene at the end of it, but in these shorter writings every page must have its merit. The author must be continually piquant—woe to him if he makes an awkward sentence or writes a stupid page; the critics are sure to pounce upon it. Yet if he succeed, the very variety & piquancy of his writings, nay their very brevity, makes them frequently recurred to—and when the mere interest of the story is exhausted, he begins to get credit for his touches of pathos or humor, his points of wit or turns of language. I give these as some of the reasons that have induced me to keep on thus far in the way I have opened for myself . . . ."

It may be useless to conjecture whether or not he could have written a novel. Certainly he never did (though he started at least one), and there is reason for believing he did not possess the requirements for writing a good play—sustained concentration, searching analysis of character, strict construction of plot, and fine adjustment of numberless details into a continuous fabric of thought. *The Sketch*

[1] *Letters of Washington Irving to Henry Brevoort,* ed. George S. Hellman (Library ed., 2 vols. in 1, New York, 1918), pp. 398–400.

Book is precisely what the title implies—a collection of sketches, odds and ends, many of them good enough in themselves, but without cohesion, one with another. *Bracebridge Hall* is a collection of stories gleaned from various sources and held together by the mechanical device, as old as *The Arabian Nights,* of having them all related by members of a hunting party marooned in Bracebridge Hall. By the time he wrote *Tales of a Traveller,* he was encountering real difficulty managing his heterogeneous materials, and the result is a hodgepodge in four parts, none of which has any relationship to the others. Irving resented the severity of the critics who took the book apart, but he was fully aware that he had exploited the sketch-book vein to the limit. The result was another change of climate and scene —a trip to and residence in Spain, where once more, under the stimulus of romantic surroundings, he produced something akin to *The Sketch Book's* excellence. Among the productions of his middle and more creative period, *The Alhambra* comes near being a book, in the sense that it is all of a piece, so far as least as atmosphere and tone could make it so. Thereafter he wisely limited himself mainly to biography (interwoven with history) or to the literature of exploration and adventure, chiefly as associated with the western United States. But in any case, the materials for these later works came ready to hand, and except for that inimitable style that was Irving's he did little more than transcribe what lay before him. When he tried for more, as he did in *Goldsmith,* it was his basic sympathy for the man, in so many ways like himself, that made it an engaging biography. *Washington,* his most ambitious undertaking, is better in details than in conception. It exhibits no great structural skill; the incidents crystallize more around the man than around principles. For the method of the philosophical historian or the critical biographer he had little aptitude; he was at his best when he grasped his subject by his sympathies rather than by rationalization from causes to effects. All in all, his first book, properly so-called, namely *Diedrich Knickerbocker's History of New York,* came nearest to meeting the Aristotelian requirements of unity—in inception, in organization, and in execution; but cold analysis reduces even it to what is basically an aggregation of tales told in chapters and books rather than a continuous story or history.

However readily Irving composed his first literary efforts, he began to encounter trouble about the time he wrote *The Sketch*

Book. Congenitally a man of moods, he was given to feelings of indolence, indirection, ineffectuality, melancholy, self-depreciation, insecurity, enervation, sterility, and despair. For months he did little more than register the state of his personal thermometer ten times daily. This preoccupation with the moody state of his mind first, last, and all the time becomes positively torturous for the reader of his journals, and belies the reputation he had of being habitually and by nature the soul of gaiety and geniality. If he managed to show the world the brighter side of himself, it was because he instinctively and consciously withdrew from social intercourse when he felt the dark moods coming on. So he carefully watched himself and nursed his oversensitive disposition. Following the great success of *The Sketch Book* he confided to his friend Leslie, "Now you suppose I am all on the alert, and full of spirit and excitement. No such thing. I am just as good for nothing as ever I was; and, indeed, have been flurried and put out by these puffings. I feel something as I suppose you did when your picture met with success—anxious to do something better, and at a loss what to do."[2]

"What to do next" became from now on a haunting worry and the natural cause for many ill-conceived plans, misdirected efforts, or false starts. At the time he refused Scott's offer to turn editor, he confessed, "My whole course of life has been desultory, and I am unfitted for any periodically recurring task, or any stipulated labor of body or mind. I have no command of my talents such as they are, and have to watch the varyings of my mind as I would a weather cock. Practice and training may bring me more into rule; but at present I am as useless for regular service as one of my own country Indians or a Don Cossack. I must, therefore, keep on pretty much as I have begun—writing when I can, not when I would. I shall occasionally shift my residence and write whatever is suggested by objects before me, or whatever runs in my imagination, and hope to write better and more copiously by and by."[3] He probably never wrote better than he did just then. This much is certain: whenever he wrote "more copiously," he did not compose as well. Often he gave way to

---

[2]Pierre M. Irving, *The Life and Letters of Washington Irving* (New York, 1862–1864), I, 415.
[3]*Ibid.,* I, 441-442.

distractions, if only to avoid the ordeal of sitting at the table unable to do more than chew his pen; and so he spent as much time preparing to write as in writing. These hesitations and doubts and the variety of uncongenial works undertaken, always with little satisfaction to himself, give evidence of the uncertainty of mind that never ended but did subside somewhat after he was fairly launched on the routine work of his biographical and historical research in Spain—that is, after he turned from composition to compilation. Routine proved a good wall to which to retreat. Even so, writing remained for him hard, agonizing work, and he had to drive himself mercilessly. During his last illness, when he was given the fifth and last volume of *Washington,* just arrived from the printer, he said with obvious and heartfelt relief, "Thank Heaven! Henceforth I give up all tasking with the pen!" Under these circumstances, the dilettante or tyro would never have produced the stout twenty-seven volumes that comprise Irving's literary output; only Irving the professional could pull it off. And the wonder is, as Dr. Samuel Johnson might have said, not that he did it so well, but that he did it at all.

We need not quarrel with Irving for not attempting what he could not and *knew* he could not do well. It is enough if we are to appreciate his doing so well with so little. His success is owing largely to his husbanding his slender store of genius and measuring out carefully his slim stock-in-trade. This studied procedure bespeaks the craftsman who knows his business rather than the divine amateur who expects a miracle. He believed he could do his countrymen a greater service chronicling Hudson River legends and bringing to them a touch of merry England and romantic Spain than by overtaxing his talents and tiring his readers' patience with moral or philosophical disquisitions; he calculated correctly that as an intermediary between old-world culture and new-world rawness and as a romancer in the sphere of belles-lettres he would speak to better purpose than as politician or preacher. "I have attempted no lofty theme, nor sought to look wise and learned, which appears to be very much the fashion among our American writers at present. . . . I seek only to blow a flute accompaniment in the national concert, and leave others to play the fiddle and French horn."[4] This careful calculation of his

⁴*Ibid.,* I, 415, 416.

own potential labels him less the amateur toying with esoteric aspirations beyond his reach than the canny professional gauging his grasp by his reach.

From
"General Introduction
To Journals"

BY NATHALIA WRIGHT

Nathalia Wright, after a Yale doctorate and teaching at Maryville College, has been a member of the University of Tennessee faculty since 1949. A Professor of English there since 1962, earlier she held a Guggenheim fellowship in 1953, and an American Association of University Women fellowship in 1959. A poet and former president of The Melville Society, her scholarly publications include *Melville's Use of the Bible* (1949), *Horatio Greenough: The First American Sculptor* (1963), and *American Novelists in Italy* (1965). Included here is the first section of the "General Introduction," taken from Volume I, 1803–1806, of the *Journals And Notebooks,* which in 1969 was the first volume to appear of *The Complete Works of Washington Irving,* an edition still in progress, sponsored by the Center for Editions of American Authors. As editor of this initial volume, Professor Wright here introduces the reader to Irving as diarist, and to matters of technique being employed by those editing Irving's manuscripts in this CEAA project.

This edition of Irving's journals and notebooks is planned to appear in five volumes of *The Complete Works of Washington Irving* sponsored by the Center for Editions of American Authors. The journals begin in 1803, Irving's twentieth year, and continue at irregular intervals through his life until 1842. Perhaps the most striking fact about them, besides their intermittent and often fragmentary nature, is their distribution. Most of the journals were written while Irving was traveling. Indeed, he made no journey of any length (on land) of which he did not keep a record, a noteworthy fact, inasmuch as he seemed to need, as a professional writer, a frequent change of scene.

It is also significant that most of Irving's journals were written while he was abroad—a total of twenty-two and a half years. Except for the youthful New York Journal of 1803 and the Western Journal, he apparently kept none during his thirty-two adult years in America: 1806–1815, 1832–1842, 1846–1859. The subject matter of his printed books is correspondingly divided. He wrote only some half dozen books entirely about his native land. The first American writer after the Revolution to come into extended contact with European culture, he did not seem to be consciously a discoverer of that culture. His European journals lack the penetrating analysis of American and European character and also the tension of a strong attraction to, and repulsion by, Europe found in the travel books of Cooper and James and in the European notebooks of Hawthorne. Nor, unlike these authors, did Irving write anything resembling an international novel, in which Americans, confronted with European experience, emerge both losers and gainers. He did, however, in both his journals and his printed works, draw the main outlines of the Old World scene—picturesque, often dangerous, and legendary—whereon in later American literature representatives of the New World repeatedly enact dramas of self-discovery.

About half the original manuscript volumes are journals and notebooks that contain some account of Irving's daily activities; the others are collections of miscellaneous notes, including expense accounts, excerpts from other authors, anecdotes, observations, and reminiscences. Although the journals and several of the notebooks have more biographical than literary value, their relationship to his other writing is nevertheless significant.

The known dates covered by these volumes are 1803–1806, 1810, 1815, 1817–1833, 1835, and 1840–1843: about half the mature period of Irving's seventy-six year life. The longest sequence of journals covers seven years—from August 1822 to August 1829—which Irving spent mostly in France, Germany, and Spain (where he served for two and a half years as a member of the American Legation). Next in length comes his account of his first European journey, from July 1804 to about January 1806. The remaining journals represent trips of a few months at most: that which he took as a young man in New York State in 1803, his tour in Wales in 1815, his tour in Scotland in 1817, his trip through the American West in 1832, and his travels from New York to Bayonne in 1842. About a third of the miscellaneous notebooks belong to the period 1817–1823, when he was emerging as a professional writer—the author of *The Sketch Book* and *Bracebridge Hall*. About the same number cannot be dated with certainty.

Washington Irving's nephew, Pierre Munro Irving, notes in the Preface to his *Life and Letters of Washington Irving* (1862) that his uncle "placed in my possession a mass of material, consisting of journals, note-books, diaries at scattered intervals. . . ." It was in the nephew's book that use was first made of the journals and notebooks. The four-volume biography, appearing two decades and more before Irving's literary compeers became the subjects of "official" or "authorized" biographers, in a manner set tone and scope for the others to follow.

But being first in any field often incurs its own drawbacks. Although Pierre M. Irving quoted at some length from his uncle's journals and letters, their separate collection lagged far behind most of the others, presumably on the assumption that the samplings which the official biography provided were sufficient. And so they were until the demands of twentieth-century scholarship encouraged a first generation of serious Irving scholars to supply some of the more significant lacunae in Irving's notebooks and journals.[1]

Good as they are, they followed varying standards and methods of transcription and editing, besides leaving a considerable gap of some two dozen separate manuscript volumes of miscellaneous journal material. This anomalous situation a half-dozen students of Irving set themselves to rectify when, at an informal meeting during the 1959 sessions of the Modern Language Association, they projected a complete and accurate edition of Irving's journals and letters, to be prepared in accord with modern editorial standards. When the Center for Editions of American Authors was formed, the project was included in the editions sponsored by the Center. The editors' intention has been to produce a text as close as possible to what Irving actually wrote, including his cancellations, insertions, and eccentric variations upon standard spelling, punctuation, and capitalization.

It goes without saying that in adopting the "Editorial Principles" as defined by the Center, the reticences, scruples, and restrictions under which the nineteenth-century editor labored are removed. Pierre M. Irving's constraints to present an image of his uncle in accord with the genteel tradition then in the making and the compulsion under which he felt himself to tidy up the portrait by making judicious deletions, even erasures, and to present an unblemished picture no longer obtain. The Irving that appears from a reproduction of the journals as he wrote them presents a far more engaging personality, subject, to be sure, to the common human frailties but also with many admirable traits, alternately succeeding and failing in rising to the occasions that presented themselves. The gaps now first filled in, in so far as the extant manuscripts permit, round out the picture with a wealth of interesting and meaningful detail that presents a better understanding of the man and eventually a sounder interpretation and appraisal of his voluminous writings.

[1]To be enumerated are the following (in chronological order):

Journal, 1803, by Washington Irving, ed. Stanley T. Williams, New York, 1934.

Notes and Journal of Travel in Europe, 1804–1805, by Washington Irving, ed. William P. Trent. 5 vols. New York, 1921.

Stanley T. Williams, "Washington Irving's First Stay in Paris, [1805]," *American Literature,* II (March 1930), 15-20.

Barbara D. Simison, "Washington Irving's Notebook of 1810," *Yale University Library Gazette,* XXIV (1949), 1–16, 74–94.

The Journals of Washington Irving, from July, 1815, to July, 1842, ed. William P. Trent and George S. Hellman. 5 vols. Boston, 1919.

Notes While Preparing Sketch Book, &c. . . . 1817, by Washington Irving, ed. Stanley T. Williams. New Haven, 1927.

Tour in Scotland, 1817, and Other Manuscript Notes by Washington Irving, ed. Stanley T. Williams. New Haven, 1927.

Journal of Washington Irving, 1823–1824, ed. Stanley T. Williams, Cambridge, 1931.

Myers, Andrew B., "Washington Irving's Madrid Journal, 1827–1828, and Related Letters," *Bulletin of the New York Public Library,* LXII (1958), 217–27, 300–311, 407–19, 463–71.

Journal of Washington Irving, 1828, and Miscellaneous Notes on Moorish Legend and History, ed. Stanley T. Williams, New York, 1937.

Washington Irving Diary: Spain, 1828–1829, ed. Clara L. Penney, New York, 1926.

The Western Journals of Washington Irving [1832–1833], ed. John F. McDermott. Norman, Okla., 1944.

Brief portions of other journals and notebooks were quoted by Stanley T. Williams in his *The Life of Washington Irving.* 2 vols. New York, 1935.

"Washington Irving: Nonsense, the Fat of the Land and the Dream of Indolence"

BY WILLIAM L. HEDGES

William L. Hedges, whose Harvard dissertation was "The Fiction of History: Washington Irving Against a Romantic Transition," taught there and at the Universities of Wisconsin and California. An American Council of Learned Societies fellow (1963–1964), he has since 1967 been Professor of English at Goucher College, where, after chairing the department, he serves as head of the American Studies Program. His Irving essay in Volume I of *Major Writers of America,* Perry Miller *et al.,* eds. (1962), was a judicious analysis of an author whose complexities, as man and native artist, Hedges treated even more thoroughly in *Washington Irving: An American Study, 1802– 1832* (1965). This selection, which takes a fresh view of Irving's humor in particular, is Chapter 7 of *The Chief Glory of Every People,* ed. Matthew Bruccoli (1973).

Any serious consideration of Washington Irving (b. 1783) must
begin with his humor. That's a kind of joke, daughter. Or to say it's a
joke's a joke—to get you into the right mood for the nonsense to
come. After all, as Psalmanazar the imposter says on the title-page of
*Salmagundi; or, the Whim-whams and Opinions of Launcelot Lang-
staff, Esq., and Others,* "In hoc est hoax." Psalma is close to being
Salma. And Langstaff and others are Washington Irving, his brother
William and James Kirke Paulding.

Now hear one of the most beautiful paragraphs in American literature, from *Salmagundi,* No. 1, January 24, 1807.

> As everybody knows, or ought to know, what a SALMA-
> GUNDI is, we shall spare ourselves the trouble of an explana-
> tion—besides, we despise trouble as we do everything that is
> low and mean; and hold the man who would incur it unneces-
> sarily, as an object worthy our highest pity and contempt. Neither
> will we puzzle our heads to give an account of ourselves, for two
> reasons; first, because it is nobody's business; secondly, because
> if it were, we do not hold ourselves bound to attend to any-
> body's business but our own; and even *that* we take the liberty
> of neglecting when it suits our inclination. To these we might
> add a third, that very few men *can* give a tolerable account of
> themselves, let them try ever so hard; but this reason, we can-
> didly avow, would not hold good with ourselves.[1]

I am perfectly serious in my admiration for the precariously con-
trolled flippancy of this paragraph, the mad consistency and symme-
try of its illogic, the sudden illumination of "very few men *can* give a
tolerable account of themselves."

Between 1800 and 1810, or even 1820, American intellectual
life, caught in the conservative reaction to revolution and terror in
France and general war in Europe, stultified considerably. The widespread fear of anarchy and atheism that swept the country at the turn
of the century brought in its wake suspicion of new ideas generally.
The early work of the English romantics, as we know, was very
coolly received for the better part of a generation. Official culture
tended to retreat into ponderous justifications of well-established attitudes and "truths." This was particularly the case in Federalist New
England. In New York, however, a booming city with a heteroge-

neous population, it was not so easy to maintain an official culture. There upstarts like the Irvings could get a hearing. *Salmagundi* and *Diedrich Knickerbocker's History of New York* (1809) both preserve certain amenities. They hold on to the fiction of affiliation with a tradition of gentility, to which Irving was powerfully attracted. But it is a feeble fiction, borne on the stooped shoulders of a few old bachelors and constantly threatened by the leveling energy of bourgeois republicanism, from which Irving could not divorce himself, try as he might.

That energy affronts readers in the first number of *Salmagundi* with the ambiguous threat of shock and confusion: "we *care* not what the public think of us; and we suspect, before we reach the tenth number, they will not *know* what to think of us." And it burlesques the form of the periodical essay almost into extinction: "Our intention is simply to instruct the young, reform the old, correct the town, and castigate the age; this is an arduous task, and therefore we undertake it with confidence." The anti-didacticism of the first number is jubilant and defiant: "In two words—we write for no earthly purpose but to please ourselves."

As a matter of fact, in its distaste for bourgeois vulgarity and the petty corruption and demagoguery associated with republican politics *Salmagundi* occasionally succumbs to a didactic urge, shows more interest in getting a message across than in mocking the medium. But even when most bent on correcting the town and castigating the age, the voices that speak through the masks of Launcelot Langstaff, Anthony Evergreen, and Will Wizard, the old-bachelor "editors," or Mustapha Rub-a-Dub Keli Khan, *Salmagundi's* "citizen of the world," are never for long gentlemanly, urbane, self-assured. The voices are too young, at times too shrill and raucously vituperative. Unconsciously the Irvings and Paulding violate the identities of their personae even when they are not trying deliberately to do so.

Playing with the worn-out periodical-essay apparatus they begin to develop the nonsense comedy which *Knickerbocker* brings to fulfillment. It is a comedy of distraction and disorientation in which the pretense of composure and authority maintained on the surface is systematically undermined and the reader is subjected to what at times becomes a deluge of non sequiturs and digressions, reversals and contradictions, abrupt shifts of style and tone, and jumblings of fact and fiction. Characters in this comedy tend, as we now so appropriately say, to self-destruct before the reader's eye—which is what happens most dramatically with that supposedly knowing or knowledgeable persona, Diedrich Knickerbocker, his ineptitude occasionally reducing him to a kind of blathering idiocy. At its best— which is generally *Knickerbocker*—this comedy offers burlesque going berserk, satire and social comment dissolving into mystification, the impulse to mock and criticize being overtaken by a delight in fantasizing.

In an article in the sixth number of *Salmagundi,* for instance, which starts as parody of inept drama criticism, Will Wizard describes going to a performance of *Othello* and getting into a three-cornered argument on several trivial issues. Though his own critical credentials have been mocked in an earlier number, he begins this evening as the voice of sanity, while his two friends strain at the text to discover "new Readings" of particular lines in the play. When Wizard offers an outlandish interpretation of his own, the reader initially takes it as an ironic rebuke of the two pedants. But then Wizard embarks on a baffling hyperbolic spiel which weaves in and out of seriousness and lasts until the end of the article—whereupon he announces in a P.S. that he's just been informed that *Othello* hasn't been produced in New York for years.

Salmagundi is a sequence of fun-house mirrors which distort reality into scarcely recognizable shapes. It wastes hard-hitting satire on embodiments of folly and vice broadly caricatured into pure fictions. Except for a few actual people like Cooper the actor and two dress-designers, Mrs. Toole and Mrs. Bouchard, New York in *Salmagundi* is a city inhabited by a diminutive breed afflicted with names like Dimple, Sparkle, Dashaway, and Ding-Dong, Shivers and 'Sbidlikensflash, Pindar Cockloft and Ichabod Fungus—and Langstaff et al. This is a society of pompous nonentities strutting and fretting to become "little great" men and women. The trick is to look, act, and sound important. Everything is show, gaudy style, and empty rhetoric. The magazine carries a fairly standard satirical awareness to an extreme by turning democracy into "logocracy," a government of words. Partisan newspaper editors become "slang-whangers." And the chief logocrat, President Jefferson, a "man of superlative ventosity," who, in the face of the British and French threat to American commerce, "talks of vanquishing all opposition by the force of reason and philosophy," becomes "a huge bladder of wind."[2]

But *Salmagundi* is implicated in the linguistic overkill which it satirizes. Its appetite for words is insatiable. It laps them up wherever it finds them, mixes them together (into a salmagundi) and regurgitates them with joyful abandon—old words and new, proverbs and Latin phrases, scraps of verse from Shakespeare or anywhere, and, as part of its pseudo erudition, an endless string of names, especially of books, authors, and characters. Burlesque and travesty serve *Salmagundi* in part as an excuse for verbal incontinence. Irving had written slang-whang himself a few years earlier for his brother Peter's newspaper *The Corrector* in support of Aaron Burr. And *Salmagundi's* attacks on logocracy and little great men in politics descend at times almost to that level, though, for the most part the abuse is not personal. Reducing words to nonsense, the magazine at once suggests the vanity of most verbalizing and testifies to the determination of a provincial society to make itself heard whatever proprieties it violated.

Knickerbocker is Irving's masterpiece, his best book—which is not to deny the superiority of a few individual stories and sketches in later works. Begun with his brother Peter as a burlesque of a guidebook to New York City, it turned into a sustained mock-history, structurally unified around its subject and held together in spite of Knickerbocker's eccentricity by Irving's ability (Peter dropped out before the project advanced very far) to modulate effectively through perpetual shifts of style and tone. Deflating the myth of the greatness of the American past, *Knickerbocker* reduces the New Netherlands to insignificance by establishing its golden age as the reign of indolence under Governor Van Twiller, when fat Dutchmen lolled in the lap of an abundant land, smoked their pipes, kept their mouths shut and were not unduly bothered by the outside world. Troubles began under Governor Kieft (William the Testy), who lost his Dutch cool as political factions arose (the beginnings of logocracy) and tensions with New England developed. Like Jefferson, Kieft tried to govern and defend the land by speeches and proclamations—to no avail. In the end came valiant Peter Stuyvesant, peg-legged and doomed to defeat, a strong executive who rose above faction, fortified the city, fought a furious and insignificant war with New Sweden (described in low-burlesque mock-epic style), prepared to make a heroic stand against the British—and was forced into an ignominious capitulation.

Knickerbocker exposes, as no American book had dared to before and not many others did for a long time afterward, the gross, overdeveloped appetites—for land, wealth, food, drink, sex, pleasure generally—the "frank evaluation of progress in terms of exploitation," as Parrington called it,[3] which has shaped America as much as have its humane aspirations. Though the focus is on New York, the satire manages to take in every section of the country, especially New England. Some of it is sharp, biting sarcasm—against puritan bigotry, for instance, or European exploitation of the Indians—but, over all, the humor is tolerant. The nonsense will not allow characters to be taken very seriously, but from time to time the reader's natural longing for someone or something to identify with converts hints of pathos or quaint dignity in a ludicrous posture into authentic sentiment —which of course never sustains itself for long.

In a larger sense the action of the *History* is Knickerbocker's distracted effort to salvage something from the past—to create a past out of nothing, if he has to—and glorify the accomplishments of his ancestors. He comments garrulously as he goes along on the perils of being a historian—and on anything else that occurs to him. The reader follows the combined narrative and commentary almost as distracted as the historian, seldom sure whether what is being said represents total misunderstanding or ingenious insight, whether Knickerbocker is being serious or ironic, or simply can't make up his mind. At times, however, he comes into odd focus as the image of all of us—humanity—pathetic, broken-backed, nearsighted and yet, absurdly, still cheerful, groping through the rubbish of the past (that is, all previous human experience) for clues to an understanding of the present. When he comes to his senses, or almost does, it seems like an heroic achievement, and the commonplace observations he makes —on fame, pride, tranquility, natural beauty, death—take on a strange profundity. Conventional wisdom is revitalized in our odd reenactment with Knickerbocker of humanity's struggle to acquire it.

At the same time, however, one must recognize the nonsense of Knickerbocker humor as psychologically regressive, part of an escape from responsibility and conflict which is characteristic of Irving generally and which is at once the great strength and weakness of his work. Writing for *Salmagundi* was at least temporarily a release from the tedium and learned logic (or was it rationalization?) of the law (he had just passed his bar examination) and the urgings of his family—his father, the rather rigid Presbyterian deacon, and his business-minded brothers—that he apply himself seriously to something. And behind *Knickerbocker* lies perhaps both his grief at the recent death of his fiancée Matilda Hoffman, and a not consciously admitted relief at not having to settle down to business and make himself a good provider. More important, though, the nonsense of the early Irving is a way of registering the confusions of the period without having to take a definite stand on a controversial issue when he doesn't want to. It was a period in which, with the United States still testing new political institutions and Europe still torn by revolutionary upheaval, western intellectual life, having lost its eighteenth-century assurances, had not yet attained those that were to see it through the nineteenth.

To what extent, one wonders, has humor in the United States, the humor of a young culture unsure of itself, been a mechanism of evasion? Discussion of American humor customarily gives Irving short shrift. His comedy is not supposed to be indigenous enough, the language not sufficiently vernacular and the characters by and large not sufficiently distinguished from English comic stereotypes. But the theory which ties "native" American humor so closely to folk experience and the oral narrative tradition seems unnecessarily restrictive. American culture has been urban as well as rural, eastern as well as western, and for many it has been a mixture of influences from several discordant sources against a background of acute awareness of the European past. Even at the pole where American humor seems most to belong to the backwoods it has had one eye cocked uneasily to the East, the intrusion of the dude being apparently one of the major factors which provokes it.

Daniel Hoffman sees in "The Legend of Sleepy Hollow" the "native" pattern of the squatter frightening the dandy reenacted by Brom Bones and Ichabod Crane.[4] But there is an analogous assault on pretensions to cultural authority in *Salmagundi* when the young voices take over the old-bachelor personae—notwithstanding Irving's characteristic ambivalence in the face of the conflict between bumptious vulgarity and overblown gentility. However much subtlety the deadpan innocence of the storyteller in the oral tradition may give it, American humor is nonetheless often hard to distinguish from boorish anti-intellectualism. Its irrepressible low-burlesque energy keeps driving it toward nonsense.

But if the basic motive is hostility to highbrow cultural encroachment, that energy often becomes a relatively detached comic exuberance, a delight almost for its own sake in hyperbolic improvisation or in what Mark Twain in "How to Tell a Story" called the "innocently unaware" stringing together of "incongruities and absurdities." *Salmagundi* and *Duck Soup* are apt titles for the roaring mishmash of verbal styles, screwball characters, and slapstick that American comedy is apt to become—not only in print but in vaudeville, the movies, radio and television as well. The basic and continuing relevance of Irving's humor is clearly evident in the striking similarity between the nonsense of the *Knickerbocker History* and that of *Catch-22*, a resemblance which Joseph Heller seems at least unconsciously to acknowledge when he has Major Major Major, a bored, inept, and insecure squadron commander, in "an act of impulsive frivolity and rebellion" begin signing Washington Irving's name to official documents.[5]

The Irving who wrote *The Sketch Book* (1819–20) and emerged almost overnight as an international success had lived the ten years since *Knickerbocker* torn between the desire to make literature a full-time commitment and the fear of abandoning a career in law and business. Living in England now (he had been working in the Liverpool branch of the family importing firm), he was cut off from the only society which he knew intimately. And financially, since he was now to write for profit, he was in no position to antagonize an audience (as *Knickerbocker* had some of the old Dutch families in New York) by taking a tone of easy familiarity with it—particularly with the English at a time when English criticism was generally scornful of American literary efforts.

But Irving was able to adapt to the exigencies of the situation. He developed a more graceful prose style, spry, rhythmic, concrete, laced with subdued humor and purged of obvious crudities and provincialisms, a style the English especially were comfortable with. And he created the persona of Geoffrey Crayon, Gent., an American traveler and "humble" lover of "the picturesque," who, like an artist following the "bent of his vagrant imagination," has sketched in "nooks, and corners, and by-places" and sadly missed all the obvious impor-

tant subjects.[6] Crayon is the mildly self-mocking image of Irving himself, now nearly forty years old, unmarried and without a permanent
home. Injecting Crayon's personality into his sketches, he both capitalized on and compensated for the superficiality of his genial tourist's view of Europe.

There is something slightly false about Irving's position as a writer from *The Sketch Book* on. He has lost the freedom to speak out
bluntly on anything he chooses. Too often now he says things that he
thinks readers want him to say. He becomes more of a sentimentalist,
for instance, more committed to titillating female readers with stories
of broken hearts and lost loves, than he perhaps intended. But much
of what he wrote during his long European period (1815–32) is re-
deemed by his eye for the ludicrous, his affection for mundane reality, and his natural antididacticism.

A low-keyed approach to short fiction was precisely what was
needed at a time when, as he well knew, "strange incident and high-
seasoned narrative" were all the "rage."[7] Irving was not above trying
for gothic or sentimental intensity, but he was much more comfortable in a manner which at least implicitly mocked the sensation-seek-
ing reader. Whole sequences of fiction in *Tales of a Traveller*
(1824), for instance, are arranged so that early pieces, much to the
annoyance of reviewers at the time, prove to be burlesques of ghost
story formulae or of romantic tales of action. They break off abruptly
in mystification or risqué humor. Only after trying to jolt readers out
of passivity and literal-mindedness and denying them gratuitous horror, is Irving willing to venture on something more serious.

For Crayon to say that Diedrich Knickerbocker wrote "Rip Van
Winkle" and swore to the truth of it is to make clear that the story is
a fabrication, at bottom a sort of tall tale—"There was this henpecked husband up in the Catskills. His wife pestered him all day
long and left him no peace anywhere in the village. So one day he
went off into the mountains to do a little light hunting and ran into
some little old boys with a keg. They got him drunk and he fell into a
nice deep sleep on a beautiful grassy knoll. It was so peaceful, he
slept for 20 years. When he woke up and went home, his wife was
dead, and he lived happily ever after." Or perhaps the story is something Rip made up to avoid having to tell what really happened during his long absence. The reader's desire for rational explanation is
frustrated. But as sheer fantasy, the tale is not so easily laughed off.

Lovable and amusing as Rip is, his account of his experience is full of hints of impotence, wasted life, and loss of identity.

Similarly "The Legend of Sleepy Hollow" offers instead of a ghost the very palpable reality of a pumpkin and, presumably, Brom Bones. The man who tells the story to Knickerbocker says he doesn't believe half of it himself and, when asked about its moral, responds with platitudes and nonsense. And yet at its climax Ichabod Crane's terror is something we can identify with and believe in, as we can not in the case of the victim of an overwrought gothic tale. With Irving in *The Sketch Book, Bracebridge Hall* (1822), *Tales of a Traveller,* and *The Alhambra* (1832) we are in at the birth of the short story as a literary form, although he was not himself fully aware of what was happening and was never quite able to duplicate the startling and somewhat fortuitous achievement of "Rip Van Winkle" and "The Legend of Sleepy Hollow." His seriocomic manner slows down action, gives character, though viewed ironically, a chance to manifest itself, and makes setting a vital part of the characters' lives. His best stories (chiefly those with American settings) seem to be conceived as extensions of his sense of locale, of the characteristic atmosphere of a region; and his sketches—of Westminster Abbey or the reading room of the British Museum or a ride in an English stagecoach—presented not as inert description but as Crayon's response to immediate experience, have a way of turning into slight fictions about an entranced but somewhat unsettled traveler. And time is as important as place in his better fiction. With the action slowed down, the illusion of time passing at a natural rate becomes stronger ("The Legend of Sleepy Hollow" is a small triumph in this regard). Stories begin to be structured to a greater extent around single climactic episodes or a few key moments. The sketches are often actually little one-scene narratives.

But Irving did not have a particularly inventive imagination. He relied heavily on stereotyped characters and plots culled from old stories, plays, legends, and folk tales. In "Rip Van Winkle" and "Sleepy Hollow" he successfully adopted German legends to the landscape of the Hudson valley. But he was not always able to revitalize his borrowings. Some of his stories are thin, insufficiently fleshed out, nothing but old stories. The range of experience, activity and feeling he is capable of exploring in fiction is limited. He has a few simple things to say about desire, fulfillment, and frustration. On occasion he says them compellingly but not enough so to bear constant repetition.

As he grew older he found it easier to write history and biography than fiction—one wishes that he had returned in earnest to satire, burlesque, and nonsense. The historical writing is uneven. Some of it was done in haste and is backed by a minimum of original research. He had trouble deciding whether he was writing primarily for a scholarly or a popular audience. And half-consciously he tended to turn history into fiction, not in the crude sense of fabricating events for which he had no documentary evidence, but by largely neglecting or minimizing the importance of social, political, economic, and psychological factors, the particulars of an age or a time, and reducing the record of the past to the perpetual reenactment, by individuals curiously almost suspended above time, of the drama of human destiny. Thus as Stanley Williams said, *Life and Voyages of Christopher Columbus* (1828), the first and best of Irving's historical works, is really a romance.[8] It transforms its hero into an archetypal pilgrim and martyr— or rather it resurrects those images from some of the early accounts of Columbus. His lot is to suffer almost constant travail on what is more a sustained allegorical journey, a religious quest, than a series of voyages of discovery. Biblical overtones in rhythm and phrasing and an abundance of Christian imagery create the feeling at times of a gospel story. The biography has considerable poetic power.

But Irving lacked the depth of moral insight demanded by a work of such pretensions. His view of the world was always pathetic, the view of Geoffrey Crayon: things don't last. Mutability is the major theme. He never hints at outrage or rebellion as a conceivable response to the absurdity and indignity of man's fate. Neither does he envision active acceptance of that fate as a means of transcending it. Laughing "right merrily at the farce of life" is still Irving's "wisdom,"[9] reducing the world to nonsense his instinctive way of coping with the reality of experience. But writing what he alleged to be history did not offer many opportunities for humor.

Irving lived until 1859, becoming increasingly identified with what Santayana was eventually to call the genteel tradition. Travel and voracious reading had made him a learned man. He was a celebrity used to associating with people of distinction and status. Walter

Scott had received him at Abbotsford even before *The Sketch Book*. Back home John Jacob Astor was his friend. He had fraternized with royalty in Dresden in 1822–23. A Russian prince had been his traveling companion in Spain, and he had toured the western American prairies with a Swiss count. The external trappings of the latter part of his life comport with the diplomatic dignity and cordiality implied in his being appointed American minister to Madrid, a post he held from 1842 to 1845. Though he did not live ostentatiously, he remodeled an old farmhouse into the modest but stylish mansion, Sunnyside, overlooking the Hudson at Tarrytown. He spent several years after his return from Madrid in bringing out a revised edition of his works touched up to conform to Victorian notions of elegance and propriety. And he labored his last several years putting together the five-volume biography of his namesake, the American patriarch, George Washington (1855–59).

But Irving did not succumb to gentility without putting up resistance. One should not forget that Squire Bracebridge, his idealized English country gentleman, is gently spoofed in *The Sketch Book* and *Bracebridge Hall* as a hobbyhorse-riding anachronism in a way that to a degree recalls the mocking of the old bachelors of *Salmagundi* with their whim-whams and whalebone habits. The follies of the gentry remained for Irving part of the farce of life. He was not by temperament or doctrine an aristocrat. He enjoyed the comforts his success allowed. By and large he simply adopted the conservative political and social attitudes of the wealthy and influential people with whom he associated. In the late thirties, the forties, and the fifties his position was basically Whiggish but not so much so as to preclude his being wooed politically by Martin Van Buren as well as by Daniel Webster—though one may wonder how much less responsive in this expansionist period Democrats were than Whigs to the idea that what's good for business is good for the country.

All his life Irving affected a patrician disdain for the "cares and sordid concerns of traffic,"[10] but he objected more to the cares than to the traffic. His commercial success, which has always from the point of view of literary history been taken as his chief significance, is symbolic of a central impulse in his work, the source, I think, together with his humor, of his limited but enduring appeal. By becoming a writer he to a large extent escaped the necessity for "any periodically recurring task, or any stipulated labor of body or mind," for which, he told Walter Scott, he was "peculiarly unfitted."[11] And yet he managed to make a comfortable living for himself. There is a strong element of frank hedonism in his work. He was certainly interested in making money, went to elaborate efforts, in fact, to prevent piracy of his works and make sure that he got royalties from them on both sides of the Atlantic. Nor was he above taking flyers on investments—in a steamboat company, for instance, or a South American copper mine.[12] It was the drudgery of business that was apt to make it a "sordid, dusty, soul killing way of life."[13]

He might be appalled by America's pursuit of the "almighty dollar," a term he coined in describing young western communities gripped by speculative fever.[14] But he was intrigued as well. Something in him responded to the excitement of flush times and the general spectacle of American money-making and conspicuous consumption. In his earliest journal (1803) he recorded his "amusement" at the "outrageous extravagance" of the manners and clothes of the wife of a nouveau-riche Boston tradesman, a woman he encountered at the Ballston spa near Albany. But he also had a grudging admiration for her: "Amidst all her vanity she shews no foolish pride respecting her origin but takes great pleasure in telling how they first entered boston in Pedlars trim."[15] He was on a trip with his boss, Judge Josiah Ogden Hoffman, to inspect a large speculation in land in upstate New York in which the latter was involved. This was the life Irving matured in, a life centered on commerce, finance, and their relation to politics. Electing candidates favorable to business interests was important. Thus the slang-whangers, thus the need to attack Jefferson, whose neutralist policies were depressing New York business. At this period in his career Irving was not too choosy about how he sought to get ahead. He was willing, for instance, to take a political appointment, if he could get it, from a governor whose candidacy he had furiously attacked in *The Corrector*.[16] He might shy away from business and politics, but he never really turned his back on them. He was too close to the gross appetites he satirized. Progress even for him was to some extent exploitation.

In his 1803 journal he also describes, with absolutely no sympathy for the victim (or victims) but considerable enthusiasm for the sport, the three or four-way competition in which he participated to capture and kill a doe trapped in a river in the backwoods. All dignity was abandoned, as several people (including Hoffman and himself) fell or deliberately plunged into the water *"to get in at the death."* A woman came close to drowning, and the doe was divided between two of the parties (Irving's included), the other hunters getting nothing for their trouble.[17] Thirty years later in what eventually became Oklahoma he engaged in a buffalo hunt with the same avidity and, though after making his kill he had a moment of remorse, he took away the buffalo tongue as a trophy and left the carcass behind on the prairie.[18]

For Irving, the American continent was both beautiful and exploitable—at least up to a certain point. As works like "A Tour on the Prairies," *Astoria* (done with Astor's cooperation, 1836), and *Adventures of Captain Bonneville, U. S. A.* (1837) show, he admired the hunters, the explorers, the trappers, the adventurers—the man who made a fortune in the fur trade. All things in moderation, of course. He knew that money corrupts. He knew the voraciousness of both nature and man. His work is full of homilies on how paradises are perverted by greed. But it was not always easy to distinguish between greed and a healthy appetite for affluence. There was a fundamental moral problem here, which Irving never faced—most Americans were not forced to face it until the frontier closed.

In the meantime he wrote repeatedly about dreams of gold, easy money, buried treasure—or better still the escape to the drowsy indolence of rural comfort and abundance, to Communipaw, the village in *Knickerbocker* lost in the American landscape, left behind by history, enviably ignorant "of all the troubles, anxieties, and revolutions of this distracted planet."[19] Irving gives us fantasies of flagrant wish-fulfillment, direct appeals to the regressive instinct—the American dream as a return to the womb, the desire to escape the grind of daily work and the Protestant ethic of frugality and the postponement of gratification, the desire to evade responsibility and remain disengaged, to steer clear of controversy.

This is Rip Van Winkle's escape from his wife. It is the dream lean Ichabod Crane dreams—to marry plump Katrina Van Tassel, gorge himself on her pastries, and gain possession of a rich farmland, all in exchange for singing a few psalms, telling a few ghost stories, and being generally charming. The reader sympathizes with the dream and has the consolation of knowing that, if Ichabod doesn't deserve Katrina, Brom Bones does. The easygoing youth ("Dolph Heyliger," "Buckthorne," Dirk Waldron in "Wolfert Webber") gets the girl—and often the gold or its equivalent—in Irving's mythology, which as his perennial habit of collecting and adapting legends shows, is, in some important respects, a duplication of aspects of folk mythology. The water carrier outwits the avaricious alcalde in a typical story of hidden treasure in *The Alhambra* ("Legend of the Moor's Legacy").

Always in the background, of course, lurks the awareness that contentment and gratification are usually fleeting or illusory. The devil comes on his white horse for Tom Walker in the counting house just as he is foreclosing on a mortgage. The reality of "the dusty world" of "bustle and business" awaits Irving after the "repose and reverie" of his sojourn in the "oriental luxury" of the Alhambra.[20] The tranquility of New Amsterdam under Van Twiller cannot last. Beyond the infantile illusion of peace, harmony, good fellowship, and repose is, obviously, the reality of competition and conflict, where one risks failure—the American nightmare, the haunting fear of loneliness, uselessness, impotence, particularly in Irving's old bachelors—even if beyond failure there is the vision which his sentimentality projects, above all in *The Sketch Book,* of death as a coming home to mother, a delicious surrender to the binder-up of wounds, to comforting arms and consoling words, death as a recovery of the womb.

But the basic dream persists in Irving, the dream of repose on what Fitzgerald called at the end of *The Great Gatsby* the "fresh, green breast of the new world." Irving knows something about ruthless exploitation, about the sorrow of Columbus and its relation to the cunning of men like Tom Walker. But he does not turn John Jacob Astor into a Gatsby or a Sutpen or an Ahab. What he sees and feels most is that gross hedonism which Faulkner was finally to depict definitively in *The Hamlet,* paying as he did so conscious and perhaps also unconscious tribute to Irving. From Katrina Van Tassel to Eula Varner in the bottomland of Mississippi the myth of American fertility runs its course, Ichabod's and Brom's lust for the farmer's daughter, the eatables and the farm hilariously metamorphosed into Frenchman's Bend's dumb wonder at Eula's indolent mammalian splendor and Ike Snopes's love affair with the cow. Faulkner's schoolmaster, the football player from Ole Miss, is Ichabod and Brom combined. Even so, however, he loses Eula. For in Faulkner the dream of abundance in America has given way to the reality of the rape of the landscape. Blem Snopes cannot be laughed off like Tom Walker. And the hope of buried treasure at the Old Frenchman place is nothing but another of Flem's schemes for disposing worthless property.

[1]Until the badly needed CEAA edition of Irving, now beginning to appear, is fully published, we lack a readily available "standard" text of his works. My quotations from those works, except for the first, are brief. I have identified them therefore not by citing page numbers but by citing particular stories, essays, chapters, etc. I have in every case quoted from texts published by Putnam, his American publisher. And I have always used the "author's revised" version of a work, except where none exists. The revisions were published 1848–50. *Salmagundi* was not revised. Neither was *Wolfert's Roost*, which came out in 1855, after the revision.

[2]"Letter from Mustapha," *Salmagundi*, no. 7.

[3]Vernon L. Parrington, *Main Currents of American Thought*, vol. 2, *The Romantic Revolution in America* (New York: Harcourt, Brace, 1927), p. 193.

[4]*Form and Fable in American Fiction* (New York: Oxford University Press, 1961), pp. 83–96.

[5]Heller, *Catch–22* (New York: Simon and Schuster, 1961), p. 91.

[6]"The Author's Account of Himself," *The Sketch Book of Geoffrey Crayon, Gent.*

[7]"The Pride of the Village," *The Sketch Book*.

[8]"Washington Irving," in *Literary History of the United States*, 3 vols., ed. Robert E. Spiller et al. (New York: Macmillan Co., 1948), 1:249.

[9]"From the Elbow-Chair," *Salmagundi*, no. 1.

[10]Pierre M. Irving, *The Life and Letters of Washington Irving*, 4 vols. (New York, 1863–64), 1:393.

[11]"Preface to the Revised Edition" (1848), *The Sketch Book*.

[12]Williams, *The Life of Washington Irving*, 2 vols. (New York: Oxford University Press, 1935), 1:288; Pierre M. Irving, 2:240–41.

[13]*Letters of Henry Brevoort to Washington Irving*, 2 vols., ed. George S. Hellman (New York, 1916), 2:185–86.

[14]"The Creole Village" (1837), republished in *Wolfert's Roost*.

[15]*Journals and Notebooks, Volume I, 1803–1806,* ed. Nathalia Wright (Madison: University of Wisconsin Press, 1969), pp. 7–8.

[16]Martin Roth, ed., *Washington Irving's Contributions to "The Corrector"* (Minneapolis: University of Minnesota Press, 1968), p. 7.

[17]*Journals and Notebooks,* pp. 15–16.

[18]"A Tour on the Prairies," chapters 29–30, *The Crayon Miscellany* (originally published, 1835).

[19]*Knickerbocker,* bk. 2, chap. 2.

[20]"The Author's Farewell to Granada," *The Alhambra.*

"Fallen From Time: Rip Van Winkle"

Philip Young, whose doctorate in English is from the State University of Iowa, has taught there, at New York University, and at Kansas State University. Since 1966 he has been Research Professor of English at Pennsylvania State University. An American Council of Learned Societies scholar, 1950–1951, he was a Fulbright fellow in Italy, 1962–1963. Westminster College (Pa.) awarded him an honorary D.H.L. in 1971. His published works include *Ernest Hemingway: A Reconsideration* (1967) and *Three Bags Full: Essays in American Fiction* (1973), from which this wide-ranging piece, on the manifold mythical aspects of "Rip" was chosen. It appeared originally as "Fallen from Time: The Mythic Rip Van Winkle," illustrated, in *Kenyon Review,* Vol. XXII (1960), 547–73.

"Black wing, brown wing, hover over;
Twenty years and the spring is over;
To-day grieves, to-morrow grieves,
Cover me over, light-in-leaves . . ."

—T. S. Eliot, Landscapes

Washington Irving is reported to have spent a June evening in 1818 talking with his brother-in-law about the old days in Sleepy Hollow. Melancholy of late, the writer was pleased to find himself laughing. Suddenly he got up and went to his room. By morning he had the manuscript of the first and most famous American short story, and his best single claim to a permanent reputation.

Nearly a century and a half have elapsed, and the name of Rip Van Winkle, one of the oldest in our fiction, is as alive as ever. The subject of innumerable representations—among them some of the country's finest paintings—America's archetypal sleeper is almost equally well known abroad. Nor is his fame simply popular, or commercial. The most complex of poets, as well as the least sophisticated of children, are attracted to him.

But there is something ironic here, for at its center Rip's story is every bit as enigmatic as it is renowned, and the usual understanding of Rip himself, spread so wide, is shallow. Very few of the millions of people who have enjoyed his tale would be comfortable for long if pressed to say exactly what "happened" to him, or if asked to explain what there is about the "poor, simple fellow" that has exerted so general and deep a fascination. Thanks to Irving, the thunder Rip heard is still rolling out of the Catskills. And it is pregnant thunder, charged with meaning. Perhaps it is time someone tried to make out what it has to say.

Irving's story may not be an easy one, but it can easily be told in such a way as to refresh the memories of those who have not encountered it of late. The hero of the tale was a good-natured, middle-aged fellow, and a henpecked husband, who lived with his Dutch neighbors in a peaceful village in the Catskill mountains along the Hudson River in the period immediately preceding the American Revolution. The trouble with Rip was that although he would hunt and fish all day, or even do odd jobs for the neighborhood women, and entertain their children, he was "insuperably averse" to exerting himself for his own practical benefit. He had lost an inheritance, his farm was in the worst condition of any in the vicinity and, worst of all, his termagant wife was always upbraiding him about these things. He had only one "domestic adherent," his dog Wolf, and one comfortable retreat, a bench outside the local inn, where under the sign of His Majesty George the Third met a kind of "perpetual club." But he was driven eventually even from this refuge, and forced to the woods for peace. On a fine fall day it happened.

Rip was shooting squirrels in a high part of the mountains. Tiring in the late afternoon, he rested on a green knoll beside a deep glen, with a sleepy view of miles of forest and the Hudson moving drowsily through it. Suddenly he heard the distant sound of his name. He saw a crow winging its way across the mountain, and Wolf bristling, and then he made out an odd figure, and short old fellow in antique Dutch clothes, coming up from the ravine with a heavy keg on his back. Rip quickly gave him a hand, and as they labored he heard distant thunder coming from a cleft in the rocks. They passed through this crevice, and came into a kind of amphitheatre, walled by precipices. Stunned with awe, Rip saw in the middle of the space a group of odd-looking men playing at nine-pins. They had peculiar, long-nosed faces; all wore beards; one man, stout and old, appeared to be their commander. "What seemed particularly odd," however, was that "although these folk were evidently amusing themselves, yet they maintained the gravest faces, the most mysterious silence, and were, withal, the most melancholy party of pleasure he had ever witnessed." The only sound was the thunder of the balls as they rolled.

When the men saw Rip they stopped their play and stared at him as if they were statues. His heart turned within him; trembling, he obeyed his guide and waited on the company. They drank from the keg in silence, and then went on with their game. Soon Rip was trying the liquor, but he drank more than he could hold, and passed into a profound sleep.

When he woke he was back on the green knoll. It was morning and an eagle wheeled aloft. His gun was rusted away, Wolf was gone, and there was no sign of the opening in the cliffs. He called his dog, but the cawing of crows high in the air was the only answer, and he headed lamely for home. As he approached his village he saw no one he knew. People kept stroking their chins when they looked at him, and when he picked up the gesture from them he discovered that his beard was now gray and a foot long. As he entered town he saw that the village itself had grown. But his own house was in ruins, and a half-starved dog that looked like Wolf skulked about the wreckage and snarled at him. In town the inn was gone, replaced by an ugly building called Jonathan Doolittle's Union Hotel, and on the old sign King George's portrait had new clothes, and beneath it a new legend: George Washington. Even the nature of the people seemed changed: their drowsy ways had become disputatious. Rudely challenged to state his affiliations, "Federal or Democrat," Rip can only protest that he is loyal to his king, whereupon he is taken by some for a spy. No one knows him, the friends he asks for are dead, and he comes to doubt his own identity, until his daughter Judith's recognition confirms it. Now he is welcomed home, learns that his wife is dead ("in a fit of passion at a New England peddler"), and that he has unaccountably been gone for twenty years. The oldest and most learned member of the community is able to throw a little light on the story he tells: it is every twenty years that Hendrik Hudson, the river's discoverer, keeps a sort of vigil in the Catskills with the crew of the *Half-Moon,* and playing at nine-pins they make the mountains ring with the distant peals of thunder. And so Rip—idle, revered and happy—retires to his place on the bench at the door of the inn.

To be sure this story, though a fine one, is not perfect. For one thing, although Irving's Federalism enables him to jab in mildly amusing fashion at the shabby and pretentious republicanism of Rip's new village, such pleasantries come at the expense of our being wholly convinced of what he is trying to tell us—that Rip at the end is in clover. But the village is no longer entirely the place for him, and the fine old inn where he sits is just not there any more.

That this is, however, the rare sort of story that both satisfies and stimulates is shown by the fact that it has been so often retold, chiefly for the stage. There have been at least five plays—beginning with John Kerr's, which first appeared in Washington in 1829—and three operas, and several children's versions. But none has added anything important to our understanding of the story. Joseph Jefferson, who played the role of Rip for forty-five years in his own extraordinarily popular interpretation, had a few sensible ideas about the material, but he also failed to throw out much of the nineteenth-century baggage handed down from Kerr.

Though Joyce and Dylan Thomas have punned elaborately on Rip's name, most of the poets who have invoked him have done nothing much either to interpret the story or the character, and only Hart Crane has given him serious and extended attention. *The Bridge* (1930) has a section called "Van Winkle," whom Crane thought of as "the muse of memory"—or, as he put it to his sponsor, Otto Kahn, "the guardian angel of the trip to the past." Here Rip is a figure evoked from recollection of the poet's childhood and the nation's; since this is to introduce Rip in a thoughtful and promising way, it is too bad that very little is really done with him in the poem.

This is unfortunate partly for the reason that Rip is, potentially, a truly mythic figure. He is conceivably even more: *ur*-mythic. At any rate a primal, primeval myth has been postulated (by Joseph Campbell in his *Hero with a Thousand Faces*), and has been described—as "a separation from the world, a penetration to some source of power, and a life-enhancing return." And this is a most excellent description of what happens in "Rip Van Winkle." But no one has elevated the story to this status. As Constance Rourke wrote of it twenty-five years ago, the tale "has never been finished, and still awaits a final imaginative re-creation." If, then, we are to be helped to understand the story more deeply by considering what has been done with it, we had better consider what had been done with it before Irving wrote it.

II

In 1912 an eminent Dutch historian, Tieman De Vries by name, published under the title of *Dutch History, Art and Literature for Americans* a series of lectures he had delivered at The University of Chicago. A large part of this book is devoted to a monumentally inept attack on Washington Irving for having, in "Rip Van Winkle," characterized the Dutch people as stupid, lazy, and credulous. For his overwhelming blow the author, protesting great reluctance and sadness, brings forth the revelation that "Rip" is not the "original" story that Irving is "generally given credit for," anyway. The bitter truth, he discloses, is that the tale had been told before: its embryo is a myth about an ancient Greek named Epimenides, and this germ was "fully developed" by Erasmus (a citizen of Rotterdam) in 1496. In the myth Epimenides was sent to look for a sheep, lay down in a cave, slept for fifty-seven years and waked to find everything changed and himself unrecognized until a brother identified him. Erasmus used this story, then, to attack the Scotist theologians of his day (whom he thought asleep) as Irving used it on the Dutch. The fact that Irving never admitted knowing Erasmus's story, says De Vries, "touches too much the character of our beloved young author to be decided in a few words," and thus, having written the words, he drops the subject.

Quite aside from the foolishness about the Dutch, who are fondly treated in the story, there are two real blunders here. First, Irving's indebtedness was so widely recognized when the story first appeared as to be a subject for newspaper comment and, second, his source was not Erasmus, whose tale is in no sense "fully developed," but an old German tale published by Otmar, the Grimm of his period, in his *Volke-Sagen* of 1800. Actually Irving was on this occasion very noisily accused of plagiarism. At the end of his story he had appended a note in which he hinted that Rip's origin was "a little German superstition about Frederick *der Rothbart* and the Kypphauser mountain," but this has always been regarded as a red herring—so freely had he borrowed from another, and adjacent, story in Otmar: the folk tale of Peter Klaus. About the only thing Irving could do when this was pointed out he did: threw up his hands and said that of course he knew the tale of Peter Klaus; he had seen it in *three* collections of German legends.

There were probably still other sources for "Rip Van Winkle." We know, for instance, that in 1817 Sir Walter Scott told Irving the story of Thomas of Erceldoune ("Thomas the Rhymer"), who was bewitched by the Queen of the Fairies for seven years. "Doldrum" —a farce about a man's surprise at the changes he found after waking from a seven-year slumber—was played in New York when Irving was fourteen. It is almost certain, moreover, that Irving knew at least a couple of the other versions of the old tradition.

The idea of persons sleeping for long periods is, of course, very common in myth, legend, and folklore. So sleep Arthur and Merlin and John the Divine, and Charlemagne and Frederick Barbarossa (or Rothbart, or Redbeard) and Wilhelm Tell, and Odin (or Woden), the Norse (or Teutonic) god, and Endymion the shepherd, and Siegfried and Oisin and several dozen other heroes of many lands, as well as Sleeping Beauty and Bruennhilde and other mythical ladies—and also the protagonists of many novels, who wake to their author's vision of utopia, or hell. And there are several myths and legends about these sleepers which come pretty close to the story Irving told. Probably the best known of these concerns the Seven Sleepers. These men, natives of Ephesus, were early Christians persecuted by the Emperor Decius. They hid in a mountain and fell asleep. On waking they assumed that a night had passed, and one of them slipped into town to buy bread. When he got there he was stunned to see a cross over the gate, and then to hear the Lord's name spoken freely. When he paid for the bread his coins, now archaic, gave him away, and he discovered he had slept for 360 years.

This myth has spread widely, and found its way into books so different as the Koran, where Mohammed adapted it and introduced a dog who sleeps with the seven men, and Mark Twain's *Innocents Abroad,* where Twain tells the story at considerable length (and says he knows it to be a true story, as he personally has visited the cave). Somewhat similar myths are also known in the religious literature of the Jews. In a section on fasting in the Babylonian Talmud, to choose a single instance, appears one of several stories about Honi the Circle Drawer, lately thrust into prominence as a candidate for identification with the Teacher of Righteousness of the Dead Sea Scrolls. One day Honi sat down to eat, the story goes, and sleep came; a rocky formation enclosed him, and he slept for seventy years. When he went home nobody would believe he was Honi; greatly hurt, he prayed for death and died.

The thing that is really vital to "Rip Van Winkle," but missing from all these other stories, is a revelation—some kind of mysterious activity witnessed by the sleeper. But such tales also exist—for instance, the Chinese story of Wang Chih, who comes upon some aged men playing chess in a mountain grotto, is given a date-stone to put in his mouth, and sleeps for centuries, finally waking to return home to practice Taoist rites and attain immortality.

More akin to Rip's is the misadventure of Herla, King of the Britons. He is approached by an ugly dwarf, somewhat resembling Pan, who tells him that he will grace Herla's wedding to the daughter of the King of France, and that Herla will in turn attend the wedding of the dwarf-king. At the Briton's marriage ceremony, the dwarf-guests serve food and drink from precious vessels. A year later, at the wedding of the dwarf-king in a mountain cavern, Herla takes a bloodhound in his arms, and he and his men are enjoined not to dismount until the bloodhound jumps. Some who try are turned to dust, but the hound never jumps and Herla thus wanders hopelessly and "maketh mad marches" with his army for the space of two hundred years. At last he reaches the sunlight and meets a shepherd who can scarcely understand the language the king speaks.*

Closer still, in one way, is the story of a blacksmith recorded in the Grimms' *Teutonic Mythology*. While trying to find wood to make a handle for his hammer, he gets lost; there are the familiar rift in the mountains, some mysterious bowlers, and a magic gift—this time a bowling ball that turns to gold. (Others who have entered this cliff have seen an old man with a long white beard holding a goblet.)

The most detailed precedent for Irving, however, and beyond a doubt his principal source, is the tale of Peter Klaus, which appeared in Otmar's collection.† This is a story of a goatherd from Sittendorf who used to pasture his sheep on the Kyfhauser mountain in Thuringia. One day he discovered that a goat had disappeared into a crack in a cliff and, following her, he came to a cave where he found her eating oats that fell from a ceiling which shook with the stamping of horses. While Peter stood there in astonishment a groom appeared and beckoned him to follow; soon they came to a hollow, surrounded by high walls into which, through the thick overhanging branches, a dim light fell. Here there was a rich, well-graded lawn, where twelve serious knights were bowling. None of them said a word. Peter was put to work setting pins.

---

*This is the only story of its kind, except for "Rip," that can be attributed to anyone—in this case to Walter Map, author of the early thirteenth century *De Nugis Curialium* ("Courtier's Trifles"), in which it appears. An intolerant but witty feudal aristocrat, probably Welsh, Map is best known for his "Dissuasion from Matrimony," long attributed to a Latin writer of a thousand years before him. In this essay he counsels young men that women are monsters and vipers (do not look for exceptions, he says: "Friend, fear all the sex"). Thus Map provides a precedent both for Rip's adventure and for Irving's whimsical antifeminism. It is very doubtful, however, if not impossible, that Irving knew of him; Herla's story has been cited as the true source of "Rip Van Winkle," but Map's book was not available to Irving until some three decades after the Irving story had been published.

†Otmar's book is very hard to come by, but Henry A. Pochmann's "Irving's German Sources in *The Sketch Book*," *Studies in Philology*, XXVII (July, 1930), 489–94, prints the most relevant portions of it.

At first his knees shook as he stole glimpses of the silent, long-bearded knights, but gradually his fear left him, and finally he took a drink from a tankard. This was rejuvenating, and as often as he felt tired he drank from the vessel, which never emptied. This gave him strength, but sleep overcame him nonetheless, and when he woke he was back at the green spot where he grazed his goats. The goats, however, were gone, and so was his dog. There were trees and bushes he couldn't remember, and in bewilderment he went into Sittendorf, below him, to ask about his herd.

Outside the village the people were unfamiliar, differently dressed and strange-spoken. They stared at him and stroked their chins as he asked for his sheep; when involuntarily he stroked his own chin he found that his beard had grown a foot long. He went to his house, which was in decay, and there he saw an emaciated dog which snarled at him. He staggered off, calling vainly for his wife and children. The villagers crowded around him, demanding to know what he was looking for, and when he asked about old friends he learned that they were dead. Then he saw a pretty young woman, who exactly resembled his wife, and when he asked her father's name she answered, "Peter Klaus, God rest his soul. It is more than twenty years since . . . his sheep came back without him." Then he shouted, "I am Peter Klaus, and no other," and was warmly welcomed home.

Since this elaborate parallel with Irving epitomizes the process whereby a national literature adapted foreign materials and began to function, it is somewhat appropriate that our first short story should owe so large a debt to European source. But it is not at all clear why this *particular* story should have come down to us across a span of some twenty-five centuries—from the time, say, of Epimenides. Some of its charm is obvious; the idea of falling clean out of time, for instance, must be universally fascinating. But the very heart of "Rip Van Winkle," and of "Peter Klaus"—the strange pageant in the mountain—is still, from whatever version of it may be the earliest on down to the present time, enigmatic.

In the scene with the "dwarfs"—to focus again on Irving—it is not even clear what is going on. When the silent men of outlandish appearance and their leader go through their motions, the feeling is very strong that their actions are intended to convey something. But what? They are bowling, of course, and producing the sound of thunder, but why are they doing this? Why are they so sad and silent as they do it? Why so odd-looking? And why does Rip's participation cost him a generation of his life? The action is fairly pulsing with overtones: the men are speaking in signs; their motions cry out for translation as vigorously as if this were, as it seems, some strangely solemn charade. The question, which seems never even to have been asked, is what are we to make of this thundering pantomime? What have the gods to impart?

The notion that somewhere in the story lurks a secondary, or symbolic, meaning is by no means new. Walter Map, for instance, intended the latter part of his story about Herla to be a satire on the court of King Henry II, which he thought unstable. Erasmus, as already noted, attacked the Scotists through his; and the Talmud draws a moral from Honi's lonely end: "Either companionship or death." More interesting, however, is Arnold Toynbee's interpretation of "Rip Van Winkle" in the third volume of his *Study of History*. There is likely to be, he feels, something "old-fashioned" about any given colonial ethos, and his theory comes to a generalization: "Geographical expansion [of a civilization] produces social retardation." Toynbee thinks Rip an expression of his principle, the long sleep symbolizing the slumber of social progress in a newly settled place. Irving "was really expressing in mythological imagery the essence of the overseas experience. . . ."

The trouble with the interpretations of Map, Erasmus, and the Talmud is that they are forced and arbitrary, and the trouble with Toynbee's is that the story doesn't fit the theory it is supposed to express. If we ever had a period during which social progress was not retarded then it was exactly the period Rip slept through. In that generation we were transformed from a group of loosely bound and often provincial colonies into a cocky and independent republic with a new kind of government and—as the story itself makes clear enough—a whole new and new-fashioned spirit. In order to fit the thesis Irving must have had Rip return to a village where nothing much had happened or changed, and thus he must have written a different story. But he chose instead to write a story on the order of the myth about Honi the Circle Drawer who, according to one tradition, slept through the destruction of the First Temple and the building of the second, or like the one about the Seven Sleepers, who slept through the Christian revolution.* In all these tales the startling developments that have taken place during the sleep are a large part of the "point." And even if to Toynbee nationalism is—and was even in eighteenth-century America—a thoroughly deplorable thing, it was not a sign of social retardation.

Since such explanations as these will not help much more than the poets and playwrights have done to show us what is going on in "Rip Van Winkle," and since there is nowhere else to look, we are forced at long last to squint for ourselves through that crevice in the mountain. There, in the shadows, lurk figures and images which take us back, along a chronological line, to a time before the beginnings of recorded history. And if we could identify and understand these figures and images we should have, finally, the answers to most of our questions.

Many editions of Irving's story carry as an epigraph some lines he took from the seventeenth-century poet William Cartwright:

> By Woden, God of Saxons,
> From whence comes Wensday, that is Wodensday,
> Truth is a thing that ever I will keep
> Until thylke day in which I creep into
> My sepulchre—.

The most plausible reading of these lines is: "By God it's a true story I'm telling." But this makes Irving's two notes—in which he calls this a true tale—redundant. Less simply read, it might be the story itself saying, "By God, I'll keep to myself the truth about this thing as long as I live." At any rate, it is either a curious coincidence or an obscure clue that, in swearing by Woden, Irving has pointed to the

---

*Indeed Irving may have got some specific ideas from the Seven Sleepers myth, for there the surprising changes in the speech of the people, and the prominent new sign over the gate of the town, are precedents for two of the very few important details to be found in "Rip" but not in "Peter Klaus." Elsewhere there is an exact precedent for the form Irving's change of signs took. In the famous *New England Primer,* with its alphabetical rimes ("In Adam's fall we sinned all"), a woodcut of King George that appeared in early editions eventually became very smudged; when this happened the portrait began to carry the name of our first President ("By Washington, great deeds were done").

remotest origins of his story that can be uncovered. To bare these origins would be to force the story, at last, to give up its secrets.

Here is a grab bag of traditional elements—folk, legendary, and mythic. The green knoll on which Rip sits when he hears his name has behind it the Green Mounds of Irish fairy tales—often prehistoric burial mounds. It is an appropriate spot for his bewitching and approximate to the "buried men" he is about to visit. Magic potions and sacred drinks are so standard in mythology, folklore, and religion as to suggest parallels automatically as Rip plays Ganymede, wine-pourer to the gods. A less familiar little tradition lies behind those dogs, which Rip and Peter find barely and implausibly alive after so many years—this takes us all the way back to Odysseus, returning after a generation's absence to find his dog Argos in Ithaca, still half-alive and lying on a heap of dung.

But the most important recognition in Irving's story concerns the identity of the men Rip meets in the mountain, and of their leader. These are "Hendrik Hudson" and his crew.* The blacksmith and Peter Klaus never identify their strange mountain men, and the unnamed leaders never appear. Nevertheless, it is not hard to guess with considerable assurance of being right both who they are and by whom they are led. It was the Odensberg that the blacksmith entered, and the Kyfhauser that Peter wormed his way into; it is in the Odensberg, according to legend, that Charlemagne and his knights are sleeping, and the Kyfhauser where sleep Frederick Barbarossa and his.† Hudson, then, is playing the role of the great kings of Euro-

---

*It should, of course, be "Henry": Hudson sailed from Holland but was English. Of all the people Irving could have put in the Catskills, however, Hudson was a fine choice, not only because the river below him was named for him and discovered by him, but because he was (in 1611 on another trip) the victim of a mutiny near Hudson Bay, was abandoned there, and disappeared for good. Thus he is like the heroes of myth and legend who sleep in mountains; no one knows where, or if, he was buried, and it is easier to think of him as not entirely dead.

†This is clear in the story that lies, in Otmar's collection, adjacent to the one of Peter Klaus—the "little German Superstition about Frederick *der Rothbart*" that Irving claimed as the origin of "Rip." It is almost certain, then, that Irving knew who led the knights Peter saw, and who Hudson's most immediate ancestor was. How much more he may have known about the origins of the materials he was borrowing is very difficult to say.

pean countries, as Arthur plays it in England, and is a survival of this tradition. This recognition opens the door.

Part of the Barbarossa legend, which is better known and more detailed than the one of Charlemagne, concerns the conditions under which he can return to active life. Around the Kyfhauser a flock of ravens is said to fly, and each time the king wakes he asks if they are still there (they are, and this means the time has not come). Another important detail of the story is his beard: it is extraordinarily long already, and when it has grown three times around the table where he sits, his time will have come. It is very likely, then, that the black wings hovering over Rip just before he enters the mountain, and just after he emerges into consciousness, are the ravens of Barbarossa—just as the beards which are prominent in his story and Peter's (although the natural enough consequences of not shaving for twenty years) come down to us from this legend.

But the most important detail of all is a game, common to so many of these stories—the Chinese and Japanese versions, and Peter Klaus and the blacksmith and Rip. And the fact that the game in the stories that primarily concern us here is always bowling, which makes the sound of thunder, gives the whole show away: we are dealing, ultimately, with the gods, and in the farthest recess of this cave the figure with the red beard (to represent lightning), that helped to identify him with Frederick the Redbeard, is the god of thunder—Thor, God of Saxons, whence comes Thorsday, that is, Thursday.

More clearly the prototype of all these sleeping heroes, however, is the magnificently white-bearded Woden, or Odin, the god of the dead whom Cartwright swore by. In the legend about Charlemagne, the people who saw the king described him as a man with a white beard, and the name of the mountain Charlemagne inhabits, the Odensberg, suggests all by itself his ancestor. But the fact that the blacksmith on the Odensberg is in search of wood for a handle to an instrument of power which was the very emblem of the god of thunder, a hammer, suggests Thor just as strongly. So thoroughly have the two gods been confused in these myths that the king who is buried in Odin's mountain has in some stories the red coloring and the red horse that are really appropriate to Thor. On this horse the god issues from the mountain with his men, every so-many years, and in this activity he is again Odin, the leader of the Wild Hunt.

These confusions between Thor and Odin are not surprising, since the two figures are cofused in Norse mythology itself. Although Thor was the son of Odin, he was also sometimes an older god than Odin; often he was a god superior to Odin, and sometimes they were thought of as exactly the same god. The direct ancestor of the Hudson Rip saw, then, was a Thor who has many of the attributes of Odin, and recognizing this takes us to the source of the traditions out of which Irving's scene is principally compounded. Recognizing these traditions, in turn, enables us to understand the subliminal richness of its materials, buried under the detritus of centuries.

The ravens which fly about the Kyfhauser, and the crows and eagle of the Catskills, are lineal descendants of the ravens Thought and Memory who sat on Odin's shoulder and kept him informed, or of the eagle that hovered over Odin's own retreat, or of the flight of ravens, "Odin's messengers" (without whose message Frederick cannot emerge)—or of all three. The dogs in the stories, mixing Greek myth with Teutonic, are progeny of the wolves Geri and Freki who sat at Odin's feet, or of the totem wolf which hung over the west door of his residence—in honor of which ancestry Rip's dog gets his name, Wolf. The drink which both invigorated and overpowered Rip is the same drink Barbarossa's knights gave Peter; it belongs also in the goblet Charlemagne was seen holding, and, despite all the magic drinks of folklore and myth, it is ultimately "Odin's mead," from which Odin got wisdom, and inspired poets; it was a magic draft related to the drink always available in the Abode of the Blest, the drink that rejuvenates, and obliterates all sorrow.

In a like manner, the odd appearance of Hudson's crew, those ugly, drab, short and curious creatures (one fellow's face is comprised entirely of his nose) are echoes of the dwarfs Herla met—although those dwarfs also looked like Pan, mixing Greek and Teutonic (and probably Welsh) mythology again. But Hudson's men get their appearance from the Night-Elves who made Thor's hammer—those ugly little long-nosed people, dirty-brown in color, who lived in caves and clefts. Beneath this effective disguise the crewmen of the *Half-Moon* are really the knights of Barbarossa and Charlemagne, who are the brave dead warriors brought back from the battlefields by the Valkyries to Odin's hall of the dead: Rip has really been in Valhalla and seen the slain collected around their god, who by the old confusion is now Thor, whose men they have become. The reason for the oddness of their behavior—their melancholy and their lacklustre stares—has become completely obvious, if indeed it was not before: they are dead. And one of Odin's chief characteristics, his extreme aloofness, accounts for the fact that Rip got but a glimpse of their leader, while neither Peter nor the blacksmith ever saw him at all.

Why such pagan gods should have been imagined as sleeping in mountains can be plausibly explained. When converted to Christianity, the people who had worshipped these figures could not quickly and completely reject the faith of their fathers. To them the outmoded gods lingered on, wandering, sleeping, and appearing infrequently. Later, vanished but actual heroes like Charlemagne, Frederick, Sir Francis Drake, Prince Sebastian of Portugal, and Arthur, were given attributes of the earlier gods. It was most common as well to place them in a mountain, where they were in earth, like the dead, but not under it—not under level ground, that is—like the really dead. Here they are sequestered in their slumbers, but the gods can be thought of as not entirely departed, and the heroes as in a position to return.

Occasionally mortals get to visit the legendary heroes who have taken over the attributes of vanished gods. When this happens, the visitor suffers a magic sleep and a long lacuna in his life: he has lapsed into a pagan world, got himself bewitched, and trafficked with a forbidden god. The punishment is severe. Thus Herla lost everything and Peter lost his flock, wife, home, and twenty years of life—though Rip, to be sure, in Irving's half-convincing happy ending, doesn't suffer so badly. The reason for the punishment is nevertheless clear: it is Christianity's dire objection to traffic with such cults as attached to those gods, as with any intercourse with fairies. This centuries-old element of the story is an historical, symbolic, and didactic expression of the church's long struggle with paganism—and has nothing to do with any social retardation of progress in colonies. Look what happened to Herla and Peter, Christian instruction could say. They were kind and ingenuous men. What then could happen to you? And then because the story is compelling in its own right it survives past the need for it, even after the knowledge of its purpose is centuries forgotten.

Is there any other connection between the visit and the great changes that follow in the life of the man who made it? And what are these visitors doing where they are not supposed to be? The sleeping gods and heroes could be described, and have been, without any mortal to intrude on them, and it doesn't look as though the mortals had just happened in: most of them appear to have been approached and led. And Rip was called by name.

Almost all of the protagonists of these stories, if they witnessed anything within the mountain, saw some kind of game. The fact that the origins of many games fade into ritual and ritual dance suggests that the games in these legends and myths might have their origin in some rite. And some authorities (Jane Harrison and Lord Raglan are notable examples) believe that all myths have their origin in ritual —that a myth is never a folk-explanation of natural phenomena, or anything of the sort, but a narrative that was once linked with a ritual —is the story, in other words, which has outlived the ritual, that the ritual once enacted. Frazer had a more moderate view, and felt that there is a *class* of myths which have been dramatized in ritual, and that these myths were enacted as magical ceremonies in order to produce the natural effects which they describe in figurative language. This hypothesis has it further that the core of such a myth traces back, finally, to the divinity who is imagined to have founded the rite. The actors are simply impersonating an activity of the originator and worshipping him in this way, his acts being the prototype of the rite. Gradually, then, the rite may be performed more out of piety than from any belief in its efficacy, and finally may be forgotten while the myth endures.

Whatever the merits of this theory one thing seems fairly sure: if it explains the origins of any myths, Rip descends from one of them. The bowlers of the Catskills are impersonating a disguised Thor, in a figurative or symbolic way, in his principal role as God of Thunder, and the actions of these resurrected men are the means of their worship. The solemnity Rip and Peter felt, in the presence of a mystery, is entirely appropriate to so sacred and secret an occasion. "Rip Van Winkle," then, is our version of a myth that survives as a description of a nearly forgotten ceremony in the worship of Thor for the production of rain. It proceeds by a symbolic imitation of how rain is made. The ritual is of the magical sort, and is intended to influence nature through the physical sympathy, or resemblance, between the ceremony and the effect it is supposed to produce.* Indeed the story is an example of what Robert Graves has called "true myth": it is an instance of "the reduction to narrative shorthand of ritual mime."

Exactly *why* Rip was allowed to witness this mystery is a secret which, since he was ignorant of the reason himself, he has been able to keep for many generations. So, in all likelihood, was Irving unaware of the original reason for the outsider's presence at the ceremony: even by Peter Klaus's time the myth had so badly deteriorated into folklore that only the fragments we are deciphering remained. But the secret is out by now: Rip and Peter were initiates. Rip goes right through the steps. While he sits dreamily and alone on the green knoll the period of preliminary isolation passes; then he is summoned by name. Helping to carry the heavy keg up the side of the ravine, which he may have had to volunteer to do, is a sort of test. There followed a kind of procession, and something like a vigil, and finally the experience of communication with the divinity and his disciples. Rip is even given a magic drink, which as a novice he is first required to serve, and after this he is plunged into the magic sleep. When he wakes he is in a new phase of life, and on this level the great changes he finds about him are symbols of the changes in him, and of the differences in his situation, now that he is initiate.

Rip has also been reborn in another, reinforcing way, for the imagery of his emergence into a new life inevitably and unavoidably suggests an issue "from the womb." This concept, which is often thrown about gratuitously, really urges itself here, for Irving's description of the entrance to the mountain, taken from "Peter Klaus," is extremely arresting—almost as pointed, say, as accounts anthropologists have given of pits dug in the ground by primitive tribesmen, and trimmed about the edges with overhanging shrubbery (which ditches the men dance about in the spring, while brandishing their spears and chanting that these are no ditches, but what they were

---

*The thunder that Thor made came ordinarily from the roar of his chariot, of course, but the method described in the myth Irving drew on is by no means unknown. Grimm reported that on hearing thunder North Germans were likely to remark, "the angels are playing at bowls"; and in our own country there is a close parallel in the mythology of the Zuni Indians of New Mexico, whose warriors when they die go off to make lightning in the sky, where rainmakers cause thunder with great "gaming stones."

built to represent). The imagery is the same when Rip is led eerily through the ravine till he comes to the bottom of a hollow, surrounded by perpendicular precipices, over the brinks of which hang the branches of trees.

From this setting he is delivered into his old age. Ripe for escape before, he has experienced an escape only one step short of death. Apparently well into middle age, and saddled with a wife who had completely lost her desirability, he laid down his gun and entered the mountain. Here he witnessed some symbolical activity—which, in the severely censored form of the pins and bowling balls, has overtones of human, as well as vegetable, fertility—and he saw it all as joyless and melancholy. Magically confirmed in his own feeling about the matter, he drank, slept like a baby, and was released into the world he had longed for—into an all-male society, the perpetual men's club that used to meet at the inn, which his wife can no longer violate as, unforgivably, she had done before. His gun is ruined and useless, and his wife is gone. But it makes no difference now; he has slept painlessly through his "change of life."

The trouble with this story as some kind of "male-menopause myth" is that the reading is partly based on a misinterpretation attributed, perhaps unfairly, to Rip. Lacking the information we have, he made a mistake: the men were lifeless and unhappy at their bowling because they were dead. More than that, they were still the followers of Thor, whose sign was lightning and whose emblem was a hammer. Thor was god of power, and of human as well as vegetable fertility. He was god of the vital moistures in general, an ithyphallic, not a detumescent, god. Even dead, his worshippers made a great deal of noise in his service. In short, the bowling which sends thunder across the Catskills is violently masculine symbolic activity in a very feminine mountain. And in this last vague but massive symbol is a final irony, for the mystery revealed to Rip had thus two aspects, animal or human, and vegetable—one for each of Thor's two fertility powers.

Of what pertinence were all these revelations to Rip? What does it mean to him that the strange men he saw have come down to us from the men of Thor, or that he was initiated into an ancient mystery and shown the sacred secrets of all life? No relevance at all to him and no meaning whatever. And that is the ironical point. Befuddled, unwitting, and likeable old Rip: no man in the valley, luxuriantly green already, thought less or as little about the crops, and no man he knew could have been chosen to witness the secrets of human fertility and found them more sleep-provoking.

III

What would have interested him, and what did he want? Concentrating somewhat anthropologically on the story's central scene in an attempt to get at the bottom of it, we have not got to the bottom of the character. But if for a moment we will think more as psychologists, and consider the story as a sort of dream—as a product of the unconscious, itself a kind of anthropologist—we open a whole new and remarkable area of meaning. Suddenly everything seems illusive, unreal; time goes into abeyance and the sense of history is lost; the very identity of the central figure is shaken, and reason dissolves.

The easiest entry to the dream level of "Rip Van Winkle" passes through that inn where Rip once sat with his friends—the inn which was "gone," and replaced by a hotel straight out of nightmare: "a large rickety wooden building . . . with great gaping windows . . . mended with old hats and petticoats"—and in front a sign with a familiar face all out of place in its setting. Soon, however, "idle with impunity" and "reverenced as one of the patriarchs of the village," Rip "took his place once more on the bench at the inn door." A conflict in Irving explains the confusion. He wanted to show the great changes a revolution had brought, but wished more deeply to feel, and wanted us to feel, that aside from the happy loss of his wife nothing had really happened to Rip. Toynbee, responding fully to this ab-sense of time and change, made what amounts to the same mistake. But it is a meaningful slip, and on one level they are both right. For Rip, time and history *have* ceased operation. Nothing *has* happened, and the inn is there to signal the fact.

What, then, are we to think when we come to the start of the very next paragraph and are told (in a kind of preliminary postscript at the end of the tale proper) that Rip is now telling his story "to every stranger that arrived at Mr. Doolittle's hotel"? The inn is there, is gone and replaced, is there again, is gone again. Reality is slithering away; and so it must eventually do, for this is not ultimately its world. Nor is this truly the world of fiction, unless of Kafka's. It is the world of the unconscious, where time and history are not sus-

pended, exactly, but do not exist—where everything exists at once. It
is the region where people and things are always appearing in unrea-
sonable places, and everything is passing strange: but distorted toward some hard-to-recognize truth. The recurring transformation of
Irving's hostelry belongs in this night world. It represents a "willful
accident," and as such makes its own kind of sense. Irving was groping very darkly in a world of symbol, myth, and dream for meanings
beyond awareness.

In this strange new world Rip's identity is harder to establish
than the identity of that shifting meeting place. Removed as he is
from time, the confusion of generations is appalling, and he is hard
pressed to know in which of at least three generations he really "belongs." It will be next to impossible to know for sure, for the truth is
he had almost as little part in his own generation as the one he slept
through. This was entirely clear, had we the wit to see it, when we
first met him. He was not an adult, but a child playing with children,
a kid with a dog. He lived with his wife, to be sure, but only in a
manner of speaking, for he accepted instead his "only alternative";
"to take gun in hand and stroll away into the wood." Or, more striking, he would escape her by sitting on a wet rock with a rod in his
hand "as long and heavy as a Tartar's lance, and fish all day . . . even
though he should not be encouraged by a single nibble." "A great favorite among all the good wives of the village," he ran their errands
and did "such little jobs as their less obliging husbands would not do
for them"—not, by pointed implication, what their husbands would
do: "As to doing family duty . . . he found it impossible."

At the inn with the menfolk, Rip shows that he wants to be a
father. But at home he is a son, and not up to it: he is the son who
wants to be the father but his mother won't let him. He represents, to
be technical for a moment, the ego arrested at the infantile level in an
Oedipal situation; under pressure he reverts all the way back to the
sleep of the womb.

The scene in the mountain now takes on a new and different
suggestiveness. It is at once the dream of a child and an adult dream
reflecting Rip's own predicament. The great noses of the mountain
men give the next phallic clue, as they must likewise have done in the
ancient Teutonic mythology. (The psychoanalytic and the anthropo-
logical mix well: they are both—the first personally, the second culturally—"regressive.") From this viewpoint the dwarfs are really dis-

guised little boys with pins and balls practicing, in highly activated silence, a forbidden rite; Rip is not invited to play, too, and they make him work, so he sneaks their drink and goes off to sleep. On the other hand the dwarfs are also so many mirrors to the "adult" Rip, held up as revelations which his consciousness is not likely to read: they are aged little men playing games, who have grown old but not up. Our protagonist, then, is both gerontion and child—or is neither, precisely. He has nor youth nor age, but as it were an after-dinner's sleep, dreaming on both.

On his return to the village, the sense of the decomposition of his "self" becomes even more awesome. His wife-mother is gone, but he is still a child as much as he is anything, and as such he must find his role in a relationship to someone else. But now it is completely bewildering. He is soon confronted with the very "ditto of himself," a negligent loafer named Rip—actually his son. Worse, he faces a woman who seems both strange and, as his poor mind struggles into recollection, hauntingly familiar. She had, she says, a father named Rip, and she carries in her arms a child of that name. Who, then, is our protagonist? His own unaccepted and "impossible" self, or the son of his wife that he used to be and emotionally remains? Or his own son, the loafer leaning there against the tree, or the son of his wife that used to be and emotionally remains? Or his own son, the loafer leaning there against the tree and, after the ravages of twenty years that passed as as a night, looking more like the man Rip impersonated than he suddenly does himself? Or perhaps another Rip, the child of his daughter, now surrogate for his departed wife, and the sign of his true emotional state? Or even, conceivably, the husband of this replacement wife-mother, and the father of this son—or of that one, or of himself? The sense of generation is shattered; his daughter's house, in which he lives, is a whole house of mirrors, and everywhere he looks he sees a different distortion. He has one moment of panicked insight: "God knows . . . I'm not myself—I'm somebody else—that's me yonder—no—that's somebody else got into my shoes. . . ." Small wonder he takes his leave of all these people for the security of the role he can play at Mr. Doolittle's.

It is clear now that Rip escaped no change of life, but his very manhood—went from childhood to second childhood with next to nothing in between. It is not just his wife he has dodged, either, but all the obligations of maturity: occupation, domestic and financial responsibility, a political position, duty to society in a time of war. His relation to history is so ambiguous that—ridiculous suspicion—he is thought a spy. Charming and infantile, he narcissistically prefers himself; he will tell his tale of twenty years' sleep at Mr. Do-little's, where Irving leaves him for the last time. It has become a symbol for the sleep that has been his life.

Considering the universality of his fame, it is a wonder that no European, say, has pointed gleefully to this figure as a symbol of America, for he presents a near-perfect image of the way a large part of the world looks at us: likeable enough, up to a point and at times, but essentially immature, self-centered, careless, and above all—and perhaps dangerously—innocent. Even more pointedly, Rip is a stereotype of the American male as seen from abroad, or in some jaundiced quarters at home: he is perfectly the jolly overgrown child, abysmally ignorant of his own wife and the whole world of adult men —perpetually "one of the boys," hanging around what they are pleased to think of as a "perpetual men's club"; a disguised Rotarian who simply will not and cannot grow up. In moments of candor we will probably admit that a stereotype with no germ of truth in it could not exist: some such mythic America, some such mythic American, exist both actually and in the consciousness of the world. Rip will do very well as their prototype.

"Rip Van Winkle" is then, and finally, a wonderfully rich tale —the richest in our literature—and an astonishingly complex experience arising from a struggle among many kinds of meaning. On the "prehistoric" level we are dimly aware of immemorial ritual significance, on the psychological of an extraordinary picture of the self arrested in a timeless infancy—rich appeals, both, to the child and primitive in everyone that never grow up and never die in anyone. These awarenesses conflict in the story, as they do in life, with the adult and rational perception that we do indeed grow old, that time and history never stop. In much the same way, our affection for Rip himself must oppose our reluctant discovery that as a man we cannot fully respect him.

But in addition to all his other sides, this remarkable Van Winkle also, of course, projects and personifies our sense of the flight— and more: the ravages—of time. And this is what wins us ultimately to his side. We know perfectly well that as an adult this darling of generations of Americans will not entirely do. But if he does seem, finally, meek, blessed, pure in heart, and if we mock him for what he has missed we do it tenderly—partly because it is something hidden in ourselves we mock. And this is not just our own hidden childishness. It is all our own lost lives and roles, the lives and roles that once seemed possible and are possible no more. In twenty years all springs are over; without mockery it might be too sad to bear. Today would grieve, and tomorrow would grieve; best cover it over lightly.

And so here is Rip at the end: Lazarus come from the dead, come back to tell us all. He will tell us all, and badgering any who will listen, he tries: Well now—have you heard what happened to *me?* But it won't do; he doesn't know. And that is a pity, truly. Here is a man in whom rest complexities and deficiencies a lifetime might contemplate, as the world has done; a man who has peered toward the dawn of civilization, witnessed ancient mysteries, and stared at his essential nature; a man who now in town is looking at the future and realizing a dream of the ages. And he cannot communicate his visions.

But supposing that he could, that he could tell us all: would it have been worthwhile? Visions, revelations like these are private. To translate what the thunder meant, to confront the meaning of life and the future of all our childish selves, we all have to go up into our own mountains.

Introduction to
Rip Van Winkle & The Legend of Sleepy Hollow

BY HASKELL SPRINGER

Haskell Springer, whose Ph.D. dissertation at Indiana was a critical edition of *The Sketch Book,* has been since 1968 on the faculty of the University of Kansas, where he is now an Associate Professor of English. His CEAA edition of *The Sketch Book* awaits publication as a key volume in *The Complete Works of Washington Irving.* Also forthcoming, in 1976, is his annotated bibliography of selected criticism, *Washington Irving: A Reference Guide.* The "Introduction" printed here is the preface to *Rip Van Winkle & The Legend of Sleepy Hollow* (1974), published by Sleepy Hollow Restorations, with illustrations, originally by F. O. C. Darley, now colored by the equally gifted Fritz Kredel. Springer's conclusion makes a proper coda to the present collection, for he emphasizes Irving's talents as storyteller, an American storyteller, in his two best tales.

"Rip Van Winkle" and "The Legend of Sleepy Hollow" Washington Irving's most widely loved and respected stories, appeared in 1819–20 in *The Sketch Book of Geoffrey Crayon, Gent.,* the first book by an American author to win international acclaim. From the time of its publication Iriving became a celebrity; and by 1848, when G. P. Putnam began issuing the volumes of the Author's Revised Edition of Irving's complete works, the titles of these tales were such a familiar part of American life that reviewers assumed that anyone who could read at all had read them. Now, more than one hundred fifty years after the appearance of *The Sketch Book,* "Rip" and "The Legend" seem so basically American that it is hard to realize that Irving borrowed the ideas from German sources. He so successfully transformed them that they fit their American dress better than he could have imagined.

Anyone who has driven around the United States, and seen, in state after state, Rip Van Winkle Motels and Sleepy Hollow Motor Inns, realizes that the stories have become, in that superficial way at least, part of modern America. But their great popularity and enduring appeal to all ages, and to students of literature as well as to motel keepers, is not explained merely by the sleepiness and dreaminess of Irving's narrations. The stories reveal as well Irving's special ability to entertain and delight by means of his remarkable control of the English language, combined with his witty, perceptive insight into human nature and the American scene.

Irving's light, genial humor has always been highly admired and imitated, and these two tales are perhaps the finest illustrations of his skill. In "The Legend of Sleepy Hollow," for example, we hear the well-modulated, kindly, yet ironic voice of Irving's narrator saying, "In this by-place of nature there abode in a remote period of American history, that is to say, some thirty years since, a worthy wight of the name of Ichabod Crane. . . ." and we smile, both at the diction and the American self-awareness. Ichabod, "though lank, had the dilating powers of an anaconda," and Balt Van Tassel "loved his daughter better even than his pipe." In such perfectly phrased comments Irving excels. And his longer passages, commenting on human quirks and eccentricities, building subtly-colored word pictures of scenes and characters such as Rip's old town and dream-haunted Catskill Mountains or the pedagogical Ichabod, whose vision is clouded by dollar signs and who dwells not in wonder but in fearful

superstition, are so gracefully created that there is not the slightest
strain or stumble in their wit, wisdom, and affection.

Just as engaging, and in addition a key to the timeless excellence of both stories, is what might be called Irving's technique of deliberate contradiction. Irving insists on the absolute reality of the unreal in one story, while in the other he treats perfectly rational, realistic events as mysterious and legendary. "Rip Van Winkle," whose
central events (a meeting with Henry Hudson and a twenty-year
sleep) are, of course, tolerantly disbelieved by the reader, is full of
assertions of truthfulness. From the bland lie in the headnote about
the "unquestionable authority" of Diedrich Knickerbocker's *A History of New York,* through the epigraph which asserts that "Truth is
a thing that ever I will keep," until the endnote which supports Mr.
Knickerbocker's tale as "an absolute fact, narrated with his usual
fidelity," the story declares its literal factuality. Of course (tongue in
cheek), we know we can believe these assertions because Knickerbocker himself saw an affidavit on the matter, "taken before a country
justice and signed with a cross in the justice's own handwriting."
"The story, therefore is beyond the possibility of doubt" [!].

Complementing the strategy in "Rip Van Winkle" is the narrative ploy of "The Legend of Sleepy Hollow," which is to call the key
events of the tale mysterious, even though the story clearly intends us
to understand that Brom Bones (not the Hessian) threw the pumpkin (not his head) at Ichabod Crane. Here Irving is intentionally
calling legendary something which he himself has made clear and rational. He even has his narrator, when questioned by the literal-
minded doubter, state that he does not "believe one-half" of the story
himself. In both stories the result of this deliberate self-contradiction
is to leave the reader somewhere between the real and the imaginary.
But where, and why?

When the anonymous narrator of "The Legend of Sleepy Hollow" confounds the doubting old gentleman with a false syllogism
supposedly explaining his tale, or when the self-important, disbeliev-
ing man in the three-cornered hat in "Rip Van Winkle" is utterly defeated, we are all on the side of the narrator and Rip. We enjoy the
skeptic's discomfort and laugh at it. But the two stories do not tell us
to replace logic with fantasy. Rather, Irving's method is to mingle the
two, to let one humorously contradict the other, until a sort of imaginative middle ground is established, in which we need neither search

irritably for the "truth" of the matter nor relinquish completely our hold on reality for the sake of fancy.

What Irving does is show us the value of imagination in bringing wonder and enjoyment into our logic-bound lives. The excitement and wonder in the lives of the Sleepy Hollow folk are created by that "Visionary propensity" of theirs, and we ourselves should have, Irving suggests, a similar ability. For just as Rip's mountaintop encounter and long sleep do not remove him from reality forever, we all come back from excursions into imagination, and if we can, like Rip, bring back with us the fruits of that experience, or like Irving, find where reality and fantasy mix and mingle, perhaps we can supply ourselves and our rationalistic, skeptical society with an imaginative freedom it needs and enjoys.

So it has been through classic American literature, as Irving, Edgar Allan Poe, Nathaniel Hawthorne, and other fine writers have created their own imaginative borderlands and have shown Americans the creative use of their imaginations. These realms conceived by some of our best writers are really not very far from our ordinary mental geography; and these authors of ours, including Irving, have a great deal to tell us about life as we know it. Now, in fact, in the last third of the twentieth century, Washington Irving's two fine stories have a special meaning for us. The main clue to that meaning is in the return scene in "Rip Van Winkle."

After twenty years of sleep on the mountain Rip comes home to find everything changed. The absence of his shrewish wife does not, to be sure, disturb him very much, but the whole character of the place has been altered; and to Rip as well as to the narrator (Diedrich Knickerbocker, alias Geoffrey Crayon, alias Washington Irving) this change is very disturbing. What has happened? The village has expanded and strangers abound; the old drowsy tranquillity has disappeared and the people have become "busy, bustling, disputatious"; the sedentary, patriarchal Nicholas Vedder and his small "junto" have been replaced by a "self-important," browbeating, cowardly old man who controls the opinions of the *crowd*.

Irving's whole description of the village clearly implies that the community has lost rather than gained by the transformation; and in this changed world Rip has also lost something—his very identity. Not only is he out of his time, but his son, whom we saw earlier as a little boy tagging along behind his mother, has now grown into a perfect model of Rip in his younger days, and is to the town their Rip Van Winkle. To use a term from our own day, old Rip suffers from "future shock"; the suddenness of the change has made the world incomprehensible. In his own home town Rip is a stranger in a strange land. But what has really occurred to that village in the Catskills? It has merely experienced what virtually all of America from before Irving's day to ours has known, immigration, population boom, building boom, constantly accelerating change—in a word, *progress.*

In recent times we have come to be a bit dubious about the benefits of material progress, because we have seen its frequently catalogued ill effects, from alienation to pollution. And in response to the pressures created by these results of progress, more and more we try to escape. We go to the woods, and to the few small towns that somehow have managed to retain the peace and charm of an earlier day, or have been restored to give at least the semblance of a simpler, quieter life. In this we are very much like the villagers in that bustling Catskill town. To them Rip is a valuable asset: he is a story-telling link with the past, with a slower, simpler way of life. And that is one reason why Washington Irving himself is our own valuable asset. He is *our* storyteller, preserving for us the ambience of an earlier way of life in America, one we cherish more dearly the more remote and irreclaimable that past simplicity becomes.

A related scenario is played out in "The Legend of Sleepy Hollow." This time Diedrich Knickerbocker tells us the story of a would-be Yankee entrepreneur, not a Dutch dreamer. Ichabod Crane is certainly associated with "progress," and this story takes a similarly dim view of its implication. Ichabod, whose name means "inglorious," is a Connecticut Yankee who falls in love with the beautiful Katrina Van Tassel, not under the spell of her loveliness, but because of her father's wealth. He views the pewter, the china and silver, the mahogany furniture, and the other riches of the Van Tassel house, and "from the moment [he] laid his eyes upon these regions of delight, the peace of his mind was at an end, and his only study was how to gain the affections of the peerless daughter of Van Tassel." In fact, Ichabod's mind even confuses love and marriage with consumption of goods; as he sees the abundance of the Van Tassel farmyard, he conjures up mental pictures: ". . . the pigeons were snugly put to bed in a comfortable pie, and tucked in with a coverlet of crust . . . and the ducks pairing cosily in dishes, like snug married couples, with a decent competency of onion sauce."

Irving writes one especially significant paragraph in which Ichabod is made to embody a particularly American, entrepreneurial idea of progress:

> As the enraptured Ichabod fancied all this, and he rolled his great green eyes over the fat meadow lands, the rich fields of wheat, of rye, of buckwheat, and Indian corn, and the orchards burthened with ruddy fruit, which surrounded the warm tenement of Van Tassel, his heart yearned for the damsel who was to inherit these domains, and his imagination expanded with the idea, how they might be readily turned into cash, and the money invested in immense tracts of wild land, and shingle palaces in the wilderness. Nay, his busy fancy already realized his hopes, and presented to him the blooming Katrina, with a whole family of children, mounted on the top of a wagon loaded with household trumpery, with pots and kettles dangling beneath; and he beheld himself bestriding a pacing mare, with a colt at her heels, setting out for Kentucky, Tennessee, or the Lord knows where.

Here is prefigured Daniel Boone, and a whole host of succeeding pioneers, settlers, land speculators, developers, and others with a particular kind of vision, who, like Ichabod, wanted to turn beautiful abundance into cash in order to buy more of nature's bounty and do the same once again. A sad version of the American Dream! But Irving shows us how, in fiction at least, that exploitive dream is frustrated, as Brom Bones, who values Katrina for herself, drives his rival from the scene.

Irving greatly values such victories made possible by literature, and makes them the focus of a number of his writings. Other themes and interests also recur in Irving's sketches. His preference for the "shadowy grandeurs of the past" over the "commonplace realities of the present," central to "Rip Van Winkle," is one of the most persistent. Other such prominent, repeated concerns are the delights of romance; the love of home, hearth, marriage, and children; the trials of bachelorhood; the superiority of rural to city life, and of the natural to the artificial; and the close relationship between literature and life.

Most pervasive, though, is the idea of mutability: All things must succumb to inexorable, destructive time; the familiar present will give way to the strange future; life and love are governed by the inevitability of change. With both sadness and humor Irving pursues this theme in his *Sketch Book,* and, in "Rip Van Winkle" at least, the problem is resolved happily. In light of the idea that perpetual change is the order of the world, we might reflect on the stability and security supplied us by our literature—by works such as "Rip Van Winkle" and "The Legend of Sleepy Hollow" and writers such as Irving—whose perennial freshness and relevance permit us to communicate with the past and better understand the present. That service to the future has not been rendered by many. Washington Irving, as one of the few, deserves our respect, admiration and gratitude.

CHRONOLOGY

1783 April 3	Born in New York City.
1802	After secondary schooling and earlier clerkships, enters law office of former Attorney General J. O. Hoffman.
1802–03	Contributes nine essays by "Jonathan Oldstyle, Gent." to the *Morning Chronicle* newspaper. Travels to the St. Lawrence River and Montreal.
1804–06	Travels in Europe.
1806 March 24	Arrives at New York; November 21, passes state bar examination.
1807–08	Contributes pseudonymously to *Salmagundi,* published in 20 numbers.
1809	"Diedrich Knickerbocker's" *A History of New York* published in U.S.
1812–14	Edits the *Analectic Magazine,* published in Philadelphia.
1814	In autumn, colonel of state militia and aide to Gov. Daniel D. Tompkins.
1815 May 15	Sails to England. Family import firm in Liverpool bankrupt in 1818; Irving turns to professional authorship.
1819–20	*The Sketch Book of Geoffrey Crayon, Gent.* published serially in U.S.; 1820, two volumes published in England.
1822	*Bracebridge Hall* published. Irving resides in Dresden.

1824	*Tales of a Traveller* published.
1826	Moves from Paris and Bordeaux to Madrid at invitation of the American Minister.
1828–29	Madrid, Seville, Granada.
1828	*Life and Voyages of Christopher Columbus* published.
1829	*The Conquest of Granada* published. Secretary to U.S. Embassy, London.
1831	Oxford confers a Doctor in Civil Law (D.C.L.) degree. *Voyages and Discoveries of the Companions of Columbus* published.
1832	*The Alhambra* published. May, returns to New York. Tours western part of country.
1835	*The Crayon Miscellany* published in three parts.
1836	*Astoria* published. Settles into Sunnyside, purchased the year before.
1837	*The Adventures of Captain Bonneville* published.
1838	Declines President Van Buren's offer of cabinet post, and also Tammany Hall nomination as Mayor of New York.
1841	*Biography . . . of Margaret Davidson* published.
1842	Appointed Minister to Spain and reaches Madrid, July 25.
1846	Returns to Sunnyside.
1848	Publication begins by G. P. Putnam of the Author's Revised Edition, to be completed in 15 volumes in 1851. It includes a revised *Oliver Goldsmith* (1949) and

a new *Mahomet and His Successors* (1850).

1849   February 14   Elected President of the first Board of Trustees of the Astor Library. *A Book of the Hudson* published.

1855   *Wolfert's Roost* published, also Volume I of the *Life of George Washington,* to be completed by Volumes II and III (1856), Volume IV (1857), and Volume V (1859).

1859   November 28   Dies at Sunnyside. Burial in Sleepy Hollow Cemetery in Tarrytown.

ADDITIONAL BIBLIOGRAPHY

WORKS

Irving's collected works are at present best looked for in the Author's Uniform Revised Edition, published in 21 volumes as *The Works of Washington Irving* (New York: G. P. Putnam's Sons, 1860–1861). In progress under the direction of the Center for Editions of American Authors, of the Modern Language Association, is a full-scale, scholarly edition of the published works and private papers, *The Complete Works of Washington Irving*. Three volumes were put out by the University of Wisconsin Press (1969–1970). The remaining volumes will be published, beginning at once, by Twayne Publishers, a division of G. K. Hall Corporation of Boston. For descriptive bibliography, combine Langfeld and Blackburn (see Part III, above) and Volume 5 (1969) of the *Bibliography of American Literature,* ed. Jacob Blanck.

HISTORIES AND STUDIES

It is worth noting here that the standard biography by Stanley T. Williams (see Part III, above), published as long ago as 1935, is beginning to show the gap in time between Williams's research and interpretations and the numerous subsequent scholarly contributions to the study of Irving's life and works. Some useful titles, not previously mentioned or excerpted in this volume, include:

Aderman, Ralph M., ed., *Washington Irving Reconsidered: A Symposium* (Hartford: Transcendental Books, 1969).

Leary, Lewis, *Washington Irving* (Minneapolis: University of Minnesota Press, 1963).

McClary, Ben H., ed., *Washington Irving and the House of Murray* (Knoxville: University of Tennessee, 1964).

Myers, Andrew, B., ed., *The Worlds of Washington Irving* (New York: New York Public Library, and Tarrytown: Sleepy Hollow Restorations, 1974).

———, ed., *Washington Irving, A Tribute* (Tarrytown: Sleepy Hollow Restorations, 1972).

Nye, Russel B., *The Cultural Life of the New Nation, 1776–1830* (New York: Harper and Row, 1960).

———, *Society and Culture in America, 1830–1860* (New York: Harper and Row, 1974).

Quinn, Arthur H., *et al*, *The Literature of the American People* (New York: Appleton-Century-Crofts, 1951).

Spiller, Robert E., ed., *The American Literary Revolution, 1783–1837* (Garden City, N.Y.: Doubleday, 1967).

Taft, Kendall B., ed., *Minor Knickerbockers* (New York: American Book, 1947). Reprinted, 1972. Books for Libraries Press, Inc.

Williams, Stanley T., and Edge, Mary A., eds., *A Bibliography of the Writings of Washington Irving, A Check List* (New York: Oxford, 1936). Reprinted, 1970. Burt Franklin & Company, Inc.

PERIODICAL CRITICISM

For single articles, etc., consult the regular bibliographies in *American Literature,* and *PMLA,* and also the bibliography supplements to the *Literary History of the United States* (1948–   ). See also Lewis Leary, ed., *Articles on American Literature, 1900–1950* (Durham, N. C.: Duke, 1954), and his *Articles on American Literature, 1950–1967* (Durham, N. C.: Duke, 1970). The only extensive separate annotated collection of titles is by Haskell S. Springer, *Washington Irving: A Reference Guide* (Boston: G. K. Hall, 1976). An older annotated list was included in Henry A. Pochmann, ed., *Washington Irving: Representative Selections* (New York: American Book, 1934). Reprinted, 1971. Scholarly Press, Inc.

INDEX

Sleepy Hollow Restorations, Incorporated, is a non-profit educational institution chartered by the *Board of Regents of the University of the State of New York*. Established under an endowment provided, in large part, by the late John D. Rockefeller, Jr., Sleepy Hollow Restorations owns and maintains *Sunnyside*, Washington Irving's picturesque home in Tarrytown; *Philipsburg Manor, Upper Mills*, in North Tarrytown, an impressive example of a colonial commercial mill complex and *Van Cortlandt Manor*, in Croton-on-Hudson, a distinguished eighteenth-century family estate.